Empire and Community

Empire and Community

*Edmund Burke's Writings and Speeches
on International Relations*

EDITED BY

David P. Fidler

AND

Jennifer M. Welsh

Westview Press
A Member of the Perseus Books Group

Permissions
The edited selections from Burke's writings and speeches in this book
are taken from *The Writings and Speeches of Edmund Burke,* gen. ed.
Paul Langford (Oxford: Clarendon Press, 1981–   ) and are reprinted
by permission of Oxford University Press.

Published in 1999 in the United States of America by Westview Press,
5500 Central Avenue, Boulder, Colorado 80301-2877, and in the
United Kingdom by Westview Press, 12 Hid's Copse Road, Cumnor
Hill, Oxford OX2 9JJ

Find us on the World Wide Web at www.westviewpress.com

Library of Congress Cataloging-in-Publication Data
Burke, Edmund, 1729–1797
    [Selections.   1999]
    Empire and community: Edmund Burke's writings and speeches on
international relations / edited by David P. Fidler, Jennifer M. Welsh.
        p.   cm.
    Includes bibliographical references and index.
    ISBN 0-8133-6830-8 (hc).—ISBN 0-8133-6829-4 (pbk.)
    1. International relations.   2. Burke, Edmund, 1729–1797—
Contributions in international relations.   3. Burke, Edmund,
1729–1797. Reflections on the Revolution in France.   I. Fidler.
David P.   II. Welsh, Jennifer M.   III. Title.
JZ1345.B87   1999
327.41'009'033—dc21   99-34902
                                                         CIP

The paper used in this publication meets the requirements of the American National Standard for Permanence of Paper for Printed Library
Materials Z39.48-1984.

10   9   8   7   6   5   4   3   2   1

*David Fidler would like
to dedicate this book to his wife, Shari,
who supports his endeavors with a patience
that is sublime and beautiful.*

*Jennifer Welsh would like to dedicate this book to her
"little platoon" of support—the Welsh family.*

Contents

Editors' Notes

Note on the Selections

Given the enormous amount of material available to Burke scholars, any selection of relevant writings and speeches inevitably leaves out many important works. For example, we have not included in this collection some of Burke's most famous pieces, such as *Reflections on the Revolution in France* or *An Appeal from the New to the Old Whigs*. Although these tracts marked seminal moments in Burke's political career and intellectual development, they are not necessarily the most illustrative of his thinking on international relations. Instead, we have chosen a few of Burke's lesser-known writings and speeches, such as *Two Letters on the Trade of Ireland* and *Thoughts on French Affairs,* which better reveal the key aspects of his international theory. Nonetheless, Part 1 frequently cites and discusses key works not included in this collection and refers to personal correspondence and parliamentary debates. For those wishing to pursue Burke's thinking in greater detail, we invite them to delve into these additional sources. Much more Burke awaits the eager mind.

We have provided some explanatory notes, as well as most of Burke's published notes, to help the reader better understand references to people and events and other allusions Burke made in his writings and speeches. We tried to keep these notes to a minimum in order not to distract the reader from Burke's arguments.

Bibliographic Abbreviations

Corr.	*The Correspondence of Edmund Burke,* ed. T. W. Copeland, 10 vols., Chicago, 1958–1978.
Parl. Hist.	*The Parliamentary History of England from the Earliest Period to the Year 1803,* ed. W. Cobbett, 36 vols., London, 1806–1820.
Works	*The Works of the Right Honourable Edmund Burke,* 6 vols. (Bohn's British Classics), London, 1854–1856.
WSEB	*The Writings and Speeches of Edmund Burke,* gen. ed. P. Langford, Oxford, 1981– (Clarendon Press series, vols. 2, 3, 5, 6, 8, and 9 published to date).

Editorial Note

In the selections of Burke's writings and speeches, we have used ellipsis points (. . .) to show that we have left material out of a sentence or paragraph. The symbol ⌇ indicates that we have omitted an entire paragraph or more.

David P. Fidler
Jennifer M. Welsh

Acknowledgments

We would like to thank Tim Dunne, Andrew Hurrell, Adam Roberts, and Paul Langford for all the advice and support they have given us in our labors on this project. We have also been sustained in our efforts by the encouragement we initially received from the late John Vincent, who first brought our mutual interests in Burke together and gave us momentum that helped carry us through to the end. We also express our gratitude to a host of people at the Indiana University School of Law—Bloomington for helping in so many ways: Jennifer Bryan, Hermine Cohen, Debbie Eads, Marie Edwards, Ralph Gaebler, Jeanine Hullinger, Rose Serot, Laura Winninghoff, and Marjorie Young. Oxford University Press has been very accommodating in allowing us to use material from its *Writings and Speeches of Edmund Burke* series. Finally, we would like to acknowledge Leo Wiegman and his staff at Westview Press for guiding us through the publication process.

D. P. F.
J. M. W.

Chronology of Burke's Life and Times

1767	Parliament again imposes taxes on the American colonies
1767–1774	Opposes all bills to reform the East India Company
1768	Purchases Beaconsfield estate in Buckinghamshire
1769	Parliament repeals all taxes on the American colonies except for the tax on tea
	Publishes *Observations on a Late State of the Nation*
1770	Publishes *Thoughts on the Cause of the Present Discontents,* in which he defends the Rockingham government's record
	Lord North forms his administration
1770–1775	Serves as the New York Assembly's agent to the British government
1773	Boston Tea Party
1774	Delivers *Speech on American Taxation;* elected MP for Bristol
1775	Delivers *Speech on Conciliation with America* in March
	American rebellion begins in April in Massachusetts
	Adam Smith elected to "the Club"
	Begins to study East India Company records
1776	Greets American Declaration of Independence with pessimism about British imperial policy
	Adam Smith publishes *Wealth of Nations*
1777	Publishes *Letter to the Sheriffs of Bristol* on the war in America and delivers *Speech on Restoring Lord Pigot,* which suggests his attitude toward the East India Company has changed
1778	Writes *Two Letters on the Trade of Ireland* to Bristol constituents
1779	With William Burke, publishes *Policy on Making Conquests for the Mahometans* criticizing behavior of the East India Company
1780	Riots in London over proposed easing of oppressive Irish laws
	Withdraws from reelection for Bristol seat in Parliament in controversy over his views on Ireland; elected MP for Malton
1781	War in America effectively ends with British defeat at Yorktown
1782–1783	Works on the select committee investigating the activities of the East India Company; authors the *Ninth* and *Eleventh Reports of the Select Committee*
1782	Joins the second Rockingham government as paymaster of the forces; Rockingham dies
1783	Delivers *Speech on Fox's India Bill*
1784	Fox-North coalition dissolves; William Pitt forms new government and wins general election
1785	Delivers *Speech on the Nabob of Arcot's Debts;* begins to formulate strategy to impeach Warren Hastings
1786	Begins process of impeaching Hastings in the House of Commons
1787	Succeeds in having the House of Commons impeach Hastings
1788	Trial of Hastings before the House of Lords begins with Burke's *Speech on Opening of Impeachment*
1789	French Revolution begins; French royal family captured at Versailles in October

1790   Warns fellow Whigs of his opposition to the French Revolution;
            publishes *Reflections on the Revolution in France*
1791   Publicly breaks his friendship and collaboration with Charles Fox over
            Fox's support for the French Revolution; publishes *An Appeal from the
            New to the Old Whigs* and *Letter to a Member of the National Assembly;*
            and writes *Thoughts on French Affairs* to challenge the Pitt
            government's handling of revolutionary France
1792   France declares war on Austria and Prussia; French Republic established
            after overthrow of the monarchy; French armies defeat Prussian forces
            at Valmy
            Writes *Letter to Sir Hercules Langrishe* on Irish affairs and *Heads for
            Consideration on the Present State of Affairs* on the situation with
            revolutionary France
1793   Louis XVI executed; France declares war on Britain; Reign of Terror
            begins in France
            Writes *Remarks on the Policy of the Allies* to convince the Pitt government
            to intervene against revolutionary France
1794   Retires from Parliament and mourns the death of his son, Richard
1795   House of Lords acquits Hastings
            Writes *Thoughts and Details on Scarcity* for the Pitt government
1796   Writes *Letter to a Noble Lord*
            Storms prevent French forces from landing at Bantry Bay, Ireland
1796–1797   Writes *Letters on a Regicide Peace* criticizing Pitt government's handling of
            the war with revolutionary France
1797   Dies at Beaconsfield on July 9

Empire and Community

PART ONE

Introduction

Burke and
International Relations

Edmund Burke poses a great challenge to those who approach his genius. Burke's political thinking has remained relevant long after his contemporaries recognized him as one
of the greatest politicians of his age. Although considerable attention has been focused
on Burke, his views on international relations have not attracted substantial discussion.
Vincent sought to redress this paucity of analysis because he knew "of no treatment of
Burke's theory of international relations except as incidental to his attitude to the French
Revolution, or to America or to any other of the great issues on which he occupied himself."[1] This neglect is curious because four of the most important issues Burke addressed
in his political career were largely international: British policy in Ireland, the treatment
of the American colonies, British imperial activity in India, and the French Revolution.[2]
In his involvement with these issues, Burke handled many aspects central to the study of
international relations. This book provides students both of Burke and of international
relations with a resource for understanding Burke's thinking on international relations.

Explaining Burke's perspective on international relations poses a number of problems.
The first is logistical. Burke produced a tremendous body of speeches, writings, and correspondence, which Vincent described as Burke's "great mine."[3] Looking at only part of
such a vast array shortchanges the quality and texture of Burke's ideas, which is why our
efforts are only a beginning.[4]

A second difficulty concerns whether to categorize Burke as a political philosopher at
all. Burke's disdain for abstract thinking, his skepticism about the power of reason, and
his partisan involvement in the politics of his day caution against such a label. As Vincent observed, "Burke did not count himself a theorist."[5] But even if we take the most
extreme view of Burke as antitheorist, we are obliged to accept this stance as a political
theory: "Burke's position is itself a theory of politics which exalts practice above every
other thing."[6] This problem, however, does not make unraveling Burke's perspective on
international relations impossible; it requires that we explain his outlook carefully.

Burke's contemporaries recognized his penchant for infusing discussion of political issues with a search for and explanation of guiding principles. His mind was interested not
merely in the cut and thrust of parliamentary politics; his thought, deeply versed in the

circumstances and historical development of any issue, transcended the ephemera of current affairs.[7] The object of Burke's scorn was thinking devoid of historical sensibility and founded on speculative reason alone.[8] His aversion to abstract thinking resulted from his belief in the practical and theoretical importance of what Montesquieu, whom Burke revered, called "the empire of circumstance."[9] Burke wrote that "[c]ircumstances (which with some gentlemen pass for nothing) give in reality to every political principle its distinguishing colour, and discriminating effect. The circumstances are what render every civil and political scheme beneficial or noxious to mankind."[10]

Burke's emphasis on circumstance, however, creates another challenge: the current relevance of Burke's ideas. One scholar stated that "[b]y his insistence on the importance of circumstances Burke ruled himself out of court for the late twentieth century."[11] We address the problem of Burke's relevance regarding contemporary international relations in Chapter 4.

Yet another problem is that Burke has been claimed as a representative of different schools of political thought and practice.[12] Depending upon what source is handy, Burke can be placed within either the British empiricist or the natural law traditions. Burke has also been called both a prophet of liberalism and the father of modern conservative thought. He has been described as an apostle of moderation and as the high priest of crusading holy war. Cobban even claimed that "there is only one school of politics for which Burke can be legitimately claimed, and that is the school of Burke."[13] For our purposes, this seeming chaos in critical commentary poses difficulties because Burke's international thinking forms part of his political philosophy.

Our aim is not to resolve these controversies but to show that a grasp of Burke's perspective on international relations is critical to understanding his political thinking. Hints about this link appear in some commentaries.[14] Macpherson, for example, noted that "[n]o one was more aware than Burke that national policies needed to be framed in the light of the international situation."[15] Similarly, Hampsher-Monk commented that "[t]hrough the causes to which Burke addressed himself during his career—the government of Ireland, the relationship with America, the administration of India, the reform of the Crown's finances, the defence of free trade within the empire—there runs the theme of empire and how to accommodate it to domestic politics."[16] Stanlis argued that "[o]ne of the greatest omissions in scholarship on Burke has been the failure to consider the vital position of the law of nations in his political philosophy."[17]

Although much promising territory awaits in Burke's commentary on international relations, we hope to avoid constraining his thought by the conventions of international relations study. Our approach would be sterile if we argued that Burke was definitively a realist, rationalist, or revolutionist. As international relations scholars have observed, aspects of all three traditions appear in Burke's international thought.[18] Our task is to explicate as much as possible the full range and power of Edmund Burke on international relations.

CHAPTER TWO

Burke's Life and International Affairs

As a first step, we present Burke's biography to show how deeply he involved himself in international issues. This overview serves as a prelude to Chapter 3, where we develop a theoretical framework for Burke's ideas on international relations.

Burke's Preparliamentary Years

Burke was born, reared, and educated an Irishman.[19] He was born in 1729 in Dublin to Richard Burke, a Protestant attorney, and Mary Burke, a Catholic. According to Ayling, "That the marriage of Burke's parents was in this religious sense mixed was to be of the highest importance in influencing his adult opinions and sentiments, especially concerning those two linked issues never absent from the politics of his adult years, the Catholic question and the governing of Ireland."[20] If O'Brien is correct that Richard Burke was Protestant by conversion rather than by birth, the pressures of religious politics in eighteenth-century Ireland scarred the Burke household.[21]

Significant to the formation of Burke's thinking was the oppressive English colonial rule over Ireland. Burke's Irish roots shaped his political thinking in two ways: (1) Mitigation of Irish suffering under English colonial rule became a priority in his political career, and (2) English policy toward Irish Catholics and Irish trade provided material for his overall ideas about British imperial policy. Burke's Irish background also affected his personal political fortunes: He never held a position of cabinet rank in the administrations he joined, despite his talent.[22] The frustration he encountered as an alien or "Irish adventurer" among the British establishment is revealed in one of his last works, *Letter to a Noble Lord* (1796), where he contrasted how the duke of Bedford (who had criticized the granting of a state pension to Burke) had been "swaddled, and rocked, and dandled into a Legislator" while "[a]t every step of my progress in life (for in every step was I traversed and opposed), and at every turnpike I met, I was obliged to shew my passport, and again and again to prove my sole title to the honour of being useful to my Country, by a proof that I was not wholly unacquainted with it's laws, and the whole system of it's interests both abroad and at home."[23]

Burke attended a Quaker boarding school in County Kildare (1741–1744) and then studied at Trinity College, Dublin (1744–1748). His activities at Trinity College showed that he was already following political affairs. With some Trinity College friends, Burke produced a weekly paper called *The Reformer*, which includes "remarkable outbursts" on the topic of British treatment of the Irish:

> He saw, and resented, the worse than colonial status to which the bulk of the population of Ireland was reduced by the heavily aristocratic establishment. He was deeply angered by the brutal poverty in which the peasantry were, as he saw it, kept by the decadent aristocratic rich, who made no effort to manage their estates efficiently and did nothing to encourage . . . their tenants becoming industrious yeomen.[24]

Burke was not, however, an Irish radical harboring aspirations for a free and independent Ireland. He expressed in these early writings no revolutionary propositions as to the redistribution of wealth in Ireland or the dependent status of Ireland as a colony. If Burke "was merciless at that time towards the idle rich he was by no means a leveller."[25] He valued the security of property and believed that owners had a duty "to improve their properties so as to increase the wealth of the nation for the benefit of all classes."[26] He saw the suffering and economic waste produced in Ireland by a sterile conception of property embraced by corrupt, ruthless, or absentee British landowners. Similarly, strong suggestions about the future of Burke's attitude on British imperial policy appear in his conclusion that independence would be fatal to Ireland.[27]

After graduating from Trinity College, Burke reluctantly began legal studies in London at Middle Temple in 1750. It was clear, however, that he had his heart set on a literary career and found studying for the bar little to his liking.[28] By 1755 he had given up his legal studies.[29]

Yet Burke's five years at Middle Temple mixed with other aspects of his education. First, Burke's emphasis on tradition, custom, and precedent in his mature political thought echoes the English common law, which Burke would have absorbed at Middle Temple.[30] Second, his legal studies gave him detailed appreciation of the British constitution, another great theme of his later political thinking. Third, during his time at Middle Temple Burke may have developed his penchant for extracting principles from the play of circumstances. Burke's own character appears in his later description of the legally educated American colonial leaders who "anticipate the evil and judge of the pressure of the grievance by the badness of the principle" and who "augur misgovernment at a distance; and snuff the approach of tyranny in every tainted breeze."[31] Finally, Burke's legal studies provided him with experience from which he could develop his opinions about the nature and purpose of law in a nation and an empire.

With the publication of *A Vindication of Natural Society* (1756) and *A Philosophical Inquiry into the Origin of Our Ideas of the Sublime and Beautiful* (1757), Burke achieved success and recognition.[32] For our purposes, *Vindication* and *Philosophical Inquiry* stand out as examples of the way in which Burke's thought was developing. In both works, Burke exhibited his skepticism about the power of human reason in shaping human experience. Such skepticism plays a central role in Burke's approach to political theory and practice.

On the heels of *Philosophical Inquiry,* Burke began two other projects. First, he contracted to write an *Abridgment of English History,* declaring that he would adhere to the historical approach of Montesquieu.[33] In *Abridgment* Burke used history not only to narrate but also to discover guiding principles. He wanted to show "that behind the complexity of events he was describing, there had been a steadfast love of liberty in the nation, which had been a unifying force, moulding in its own fashion not only incidental events, but also the character and institutions of the nation."[34] For Burke, history was not a parade of horrors; it was instead the crucible of a people's political, moral, and spiritual essence.

The second project Burke undertook in 1758 was editing the *Annual Register,* which reviewed the year's major political, literary, and social events.[35] Interest in such a publication directly related to England's participation in the Seven Years' War (1756–1763) with France over control of Canada. According to Osborn, "Pitt's stirring appeal to the patriotism of his countrymen and his spectacular success in the conduct of the war caused the average Englishman to express a desire to understand more clearly the significance of events as far as they concerned England's imperial affairs."[36] Britain was entering a new era of international power, and Burke, sensitive to issues of empire and domestic politics, decided to play a role in educating the public about Britain's contemporary affairs.[37]

Not long after he became editor of the *Annual Register,* Burke took his first steps in the political world in 1759 as assistant to William Hamilton, member of Parliament (MP) for Pontefract in Yorkshire. It is not clear if Burke's employment by Hamilton marked a change of direction for Burke's career. Indeed, some evidence indicates that he still wanted to be a man of letters. Horace Walpole wrote in 1761 that "young Mr Burk . . . thinks there is nothing so charming as writers and to be one."[38] Further, the eventual break with Hamilton in 1765 came after he accused Burke of unkindness in rejecting his offer of more permanent employment, a prospect Burke found intolerable for a "gentleman, a freeman, a man of education, and one pretending to literature."[39] Other evidence, however, suggests that a passion for the political was overtaking Burke's literary ambition. Why, after all, would a man who had won the praise of such leading lights as Adam Smith, David Garrick, Joshua Reynolds, and Samuel Johnson toil for nearly six years as a personal assistant to an MP? Moreover, Burke angled for a more substantial political post not long after Hamilton retained his services: In 1759 he attempted to solicit the influence of Elizabeth Montagu with the Elder Pitt in relation to Burke's application for the consulship in Madrid.[40]

Burke's break with Hamilton in 1765 left him bitter and frustrated: "[S]ix of the best years of my life he took from me every pursuit of literary reputation or of improvement of my fortune. . . . In all this time you may easily conceive how much I felt at seeing myself left behind by almost all my contemporaries."[41] His efforts at securing alternative employment foundered.[42] Burke was at this time thirty-six, and nearly ten years had passed since he had published the works that brought him recognition. At this personal crossroads, he searched for an opportunity to satisfy his talents and ambitions. As Macpherson put it, "His future seemed gloomy, but his merits were not unknown."[43]

Burke's Parliamentary Career

In 1765 King George III dissolved the administration led by George Grenville and asked Lord Rockingham to form a new government. Rockingham needed a reliable and skilled personal secretary. Upon advice from parliamentary supporters Lord Cavendish and William Fitzherbert, he hired Burke. Quick on the heels of becoming private secretary to the prime minister, the Whig magnate Lord Verney returned Burke as MP for Wendover in Buckinghamshire. His initial speech to Parliament in January 1766 brought him admiration from fellow MPs and society figures.

Burke's successful start as an MP was fitting for a man whose involvement in the major issues facing Britain at home and abroad would permeate political and parliamentary history for more than thirty years. In order to organize Burke's parliamentary career as it relates to his perspective on international relations, we concentrate on four issues: Ireland, America, India, and the French Revolution.

Irish Policy: Catholicism and Trade

Ireland constituted one of Burke's lasting concerns throughout his public life. It is a measure of the man that he "wished to alleviate the condition of his countrymen" even at the risk of political credibility and, at one point, life and limb.[44] Nevertheless, his efforts should not be considered as blind love for his native land. He proceeded on Irish policy within a framework that represented his perspective on imperial policy: toleration of the colony's traditions, customs, and culture; recognition of empire as a unity of purpose and interest; the importance of imperial free trade; the effect on English liberties of imperial activity; and the military and strategic dangers lurking in disgruntled colonies.

The concern Burke had demonstrated at Trinity College about British rule in Ireland continued as his political career developed. Burke's time with Hamilton allowed him to focus again on Ireland. Hamilton was appointed chief secretary to Lord Halifax, the lord lieutenant in Ireland; so Burke accompanied Hamilton to Dublin from 1761 to 1762 and again between 1763 and 1764. During this time Burke drafted some fragments on the impact of anti-Catholic legislation in Ireland, which were published after his death under the title *Tracts Relating to Popery Laws*.[45] After outlining the nature of British rule in Ireland, Burke declared that this "system . . . is unjust, impolitick, and inefficacious; that it has the most unhappy influence on the prosperity, the morals, and the safety of that country."[46] Burke objected to the popery laws because they were wrong in their "erroneous principle": They were laws "against the majority of the people" that represent "not particular injustice, but general oppression."[47] The British nation's love of liberty that Burke discerned in *Abridgment* paled against British oppression in Ireland. Burke was defiant: The British "have no right to make a Law prejudicial to the whole community."[48]

One reason for the harsh anti-Catholic laws was Britain's fear that Ireland, dangerously proximate to Britain, would serve as a springboard for renewed efforts by Catholic absolutists to strangle British liberties. Such realpolitik reasoning left Burke cold and indignant: "No arguments of policy, reason of State, or preservation of the Constitution, can be pleaded in favour of such a practice."[49] He subjected British foreign policy in Ireland to an exacting standard: "the principle of a superior Law . . . the will of Him who gave us our nature, and in giving impressed an invariable Law upon it."[50]

This appeal to divine principle suggests that Burke's attitude to empire encompasses not only self-interest and political prudence but also a transcendent morality. And the morality that Burke hinted at in the *Tracts* is one that cannot be confined by particular divisions in Christianity. He dismissed the British excuse that it was proper to force Catholics to realize the errors of their religion and conform to the Protestant faith because the Englishman's "pretending to determine . . . the happiness of another" and "claiming a right to use what means he thinks proper in order to bring him to a sense of it" is "the ordinary and trite sophism of oppression."[51] Burke instead referred to "our common Christianity," thus invoking a set of moral values and heritage that should unite Christian nations rather than lead one to oppress another.[52]

Burke's first significant Irish activity after he left Hamilton's service came in 1773, when he objected to a proposal to grant the Dublin parliament power to tax absentee British landlords. In a letter to the Irish MP Sir Charles Bingham, Burke spelled out his position.[53] Burke opposed the tax because he saw empire as a unity, as a single society rather than a set of disparate societies connected by the tenuous bonds of submission and domination.[54] Proponents of the tax claimed that absentee landlords drained away Ireland's wealth for enjoyment in Britain. Burke did not quarrel with the observation that money flowed from the colonies to "the metropolis"; in fact, he said this was natural and unavoidable.[55] Burke objected to thinking about the British Empire in any way that treated Britain like "a foreign country."[56] He opposed the tax because it was "a renunciation . . . of the principle of *common naturalization*, which runs through this whole empire" and an attack on "the union of the whole Empire."[57] Burke's emphasis on the common texture of imperial society must be considered in relation to his other views on imperial policy. If Ireland was not to view Britain as "a foreign country," then neither should Britain oppress Ireland. But as Burke saw it, oppression is exactly what the British meted out to the Irish.

Burke returned to Irish policy in the late 1770s, when he sought to loosen restrictions on Irish trade and mitigate the discrimination against Catholics. In 1778 Lord North's administration moved to preempt any Irish version of the American rebellion by proposing bills to ease restrictions on Irish trade. Burke, who now represented Bristol in Parliament, supported the liberalization of Irish trade despite opposition by powerful Bristol merchants. Although friends began to worry about his political prospects in Bristol, Burke never wavered. He was being true to his word, for he had told his new Bristol constituents after his election in 1774 that "[y]our Representative owes you, not his industry only, but his judgement; and he betrays, instead of serving you, if he sacrifices it to your opinion."[58] As with his opposition to the absentee landlord tax, Burke built his support for liberalizing Irish trade on some fundamental principles, most important his belief in imperial free trade.

Burke was a keen student of political economy. In a speech before the 1774 Bristol parliamentary election, Burke told his audience that commerce was a principal source of British power and "has ever been a very particular and a very favourite object of my study."[59] Burke was so conversant in matters of political economy that the leading political economist of the age, Adam Smith, once declared that Burke was the only man who on his own endeavors thought about economic matters exactly as he did.[60] It comes as no surprise, then, to find Burke supporting measures on Irish trade and even urging further liberalization two years after the publication of Smith's *Wealth of Nations* (1776).

In his support for the relief of Irish trade, Burke emphasized again the importance of viewing the empire as a single entity, and he coupled his notion of the British imperial society with a strong belief in the mutual benefits to be gained from a more liberal trading regime. In letters to Bristol constituents, Burke wrote:

Indeed, Sir, England and Ireland may flourish together. The world is large enough for us both. Let it be our care not to make ourselves too little for it. . . . I know, that it is but too natural for us to see our own *certain* ruin, in the *possible* prosperity of other people. It is hard to persuade us, that every thing which is *got* by another is not *taken* from ourselves. . . . Trade is not a limited thing; as if the objects of mutual demand and consumption could not stretch beyond the bounds of our Jealousies.[61]

The second effort Burke made for Ireland in the late 1770s was his continuing opposition to the harsh anti-Catholic laws. Burke had remained firm in his call for religious toleration in Ireland since the *Tracts*. His belief in religious toleration drew on his views of religion as the basis of civil society and the value to a society in the preservation of ancient and honored religious tradition. Such toleration, of course, meant that the British Empire would not be homogeneous in religious practices; Burke, however, saw graver threats to the unity of the empire if the British attempted to destroy something fundamental to the moral, political, and economic stability of colonial regions. His pleas for religious toleration, therefore, went beyond compassion for suffering Catholics to address the cohesion of British imperial society.

For these views, Burke and his fellow Whigs became targets of a Protestant-inspired mob that rioted throughout London in June 1780. The violence had been set off by Sir George Savile's act to repeal a 1699 statute that prohibited Catholics from bequeathing property and banned Catholic schooling and Catholic Mass. Burke reviled the 1699 statute. After the mob destroyed Savile's house, Burke emptied his own home of its books, papers, and furniture; dismissed the soldiers guarding it; and then "spent part of the day in the street amid this wild assembly into whose hands I delivered myself informing them who I was."[62]

Bristol did not return Burke as MP in the 1780 general election largely because of his support for liberalizing Irish trade and his urging toleration of the Catholic religion. In a preelection speech at the Bristol guildhall in September 1780, Burke addressed the issues that had caused his standing in Bristol to suffer, dwelling on Irish trade and relief of Irish Catholics.[63] Burke's condemnation of British policy and attitudes toward Ireland was sweeping, and the speech reflects some of the personal anguish Burke felt because of the religious stress in his family and upbringing.[64]

After the unhappy events at Bristol, Lord Rockingham arranged for Burke to be returned to Westminster as MP for Malton. Two years later, after the British debacle in America, Parliament granted many of the demands being made by Protestant leaders in the Dublin parliament, which reduced British control over Irish legislation and the judiciary. Burke wrote to the duke of Portland, then lord lieutenant, that "[e]very thing asked or even hinted at from Ireland has been yielded in the fullest measure and with the compleatest unanimity. . . . If things are prudently managed, Ireland will become a great country by degrees."[65] Ayling, however, noted that Burke's support for the Irish measures of 1782 was "lukewarm . . . and he accepted only with misgivings the concessions to the Irish."[66] What could explain this attitude?

Burke might have been uneasy about the measures for two reasons. For one, Parliament granted concessions to Ireland out of fear and weakness following the loss of America. Imperial misgovernment, as Burke had long believed, was leading to imperial disintegration.

The "union" of the empire was fraying badly. America was now "a foreign country," and the new measures gave Ireland more political independence than it had enjoyed for a very long time. Burke may have speculated that the concessions signaled the beginning of Ireland's withdrawal from the imperial society. Second, the measures of 1782 had done nothing to ameliorate the sufferings of the Irish Catholics. The reforms solidified the power of the "Protestant ascendancy" and provided no abatement of religious persecution.[67] Ireland was drifting from the imperial society with all the evils bequeathed by British oppression. Burke might have considered this the worst of all possible circumstances for his native country.

But the concessions did not settle Irish affairs. Early in his ministry, William Pitt "prepared in 1785 an elaborate plan, set out in commercial propositions, for putting Anglo-Irish economic relations on a satisfactory basis."[68] Pitt's plan contained an explicit bargain: Trade between Britain and Ireland would be liberalized if Ireland agreed to make contributions to the defense of the empire. Burke strongly opposed Pitt's commercial proposals in Parliament. Citing Burke's penchant for free trade and desire to have Ireland within the empire, McDowell attributed his opposition to his membership in "a party which was recently smarting under its recent loss of office and severe defeat at the polls."[69] McDowell claimed that Burke "attacked in misleading detail the provisions relating to the defense contribution, and . . . dwelt on the danger of exposing British industry to competition."[70] In short, McDowell portrayed Burke as a protectionist politico playing loose with the facts.

Burke's opposition to Pitt's commercial propositions, however, was consistent with his perspective on the imperial society. As further elaborated in Chapter 3, Burke did not reflexively support the principle of free trade. For him, political context—not abstract principle—was crucial. Similar to his misgivings about the Irish reforms of 1782, Burke had concerns that liberalizing Irish trade would weaken the links of the imperial society by making Ireland a "foreign country." Burke's comments in his May 1785 *Speech on Irish Commercial Propositions* about the effect of Pitt's proposals on manufacturing in Britain should be interpreted in light of his vision of empire.[71] Burke saw Britain and Ireland as parts of a greater whole, each with its role to play.[72] He stated that Britain should bear the responsibility for outfitting fleets for imperial defense and that "it should be the business of Ireland to assist her in another way; and it was astonishing how much the latter might do by pursuing a rigid plan of economy."[73] As indicated earlier, Burke worked to liberalize those aspects of Irish trade that would allow Ireland to prosper within the imperial society.

Second, Burke opposed the commercial propositions because they were conditional: liberalized trade in return for contributions to imperial defense.[74] Burke compared Pitt's policy to the tragic effort to exact revenue for imperial defense in America.[75] Burke puts the issue of imperial defense in perspective; England alone, he said,

> must bear the weight and burden of empire; she alone must pour out the ocean of wealth necessary for the defense of it; Ireland and other parts might empty their little urns to swell the tide; they might wield their little puny tridents; but the great trident that was to move the world, must be grasped by England alone and dearly it cost her to hold it.[76]

Burke believed that the subordinate parts of the imperial society would contribute more to the security of the empire if given the opportunity to prosper economically. Such contributions were indirect, unlike the attempts to raise revenue in America and Ireland, but

in Burke's mind more powerful because they arose from the deepening of common interests within the empire.

In Burke's last phase of Irish endeavors, he warned about the danger posed to disgruntled colonies by hostile states and forces in the international system. In 1790 Thomas
Hussey solicited Burke's support in winning Catholics the right to vote in Ireland. Hussey
mentioned a danger that had already registered in Burke's mind: The disaffected Catholic
majority in Ireland might emulate the French Revolution unless the burdens of British oppression were eased further. Burke dispatched his son, Richard, to act as his agent in working with the Catholic Committee in Dublin. In 1792 Burke wrote a lengthy letter to Sir
Hercules Langrishe, an Irish MP.[77] In this letter, intended for general publication, Burke
urged immediate enfranchisement for Catholics.

Characteristically, Burke's arguments work at different levels. Burke appealed to the
principles taught by history: "[N]o nation in the world has ever been known to exclude so
great a body of men (not born slaves) from the civil state, and all the benefits of the constitution."[78] He appealed to the "union" of the imperial society: "If they are not satisfied,
you have two millions of subjects in your bosom, full of uneasiness . . . because you will
not suffer them to enjoy the ancient, fundamental, tried advantages of a British constitution."[79] He argued against the dangers of intolerance and arrogance: "It is impossible that
such a state of things . . . must not produce alienation on one side, and pride and insolence on the other."[80] And Burke warned of the prospect of colonial discontent with the
"French disease" in the air:

> If two parts Catholic be driven into a close confederacy with half the third part of Protestants,
> with a view to a change in the constitution in church or state, or both; and you rest the whole
> of their security on a handful of gentlemen, clergy, and their dependents; compute the
> strength *you have in Ireland,* to oppose to grounded discontent; to capricious innovation; to
> blind popular fury, and to ambitious turbulent intrigue.[81]

Burke's efforts on behalf of the Catholics had by 1792 borne no fruit in Dublin or London. With the outbreak of war between France and Britain in 1792, however, the stature
of Burke's views—not only on France but also on Ireland rose. Burke used his influence
with the Pitt ministry to promote new measures for the emancipation of Irish Catholics.
In 1793 the Catholic Relief Act lifted most of the remaining disabilities on Catholics, except the right to sit in the Irish Parliament.[82] Although Burke had long urged this result,
he had no illusions about the healing power of this measure, which was taken with a fearful eye toward France. British policy in Ireland now had to contend with an increasingly
restless Catholic majority, Protestant minority, and the infectious Jacobin virus. The bitterness engendered by British oppression, the misgovernment by Irish Protestants, and the
radicalism of some Irish Catholics converged to spell travail for Burke's native land. As first
grief at his brother's and son's deaths and then sickness racked Burke's body and mind after
1794, Ireland's fate became part of the sorrow that accompanied him to his grave. In late
1794, when Pitt appointed as viceroy of Ireland Earl Fitzwilliam, over whom Burke held
great sway on Irish affairs, it seemed as if Burke's influence on Irish policy had reached its
peak. Burke hoped to wield that influence to dismantle the remaining prohibition on
Catholics sitting in the Irish Parliament. Burke and Fitzwilliam, however, soon discovered

that Pitt "never had any intention of allowing Fitzwilliam any scope in Ireland, to walk his Burkean way."[83] When Pitt recalled Fitzwilliam in February 1795, Burke's hopes for Ireland received another devastating blow.[84]

Fitzwilliam's recall stirred the passions of the already angry Catholic majority in Ireland. Rebellious feeling was in the air, aggravated by the example of the French Revolution. Burke had long feared this consequence of imperial misgovernment. He had throughout his public career tried to build a society between the British and Irish on the basis of the British constitution. As he became a "helpless spectator" in Irish affairs, Burke expressed in a letter to Thomas Hussey in late 1796 sympathy with the Irish Catholic rebels and exasperation at the continuance of British oppression.[85] Burke distinguished the rebellious passions of the Irish Catholics, which were based on "Penury and irritation, from scorned loyalty, and rejected Allegiance," from "Jacobinism, which is Speculative in its Origin, and which arises from Wantonness and fullness of bread."[86] The confluence of Irish Catholic defiance, which Burke thought justifiable, and French Jacobinism, which he loathed, caused him torment.[87] Revolutionary France was a menace to the commonwealth of Europe, Catholic rebels in Ireland were a threat to the imperial society, and British fear of Jacobinism in Ireland was a source of continued oppression for the people of his native land.[88] In his final days, Burke could see for Ireland "only a bitter future, and to the end it caused him angry grief."[89]

America: English Civil War

A second major international issue that Burke focused on during his parliamentary career was British policy toward the American colonies. His ideas on the proper functioning of the British imperial society strongly appear in his thinking on America. Burke's thoughts on British imperial policy toward America, however, differ somewhat from those on Irish policy. American affairs did not involve the bloody history of English conquest and oppression of a Catholic people. Burke's praise for the British constitution and his attempts to include the Catholic Irish within its principles and institutions always remained in tension with his disgust at the oppression of Irish Catholics. The American colonies, in contrast, were English and Protestant. The societal ties between Britain and America were so organic and direct that Burke viewed violent struggle between the home country and its American colonies as nothing less than civil war between Englishmen.

Burke's interest in the American colonies predates his parliamentary career. Although Burke never visited America, he displayed a keen interest in it during the 1750s. Apparently, Burke upset his father by proposing to go to America for a visit during his studies at Middle Temple.[90] After publication of *Vindication* and *Philosophical Inquiry*, Burke wrote to his childhood friend Richard Shackleton in 1757 of his desire "shortly, please God, to be in America."[91] That Burke would wish to leave his newly won literary recognition for a taste of colonial life seems curious. He may have formed this desire during his collaboration with his close friend William Burke on the publication of *Account of the European Settlements in America* (1757).[92]

As private secretary to the prime minister Lord Rockingham and as a new MP, Burke quickly put to use his knowledge of the American situation.[93] Rockingham's short administration (1765–1766) repealed the Stamp Act and liberalized trade opportunities for the colonies. As Burke's *Short Account of a Late Short Administration* (1766) makes clear, he considered both acts to be achievements, because the repeal of the Stamp Act composed the "Distractions of the *British* Empire" and the liberalization of trade with America set America "free from injudicious and ruinous Impositions" and extended its commerce "with foreign Countries."[94] Both policies also fit within Burke's overall conception of how the British imperial society should function.

Parliament imposed the Stamp Act in 1765 on the grounds that the colonists "should contribute towards the military defence of an Empire from which they derived safety and benefit."[95] The Seven Years' War with France enlarged the British Empire and Britain's financial debts. War and imperial expansion, however, encouraged English politicians to stray from one of the ancient principles of the British constitution: no taxation without representation. Burke's opposition to the Stamp Act and to all subsequent schemes for raising revenue from America rested on his fundamental attachment to the wisdom of following the British constitution in imperial policy, a belief evident when he urged Britain to allow the Irish "to enjoy the ancient, fundamental, tried advantages of a British constitution."[96] In his writings on America, this theme received major emphasis.

Burke also opposed the Stamp Act because it contravened a historical principle embedded in imperial relations with America: Britain had always asserted (and the Americans acknowledged) its right to regulate American trade, but never—until the mid-1760s—had Parliament sought to raise revenue in America.[97] The Stamp Act, in Burke's eyes, represented a failure of British politicians to ground imperial policy in a thorough understanding of British constitutional principles and the valuable lessons of historical experience. Burke conceded Britain's abstract right to tax the colonies found in the Declaratory Act of 1766, but he was convinced of the political folly of bringing that abstraction to life.

As for easing the commercial regulations on the American colonies, Burke again moved within his belief of the mutual benefits to be gained from a freer trade within the imperial society. Burke knew that Britain had long regulated American trade, and he did not question its right to do so. What Burke questioned was "the mischief and folly of a plan of indiscriminate restraint."[98] He believed that heavy regulation of American trade would negatively affect British commercial power: "Without some such scheme of enlargement, it was obvious that any benefit we could expect from these colonies must be extremely limited."[99] Burke's support for liberalizing American trade in 1766 shows his adherence to Montesquieu's belief in the beneficial economic, social, and political consequences of the "spirit of commerce."[100] As Montesquieu believed that commerce contributed to more peaceful relations between states, so Burke saw commerce as a way to strengthen the stability and prosperity of the imperial society. Burke partook of the Enlightenment belief in the virtues of commerce. Characteristically, he did not embrace the abstract principle but instead sought evidence in British imperial history to justify his advocacy of the practical principle of freer trade within the empire.

The American policy of the short Rockingham administration, however, did not guide subsequent ministries. The year after the fall of the Rockingham ministry, Lord Chatham's government brought the abstraction of the Declaratory Act to life by imposing duties on goods imported into America.[101] Continued unrest in America over such imperial taxation spawned another round of British hand-wringing in 1769 when Parliament repealed five of the six duties imposed in 1767. The remaining duty applied to tea. And it was this duty, augmented by the Tea Act of 1773, that provoked the Boston Tea Party of 1773 and the American colonial tea embargo. When Burke rose in the House of Commons to deliver his famous *Speech on American Taxation* (1774), he described the time since the repeal of the Stamp Act as nine years during which "we have been lashed round and round this miserable circle of occasional arguments and temporary expedients. I am sure our heads must turn and our stomachs nauseate with them. . . . [B]ut obstinacy is not yet conquered."[102]

Burke's *Speech on American Taxation* combined historical and political analysis in criticizing the "woeful variety of schemes" adopted to tax Americans. His historical narrative demonstrated the long-standing British practice toward America of regulating trade but not seeking tax revenues. Burke saw the taxation fetish of many parliamentarians as foolish flirtation with abstract questions of legal right. *American Taxation* illustrates his procedural conservatism, which describes the proper disposition and attitude of statesmen toward the making of foreign policy.[103] Burke urged his fellow MPs to recover "your old, your strong, your tenable position" and to use "the ancient policy and practice of the empire, as a rampart against the speculations of innovators . . . and you will stand on great, manly, and sure ground."[104] Burke continued:

> Again, and again, revert to your old principles—seek peace and ensue it—leave America . . . to tax herself. I am not here going into the distinctions of rights. . . . I do not enter into these metaphysical distinctions; I hate the very sound of them. Leave the Americans as they antiently stood, and these distinctions, born of our unhappy contest, will die along with it. They, and we, and their and our ancestors, have been happy under that system.[105]

Burke further pursued the abstract question of the right of Parliament to tax the American colonies, expounding his "idea of the constitution of the British Empire."[106] Since he played a major role in the passage of the Declaratory Act of 1766, Burke needed to make clear his position on the respective rights and privileges of Parliament and the American colonies. Burke argued that Parliament had an "*imperial character*" in which it "superintends all the several inferior legislatures, and guides, and controls them all without annihilating any."[107] Parliament had "to coerce the negligent, to restrain the violent, and to aid the weak and deficient, by the over-ruling plenitude of her power."[108] In order to fulfill its imperial role, Parliament's "powers must be boundless."[109] But this conception of "boundless" power had to be seen within the context of empire as a society, not as a relationship of domination and submission. Thus, Parliament "is never to intrude into the place of the others, whilst they are equal to the common ends of their institution."[110] Under this conception, Burke saw "the imperial rights of Great Britain, and the privileges which the Colonists ought to enjoy under these rights, to be just the most reconcileable things in the world."[111]

In *American Taxation* Burke also displayed an awareness of the interdependence of imperial policy. He observed that the American tea embargo threatened to destroy the strategy devised in 1773 to save the East India Company from financial collapse. As a way for the company to shore up its finances, Parliament allowed it to export tea to America without paying duties. The American embargo on tea left, in Burke's words, "Ten Millions of pounds of this commodity . . . locked up by the operation of an injudicious Tax, and rotting in the warehouses of the Company."[112] The strategy of using the American market to allow the East India Company to crawl out of its own financial morass was in serious trouble, meaning that Parliament might have to bear the entire burden of the company's debt. "It is through the American trade of Tea," Burke noted, "that your East India conquests are to be prevented from crushing you with their burthen."[113] Misgovernment in one part of the empire detrimentally affected efforts in another part. Burke commented bitterly: "It is the same folly that has lost you at once the benefit of the West and of the East."[114]

Burke's efforts to put the ship of imperial society on an even keel, however, were not keeping pace with the speed of events in America or Britain. When Burke gave his *Speech on American Taxation,* Parliament had already passed punitive measures against Boston and the colony of Massachusetts. Such legislation stoked the fires of American unity; more and more the Americans began to feel like and want to be "a foreign country." Yet Burke remained determined to prevent a rupture. In March 1775 Burke gave one of his most famous speeches, *Speech on Conciliation with America,* in which he clearly stated the difficulty of the task before the nation: "To restore order and repose to an Empire so great and so distracted as ours, is, merely in the attempt, an undertaking that would ennoble the flights of the highest genius, and obtain pardon for the efforts of the meanest understanding."[115]

Burke proposed "Peace . . . simple Peace."[116] He claimed that his plan was not "new and captivating" and rested on the "idea of conciliation."[117] Burke told the House of Commons that Britain had to offer concessions to the colonials to restore the *"former unsuspecting confidence of the Colonies in the Mother Country."*[118] He then reminded his colleagues about the importance of America to Britain's commercial and political power. This importance, he admitted, was not lost on many Englishmen, who believed America was "an object well worth fighting for."[119] For his part, Burke rejected the use of force to preserve the imperial society. Burke thought force a "feeble instrument" for the task at hand because its effects were temporary ("a nation is not governed, which is perpetually to be conquered"), uncertain ("[t]error is not always the effect of force; and an armament is not a victory"), counterproductive ("[t]he thing you fought for is . . . depreciated, sunk, wasted, and consumed in the contest"), and historically untested ("we have no sort of *experience* in favour of force as an instrument in the rule of our Colonies").[120] To reinforce the folly of resorting to force, Burke provided an analysis of the *"Temper and Character"* of the Americans, who as descendants of free Englishmen had developed into an energetic people in which "a fierce spirit of Liberty" had grown up.[121] Burke sensed the power of the American spirit and rejected as "desperate" notions of changing or breaking this spirit.[122]

The opening of *Conciliation* reads like a blunt piece of realism as Burke emphasized Britain's self-interest in holding onto America while warning of the tremendous obstacles of trying to do so by force. Burke changed the tone of his argument as he presented his vision of the unity of the British imperial society. He first criticized false notions about the imperial relationship between the "common head" and the "subordinate parts."[123] Burke "can scarcely conceive any thing more compleatly imprudent, than for the Head of the Empire to insist, that, if any privilege is pleaded against his will, or his acts, that his whole authority is denied; instantly to proclaim rebellion, to beat to arms, and to put the offending provinces under the ban."[124] Empire was a more complicated relationship than simple authority and subservience, particularly when it involved Englishmen on both sides. As Burke noted, the Americans first complaint was "that they have not the characteristic Mark and Seal of British Freedom. . . . [T]hey are taxed in a Parliament, in which they are not represented."[125] Burke again condemned the sterility of abstract thinking about the imperial relationship: "The question with me is, not whether you have a right to render your people miserable; but whether it is not your interest to make them happy?"[126]

As with Irish policy, Burke urged "the absolute necessity of keeping up the concord of this empire by a Unity of Spirit, though in a diversity of operations."[127] For Burke, the unity of spirit for the British imperial society found its strength and purpose in "the principles of Freedom."[128] The remedy for the American distemper, he argued, could be found where English freedoms were enshrined: the British constitution. "My idea," Burke announced, "is *to admit the people of our Colonies into an interest in the constitution.*"[129] He provided historical precedent for this idea in the history of English expansion in the British isles: "English authority and English liberties had exactly the same boundaries."[130]

Burke proposed the same unity of power and liberty in the imperial ties between Britain and America. To the procedural conservatism in *Taxation* and the stark realism at the beginning of *Conciliation,* Burke added a substantive vision of an imperial society based on liberty:

> My hold of the Colonies is in the close affection which grows from common names, from kindred blood, from similar privileges, and equal protection. These are ties which, though light as air, are as strong as links of iron. . . . As long as you have the wisdom to keep the sovereign authority of this country as the sanctuary of liberty, the sacred temple consecrated to our common faith, wherever the chosen race and sons of England worship freedom, they will turn their faces towards you.[131]

Burke's eloquence and vision could not slow the rapid descent in the relations between Britain and America. Reflecting on the news of Bunker Hill, Burke in an August 1775 letter expressed his sense that defeat or victory in America meant tragedy for Britain.[132] Burke greeted the Declaration of Independence in July 1776 with a similar sense of gloom, as he beheld the spectacle of fellow Englishmen unfurling the bloody banners of civil war.[133] In 1777 Burke called this the "fatal Aera" when "British blood was spilld by British hands."[134]

Burke's later writings on America, particularly his *Letter to the Sheriffs of Bristol* (1777), contain another theme in his international thinking: the impact on the British constitution of imperial misgovernment and oppressive behavior abroad. Burke denounced in *Address to the King* (1777) and *Letter to the Sheriffs of Bristol* the government's employment of German mercenaries and encouragement of Indian attacks on the rebellious Americans.[135] Such acts were symptoms of what Burke sensed would be a more deadly effect of the civil war. "Liberty," Burke wrote in *Letter to the Sheriffs of Bristol,* "is in danger of being made unpopular to Englishmen."[136] The great virtues of the British constitution and the British people that Burke admired seemed potential victims of the American war.[137] Although the final defeat of British forces was still to come, by 1778 Burke's "dream of a harmonious British empire linked rather than divided by the Atlantic" was completely blown away.[138]

In 1782, after the 1781 British defeat at Yorktown, Lord Rockingham, led by Burke, made American independence a precondition of forming a new administration to replace

Lord North's ministry.[139] Ironically, the man who had labored so hard to prevent the fragmentation of the British Empire forced George III to recognize American independence.[140] For Burke, preserving empire at all costs was not the ultimate objective. His notion of the imperial society rested on deeper political principles at the heart of the British constitution—principles that Burke believed British imperial policy had debased. Burke sought to preserve Britain's relationship with America not for the sake of empire itself but rather because he wanted empire to embody a community sharing the fruits of freedom. Although he tried to reconcile the ideas of empire and freedom, when British policy forced a choice between those ideas, Burke supported freedom.

India: The Path to the Hastings Impeachment

At the end of his political career, Burke considered his efforts on behalf of India to be his most important: "Let my endeavours to save the Nation from that Shame and guilt, be my monument; The only one I ever will have. Let every thing I have done, said, or written be forgotten but this."[141] Burke spent more time and energy on India than any other issue he addressed in Parliament. As a result, these efforts constitute a major aspect of his international political perspective, yet they "have been relatively ignored by students of his political thought."[142]

The early part of Burke's life and parliamentary career reveals no burning interest in British activities in India. In fact, the contrast between Burke's speeches on the East India Company in the late 1760s and early 1770s and his later pursuit of Warren Hastings, governor-general of Bengal, in the 1780s is dramatic. Burke's path to the Hastings impeachment requires careful analysis to avoid simplistic conclusions about the transformation in his thought on India. His perspectives on India contain the full richness and complexity of his overall political and moral thought. In Burke's "great mine," India is one of the richest veins.

The extent of Burke's knowledge about India before he entered Parliament in 1765 is unclear. In a speech in 1773, he admitted that he felt no mastery on the subject.[143] But Burke was not completely ignorant of India when he entered Parliament. According to Marshall, Burke "[f]rom early in his life . . . appears to have been an avid reader of travel accounts."[144] Further, shortly after becoming an MP, he was involved with his brother Richard Burke and close friend William Burke in "a highly ambitious and initially successful speculation in East India stock."[145]

Between 1767 and 1773, government and Parliament faced growing concerns about alleged misgovernment, financial difficulties, and corruption in the East India Company. During this period, Burke opposed reform of the East India Company. When Lord Clive faced investigation by a select parliamentary committee and then a full Commons debate on East India Company activities in 1773, Burke apparently was happy that Clive won the showdown.[146] Similarly, Burke attacked all East India Company reform bills between 1767 and 1774. He did so once, in the words of the *General Evening Post,* "with a vehemence uncommon amongst our modern Orators."[147] Burke's opposition to East India Company reform, therefore, was neither passive nor timid.

Dissecting the motives behind Burke's opposition is a complicated matter. A standard interpretation is that he believed in the East India Company's imperial activities and saw reform proposals only through the prism of domestic, partisan politics.[148] In February 1769 Burke referred to the Indian empire by saying that the "orient sun never laid more glorious expectations before us" and that "Europe will envy, the East will envy: I hope we shall remain an envied People."[149] He also praised the East India Company as "a great, a glorious Company."[150] In fact, in June 1773 Burke stated that the company had not been improperly managed.[151]

Evidence that Burke saw the East India Company as a domestic political issue also abounds in his speeches and letters of this time. As Langford wrote, "Indian problems, so far as he was concerned with them at this time, were seen primarily as additional symptoms of the constitutional disease at home."[152] Burke feared that the reform proposals were pretexts for the Crown and the government to gain control of the wealth and patronage opportunities in the growing Indian empire.[153] Such fears are echoed in Burke's major political writings of this period, *Observations on a Late State of the Nation* (1769) and *Thoughts on the Present Discontents* (1770), in which he developed his theory of party and argued the importance of party in the struggle against the Crown's attempts to encroach on the power and independence of Parliament.[154]

Although this standard explanation of Burke's opposition to East India Company reform between 1767 and 1774 does have merit, other considerations deserve exploration. A theme in Burke's speeches of this period relates to issues of political economy.[155] In his earliest recorded speech on India, delivered in May 1767, Burke attacked Lord Chatham's East India Dividend Bill because it represented governmental interference in commercial affairs.[156] Burke's free market predilections shone forth in this speech, as he argued that the bill threatened "to make a most important Revolution indeed in the whole Policy of this Country with regard to its Laws[,] its Commerce and its Credit" because it restricted "by a positive arbitrary Regulation the enjoyment of the profits which should be made in Commerce" and did so by taking profit from the East India Company, even though "it sinned against no *rule* prescribed *by Law.*"[157] Burke likewise had little time for the assertion that regulation was needed to prevent falls in East India Company stock prices. In his February 1769 *Speech on East India Settlement,* Burke told East India Company shareholders to "profit from your prosperity, and bear like men your adversity."[158] In the December 1772 *Speech on East India Restraining Bill,* Burke blamed government interference for bankrupting the company through "plunder" and "extorting Money."[159] Sentiments such as these cast Burke "as a friend of the company" in the early 1770s.[160]

Another theme in Burke's speeches at the time is the question of rights. As indicated by his opposition to government regulation of the East India Company, Burke defended "chartered, propertied rights against the incursions of a corrupt and avaricious government."[161] In his April 1773 *Speech on North's East India Resolutions,* Burke attacked the government's claim that it had a right to the territories acquired by the East India Company. In keeping with his distaste for abstract rights, Burke argued that a "*right* implied something settled, and established by certain known rules and maxims; it implied, in short, a *legal decision;* for to talk of a right where no legal decision had been obtained, was to talk of a non-entity."[162] Burke also claimed that the government's alleged right was imaginary because it was not based on any "maxim of law or equity."[163] He thus condemned the proposed resolutions as impolitic, unwise, "and entirely repugnant to the letter as well as the spirit of the laws, the liberties, and the constitution of this country."[164]

For Burke, the East India Company reforms threatened not only the domestic political balance of power but also the principles of the British constitution.

Burke's praise for the East India Company and his opposition to reform seem to contradict his sensitive perspective on empire developed in his Irish and American writings. The whole story, however, is yet to be told. In the same speech in which he extolled the "glorious expectations" of empire in India and the "great, glorious Company," he made a more sober and ambiguous statement: "You are plunged into Empire in the east. You have formed a great body of power, you must abide by the consequence."[165] Darker concerns shape the sentiment in these words. His *Speech on North's East India Resolutions* confirmed that Burke had such worries. He argued

> that the East India Company tied about their [the government's ministers'] necks, would, like a mill-stone, drag them down into an unfathomable abyss; that it was well if it dragged not this nation along with them, for that, for his [Burke's] part, he always had had his fears, and would now venture to prophecy his apprehensions, that this cursed Company would at last, viper, be the destruction of the country which fostered it in her bosom.[166]

Glorious expectations were now weights that could plunge Britain into the depths; the great and glorious East India Company had become a viper portending the ruin of the country. In the same speech, Burke used a theme he employed with Ireland and America: that imperialism could pose a direct threat to the spirit and constitution of the British people. He argued that the East India Company affair had already encouraged a "total want of principles . . . amongst all ranks and degrees of people" that made them "a most servile degenerate herd, destitute of capacity to distinguish, or virtue to relish, what was good."[167] Burke preferred to see the East India Company "fall to ruin about his ears, than have the *base of the English Constitution undermined, or a single pillar which contributed to the support of so excellent a structure receive the slightest fracture, or defaced in the minutest part.*"[168]

Burke's April 1773 speech suggests that his opposition to East India Company regulation was neither as complacent nor ill conceived as some have claimed.[169] Not all the strands of Burke's thought outlined above run together coherently. Perhaps he sensed this confusion. As Marshall noted, "[a]t least from the mid-1770's, he began a prolonged immersion in the copious records of the East India Company, as his papers show, taking notes of much that he read."[170] That Burke began intensive study of the India question immediately after his initial involvement (1767–1774) indicates that something about the question triggered his intellectual and moral energies. When India next appeared on the national agenda, Burke was in an entirely different frame of mind.

This new attitude first displayed itself in 1777 in the Lord Pigot affair. In 1773 the nawab of the Carnatic deposed the raja of Tanjore with the help of East India Company troops. Lord Pigot was sent to Madras in 1776 as the new governor-general with orders to restore the raja to the throne. Lord Pigot's subordinates in Madras, however, arrested him and threw him into prison after he had reinstated the raja. Those in collusion with the Madras subordinates began lobbying in London to have Tanjore returned to the nawab. William Burke acted as a London agent for the raja, and Burke himself became involved in this affair by protesting against the insubordination in Madras and the English-inspired violence against Tanjore.

In his *Speech on Restoring Lord Pigot*, delivered in May 1777, Burke explained his opposition to the previous attempts to regulate the East India Company as a case of wishing "to see the Company free from *Court influence* that it might always be under *publick Control*."[171] He admitted that the East India Company could be regulated by public law—as long as that regulation did not threaten the balance of power within the British constitutional system. To Burke the insubordination of the East India Company employees in Madras in arresting and imprisoning Lord Pigot constituted a fundamental challenge to British principles of government.[172] He addressed this theme in his American speeches, making explicit reference to the similarity of imperial problems in America and India.[173]

Burke also knew that the American rebellion and that in Madras fundamentally differed. The Americans rose up because the British government and Parliament refused to apply the wisdom of the constitution to colonials. "[I]f the people rebel," Burke said, "it may be from a sense of *grievance* and all government is subordinate to them."[174] Such a people's rebellion "*may* be right," but "the rebellion of subordinate office against the superior never can be so for they derive no authority but from him."[175] The spectacle of British subordinates overthrowing their duly appointed superior marked a dangerous turn in imperial activity. If the traditions and principles of good governance at home were questioned through private avarice in the distant imperial realms, then empire would become a rotten, corrupt endeavor. This would become one of the great themes of Burke's later pursuit of Hastings.

The Tanjore controversy allowed Burke to theorize further on the proper governance of a foreign people. An article in the November 1778 *Annual Register* condemned the invasion of Tanjore as cruel and unjust.[176] As part of the lobbying campaign for the raja of Tanjore, Burke collaborated with William Burke on a pamphlet called *Policy of Making Conquests for the Mahometans* (1779).[177] Although the pamphlet mostly engages in a duel of quotations from East India Company records between the pro- and antiraja positions, some passages touch on deeper principles. With regard to India, Burke was dealing with a part of the British Empire that was neither culturally or religiously similar nor populated by Englishmen. The vision of the imperial society he had applied to Ireland and America did not fit the circumstances of the empire in India. In *Policy of Making Conquests*, Burke took his first steps in developing principles about handling imperial power over a racially, religiously, and culturally different people.

Burke attacked the supporters of the nawab because they "confine their attention solely to Princes, and to the rights of Princes."[178] He complained that the "wretched *people* are no part of whatsoever of their consideration."[179] The crucial point in having a native government between the East India Company and the people is that such government should be "congenial to the native inhabitants, correspondent to their manners, and soothing to their prejudices."[180] Using British bayonets to force a Muslim despot on the Hindu people of Tanjore was not the kind of sensitivity to existing Indian society that Burke believed necessary for good imperial rule in India.

Burke was aware that problems would arise when a technologically superior culture came in contact with a less advanced culture. But with superiority came not only power but also responsibility. "It was our duty," Burke wrote, "in order to make some sort of compensation for the mischiefs inseparable from a foreign and commercial superiority, to keep a balance of justice and proportion in the several powers that were subordinate to us."[181] Instead, the East India Company supported the violent aggrandizement of the nawab, who merely acted to increase his own tyranny and his patronage from the British. Burke argued that "our evident duty, and our clearest interest, was to employ those [European] arts and that [European] discipline, and the power that grew out of them, to meliorate the condition of the subject and the dependent."[182]

In short, Burke believed that the East India Company had a duty to improve the lot of Indians through mutually beneficial intercourse with Britain without destroying the indigenous society. India, then, would be part not of the empire of liberty under the British constitution but of an empire of preservation and improvement.

In the *Policy of Making Conquests*, Burke called for investigation of the evils the East India Company had inflicted on Tanjore.[183] Burke became a key figure in the inquiry when in 1781 he was made a member of a parliamentary select committee charged with considering in relation to India how "the greatest Security and Advantage to this Country, and . . . the Happiness of the Native Inhabitants may best be promoted."[184] The select committee looked into the entire relationship between Britain and India and produced eleven reports between 1782 and 1783. Burke played a substantial role on the committee and authored the famous *Ninth* and *Eleventh Reports of the Select Committee*.[185]

The *Ninth Report* explained in detail "the Principles of Policy, and the Course of Conduct, by which the Natives of all Ranks and Orders have been reduced to their present State of Depression and Misery."[186] In keeping with Burke's interest in political economy, much of the *Ninth Report* discussed the economic policies and impact of the East India Company. Burke condemned both the company's own trade policies and its approach toward native trade. In his view, all the East India Company's "Regulations naturally tended to weaken, in the very original Constitution of the Company, the main Spring of the Commercial Machine, the *Principles of Profit and Loss*."[187] Burke catalogued the economic hardships meted out to native Indians in the company's policy of monopolizing "every Article of Trade, Foreign and Domestic."[188] He also analyzed the company's system of governing India.[189] And he charged the company in India with manifest insubordination and disobedience toward the company's court of directors and Parliament. Hastings drew much of Burke's fire in this part of the *Ninth Report*.[190] The governor-general Hastings similarly played the central role in the analysis of East India Company corruption that Burke detailed in the *Eleventh Report*.

The *Ninth* and *Eleventh Reports* allowed Burke to reveal the misdeeds flowing from East India Company conduct in India. But as always, Burke was interested in deeper principles. Perhaps the most important principle was respect for India's traditions, commerce, and peoples. Burke wrote in the *Ninth Report:* "Before any remedial Law can have its just Operation, the Affairs of India must be restored to their natural Order. The Prosperity of the Natives must be previously secured, before any Profit from them whatsoever is attempted."[191] For Burke, such a principle represented not softheaded sympathy for a strange and curious people but a realistic sense that imperial power finds security only in matching self-interest between the foreigner and the native. In Burke's view, such a match could occur only if imperial activity were restricted and preserved as much as possible the native society. Empire should limit itself to producing the circumstances for the development of trade and commerce in keeping with the proper principles of political economy. Any social, moral, and political changes should be encouraged only for the good of the native society. As Marshall observed, Burke thought that "British interference should be kept to a minimum, and Indian society should be left alone to recover through its own inherent strength."[192]

Burke's efforts on the select committee convinced him that Parliament had to reform the East India Company. As a result, he played a major role in drafting and fighting for what became known as Fox's India Bill. In his *Speech on Fox's India Bill* (1783), Burke introduced the reforms in Fox's proposed legislation, most important shifting power from the East India Company's court of directors to an independent commission accountable to Parliament and the Crown. Whelan noted that Fox's bill was "a relatively radical legislative proposal" that demonstrated Burke's willingness "to support radical solutions to problems when more moderate approaches appeared futile."[193]

The speech detailed the sufferings imposed on India by the East India Company, but Burke also appealed to the grander themes that give his perspective on the Indian empire originality and power. Early in the speech, he argued that a remedy for the evils propagated by the East India Company "is demanded from us by humanity, by justice, and by every principle of true policy," and he attacked the "total silence" of his fellow MPs "concerning the interest and well-being of the people of India."[194] Burke exhibited a sensitivity about native Indian society by encouraging Parliament and the nation to see Indians not as "gangs of savages" but as "a people for ages civilized and cultivated; cultivated by all the arts of polished life, whilst we were yet in the woods."[195] Although very different from European civilization, Indian society sparked in Burke a sense of common humanity. Burke compared India with the German empire so that "India might be approximated to our understandings, and if possible to our feelings; in order to awaken something of sympathy for the unfortunate natives."[196]

Burke's appreciation of India served as the foundation for his argument that "justice" demanded action against the East India Company. Burke worked his claim on two levels. First, he made the case that the company's abusive behavior meant that its charter, granted by Parliament in trust, had been broken. There is also the sense that Britain had violated the trust given it by providence in the form of technological superiority over the Indian peoples. Government and empire, in Burke's opinion, are relationships of accountability: "[A]ll political power which is set over men . . . ought to be some way or other exercised ultimately for their benefit."[197] Burke detailed how the power exercised by the East India Company worked at every level against the benefit of Indians. The lack of accountability of the East India Company meant that "the cries of India are given to the seas and winds, to be blown about, in every breaking up of the monsoon, over a remote and unhearing ocean."[198] The reforms in Fox's India Bill sought to make the East India Company accountable to Parliament.

Second, Burke claimed that Fox's bill constituted "the *Magna Charta* of Hindostan" by promising to turn Indians' natural rights, which the East India Company abused, into "the chartered rights of men."[199] Burke appealed to a common form of just treatment for the different peoples of the earth. Under this conception, imperial contact outside the imperial society remained intimately attached to universal conceptions of human justice.[200] Burke sought to use Fox's bill to make concrete the rights Indians possessed under natural law, just as the Magna Carta in England had transformed natural rights into prescriptive rights.[201]

In his speech on Fox's bill, Burke again took up themes of proper imperial policy. Echoing his realist tactic in *Conciliation,* Burke outlined the economic and strategic importance of India to Britain. Despite this importance, Burke noted the "total silence" from MPs "concerning the interest which this nation has in the commerce and revenues of that country."[202] Burke repeated the arguments made in the *Ninth Report* that East India Company government and commercial policy had succeeded in alienating the Indian people, producing violence and suffering and wasting a society and economy that, properly dealt with, could prosper to the benefit of Britain. Self-interest, in parallel with humanitarian interests, called for reform of the East India Company.

Under the existing regime, Burke believed that "there is nothing before the eyes of the natives but an endless, hopeless prospect of new flights of birds of prey and passage, with appetites continually renewing for a food that is continually wasting."[203] The head falconer of this rapacious flock, in Burke's mind, was Warren Hastings, who again came under fire from Burke for his "despotic acts."[204] In this speech Burke made Hastings a symbol of the evil being perpetrated in India.

This speech shows as well Burke's sensitivity to the dangers for the British constitution lurking in the oppression of India. Burke refuted the accusations that Fox's bill would alter the constitutional balance of power by materially increasing or decreasing the influence of the Crown. Still, although he had opposed earlier reform efforts, Burke stated that if expanding the power of the Crown would bring relief to suffering Indians, then he was ready to embrace such influence.[205] Given his vigilance toward the British constitution, this change of heart might seem like the triumph of sympathy over principle. But such a perception would be mistaken, because Burke had by 1783 come to believe that the continued exercise of arbitrary power by the East India Company posed a greater threat to the British constitution than reform proposals. He stated early in his speech, "I am certain that every means, effectual to preserve India from oppression, is a guard to preserve the British constitution from its worst corruption."[206]

Burke, however, pushed the relationship of empire and constitution further. Although he believed that the demands of constitutional politics and enlightened imperial policy could be reconciled, he argued that if such a reconciliation were not possible, Britain would have to disengage from its Indian empire: "[I]f we are not able to contrive some method of governing India *well,* which will not of necessity become the means of governing Great Britain *ill,* a ground is laid for their eternal separation; but none for sacrificing the people of that country to our constitution."[207]

Despite Burke's efforts on the Fox bill, it failed, and its failure largely precipitated the fall of the Fox-North coalition in 1784.[208] William Pitt formed a new administration and won the general election of 1784 with financial help from the East India Company. These developments left Burke distraught. All his attempts to change the course of Indian policy produced only a new administration, carried to power through the defeat of Fox's bill and the money of the East India Company. Although Burke's own political fortunes were at a low point and he perceived himself surrounded by political enemies, such worries could not shake his determination to help shape Indian policy.[209]

Burke demonstrated this determination in his February 1785 *Speech on Nabob of Arcot's Debts.*[210] The issue at hand was the government's proposal to pay from public funds debts owed by the nabob of Arcot to private individuals, most of whom were East India Company servants. He attempted to expose the debts as fraudulent, and he accused Pitt's administration of colluding with the corrupt figures in the East India Company.[211] Contrary to the suggestions of some commentators, what prompted Burke to issue this "great philippic"[212] was less his general political frustration than his incredulity that the government wanted to compensate East India Company servants for destroying India.[213] This proposal was all the more outrageous to Burke because Henry Dundas, chairman of the secret committee that had uncovered so much evil perpetrated by the East India Company in India, was the main mover of the government's policy.[214]

Burke sensed in the proposal, in Dundas's change of attitude, and in the alleged collusion between the government and the East India Company the danger to the British nation that he always saw in imperial misgovernment. He charged that this unseemly episode revealed that British rapacity in India may "have dulled, if not extinguished, the honour, the candour, the generosity, the good-nature, which used formerly to characterize the people of England."[215] "[A]n unnatural injection, a pestilential taint fermenting in the constitution of society," said Burke, had polluted the glory of Britain and its empire so that "instead of what was but just now the delight and boast of the creation, there will be cast out in the face of the sun, a bloated, putrid, noisome carcass, full of stench and poison, an offence, a horror, a lesson to the world."[216] The ferocity of Burke's rhetoric in the *Speech on Nabob of Arcot's Debts* revealed that he had not lost his passion for helping India, despite the enmity and political frustration that it brought him.[217]

Since he could not as a member of a fragmented opposition enact reforming legislation, Burke decided to initiate an impeachment against Hastings.[218] Burke had no illusions about successfully impeaching Hastings, for he wrote in correspondence that he was interested only in "what will acquit and justify myself to those few persons and to those distant times, which may take a concern in these affairs and the Actors in them."[219] Some have suggested that this statement meant Burke was concerned mainly with his own name.[220] But however much Burke worried about his reputation, the statement should more accurately be seen as an indication of Burke's desire to preserve for posterity the principles he had tried to support in his Indian efforts.

Burke launched his campaign against Hastings in February 1786, when he called for East India Company records to be handed over to Parliament as part of an investigation leading to the impeachment of the governor-general.[221] To Burke's surprise, the House of Commons and the government favorably received his speech and motions.[222] Obtaining East India Company records and starting a parliamentary investigation meant that Burke, for reasons of procedural justice, needed to draw up and present impeachment charges. Working with sympathetic friends and MPs, Burke presented to the House of Commons twenty two articles of charge of high crimes and misdemeanors during April and May 1786. In keeping with his desire to teach a lesson for posterity's sake, Burke formulated the charges not in proper legal terms but in a manner comprehensible to the public.[223] Ironically, this tactic later backfired when Burke actually succeeded in bringing Hastings before a trial of impeachment in the House of Lords.

Hastings helped Burke's cause by providing the House with a defense of his actions that seemed to confirm Burke's accusations. The momentum for impeachment in the House grew stronger. On June 1, 1786, Burke formally opened the articles of charge with a speech on the first charge, concerning the Rohilla war.[224] In this speech, Burke made clear that his purpose in pursuing Hastings was not personal but an exposition and affirmation of the fundamental principles upon which imperial policy in India should be founded.[225] Burke outlined the structure of imperial justice that he more fully developed in his opening speech of the impeachment trial in February 1788. For Burke, the misdeeds of the East India Company were a question of *justice* at the individual, national, and universal levels.

Burke accused Hastings of basing his behavior in India on the principles of avarice, corruption, and bribery. Further, Hastings allegedly embraced these principles for personal gain at the expense of the East India Company, Britain, and the Indian people. Burke argued that the *"spirit of Avarice"* prevailed so strongly in Hastings that he resorted even to war to satiate the appetite of individual corruption.[226] This appetite, according to Burke, could not resist the tempting spoils of the Rohilla's "luxuriant garden."[227] In precipitating this war, Hastings used his avarice "as a sword of vengeance, cruelty, and murder!"[228] Although the impeachment was not "personal," Burke's focus on the triumph of individual greed shows his concern about the importance of honorable and exacting personal behavior in lands far from home, in which moral weakness can lead to human catastrophe. The Englishman could not leave his virtue behind when he went forth into empire.

Hastings's defense that his actions were justified because "the history of Asia is nothing more than precedents to prove the invariable exercise of arbitrary power"[229] suggested that Hastings believed that a different individual and national morality prevailed in India. In the Rohilla war speech, Burke was scathing about Hastings's claim because it directly contradicted proper notions of virtue as well as bedrock principles of British government. Hastings's exercise of arbitrary power repulsed Burke as an attempt "repugnant to any principles of government . . . and most especially where the constitution of the superintending government at home was free."[230] Hastings had claimed that British imperial servants, though ultimately responsible to Parliament, could ignore the principles of government enshrined in the British constitution. It was in such attitudes that Burke saw dangers to the British constitution from imperial activities. Burke, however, knew that the servants of the East India Company "could not be expected . . . [to] practise Magna Charta."[231] So Burke added a third layer of justice for imperial thinking: maxims of international and universal justice. Burke asserted that Hastings and his cohorts should have relied on "the law of nature and nations, the great and fundamental axioms on which every form of society was built."[232]

Although the House of Commons rejected the article of charge against Hastings on the Rohilla war, the House eventually accepted seven of the charges against Hastings and in May 1787 voted to impeach him. Burke had won a great personal and political achievement in moving the impeachment successfully through the House. His political credibility had recovered since its nadir after the defeat of Fox's India Bill.[233] Now came the final and most difficult test in Burke's strategy to resurrect proper principles of imperial policy: the impeachment trial before the House of Lords.

The trial began on February 15, 1788. Burke's opening speech became the centerpiece of this unusual but solemn political theater. This speech lasted four days, during which Burke attempted to condense his knowledge of India and East India Company affairs and his opinions on the principles that should inform British policy in India. Burke moved between the details of Hastings's actions in India to the principles guiding the spirit of the impeachment. Within this massive effort lives the refined wisdom of Burke's thought about imperial policy in India.

The theme upon which all the details about Hastings and his subordinates build is the elevation of the Indian peoples to a moral and social equality with European civilization. Burke created a conception of a world community imbued with cultural sensitivity and common principles of law and justice. And he firmly included respect for this community as a critical element not only of British self-interest but also honor and virtue.

On the first day of the speech, Burke declared that the issue of Hastings's guilt was subordinate to the question "whether millions of mankind shall be made miserable or happy."[234] The answer to this question would decide "the credit and honour of the British nation itself."[235] Burke expressed his belief that the British constitution "is deeply involved in the event of this Cause" and his hope that the House of Lords proved capable of approaching the fateful question "upon solid principles of State morality," referring to no "rules whatever except those of natural, immutable and substantial justice."[236] Anticipating the strategy of legal technicalities planned by Hastings's counsel, Burke urged the lords to think in terms of "Imperial justice" rather than "municipal maxims" because "you try the Cause of Asia in the presence of Europe."[237] The first step in rendering imperial justice, according to Burke, was "to enlarge the circle of justice to the necessities of the Empire that we have obtained."[238] Burke's message is that the justice of imperial and foreign policy could not be determined solely by reference to the narrow confines of national law. Justice could be rendered to the Irish Catholics and the American colonists by extending the British constitution to them; justice for Indians required a different conception.

In the second day of the speech, Burke used the British constitution as the bridge to the overarching doctrine of imperial justice for India. He contended that Hastings "ought to govern upon British principles, not by British forms," which consist of "that spirit of equity, that spirit of justice, that spirit of safety, that spirit of protection, [and] that spirit of lenity."[239] He argued that Hastings's claim that arbitrary power was the political morality in India should be rejected. Burke found the Indian peoples deserving of the morality of British principles for two reasons. First, the spirit of these principles reflected a greater morality and law: "We are all born in subjection,—all born equally, high and low, governors and governed, in subjection to one great, immutable, pre-existent law, prior to all our devices, and prior to all our contrivances, paramount to our very being itself, by which we are knit and connected in the eternal frame of the universe, out of which we cannot stir."[240] Hastings's conception of "Geographical morality" violated this higher law.[241]

Second, Burke argued that the Indian peoples have an equal place under this law with Europeans. This is what Burke meant on the first day of the impeachment speech when he said there was a "law of common justice which cements them to us and us to them."[242] Despite the cultural, religious, and political differences between the British and Indian peoples, Burke believed that a common humanity bound them. Indians deserved as much respect and concern as did Englishmen in terms of the morality of power and government.

Burke was aware of the prejudices held by his contemporaries toward India; as we have seen, in the speech on Fox's India Bill he tried to make India comprehensible to the moral sensibilities of British people. His purpose in his opening impeachment speech was to demonstrate that Indian morality did not embrace arbitrary power as Hastings claimed. Burke spent a great deal of time explaining to the House of Lords the history, culture, laws, and society of the people who suffered during Hastings's regime. He attempted to bring to life the diversity, complexity, traditions, and beauty of Indian society. "[W]e, if we must govern such a Country," urged Burke, "must govern them upon their own principles and maxims and not upon ours, that we must not think to force them to our narrow ideas, but extend ours to take in theirs."[243] Burke devoted an important part of his speech on the second day to demonstrating that Indians held rulers responsible to the law and to the welfare of the people.[244]

Burke's study of Indian society led him to a conclusion that no doubt raised the eyebrows of his contemporaries: "I assert that their morality is equal to ours as regards the morality of Governors, fathers, superiors; and I challenge the world to shew, in any modern European book, more true morality and wisdom than is to be found in the writings of Asiatic men in high trusts, and who have been Counsellors to Princes."[245] He noted that Britain gained empire in India at a time when the fortunes of Europe were better than those of Asia—but that conquest by a surging European power did not alter the moral and political equality the Indian peoples held under the great common law and the example of their unique civilization.[246]

According to Burke, Hastings's high crimes and misdemeanors grew out of disrespect for law on all levels: the law of common humanity emanating from the divine, the principles and laws of Britain, and the laws and principles of India.[247] Burke provided detailed accusations of how Hastings's disrespect for the virtue of imperial justice produced in Indian society destruction of a most thorough and cruel kind. Burke accused Hastings of dispossessing landowners from their property, forcing people to lose their traditional castes, and torturing indiscriminately the poor and powerless. Burke considered that British avarice in India had in its rapacity despoiled traditional, native forms of government, economic relations, and social stability.

Burke's conception of imperial justice in relation to India combines ancient and modern aspects. The appeal to universal, binding principles and laws reflects Roman ideas.[248] Unlike the Romans, who believed in extending Roman citizenship to conquered peoples, however, Burke rejected traditional images of non-European peoples and devoted himself to convincing his contemporaries that justice between different peoples required not assimilation of the weaker to the stronger but the preservation of difference. This conservative perspective parallels Burke's efforts to impress upon the House of Commons the importance of recognizing Irish or American characteristics and tolerating such national traits. In this sense, Burke's perspective on international relations is consistent with his strong attachment to the domestic traditions and customs that provided the fiber of the British constitutional system. The spirit of Burke's conception of imperial justice is a tolerant conservatism, which finds virtue in attachment to a common humanity. Toward the end of the opening impeachment speech, Burke implored the lords to acknowledge "that the sun in his beneficent progress round the world does not behold a more glorious sight than that of men, separated from a remote people by the material bounds and barriers of nature, united by the bond of a social and moral community, all the Commons of England resenting as their own, the indignities and cruelties that are offered to all the people of India."[249]

It was this spirit that maintained Burke in the lengthy impeachment process, which did not finish until 1795. The momentum Burke had gathered by 1788, however, disappeared as the impeachment trial dragged on. As Burke had suspected, Hastings's counsel mounted a defense based on legal technicalities. Meanwhile, Hastings conducted a press campaign seeking to bring Burke into disrepute for his attacks on the British Empire.

Hastings's press campaign struck responsive chords in the British public, as the 1790s witnessed increasing pride in the British Indian empire.[250] Although Hastings's acquittal became a foregone conclusion, Burke fought until the bitter end for his conception of imperial justice. At the close of his life, however, Burke put this "failure" into perspective against his long political career.[251] He wanted his Indian endeavors to be his "only monument." His spirit of solidarity with a people he had never seen but had nonetheless come to honor never faltered.

The Crusade Against the French Revolution

The last and most famous of Burke's international concerns was his reaction and fierce opposition to the French Revolution. Although Burke wanted to be remembered for his work on relieving the sufferings of India, he considered the Jacobinism released by the French Revolution as "the greatest evil" he had encountered in his lifetime.[252] Indeed, fighting the effects of the French Revolution brought him the greatest blame and praise after his death.

The man who would eventually lead the call for a war of intervention and annihilation against the French Revolution found himself surprised and fascinated by the happenings in France in July 1789. In August 1789 Burke wrote to the earl of Charlemont: "As to us here our thoughts of every thing at home are suspended, by our astonishment at the wonderful Spectacle which is exhibited in a Neighboring and rival Country—what Spectators, and what actors! England gazing with astonishment at a French struggle for Liberty and not knowing whether to blame or to applaud!"[253] Even in these early days, however, we find the seeds of worry and doubt about the nature of the political upheaval in France that later grew into Burke's crusade against Jacobinism.

First, as he wrote to Charlemont, Burke feared that if the revolution in France "should be character rather than accident, then that people are not fit for Liberty, and must have a Strong hand like that of their former masters to coerce them."[254] He suspected that the revolution would not yield any liberty to the French but merely deliver up a new form of tyranny. Second, the rapid movement from order to chaos in revolutionary France troubled Burke because of the potentially destabilizing consequences for the European balance of power. "I should certainly wish to see France," wrote Burke to Earl Fitzwilliam, "circumscribed within moderate bounds. The interest of this Country requires, perhaps the Interests of mankind require, that she should not be in a condition despotically to give the Law to Europe."[255] Third, Burke hinted at what later became a prevailing theme in his anti-Jacobin crusade: the novel threat posed by the revolution to Britain and the rest of Europe. Unlike the military menace France represented at the beginning of the eighteenth century, revolutionary France threatened the very nature of the political, social, and moral order in Europe, through its proclamation and violent pursuit of the "rights of man." In November 1789 Burke's response to a letter from Charles-Jean-François Depont previews the *Reflections on the Revolution in France* in its sharp critique of the revolutionary attempt to destroy the ancien régime institutions of property, religion, nobility, monarchy, and law.[256] Furthermore, the letter emphasized the transnational challenge of the revolutionary ideology, reflected in its universalist proclamations that recognized no settled border.

As Burke's private correspondence suggests, he had by the end of 1789 "made up his mind, in a decidedly negative way, about the character and probable future course of the

French Revolution."[257] In early 1790 he voiced this opposition publicly through his parliamentary duties and literary endeavors. In January 1790 Burke received direct provocation that ignited his spirit against the revolution in France and confirmed his fear that the philosophy it promulgated would infect and corrupt other societies in Europe, particularly Britain. The challenge came from a sermon delivered by Dr. Richard Price to the Revolution Society of Britain in November 1789, in which Price welcomed the French Revolution and encouraged the adoption of its ideas in Britain.

In February 1790, in response to Price's sermon, Burke proclaimed in Parliament "his uncompromising and comprehensive hostility to the French Revolution, and his fears of British friendship towards it."[258] More significant, Burke was firing salvos across the bows of fellow Whigs, particularly Charles Fox, who were sympathetic toward the revolution. Burke made it clear that the principles at stake were so fundamental that he would sever his hard-won connections with the Whig party and with his friends in Parliament.[259] Events were to prove that he was not bluffing.

Burke reinforced his parliamentary efforts to warn of the dangers inherent in the French Revolution with his most famous literary work, *Reflections on the Revolution in France*, published in November 1790.[260] Broadly speaking, *Reflections* addressed the nature and consequences of political change. Burke set out in the first section of the *Reflections* to destroy the parallels Price had drawn between England's Glorious Revolution of 1688 and the French Revolution. Burke argued that the Glorious Revolution

> was made to preserve our *antient* indisputable laws and liberties, and that *antient* constitution
> of government which is our only security for law and liberty. . . . We wished at the period of
> the Revolution, and do now wish, to derive all we possess *as an inheritance from our forefathers*.
> . . . All the reformations we have hitherto made, have proceeded upon the principle of reference to antiquity.[261]

According to Burke, the Glorious Revolution proceeded not only on the basis of the principle of reference to antiquity but also upon the "principles of conservation and correction" that allowed Britain to regenerate "the deficient part" without dissolving "the whole fabric" of the country.[262]

The spirit and principles of the French Revolution, by contrast, manifested a different type of political change.[263] There was no hint of or reference to antiquity. History, culture, and prejudice counted for nothing in the passion of the revolutionaries, who chose to act as if they "had never been moulded into civil society, and had every thing to begin anew."[264] Moreover, there was no evidence of Burke's cherished principle of conservation: "Your constitution, it is true, . . . suffered waste and dilapidation; but you possessed in some parts the walls and, in all, the foundations of a noble and venerable castle. You might have repaired those walls; you might have built upon those old foundations. Your constitution was suspended before it was perfected."[265] Finally, Burke attacked the revolutionaries for rejecting the principle of correction: "Rage and phrenzy will pull down more in half an hour, than prudence, deliberation, and foresight can build up in an hundred years."[266]

The *Reflections* dealt with not only how the revolutionaries effected political change but also the substance of the change intended. Burke attacked the French Revolution for savaging the ancient institutions of monarchy, religion, property, and chivalry—pillars of the commonwealth of Europe—in order to realize an abstract form of democracy and egalitarianism. Such a program of "levelling," Burke believed, "destroyed all the balances and counterpoises which serve to fix the state, and to give it a steady direction" and melted "down the whole in to one incongruous, ill-connected mass."[267] Into this political and social vacuum, he predicted, would rush military despotism.[268] In the end, the dangerous ideology of the French Revolution would spread not only by example but also by the sword.

Burke warned that the supposed new dawn for humankind inaugurated in France was not novel at all. It was merely another historical misery "brought upon the world by pride, ambition, avarice, revenge, lust, sedition, hypocrisy, ungoverned zeal, and all the train of disorderly appetites, which shake the public with the same 'troublous storms that toss/The private state, and render life unsweet.'"[269] The "rights of man," Burke suggested, represented only the latest "pretext" of the evil lurking in human nature. "Wickedness," he observed, "was in this case just "a little more inventive."[270]

The *Reflections* became internationally controversial, provoking sympathizers of the French Revolution to answer his challenge.[271] After publication of the *Reflections*, Burke directed his energies toward two main enemies: those contributing to the spread of Jacobinism in Britain and those within the British government who refused to countenance a counterrevolutionary war against France.

The most celebrated episode in Burke's efforts to protect the British constitution from the "French disease" was his quarrel with the Whig party leader, Charles Fox, in 1791. Fox sympathized with the French Revolution both as an event and as an example for Britain. In Parliament on April 15, 1791, Fox proclaimed his admiration for "the new constitution of France, considered altogether, as the most stupendous and glorious edifice of liberty, which had been erected on the foundation of human integrity in any time or country."[272] As O'Brien pointed out, Fox must have realized that after the publication of the *Reflections*, such a public embrace of the French Revolution would constitute a grave provocation to Burke.[273] The final break between the two men came in the House of Commons in May 1791, when Burke ended his twenty-plus-year friendship and collaboration with Fox. Burke cast aside his connections with the Whig party and its leader because he felt himself engaged in "a struggle, not to support any man, or set of men, but a struggle to support the British constitution."[274] He insisted that he held "his duty far beyond any friendship, any fame, or any other consideration" and he would—despite the loss of friends, party, and reputation—"tell all the world that the constitution was in danger."[275]

In the cases of Ireland, America, and India, Burke saw the British constitution threatened from within by imperial misgovernance. The French Revolution, however, constituted a triple threat to the British constitution, working through external as well as internal elements. For one, the principles of the revolution found favor with British politicians and radicals.[276] He opposed such sympathizers in Parliament and with his pen.[277] Burke considered any cry for reform of political, religious, and social institutions in Britain as evidence of a larger Jacobin conspiracy. Further, the French Revolution threatened to undermine the greater historical and cultural framework of the commonwealth of Europe, of which the British constitution formed a part. Success in stifling revolutionary sympathies at home would ultimately be hollow if the rest of the continent broke with its shared European heritage to embrace the "rights of man." Burke contended that foreign politics are "foreign only in name; for they are not only connected with our domestic Politics, but the domestic Politics are actually included in them."[278] Hence, in contrast to Pitt's government, he could not view the revolution in France as an event from which the British constitution was isolated or indeed neutral. However unique the British constitution, it was embedded in a larger political, social, and moral order—the security of which directly implicated its fate.

The third danger inherent in the French Revolution was more traditional. British national security and its interests both on the European continent and with its colonies faced serious danger from the spread of the influence of revolutionary France. Burke believed the "rights of man" were merely a pretext for more ancient and less noble passions. His prediction that France would eventually fall into the grip of military despotism indicated his concern that France would upset the balance of power in Europe and jeopardize Britain's traditional interests, particularly in the Low Countries. Such threats had been a constant feature of Anglo-French relations before the French Revolution.[279] The strategic and military challenges from revolutionary France, however, promised to disturb not only the traditional European balance of power but also the entire transnational order in Europe on which the balance depended. The entire pattern of European international relations, Burke forecast, would be forever altered by the success of the revolutionaries in France.

Burke's perception of the nature of the domestic and international threats posed by the French Revolution led him to go beyond opposing British sympathizers of the revolution. Not long after the *Reflections,* Burke advocated that Britain lead or participate in a war of intervention against revolutionary France. In January 1791 Burke wrote in a letter to the comtesse de Montrond, a French émigré, that "[s]omething must be done. You have an armed Tyranny to deal with; and nothing but arms can pull it down."[280] Burke was convinced that whatever counterrevolution was mounted, only one utilizing the combined forces of the commonwealth of Europe would suffice.[281]

Burke did not reserve his interventionary rhetoric for private correspondence. In his *Letter to a Member of the National Assembly* (1791), Burke argued that it was in the collective interest of the European powers to intervene by armed force to preserve the commonwealth of Europe before the revolution exported its theories by the point of a bayonet.[282] It is important to note that Burke began his determined effort for intervention *before* it became apparent from events in France that the revolution contained a tyrannical character. At a time when the revolution was in an ostensibly stable period of constitution-making, Burke predicted in *Letter to a Member* the execution of Louis XVI and Marie Antoinette and the rise to power of a violent faction within the revolutionary movement. The unsuccessful escape of the French king and queen in June 1791 confirmed the revolution's descent into extremism. So confident was Burke of his analysis of the French Revolution that he had drafted for Pitt's government before the June 1791 escape attempt an aide-mémoire "which would be a preliminary to the breaking off of diplomatic relations between Britain and France."[283]

As he expected, Burke came under attack for his positions on the French Revolution. Fox and his Whig supporters criticized Burke for inconsistency with his previous parliamentary endeavors and with liberal Whig principles in general. This charge had been very common since the publication of *Reflections.* Thomas Paine in *The Rights of Man* marveled at Burke's "change of principles," and Thomas Jefferson remarked after reading the *Reflections* that "[t]he Revolution in France does not astonish me so much as the Revolution of Mr. Burke."[284] Burke's *Appeal from the New to the Old Whigs,* published anonymously in August 1791, contained his defense against the charge of inconsistency.[285] In this work Burke demonstrated the coherence of his views on the British constitution, the American Revolution, and the French Revolution. In each case he had set out to combat the rise and exercise of arbitrary power. *An Appeal,* therefore, provides insight into the entire texture of Burke's political thinking and shows how his principles worked within the different contexts of the imperial society and commonwealth of Europe.

Burke's call to arms, however, was ignored in Britain and among France's continental neighbors. Burke referred to the general inaction of the major powers as the "blindness of the States of Europe."[286] In the summer of 1791, Charles-Alexander de Calonne, military adviser to the exiled prince de Condé, visited London to ask for British support for intervention in France. Calonne sought out Burke when the Pitt government proved unsympathetic. After this meeting Burke sent his son, Richard, to Koblenz to assist in building a military force among the émigrés.[287] The émigrés responded by appointing the Chevalier de la Bintinaye as a representative "auprès de M. Burke," a quasi-diplomatic arrangement that amazed Burke's contemporaries.[288] Indeed, Sir Gilbert Elliot wrote that "Burke is in himself a sort of *power* in the State. It is even not too much to say that he is a sort of *power* in *Europe.*"[289]

In September 1791 Burke began a concerted effort to persuade the Pitt government to abandon its neutrality and support armed intervention. In doing so, he condemned the government's policy of trying to stop Jacobinism only within Britain: "Very little can be done *at home* in my opinion. . . . [T]he root of the Evil is *abroad;* and the way to secure us at *home* is to deprive mischeivous factions of the *foreign* alliances."[290] Burke found the moment propitious for Britain to lead the crusade against revolutionary France: "All [Europe's] powers are, with an unanimity without example, indisposed to this French System. A few months may change a situation and dispositions so rarely found and combined."[291]

Frustrated by the refusal of the Pitt government to change its policy, Burke in December 1791 prepared a memorandum for the government on the need for intervention, which was published posthumously as *Thoughts on French Affairs.*[292] In this memorandum he explored the policy options open to Britain (that is, recognition of the French revolutionary regime versus armed intervention to reverse the revolution) and argued that the French Revolution required a different approach to traditional foreign-policy making: "The conduct which prudence ought to dictate to Great Britain will not depend . . . upon merely *external* relations; but, in a great measure also upon the system which we may think it right to adopt for the internal government of our country."[293] In other words, a policy decision taken abroad had the potential to affect the fate of the British constitution.

For Burke, the fates of all members of the commonwealth of Europe were no less implicated. In *Thoughts* he contrasted the Glorious Revolution in England, which "did not extend beyond its territory," with the French Revolution, which "*is a Revolution of doctrine and theoretick dogma*" not unlike the religious upheaval of the Reformation.[294] As with the religious wars of the seventeenth century, the French Revolution had the power to "*introduce other interests into all countries, than those which arose from their locality and natural circumstances.*"[295] Burke warned that the "spirit of proselytism" burned as strongly in the hearts of the French revolutionaries as it did for the religious factions of the Reformation: "The intention of the several actors in the change in France, is not a matter of doubt. It is very openly professed."[296]

Given this characterization of the French revolutionary zeal, Burke advised the government that an internal counterrevolution in France was unlikely to occur. Moreover, he predicted "that the longer the present system exists, the greater will be it's strength."[297] He concluded that the only effective policy option to the novel challenge of the French Revolution was armed intervention: "I wind up in a full conviction within my own breast . . . that the state of France is the first consideration in the politicks of Europe, and of each state, externally as well as internally considered."[298]

Thoughts on French Affairs did not succeed in shifting the Pitt government from its neutrality.[299] Events in 1792, however, began to demonstrate that the French Revolution did indeed possess the dark and violent intentions Burke had sensed as early as 1790. In April 1792 the French National Assembly declared war on Austria and Prussia, and the leader of the dominant faction in the assembly hailed the coming war as a "universal crusade for liberty."[300] In response, Burke intensified his campaign to persuade the Pitt government to abandon the policy of nonintervention. He began as well to attack the foreign policies of Prussia and Austria for viewing their war with France in realpolitik rather than counterrevolutionary terms. In *Heads for Consideration on the Present State of Affairs,* written in November 1792, Burke criticized the Prussians and Austrians for "admitting, that they had nothing to do with the interiour arrangements of France."[301] For Burke, the war against France could not be waged on limited views of strategy or security, for the entire fabric of Europe's political, social, and moral order was under malignant stress from its revolution.

Burke had the same harsh criticism for Britain. After Prussia's defeat at Valmy, Burke asserted that there is no "rational hope of making an impression on France by any Continental Powers, if England is not a part, is not the directing part, is not the soul, of the whole confederacy against it."[302] Although Burke spiced arguments for intervention with traditional appeals to Britain's self-interest, his major concern at this time was the apparent ambivalence of the Pitt government to Britain's societal heritage with Europe:

> The Ministers by their neutrality . . . had broken the continuity and chain of their connexions with the continent; and of course there was no sort of reciprocal confidence or communication between this Court and any other in Europe. An universal weakness appeared to me to be the result of that neutrality, which by taking away the connexion with Great Britain, took away the cement which held together all other States.[303]

For Burke, state interests and the traditional system of interstate relations made sense only in the context of a broader European framework. The French Revolution, in his view, threatened not only individual European nations but also this deeper historical, religious, and cultural European society.[304]

The opening of the trial for treason of Louis XVI in December 1792 marked the beginning of the fulfillment of Burke's prediction of regicide. Burke had already forecast the seizure of power of "a new generation of revolutionaries, harder and more purposeful"[305] and revolutionary France's military expansionism. With the French monarch's execution in

January 1793, only the dramatic rise of Napoleon was left to realize Burke's prophecy that the revolution would descend into military despotism.

Soon after the execution of Louis XVI, Britain broke off diplomatic relations and presented a set of ultimatums to the French, who ignored the demands and proceeded to declare war on Britain. Burke's lonely efforts to warn of the peril of the French Revolution were vindicated—but the peril was now far stronger and the task ahead more arduous than when Burke first sounded the alarm in 1790. Burke succeeded in splintering the Whig party in 1793 when Earl Fitzwilliam and the duke of Portland broke with Fox to form the Portland Whigs. This group worked and voted "in favour of the war and of measures of repression against Jacobin propaganda" in both Houses of Parliament.[306] Pitt, so long cool to Burke's warnings and advice, now consulted Burke on the unfolding European crisis.[307]

Despite this tacit alliance with Pitt's government, Burke remained skeptical about the prime minister's commitment to the struggle against revolutionary France.[308] In particular, he questioned Pitt's reluctance to wage a counterrevolutionary war in the heart of French territory in cooperation with royalist and émigré forces.[309] In addition, he criticized British fighting strategy, which remained predominantly colonial and naval, as "inert, passive and overly defensive."[310] Pitt's attempts to negotiate a peace with France beginning in autumn 1795 confirmed Burke's suspicions about the prime minister's commitment to counterrevolution and provoked Burke's last literary effort against the French Revolution, the four *Letters on a Regicide Peace*.[311] In those letters, Burke poured scorn on the argument of the peace proponents that France had been "tamed" and had returned to the traditional modes of domestic and international politics. "The word France," wrote Burke, "is slipped in just as if the government stood exactly as before that revolution which has astonished, terrified, and almost overpowered Europe."[312] Burke was stunned that Pitt's ministry contemplated negotiating with the French regime as if the revolution and its doctrines had never existed. Returning to a theme he argued often in the past, Burke concluded, "We are at war with a system, which, by it's essence, is inimical to all other Governments. . . . It is with an *armed doctrine*, that we are at war."[313] As a result, Burke rejected any possibility of accommodation or compromise. In dealings with the "Ambassadors of Infamy,"[314] he wrote, all the traditional diplomatic discourse and tools of foreign policy are ineffective: "To talk of the balance of power to the governors of such a country, was a jargon which they could not understand even through an interpreter."[315]

Burke predicted a long and bloody "Holy War" against the revolutionary regime. He chastised Pitt and his colleagues for failing to grasp that the war against revolutionary France was really "a *civil war* . . . between the partizans of the antient, civil, moral, and political order of Europe against a sect of fanatical and ambitious atheists which means to change them all."[316] More important, it was a struggle in which the "manners and principles" and "mode of civilized war" could no longer be practiced.[317] Throughout the *Letters on a Regicide Peace*, he retained this uncompromising position:

[T]hat this new system of robbery in France, cannot be rendered safe by any art; that it *must* be destroyed, or that it will destroy all Europe; that to destroy that enemy, by some means or other, the force opposed to it should be made to bear some analogy and resemblance to the force and spirit which that system exerts. . . . In one word, with this Republick nothing independent can co-exist.[318]

The Directory in Paris rejected Pitt's peace initiative in fall 1796, and the war continued. And as Burke predicted, it continued for a long while. At the time of Pitt's failed peace initiative, Burke had less than a year to live. The struggle with revolutionary France cast dark shadows across the last months of his life. In January 1797 Burke learned that storms had thwarted the landing of a French army in Bantry Bay, Ireland. During the same month, a pro-Jacobin mob stoned a school for the sons of French refugees founded by Burke near Beaconsfield. Burke's personal struggle against the French Revolution was nearing an end as his health deteriorated during 1797. He recognized, however, that this war would not end upon his death. Three days before dying, on July 9, 1797, Burke requested to be buried "unknown, the spot unmarked and separate from his son, wife, and Brother on *account of the French Revolutionists.*"[319] Should the commonwealth of Europe crumble and Jacobinism prevail in Britain, Burke wanted to deny his hated foes the opportunity to desecrate his grave and thus demean and degrade what he had long and passionately believed: that the French Revolution was a modern incarnation of ancient evil deadly to European civilization.

CHAPTER THREE

Burke and the Theory of International Relations

Burke as an International Relations Theorist?

Having introduced the main international themes that Edmund Burke addressed during his parliamentary career, we now turn to Burke as a theorist of international relations. Such analysis may seem problematic given Burke's career as an active politician and his contempt for abstract theorizing. Nonetheless, the previous chapter's overview of Burke's career demonstrates that he grappled with many of the classic and perennial issues of international relations: war, diplomacy, trade, international law, and the balance of power. Wight, for example, remarked that the "only political philosopher who has turned wholly from political theory to international theory is Burke."[320]

A serious challenge in addressing Burke as a theorist of international relations relates to the issue of "textual" interpretation. Scholars such as Skinner have asserted that an endeavor such as ours, the analysis of a classical thinker in relation to modern-day issues and debates, is methodologically flawed and tainted with partiality. According to Skinner, our treatment of Burke in relation to traditions of international theory or "perennial questions" of international relations threatens to overlook the "overwhelming element of contingency" that accompanies Burke's writings and speeches.[321] By contrast, Skinner's "contextual" approach treats classical works as historical events, happening within a particular social, political, and intellectual context that few scholars today can hope to reconstruct.[322]

Although we share Skinner's concern for historical context and have tried in Chapter 2 to situate Burke firmly within his historical era, we contest Skinner's suggestion that Burke or other classical thinkers have nothing to add to current debates about theory and practice of international relations.[323] The specific intentions of a great thinker are only part of the picture; there is also an objective dimension to historical texts that take on a life of their own as succeeding generations explore political, social, and economic problems.[324] Consulting the wisdom of classical thinkers is not the only way to learn about international relations, but we contend that it is still a legitimate approach. In this chapter we focus on aspects of Burke's thought that have transcended his time to inform important discussions in international relations today: sovereignty, war, the balance of power, international political economy, international law and morality, empire, intervention, and the role of culture. Although Burke's analysis of these topics is influenced by eighteenth-century language and concepts, it is grounded in principles and ideas that are still recognizable and relevant in our own time. Burke's treatment of the great issues of his day challenges us to question the very nature of international order and society and the traditional distinction between domestic and international politics.

Burke and the Three Traditions

As mentioned earlier, few commentators have systematically attempted to provide a framework through which to understand Burke's views on international relations. And several of those who have addressed the international dimension of his thinking have tended to do so with a particular agenda in mind.[325] Our goal is to provide a more general examination of Burke's ideas on international relations and the implications of those ideas for current debates and theories. This is the focus of Chapters 3 and 4.

Before we begin this analysis, we introduce some important concepts from international relations theory. We often compare Burke's ideas to realism, rationalism, and revolutionism—the three main traditions of international relations theory formulated by Martin Wight.[326] Our use of these three traditions does not imply that other theories or schools of international relations theory do not exist, but we believe that Wight's traditions are a powerful analytical tool in connection with assessing Burke's place in international relations theory.

First, these traditions have frequently been employed by scholars working within the so-called English School of international relations theory, which is also referred to as the international society tradition.[327] International relations analysis of Burke to date has come largely from scholars within the English School, such as Wight, Vincent, and Welsh, which suggests that the three traditions have become important in explaining Burke. Second, use of the three traditions generally shows an appreciation for "the interplay of the theory and practice of the states system," which is an appreciation close to Burke's dislike for abstract theory and emphasis on practical statesmanship.[328]

Third, the richness of Burke's thinking suggests that the traditions are permeable and not absolute categories because he displays aspects of all three. Finally, the three traditions are convenient and efficient devices for analyzing Burke because other theoretical approaches to international relations often use them as departure points for their analysis, making the traditions important background material even for nontraditional approaches.[329]

Realism, rationalism, and revolutionism each represent a distinct approach to explaining international relations. Realism describes the thinking of "those who emphasize in international relations the element of anarchy, of power-politics, and of warfare."[330] Realists focus "on the actual, what is, rather than the ideal, or what ought to be; on facts rather than obligations."[331] Niccolò Machiavelli, Thomas Hobbes, Jean-Jacques Rousseau, E. H. Carr, Hans Morgenthau, and Henry Kissinger all are placed in the realist camp.

Rationalists differ from realists because they "concentrate on, and believe in the value of, the element of international intercourse in a condition predominantly of international anarchy."[332] Rationalism shares with realism a focus on the state as the primary unit of analysis and the acceptance of the condition of interstate anarchy. Rationalism differs from realism by positing that through reasoned accommodation of national interests states can create rules, institutions, and values that bring some order and morality to international relations. Hugo Grotius, Emer de Vattel, Thomas Jefferson, Woodrow Wilson, Martin Wight, and Hedley Bull are generally considered to be rationalists.

Revolutionism emanates from "those who believe so passionately in the moral unity of the society of states, or international society, that they identify themselves with it, and therefore they both claim to speak in the name of this unity, and experience an overriding obligation to give effect to it, as the first aim of their international policies."[333] Revolutionism is a broad tradition because it encompasses thinkers as diverse as the French revolutionaries, Immanuel Kant, and Karl Marx. Revolutionism rejects realism's disdain for the ideal and rationalism's acceptance of the halfway house of a mere society of states. As Wight observed, "It is characteristic of Revolutionism . . . to deny its past, to try to start from scratch, to jump out of history and begin again."[334]

The Golden Mean

Critical to understanding Burke's international thinking is the notion of prudence—what he referred to as the "first of Virtues" and "the God of this lower world."[335] For Burke, harmony and stability are set out as the standards of virtue, whereas excess and discord are considered the essences of evil. Burke's ideal statesperson is one who can carve out the golden mean between polar positions: "[He] forms the best judgment of all moral disquisitions who has the greatest number and variety of considerations in one before him, and can take them in with the best possible consideration of the middle results of all."[336]

In much of his writing, Burke championed this conservative ideal of the via media.[337] He was quick to condemn thinkers such as Rousseau, whom Burke saw as prone to extremism: "[Rousseau] seldom can discover that precise point in which excellence consists, where to exceed is almost as bad as to fall short, and which every step you go beyond, you grow worse and worse."[338] Burke, by contrast, injected political thought and action with a spirit of balance, conciliation, and moderation. In *Reflections* he described himself as one who "when the equipoise of the vessel in which he sails, may be endangered by overloading it upon one side, is desirous of carrying the small weight of his reasons to that which may preserve its equipoise."[339]

In Burke's general political theory, this tendency to conciliate can be seen most clearly in his writings on the British constitution. For him, the British constitution embodied the golden mean. In particular, he praised its ability to balance monarchical, aristocratic, and popular principles of government. "The whole scheme of our mixed constitution," Burke explained, "is to prevent any one of its principles from being carried as far, as, taken by it self, and theoretically, it would go."[340]

Burke's desire to straddle a middle line is also evident in his treatment of human nature. His theory of human nature represents a compromise between particularism and universalism.[341] Although he acknowledged the distinctions among individuals resulting from geography, culture, history, and religion, he observed that human nature remains in some respects constant.[342] From a moral point of view, human nature is fixed: It has potential for good as well as evil.[343] Political and social institutions can, however, be constructed to alter the amount of that good or evil. If human beings can never be perfect, neither are they wholly beyond redemption.

At the heart of Burke's theory of human nature is a belief in the basic social impulse—or sociability—of human beings, which resembles the Grotian perspective.[344] In fact, Burke was a critic of social contract theorists and their depiction of human beings in an imaginary state of nature. "The state of civil society," he wrote "is a state of nature; and much more truly so than a savage and incoherent mode of life."[345] Burke's catalogue of individual rights does not include abstract or "presocial" liberties, such as rebellion. Instead, his thinking gives prominence to "social rights," such as the right to property by descent, the right to education, and the right to due process.[346] These civil rights, he contended, constitute the "*real* rights of men."[347]

Finally, Burke's theorizing on the origins of the state follows his search for the golden mean. At times he accepted rather than accounted for the existence of political authority, claiming that there is a "sacred veil to be drawn over the beginnings of all governments."[348] Nevertheless, although Burke suggested that government ultimately emanates from God's will, he also sought to endow it with a human dimension. His aversion to the pure thesis of "divine right" led him to adopt the contractarian language of eighteenth-century political discourse.[349]

Burke did not accept, however, the revolutionary implications of such Enlightenment contract theories, especially the notion that government is an act of legal agreement or arbitrary choice. He denounced John Locke's revolutionary notion that each individual must decide anew, from an imaginary "state of nature," whether to accept the social contract. Such an idea, he argued, "supposes in any strong combination of men a power and right of always dissolving the social union," rendering them "a mere unconnected multitude."[350] As Cobban argued, Burke transformed the social contract from its Lockean form as a basis of resistance into a "bulwark of conservatism."[351] For Burke, the state was a prescriptive and historic as well as a divine institution. It had to be treated with caution and reverence.

Burke also challenged the contractarian attempt to define the nation in purely territorial terms. He described the nation as a "moral essence, not a geographical arrangement, or a denomination of the nomenclator."[352] Thus, he argued that the "real" France—the pre-1789 society and culture, though stripped of territorial possession by the revolutionaries—still existed.[353] In this sense, Burke occupies an intermediary stage in the evolution of ideas about nationhood occurring in the late eighteenth century. His depiction of the nation as a historical community places him between what Hinsley called a territorial and institutional concept of nation, which grew out of contract theory, and the later romantic idea of the nation as a cultural and ethnic community.[354]

In Burke's thinking, a state (or nation) is "not an idea only of local extent, and individual momentary aggregation," but "an idea of continuity, which extends in time as well as in numbers, and in space."[355] In *Reflections* he depicted the social contract as a "partnership not only between those who are living, but between those who are living, those who are dead, and those who are to be born."[356] Moreover, each separate social partnership was but "a clause in the great primeval contract of eternal society which holds all physical and all moral natures, each in their appointed place."[357]

Sovereignty and War

Burke's belief in the state as a historic contract and as part of a larger "chain of being" led him to place less importance on the absolute exercise of state autonomy and independence. In keeping with his preference for balance and moderation, he insisted that a healthy society was one with some means of restraining the exercise of liberty. For him, absolute freedom was the "greatest of all possible evils."[358] In contrast to many of his Enlightenment peers, who were convinced that the pursuit of individual happiness did not conflict with the goals of society at large, Burke stressed the need to balance liberty with other ingredients of social order. The kind of liberty he advanced is not "solitary" or "unconnected," but a "social freedom" in which "[l]iberty . . . must be limited in order to be possessed."[359] In this way, individual action is no longer random or isolated but part of a greater, interdependent social matrix.

As Vincent noted, this qualified definition of individual liberty parallels a weak conception of state sovereignty.[360] Just as Burke refused to assume the absolute freedom of individuals, so he refused to assume the absolute autonomy of states. As we argue later in the chapter, Burke viewed European states not as isolated enclaves but as partners in a larger interdependent society—the "commonwealth of Europe." Within this greater whole, states must fulfill their duties as well as exercise their rights and must balance their individual objectives against the larger objective of European order. Since he conceived of individuals, groups, and states as part of a wider "chain of being," Burke claimed that it was permissible to take action within the sovereign realm of another state. "A more mischievous idea cannot exist," he wrote, "than that any degree of wickedness, violence, and oppression may prevail in a Country, that the most abominable, murderous and exterminatory Rebellions may rage in it, or the most atrocious and bloody tyranny may domineer, and that no neighbouring power can take cognizance of either, or afford succour to the miserable Sufferers."[361]

Burke's understanding of sovereignty directly affects his attitude toward the use of force in international relations.[362] At first glance, he appears to be a realist, claiming that wars are "inevitable in every state of human nature" and accepting force as "the sole means of justice among nations."[363] Nonetheless, he added that the causes and effects of war should be tempered through legal and moral regulation. "[It] is one of the greatest objects of human wisdom," he wrote, "to mitigate those evils which we are unable to remove."[364]

Burke's characterization of war as a necessary evil resembles the position of rationalists such as Grotius and Vattel.[365] Following these international lawyers, he argued that war should be waged only for specific and just causes and "never entered into without mature deliberation."[366] In addition to distinguishing between just and unjust wars, Burke obeyed the legal precepts of *jus in bello* by suggesting that "the rights of war were not unlimited."[367] Therefore, during the rupture between Holland and Britain over the island of St. Eustatius in 1781, he condemned Britain's violation of neutrality and confiscation of property as "contrary to the law of nations."[368] He also pleaded for moderation during Britain's conflict with America, criticizing British use of German mercenaries and Native American tribes in the fighting and instructing the British government to inflict punishment in proportion to the crime.[369]

In short, Burke's outlook on war finds a via media somewhere between pacifism and militarism. Although he believed some forms of war are outlawed in international society, other kinds may be sanctioned by it. Furthermore, prudence and moderation were virtues to be practiced in war and peace. Simply because the structure of the international system is anarchical, leading to clashes among its members, does not mean this sphere lacks moral and legal rules. War formed part of Burke's mix of elements that contributes to the maintenance of international order, an objective he considered critical to the moral fiber of humankind.

The Balance of Power

As shown in his reflections on India, America, and Ireland, Burke feared the abuse of power. Throughout his writings and speeches, he discussed how to control, direct, and balance power so that it served as a source of stability rather than instability.[370] In the domestic arena, a mixed constitution would lead to a balance of power. In the international arena, a single nation's power was to be tamed through the balance of power among all nations—that "known common law of Europe at all times, and by all powers."[371]

Burke noted that whereas other civilizations crumbled because of their imperial ambitions, Europe owed its survival and superiority to its system of balancing power.[372] He described this overall equilibrium in Europe as based on four regional balances: (1) the great middle balance of Britain, France, and Spain; (2) the balance of the north; (3) the internal balance between Austria and Prussia; and (4) the balance of Italy. France was the linchpin of this formula—a "natural guardian" of European stability.[373] Hence, even at the height of his counterrevolutionary campaign, Burke insisted that the French state remain a player in the European balance of power.[374]

Burke's portrayal of the balance of power as part of the "public law of Europe" renders his interpretation rationalist rather than realist.[375] As he saw it, the balance in Europe was more than a haphazard outcome of uncoordinated efforts or an expedient rule to be followed by individual states.[376] Burke also did not believe, as some realists do, that a balance of power comes into being automatically as an inherent feature of a system of states. Instead, it is a collective or social good, requiring constant attention from all European sovereigns. "The same principles that make it incumbent upon the patriotic member of a republic to watch with the strictest attention the motions and designs of his powerful fellow citizens," Burke stated, "should equally operate upon the different states in such a community as Europe."[377] As Wight described it, Burke saw the balance of power as a "moral objective" rather than "an objective relationship of forces."[378]

Despite Burke's veneration for the balance of power as an institution, he acknowledged that it had also been "the original of innumerable and fruitless wars" and has frequently been "made an engine subservient to the designs of interested and ambitious persons, and perhaps thereby been productive of some unnecessary wars."[379] Burke expressed these sentiments in his critique of the 1772 partition of Poland, an event he described as "the first very great breach in the modern political system of Europe."[380]

For Burke, the balance of power was to serve not as a pretext for state aggrandizement but as an instrument for the European powers to express their unity against potential hegemons or disintegrating forces.[381] He counseled the guardians of this balance to practice restraint and moderation, with an eye to both their separate political interests and the health of international society at large.

International Political Economy

Prudence and moderation are also apparent in Burke's approach to economic intercourse between states.[382] As Coniff pointed out, the popular view of Burke is that he was a staunch advocate of laissez-faire in economic matters.[383] This case for Burke as a laissez-faire political economist rests on three major points. First, in writings such as *Speech on*

Economical Reform (1780) and *Thoughts and Details on Scarcity* (1795) Burke argued for restricting government expenditures and intervention in the marketplace.[384] Then, too, as noted before, Burke strongly advocated for free trade between Britain and its Irish and American colonies. According to Barrington, Burke "was the first great English statesman to preach Free Trade."[385] And finally, Burke's relationship with and admiration for Adam Smith enhance his credentials as a free marketeer.[386] What these laissez-faire credentials mean in terms of Burke's perspective on international political economy is, however, more complex than any label suggests.

One clue that Burke should not be considered fully within the liberal perspective on international political economy is that he did not completely ascribe to the liberal notion that trade and commerce breed peace within the international system.[387] Burke, for example, defended the use of restrictions on trade for reasons of imperial defense. In *American Taxation* he did not condemn the restrictive Navigation Acts as measures improperly restricting free trade between Britain and the American colonies. Although he favored more open trade with the colonies, Burke was not dogmatic about the free trade principle. He recognized that strategic and security concerns were as important in trade policy as strictly economic questions. Similarly, Burke did not advocate replacing the East India Company monopoly with a trade system open to all British merchants. Nor is there any suggestion that he believed in allowing foreign merchants to compete with the British in Indian trade.[388] Further, in arguing that the other members of the commonwealth of Europe should intervene militarily to quell the French Revolution, he never suggested that economic intercourse offered an alternative path toward peace.

Free trade was most important to Burke in relation to his conception of the imperial society encompassing Britain, America, and Ireland. Within the imperial society, Burke opposed many of the restrictions imposed from London on the ground that they fostered the perception that Britain's colonial possessions were "foreign countries." Freer trade, in Burke's view, would generate an attitude of imperial unity, a feeling of solidarity, a true sense of society. In this way, Burke's vision of the imperial society reflects many of the liberal arguments about the power of commerce in the international system. Burke's writings and speeches on India, however, demonstrate that the imperial society was limited. Whereas liberal thinkers such as Kant considered trade as a way of facilitating the spread of democracy globally, Burke showed no interest in carrying the British constitution to India on the sails of British merchants ships.

Burke's perspective on international political economy has four main elements, each relating to a different historical and political context. To begin with, Burke showed concern about protecting British commercial and strategic interests against foreign enemies in his support of the Navigation Acts and the British monopoly on Indian trade. Second, Burke conceived of trade and commerce differently within the imperial society, not only as a source of national power against competing states but also as a method of building community around the central values represented in the British constitution. Third, Burke viewed trade among members of the commonwealth of Europe as a reflection and a vital component of the historical heritage that gave life to the concept of Europe. And last, he believed that economic contact between Britain and cultures outside the imperial society and the commonwealth of Europe should be confined to limited contact for purposes of mutual material exchange. This more complex interpretation of Burke's international economic thinking suggests that the images of Burke as a classical laissez-faire economist are incomplete and misleading.[389]

As with other areas of Burke's thought, the prudential, contextual approach to international political economy contains strong moral sentiment. We have already mentioned Burke's attitude toward Britain's economic policy in Ireland. We have reviewed as well Burke's many pleas for Britain to change its trade and taxation policies toward America. Morality led Burke to oppose the East India Company's commercial policies in India. Burke also formulated a code to regulate and phase out the international slave trade.[390] As his efforts on India and the slave trade demonstrate, he did not shy away from advocating "broad and positive government action in some areas of social and economic concern."[391] Burke's strong moral sentiment prevented him from becoming dogmatic on abstract principles and gave him flexibility to shape his economic thinking against historical, political, cultural, and moral circumstances.

Although Burke echoed different schools of thought and yet belonged to none, his eclecticism is neither incoherent nor empty. Burke's perspective on international political economy is procedurally and substantively conservative: It takes a prudential approach to fostering political and moral development through economic relations without eroding the stability provided by the historical wisdom and heritage of different communities in the international system.[392]

International Law and Morality

As did many conservative thinkers, Burke accorded law a critical role in restraining excess and achieving social harmony. In his thinking, natural law and legal regulation are fundamental components of international as well as domestic order. Hence, in the opening speech in the Hastings impeachment, Burke referred to "one great, immutable, pre-existent law."[393] According to Burke, the law of nations derived from the attempt to apply these imperatives of natural law to the real circumstances of individuals and nations.[394] Though he admitted that "there was no positive law of nations . . . established like the laws of Britain in black letter, by statute and record," he insisted that "there was a law of nations as firm, as clear, as obligatory, as indispensable":

> [T]here were certain limited and defined rights of war recognized by civilised states, and practised in enlightened Europe. . . . [T]hey were established by reason, in which they had their origin . . . by the convention of parties . . . by the authorities of writers, who took the laws and maxims . . . from the consent and sense of ages; and lastly, from the evidence of precedent.[395]

As Davidson pointed out, this reliance on custom as a source for international law is yet another instance of Burke's search for the via media, this time between naturalism and positivism.[396]

Most of Burke's thoughts on international law are restricted to the norms and rules that operated within European civilization.[397] Although he believed in a universal natural law, he identified a particular "public law of Europe" to regulate relations among the members of European international society. Burke called this customary international law the "great ligament of mankind,"[398] and he usually had this in mind when using the term "law of nations." Nonetheless, he believed that wider principles of justice should govern all political action, whether within the boundaries of Europe or outside. This view, as noted earlier, informed his attack on Hastings's doctrine of "geographical morality."

His faith in overarching standards of law and morality fueled Burke's contempt for the realist doctrine of *raison d'état*, described sarcastically in his *Vindication of Natural Society*.[399] It was callous devotion to individual interest and aggrandizement that he found so distasteful in policies such as the partition of Poland. Burke's critique of realist amorality did not, however, translate into the revolutionist dream of a single world community, with its moral imperative requiring "all men to work for human brotherhood."[400] For him, the sovereign state remained a mediating moral influence.

Burke's greater concern was to infuse the exercise of state power with caution, humility, and sensitivity. Commenting on British foreign policy during the French Revolution, he wrote: "Among precautions against ambition, it may not be amiss to take one precaution against our *own*. . . . I dread our *own* power, and our *own* ambition; I dread our being too much dreaded."[401] In addition, he rejected the view that the morality applicable to policymakers in the conduct of foreign relations was somehow different from that observed by citizens in their domestic relationships. His belief in prudence and natural law produces a certain "ethical temper" that encourages leaders to see the moral context of their political action and to recognize that the upholding of moral standards will strengthen both domestic and international society.[402]

Burke's understanding of international morality, therefore, is focused primarily on individual sovereigns rather than states. This is evident in his doctrine of political trusteeship, in which those who govern become stewards or trustees for their constituents and for future generations.[403] Burke acted on this principle as an MP when he refused to succumb to the vagaries of public opinion. In Burke's international theory, he extrapolated the notion of trusteeship: Duties are owed not only by each government to its subjects but also by one government and people to another.[404]

In sum, Burke's writings on international affairs tread a middle path between realism, which depicts international relations as a state of war, and revolutionism, which views international relations as the chrysalis for a peaceful community of humankind. His more rationalist position conceives of a European international society characterized by both cooperation and conflict and regulated by moral and legal maxims. This society embraces sovereign states in a larger whole and endows them with collective duties as well as rights. Beyond the commonwealth of Europe, Burke's thinking retains its rationalist hue in his appeal to natural law and his efforts to reform British imperial behavior in India.

"Unity of Spirit, Diversity of Operations"

Burke's appeal to the larger collective in international relations has led some scholars to characterize him as a "medieval" thinker.[405] In fact, his historical and political works frequently refer to the model of Western Christendom. Burke was attracted to the medieval conception of social order because it achieved a healthy balance between unity and diversity. Although medieval societies permitted a certain degree of decentralization and autonomy, they insisted on a core of cultural and political uniformity.[406]

Burke and Empire

As discussed in Chapter 2, diversity and devolution figured prominently in Burke's approach to imperial policy. Burke did not conceive of the British Empire as monolithic.[407] Nevertheless, his efforts on Ireland and America reveal a different notion of empire than do his Indian endeavors.

The Imperial Society. As elaborated before, Burke incorporated Britain, Ireland, and America into an imperial society characterized by a respect for diverse traditions, a toleration of local autonomy, and an aversion to heavy-handed central control. The imperial society was an "aggregate of many States under one common head" in which the "subordinate parts have many local privileges and immunities."[408] Although Burke's proclivity for diversity and devolution in the imperial society stemmed from practical considerations, such as the immense ocean expanse between Britain and America, his obedience to the "eternal Law, of extensive and detached Empire" arose from his general preference for diluted authority.[409] Within the imperial society, Burke accepted the theoretical premise that Britain's powers were "boundless," but he rejected any attempt to implement that premise and to make the relationship between the colonies and the metropolis merely one of domination and submission.

Whenever British imperial policy demanded submission rather than fostered community, Burke was sympathetic toward the grievances of the colonists. This was demonstrated in his eventual support for American independence and his sympathy for rebelliousness among Irish Catholics in the 1790s. Burke's imperial society was not indivisible; imperial misgovernment could provide the grounds for a just rebellion. Relationships within the imperial society always operated in a context governed by fundamental British principles of political and moral action. As demonstrated earlier, Burke included natural law as part of the governing framework of the imperial society. When the homeland ignored fundamental principles, all that remained was its exercise of superior, arbitrary power. Burke denounced this exercise of power, whether in Ireland or America, and he warned that in the long run it was corrosive both to the operation of natural law and to national principles in Britain. As shown later in the chapter, Burke's reliance on common principles and values within the imperial society parallels his conception of order in international society.

Empire of Preservation and Improvement. Burke's notion of an "imperial society," however, did not include Britain's imperial relationship with India. In contrast to the sense of community Burke attempted to foster among Britain, Ireland, and America, he conceived of empire in India in a very limited sense. For Burke, Britain's empire in India was to serve only two purposes: (1) to generate economic wealth for Britain and India through trade and (2) to deny such economic wealth to rival great powers, namely, France. His proposals for reforming the East India Company attempted to preserve this trading monopoly for Britain in India.

Burke further qualified this limited sense of empire by insisting that Britain's monopoly operate in conformity with strict principles drawn from the British constitution, natural law, and the customs, laws, and values of the Indian peoples. Even though Burke did not desire to give the Indian peoples an interest in the British constitution, British imperial conduct was to be based on sound principles—not raw force. The British Indian empire, then, was to be a commercial endeavor conducted according to constitutional rules and principles of a common humanity. Only in this way would the confluence of the British and Indian cultures preserve the traditions and values of the weaker party and improve the material wealth of both. Burke thus conceived of empire between two different cultures within a societal milieu: Imperial conduct should reflect the highest standards of the metropolis and respect the periphery as an equal member of the common humanity.

Burke's reform proposals for the East India Company and his pursuit of Hastings were designed to contain British imperial power in India within the tempering bonds of the British constitution, respect for Indian culture, and universal justice. If such tempering could not be achieved, then Burke advocated the termination of the imperial relationship. There is a symmetry between this sentiment concerning imperial misgovernment in India and Burke's perspective on just rebellion within the imperial society. Burke acknowledged that Britain might have to lose the strategic advantage of empire vis-à-vis other great powers and thus rejected any realist premise for having empire merely as an aspect of great power politics.

Origins of Empire and the Threat to the Constitution.　As with his view on the origins of the state, Burke drew a "sacred veil" over the beginnings of the British Empire.[410] In this case, however, his reliance on the veil lacks a certain historical sensibility. The British Empire was, in contrast to the British nation-state, a recent historical development. The imperial veil was less opaque and the mists of time less dense when Burke was dealing with empire. Rather than challenging the legitimacy of empire, Burke focused on making the management of that empire compatible with British constitutional principles, the culture and spirit of the colonial peoples, and the norms of natural law. He found empire illegitimate when imperial policy failed to live up to these standards.

Although Burke in general relied on this sacred veil in proceeding with his case for imperial reform, his arguments revealed a disquiet about the establishment of empire in Ireland and India. His disgust at the nature of British rule in Ireland seeped through his attachment to the notion of an imperial society. Similarly, his efforts on India suggested concerns about the consequences of uncontrolled and arbitrary action on the part of a chartered trading company.

Burke's discomfort about the origin of parts of the British Empire relates not only to the sufferings of colonial peoples but also to the threat to the British constitution. Ocean expanses served as no defense to the contagion of the abuse of power flowing from imperial arrogance back into the halls of Westminster and the vaults of the City of London. In this sense, Burke's linkage of domestic and international politics pushed beyond standard analyses of empire, which concentrate on the impact in the colonies, to warn about the malignant dangers to the metropolis from possession of empire.

The Commonwealth of Europe

Burke's thoughts on diversity and unity come together most vividly in his vision of European international society, what he called the commonwealth of Europe.[411] Although Burke acknowledged the strength of "national character" in Europe, he believed this autonomy and diversity was made possible because of an underlying sense of community among European states and a collective commitment to maintaining order. As Vincent observed, "The system worked within a society; pluralism worked because of a deeper solidarity."[412]

For Burke, a fundamental social, political, and cultural homogeneity extending across sovereign frontiers sustained order among the members of European international society. In his *Letters on a Regicide Peace,* he portrayed Europe as "virtually one great state" marked by the "same basis of general law; with some diversity of provincial customs and local establishments."[413] More specifically, he accentuated the common European dedication to the Christian religion, monarchical principle of government, Roman law heritage, and feudal custom.[414] This consensus was capped off by a long tradition of trade and economic interaction. In contrast to Rousseau, who criticized the increasing economic ties among European states, Burke believed the individual members of European international society could be strengthened by economic interdependence.[415]

Although this political, legal, and economic convergence is critical to Burke's picture of European international society, he gave greater weight to the cultural mores, or "manners," shared by European peoples.[416] It is this "ancient system of opinion and sentiment," he argued, that accounted for Europe's preponderance and distinguished it from other parts of the world.[417] Such manners, which grew out of the feudal traditions of nobility and chivalry, "softened, blended, and harmonized the colours of the whole," providing a deeper foundation for laws and institutions. "The law touches us but here and there," Burke remarked, but manners "are what vex or sooth . . . barbarize or refine us, by a constant steady, uniform, insensible operation, like that of the air we breathe in."[418] The common system of education for Europeans perpetuated this common set of manners. As a result, he concluded, "no citizen of Europe could be altogether an exile in any part of it. . . . When a man travelled or resided for health, pleasure, business or necessity, from his country, he never felt himself quite abroad."[419]

As Burke saw it, Europe had cultural and historical connotations that transcended physical or legal barriers. In spite of the lack of any formal or binding compact uniting the members of the commonwealth, a deep affection arose from their historical experience of coexistence. This emphasis on culture—as opposed to more institutional factors—is crucial to appreciating Burke's approach to international order:

> In the intercourse between nations, we are apt to rely too much on the instrumental part. . . . Men are not tied to one another by papers and seals. They are led to associate by resemblances, by conformities, by sympathies. It is with nations as with individuals. Nothing is so strong a tie of amity between nation and nation as correspondence in laws, customs, manners, and habits of life. They have more than the force of treaties in themselves. They are obligations written in the heart. . . . The secret, unseen, but irrefragable bond of habitual intercourse holds them together, even when their perverse and litigious nature sets them to equivocate, scuffle, and fight, about the terms of their written obligations.[420]

Although Burke's conception of international order invokes all of the traditional procedures for maintaining stability among European states—the balance of power, trade, international law, and diplomacy—of greater significance is an underlying cultural homogeneity. He admitted that cultural solidarity among European states would not eliminate conflict, but he was confident that their "conformity and analogy . . . has a strong tendency to facilitate accommodation, and to produce a generous oblivion of the rancour of their quarrels."[421]

Burke's conception of international order, which had a strong cultural foundation, distinguishes him from more "pluralist" eighteenth-century international thinkers, such as Vattel.[422] The pluralists conceived of Europe first in terms of its separation into sovereign states and only second as a voluntary and consensual association of those states into an international society. The development of a positive international law to codify interstate relations and achieve an *external* order among sovereign units reflected this emphasis on division. Burke's concern for *internal* as well as external order more closely approximates those medieval philosophers who wrote about the "right ordering of Christendom" or later peace theorists such as the Abbé de Saint Pierre, whose projects sought to guarantee European monarchs not merely a territorial equilibrium but also a political and social status quo within their frontiers.[423] In the end, although Burke often consulted the works of contemporaries, particularly Vattel, his notion of the commonwealth of Europe drew heavily on the Middle Ages for inspiration.

Intervention

Burke's views on the nature of order in European international society informed his perspective on one of the most important norms of that society: nonintervention. As Wight suggested, the notion of intervention has been a prominent feature of Western ideas concerning international relations.[424] On one side are persons who exalt the right and duty of intervention as a way of preserving order in the international system or of reforming that system and enshrining democratic or other political principles within its component states.[425] On the other side are those who accord a moral value to sovereignty and therefore deny the right of intervention except in extreme cases of self-preservation.[426]

Burke advanced a kind of conservative interventionism.[427] Although he permitted diversity within the commonwealth of Europe, his theory of international order could not tolerate heterogeneity regarding the fundamental social, political, and cultural precepts of European civilization. In other words, Burke's theory posits an important interrelationship between a homogeneous and stable international society and the preservation of a domestic status quo. Consequently, he asserted that foreign states have not only a right but "an indispensable duty" to monitor changes occurring elsewhere in Europe.

During Burke's career the greatest threat to the solidarity and stability in the commonwealth of Europe came in the form of the French Revolution. In contrast to the Pitt government's neutral and noninterventionary posture, Burke perceived the revolution as a threat to the foundations of order in Europe because it challenged established religion, property, and dynastic legitimacy. The novel "armed doctrine" of the Jacobins reached the minds of human beings, whatever state they inhabited.[428] For Burke, this "violent breach in the community of Europe" blurred the traditional lines of international politics and demanded suspension of the ordinary rules of the game.[429]

Interspersed in Burke's writings and speeches are three theoretical arguments to rationalize intervention in the affairs of the French state: (1) the pretext of preventive war, derived from his understanding of the balance of power; (2) the rights of intervention in civil conflict, taken from his reading of international law; and (3) the right of "vicinage," extrapolated from the Roman civil law notions of vicinity and neighborhood. We explore each of these in the sections below.

Intervention to Maintain the Balance of Power

Burke's promotion of intervention against revolutionary France was an extension of his views on the balance of power. In fact, many eighteenth-century thinkers and statesmen considered intervention to be one means of maintaining the balance of power, despite recognition of the merits of noninterference.[430] This hierarchical relationship between the balance of power and the principle of nonintervention reflected the conviction that an equilibrium among European states was something that should actively be sought, as opposed to a phenomenon that spontaneously occurred.[431] As shown in our earlier references to Poland, Burke adopted this rationalist rather than realist approach to the balance of power, calling on the prudent and "unremitting attention" of European statesmen to disturbing developments in any part of Europe.[432] Indeed, he argued that cases of intervention on behalf of the balance of power "fill half the pages of history," referring in particular to the treaties of guarantee to the Protestant Succession in England.[433]

But Burke went a step further. He asserted that prudent balance of power politics may require intervention in the face of the threat of imminent attack as well as de facto aggression. In his mind, the Jacobin menace was not primarily military but ideological, based on subversive and contagious principles. He extended Vattel's legal interpretation to encompass political and social as well as military threats, and he concluded that international law allowed for such preemptive action in cases of "hostile intention."[434] For Burke, the "pernicious maxims" of the French revolutionaries were equally threatening as the "formidable forces" of a mobilized army.[435] France "by the very condition of its existence" and "by its essential constitution" was already "in a state of hostility with us, and with all civilized people."[436]

Intervention and Civil War

Burke's treatment of intervention also drew on Vattel's ideas on aiding the just side in a civil war.[437] Extrapolating from Vattel, however, Burke argued that the law of nations permitted "a neighbour to support *any* of the parties according to his choice."[438] In other words, he did not define the "just side" only in terms of the forces of rebellion but extended the right of intervention to the benefit of the ancien régime. In response to his noninterventionist critics in the House of Commons, such as Fox, Burke contended that this policy of aiding the royalist cause was consistent with historical and legal precedent. Fox and his compatriots, he explained, confused the law of nations by failing to differentiate between two kinds of interference: stirring up dissension in another country and taking part in a civil war already commenced. "In the first Case there is undoubtedly more difficulty than in the second," Burke stated, "in which there is clearly no difficulty at all."[439] Although interference in civil conflicts always required "great prudence and circumspection," Burke concluded, there was no "abstract principle of public law, forbidding such interference."[440]

This endeavor to demonstrate the legality of intervention in France within the terms of the existing law of nations reflects Burke's conservative respect for "established wisdom." Nevertheless, he moved beyond conventional interpretations when arguing his case for intervention against the French Revolution. Burke conceived armed action by the European powers against the Jacobins not as a war against the French *state* but as a crusade against a revolutionary *faction* threatening to tear apart the commonwealth of Europe. He insisted that such intervention should not be portrayed as foreign as such; rather, it was part of a larger, European civil war.[441] The forces of the status quo in all parts of Europe had to join forces to defend the historical pillars of European order.

Vicinity and Neighborhood

To develop further his argument that the French revolutionaries ignited a civil war in Europe, Burke turned to the Roman law principles of vicinity and neighborhood. This reliance on civil law reflected his anxiety over the survival of the commonwealth of Europe and his frustration with the noninterventionist approach of his fellow parliamentarians.

The law of vicinity, as Burke portrayed it, was essentially the circumstance of connectedness. Proximity and habitual intercourse carried certain rights and responsibilities.[442] As we have shown, Burke frequently highlighted this phenomenon of vicinage for the members of his European commonwealth, who were joined together by factors of geography, politics, economics, religion, and culture and who took an interest in developments occurring in any part. The law of vicinity also factored into Burke's attitude toward Ireland as part of the imperial society.

The partner of the law of vicinity is the law of neighborhood: the right of a neighbor to protest when he "sees a *new erection,* in the nature of a nuisance, set up at his door."[443] Burke applied this precept of civil law to the relations among European states:

> Now where there is no constituted judge, as between independent states there is not, the vicinage itself is the natural judge. It is, preventively, the assertor of its own rights; or remedially, their avenger. . . . This principle, which, like the rest, is as true of nations, as of individual men, has bestowed on the grand vicinage of Europe, a duty to know, and a right to prevent, any capital innovation which may amount to the reaction of a dangerous nuisance. . . . What in civil society is a ground of action, in politick society is a ground of war.[444]

In his mind, the "nuisance" created by the contagious principles of the French Revolution activated the right of intervention for all of France's neighbors in Europe.

To conclude, Burke conceived the problem of international order as involving both external and internal elements. His international thinking did not posit state sovereignty as an absolute value or as the guiding principle of order. Instead, he held to a weak and qualified idea of sovereignty, which balances the needs of international society as a whole against the absolute liberty and independence of its individual members. Hence, he was prepared to override the pluralist doctrine of reciprocal noninterference if the more fundamental components of European order were threatened.

Burke's Place in International Relations Theory

Some international relations scholars have already shown the difficulty of pigeonholing Burke in any one of Wight's three traditions of realism, rationalism, and revolutionism.[445]

Though Burke supported some of the tenets of realism, he contested its portrayal of the international system as a state of war, its ruthless interpretation of the balance of power, and its tendency to downplay the role of international morality.[446] Second, if Burke shared the rationalists' interest in the nature of international society, his theory demands more homogeneity and solidarity than do rationalists who stress the institutional features of international relations.[447] Burke saw the "obligations written in the heart" as more reliable than the "formality of treaties and compacts."[448] Nonetheless, his vision of international society, based on cultural similitude, stops short of the complete doctrinal uniformity advocated by the revolutionists.

The closest Burke's thinking comes to forming part of any theoretical club is what has been referred to as the English School of international relations theory, or the international society tradition.[449] In many ways, Bull's definition of international society as "a group of states, conscious of certain common interests and common values . . . that conceive themselves to be bound by a common set of rules in their relations with one another, and share in the working of common institutions" captures much of Burke's international thinking.[450] Indeed, his account of international society sparks some of the most interesting debates within this tradition.

Burke "forces us to consider whether order is founded on the 'instrumental part' of international society—its procedural rules and institutions—or on its deeper 'correspondence in customs, manners, and habits of life.'"[451] More specifically, his writings draw our attention to those political, social, and cultural values that lie within the realm of the domestic but are nonetheless indispensable for the maintenance of an international "equipoise." As Vincent pointed out, Burke treated international politics as a branch of all politics. His main point "is that we must grasp what it is that is common to all European societies before we can gain an appreciation of the relations among them."[452] The same encompassing political perspective appears in Burke's efforts to improve British imperial policy in Ireland, America, and India. He showed deep interest in not only the external features of empire but also its internal political, economic, and moral aspects in core and periphery alike.

Looking at Burke through the international society lens helps illuminate aspects of his thinking as well as difficult questions his thought raises for the concepts of order and society in international relations. Within the international society tradition, at least two distinct attitudes exist: the institutional (or pluralist) approach and the cultural (or solidarist) perspective. The pluralist conception of international society is transcultural: It highlights the procedural and institutional features of the international system that are not culturally specific, such as the exchange and treatment of diplomats, treaty law, the requirement of reciprocity, and the principle of nonintervention.[453] It is this set of principles and institutions, pluralists argue, that maintains order in an otherwise anarchical system of states. This pluralist perspective on international society does not exclude states and equivalent entities from participation on the basis of religion, culture, or ideology. But the pluralist approach also maintains that international institutions and principles of international law represent social *values* among states and provide a framework for implementing them internationally.[454] For the pluralists, then, international society functions as a pragmatic dynamic that accommodates cultural difference.

The solidarist perspective on international society focuses on a shared political, economic, religious, and social heritage among *peoples*—and not just states—that affects the way in which states interact. "Nothing is so strong a tie of amity between nation and nation," wrote Burke, "as correspondence in laws, customs, manners, and habits of life."[455] The common values in Burke's commonwealth of Europe—a culturally based international society—differ from the interstate values of the pluralist model of international society because those values exist transnationally at the substate level. Moreover, this deeper consensus at a substate level is what makes possible the interstate rules and institutions of pluralism. Without a strong cultural consensus, solidarists argue, the efficacy of the instruments of state relations will rest only on the convergence of interests, which is a weaker basis for international order.[456]

A number of issues arise from the solidarist conception of international society. The first concerns the nature of sovereignty. As we have shown, Burke's commonwealth of Europe was a strong international society, rooted in the shared manners, customs, and practices of European peoples. The transnational links consequently qualified and weakened the sovereignty of the state.[457] For Burke, sovereignty was not a value in itself but became subordinate to the continuation of a shared cultural heritage. In the pluralist perspective of international society, sovereignty is a legal status that gives meaning to the rules and institutions of state coexistence. Sovereignty cannot be qualified to the extent that it is under solidarism, for the very foundation of international law and institutions is state consent. As a result, pluralism yields a weaker sense of international society than solidarism.

Burke's emphasis on solidarity and culture also has implications for setting the boundaries of international society. For Burke, international society was an inherently limited concept because the type of cultural homogeneity that he idealized did not extend throughout the international system. Burke contended, for example, that Europe's "antient system of opinion and sentiment" distinguished it from other parts of the world.[458] Hence, he hinted that the "wholly Asiatic" Ottoman Empire remained outside the bounds of European international society and the balance of power.[459] The pluralist view of international society, by contrast, has the potential to expand globally because it concentrates on the sovereign state and relations among states, without reference to the cultural connections among them.[460]

The solidarist perspective on international society, therefore, raises the question of the "other"—those who belong to different cultural traditions. Burke confronted this problem of the "other" in his efforts to reform British imperial policy in India. He did not refer to the standards of the commonwealth of Europe to condemn the practices of the East India Company, nor did he construct obligations on the basis of an institutional view of an international society between Britain and the Indian provinces. As noted earlier, Burke regarded India as outside the area where the "law of nations" applied because his conception of international law was influenced by the common cultural heritage of Europe. Burke appealed instead to notions of universal justice and natural law in criticizing British imperial policy in India.

Further reflection on Burke's ideas, however, suggests that the distinction between pluralism and solidarism may be a false one. What Burke helps us see is that the pluralist perspective is not culture-neutral. It, too, is culturally bound because it arose from the particular circumstances within post-Renaissance Europe. The "expansion of international society" to non-European areas was a cultural expansion, not just an expansion of pragmatic, value-neutral interstate institutions of diplomacy and commerce.[461] The world today reflects the expansion of the institutions of post-Renaissance Europe—states, sovereignty, diplomacy, trade, and interstate war—into areas with cultures vastly different from those in Europe. In the late twentieth century, formalistic pluralism coincides with shallow solidarity. This state of affairs creates, in Kingsbury's words, "the problem of reaching normative judgments in a heterogeneous world while simultaneously accommodating deep cultural, social, and religious differences."[462]

Burke's solidarist conception of international society has different implications for each of Wight's three traditions. First, it rejects realism's rigid focus on the state and disinterest in matters beneath the state that might affect international relations. Solidarism helps explain the success of international law and organizations among like-minded states, as noted by current scholars analyzing the special international political dynamics among liberal states.[463] Second, solidarism limits the potential of rationalism outside the context of cultural homogeneity. And finally, the importance of cultural solidarity calls into question practically and morally the universal aspirations of revolutionism.

The solidarist perspective in Burke's thinking also raises questions for so-called new approaches to international relations theory. According to Smith, a common feature of approaches that have developed since the 1970s is that they are "postpositivist"; they reject some or all of the assumptions made by mainstream theoretical approaches, such as realism and liberalism.[464] Smith included in these postpositivist approaches normative theory, feminist theory, critical theory, historical sociology, and postmodernism.[465] The nature of international society represents an important issue for each of these theories.

The rebirth of normative theory has been a key development in international theory since the late 1980s.[466] According to Brown, normative theory "addresses the moral dimensions of international relations and . . . the ethical nature of the relations between communities/states, whether in the context of the old agenda, which focused on violence and war, or the new(er) agenda, which mixes these traditional concerns with the modern demand for international distributive justice."[467] The main foci for contemporary normative theory—state autonomy, the ethics of the use of force, and international justice[468]—are also key issues for the international society tradition, and Burke himself addressed each of them in his writings and speeches. More specifically, Burke's perspective on international society relates to a prominent debate in normative theory between cosmopolitanism and communitarianism.[469] Although Burke appealed to a universal natural law applicable to humanity, his emphasis on cultural similitude as an underpinning for international society (particularly in Europe) parallels communitarianism as a normative approach to international relations.

Feminist theory, too, grapples with the role of culture in international relations. Feminists see the domestic and the international as fundamentally connected, a link realism denies. Feminist theorists argue that realism denies women a role in international relations because it associates femininity with the realm of the domestic. Similarly, gender issues historically have been outside the purview of the instruments of rationalism, namely, international law and organizations. With the treatment of women closely intertwined with cultural mores and traditions, feminist international relations theorists echo Burke in breaking down the distinction between domestic "private space" and international "public space."

Burke's emphasis on customs, manners, and mores as pillars of international order made his attitudes toward women part of his international thinking. Of course, feminists do not agree with *how* Burke connected gender and international order. Burke's famous anger about the treatment of the begums (princesses) of Oudh and other Indian women by the

East India Company and Marie Antoinette by the French revolutionaries has caught the critical eye of feminist analysis.[470] According to Zerilli, "The figure of a lady in distress is an all too common trope in Burke's writings and speeches."[471] The chivalric nature of Burke's prose in the Antoinette passage stems largely from his veneration of antiquity, especially the Middle Ages.[472] In defending the begums of Oudh, Burke highlighted the "reverence of 'eastern' people for women and the powerful influence that certain women exercise in such societies. The Begums of Oudh were such women and should have been treated with proper reverence by the East India Company."[473] Kramnick noted the parallel in Burke's writings on women in the French and Indian contexts, observing that "[t]he treatment of these [Indian] princesses becomes the grand metaphor for all that India represented for Burke just as the treatment of Marie Antoinette . . . would symbolize the passing of chivalry and the old order."[474] Although not feminist, the cultural foundations of Burke's international thinking do raise many issues at the heart of feminist approaches to international relations. The influence of culture in the gendering of social and political structures and interactions forms part of feminist analysis. In addition, much of the normative force of feminist theory seeks to liberate women from male-determined culture.[475]

Like normative theory, critical theory seeks "to improve human existence by abolishing injustice" by stimulating "alternative visions of world order."[476] According to critical theory, the existing structure of sovereign states causes injustice. But there is potential for change immanent in current political, economic, and social dynamics.[477] In examining the status quo, critical theorists focus on multiple forms of power and oppression, not just interstate relations, in order "to take account of the full impact of modernity, especially those structures formed and sustained under processes of globalization."[478] The ultimate goal of critical theory is to facilitate "the possibility of overcoming the sovereign state and inaugurating post-sovereign world politics."[479]

How culture factors into critical theory is a complicated matter. To a critical theorist, Burke is the quintessential "problem solver," the type of theorist who takes the existing structures as givens and merely tinkers with specific problems that arise within them.[480] Nothing exemplifies this as much as Burke's attachment to cultural similitude. Critical theorists, by contrast, aim to emancipate humanity, not merely to rearrange existing injustices. Emancipation on a global scale "involves the evolution of more inclusionary, less particularistic, forms of political association."[481] Critical theory seeks a form of global politics that is universal in scope and democratic in process, yet sensitive to diversity in practice. Although this sounds like Burke's "unity of spirit, diversity of operations" concept, it is fundamentally different. His concept was based on cultural similitude and is exclusionary from a critical theorist's point of view. Human emancipation must also involve emancipation from cultural practices that reinforce the oppressive and unfair system of sovereign state politics. In fact, it seeks a universal culture that liberates people from their exclusionary traditions. Whether this "liberation culture" is reminiscent of abstract radicalism or is a necessary precondition for progress in a globalized world remains an open question.

Culture features prominently in historical sociology as an approach to international relations. Historical sociologists are interested "in the ways in which societies develop through history."[482] In terms familiar to the student of Burke, they attempt to "show that there can be no simple distinction between international and domestic societies" and "that the state is created by international and domestic forces, and that the international is itself a determinant of the nature of the state."[483] There is much in Burke to support historical sociologists' claim that "[s]ocieties are structured primarily by entwined ideological, economic, military, and political power."[484] From the Burkean perspective, culture is at the center of the historical process that shapes domestic and international societies, and culture is in turn shaped by national and transnational forces.

Postmodernism asserts that nothing can be established as true outside a particular discourse.[485] For postmodernists, it would seem, culture is merely a "truth regime."[486] According to these theorists, cultural clashes in international relations are intersubjective contests between regimes of truth for which there is no arbiter. Domination and oppression exist as these different regimes rise and fall through history. Burke's use of natural law to defend Indian culture from British imperialism was simply an exportation of a European "truth regime"; it represented European domination, not moral sensitivity. Solidarism, as exhibited in Burke's perspective on international society, similarly has no objective value. Thus, what for Burke was the source of stability in international relations postmodernism seeks to destabilize.

A final "new approach" that grapples with cultural issues related to international society is social constructivism. The essence of this theory is captured in Wendt's argument that "anarchy is what states make of it."[487] The basic thrust of social constructivists is that the selfish, often violent behavior of states is not a natural, predetermined, or fixed outcome of a structural condition of interstate anarchy (as realists would have us believe). Instead, the type of anarchy witnessed in international relations is constructed by states themselves through their habitual interaction. State actors become "socialized" through the international system to act in ways that preclude deeper collaboration.

Social constructivism seems to parallel rationalism and its pluralistic approach to international society. It highlights the importance of the state and the interstate system simultaneously. Moreover, it recognizes the need and opportunity for reconstructing state interests and deepening the sense of society through international politics. Wendt developed his social constructivist approach "on behalf of the liberal claim that international institutions can transform state identities and interests."[488] As we have shown, this approach to building international society is incomplete from the Burkean perspective. Burke's thought stressed cultural homogeneity more prominently than the "instrumental parts" of international relations valued by social constructivists. The power of international institutions depends, claimed Burke, on cultural like-mindedness, not merely the existence of procedures such as international law. Burkean solidarism, therefore, poses challenges for social constructivism because it drills more deeply into the transnational, national, and subnational aspects of culture that influence peoples, states, and international institutions—for better or worse.

Our use of Burke's solidarism to explore the international society tradition and new theoretical approaches does not exhaust the ways his thinking might help illuminate current debates in the discipline of international relations. Our modest objective was to show that the Burkean perspective on international relations provides food for thought for both traditional and nontraditional international relations theorists. In other words, Burke's writings and speeches have not become theoretically soggy in the 200-plus years since his death. His continuing theoretical crispness forms part of his sustained relevance for thinking about contemporary international relations, to which we now turn in more detail.

ᗌ CHAPTER FOUR ᗌ

Burke's Relevance

Edmund Burke's eighteenth-century contemporaries recognized the great expanse of his political thinking and oratorical and literary powers. On a day when he was feeling under the weather and Burke became the topic of discussion, Samuel Johnson remarked: "That fellow calls forth all my powers. Were I to see Burke now, it would kill me."[489] George Canning summed up Burke's stature by writing upon the day of Burke's death: "There is but one event, but it is an event for the world. Burke is dead."[490] Even if his critics sometimes outnumbered his admirers, Burke's relevance to the great affairs of his time cannot be questioned. But how does Burke's thinking live for us today? This question, like so many others in Burke studies, has been controversial.

As discussed in the previous chapter, Burke's solidaristic perspective on international society remains relevant to the discipline of international relations. The debate about the nature of international society as either pluralist or solidarist continues to be important. We believe that Burke's contribution to this debate should also be briefly highlighted in connection with specific problems on the current landscape of world politics. Although scholars such as Macpherson find no present-day value in Burke's thought, others argue that he ought not to be forgotten.[491] We aim to establish a relevance for Burke that is deeper than his constant appropriation and reappropriation by the political left, right, and center.[492] Laski aptly captured Burke's importance to today's policymakers and scholars: "There is no wise man in politics, with an important decision to make, who would not do well to refresh his mind by discussion with Burke's mind."[493]

Burke During and After the Cold War

American scholars and conservatives led a renaissance in Burke studies in the 1950s as they searched his crusading counterrevolutionary writings to support the tenets of anti-communism. As O'Brien pointed out, enlisting Burke in the anti-Communist effort often produced distortions and abuses in the presentation of Burke's political philosophy.[494] One such distortion is that Burke is relevant only for counterrevolutionary purposes, which the collapse of communism and the end of the cold war have now drained of urgency and significance.

As Bolton observed, "The problem many [American] foreign policy analysts have today is that our 'French Revolution' problem is over."[495] In the late 1990s, "[i]nstead of the bright distinctions and clear battles to fight, we now have to face the ambiguities that Burke understood so well in contexts as disparate as colonial America, imperial India, and neighboring Ireland."[496] Burke's "understanding of the importance of circumstances in setting policy, his emphasis on prudence and 'rational, cool endeavors', and his devotion to practicality over abstraction" make his pragmatism a fitting model for American foreign-policy making in the era of globalization.[497] From this perspective, Burke's continued resonance flows from the prudential approach to politics he rigorously upheld as a model for one of the leading great powers of the eighteenth century. In his fight to temper the exercise of British might, he advocated a policy that melded self-interest, moral responsibility, and a concept of common humanity.

Burke's prudential approach to politics is particularly appropriate for the United States as the world's military, economic, and cultural hegemon because it would not only shield the United States from dogmatism but also protect its foreign and domestic interests. Burke's warning to Britain in *Remarks on the Policy of the Allies* is strikingly germane for the United States today:

> Among precautions against ambition, it may not be amiss to take one precaution against our *own*. I must fairly say, I dread our *own* power and our *own* ambition; I dread our being too much dreaded. It is ridiculous to say we are not men; and that, as men, we shall never wish to aggrandize ourselves in some way or other. Can we say, that even at this very hour we are not invidiously aggrandized? We are already in possession of almost all the commerce of the world. . . . If we should come to be in a condition not only to have all this ascendant in commerce, but to be absolutely able, without the least controul, to hold the commerce of all other Nations totally dependent upon our good pleasure, we may say that we shall not abuse this astonishing, and hitherto unheard of power. But every other Nation will think we shall abuse it. It is impossible but that sooner or later, this state of things must produce a combination against us which may end in our ruin.[498]

The virtue of prudence further prevents the conduct of foreign policy from corrupting domestic principles and ideals. A central theme of our treatment of Burke's theory of international relations is the importance of the British constitution and the threat to it created by British imperial behavior. His constant appeals to the British constitution reflected a belief that international relations are not a separate branch of politics but are intimately connected with all politics. Traces of this Burkean message can be found in twentieth-century thinkers such as George Kennan, who warned against the degradation of American domestic constitutional principles through corrupt and adventuristic foreign policies.

In the cases of Ireland, America, and India, Burke was dismayed that Britain acted as if its national principles and character changed the moment its ships left British shores. As we have shown, for Burke the nation was a "moral essence, not a geographical arrangement"; it could not change that essence when it exercised power beyond its borders without endangering the domestic political and moral order.[499] This "constitutional" perspective on foreign policy is sensitive to dangers to constitutional order lurking in the conduct of foreign affairs. Burke was always vigilant about the proper balance of power between the House of Commons and the Crown, and he believed, especially in the case of India, that foreign policy provided a dangerous means for the Crown to gain the upper hand on the Commons. The struggle between the U.S. executive and legislative branches for control over foreign affairs, present since the creation of the American republic, echoes Burke's constitutional insight.

Burke, Culture, and Contemporary International Relations

Although Burke's discussion of power—and how to balance it—is interesting for international relations today, it is ultimately a procedural rather than a substantive issue. What is more important, we believe, is Burke's solidarist conception of international society based on cultural homogeneity. We need to explore the relevance of this central aspect of Burke's thought to understand more fully his contribution to contemporary debates.

The Burkean perspective on international society heightens our sensitivity to the cultural landscape of international relations. Further, his conservative solidarism draws our attention to the fate of traditions, customs, manners, and mores and their importance in contemporary international affairs. Much scholarly and popular discourse today centers on the question whether cultural heterogeneity is a positive or negative force in international relations. Some commentators, such as Huntington, have predicted that civilizational differences will be the focal point for future warfare in the international system.[500] Others, such as the proponents of "Asian values," insist that the uniqueness of Asian culture explains why some societies have enjoyed economic success without the social ills suffered in Western nations.[501] Indeed, some critics of globalization fear that its processes are homogenizing (or Americanizing) culture around the world to the detriment of non-Western cultures. Barber argued, for example, that cultural homogenization and renewed ethnic tensions are occurring simultaneously in a dialectical "jihad versus McWorld."[502]

If, in Zakaria's words, "culture is in" for the study of international relations, what does the Burkean perspective have to add to contemporary discourse?[503] In linking Burke's observations about cultural similitude to today's world, a fundamental question emerges. What potential exists for deepening solidarity in an international system characterized by cultural heterogeneity? This question drives to the heart of both Burke's thinking and its relevance for contemporary international affairs.

We have shown that Burke believed that international order and justice depended on the existence of deep cultural solidarity among states and peoples. This solidarity in the imperial society flowed from the British constitution and the role it played in British society, at home and abroad. The commonwealth of Europe rested on the foundation of a shared political, economic, legal, and religious heritage. Outside these two contexts, whatever solidarity existed between Britain and India depended on the concept of natural law, a much less solid foundation. Despite the massive changes in international relations since Burke's time, his focus on the need for solidarity remains relevant. Much of the debate between solidarism and pluralism in international relations theory involves a continuing desire to establish international order and justice on foundations firmer than what Burke called "papers and seals." This desire can even be seen animating the thinking of key theorists of the English School, such as Hedley Bull. Wheeler and Dunne demonstrated how Bull struggled to reconcile pluralism and solidarism in his own thinking.[504] In *The Anarchical Society,* Bull concluded:

The future of international society is likely to be determined . . . by the preservation and extension of a cosmopolitan culture, embracing both common ideas and common values, and rooted in societies in general as well as in their elites, that can provide the world international society of today with the kind of underpinning enjoyed by the geographically smaller and culturally more homogeneous international societies of the past.[505]

Burke's emphasis on the constitutional principles of one great power and the cultural heritage of a particular geographic region today seem inappropriate as paradigms for establishing cosmopolitan solidarity. In contemporary international affairs, liberalism is the leading candidate for fostering solidarism among states and peoples through the creation of transnational liberal values. Scholars such as Doyle and Fukuyama believe that the unique relations liberal states enjoy with each other carry the potential to promote more order and justice domestically and internationally.[506] Unlike Burkean conservatism, liberalism has universal potential as well, addressing the need for what Bull called a "cosmopolitan culture."

Whether liberalism really can create deeper solidarity in this culturally heterogeneous world remains controversial for many reasons.[507] We focus here on concerns raised from within the Burkean perspective to demonstrate its continued relevance. First, the unique nature of the "liberal peace" can be seen to stem from not only philosophical like-mindedness but also cultural similitude. Established liberal states are, by and large, connected directly to the cultural heritage Burke identified as the core of the commonwealth of Europe. The special nature of interliberal state relations is, therefore, not solely the product of culturally heterogeneous nations' dedicating themselves to abstract propositions concerning democracy, the rule of law, economic interdependence, and human rights. Cultural similitude still factors strongly into the special place liberalism holds in contemporary international affairs.

Second, the resurgence of interest in culture as a factor in international relations reveals great friction in the dominance of liberal values and interests in international institutions. Some of this resentment represents suspicion and opposition to liberal institutions and values in non-Western societies.[508] But the friction also reflects fear about liberalism's potential to transform traditional cultures in the image of Western societies.[509] Part of the angst over the prominence of liberalism is driven by liberal states' use of international law and institutions as instruments of liberal solidarism. Embedding the liberal objectives of democracy, the rule of law, free trade, and human rights into international law and the dynamics of international institutions changes the instruments of pluralistic rationalism into potential weapons of revolutionary solidarism.

Finally, Burke's conception of international society encourages us to question the substantive reality of any emerging liberal cosmopolitan culture. Liberal concepts such as democracy, capitalism, the rule of law, and human rights often find shallow expression in nonliberal cultures, suggesting that liberal "solidarity" is not so deep. In fact, it can appear remarkably fragile. Commentators have used terms such as "pseudo-capitalism" and "low-intensity democracy" to describe the thin liberal veneer applied in many nonliberal cultures.[510] In addition, it is clear that liberal values are not penetrating at equal speeds. Market reforms often occur readily, whereas political reforms lag far behind, reinforcing existing problems within the society in question. Indeed, the advocates of "Asian values" maintained that Asian countries could be capitalistic without the political or social aspects of liberalism.[511] Seen through a Burkean lens, today's vision of deeper solidarity through liberalism remains at best a distant dream. As a cultural matter, international society is currently lumpy; it has pockets of deep homogeneity amid general heterogeneity.

From the Burkean perspective, the "liberal peace" thesis remains culturally bounded, as were Burke's concepts of the imperial society and the commonwealth of Europe. In many ways the special nature of the relations among liberal states rests on cultural solidarity—common political, economic, legal, religious, and social values and practices. To paraphrase Burke, when a citizen of a liberal state travels or resides for health, pleasure, business, or necessity within any country within the liberal alliance, he or she never feels quite abroad. The limited scope of Burkean solidarism better explains the "liberal peace" than does the cosmopolitan ambition of liberal solidarism. There is perhaps no more fitting example of this than the European Union, the modern-day expression of so much of what Burke found important about the commonwealth of Europe. As with the commonwealth of Europe, the pillars of the European Union are shared concepts of political legitimacy, mutual security concerns, common culture, economic intercourse, and geographical proximity. Although the shared view of political legitimacy has changed dramatically since Burke's day, Burkean solidarism can help explain the extraordinary status the European Union has in international relations.

Two particular aspects of the liberal agenda reinforce Burkean skepticism about the potential of liberalism to foster deeper solidarity in international relations: human rights and economic interdependence. The liberal attachment to human rights continues to create cultural tension in international society. Human rights embedded in international law are proclaimed to be universal, but many countries and commentators continue to reject the universality of "Western" conceptions of human rights in the name of cultural relativism.[512] As Vincent argued, "[W]hat the doctrine of cultural relativity allows in practice is a surrender to what John Stuart Mill called the 'despotism of custom.'"[513] Burke's attacks on Hastings's geographical morality indicate that he rejected cultural relativism in favor of a universal sense of justice that governments (and nonstate actors) could not violate in their policies. Burke's use of natural law to affirm the legitimacy of Indian culture should not be stretched to claim that he placed Indian governments beyond the pale of criticism for the treatment of their subjects. Characteristically, Burke found natural law reflected in the specific religious and political laws that developed in India. As he stated in *Speech on Opening of Impeachment,* he "would as willingly have him [Hastings] tried upon the law of the Koran, or the Institutes of Tamerlane, as upon the Common Law or the Statute Law of this Kingdom."[514] Today's cultural relativist critics of international human rights law often use culture to shield the arbitrary, unrestrained application of government power from transnational scrutiny.[515] This is a practice that Burkean thinking does not support. As we have shown, Burke's weak sense of sovereignty and belief that states formed part of a greater "neighborhood" provide sufficient ground on which to challenge a government for mistreating its citizens. He in fact argued that states can intervene to "afford succour to the miserable Sufferers" who live under "atrocious and bloody tyranny."[516]

Burke's appeal to natural law does not, however, mean his thinking upholds universalism in contemporary human rights. Burke's interest in concrete circumstances and his respect for how natural law is differently reflected in diverse cultures raise questions for the universal aspirations of today's human rights discourse. The protection of human rights became an issue in international law after World War II because states came to believe that a government's treatment of its citizens was a matter of concern for international peace and order. Burke's opposition to the French Revolution was based on the belief that the tyrannical behavior of the Jacobins threatened international peace and security. Like contemporary proponents of human rights law, he drew a connection between the domestic and the international. But central to Burke's reaction to the French Revolution was his concept of the commonwealth of Europe, an entity that was culturally specific. In addition, his opposition to the French Revolution was based not on how the Jacobins were mistreating the French "people" but rather on the Jacobin threat to monarchy, religion, and property—the pillars of national and international order. His ideas on permeable sovereignty and intervention stemmed from a deeper confidence in a definable set of common values and practices among European states. In the French context, "[h]is intervention is in the name of legitimism rather than progressivism."[517] Burke's view thus does not champion an energetic doctrine of humanitarian intervention.

Burke's conservative solidarism is interesting today given the controversies surrounding the punishment of individuals under international law for violating human rights. The detention and extradition proceedings against former Chilean dictator Augusto Pinochet in 1998–1999 brought this issue to prominence. Many, including nongovernmental organizations such as Amnesty International and Human Rights Watch, have urged that Pinochet be extradited and punished for the human rights violations committed under his regime in Chile. This position stands firmly on the universalism of human rights, particularly the concept of universal jurisdiction of perpetrators of human rights abuses.[518] Others, such as Bolton, believe that those seeking to prosecute persons accused of violating international human rights norms have in their "utopian zeal" lost sight of the political context of such violations.[519] Perhaps revealing his Burkean sympathies, Bolton has argued that "[n]either the 'one size fits all' prosecutorial strategy, nor a uniform preference for amnesty or some non-juridical alternative in every case, would be justifiable. Circumstances differ, and circumstances matter."[520]

Two cases from Burke's writings and speeches are particularly instructive in this context: (1) his comments on the appropriate handling of persons associated with the revolutionary atrocities in France and (2) his belief, expressed in the Hastings impeachment, that individuals are accountable for committing atrocities.[521] In the case of punishing the French revolutionaries, Burke's foremost concern was the restoration of the ancien régime and the return of France to its rightful place in the commonwealth of Europe and European balance of power.

Once the recovery of France was complete, retribution could be pursued, but in a very particular way. Burke first disclaimed "the interference of foreign powers in a business that properly belongs to the Government which we have declared legal."[522] Later he remarked that "I am not for a total indemnity, nor a general punishment" and proceeded to analyze the contexts in which amnesty should be granted or punishment warranted.[523] He characteristically singled out for punishment individuals guilty of regicide and destruction of property and religion after the conduct of fair trials.[524] Burke combined the need for both social stability and justice, but with a clear emphasis on restoration of order.

In connection with his pursuit of Hastings, Burke's overriding goal was to hold the East India Company and its officials accountable for their atrocities in India. Even though he knew from the earliest days of his campaign that Hastings would be acquitted, Burke conceived of his task less as punishment than instruction for posterity. In this case Burke serves as an ally for those who believe the task of exposing atrocities and calling people into account for them has value whether or not the wrongdoers are ever actually punished.

Burke's thinking in these two cases reminds us of the search to balance domestic order and justice through truth and reconciliation processes that many countries have undertaken during transitions from dictatorships to democracies. Although many human rights activists dislike these processes because perpetrators of atrocities sometimes escape punishment, Burke's emphasis on order and stability as a primary objective supports these attempts to balance order and justice and to expose accountability for evil acts. The decision to punish should, under the Burkean view, be left in the hands of the legitimate government and should not be the business of other countries.

Taking all these observations on Burke's solidarism into account, the challenge with international human rights law is that it is a culturally inspired project on a global rather than regional scale. As such, it confronts deep cultural heterogeneity around the world. From the Burkean perspective, the extensive use of international law to prescribe human rights represents lots of "papers and seals" absent the all-important "obligations written in the heart." The weakness of contemporary international human rights law is not a function of weak institutions (e.g., no adequate enforcement mechanisms) but of cultural dissonance. As a result, this body of law does not yet signal growing cosmopolitan solidarity among states or peoples.

The second aspect of the liberal agenda for cosmopolitan solidarity—economic interdependence—triggers Burkean concerns as well. With the end of the cold war, international economic and commercial issues occupy a more prominent place in international relations. The failure of communism as an economic theory and a political system has precipitated the global ascendance of liberal economic thinking, both within states and in international law and organizations.[525] A driving force behind the globalization of markets is liberal and neoliberal economic thought and policy, reflected in such institutions as the World Trade Organization, World Bank, and International Monetary Fund. The growing literature and controversy about globalization reveals the disquiet about this rise of liberal thinking. Although globalization is much more than an economic phenomenon, the globalization of markets for goods, services, and capital has captured the lion's share of attention in current analyses. As Walker and Fox argued, "The key feature which underlies the concept of globalization . . . is the erosion and irrelevance of national boundaries in markets which can truly be described as global."[526]

Burke's name does not instantly come to mind in the globalization debate. After all, the historical circumstances of the era of globalization, with the growing influence of new information technologies and new "territories" of competition in cyberspace, seem far removed from eighteenth-century Europe. Burke's thinking, however, is surprisingly helpful in understanding the discourse about the globalization of markets. His weak conception of sovereignty is a handy reference for those who express concern about globalization's corrosive effect on statehood. As noted in Chapter 3, Burke conceived of the state and sovereignty as less than absolute and permeable to all kinds of political, economic, and moral influences. He constantly reminded his audiences of the interdependence between the domestic and international, which is a key theme in globalization literature.

Then, too, Burke's pragmatic rather than ideological support for free trade connects with modern complaints about the ideological imposition of liberal economics on states and within international regimes.[527] Maynes wrote, for example, that the "fundamental truth" that open economies perform better than closed economies "was transformed during the 1990s into an increasingly rigid ideology that blinded otherwise intelligent people to some of the inherent shortcomings of a free market."[528] In Burke-like language, Maynes suggested that "[t]he new [liberal] orthodoxy's command of economics was better than its command of politics; [and] it overestimated the power of logic while underestimating the power of psychology."[529] Burke's writings and speeches on free trade teach us about the need for prudence and sensitivity to context when applying economic theory.[530] Above all, his approach frowns upon the penchant to prescribe abstract liberal economic theory as the cure-all for every national and global economic problem.

Third, Burke's views on free trade and market economics contained a social element that speaks to current angst about globalization. The "market" for Burke was not merely a place to exchange goods and resources; it was the very stuff of social relations. Through economic behavior people exercised their liberty and formed the "little platoons" that provided a buffer between the state and the individual. A similar conception of the market permeates his international thinking. In keeping with his pragmatic approach to economics, Burke saw trade as an instrument of social cohesion within and across borders. For example, central to Burke's support for liberalized trade with Ireland and America was his belief that commerce would serve the greater cause of reinforcing bonds among the peoples within the imperial society. Burke's ideas are therefore relevant to concerns that the globalization of markets is weakening social relations within and among nations. Increasing aggregate world wealth through free trade and the globalization of markets will ultimately prove sterile or dangerous if the social aspects of such economic activities are ignored.

Finally, Burke's efforts on India demonstrate that he possessed moral sensibility in connection with economic intercourse among peoples of different cultures. His writings on India would make relevant reading for those struggling with the fate of developing countries. Although Burke acknowledged that trade and commerce translate into power, he also knew that economically powerful states ran the risk of abusing their power through either fear or arrogance. Burke's writings on America and Ireland are germane for those who view international economic discourse, particularly among industrialized democracies, as a zero-sum game. Within a community of like-minded states, economic power fluctuates. But the point often overlooked is that the fluctuations benefit all members of the community in the long run provided that other bases of social cohesion remain strong. As Burke understood, to look beyond short-term trends in economic relations takes historical perspective and often enlightened self-interest.

Another aspect of moral responsibility in Burke's economic thinking arises when the strong interact with the weak in a context of cultural difference. Burke's writings on India send the message that material inequality among peoples does not translate into moral inequality. Even though India was outside the imperial society and the commonwealth of Europe, he struggled to ensure that economic relations between Britain and India retained moral sensitivity. Surveying the post–cold war "bourgeois triumphalism," Almond wrote:

Burke surely would have considered the subordination of all policy to the selfish interests of individuals as not just short-sighted in the extreme, but as the denial of the proper rôle of statesman and merchant. The interpenetration of élites, post-communist and post-Burkean, across the northern hemisphere is not producing the well-ordered society and economy advocated by Burke.[531]

Burke's respect for the Indian peoples, culture, and society stands as a warning against affluence-inspired arrogance and hubris in the dynamics of the global economic system. This message is much needed in a time when the developing world is being transformed from a battleground in a strategic and ideological struggle into a new playing field for the rich and powerful in the search for global economic competitive advantage.

Burke's wrath against Warren Hastings and the East India Company should also inform the behavior of individuals and private companies in the conduct of global business. Burke set out to expose not only official British policy but also the immoral activities of nonstate actors. He was determined to see the East India Company held publicly accountable for its actions. The exposure by nongovernmental organizations that Western multinational corporations (MNCs) are engaging in various forms of economic exploitation and environmental degradation in developing countries echoes Burke's tireless campaign against the rapacious acts of the servants of the East India Company and attempts to hold them accountable. In addition, Burke's involvement with India draws attention to the issue of governmental complicity and corruption in allowing such abuses to occur and continue. His call for British behavior in India to be informed not only by British law but also the spirit of British principles of fairness and justice transcends the context of the eighteenth century. It speaks to personal, corporate, and governmental conduct in the era of globalization.

Burkean skepticism about the potential of liberalism to build deeper solidarity in international relations also contains the more general position that deeper solidarity in a culturally heterogeneous world is an illusory goal. This doubt can be read as a virtue and a vice in connection with contemporary international affairs. The virtue is that it produces tolerance of cultural differences among states in the international system. Burke's struggle to reform British imperial policy in Ireland, America, and India was largely about getting the British government to respect diversity, whether in the form of the American national character, Irish Catholicism, or traditional Indian culture.

The vice is that for many scholars in the international society tradition it fails to provide a sufficient moral vision for international society.[532] For those within this tradition who are disillusioned with pluralism and are seeking to advance solidarism globally, Burke's perspective seems to offer little help. If cultural heterogeneity continues to throw international society back toward pluralism, then the moral contribution of the society of states to both international order and justice may be undermined in the long run. Indeed, for modern-day international relations scholars, Burke's conception of international society provides a weak foundation for pluralism; any rules of coexistence between culturally heterogeneous states simply reflect the temporary convergence of selfish interests or the vague tenets of natural law. How different, it may be asked, is this conception from the weakest forms of rationalism or even realism?

The importance of Burkean skepticism about the potential for cosmopolitan solidarity is not, however, diminished because it moves against the normative trends in the international society tradition. To date, the search for cosmopolitan solidarity has not proved very successful practically or theoretically. In fact, an interesting feature of recent writing in the international society tradition serves to underscore the continuing power of the Burkean view. Within "critical international society theory," the pressure for cosmopolitan solidarism comes not from states but from civil society mobilized transnationally.[533] As Wheeler and Dunne observed, "The limitations of governments as agents of humanity lead critics of the society of states to invest their hopes in non-governmental agencies and the conscience of world public opinion."[534] This position reflects a rejection of the distinction between domestic and international politics, something that was already fundamental to Burke's thinking.[535] Nonetheless, there is no guarantee that the development of global society will be any less "elitist" than the current society of states. In Burke's time it was less significant that those who enjoyed the benefits of transnationalism belonged to a small sliver of the European population. For today's critical international society theorists, however, an elitist global civil society falls far short of the kind of cosmopolitan solidarity they seek.

From a Burkean perspective, what may be more significant than either states or nongovernmental organizations pushing solidaristic projects is the cultural homogenization being fostered below the state by the processes of globalization, especially in the economic context. As we noted earlier, globalization is accelerating the blurring of the domestic and the international and may be fostering a globalized culture by allowing Western ways of life to penetrate deeply into non-Western societies. Because private as well as public forces drive globalization, its cultural ramifications have been prominent. "The dilemma that emerged right across the world," wrote Murden, "was the extent to which engaging with the world market economy threatened existing patterns of culture and social order."[536]

Will globalization lay the groundwork for the deep, transcultural solidarism that states and nongovernmental organizations have found so difficult to create? Burke's thinking on culture suggests a negative answer to this question. Although Burke stressed the social context of economic activity, his sensitivity to cultural differences in connection with economic intercourse suggests that he saw limits to the "community-building" potential of commerce. To produce "obligations written on the heart" on a truly global scale will require more than inculcating non-Western peoples with consumerism. Cultural solidarity for Burke involved a complex set of historical, political, legal, economic, moral, and religious factors that globalization by itself cannot replicate.

More important for Burke's theory are conservative concerns about the culture-destroying potential of globalization. As we have shown, Burke maintained that the British had moral responsibility in their encounters with a poorer, less technologically powerful people that encompassed both respecting what existed in India and adding to its cultural stock through peaceful commercial intercourse with Britain. Burke's rhetorical questions in *Speech on Nabob of Arcot's Debts*, about British behavior in India, remain important as we consider the effects of the processes of globalization on developing countries today:

What are the articles of commerce, or the branches of manufacture which those gentlemen [of the East India Company] have carried hence to enrich India? What are the sciences they beamed out to enlighten it? What are the arts they introduced to chear and adorn it? What are the religious, what the moral institutions they have taught among that people as a guide to life, or as a consolation when life is to be no more . . . ?[537]

Whether the processes of globalization enrich, enlighten, cheer, adorn, teach, or console traditional cultures in the developing world remains very much open to debate. Whether globalization helps transform the "papers and seals" between states into "obligations written in the hearts" of culturally heterogeneous peoples constitutes one of the great but enigmatic questions for the new millennium.

Conclusion

Looking back into the wisdom of history and the thinking of Burke may not, in the end, help us meet future challenges that await states and peoples. So much of what is shaping the world today was not foreseen even fifteen years ago, let alone in the context of Burke's age. Burke himself recognized the limits of history as a guide for future action. Reflecting on the French Revolution, he wrote:

> But these things history and books of speculation . . . did not teach men to foresee, and of course to resist. Now that they are no longer a matter of sagacity, it would be unjustifiable to go back to the records of other times, to instruct us to manage what they never enabled us to foresee.[538]

These cautionary sentiments about history's wisdom can also apply to how we use Burke in the future. Burke endeavored in "other times" to improve empire and build community, and we can learn much from his thinking, which remains highly relevant to this day. But he would have been the first to chastise those who confuse his theoretical and historical relevance for substantive policy in the world of current circumstances. Such confusion, he might have observed, would not be prudent.

PART TWO

Writings and Speeches

Selections

CHAPTER FIVE

On Ireland

Introductory Note to
Two Letters on the Trade of Ireland
(1778)

Burke sent Two Letters on the Trade of Ireland *to merchants in his Bristol constituency to answer concerns about his support in Parliament for limited measures to liberalize Irish trade. These measures were proposed after Britain had suffered setbacks in the war in the American colonies, including the entry of France into the war on the side of the Americans. Burke used the American crisis to point out that liberalizing trade was a small, incomplete step toward healing the relations between Britain and* "those parts . . . which are still content to be governed by our councils." *Burke told his constituents that the* "evils" *that arose from the American policy would be aggravated by the rejection of the Irish trade measures. As the American crisis destroyed Burke's vision of the transatlantic imperial society, his support of the Irish trade measures resulted in part from his desire to preserve what remained of the imperial society. Although the revolution in America weighed heavily on Burke's mind in relation to the Irish trade measures,* Two Letters on the Trade of Ireland *also contained Burke's strong belief in the benefits of imperial free trade.*

As can be sensed from the defensive posture of these two letters, Burke's attachment to the preservation of the British imperial society and his belief in free trade within such society did not win him many friends in Bristol. Burke lost his seat in Bristol in the election of 1780, and he attributed his problems with his constituents to his efforts on behalf of free trade with Ireland and relief of Irish Catholics.[1] As O'Brien commented, "He put free trade principles, in relation to trade between Ireland and Britain, ahead of the perceived interests of his most powerful constituents."[2] *Burke concluded the first of the two letters with his creed that the elected leader* "speaks the language of truth and sincerity; and that he is not ready to take up or lay down a great political system for the convenience of the hour; that he is in parliament to support his opinion of the public good, and does not form his opinion in order to get into parliament, or to continue in it." ~

---

[1]One month after he wrote *Two Letters on the Trade of Ireland,* Burke vigorously supported measures to relax the Penal Laws against Irish Catholics, measures that became the Catholic Relief Act of 1778. See Burke's discussion of his efforts on behalf of Irish free trade and the Irish Catholics in his 1780 *Speech at Bristol Previous to the Election, WSEB,* iii, 620–664.

[2]O'Brien, *The Great Melody,* 71.

Two Letters on the Trade of Ireland (1778)

First Letter

To Samuel Span, Esq.: Master of the Society of Merchants Adventurers of Bristol.

Sir,

I am honoured with your letter of the 13th, in answer to mine, which accompanied the resolutions of the House relative to the trade of Ireland.

෴

The fault I find in the scheme is,—that it falls extremely short of that liberality in the commercial system, which, I trust, will one day be adopted. If I had not considered the present resolutions, merely as preparatory to better things, and as a means of shewing experimentally, that justice to others is not always folly to ourselves, I should have contented myself with receiving them in a cold and silent acquiescence. Separately considered, they are matters of no very great importance. But they aim, however imperfectly, at a right principle. I submit to the restraint to appease prejudice: I accept the enlargement, so far as it goes, as the result of reason and of sound policy.

We cannot be insensible of the calamities which have been brought upon this nation by an obstinate adherence to narrow and restrictive plans of government. I confess, I cannot prevail on myself to take them up, precisely at a time, when the most decisive experience has taught the rest of the world to lay them down. The propositions in question did not originate from me, or from my particular friends.

But when things are so right in themselves, I hold it my duty, not to enquire from what hands they come. I opposed the American measures upon the very same principle on which I support those that relate to Ireland. I was convinced, that the evils which have arisen from the adoption of the former, would be infinitely aggravated by the rejection of the latter.

Perhaps Gentlemen are not yet fully aware of the situation of their country, and what its exigencies absolutely require. I find that we are still disposed to talk at our ease, and as if all things were to be regulated by our good pleasure. I should consider it as a fatal symptom, if, in our present distressed and adverse circumstances, we should persist in the errors which are natural only to prosperity. One cannot indeed sufficiently lament the continuance of that spirit of delusion, by which, for a long time past, we have thought fit to measure our necessities by our inclinations. Moderation, prudence, and equity, are far more suitable to our conditions, than loftiness, and confidence, and rigour. We are threatened by enemies of no small magnitude, whom, if we think fit, we may despise, as we have despised others; but they are enemies who can only cease to be truly formidable, by our entertaining a due respect for their power. Our danger will not be lessened by our shutting our eyes to it; nor will our force abroad be encreased by rendering ourselves feeble, and divided at home.

There is a dreadful schism in the British nation. Since we are not able to reunite the empire, it is our business to give all possible vigour and soundness to those parts of it which are still content to be governed by our councils. Sir, it is proper to inform you, that our measures *must be healing.* Such a degree of strength must be communicated to all the members of the state, as may enable them to defend themselves, and to co-operate in the defence of the whole. Their temper too must be managed, and their good affections cultivated. They may then be disposed to bear the load with chearfulness, as a contribution towards what may be called with truth and propriety, and not by an empty form of words, *a common cause*. Too little dependence cannot be had, at this time of day, on names and prejudices. The eyes of mankind are opened; and communities must be held together by an evident and solid interest. God forbid, that our conduct should demonstrate to the world, that Great Britain can, in no instance whatsoever, be brought to a sense of rational and equitable policy, but by coercion and force of arms!

I wish you to recollect, with what powers of concession, relatively to commerce, as well as to legislation, his Majesty's Commissioners to the United Colonies have sailed from England within this week.[3] Whether these powers are sufficient for their purposes, it is not now my business to examine. But we all know, that our resolutions in favour of Ireland are trifling and insignificant, when compared with the concessions to the Americans. At such a juncture, I would implore every man, who retains the least spark of regard to the yet remaining honour and security of this country, not to compel others to an imitation of their conduct; or by passion and violence, to force them to seek in the territories of the separation, that freedom, and those advantages, which they are not to look for whilst they remain under the wings of their ancient government.

After all, what are the matters we dispute with so much warmth? Do we in these resolutions *bestow* any thing upon Ireland? Not a shilling. We only consent to *leave* to them, in two or three instances, the use of the natural faculties which God has given to them, and to all mankind. Is Ireland united to the crown of Great Britain for no other purpose, than that we should counteract the bounty of Providence in her favour? And in proportion as that bounty has been liberal, that we are to regard it as an evil, which is to be met with in every sort of corrective? To say that Ireland interferes with us, and therefore must be checked, is, in my opinion, a very mistaken, and a very dangerous principle. I must beg leave to repeat, what I took the liberty of suggesting to you in my last letter, that Ireland is a country, in the same climate, and of the same natural qualities and productions, with this; and has consequently no other means of growing wealthy in herself, or, in other words, of being useful to us, but by doing the very same things which we do, for the same purposes. I hope that in Great Britain we shall always pursue, without exception, *every* means of prosperity; and of course, that Ireland *will* interfere with us in something or other; for either, in order to *limit* her, we *must restrain* ourselves, or we must fall into that shocking conclusion, that we are to keep our yet remaining dependency, under a general and indiscriminate restraint, for the mere purpose of oppression. Indeed, Sir, England and Ireland may flourish together. The world is large enough for us both. Let it be our care, not to make ourselves too little for it.

I know it is said, that the people of Ireland do not pay the same taxes, and therefore ought not in equity to enjoy the same benefits with this. I had hopes, that the unhappy phantom of a compulsory *equal*

---

[3]Parliament authorized King George III in March 1778 to appoint commissioners to negotiate with the Americans. The commissioners sailed for the colonies in April 1778.

taxation had haunted us long enough. I do assure you, that until it is entirely banished from our imaginations, . . . we shall never cease to do ourselves the most substantial injuries. To that argument of equal taxation, I can only say,—that Ireland pays as many taxes, as those who are the best judges of her powers, are of opinion she can bear. To bear more she must have more ability; and in the order of nature, the advantage must *precede* the charge. This disposition of things, being the law of God, neither you not I *can* alter it. So that if you will have more help from Ireland, you must *previously* supply her with more means. I believe it will be found, that if men are suffered freely to cultivate their natural advantages, a virtual equality of contribution will come in its own time, and will flow by an easy descent, through its own proper and natural channels. An attempt to disturb that course, and to force nature, will only bring on universal discontent, distress and confusion.

You tell me, Sir, that you prefer an union with Ireland to the little regulations which are proposed in Parliament. This union is a great question of state, to which, when it comes properly before me in my parliamentary capacity, I shall give an honest and unprejudiced consideration. However, it is a settled rule with me, to make the most of my *actual situation;* and not to refuse to do a proper thing, because there is something else more proper, which I am not able to do. This union is a business of difficulty; and on the principles of your letter, a business impracticable. Until it can be matured into a feasible and desirable scheme, I wish to have as close an union of interest and affection with Ireland, as I can have; and that, I am sure, is a far better thing than any nominal union of government.

France, and indeed most extensive empires, which by various designs and for-

tunes have grown into one great mass, contain many Provinces that are very different from each other in privileges and modes of government; and they raise their supplies in different ways; in different proportions; and under different authorities; yet none of them are for this reason, curtailed of their natural rights; but they carry on trade and manufactures with perfect equality. In some way or other the true balance is found; and all of them are properly poised and harmonised. How much have you lost by the participation of Scotland in all your commerce? The external trade of England has more than doubled since that period;[4] and I believe your internal (which is the most advantageous) has been augmented at least four-fold. Since virtue there is in liberality of sentiment, that you have grown richer even by the partnership of poverty.

If you think, that this participation was a loss, commercially considered, but that it has been compensated by the share which Scotland has taken in defraying the public charge—I believe you have not very carefully looked at the public accounts. Ireland, Sir, pays a great deal more than Scotland; and is perhaps as much, and as effectually united to England as Scotland is. But if Scotland, instead of paying little, had paid nothing at all, we should be gainers, not losers by acquiring the hearty cooperation of an active intelligent people, towards the increase of the common stock; instead of our being employed in watching and counteracting them, and their being employed in watching and counteracting us, with the peevish and churlish jealousy of rivals and enemies on both sides.

I am sure, Sir, that the commercial experience of the merchants of Bristol, will

---

[4]England and Scotland were united under the name "Great Britain" in 1707.

soon disabuse them of the prejudice, that they can trade no longer, if countries more lightly taxed, are permitted to deal in the same commodities at the same markets. You know, that in fact you trade very largely where you are met by the goods of all nations. You even pay high duties, on the import of your goods, and afterwards undersell nations less taxed, at their own markets; and where goods of the same kind are not charged at all. If it were otherwise, you could trade very little. You know, that the price of all sorts of manufacture is not a great deal inhanced, (except to the domestic consumer) by any taxes paid in this country. This I might very easily prove.

The same consideration will relieve you from the apprehension you express, with relation to sugars, and the difference of the duties paid here and in Ireland. Those duties affect the interior consumer only; and for obvious reasons, relative to the interest of revenue itself, they must be proportioned to his ability of payment; but in all cases in which sugar can be an *object of commerce,* and therefore (in this view) of rivalship, you are sensible, that you are at least on a par with Ireland. As to your apprehensions concerning the more advantageous situation of Ireland, for some branches of commerce, . . . I trust you will not find them more serious. Milford Haven, which is at your door, may serve to shew you, that the mere advantage of ports is not the thing which shifts the seat of commerce from one part of the world to the other. If I thought you inclined to take up this matter on local considerations, I should state to you, that I do not know any part of the kingdom so well situated for an advantageous commerce with Ireland as Bristol; and that none would be so likely to profit of its prosperity as our city. But your profit and theirs must concur.

Beggary and bankruptcy are not the circumstances which invite to an intercourse with that or with any country; and I believe it will be found invariably true, that the superfluities of a rich nation furnish a better object of trade than the necessities of a poor one. It is the interest of the commercial world that wealth should be found every where.

~

I have written this long letter, in order to give all possible satisfaction to my constituents with regard to the part I have taken in this affair. It gave me inexpressible concern to find, that my conduct had been a cause of uneasiness to any of them. Next to my honour and conscience, I have nothing so near and dear to me as their approbation. However, I had much rather run the risque of displeasing than of injuring them;—if I am driven to make such an option. You obligingly lament, that you are not to have me for your advocate; but if I had been capable of acting as an advocate in opposition to a plan so perfectly consonant to my known principles, and to the opinions I had publicly declared on an hundred occasions, I should only disgrace myself, without supporting with the smallest degree of credit or effect, the cause you wished me to undertake. I should have lost the only thing which can make such abilities as mine of any use to the world now or hereafter; I mean that authority which is derived from an opinion, that a member speaks the language of truth and sincerity; and that he is not ready to take up or lay down a great political system for the convenience of the hour; that he is in parliament to support his opinion of the public good, and does not form his opinion in order to get into parliament, or to continue in it. It is in a great measure for your sake, that I wish to preserve this character.

Without it, I am sure, I should be ill able to discharge, by any service, the smallest part of that debt of gratitude and affection, which I owe you for the great and honourable trust you have reposed in me. I am, with the highest regard and esteem,

Sir,
Your most obedient
And humble Servant

E.B.
Beaconsfield
23d April, 1778

Second Letter

Gentlemen

It gives me the most sensible Concern to find, that my Vote on the Resolutions relative to the Trade of Ireland, has not been fortunate enough to meet with your approbation. I have explained at large the Grounds of my Conduct on that occasion in my Letters to the Merchants Hall. But my very sincere regard and Esteem for you will not permit me to let the matter pass without an explanation, which is particular to yourselves, and which I hope, will prove satisfactory to you.

↫

The reason, Gentlemen, for taking this step, at this time, is but too obvious, and too urgent. I cannot imagine, that you forget the great War, which has been carried on with so little success (and as I thought with so little Policy) in America; or that you are not aware of the other great Wars, which are impending. Ireland has been called upon, to repel the attacks of Enemies of no small power, brought upon her by Councils, in which she has had no share.

The very purpose and declared object of that Original War, which has brought other Wars, and other Enemies on Ireland,[5] was not very flattering to her dignity, her Interest, or to the very principle of her Liberty. Yet she submitted patiently to the Evils she suffered from an attempt, to *subdue* to your obedience, Countries, whose very Commerce was not open to her. America was to be conquered, in order that Ireland should *not* Trade thither; whilst the miserable Trade, which she is permitted to carry on to other places, has been torn to pieces in the struggle. In this situation, are we neither, to suffer her to have any real Interest in our quarrel; or to be flatter'd with the hope of any future means of bearing the Burthens, which she is to incurr in defending herself against Enemies which we have brought upon her?

I cannot set my face against such Arguments. Is it quite fair to suppose, that I have no other Motive for yielding to them, but a desire of acting *against* my Constituents? It is *for* you, and *for* your Interest, as a dear, cherished, and respected part, of a valuable whole, that I have taken my share in this question. You do not; you cannot suffer by it. If Honesty be true policy with regard to the transient Interest of Individuals; it is much more certainly so with regard to the permanent interests of communities. I know, that it is but too natural for us to see our own *certain* ruin, in the *possible* prosperity of other people. It is hard to persuade us, that every thing which is *got* by another is not *taken* from ourselves. But it is fit, that we should get the better of these Suggestions, which come from what is not the best and soundest part of our Nature; and that

---

[5]Burke is referring to the war with the American colonists that produced the French-American alliance in March 1778, which created a state of war between Britain and France.

we should form to ourselves a way of thinking, more rational, more just, and more religious. Trade is not a limited thing; as if the objects of mutual demand and consumption, could not stretch beyond the bounds of our Jealousies. God has given the Earth to the Children of Man; and he has undoubtedly, in giving it to them, given them what is abundantly sufficient for all their Exigencies; not a scanty, but a most liberal provision for them all. The author of our Nature has written it strongly in that Nature, and has promulgated the same Law in his written Word, that Man shall eat his Bread by his Labour; and I am persuaded, that no man, and no combination of Men, for their own Ideas of their particular profit, can, without great impiety, undertake to say, that he *shall not* do so; that they have no sort of right, either to prevent the Labour, or to withhold the Bread. Ireland having received no *compensation,* directly or indirectly, for any restraints on their Trade, ought not, in Justice or common honesty, be made subject to such restraints. I do not mean to impeach the Right of the Parliament of Great Britain to make Laws for the Trade of Ireland. I only speak of what Laws it is right for Parliament to make.

It is nothing to an oppressed people, to say, that in part they are protected at our Charge. The Military force, which shall be kept up in order to cramp the natural faculties of a people, and to prevent their arrival to their utmost prosperity, is the instrument of their Servitude, not the means of their protection. To protect Men is to forward, and not to restrain, their improvement. Else what is it more than to avow to them and to the world, than that you guard them from others, only to make them a prey to yourself. This fundamental Nature of protection does not belong to free, but to all Governments; and is as valid in Turkey as in Great Britain. No

Government ought to own it exists for the purpose of checking the prosperity of its people; or that there is such a principle involved in its policy.

Under the impression of these Sentiments, . . . I voted for these Bills which give you so much trouble. I voted for them, not as doing compleat Justice to Ireland; but as being something less unjust, than the general prohibition which has hitherto prevailed. I hear some discourse, as if, in one or two paltry duties on Materials, Ireland had a preference; and that those who set themselves against this Act of scanty Justice, assert that they are only contending for an *equality.* What Equality? Do they forget, that the whole Woollen Manufacture of Ireland, the most extensive and profitable of any, and the natural Staple of that Kingdom, has been in a manner so destroyed by restrictive Laws of *ours,* and (at our persuasion, and on our promises) by restrictive Laws of *their own,* that in a few years, it is probable, they will not be able to wear a Coat of their own Fabrick? Is this Equality? Do Gentlemen forget, that the understood faith, upon which they were persuaded to such an unnatural Act, has not been kept; but a Linen Manufacture has been set up and highly encouraged against them? Is this Equality? Do they forget, the State of the Trade of Ireland in Beer, so great an Article of consumption, and which now stands in so mischievous a position with regard to their Revenue, their Manufacture, and their Agriculture? Do they find any equality in all this? Yet if the least step is taken towards doing the common justice in the lightest Articles for the most limited Markets, a Cry is raised as if we were going to be ruined by partiality to Ireland.

Gentlemen, I know, that the deficiency in these Arguments, is made up (not by you but by others) by the usual resource on such occasions, the confidence in Military force and superior powers. But that ground of confidence, which at no time was perfectly just, or the avowal of it tolerably decent, is at this time very unreasonable. Late experience has shewn, that it cannot be altogether relied upon; and many if not all our present difficulties have arisen from putting our Trust in what may possibly fail; and if it should fail, leaves those who are hurt by such a reliance, without Pity. Whereas Honesty, and justice, Reason and equity, go a very great way in securing prosperity to those who use them; and in case of failure, secure the best retreat and the most honorable consolations.

It is very unfortunate, that we should consider those as Rivals, whom we ought to regard as fellow labourers in a common Cause. Ireland has never made a single step in its progress towards prosperity, in which you have not had a share and perhaps the greatest Share in the Benefit. That progress has been chiefly owing to her own natural advantages, and her own Efforts; which, after a long time, and by slow degrees, have prevailed in some measure over the Mischeivous Systems, which have been adopted. Far enough she is still from having arrived even at an ordinary state of perfection; and if our Jealousies were to be converted into Politicks as systematically as some would have them, the Trade of Ireland would vanish out of the System of Commerce. But believe me, if Ireland is beneficial to you, it is so, not from the parts in which it is restrained; but from those in which it is left free, though not unrivalled. The greater its freedom the greater must be your advantage. If you should lose in one way, you will gain in twenty.

Whilst I remain under this unalterable and powerful conviction, you will not wonder at the *decided* part I take. It is my

custom so to do, when I see my way clearly before me; and when I know that I am not misled by any passion or any personal Interest; which in this Case, I am very sure, I am not. I find that disagreeable things are circulated among my Constituents; and I wish my Sentiments, which form my justification, may be equally general with the Circulation against me. I have the honour to be with the greatest regard and Esteem

Gentlemen
your most Obedient
and Humble Servant

EDM BURKE
Westminster May 2d 1778
To
Messrs Harford Coules & Co.
Bristol.

Introductory Note to
Letter to Sir Hercules Langrishe
(1792)

Burke wrote his Letter to Sir Hercules Langrishe *in the midst of a campaign to win the franchise for Irish Catholics, and according to O'Brien, it represented Burke's first major public statement on Irish affairs.[6] Langrishe, who advocated limited Catholic emancipation short of enfranchisement, apparently wrote Burke in December 1791 to get his views on proposed measures to ease restrictions on Catholics. Burke used the opportunity to argue powerfully for Catholic enfranchisement.*

In Letter to Sir Hercules Langrishe, *Burke systematically attacked the various ra-*

---

[6]O'Brien, *The Great Melody,* 476.

tionales used to justify the exclusion of the Irish Catholics from the franchise and the full benefits of the British constitution. His conception of a tolerant, imperial society between Britain and Ireland comes through clearly in his condemnation of British oppression of the Catholics and his compassion for the Catholic desire to partake of the advantages of the British constitution. Although he condemned the growing radicalism in elements of both the Protestant and Catholic communities in Ireland, Burke noted that such radicalism had its source in British imperial misgovernment and mistreatment of the Irish.

The Letter to Sir Hercules Langrishe *is interesting as well because in it Burke weaves together Ireland, America, India, and the French Revolution—all the strands of Burke's international thinking. The letter, of course, is primarily about Burke's deep hatred of the British treatment of the Irish Catholics and his concern for the health of the British imperial society. Burke explicitly linked what was happening in Ireland with Britain's humiliating loss of America. Burke also connected his efforts on Irish Catholic emancipation with his continuing endeavors on behalf of the people of India, whom Burke referred to as "another distressed people, injured by those who have vanquished them, or stolen a dominion over them." Finally, Burke expressed his anxiety that the continued oppression of the Irish Catholics would drive them, arm in arm with radical Irish Protestant factions, into embracing the tenets of the French Revolution. Burke wrote the* Letter to Sir Hercules Langrishe *closely on the heels of* Thoughts on French Affairs *(December 1791), in which he urged the Pitt government to intervene militarily against revolutionary France, and the letter demonstrates that the French threat weighed heavily on his mind in connection with Ireland's future.* ~

Letter to Sir Hercules Langrishe (1792)

MY DEAR SIR,

↫

You see by the paper I take that I am likely to be long, with malice prepense. You have brought under my view, a subject, always difficult, at present critical.—It has filled my thoughts, which I wish to lay open to you with the clearness and simplicity which your friendship demands from me. . . .

The case upon which your letter of the 10th of December turns, is hardly before me with precision enough, to enable me to form any very certain judgment upon it. It seems to be some plan of further indulgence proposed for Catholics of Ireland.[7] . . .

In my present state of imperfect information, you will pardon the errors into which I may easily fall. The principles you lay down are, "that the Roman Catholics should enjoy every thing *under* the state, but should not be *the state itself.*" And you add, "that when you exclude them from being *a part of the state,* you rather conform to the spirit of the age, than to any abstract doctrine;" but you consider the constitution as already established—that our state is Protestant. . . .

As to the plan to which these maxims are applied, I cannot speak, as I told you, positively about it. Because, neither from your letter, nor from any information I have been able to collect, do I find any thing settled, either on the part of the

---

[7]Burke is alluding to the December 1791 petitions from the Irish Catholic Committee to the British Parliament for further relief of the Irish Catholics, including limited franchise.

Roman Catholics themselves, or on that of any persons who may wish to conduct their affairs in Parliament. But if I have leave to conjecture, something is in agitation towards admitting them, under *certain qualifications* to have *some share* in the election of members of parliament. . . .

. . . You, who have looked deeply into the spirit of the Popery laws, must be perfectly sensible, that a great part of the present mischief, which we abhor in common . . . has arisen from them. Their declared object was to reduce the Catholics of Ireland to a miserable populace, without property, without estimation, without education. The professed object was to deprive the few men who, in spite of those laws, might hold or obtain any property amongst them, of all sort of influence or authority over the rest. They divided the nation into two distinct bodies, without common interest, sympathy or connexion; one of which bodies was to possess *all* the franchises, *all* the property, *all* the education: The other was to be composed of drawers of water and cutters of turf for them. Are we to be astonished that when, by the efforts of so much violence in conquest, and so much policy in regulation, continued without intermission for near an hundred years, we had reduced them to a mob; that whenever they came to act at all, many of them would act exactly like a mob without temper, measure, or foresight? Surely it might be just now a matter of temperate discussion, whether you ought not apply a remedy to the real cause of the evil. If the disorder you speak of be real and considerable you ought to raise an aristocratic interest; that is, an interest of property and education amongst them: and to strengthen by every prudent means, the authority and influence of men of that description. It will deserve your best thoughts, to examine whether this can be

done without giving such persons the means of demonstrating to the rest, that something more is to be got by their temperate conduct, than can be expected from the wild and senseless projects of those, who do not belong to their body, who have no interest in their well being, and only wish to make them the dupes of their turbulent ambition.

If the absurd persons you mention find no way of providing for liberty, but by overturning this happy constitution, and introducing a frantic democracy, let us take care how we prevent better people from any rational expectations of partaking in the benefits of that constitution *as it stands*. The maxims you establish cut the matter short. They have no sort of connexion with the good or ill behaviour of the persons who seek relief, or with the proper or improper means by which they seek it. They form a perpetual bar to all pleas and to all expectations.

You begin by asserting that "they ought to enjoy all things *under* the state, but that they ought not to *be the state*." A position which, I believe, in the latter part of it, and in the latitude there expressed, no man of common sense has ever thought proper to dispute: because the contrary implies, that the state ought to be in them *exclusively*. But before you have finished the line, you express yourself as if the other member of your proposition, namely, that "they ought not to be *a part* of the state," were necessarily included in your first—Whereas I conceive it to be as different, as a part is from the whole; that is just as different as possible. I know indeed that it is common with those who talk very different from you, that is with heat and animosity, to confound those things, and to argue the admission of the Catholics into any, however minute and subordinate parts of the state, as a surrender into their hands of the whole government of the kingdom. To them I have nothing at all to say.

Wishing to proceed with a deliberative spirit and temper in so very serious a question, I shall attempt to analyze, as well as I can, the principles you lay down, in order to fit them for the grasp of an understanding so little comprehensive as mine— 'State'—'Protestant'—'Revolution' these are terms, which, if not well explained, may lead us into many errors—In the word *State*, I conceive there is much ambiguity. The state is sometimes used to signify *the whole common-wealth*, comprehending all its orders, with the several privileges belonging to each. Sometimes it signifies only *the higher and ruling part* of the common-wealth; which we commonly call *the Government*. In the first sense, to be under the state, but not the state itself, *nor any part of it*, is a situation perfectly intelligible: but to those who fill that situation, not very pleasant, when it is understood. It is a state of *civil servitude* by the very force of the definition. . . . This servitude, which makes men *subject* to a state without being *citizens*, may be more or less tolerable from many circumstances: but these circumstances, more or less favourable, do not alter the nature of the thing. The mildness by which absolute masters exercise their dominion, leaves them masters still. We may talk a little presently of the manner in which the majority of the people of Ireland (the Catholics) are affected by this situation; which at present undoubtedly is theirs, and which you are of opinion, ought to continue for ever.

In the other sense of the word *State*, by which is understood the *Supreme Government* only, I must observe this upon the question: that to exclude whole classes of men entirely from this *part* of government, cannot be considered as *absolute slavery*. It only implies a lower and degraded state of citizenship; such is . . . the condition of all countries, in which an hereditary nobility possess the exclusive rule. This may be no bad mode of government; provided that the personal authority of individual nobles be kept in due bounds, that their cabals and factions are guarded against with a severe vigilance, and that the people, (who have no share in granting their own money) are subjected to but light impositions, and are otherwise treated with attention, and with indulgence to their humours and prejudices.

↜

In all considerations which turn upon the question of vesting or continuing the state solely and exclusively in some one description of citizens; prudent legislators will consider, how far *the general form and principles of their common-wealth render it fit to be cast into an oligarchical shape, or to remain always in it*. We know that the government of Ireland (the same as the British) is not in its constitution *wholly* Aristocratical; and as it is not such in its form, so neither is it in its spirit. If it had been inveterately aristocratical, exclusions might be more patiently submitted to. The lot of one plebeian would be the lot of all; and an habitual reverence and admiration of certain families, might make the people content to see government wholly in hands to whom it seemed naturally to belong. But our constitution has *a plebeian member*, which forms an essential integrant part of it. A plebeian oligarchy is a monster in itself: and no people, not absolutely domestic or predial slaves, will long endure it. The Protestants of Ireland are not *alone* sufficiently the people to form a democracy; and they are *too numerous* to answer the ends and purposes of *an aristocracy*. Admiration, that first source of obedience, can be only the claim or the imposture of the few. I hold it to be absolutely impossible for two millions of plebeians, composing certainly, a very clear and decided majority in that class, to become so far in love with six or seven hundred thousand of their fellow-citizens (to all outward appearance plebeians like themselves, and many of them tradesmen, servants, and otherwise inferior to some of them) as to see with satisfaction, or even with patience, an exclusive power vested in them, by which *constitutionally* they become the absolute masters; and by the *manners* derived from their circumstances, must be capable of exercising upon them, daily and hourly, an insulting and vexatious superiority. Neither are the majority of the Irish indemnified (as in some aristocracies) for this state of humiliating vassalage . . . by having the lower walks of industry wholly abandoned to them. They are rivalled, to say the least of the matter, in every laborious and lucrative course of life: while every franchise, every honour, every trust, every place down to the very lowest and least confidential (besides whole professions), is reserved for the master cast.

Our constitution is not made for great, general, and proscriptive exclusions; sooner or later, it will destroy them, or they will destroy the constitution. In our constitution there has always been a difference made between *a franchise* and *an office*, and between the capacity for the one and for the other. Franchises were supposed to belong to the *subject, as a subject,* and not *as a member of the governing part of the state.* The policy of Government has considered them as things very different: for whilst Parliament excluded by the test acts[8] (and

for a while these test acts were not a dead letter, as now they are in England) Protestant dissenters from all civil and military employments, they *never touched their right of voting for members of Parliament, or sitting in either House;* a point I state, not as approving or condemning, with regard to them, the measure of exclusion from employments, but to prove that the distinction has been admitted in legislature, as, in truth, it is founded in reason.

I will not here examine, whether the principles of the British constitution, be wise or not. I must assume that they are; and that those who partake the franchises which make it, partake of a benefit. They who are excluded from votes . . . are excluded, not from the *state,* but from *the British constitution.* They cannot by any possibility, whilst they hear its praises continually rung in their ears, and are present at the declaration which is so generally and so bravely made by those who possess the privilege—that the best blood in their veins ought to be shed, to preserve their share in it; they, the disfranchised part cannot, I say, think themselves in an *happy* state, to be utterly excluded from all its direct and all its consequential advantages. The popular part of the constitution must be to them, by far the most odious part of it. To them it is not *an actual,* and, if possible, still less a *virtual* representation. It is indeed the direct contrary. It is power unlimited, placed in the hands of *an adverse* description, *because it is an adverse description.* And if they who compose the privileged body have not an interest, they must but too frequently have motives of pride, passion, petulance, peevish jealousy, or tyrannic suspicion, to urge them to treat the excluded people with contempt and rigour.

This is not a mere theory; though whilst men are men, it is a theory that cannot be false. I do not desire to revive all the particulars in my memory; I wish them to sleep for ever; but it is impossible I should wholly forget, what happened in some parts of Ireland, with very few and short intermissions, from the year 1761 to the year 1766, both inclusive.[9] In a country of miserable police, passing from the extremes of laxity to the extremes of rigour, among a neglected, and therefore disorderly populace—if any disturbance or sedition, from any grievance real or imaginary happened to arise, it was presently perverted from its true nature (often criminal enough in itself to draw upon it a severe appropriate punishment), it was metamorphosed into a conspiracy against the state, and prosecuted as such. Amongst the Catholics, as being, by far, the most numerous and the most wretched, all sorts of offenders against the laws must commonly be found. The punishment of low people for the offences usual amongst low people, would warrant no inference against any descriptions of religion or of politicks. Men of consideration from their age, their profession, or their character; men of proprietary landed estates, substantial renters, opulent merchants, physicians, and titular bishops, could not easily be suspected of riot in open day, or of nocturnal assemblies for the purpose of pulling down hedges, making breaches in park walls, firing barns, maiming cattle, and outrages of a similar nature, which characterize the disorders of an oppressed or a licentious populace. But when the evidence given on the trial for such misdemeanours, qualified them as overt acts of high treason, and when witnesses were found (such witnesses as they were) to depose to the taking of oaths of allegiance by the rioters to the king of France, to their being paid by his money, and embodied and exercised under his officers, to overturn the state for the purposes of that potentate; in that case, the rioters might (if the witness was believed) be supposed only the troops, and persons more reputable, the leaders and commanders in such a rebellion. All classes in the obnoxious description, who could not be suspected of the lower crime of riot, might be involved in the odium, in the suspicion, and sometimes in the punishment, of a higher and far more criminal species of offence. These proceedings did not arise from any one of the Popery laws since repealed, but from this circumstance, that when it answered the purposes of an election party, or a malevolent person of influence to forge such plots, the people had no protection. The people of that description have no hold on the gentlemen who aspire to be popular representatives. The candidates neither love, nor respect, nor fear them individually or collectively. I do not think this evil (an evil amongst a thousand others) at this day entirely over; for I conceive I have lately seen some indication of a disposition perfectly similar to the old one; that is, a disposition to carry the imputation of crimes from persons to descriptions, and wholly to alter the character and quality of the offences themselves.

This universal exclusion seems to me a serious evil—because many collateral oppressions, besides what I have just now stated, have arisen from it. . . . They who consider also the state of all sorts of tradesmen, shopkeepers, and particularly publicans in towns, must soon discern the disadvantages under which those labour who have no votes. It cannot be otherwise, whilst the spirit of elections, and the tendencies of human nature continue as they

---

[9]Burke has in mind the "White Boy" disturbances in Ireland, which Protestant gentry in Ireland claimed were inspired by France (with which Britain was at war until 1763) and thus seditious.

are. If property be artificially separated from franchise, the franchise must in some way or other, and in some proportion, naturally attract property to it. Many are the collateral disadvantages, amongst a *privileged* people, which must attend those who have *no* privileges. Among the rich, each individual, with or without a franchise, is of importance; the poor and the middling are no otherwise so, than as they obtain some collective capacity, and can be aggregated to some corps. If legal ways are not found, illegal will be resorted to; and seditious clubs and confederacies, such as no man living holds in greater horror than I do, will grow and flourish, in spite, I am afraid, of any thing which can be done to prevent the evil. Lawful enjoyment is the surest method to prevent unlawful gratification. Where there is property, there will be less theft; where there is marriage, there will always be less fornication.

I have said enough of the question of state, *as it affects the people, merely as such.* But it is complicated with a political question relative to religion, to which it is very necessary I should say something; because the term *Protestant,* which you apply, is too general for the conclusions which one of your accurate understanding would wish to draw from it, and because a great deal of argument will depend on the use that is made of that term.

It is *not* a fundamental part of the settlement at the revolution,[10] that the state should be protestant without *any qualification of the term.* With a qualification it is unquestionably true; not in all its latitude. With the qualification, it was true before the revolution. Our predecessors in legislation were not so irrational (not to say im-

pious) as to form an operose ecclesiastical establishment, and even to render the state itself in some degree subservient to it, when their religion (if such it might be called) was nothing but a mere *negation* of some other—without any positive idea either of doctrine, discipline, worship, or morals, in the scheme which they professed themselves, and which they imposed upon others, even under penalties and incapacities—No! No! This never could have been done even by reasonable Atheists. They who think religion of no importance to the state have abandoned it to the conscience, or caprice of the individual; they make no provision for it whatsoever, but leave every club to make, or not, a voluntary contribution towards it support, according to their fancies. This would be consistent. The other always appeared to me to be a monster of contradiction and absurdity. . . . There never has been a religion of the state . . . but that of *the episcopal church of England;* the episcopal church of England, before the reformation, connected with the See of Rome, since then, disconnected and protesting against some of her doctrines, and against the whole of her authority, as binding in our national church: nor did the fundamental laws of this kingdom (in Ireland it has been the same) ever know, at any period, any other church *as an object of establishment;* or in that light, any other Protestant religion. . . . So little idea had they at the revolution of *establishing* Protestantism indefinitely, that they did not indefinitely *tolerate* it under that name. I do not mean to praise that strictness, where nothing more than merely religious toleration is concerned. Toleration being a part of moral and political prudence, ought to be tender and large. A tolerant government ought not to be too scrupulous in its investigations; but may bear without blame,

---

[10]Burke is referring to the constitutional and legislative acts taken after the Glorious Revolution of 1688 in England.

not only very ill-grounded doctrines, but even many things that are positively vices, where they are *adulta et praevalida*.[11] The good of the common-wealth is the rule which rides over the rest; and to this every other must completely submit.

❧

As to the coronation oath, to which you allude as opposite to admitting a Roman Catholic to the use of any franchise whatsoever, I cannot think that the king would be perjured if he gave his assent to any regulation which Parliament might think fit to make, with regard to that affair. The king is bound by law, as clearly specified in several acts of Parliament, to be in communion with the church of England. It is a part of the tenure by which he holds his crown; and though no provision was made till the revolution, which could be called positive and valid in law, to ascertain this great principle; I have always considered it as in fact fundamental, that the king of England should be of the Christian religion, according to the national legal church for the time being. I conceive it was so before the reformation. Since the reformation it became doubly necessary; because the king is the head of that church; in some sort an ecclesiastical person; and it would be incongruous and absurd, to have the head of the church of one faith, and the members of another. The king may *inherit* the crown as a *Protestant,* but he cannot *hold it* according to law, without being a Protestant *of the church of England.*

Before we take it for granted, that the king is bound by his coronation oath, not to admit any of his Catholic subjects to the rights and liberties, which ought to belong to them as Englishmen (not as reli-

gionists) or to settle the conditions or proportions of such admission by an act of Parliament; I wish you to place before your eyes that oath itself, as it is settled in the act of William and Mary.

"Will you to the utmost of your power maintain—The laws of God, the true Profession of the gospel—and The protestant reformed religion *as it is established by law.*—And will you preserve unto *bishops* and clergy, and the churches committed to *their* charge, all such rights and privileges as by law do, or shall appertain to them, or any of them.—All this I promise to do."

Here are the coronation engagements of the King. In them I do not find one word to preclude his Majesty from consenting to any arrangement which Parliament may make with regard to the civil privileges of any part of his subjects.

❧

There is no man on earth, I believe, more willing than I am to lay it down as a fundamental of the constitution, that the church of England should be united and even identified with it: but allowing this, I cannot allow that all *laws of regulation,* made from time to time, in support of that fundamental law, are, of course, equally fundamental and equally unchangeable. This would be to confound all the branches of legislation and of jurisprudence.—The *Crown* and the personal safety of the monarch are *fundamentals* in our constitution: Yet, I hope that no man regrets, that the rabble of statutes got together during the reign of Henry the Eighth, by which treasons are multiplied with so prolific an energy, have been all repealed in a body; although they were all, or most of them, made in support of things truly fundamental in our constitution. . . . None of this species of *secondary and subsidiary laws* have been held funda-

---

[11]"Deeply rooted and prevalent."

mental. They have yielded to circumstances; particularly where they were
thought, even in their consequences, or
obliquely, to affect other fundamentals.
How much more, certainly, ought they to
give way, when, as in our case, they effect,
not here and there, in some particular
point, or in their consequence, but universally, collectively, and directly, the fundamental franchises of a people equal to the
whole inhabitants of several respectable
kingdoms and states; equal to the subjects
of the kings of Sardinia or Denmark; equal
to those of the United Netherlands; and
more than are to be found in all the states
of Switzerland. This way of proscribing
men by whole nations, as it were, from all
the benefits of the constitution to which
they were born, I never can believe to be
politic or expedient, much less necessary
for the existence of any state or church in
the world. Whenever I shall be convinced,
which will be late and reluctantly, that the
safety of the church is utterly inconsistent
with all the civil rights whatsoever of the
far larger part of the inhabitants of our
country, I shall be extremely sorry for it;
because I shall think the church to be truly
in danger. It is putting things into the position of an ugly alternative, into which, I
hope in God, they never will be put.

↜

. . . I . . . come to what seems to be a serious consideration in your mind; I mean
the dread you express of "reviewing, for
the purpose of altering, the *principles of the
Revolution.*" This is an interesting topic;
on which I will, as fully as your leisure and
mine permits, lay before you the ideas I
have formed.

First, I cannot possibly confound in my
mind all the things which were done at the
Revolution, with the *principles* of the Revolution. As in most great changes many

things were done from the necessities of
the time, well or ill understood, from passion or from vengeance, which were not
only, not perfectly agreeable to its principles, but in the most direct contradiction
to them. I shall not think that the *deprivation of some millions of people of all the rights
of the citizens, and all interest in the constitution, in and to which they were born,* was
a thing conformable to the *declared principles* of the Revolution. This I am sure is
true relatively to England (where the operation of these *anti-principles* comparatively
were of little extent), and some of our late
laws, in repealing acts made immediately
after the Revolution, admit that some
things then done were not done in the true
spirit of the Revolution. But the Revolution operated differently in England and
Ireland, in many, and these essential particulars. Supposing the principles to have
been altogether the same in both kingdoms, by the application of those principles to very different objects, the whole
spirit of the system was changed, not to say
reversed. In England it was the struggle of
the *great body* of the people for the establishment of their liberties, against the efforts of a very *small faction,* who would
have oppressed them. In Ireland it was the
establishment of the power of the smaller
number, at the expence of the civil liberties
and properties of the far greater part; and
at the expence of the political liberties of
the whole. It was, to say the truth, not a
revolution, but a conquest, which is not to
say a great deal in its favour. To insist on
every thing done in Ireland at the Revolution, would be to insist on the severe and
jealous policy of a conqueror, in the crude
settlement of his new acquisition, as a *permanent* rule for its future government.
This, no power, in no country that ever I
heard of; has done or professed to do—except in Ireland; where it is done, and pos-

sibly by some people will be professed. Time has, by degrees, in all other places and periods, blended and coalited the conquered with the conquerors. . . .

For a much longer period than that which had suffered to blend the Romans with the nation to which of all others they were the most adverse, the Protestants settled in Ireland, considered themselves in no other light than that of a sort of a colonial garrison, to keep the natives in subjection to the other state of Great Britain. The whole spirit of the revolution in Ireland, was that of not the mildest conqueror. In truth, the spirit of those proceedings did not commence at that aera, nor was religion of any kind their primary object. What was done, was not in the spirit of a contest between two religious factions; but between two adverse nations. The statutes of Kilkenny[12] shew, that the spirit of the popery laws, and some even of their actual provisions, as applied between Englishry and Irishry, had existed in that harassed country before the words Protestant and Papist were heard of in the world. If we read Baron Finglas, Spenser, and Sir John Davis,[13] we cannot miss the true genius and policy of the English government there before the revolution, as well as during the whole reign of Queen Elizabeth. Sir John Davis boasts of the benefits received by the natives, by extending to them the English law, and turning the whole kingdom into shire ground. But the appearance of things alone was changed. The original scheme was never deviated from for a single hour. Unheard of confis-

cations were made in the northern parts, upon grounds of plots and conspiracies, never proved upon their supposed authors. The war of chicane succeeded to the war of arms and of hostile statutes; and a regular series of operations were carried on . . . in the ordinary courts of justice, and by special commissions and inquisitions; first, under pretence of tenures, and then of titles in the crown, for the purpose of the total extirpation of the interest of the natives in their own soil—until this species of subtile ravage, being carried to the last excess of oppression and insolence under Lord Strafford,[14] it kindled at length the flames of that rebellion which broke out in 1641. By the issue of that war, by the turn which the Earl of Clarendon[15] gave to things at the restoration, and by the total reduction of the kingdom of Ireland in 1691;[16] the ruin of the native Irish, and in a great measure too, of the first races of the English, was completely accomplished. The new English interest was settled with as solid a stability as any thing in human affairs can look for. All the penal laws of that unparalleled code of oppression, which were made after the last event, were manifestly the effects of national hatred and scorn towards a conquered people; whom the victors delighted to trample upon, and were not at all afraid to provoke. They were not the effect of their fears but of their security. They who carried on this system, looked to the irre-

---

[12]These were measures passed in 1366 that attempted to separate the English and Irish races in Ireland.

[13]Patrick Finglass, Edmund Spenser, and Sir John Davis wrote on Ireland in the sixteenth and seventeenth centuries.

---

[14]Thomas Wentworth, first earl of Strafford and governor of Ireland from 1633 to 1641.

[15]Edward Hyde, first earl of Clarendon, who wrote the *True Historical Narrative of the Rebellion and Civil Wars in England,* which was published in 1702–1704.

[16]Burke is referring to the destructive aftermath of the English defeat of the Irish Catholics under James II by the forces of William of Orange in 1690.

sistible force of Great Britain for their support in their acts of power. They were quite certain that no complaints of the natives would be heard on this side of the water, with any other sentiments than those of contempt and indignation. Their cries served only to augment their torture. Machines which could answer their purposes so well, must be of an excellent contrivance. Indeed at that time in England, the double name of the complainants, Irish and Papists (it would be hard to say, singly, which was the most odious) shut up the hearts of every one against them. Whilst that temper prevailed, and it prevailed in all its force to a time within our memory, every measure was pleasing and popular, just in proportion as it tended to harass and ruin a set of people, who were looked upon as enemies to God and man; and indeed as a race of bigotted savages who were a disgrace to human nature itself.

However, as the English in Ireland began to be domiciliated, they began also to recollect that they had a country. The *English interest* at first by faint and almost insensible degrees, but at length openly and avowedly, became an *independent Irish interest;* full as independent as it could ever have been, if it had continued in the persons of the native Irish; and it was maintained with more skill, and more consistency than probably it would have been in theirs. With their views, the *Anglo-Irish* changed their maxims—it was necessary to demonstrate to the whole people, that there was something at least, of a common interest, combined with the independency, which was to become the object of common exertions. The mildness of government produced the first relaxation towards the Irish; the necessities, and, in part too, the temper that predominated at this great change, produced the second and the most important of these relaxations. English government, and Irish legis-

lature felt jointly the propriety of this measure. The Irish parliament and nation became independent.

↬

Great Britain finding the Anglo-Irish highly animated with a spirit, which had indeed shewn itself before, though with little energy, and many interruptions, and therefore suffered a multitude of uniform precedents to be established against it, acted in my opinion, with the greatest temperance and wisdom. She saw, that the disposition of the *leading part* of the nation, would not permit them to act any longer the part of a *garrison*. She saw, that true policy did not require that they ever should have appeared in that character; or if it had done so formerly, the reasons had now ceased to operate. She saw that the Irish of her race, were resolved, to build their constitution and their politics, upon another bottom. With those things under her view, she instantly complied with the whole of your demands, without any reservation whatsoever. She surrendered that boundless superiority, for the preservation of which, and the acquisition, she had supported the English colonies in Ireland for so long a time, and at so vast an expence . . . of her blood and treasure.

When we bring before us the matter which history affords for our selection, it is not improper to examine the spirit of the several precedents, which are candidates for our choice. Might it not be as well for your statesmen, on the other side of the water, to take an example from this latter, and surely more conciliatory revolution, as a pattern for your conduct towards your own fellow-citizens, than from that of 1688, when a paramount sovereignty over both you and them, was more loftily claimed, and more sternly exerted, than at any former, or at any subsequent period? Great Britain in 1782, rose above the vulgar ideas of policy, the ordinary jealousies of state, and all the sentiments of national pride and national ambition.[17] If she had been more disposed than, I thank God for it, she was, to listen to the suggestions of passion, than to the dictates of prudence; she might have urged the principles, the maxims, the policy, the practice of the revolution, against the demands of the leading description in Ireland, with full as much plausibility, and full as good a grace, as any amongst them can possibly do, against the supplications of so vast and extensive a description of their own people. A good deal too, if the spirit of domination and exclusion had prevailed in England, might be excepted against some of the means then employed in Ireland, whilst her claims were in agitation; they were, at least, as much out of ordinary course, as those which are now objected against admitting your people to any of the benefits of an English constitution.

⤳

Compare what was done in 1782, with what is wished in 1792; consider the spirit of what has been done at the several periods of reformation; and weigh maturely, whether it be exactly true, that conciliatory concessions, are of good policy only in discussions between nations; but that among descriptions in the same nation, they must always be irrational and dangerous. What have you suffered in your peace, your prosperity, or, in what ought ever to be dear to a nation, your glory, by the last act by which you took the property of that people under the protection of the *laws?* What reason have you to dread the consequences of admitting the people possessing that property to some share in the protection of the *constitution?*

I do not mean to trouble you with any thing to remove the objections, I will not call them arguments, against this measure, taken from a ferocious hatred to all that numerous description of Christians. It would be to pay a poor compliment to your understanding or your heart. Neither *your* religion, nor *your* politics consist "in odd perverse antipathies." You are not resolved to persevere in proscribing from the constitution, so many millions of your countrymen, because, in contradiction to experience and to common sense, you think proper to imagine, that their principles are subversive of common human society. To that I shall only say, that whoever has a temper, which can be gratified by indulging himself in these good-natured fancies, ought to do a great deal more. For an exclusion from the privileges of British subjects, is not a cure for so terrible a distemper of the human mind, as they are pleased to suppose in their countrymen. I rather conceive a participation in those privileges to be itself a remedy for some mental disorders.

As little shall I detain you with matters that can as little obtain admission into a mind like yours; such as the fear, or pretence of fear, that in spite of your own power, and the trifling power of Great Britain, you may be conquered by the Pope; or that this commodious bugbear (who is of infinitely more use to those who pretend to fear, than to those who love him) will absolve his Majesty's subjects from their allegiance, and send over the cardinal of York to rule you as his viceroy; or that, by the plenitude of his power, he will take that fierce tyrant, the king of the

---

[17]In 1782 the British Parliament repealed the Irish Declaratory Act of 1719 that proclaimed Britain's legislative supremacy over Ireland, thus giving the Irish Parliament more legislative autonomy.

French, out of his jail,[18] and arm that nation (which on all occasions treats his Holiness so very politely) with his bulls and pardons, to invade poor old Ireland, to reduce you to popery and slavery, and to force the freeborn, naked feet of your people into the wooden shoes of that arbitrary monarch. I do not believe that discourses of this kind are held, or that any thing like them will be held, by any who walk about without a keeper. Yet, I confess, that on occasions of this nature, I am the most afraid of the weakest reasonings; because they discover the strongest passions. . . . But I know, and am sure, that such ideas as no man will distinctly produce to another, or hardly venture to bring in any plain shape to his own mind—he will utter in obscure, ill explained doubts, jealousies, surmises, fears, and apprehensions; and that in such a fog, they will appear to have a good deal of size, and will make an impression; when, if they were clearly brought forth and defined, they would meet with nothing but scorn and derision.

There is another way of taking an objection to this concession, which I admit to be something more plausible, and worthy of a more attentive examination. It is, that this numerous class of people is mutinous, disorderly, prone to sedition, and easy to be wrought upon by the insidious arts of wicked and designing men; that conscious of this, the sober, rational, and wealthy part of that body, who are totally of another character, do by no means desire any participation for themselves, or for any one else of their description, in the franchises of the British constitution.

I have great doubt of the exactness of any part of this observation. But let us

admit that the body of the Catholics are prone to sedition (of which, as I have said, I entertain much doubt), is it possible, that any fair observer or fair reasoner, can think of confining this description to them only? I believe it to be possible for men to be mutinous and seditious who feel no grievance: but I believe no man will assert seriously, that when people are of a turbulent spirit, the best way to keep them in order, is to furnish them with something substantial to complain of.

You separate very properly the sober, rational, and substantial part of their description from the rest. You give, as you ought to do, weight only to the former. What I have always thought of the matter is this—that the most poor, illiterate, and uninformed creatures upon earth, are judges of a *practical* oppression. It is a matter of feeling; and as such persons generally have felt most of it, and are not of an over-lively sensibility, they are the best judges of it. But for the *real cause,* or the *appropriate remedy,* they ought never to be called into council about the one or the other. They ought to be totally shut out; because their reason is weak; because when once roused, their passions are ungoverned; because they want information; because the smallness of the property which individually they possess, renders them less attentive to the consequence of the measures they adopt in affairs of moment. When I find a great cry amongst the people, who speculate little, I think myself called seriously to examine into it, and to separate the real cause from the ill effects of the passion it may excite; and the bad use which artful men may make of an irritation of the popular mind. Here we must be aided by persons of a contrary character; we must not listen to the desperate or the furious; but it is therefore necessary for us to distinguish who are the *really* indigent, and the *really* intemperate. . . .

---

[18]Burke means Louis XVI, king of France, who was at that time held captive by the French revolutionaries.

～

The object pursued by the Catholics is, I understand, and have all along reasoned as if it were so, in some degree or measure to be again admitted to the franchises of the constitution. Men are considered as under some derangement of their intellects, when they see good and evil in a different light from other men; when they choose nauseous and unwholesome food; and reject such as to the rest of the world seems pleasant, and is known to be nutritive. I have always considered the British constitution, not to be a thing in itself so vitious, as that none but men of deranged understanding, and turbulent tempers could desire a share in it: on the contrary, I should think very indifferently of the understanding and temper of any body of men, who did not wish to partake of this great and acknowledged benefit. I cannot think quite so favourably either of the sense or temper of those, if any such there are, who would voluntarily persuade their brethren that the object is not fit for them, or they for the object. . . .

～

It is known, I believe, that the greater, as well as the sounder part of our excluded countrymen, have not adopted the wild ideas, and wilder engagements, which have been held out to them; but have rather chosen to hope small and safe concessions from the legal power, than boundless objects from trouble and confusion. This mode of action seems to me to mark men of sobriety, and to distinguish them from those who are intemperate, from circumstance or from nature. But why do they not instantly disclaim and disavow those who make such advances to them? In this too, in my opinion, they shew themselves no less sober and circumspect. In the pres-

ent moment, nothing short of insanity could induce them to take such a step. Pray consider the circumstances. Disclaim, says somebody, all union with the Dissenters;—right—But, when this your injunction is obeyed, shall I obtain the object which I solicit from *you?*—Oh, no—nothing at all like it!—But, in punishing us by an exclusion from the constitution through the great gate, for having been invited to enter into it by a postern, will you punish by deprivation of their privileges; or mulct in any other way, those who have tempted us?—Far from it—we mean to preserve all *their* liberties and immunities, as *our* life blood. We mean to cultivate *them,* as brethren whom we love and respect—with *you,* we have no fellowship. We can bear, with patience, their enmity to ourselves; but their friendship with you, we will not endure. But mark it well! All our quarrels with *them,* are always to be revenged upon you. Formerly, it is notorious, that we should have resented with the highest indignation, your presuming to shew any ill-will to them. You must not suffer them, now, to shew any good-will to you. Know—and take it once for all—that it is, and ever has been, and ever will be, a fundamental maxim in our politics, that you are not to have any part, or shadow, or name of interest whatever, in our state. That we look upon you, as under an irreversible outlawry from our constitution— as perpetual and unalliable aliens.

～

Observe, on these principles, the difference between the procedure of the Parliament and the Dissenters, towards the people in question. One employs courtship, the other force. The Dissenters offer bribes, the Parliament nothing but the *front negative* of a stern and forbidding authority. A man may be very wrong in his ideas of what is good for him. But no man affronts me, nor can therefore justify my affronting him, by offering to make me as happy as himself, according to his own ideas of happiness. This the Dissenters do to the Catholics. You are on the different extremes. The Dissenters offer, with regard to constitutional rights and civil advantages of all sorts, *every thing*—you refuse *every thing*. With them, there is boundless, tho' not very assured hope; with you, a very sure and very unqualified despair. The terms of alliance, from the Dissenters, offer a representation of the Commons, chosen out of the people by the head. This is absurdly and dangerously large, in my opinion; and that scheme of election is known to have been, at all times, perfectly odious to me. But I cannot think it right of course, to punish the Irish Roman Catholics by an universal exclusion, because others, whom you would not punish at all, propose an universal admission. . . .

I am not at all enamoured, as I have told you, with this plan of representation; as little do I relish any bandings or associations for procuring it. But if the question was to be put to you and me—*universal* popular representation, or *none at all for us and ours*—we should find ourselves in a very awkward position. I don't like this kind of dilemmas, especially when they are practical.

Then, since our oldest fundamental laws follow, or rather couple, freehold with franchise; since no principle of the Revolution shakes these liberties; since the oldest and one of the best monuments of the constitution, demands for the Irish the privilege which they supplicate; since the principles of the Revolution coincide with the declarations of the Great Charter; since the practice of the Revolution, in this point, did not contradict its principles; since, from that event, twenty-five years

had elapsed, before a domineering party, on a party principle, had ventured to disfranchise, without any proof whatsoever of abuse, the greater part of the community; since the King's coronation oath does not stand in his way to the performance of his duty to all his subjects; since you have given to all other Dissenters these privileges without limit, which are hitherto withheld, without any limitation whatsoever, from the Catholics; since no nation in the world has ever been known to exclude so great a body of men (not born slaves) from the civil state, and all the benefits of its constitution; the whole question comes before Parliament, as a matter for its prudence. I do not put the thing on a question of right. . . . Supplicants ought not to appear too much in the character of litigants. If the subject thinks so highly and reverently of the sovereign authority, as not to claim any thing of right, so that it may seem to be independent of the power and free choice of its government: and if the sovereign, on his part, considers the advantages of the subjects as their right, and all their reasonable wishes as so many claims; in the fortunate conjunction of these mutual dispositions are laid the foundations of a happy and prosperous commonwealth. For my own part, desiring of all things that the authority of the legislature under which I was born, and which I cherish, not only with a dutiful awe, but with a partial and cordial affection, to be maintained in the utmost possible respect, I never will suffer myself to suppose, that, at bottom, their discretion will be found to be at variance with their justice.

The whole being at discretion, I beg leave just to suggest some matters for your consideration—Whether the government in church or state is likely to be more secure by continuing causes of grounded discontent, to a very great number (say two millions) of the subjects? or, Whether the constitution, combined and balanced as it is, will be rendered more solid, by depriving so large a part of the people of all concern, or interest, or share, in its representation, actual or *virtual?* I here mean to lay an emphasis on the word *virtual*. Virtual representation is that in which there is a communion of interests, and a sympathy in feelings and desires between those who act in the name of any description of people, and the people in whose name they act, though the trustees are not actually chosen by them. This is virtual representation. Such a representation I think to be, in many cases, even better than the actual. It possesses most of its advantages, and is free from many of its inconveniences: it corrects the irregularities in the literal representation, when the shifting current of human affairs, or the acting of public interests in different ways, carry it obliquely from its first line of direction. The people may err in their choice; but common interest and common sentiment are rarely mistaken. But this sort of virtual representation cannot have a long or sure existence, if it has not a substratum in the actual. The member must have some relation to the constituent. As things stand, the Catholic, as a Catholic and belonging to a description, has no *virtual* relation to the representative; but the *contrary*. There is a relation in mutual obligation. Gratitude may not always have a very lasting power; but the frequent recurrency for favours will revive and refresh it, and will necessarily produce some degree of mutual attention. It will produce, at least, acquaintance; the several descriptions of people will not be kept so much apart as they now are, as if they were not only separate nations, but separate species. The stigma and reproach, the hideous mask will be taken off, and men will see each other as they are. Sure I am, that there have been thousands in Ireland, who have never conversed with a Roman Catholic in their whole lives, unless they happened to talk to their gardiner's workmen, or to ask their way, when they had lost it, in their sports; or, at best, who had known them only as footmen, or other domestics of the second and third order: and so averse were they, some time ago, to have them near their persons, that they would not employ even those who could never find their way beyond the stable. I well remember a great, and, in many respects, a good man, who advertised for a blacksmith; but, at the same time, added, he must be a Protestant. It is impossible that such a state of things, though natural goodness in many persons would undoubtedly make exceptions, must not produce alienation on one side, and pride and insolence on the other.

Reduced to a question of discretion, and that discretion exercised solely upon what will appear best for the conservation of the state on its present basis, I should recommend it to your serious thoughts, whether the narrowing of the foundation is always the best way to secure the building? The body of disfranchised men will not be perfectly satisfied to remain always in that state. If they are not satisfied, you have two millions of subjects in your bosom, full of uneasiness; not that they cannot overturn the act of settlement, and put themselves and you under an arbitrary master; or, that they are not permitted to spawn an hydra of wild republics, on principles of a pretended natural equality in man; but, because you will not suffer them to enjoy the ancient, fundamental, tried advantages of a British constitution: that you will not permit them to profit of the protection of a common father, or the freedom of common citizens: and that the only reason which can be assigned for this disfranchisement, has a tendency more deeply to ulcerate their minds than the act of exclusion itself. What the consequence of such feelings must be, it is for you to look to. To warn, is not to menace.

I am far from asserting, that men will not excite disturbances without just cause. I know that such an assertion is not true. But, neither is it true that disturbances have never just complaints for their origin. I am sure that it is hardly prudent to furnish them with such causes of complaint, as every man who thinks the British constitution a benefit, may think, at least, colourable and plausible.

↬

Think, whether this be the way to prevent, or dissolve factious combinations against the church, or the state. Reflect seriously on the possible consequences of keeping, in the heart of your country, a bank of discontent, every hour accumulating, upon which every description of seditious men may draw at pleasure. They, whose principles of faction would dispose them to the establishment of an arbitrary monarchy, will find a nation of men who have no sort of interest in freedom; but who will have an interest in that equality of justice or favour, with which a wise despot must view all his subjects who do not attack the foundations of his power. Love of liberty itself may, in such men, become the means of establishing an arbitrary domination. On the other hand, they who wish for a democratic republic, will find a set of men who have no choice between civil servitude, and the entire ruin of a mixed constitution.

Suppose the people of Ireland divided into three parts; of these (I speak within compass) two are Catholic. Of the remaining third, one half is composed of Dissenters. There is no natural union between those descriptions. It may be produced. If the two parts Catholic be driven into a close confederacy with half the third part of Protestants, with a view to a change in the constitution in church or state, or both; and you rest the whole of their security on a handful of gentlemen, clergy, and their dependants; compute the strength *you have in Ireland,* to oppose to grounded discontent; to capricious innovation; to blind popular fury, and to ambitious turbulent intrigue. . . .

↬

I believe, nay, I am sure, that the people of Great Britain, with or without an union, might be depended upon, in cases of any real danger, to aid the government of Ireland with the same cordiality as they would support their own against any wicked attempts to shake the security of the happy constitution in church and state. But, before Great Britain engages in any quarrel, the *cause of the dispute* would certainly be a part of her consideration. If confusions should arise in that kingdom, from too steady an attachment to a proscriptive monopolizing system, and from the resolution of regarding the franchise, and, in it the security of the subject, as belonging rather to religious opinions than to civil qualification and civil conduct, I doubt whether you might quite certainly reckon on obtaining an aid of force from hence, for the support of that system. We might extend your distractions to this country, by taking part in them. England will be indisposed, I suspect, to send an army for the conquest of Ireland. What was done in 1782 is a decisive proof of her sentiments of justice and moderation. She will not be fond of making another American war in Ireland. The principles of such a war would but too much resemble the former one. The well-disposed and the ill-disposed in England, would (for different reasons perhaps) be equally averse to such an enterprize. The confiscations, the public auctions, the private grants, the plantations, the transplantations, which formerly animated so many adventurers, even among sober citizens, to such Irish expeditions, and which possibly might have animated some of them to the American, can have no existence in the case that we suppose.

Let us form a supposition (no foolish or ungrounded supposition) that in an age, when men are infinitely more disposed to heat themselves with political than religious controversies, the former should entirely prevail, as we see that in some places they have prevailed, over the latter: and that the Catholics of Ireland, from the courtship paid them on the one hand, and the high tone of refusal on the other, should, in order to enter into all the rights of subjects, all become Protestant Dissenters; and as the others do, take all your oaths. They would all obtain their civil objects, and the change; for any thing I know to the contrary, (in the dark as I am about the Protestant Dissenting tenets) might be of use to the health of their souls. But, what security our constitution, in church or state, could derive from that event, I cannot possibly discern. Depend upon it, it is as true as nature is true, that if you force them out of the religion of habit, education or opinion, it is not to yours they will ever go. Shaken in their minds, they will go to that where the dogmas are fewest; where they are the most uncertain; where they lead them the least to a consideration of what they have abandoned. They will go to that uniformly democratic system, to whose first movements they owed their emancipation. I recommend you seriously to turn this in your mind. Believe that it requires your best and ma-

turest thoughts. Take what course you please—union or no union; whether the people remain Catholics, or become Protestant Dissenters, sure it is, that the present state of monopoly, *cannot* continue.

If England were animated, as I think she is not, with her former spirit of domination, and with the strong theological hatred which she once cherished for that description of her fellow-christians and fellow-subjects; I am yet convinced, that, after the fullest success in a ruinous struggle, you would be obliged finally to abandon that monopoly. We were obliged to do this, even when every thing promised success in the American business. If you should make this experiment at last, under the pressure of any necessity, you never can do it well. But if, instead of falling into a passion, the leading gentlemen of the country themselves should undertake the business cheerfully, and with hearty affection towards it, great advantages would follow. What is forced, cannot be modified; but here, you may measure your concessions.

⌐

There is another advantage in taking up this business, singly and by an arrangement for the single object. It is, that you may proceed by *degrees*. We must all obey the great law of change, it is the most powerful law of nature, and the means perhaps of its conservation. All we can do, and that human wisdom can do, is to provide that the change shall proceed by insensible degrees. This has all the benefits which may be in change, without any of the inconveniences of mutation. Every thing is provided for as it arrives. This mode will, on the one hand, prevent the *unfixing old interests at once;* a thing which is apt to breed a black and sullen discontent, in those who are at once dispossessed of all their influence and consideration. This gradual course, on the other side, will prevent men, long under depression, from being intoxicated with a large draught of new power, which they always abuse with a licentious insolence. But, wishing, as I do, the change to be gradual and cautious, I would, in my first steps, lean rather to the side of enlargement than restriction.

It is one excellence of our constitution, that all our rights of provincial election regard rather property than person. It is another, that the rights which approach more nearly to the personal, are most of them corporate, and suppose a restrained and strict education of seven years in some useful occupation. In both cases the practice may have slid from the principle. The standard of qualification in both cases may be so low, or not so judiciously chosen, as in some degree to frustrate the end. But all this is for your prudence in the case before you. You may rise, a step or two, the qualification of the Catholic voters. But if you were, tomorrow, to put the Catholic freeholder on the footing of the most favoured forty shilling Protestant Dissenter, you know that, such is the actual state of Ireland, this would not make a sensible alteration in almost any *one* election in the kingdom. The effect in their favour, even defensively, would be infinitely slow. But it would be healing; it would be satisfactory and protecting. The stigma would be removed. By admitting settled permanent substance in lieu of the numbers, you would avoid the great danger of our time, that of setting up number against property. The numbers ought never to be neglected; because, (besides what is due to them as men) collectively, though not individually, they have great property: they ought to have therefore protection: they ought to have security: they ought to have even consideration: but they ought not to predominate.

My dear Sir, I have nearly done; I meant to write you a long letter; I have written a long dissertation. I might have done it early and better. I might have been more forcible and more clear, if I had not been interrupted as I have been; and this obliges me not to write to you in my own hand. Though my hand but signs it, my heart goes with what I have written. Since I could think at all, those have been my thoughts. You know that thirty-two years ago they were as fully matured in my mind as they are now. A letter of mine to Lord Kenmare, though not by my desire, and full of lesser mistakes, has been printed in Dublin. It was written ten or twelve years ago, at the time when I began the employment, which I have not yet finished, in favour of another distressed people, injured by those who have vanquished them, or stolen a dominion over them. It contained my sentiments then; you will see how far they accord with my sentiments now. Time has more and more confirmed me in them all. The present circumstances fix them deeper in my mind.

I voted last session, if a particular vote could be distinguished, in unanimity, for an establishment of the Church of England *conjointly* with the establishment which was made some years before by act of parliament, of the Roman Catholic, in the French conquered country of Canada. At the time of making this English ecclesiastical establishment, we did not think it necessary for its safety, to destroy the former Gallican church settlement. In our first act we settled a government altogether monarchical, or nearly so. In that system, the Canadian Catholics were far from being deprived of the advantages of distinctions, of any kind, which they enjoyed under their former monarchy. It is true, that some people, and amongst them one eminent divine, predicted at that time, that by this step we should lose our dominions in America. He foretold that the Pope would send his indulgences thither; that the Canadians would fall in with France; would declare independence, and draw or force our colonies into the same design. The independence happened according to his prediction; but in directly the reverse order. All our English Protestant colonies revolted. They joined themselves to France; and it so happened that Popish Canada was the only place which preserved its fidelity; the only place in which France got no footing; the only peopled colony which now remains to Great Britain. Vain are all the prognostics taken from ideas and passions, which survive the state of things which give rise to them. When last year we gave a popular representation to the same Canada, by the choice of the landholders, and an aristocratic representation, at the choice of the crown, neither was the choice of the crown, nor the election of the landholders, limited by a consideration of religion. We had no dread for the Protestant church, which we settled there, because we permitted the French Catholics, in the utmost latitude of the description, to be free subjects. They are good subjects, I have no doubt; but I will not allow that any French Canadian Catholics are better men or better citizens than the Irish of the same communion. Passing from the extremity of the west, to the extremity almost of the east; I have been many years (now entering into the twelfth) employed in supporting the rights, privileges, laws and immunities of a very remote people. I have not as yet been able to finish my task. I have struggled through much discouragement and much opposition; much obloquy; much calumny, for people with whom I have no tie, but the common bond of mankind. In this I have not been left alone. We did not

fly from our undertaking, because the people were Mahometans or Pagans, and that a great majority of the Christians amongst them were Papists. Some gentlemen in Ireland, I dare say, have good reasons for what they may do, which do not occur to me. I do not presume to condemn them; but, thinking and acting, as I have done, towards these remote nations, I should not know how to shew my face, here or in Ireland, if I should say that all the Pagans, all the Mussulmen, and even all the Papists (since they must form the highest stage in the climax of evil) are worthy of a liberal and honourable condition, except those of one of the descriptions, which forms the majority of the inhabitants of the country in which you and I were born. If such are the Catholics of Ireland; ill-natured and unjust people, from our own data, may be inclined not to think better of the Protestants of a soil, which is supposed to infuse into its sects a kind of venom unknown in other places.

You hated the old system as early as I did. Your first juvenile lance was broken against that giant. I think you were even the first who attacked the grim phantom. You have an exceeding good understanding, very good humour, and the best heart in the world. The dictates of that temper and that heart, as well as the policy pointed out by that understanding, led you to abhor the old code. You abhorred it, as I did, for its vicious perfection. For I must do it justice: it was a complete system, full of coherence and consistency; well digested and well composed in all its parts. It was a machine of wise and elaborate contrivance; and as well fitted for the oppression, impoverishment and degradation of a people, and the debasement, in them, of human nature itself, as ever proceeded from the perverted ingenuity of man. It is a thing humiliating enough, that we are doubtful of the effect of the medicines we compound. We are sure of our poisons. My opinion ever was (in which I heartily agreed with those that admired the old code) that it was so constructed, that if there was once a breach in any essential part of it; the ruin of the whole, or nearly of the whole, was, at some time or other, a certainty. For that reason I honour, and shall for ever honour and love you, and those who first caused it to stagger, crack, and gape.—Others may finish; the beginners have the glory; and, take what part you please at this hour, . . . your first services will never be forgotten by a grateful country. Adieu! Present my best regards to those I know, and as many as I know in our country, I honour. There never was so much ability, or, I believe, virtue, in it. They have a task worthy of both. I doubt not they will perform it, for the stability of the church and state, and for the union and the separation of the people: for the union of the honest and peaceable of all sects; for their separation from all that is ill-intentioned and seditious in any of them.

Beaconsfield,
January 3, 1792

⤙ CHAPTER SIX ⤚

On America

Introductory Note to
Speech on American Taxation
(1774)

From his earliest days in Parliament, Burke was actively involved with the formulation of Britain's policy toward America. Burke was instrumental in the repeal of the Stamp Act, which was immensely unpopular in America, and the passage of the Declaratory Act, both in 1766, during the short-lived Rockingham ministry. Parliament again attempted to raise revenue in America in 1767 by imposing six duties on goods imported into America. American opposition to these new taxes led Parliament in 1769 to repeal all but one of the duties imposed two years earlier. The only duty that remained was on tea, which eventually provoked the Boston Tea Party of 1773. This act of defiance by the Americans brought to a head the question about the nature and practice of British imperial policy in America.

Speech on American Taxation *represented Burke's first major response to the* controversy sparked by the Boston Tea Party. *In a debate on a motion to repeal the duty on tea, Burke set out to destroy the arguments made by supporters of the duty in order to hone in on the fundamental issue at stake: the legislative supremacy of Parliament, as established by the Declaratory Act, over Britain's imperial dominions. As a key figure in the repeal of the Stamp Act and the passage of the Declaratory Act, Burke had to reconcile the policy of repealing taxes with Parliament's right to impose them.*

Burke did so by showing that historically Britain regulated American trade but avoided raising tax revenue in America. Speech on American Taxation *incorporated Burke's procedural and substantive conservatism as he advised Britain to follow historical experience and to recognize the American attachment to fundamental British principles of freedom. In such an approach, Parliament would exercise supreme power in a decentralized way that respected the character and temper of the dominion peoples.* ⤳

Speech on American Taxation (1774)

SIR,

I Agree with the Honourable Gentleman who spoke last, that this subject is not new in this House. Very disagreeably to this House, very unfortunately to this Nation, and to the peace and prosperity of this whole Empire, no topic has been more familiar to us. For nine long years, session after session, we have been lashed round and round this miserable circle of occasional arguments and temporary expedients. I am sure our heads must turn, and our stomachs nauseate with them. We have had them in every shape; we have looked at them in every point of view. Invention is exhausted; reason is fatigued; experience has given judgement; but obstinacy is not yet conquered.

When Parliament repealed the Stamp Act in the year 1766, I affirm, first, that the Americans did *not* in consequence of this measure call upon you to give up the former parliamentary revenue which subsisted in that Country; or even any one of the articles which compose it. I affirm also, that when, departing from the maxims of that repeal, you revived the scheme of taxation, and thereby filled the minds of the Colonists with new jealousy, and all sorts of apprehensions, then it was that they quarreled with the old taxes, as well as the new; then it was, and not till then, that they questioned all the parts of your legislative power; and by the battery of such questions have shaken the solid structure of this Empire to its deepest foundations.

The Act of 1767, which grants this tea duty, sets forth in its preamble, that it was expedient to raise a revenue in America, for the support of the civil government there, as well as for purposes still more extensive. To this support the Act assigns six branches of duties. About two years after this Act passed, the Ministry, I mean the present Ministry,[1] thought it expedient to repeal five of the duties, and to leave (for reasons best known to themselves) only the sixth standing. Suppose any person, at the time of that repeal, had thus addressed the Minister, "Condemning, as you do, the repeal of the Stamp Act, Why do you venture to repeal the duties upon glass, paper, and painters colours? Let your pretence for the repeal be what it will, are you not thoroughly convinced, that your concessions will produce, not satisfaction, but insolence in the Americans; and that the giving up these taxes will necessitate the giving up of all the rest?" This objection was as palpable then as it is now; and it was as good for preserving the five duties as for retaining the sixth. Besides, the Minister will recollect, that the repeal of the Stamp Act had but just preceded his repeal; and the ill policy of that measure . . ., and the mischiefs it produced, were quite recent. Upon the principles therefore of the Hon. Gentleman, upon the principles of the Minister himself, the Minister has nothing at all to answer. He stands condemned by himself, and by all his associates old and new, as a destroyer, in the first trust of finance, of the revenues; and in the first rank of honour, as a betrayer of the dignity of his Country.

---

[1]Burke is referring to the government led by Lord North, the prime minister.

⤜

But I hear it rung continually in my ears, now and formerly,—"the Preamble! what will become of the Preamble, if you repeal this Tax?"—I am sorry to be compelled so often to expose the calamities and disgraces of Parliament. The preamble of this law, standing as it now stands, has the lie direct given to it by the provisionary part of the Act; if that can be called provisionary which makes no provision. I should be afraid to express myself in this manner, especially in the face of such a formidable array of ability as is now drawn up before me, composed of the antient household troops of that side of the House, and the new recruits from this, if the matter were not clear and indisputable. Nothing but truth could give me this firmness; but plain truth and clear evidence can be beat down by no ability. The Clerk will be so good as to turn to the Act, and to read this favourite preamble:

Whereas it is expedient *that a revenue should be raised in your Majesty's Dominions in America, for making a more* certain *and* adequate *provision for defraying the charge of the* administration of justice, and support of civil government, *in such Provinces where it shall be found necessary; and towards* further defraying *the expences of* defending, protecting, and securing the said Dominions.

You have heard this pompous performance. Now where is the revenue which is to do all these mighty things? Five sixths repealed—abandoned—sunk—gone—lost for ever. Does the poor solitary tea duty support the purposes of this preamble? Is not the supply there stated as effectually abandoned as if the tea duty had perished in the general wreck? Here, Mr. Speaker, is a precious mockery—a preamble without an act—taxes granted in order to be re-pealed—and the reasons of the grant still carefully kept up! This is raising a revenue in America! This is preserving dignity in England! If you repeal this tax in compliance with the motion, I readily admit that you lose this fair preamble. Estimate your loss in it. The object of the act is gone already; and all you suffer is the purging the Statute-book of the opprobrium of an empty, absurd, and false recital.

⤜

Sir, it is not a pleasant consideration; but nothing in the world can read so awful and so instructive a lesson, as the conduct of Ministry in this business, upon the mischief of not having large and liberal ideas in the management of great affairs. Never have the servants of the state looked at the whole of your complicated interests in one connected view. They have taken things, by bits and scraps, some at one time and one pretence, and some at another, just as they pressed, without any sort of regard to their relations or dependencies. They never had any kind of system, right or wrong; but only invented occasionally some miserable tale for the day, in order meanly to sneak out of difficulties, into which they had proudly strutted. And they were put to all these shifts and devices, full of meanness and full of mischief, in order to pilfer piecemeal a repeal of an act, which they had not the generous courage, when they found and felt their error, honourably and fairly to disclaim. By such management, by the irresistible operation of feeble councils, so paltry a sum as three-pence in the eyes of a financier, so insignificant an article as tea in the eyes of a philosopher, have shaken the pillars of a Commercial Empire that circled the whole globe.

Do you forget that, in the very last year, you stood on the precipice of general bankruptcy? Your danger was indeed great. You were distressed in the affairs of the East India Company; and you well know what sort of things are involved in the comprehensive energy of that significant appellation. . . . The monopoly of the most lucrative trades, and the possession of imperial revenues, had brought you to the verge of beggary and ruin. Such was your representation—such, in some measure, was your case. The vent of Ten Millions of pounds of this commodity, now locked up by the operation of an injudicious Tax, and rotting in the warehouses of the Company, would have prevented all this distress, and all that series of desperate measures which you thought yourselves obliged to take in consequence of it. America would have furnished that vent, which no other part of the world can furnish but America; where Tea is next to a necessary of life; and where the demand grows upon the supply. . . . It is through the American trade of Tea that your East India conquests are to be prevented from crushing you with their burthen. They are ponderous indeed; and they must have that great country to lean upon, or they tumble upon your head. It is the same folly that has lost you at once the benefit of the West and of the East. This folly has thrown open folding-doors to contraband; and will be the means of giving the profits of the trade of your Colonies, to every nation but yourselves. Never did a people suffer so much for the empty words of a preamble. It must be given up. For on what principle does it stand? This famous revenue stands, at this hour, on all the debate, as a description of revenue not as yet known in all the comprehensive (but too comprehensive!) vocabulary of finance—*a preambulary tax.* It is indeed a tax of sophistry, a tax of pedantry, a tax of disputation, a tax of war and rebellion, a tax for any thing but benefit to the imposers, or satisfaction to the subject.

⟿

Could any thing be a subject of more just alarm to America, than to see you go out of the plain high road of finance, and give up your most certain revenues and your clearest interests, merely for the sake of insulting your Colonies? No man ever doubted that the commodity of Tea could bear an imposition of three-pence. But no commodity will bear a three-pence, or will bear a penny, when the general feelings of men are irritated, and two millions of people are resolved not to pay. . . . It is the weight of that preamble, of which you are so fond, and not the weight of the duty, that the Americans are unable and unwilling to bear.

It is then, Sir, upon the *principle* of this measure, and nothing else, that we are at issue. It is a principle of political expediency. Your act of 1767 asserts, that it is expedient to raise a revenue in America; your act of 1769, which takes away that revenue, contradicts the act of 1767; and, by something much stronger than words, asserts, that it is not expedient. It is a reflexion upon your wisdom to persist in a solemn parliamentary declaration of the expediency of any object, for which, at the same time, you make no sort of provision. And pray, Sir, let not this circumstance escape you; it is very material; that the preamble of this act, which we wish to repeal, is not *declaratory of a right,* as some gentlemen seem to argue it; it is only a recital of the *expediency* of a certain exercise of a right supposed already to have been asserted; an exercise you are now contending for by ways and means, which you confess, though they were obeyed, to be utterly insufficient for their purpose. You are therefore at this moment in the aukward situation of fighting for a phantom; a quiddity; a thing that wants, not only a substance, but even a name; for a thing; which is neither abstract right, nor profitable enjoyment.

They tell you, Sir, that your dignity is tied to it. I know not how it happens, but this dignity of yours is a terrible incumbrance to you; for it has of late been ever at war with your interest, your equity, and every idea of your policy. Shew the thing you contend for to be reason; shew it to be common sense; shew it to be the means of attaining some useful end; and then I am content to allow it what dignity you please. But what dignity is derived from the perseverance in absurdity is more than ever I could discern. . . .

⤷

If this dignity, which is to stand in the place of just policy and common sense, had been consulted, there was a time for preserving it, and for reconciling it with any concession. If in the session of 1768, that session of idle terror and empty menaces, you had, as you were often pressed to do, repealed these taxes; then your strong operations would have come justified and enforced, in case your concessions had been returned by outrages. But, preposterously, you began with violence; and before terrors could have any effect, either good or bad, your ministers immediately begged pardon, and promised that repeal to the obstinate Americans which they had refused in an easy, good-natured, complying British Parliament. The assemblies which had been publicly and avowedly dissolved for *their* contumacy, are called together to receive *your* submission. Your ministerial directors blustered like tragic tyrants here; and then went mumping with a fore leg in America, canting, and whining, and complaining of faction, which represented them as friends to a revenue from the Colonies. I hope nobody in this House will hereafter have the impudence to defend American taxes in the name of Ministry. . . .

⤷

But still it sticks in our throats, if we go so far, the Americans will go farther.—We do not know that. We ought, from experience, rather to presume the contrary. Do we not know for certain, that the Americans are going on as fast as possible, whilst we refuse to gratify them? can they do more, or can they do worse, if we yield this point? I think this concession will rather fix a turnpike to prevent their further progress. It is impossible to answer for bodies of men. But I am sure the natural effect of fidelity, clemency, kindness in governors, is peace, good-will, order, and esteem, on the part of the governed. I would certainly, at least, give these fair principles a fair trial; which, since the making of this act to this hour, they never have had.

⤷

Permit me then, Sir, to lead your attention very far back; back to the act of navigation;[2] the corner-stone of the policy of this country with regard to its colonies. Sir, that policy was, from the beginning, purely commercial; and the commercial system was wholly restrictive. It was the system of a monopoly. No trade was let loose from that constraint, but merely to enable the Colonists to dispose of what, in the course of your trade, you could not take; or to enable them to dispose of such articles as we forced upon them, and for which, without some degree of liberty, they could not pay. Hence all your specific and detailed enumerations: hence the in-

---

[2]The "act of navigation" refers to British legislation that regulated commerce between Britain and the American colonies for the benefit of Britain.

numerable checks and counter-checks: hence that infinite variety of paper chains by which you bind together this complicated system of the Colonies. This principle of commercial monopoly runs through no less than twenty-nine Acts of Parliament, from the year 1660 to the unfortunate period of 1764.

In all those acts the system of commerce is established, as that, from whence alone you proposed to make the Colonies contribute . . . to the strength of the empire. I venture to say, that during that whole period, a parliamentary revenue from thence was never once in contemplation. . . . The scheme of a Colony revenue by British authority appeared therefore to the Americans in the light of a great innovation; the words of Governor Bernard's ninth Letter, written in Nov. 1765,[3] state this idea very strongly; "it must," says he, "have been supposed, *such an innovation as a parliamentary taxation*, would cause a great *alarm*, and meet with much *opposition* in most parts of America; it was *quite new* to the people, and had no *visible bounds* set to it." After stating the weakness of government there, he says, "was this a time to introduce *so great a novelty* as a parliamentary inland taxation in America?" Whatever the right might have been, this mode of using it was absolutely new in policy and practice.

Sir, they who are friends to the schemes of American revenue say, that the commercial restraint is full as hard a law for America to live under. I think so too. I think it, if uncompensated, to be a condition of as rigorous servitude as men can be subject to. But America bore it from the fundamental act of navigation until 1764.— Why? Because men do bear the inevitable

---

[3]Francis Bernard was governor of the Massachusetts Bay Colony.

constitution of their original nature with all its infirmities. The act of navigation attended the Colonies from their infancy, grew with their growth, and strengthened with their strength. They were confirmed in obedience to it, even more by usage than by law. They scarcely had remembered a time when they were not subject to such restraint. Besides, they were indemnified for it by a pecuniary compensation. Their monopolist happened to be one of the richest men in the world. By his immense capital (primarily employed, not for their benefit, but his own) they were enabled to proceed with their fisheries, their agriculture, their ship-building (and their trade too within the limits), in such a manner as get far the start of the slow languid operation of unassisted nature. This capital was a hot-bed to them. Nothing in the history of mankind is like their progress. For my part, I never cast an eye on their flourishing commerce, and their cultivated and commodious life, but they seem to me rather antient nations grown to perfection through a long series of fortunate events, and a train of successful industry, accumulating wealth in many centuries, than the Colonies of yesterday; than a set of miserable out-casts, a few years ago, not so much sent as thrown out, on the bleak and barren shore of a desolate wilderness three thousand miles from all civilized intercourse.

All this was done by England, whilst England pursued trade, and forgot revenue. You not only acquired commerce, but you actually created the very objects of trade in America; and by that creation you raised the trade of this kingdom at least four-fold. America had the compensation of your capital, which made her bear her servitude. She had another compensation, which you are now going to take away from her. She had, except the commercial restraint, every characteristic mark of a free people in all her internal concerns. She had the image of the British constitution. She had the substance. She was taxed by her own representatives. She chose most of her own magistrates. She paid them all. She had in effect the sole disposal of her own internal government. This whole state of commercial servitude and civil liberty, taken together, is certainly not perfect freedom; but comparing it with the ordinary circumstances of human nature, it was an happy and a liberal condition.

       ↩

Whether you were right or wrong in establishing the Colonies on the principles of commercial monopoly, rather than on that of revenue, is at this day a problem of mere speculation. You cannot have both by the same authority. To join together the restraints of an universal internal and external monopoly, with an universal internal and external taxation, is an unnatural union; perfect uncompensated slavery. You have long since decided for yourself and them; and you and they have prospered exceedingly under that decision.

This nation, Sir, never thought of departing from that choice until the period immediately on the close of the last war.[4] Then a scheme of government new in many things seemed to have been adopted. . . . At that period the necessity was established of keeping up no less than twenty new regiments, with twenty colonels capable of seats in this House. This scheme was adopted with very general applause from all sides, at the very time that, by your conquests in America, your danger from foreign attempts in that part of the world was much lessened, or indeed rather quite

over. When this huge encrease of military establishment was resolved on, a revenue was to be found to support so great a burthen. Country gentlemen, the great patrons of oeconomy, and the great resisters of a standing armed force, would not have entered with much alacrity into the vote for so large and so expensive an army, if they had been very sure that they were to continue to pay for it. But hopes of another kind were held out to them; and in particular, I well remember, that Mr. Townshend,[5] in a brilliant harangue on this subject, did dazzle them, by playing before their eyes the image of a revenue to be raised in America.

Here began to dawn the first glimmerings of this new Colony system. . . .

       ↩

After the war, and in the last years of it, the trade of America had encreased far beyond the speculations of the most sanguine imagination. It swelled out on every side. It filled all its proper channels to the brim. It overflowed with a rich redundance, and breaking its banks on the right and on the left, it spread out upon some places, where it was indeed improper, upon others where it was only irregular. It is the nature of all greatness not to be exact; and great trade will always be attended with considerable abuses. The contraband will always keep pace in some measure with the fair trade. It should stand as a fundamental maxim, that no vulgar precaution ought to be employed in the cure of evils, which are closely connected with the cause of our prosperity. . . . The bonds of the act of navigation were straitened so much, that America was on the point of having no trade, either contraband

---

[4]This was the Seven Years' War with France, which took place from 1756 to 1763.

[5]Charles Townshend, who was responsible as chancellor of the exchequer for the duties imposed on the American colonies in 1767.

or legitimate. They found, under the construction and execution then used, the act no longer tying but actually strangling them. All this coming with new enumerations of commodities; with regulations which in a manner put a stop to the mutual coasting intercourse of the Colonies; with the appointment of courts of admiralty under various improper circumstances; with a sudden extinction of the paper currencies; with a compulsory provision for the quartering of soldiers; the people of America thought themselves proceeded against as delinquents, or at best as people under suspicion of delinquency; and in such a manner, as they imagined, their recent services in the war did not at all merit. Any of these innumerable regulations, perhaps, would not have alarmed alone; some might be thought reasonable; the multitude struck them with terror.

But the grand manoeuvre in that business of new regulating the Colonies, was the 15th act of the fourth of George III.;[6] which, besides containing several of the matters to which I have just alluded, opened a new principle: and here properly began the second period of the policy of this country with regard to the Colonies; by which the scheme of a regular plantation parliamentary revenue was adopted in theory, and settled in practice. A revenue not substituted in the place of, but superadded to, a monopoly; which monopoly was enforced at the same time with additional strictness, and the execution put into military hands.

This act, Sir, had for the first time the title of "granting duties in the Colonies and Plantations of America;" and for the first time it was asserted in the preamble, "that it was *just* and *necessary* that a revenue should be raised there." Then came the technical words of "giving and granting;" and thus a complete American revenue act was made in all the forms, and with a full avowal of the right, equity, policy, and even necessity of taxing the Colonies, without any formal consent of theirs. There are contained also in the preamble to that act these very remarkable words—the Commons, &c.— "being desirous to make *some* provision in the *present* Session of Parliament *towards* raising the said revenue." By these words it appeared to the Colonies, that this act was but a beginning of sorrows; that every session was to produce something of the same kind; that we were to go on from day to day, in charging them with such taxes as we pleased, for such a military force as we should think proper. Had this plan been pursued, it was evident that the provincial assemblies, in which the Americans felt all their portion of importance, and beheld their sole image of freedom, were *ipso facto* annihilated. This ill prospect before them seemed to be boundless in extent, and endless in duration. Sir, they were not mistaken. The Ministry valued themselves when this act passed, and when they gave notice of the Stamp Act,[7] that both of the duties came very short of their ideas of American taxation. Great was the applause of this measure here. In England we cried out for new taxes on America, whilst they cried out that they were nearly crushed with those which the war and their own grants had brought upon them.

Sir, it has been said in the debate, that when the first American revenue act (the act in 1764, imposing the port duties) passed, the Americans did not object to the principle. . . .

⏪

---

[6]The Sugar Act of 1764 that imposed duties on the American colonies for the first time.

[7]The Stamp Act of 1765.

... It is said, that no conjecture could be made of the dislike of the Colonies to the principle. This is ... untrue. ... After the resolution of the House, and before the passing of the stamp-act, the Colonies of Massachuset's Bay and New York did send remonstrances, objecting to this mode of parliamentary taxation. What was the consequence? They were suppressed; they were put under the table; notwithstanding an order of council to the contrary, by the ministry which composed the very council that had made the order; and thus the House proceeded to its business of taxing, without the least regular knowledge of the objections which were made to it. But to give that House its due, it was not over desirous to receive information, or to hear remonstrance. On the 15th of February, 1765, whilst the stamp-act was under deliberation, they refused with scorn even so much as to receive four petitions presented from so respectable Colonies as Connecticut, Rhode Island, Virginia, and Carolina; besides one from the traders of Jamaica. As to the Colonies, they had no alternative left to them, but to disobey; or to pay the taxes imposed by that Parliament which was not suffered, or did not suffer itself, even to hear them remonstrate upon the subject.

This was the state of the Colonies before his Majesty thought fit to change his ministers. It stands upon no authority of mine. It is proved by uncontrovertible records. The Hon. Gentleman has desired some of us to lay our hands upon our hearts, and answer to his queries upon the historical part of this consideration; and by his manner (as well as my eyes could discern it) he seemed to address himself to me.

Sir, I will answer him as clearly as I am able, and with great openness: I have nothing to conceal. In the year sixty-five, being in a very private station, far enough from any line of business, and not having the honour of a seat in this House, it was my fortune, unknowing and unknown to the then ministry, by the intervention of a common friend, to become connected with a very noble person, and at the head of the Treasury department.[8] ... Sir, Lord Rockingham very early in that summer received a strong representation from many weighty English merchants and manufacturers, from governors of provinces and commanders of men of war, against almost the whole of the American commercial regulations; and particularly with regard to the total ruin which was threatened to the Spanish trade.[9] I believe, Sir, the noble Lord soon saw his way in this business. But he did not rashly determine against acts which it might be supposed were the result of much deliberation. However, Sir, he scarcely began to open the ground, when the whole veteran body of office took the alarm. A violent outcry of all (except those who knew and felt the mischief) was raised against any alteration. On one hand, his attempt was a direct violation of treaties and public law.—On the other, the Act of Navigation and all the corps of trade laws were drawn up in array against it.

↩

On the conclusion of this business of the Spanish trade, the news of the troubles, on account of the stamp-act, arrived in England. ... No sooner had the sound of that mighty tempest reached us in England, than the whole of the then opposi-

---

[8]Charles Watson Wentworth, second marquess of Rockingham.

[9]Burke is referring to concerns of British merchants that measures aimed at restricting the illegal commerce between the Spanish possessions in the Americas and the British West Indies would adversely affect British trade in the Caribbean.

tion, instead of feeling humbled by the unhappy issue of their measures, seemed to be infinitely elated, and cried out, that the ministry, from envy to the glory of their predecessors, were prepared to repeal the stamp-act. . . .

The first of the two considerations was, whether the repeal should be total, or whether only partial; taking out every thing burthensome and productive, and reserving only an empty acknowledgement, such as a stamp on cards or dice. The other question was, On what principle the act should be repealed? On this head also two principles were started. One, that the legislative rights of this country, with regard to America, were not entire, but had certain restrictions and limitations. The other principle was, that taxes of this kind were contrary to the fundamental principles of commerce on which the Colonies were founded; and contrary to every idea of political equity; by which equity we are bound, as much as possible to extend the spirit and benefit of the British constitution to every part of the British dominions. . . .

꘏

Sir, a partial repeal, or, as the *bon ton* of the court then was, a *modification*, would have satisfied a timid, unsystematic, procrastinating ministry, as such a measure has since done such a ministry. A modification is the constant resource of weak undeciding minds. To repeal by a denial of our right to tax in the preamble (and this too did not want advisers), would have cut, in the heroic style, the Gordian knot with a sword. Either measure would have cost no more than a day's debate. But when the total repeal was adopted; and adopted on principles of policy, of equity, and of commerce; this plan made it necessary to enter into many and difficult mea-

sures. It became necessary to open a very large field of evidence commensurate to these extensive views. But then this labour did knights service. It opened the eyes of several to the true state of the American affairs; it enlarged their ideas; it removed prejudices; and it conciliated the opinions and affections of men. . . . I think the enquiry lasted in the Committee for six weeks;[10] and at its conclusion this House, by an independent, noble, spirited, and unexpected majority; by a majority that will redeem all the acts ever done by majorities in Parliament; in the teeth of all the old mercenary Swiss of state, in despite of all the speculators and augurs of political events, in defiance of the whole embattled legion of veteran pensioners and practised instruments of a court, gave a total repeal to the stamp-act, and (if it had been so permitted) a lasting peace to this whole empire.

꘏

Sir, this act of supreme magnanimity has been represented, as if it had been a measure of an administration, that, having no scheme of their own, took a middle line, pilfered a bit from one side and a bit from the other. Sir, they took *no* middle lines. They differed fundamentally from the schemes of both parties; but they preserved the objects of both. They preserved the authority of Great Britain. They preserved the equity of Great Britain. They made the declaratory act;[11] they repealed the stamp act. They did both *fully;* because the declaratory act was *without qualification;* and

---

[10]A parliamentary committee heard evidence at the beginning of 1766 on the impact in the American colonies of the Stamp Act of 1765.

[11]The Declaratory Act of 1766 that proclaimed Parliament's legislative power and supremacy over the American colonies.

the repeal of the stamp act *total*. This they did in the situation I have described.

Now, Sir, what will the adversary say to both these acts? If the principle of the declaratory act was not good, the principle we are contending for this day is monstrous. If the principle of the repeal was not good, why are we not at war for a real substantial effective revenue? If both were bad; why has this ministry incurred all the inconveniences of both and of all schemes? Why have they enacted, repealed, enforced, yielded, and now attempt to enforce again?

Sir, I think I may as well now, as at any other time, speak to a certain matter of fact not wholly unrelated to the question under your consideration. We, who would persuade you to revert to the antient policy of this kingdom, labour under the effect of this short current phrase, which the court leaders have given out to all their corps, in order to take away the credit of those who would prevent you from that frantic war you are going to wage upon your Colonies. Their cant is this; "All the disturbances in America have been created by the repeal of the Stamp Act." I suppress for a moment my indignation at the falsehood, baseness, and absurdity of this most audacious assertion. Instead of remarking on the motives and character of those who have issued it for circulation, I will clearly lay before you the state of America, antecedently to that repeal; after the repeal; and since the renewal of the schemes of American taxation.

It is said, that the disturbances, if there were any, before the repeal, were slight; and without difficulty or inconvenience might have been suppressed. For an answer to this assertion I will send you to the great author and patron of the Stamp Act,[12] who certainly meaning well to the

---

authority of this Country, and fully apprized for the state of that, made, before a repeal was so much as agitated in this House, the motion which is on your Journals; and which . . . I will now read to you. It was for an amendment to the address of the 17th of December 1765:

To express our just resentment and indignation at the outrageous tumults and insurrections *which have been excited and carried on in North America; and at the resistance given by* open *and* rebellious *force to the execution of the laws in that part of his Majesty's dominions. And to assure his Majesty, that his faithful Commons, animated with the warmest duty and attachment to his royal person and government, will firmly and effectually support his Majesty in all such measures as shall be necessary for preserving and supporting the legal dependance of the Colonies on the Mother Country, &c. &c.*

Here was certainly a disturbance preceding the repeal; such a disturbance as Mr. Grenville thought necessary to qualify by the name of an *insurrection,* and the epithet of a *rebellious* force: terms much stronger than any, by which, those who then supported his motion, have ever since thought proper to distinguish the subsequent disturbances in America. They were disturbances which seemed to him and his friends to justify as strong a promise of support, as hath been usual to give in the beginning of a war with the most powerful and declared enemies. . . .

↬

It is remarkable, Sir, that the persons who formerly trumpeted forth the most loudly, the violent resolutions of assemblies; the universal insurrections; the seizing and burning the stamped papers; the forcing stamp officers to resign their commissions under the gallows; the rifling and pulling

---

[12]George Grenville, prime minister when Parliament passed the Stamp Act of 1765.

down of the houses of magistrates; and the expulsion from their country of all who dared to write or speak a single word in defence of the powers of parliament; these very trumpeters are now the men that represent the whole as a mere trifle; and choose to date all the disturbances from the repeal of the stamp act, which put an end to them. Hear your officers abroad, and let them refute this shameless falsehood, who, in all their correspondence, state the disturbances as owing to their true causes, the discontent of the people, from the taxes. You have this evidence in your own archives—and it will give you compleat satisfaction; if you are not so far lost to all parliamentary ideas of information, as rather to credit the lye of the day, than the records of your own House.

Sir, this vermin of court reporters, when they are forced into day upon one point, are sure to burrow in another; but they shall have no refuge: I will make them bolt out of all their holes. . . . They say, that the opposition made in parliament to the stamp act at the time of its passing, encouraged the Americans to their resistance. . . . But this assertion too, just like the rest, is false. In all the papers which have loaded your table; in all the vast crowd of verbal witnesses that appeared at your bar, witnesses which were indiscriminately produced from both sides of the House; not the least hint of such a cause of disturbance has ever appeared. . . . There was but one division in the whole progress of the bill; and the minority did not reach to more than 39 or 40. In the House of Lords I do not recollect that there was any debate or division at all. I am sure there was no protest. In fact, the affair passed with so very, very little noise, that in town they scarcely knew the nature of what you were doing. The opposition to the bill in England never could have done this mischief,

because there scarcely ever was less of opposition to a bill of consequence.

Sir, the agents and distributors of falsehoods have, with their usual industry, circulated another lye of the same nature with the former. It is this, that the disturbances arose from the account which had been received in America of the change in the ministry. No longer awed, it seems, with the spirit of the former rulers, they thought themselves a match for what our calumniators choose to qualify by the name of so feeble a ministry as succeeded. Feeble in one sense these men certainly may be called; for with all their efforts, and they have made many, they have not been able to resist the distempered vigour, and insane alacrity with which you are rushing to your ruin. But it does so happen, that the falsity of this circulation is (like the rest) demonstrated by indisputable dates and records.

~

Thus are blown away the insect race of courtly falsehoods! thus perish the miserable inventions of the wretched runners for a wretched cause, which they have flyblown into every weak and rotten part of the country, in vain hopes that when their maggots had taken wing, their importunate buzzing might sound something like the public voice!

Sir, I have troubled you sufficiently with the state of America before the repeal. Now I turn to the Hon. Gentleman who so stoutly challenges us, to tell, whether, after the repeal, the Provinces were quiet? This is coming home to the point. Here I meet him directly; and answer most readily, *They were quiet.* And I, in my turn, challenge him to prove when, and where, and by whom, and in what numbers, and with what violence, the other laws of trade, as gentlemen assert, were violated in consequence of your concession? or that even your other revenue laws were attacked? But I quit the vantage ground on which I stand, and where I might leave the burthen of the proof upon him: I walk down upon the open plain, and undertake to shew, that they were not only quiet, but shewed many unequivocal marks of acknowledgement and gratitude. . . .

~

. . . Almost every . . . part of America in various ways demonstrated their gratitude. I am bold to say, that so sudden a calm recovered after so violent a storm is without parallel in history. . . . But as far as appearances went, by the judicious sacrifice of one law, you procured an acquiescence in all that remained. After this experience, nobody shall persuade me, when an whole people are concerned, that acts of lenity are not means of conciliation.

~

I have done with the third period of your policy; that of your repeal; and the return of your ancient system, and your ancient tranquillity and concord. Sir, this period was not as long as it was happy. Another scene was opened, and other actors appeared on the stage. The state, in the condition I have described it, was delivered into the hands of Lord Chatham—a great and celebrated name; a name that keeps the name of this country respectable in every other on the globe.[13] . . .

. . . For a wise man, he seemed to me at that time, to be governed too much by general maxims. I speak with the freedom of history, and I hope without offence. One or two of these maxims, flowing from an opinion not the most indulgent to our

unhappy species, and surely a little too general, led him into measures that were greatly mischievous to himself; and for that reason, among others, perhaps fatal to his country; measures, the effects of which, I am afraid, are for ever incurable. He made an administration, so checkered and speckled; he put together a piece of joinery, so crossly indented and whimsically dovetailed; a cabinet so variously inlaid; such a piece of diversified Mosaic; such a tesselated pavement without cement; here a bit of black stone, and there a bit of white; patriots and courtiers, kings friends and republicans; whigs and tories; treacherous friends and open enemies: that it was indeed a very curious show; but utterly unsafe to touch, and unsure to stand on. . . .

Sir, in consequence of this arrangement, having put so much the larger part of his enemies and opposers into power, the confusion was such, that his own principles could not possibly have any effect or influence in the conduct of affairs. If ever he fell into a fit of the gout, or if any other cause withdrew him from publick cares, principles directly the contrary were sure to predominate. When he had executed his plan, he had not an inch of ground to stand upon. When he had accomplished his scheme of administration, he was no longer a minister.

When his face was hid but for a moment, his whole system was on a wide sea, without chart or compass. The gentlemen, his particular friends, who, with the names of various departments of ministry, were admitted, to seem, as if they acted a part under him, with a modesty that becomes all men, and with a confidence in him, which was justified even in its extravagance by his superior abilities, had never, in any instance, presumed upon any opinion of their own. Deprived of his guiding influence, they were whirled about, the

---

[13]William Pitt (the Elder), prime minister when Parliament imposed duties on America in 1767.

sport of every gust, and easily driven into any port; and as those who joined with them in manning the vessel were the most directly opposite to his opinions, measures, and character, and far the most artful and most powerful of the set, they easily prevailed, so as to seize upon the vacant, unoccupied, and derelict minds of his friends; and instantly they turned the vessel wholly out of the course of his policy. As if it were to insult as well as to betray him, even long before the close of the first session of his administration, when every thing was publickly transacted, and with great parade in his name, they made an act, declaring it highly just and expedient to raise a revenue in America. For even then, Sir, even before this splendid orb was entirely set, and while the Western horizon was in a blaze with his descending glory, on the opposite quarter of the heavens arose another luminary, and, for his hour, became lord of the ascendant.

This light too is passed and set for ever. You understand, to be sure, that I speak of Charles Townshend, officially the re-producer of this fatal scheme; whom I cannot even now remember without some degree of sensibility. In truth, Sir, he was the delight and ornament of this house, and the charm of every private society which he honoured with his presence. Perhaps there never arose in this country, nor in any country, a man of a more pointed and finished wit; and (where his passions were not concerned) of a more refined, exquisite, and penetrating a judgment. . . .

I beg pardon, Sir, if when I speak of this and of other great men, I appear to digress in saying something of their characters. In this eventful history of the revolutions of America, the characters of such men are of much importance. Great men are the guide-posts and land-marks in the state. The credit of such men at court, or in the na-

tion, is the sole cause of all the publick measures. It would be an invidious thing, . . . to remark the errors into which the authority of great names has brought the nation, without doing justice at the same time to the great qualities, whence that authority arose. . . .

That fear of displeasing those who ought most to be pleased, betrayed him[14] sometimes into the other extreme. He had voted, and in the year 1765, had been an advocate for the Stamp Act. Things and the disposition of mens minds were changed. In short, the Stamp Act began to be no favourite in this house. He therefore attended at the private meeting, in which resolutions moved by a Right Hon. Gentleman were settled; resolutions leading to the repeal. The next day he voted for that repeal; and he would have spoken for it too, if an illness, (not as was then given out a political) but to my knowledge, a very real illness, had not prevented it.

The very next session, as the fashion of this world passeth away, the repeal began to be in as bad an odour in this house as the Stamp Act had been in the session before. To conform to the temper which began to prevail, and to prevail mostly amongst those most in power, he declared, very early in the Winter, that a revenue must be had out of America. Instantly he was tied down to his engagements by some, who had no objection to such experiments, when made at the cost of persons for whom they had no particular regard. The whole body of courtiers drove him onward. They always talked as if the king stood in a sort of humiliated state, until something of the kind should be done.

Here this extraordinary man, then Chancellor of the Exchequer, found himself in great straits. To please universally

---

[14]Townshend.

was the object of his life; but to tax and to please, no more than to love and to be wise, is not given to men. However he attempted it. To render the tax palatable to the partizans of American revenue, he made a preamble stating the necessity of such a revenue. To close with the American distinction, this revenue was *external* or port-duty; but again, to soften it to the other party, it was a duty of *supply.* To gratify the *colonists,* it was laid on British manufactures; to satisfy the *merchants of Britain,* the duty was trivial, and (except that on tea, which touched only the devoted East India Company) on none of the grand objects of commerce. To counterwork the American contraband, the duty on tea was reduced from a shilling to three-pence. But to secure the favour of those who would tax America, the scene of collection was changed, and, with the rest, it was levied in the Colonies. What need I say more? This fine-spun scheme had the usual fate of all exquisite policy. But the original plan of the duties, and the mode of executing that plan, both arose singly and solely from a love of our applause. He was truly the child of the house. He never thought, did, or said any thing but with a view to you. He every day adapted himself to your disposition; and adjusted himself before it, as at a looking-glass.

↬

Hence arose this unfortunate act, the subject of this day's debate; from a disposition which, after making an American revenue to please one, repealed it to please others, and again revived it in hopes of pleasing a third, and of catching something in the ideas of all.

This revenue act of 1767, formed the fourth period of American policy. How we have fared since then—what woeful variety of schemes have been adopted; what en-

forcing, and what repealing; what bullying, and what submitting; what doing, and undoing; what straining, and what relaxing; what assemblies dissolved for not obeying, and called again without obedience; what troops sent out to quell resistance, and on meeting that resistance, recalled; what shiftings, and changes, and jumblings of all kinds of men at home, which left no possibility of order, consistency, vigour, or even so much as a decent unity of colour in any one public measure. . . .

After all these changes and agitations, your immediate situation upon the question on your paper is at length brought to this. You have an act of parliament, stating that "it is *expedient* to raise a revenue in America." By a partial repeal you annihilated the greatest part of that revenue, which this preamble declares to be so expedient. You have substituted no other in the place of it. A secretary of state has disclaimed, in the king's name, all thoughts of such a substitution in future.[15] The principle of this disclaimer goes to what has been left, as well as what has been repealed. The tax which lingers after its companions, (under a preamble declaring an American revenue expedient, and for the sole purpose of supporting the theory of that preamble) militates with the assurance authentically conveyed to the Colonies; and is an exhaustless source of jealousy and animosity. On this state, which I take to be a fair one; not being able to discern any grounds of honour, advantage, peace, or power, for adhering, either to the act or to the preamble, I shall vote for the question which leads to the repeal of both.

If you do not fall in with this motion, then secure something to fight for, consis-

---

[15]Burke is referring to a circular letter of May 1769 written by Lord Hillsborough, secretary of state for the colonies.

tent in theory and valuable in practice. If you must employ your strength, employ it to uphold you in some honourable right, or some profitable wrong. If you are apprehensive that the concession recommended to you, though proper, should be a means of drawing on you further but unreasonable claims,—why then employ your force in supporting that reasonable concession against those unreasonable demands. You will employ it with more grace; with better effect; and with great probable concurrence of all the quiet and rational people in the provinces; who are now united with, and hurried away by, the violent; having indeed different dispositions, but a common interest. If you apprehend that on a concession you shall be pushed by metaphysical process to the extreme lines, and argued out of your whole authority, my advice is this; when you have recovered your old, your strong, your tenable position, then face about—stop short—do nothing more—reason not at all—oppose the ancient policy and practice of the empire, as a rampart against the speculations of innovators on both sides of the question; and you will stand on great, manly, and sure ground. On this solid basis fix your machines, and they will draw worlds towards you.

Your ministers, in their own and his Majesty's name, have already adopted the American distinction of internal and external duties. It is a distinction, whatever merit it may have, that was originally moved by the Americans themselves; and I think they will acquiesce in it, if they are not pushed with too much logic and too little sense, in all the consequences. That is, if external taxation be understood, as they and you understand it when you please, to be not a distinction of geography, but of policy; that it is a power for regulating trade, and not for supporting establish-

ments. The distinction, which is as nothing with regard to right, is of most weighty consideration in practice. Recover your old ground, and your old tranquillity—try it—I am persuaded the Americans will compromise with you. When confidence is once restored, the odious and suspicious *summum jus* will perish of course. The spirit of practicability, of moderation, and mutual convenience, will never call in geometrical exactness as the arbitrator of an amicable settlement. Consult and follow your experience. Let not the long story with which I have exercised your patience, prove fruitless to your interests.

⌒

Let us, Sir, embrace some system or other before we end this session. Do you mean to tax America, and to draw a productive revenue from thence? If you do, speak out: name, fix, ascertain this revenue; settle its quantity; defines its objects; provide for its collection; and then fight when you have something to fight for. If you murder—rob! If you kill, take possession; and do not appear in the character of madmen, as well as assassins, violent, vindictive, bloody, and tyrannical, without an object. But may better counsels guide you!

Again, and again, revert to your old principles—seek peace and ensue it—leave America, if she has taxable matter in her, to tax herself. I am not here going into the distinctions of rights, nor attempting to mark their boundaries. I do not enter into these metaphysical distinctions; I hate the very sound of them. Leave the Americans as they antiently stood, and these distinctions, born of our unhappy contest, will die along with it. They, and we, and their and our ancestors, have been happy under that system. Let the memory of all actions, in contradiction to that good old mode, on both sides, be extinguished for ever. Be content to bind America by laws of trade; you have always done it. Let this be your reason for binding their trade. Do not burthen them by taxes; you were not used to do so from the beginning. Let this be your reason for not taxing. These are the arguments of states and kingdoms. Leave the rest to the schools; for there only they may be discussed with safety. But if, intemperately, unwisely, fatally, you sophisticate and poison the very source of government, by urging subtle deductions, and consequences odious to those you govern, from the unlimited and illimitable nature of supreme sovereignty, you will teach them by these means to call that sovereignty itself in question. When you drive him hard, the boar will surely turn upon the hunters. If that sovereignty and their freedom cannot be reconciled, which will they take? They will cast your sovereignty in your face. No body will be argued into slavery. Sir, let the gentlemen on the other side call forth all their ability; let the best of them get up, and tell me, what one character of liberty the Americans have, and what one brand of slavery they are free from, if they are bound in their property and industry, by all the restraints you can imagine on commerce, and at the same time are made pack-horses of every tax you choose to impose, without the least share in granting them? When they bear the burthens of unlimited monopoly, will you bring them to bear the burthens of unlimited revenue too? The Englishman in America will feel that this slavery—that it is *legal* slavery, will be no compensation, either to his feelings or his understanding.

A Noble Lord, who spoke some time ago, . . . has said, that the Americans are our children; and how can they revolt against their parent? He says, that if they are not free in their present state, England is not free; because Manchester, and other considerable places, are not represented. So then, because some towns in England are not represented, America is to have no representative at all. They are "our children;" but when children ask for bread, we are not to give a stone. Is it because the natural resistance of things, and the various mutations of time, hinders our government, or any scheme of government, from being any more than a sort of approximation to the right, is it therefore that the Colonies are to recede from it infinitely? When this child of ours wishes to assimilate to its parent, and to reflect with a true filial resemblance the beauteous coutenance of British liberty; are we to turn to them the shameful parts of our constitution? are we to give them our weakness for their strength; our opprobrium for their glory; and the slough of slavery, which we are not able to work off, to serve them for their freedom?

If this be the case, ask yourselves this question, will they be content in such a state of slavery? If not, look to the consequences. Reflect how you are to govern a people, who think they ought to be free, and think they are not. Your scheme yields no revenue; it yields nothing but discontent, disorder, disobedience; and such is the state of America, that after wading up to your eyes in blood you could only end just where you begun; that is, to tax where no revenue is to be found, to—my voice fails me; my inclination indeed carries me no further—all is confusion beyond it.

Well, Sir, I have recovered a little, and before I sit down I must say something to another point with which gentlemen urge us. What is to become of the declaratory act asserting the entireness of British legislative authority, if we abandon the practice of taxation?

For my part I look upon the rights stated in that act, exactly in the manner in which I viewed them on its very first proposition, and which I have often taken the liberty, with great humility, to lay before you. I look, I say, on the imperial rights of Great Britain, and the privileges which the Colonists ought to enjoy under these rights, to be just the most reconcileable things in the world. The Parliament of Great Britain sits at the head of her extensive empire in two capacities: one as the local legislature of this island, providing for all things at home, immediately, and by no other instrument than the executive power.—The other, and I think her nobler capacity, is what I call her *imperial character;* in which, as from the throne of heaven, she superintends all the several inferior legislatures, and guides, and controls them all without annihilating any. As all these provincial legislatures are only coordinate to each other, they ought all to be subordinate to her; else they can neither preserve mutual peace, nor hope for mutual justice, nor effectually afford mutual assistance. It is necessary to coerce the negligent, to restrain the violent, and to aid the weak and deficient, by the over-ruling plenitude of her power. She is never to intrude into the place of the others, whilst they are equal to the common ends of their institution. But in order to enable parliament to answer all these ends of provident and beneficent superintendance, her powers must be boundless. The gentlemen who think the powers of parliament limited, may please themselves to talk of requisitions. But suppose the requisitions are not obeyed? What! Shall there be no reserved power in the empire, to supply a deficiency which may weaken, divide, and dissipate the whole? We are engaged in war—the Secretary of State calls upon the Colonies to contribute—some would do it, I think most would chearfully furnish whatever is demanded—one or two, sup-

pose, hang back, and, easing themselves, let the stress of the draft lie on the others—surely it is proper, that some authority might legally say—"Tax yourselves for the common supply, or parliament will do it for you." This backwardness was, as I am told, actually the case of Pennsylvania for some short time towards the beginning of the last war, owing to some internal dissentions in the Colony. But, whether the fact were so, or otherwise, the case is equally to be provided for by a competent sovereign power. But then this ought to be no ordinary power; nor ever used in the first instance. This is what I meant, when I have said at various times, that I consider the power of taxing in parliament as an instrument of empire, and not as a means of supply.

Such, Sir, is my idea of the constitution of the British Empire, as distinguished from the constitution of Britain; and on these grounds I think subordination and liberty may be sufficiently reconciled through the whole; whether to serve a refining speculatist, or a factious demagogue, I know not; but enough surely for the ease and happiness of man.

Sir, whilst we held this happy course, we drew more from the Colonies than all the impotent violence of despotism ever could extort from them. We did this abundantly in the last war. It has never been once denied—and what reason have we to imagine that the Colonies would not have proceeded in supplying government as liberally, if you had not stepped in and hindered them from contributing, by interrupting the channel in which their liberality flowed with so strong a course; by attempting to take, instead of being satisfied to receive. Sir William Temple says, that Holland has loaded itself with ten times the impositions which it revolted from Spain, rather than submit to. He says true. Tyranny is a poor provider. It knows neither how to accumulate, nor how to extract.

I charge therefore to this new and unfortunate system the loss not only of peace, of union, and of commerce, but even of revenue, which its friends are contending for.—It is morally certain, that we have lost at least a million of free grants since the peace. I think we have lost a great deal more; and that those who look for a revenue from the Provinces, never could have pursued, even in that light, a course more directly repugnant to their purposes.

Now, Sir, I trust I have shewn, first on that narrow ground which the Hon. Gentleman measured, that you are like to lose nothing by complying with the motion, except what you have lost already. I have shewn afterwards, that in time of peace you flourished in commerce, and when war required it, had sufficient aid from the Colonies, while you pursued your antient policy; that you threw every thing into confusion when you made the stamp act; and that you restored every thing to peace and order when you repealed it. I have shewn that the revival of the system of taxation has produced the very worst effects; and that the partial repeal has produced, not partial good, but universal evil. Let these considerations, founded on facts, not one of which can be denied, bring us back to your reason by the road of your experience.

I cannot, as I have said, answer for mixed measures; but surely this mixture of lenity would give the whole a better chance of success. When you once again regain confidence, the way will be clear before you. Then you may enforce the act of navigation when it ought to be enforced. You will yourselves open it where it ought still further to be opened. Proceed in what you do, whatever you do, from policy, and not from rancour. Let us act like men, let us act like statesmen. Let us hold some sort of consistent conduct—It is agreed that a revenue is not to be had in America. If we lose the profit, let us get rid of the odium.

On this business of America I confess I am serious, even to sadness. I have had but one opinion concerning it since I sat, and before I sat, in Parliament. . . . I honestly and solemnly declare, I have in all seasons adhered to the system of 1766, for no other reason, than that I think it laid deep in your truest interests—and that, by limiting the exercise, it fixes on the firmest foundation, a real, consistent, well-grounded authority in parliament. Until you come back to that system, there will be no peace for England.

Introductory Note to
Speech on Conciliation with America (1775)

Relations between Britain and the American colonies continued to deteriorate after Burke's Speech on American Taxation *(1774). At the end of* Speech on American Taxation, *Burke sketched the outlines of his solution to the American troubles. In* Speech on Conciliation with America, *Burke proposed his plan for "restoring the former unsuspecting confidence of the colonies in the mother country." Burke argued that conciliation and compromise by Britain was the only rational option open to restore peace with the American colonists.*

The heart of Burke's plan for conciliation with the Americans echoed a central feature of his Irish thinking: "to admit the people of our colonies into an interest in the constitution." Here we see Burke again attempting to build the imperial society upon the foundation of the British constitution. Burke cap-

tured his vision of the British Empire in his statement that the empire should be animated by "a unity of spirit" but be characterized by "a diversity of operations." Burke contended that the "cement" and "cohesion" of the imperial society depended upon the Americans' enjoying privileges of power within the imperial framework.

Burke's conciliatory resolutions were heavily defeated in Parliament. Four weeks later, at Concord, Massachusetts, hostilities between the Americans and the British began. ⌒

Speech on Conciliation with America (1775)

I HOPE, Sir, that, notwithstanding the austerity of the Chair, your good-nature will incline you to some degree of indulgence towards human frailty. You will not think it unnatural, that those who have an object depending, which strongly engages their hopes and fears, should be somewhat inclined to superstition. As I came into the house full of anxiety about the event of my motion, I found to my infinite surprize, that the grand penal Bill, by which we had passed sentence on the trade and sustenance of America, is to be returned to us from the other House.[16] I do confess, I could not help looking on this event as a fortunate

---

[16]The Act to restrain the Trade and Commerce of the Provinces of Massachuset's Bay and New Hampshire, and Colonies of Connecticut and Rhode Island, and Providence Plantation, in North America, to Great Britain, Ireland, and the British Islands in the West Indies; and to prohibit such Provinces and Colonies from carrying on dry Fishery on the Banks of Newfoundland, and other places therein mentioned, under certain Conditions and Limitations. [Burke's note.]

omen. I look upon it as a sort of providential favour; by which we are put once more in possession of our deliberative capacity, upon a business so very questionable in its nature, so very uncertain in its issue. By the return of this Bill, which seemed to have taken its flight for ever, we are at this very instant nearly as free to chuse a plan for our American Government, as we were on the first day of the Session. If, Sir, we incline to the side of conciliation, we are not at all embarrassed (unless we please to make ourselves so) by any incongruous mixture of coercion and restraint. We are therefore called upon, as it were by a superior warning voice, again to attend to America; to attend to the whole of it together; and to review the subject with an unusual degree of care and calmness.

Surely it is an awful subject; or there is none so on this side of the grave. When I first had the honour of a seat in this House, the affairs of that Continent pressed themselves upon us, as the most important and most delicate object of parliamentary attention. My little share in this great deliberation oppressed me. I found myself a partaker in a very high trust; and having no sort of reason to rely on the strength of my natural abilities for the proper execution of that trust, I was obliged to take more than common pains, to instruct myself in every thing which relates to our Colonies. I was not less under the necessity of forming some fixed ideas, concerning the general policy of the British Empire. Something of this sort seemed to be indispensable; in order, amidst so vast a fluctuation of passions and opinions, to concenter my thoughts; to ballast my conduct; to preserve me from being blown about by every wind of fashionable doctrine. I really did not think it safe, or manly, to have fresh principles to seek upon every fresh mail which should arrive from America.

At that period, I had the fortune to find myself in perfect concurrence with a large majority in this House. Bowing under that high authority, and penetrated with the sharpness and strength of that early impression, I have continued ever since, without the least deviation, in my original sentiments. Whether this be owing to an obstinate perseverance in error, or to a religious adherence to what appears to me truth and reason, it is in your equity to judge.

Sir, Parliament having an enlarged view of objects, made, during this interval, more frequent changes in their sentiments and their conduct, than could be justified in a particular person upon the contracted scale of private information. But though I do not hazard any thing approaching to a censure on the motives of former parliaments to all those alterations, one fact is undoubted; that under them the state of America has been kept in continual agitation. Every thing administered as remedy to the public complaint, if it did not produce, was at least followed by, an heightening of the distemper; until, by a variety of experiments, that important Country has been brought into her present situation;—a situation, which I will not miscall, which I dare not name; which I scarcely know how to comprehend in the terms of any description.

↜

To restore order and repose to an Empire so great and so distracted as ours, is, merely in the attempt, an undertaking that would ennoble the flights of the highest genius, and obtain pardon for the efforts of the meanest understanding. Struggling a good while with these thoughts, by degrees I felt myself more firm. I derived, at length, some confidence from what in other circumstances usually produces timidity. I grew less anxious, even from the

idea of my own insignificance. For, judging of what you are, by what you ought to be, I persuaded myself, that you would not reject a reasonable proposition, because it had nothing but its reason to recommend it. On the other hand, being totally destitute of all shadow of influence, natural or adventitious, I was very sure, that, if my proposition were futile or dangerous; if it were weakly conceived, or improperly timed, there was nothing exterior to it, of power to awe, dazzle, or delude you. You will see it just as it is; and you will treat it just as it deserves.

The proposition is Peace. Not Peace through the medium of War; not Peace to be hunted through the labyrinth of intricate and endless negociations; not Peace to arise out of universal discord, fomented, from principle, in all parts of the Empire; not Peace to depend on the Juridical Determination of perplexing questions; or the precise marking the shadowy boundaries of a complex Government. It is simple Peace; sought in its natural course, and its ordinary haunts.—It is Peace sought in the Spirit of Peace; and laid in principles purely pacific. I propose, by removing the Ground of the difference, and by restoring the *former unsuspecting confidence of the Colonies in the Mother Country,* to give permanent satisfaction to your people; and (far from a scheme of ruling by discord) to reconcile them to each other in the same act, and by the bond of the very same interest, which reconciles them to British Government.

My idea is nothing more. Refined policy ever has been the parent of confusion; and ever will be so, as long as the world endures. Plain good intention, which is as easily discovered at the first view, as fraud is surely detected at last, is, let me say, of no mean force in the Government of Mankind. Genuine Simplicity of heart is an healing and cementing principle. My Plan, therefore, being formed upon the most simple grounds imaginable, may disappoint some people, when they hear it. It has nothing to recommend it to the pruriency of curious ears. There is nothing at all new and captivating in it. It has nothing of the Splendor of the Project, which has been lately laid upon your Table by the Noble Lord in the Blue Ribband.[17] It does not propose to fill your Lobby with squabbling Colony Agents, who will require the interposition of your Mace, at every instant, to keep the peace amongst them. It does not institute a magnificent Auction of Finance, where captivated provinces come to general ransom by bidding against each other, until you knock down the hammer, and determine a proportion of payments, beyond all the powers of Algebra to equalize and settle.

The plan, which I shall presume to suggest, derives, however, one great advantage from the proposition and registry of that Noble Lord's Project. The idea of conciliation is admissible. First, the House, in accepting the resolution moved by the Noble Lord, has admitted, notwithstanding the menacing front of our Address, notwithstanding our heavy Bill of Pains and Penalties—that we do not think ourselves precluded from all ideas of free Grace and Bounty.

The House has gone farther; it has declared conciliation admissible, *previous* to any submission on the part of America. It has even shot a good deal beyond that mark, and has admitted, that the complaints of our former mode of exerting the Right of Taxation were not wholly unfounded. That right thus exerted is al-

lowed to have had something reprehensible in it; something unwise, or something grievous: since, in the midst of our heat and resentment, we, of ourselves, have proposed a capital alteration; and, in order to get rid of what seemed so very exceptionable, have instituted a mode that is altogether new; one that is, indeed, wholly alien from all the ancient methods and forms of Parliament.

The *principle* of this proceeding is large enough for my purpose. . . . I mean to give peace. Peace implies reconciliation; and where there has been a material dispute, reconciliation does in a manner always imply concession on the one part or on the other. In this state of things I make no difficulty in affirming, that the proposal ought to originate from us. Great and acknowledged force is not impaired, either in effect or in opinion, by an unwillingness to exert itself. The superior power may offer peace with honour and with safety. Such an offer from such a power will be attributed to magnanimity. But the concessions of the weak are the concessions of fear. When such a one is disarmed, he is wholly at the mercy of his superior; and he loses for ever that time and those chances, which, as they happen to all men, are the strength and resources of all inferior power.

The capital leading questions on which you must this day decide, are these two. First, whether you ought to concede; and secondly, what your concession ought to be. On the first of these questions we have gained (as I have just taken the liberty of observing to you) some ground. But I am sensible that a good deal more is still to be done. Indeed, Sir, to enable us to determine both on the one and the other of these great questions with a firm and precise judgement, I think it may be necessary to consider distinctly the true nature and the peculiar circumstances of the object

---

[17]Lord North, the prime minister. The "Blue Ribband" refers to the Order of the Garter bestowed on North by King George III in 1772.

which we have before us. Because after all our struggle, whether we will or not, we must govern America, according to that nature, and to those circumstances; and not according to our own imaginations; not according to abstract ideas of right; by no means according to mere general theories of government, the resort to which appears to me, in our present situation, no better than arrant trifling. I shall therefore endeavour, with your leave, to lay before you some of the most material of these circumstances in as full and as clear a manner as I am able to state them.

The first thing that we have to consider with regard to the nature of the object is— the number of people in the Colonies. I have taken for some years a good deal of pains on that point. I can by no calculation justify myself in placing the number below Two Millions of inhabitants of our own European blood and colour; besides at least 500,000 others, who form no inconsiderable part of the strength and opulence of the whole. This, Sir, is, I believe, about the true number. There is no occasion to exaggerate, where plain truth is of so much weight and importance. But whether I put the present numbers too high or too low, is a matter of little moment. Such is the strength with which population shoots in that part of the world, that state the numbers as high as we will, whilst the dispute continues, the exaggeration ends. Whilst we are discussing any given magnitude, they are grown to it. Whilst we spend our time in deliberating on the mode of governing Two Millions, we shall find we have Millions more to manage. Your children do not grow faster from infancy to manhood, than they spread from families to communities, and from villages to nations.

I put this consideration of the present and the growing numbers in the front of our deliberation; because, Sir, this consideration will make it evident to a blunter discernment than yours, that no partial, narrow, contracted, pinched, occasional system will be at all suitable to such an object. It will shew you, that it is not to be considered as one of those *Minima* which are out of the eye and consideration of the law; not a paltry excrescence of the state; not a mean dependant, who may be neglected with little damage, and provoked with little danger. It will prove, that some degree of care and caution is required in the handling such an object; it will shew, that you ought not, in reason, to trifle with so large a mass of the interests and feelings of the human race. You could at no time do so without guilt; and be assured you will not be able to do it long with impunity.

But the population of this country, the great and growing population, though a very important consideration, will lose much of its weight, if not combined with other circumstances. The commerce of your Colonies is out of all proportion beyond the numbers of the people. . . .

I have in my hand two accounts; one a comparative state of the export trade of England to its Colonies, as it stood in the year 1704, and as it stood in the year 1772. The other a state of the export trade of this country to its Colonies alone, as it stood in 1772, compared with the whole trade of England to all parts of the world (the Colonies included) in the year 1704. . . .

From Five Hundred and odd Thousand, it has grown to Six Millions. It has increased no less than twelve-fold. This is the state of the Colony trade, as compared with itself at these two periods, within this century;—and this is matter for meditation. But this is not all. Examine my second account. See how the export trade to the Colonies alone in 1772 stood in the other point of view, that is, as compared to the whole trade of England in 1704.

↜

The trade with America alone is now within less than 500,000*l.* of being equal to what this great commercial nation, England, carried on at the beginning of this century with the whole world! If I had taken the largest year of those on your table, it would rather have exceeded. But, it will be said, is not this American trade an unnatural protuberance, that has drawn the juices from the rest of the body? The reverse. It is the very food that has nourished every other part into its present magnitude. Our general trade has been greatly augmented; and augmented more or less in almost every part to which it ever extended; but with this material difference; that of the Six Millions which in the beginning of the century constituted the whole mass of our export commerce, the Colony trade was but one twelfth part; it is now (as a part of Sixteen Millions) considerably more than a third of the whole. This is the relative proportion of the importance of the Colonies at these two periods: and all reasoning concerning our mode of treating them must have this proportion as its basis; or it is a reasoning weak, rotten, and sophistical.

↜

I choose, Sir, to enter into these minute and particular details; because generalities, which in all other cases are apt to heighten and raise the subject, have here a tendency to sink it. When we speak of the commerce with our Colonies, fiction lags after truth; invention is unfruitful, and imagination cold and barren.

So far, Sir, as to the importance of the object in the view of its commerce, as concerned in the exports from England. If I were to detail the imports, I could shew how many enjoyments they procure, which deceive the burthen of life; how many materials which invigorate the springs of national industry, and extend and animate every part of our foreign and domestic commerce. This would be a curious subject indeed—but I must prescribe bounds to myself in a matter so vast and various.

I pass therefore to the Colonies in another point of view, their agriculture. This they have prosecuted with such a spirit, that, besides feeding plentifully their own growing multitude, their annual export of grain, comprehending rice, has some years ago exceeded a Million in value. Of their last harvest, I am persuaded, they will export much more. At the beginning of the century, some of these Colonies imported corn from the mother country. For some time past, the old world has been fed from the new. The scarcity which you have felt would have been a desolating famine; if this child of your old age, with a true filial piety, with a Roman charity, had not put the full breast of its youthful exuberance to the mouth of its exhausted parent.

As to the wealth which the Colonies have drawn from the sea by their fisheries, you had all that matter fully opened at your bar. You surely thought those acquisitions of value; for they seemed even to excite your envy; and yet the spirit, by which that enterprizing employment has been exercised, ought rather, in my opinion, to have raised your esteem and admiration. And pray, Sir, what in the world is equal to it? Pass by the other parts, and look at the manner in which the people of New England have of late carried on the Whale Fishery. Whilst we follow them among the tumbling mountains of ice, and behold them penetrating into the deepest frozen recesses of Hudson's Bay, and Davis's Streights, whilst we are looking for them beneath the Arctic circle, we hear that they have pierced into the opposite region of polar cold, that they are at the Antipodes, and engaged under the frozen serpent of the south.[18] Falkland Island, which seemed too remote and romantic an object for the grasp of national ambition, is but a stage and resting place in the progress of their victorious industry. Nor is the equinoctial heat more discouraging to them, than the accumulated winter of both the poles. We know that whilst some of them draw the line and strike the harpoon on the coast of Africa, others run the longitude, and pursue their gigantic game along the coast of Brazil. No sea but what is vexed by their fisheries. No climate that is not witness to their toils. Neither the perseverance of Holland, nor the activity of France, nor the dextrous and firm sagacity of English enterprize, ever carried this most perilous mode of hardy industry to the extent to which it has been pushed by this recent people; a people who are still, as it were, but in the gristle, and not yet hardened into the bone of manhood. When I contemplate these things; when I know that the Colonies in general owe little or nothing to any care of ours, and that they are not squeezed into this happy form by the constraints of watchful and suspicious government, but that through a wise and salutary neglect, a generous nature has been suffered to take her own way to perfection: when I reflect upon these effects, when I see how profitable they have been to us, I feel all the pride of power sink, and all presumption in the wisdom of human contrivances melt, and die away within me. My rigour relents. I pardon something to the spirit of Liberty.

---

[18]The constellation Hydrus, visible in the Southern Hemisphere near Antarctica and represented by a serpent in astronomy.

I am sensible, Sir, that all which I have asserted in my detail, is admitted in the gross; but that quite a different conclusion is drawn from it. America, Gentlemen say, is a noble object. It is an object well worth fighting for. Certainly it is, if fighting a people be the best way of gaining them. Gentlemen in this respect will be led to their choice of means by their complexions and their habits. Those who understand the military art, will of course have some predilection for it. Those who wield the thunder of the state, may have more confidence in the efficacy of arms. But I confess, possibly for want of this knowledge, my opinion is much more in favour of prudent management, than of force; considering force not as an odious, but a feeble instrument, for preserving a people so numerous, so active, so growing, so spirited as this, in a profitable and subordinate connexion with us.

First, Sir, permit me to observe, that the use of force alone is but *temporary*. It may subdue for a moment; but it does not remove the necessity of subduing again: and a nation is not governed, which is perpetually to be conquered.

My next objection is its *uncertainty*. Terror is not always the effect of force; and an armament is not a victory. If you do not succeed, you are without resource; for, conciliation failing, force remains; but, force failing, no further hope of reconciliation is left. Power and authority are sometimes bought by kindness; but they can never be begged as alms, by an impoverished and defeated violence.

A further objection to force is, that you *impair the object* by your very endeavours to preserve it. The thing you fought for, is not the thing which you recover; but depreciated, sunk, wasted, and consumed in the contest. Nothing less will content me, than *whole America*. I do not choose to consume its strength along with our own; because in all parts it is the British strength that I consume. I do not choose to be caught by a foreign enemy at the end of this exhausting conflict; and still less in the midst of it. I may escape; but I can make no insurance against such an event. Let me add, that I do not choose wholly to break the American spirit, because it is the spirit that has made the country.

Lastly, we have no sort of *experience* in favour of force as an instrument in the rule of our Colonies. Their growth and their utility has been owing to methods altogether different. Our ancient indulgence has been said to be pursued to a fault. It may be so. But we know, if feeling is evidence, that our fault was more tolerable than our attempt to mend it; and our sin far more salutary than our penitence.

These, Sir, are my reasons for not entertaining that high opinion of untried force, by which many Gentlemen, for whose sentiments in other particulars I have great respect, seem to be so greatly captivated. But there is still behind a third consideration concerning this object, which serves to determine my opinion on the sort of policy which ought to be pursued in the management of America, even more than its Population and its Commerce, I mean its *Temper and Character*.

In this Character of the Americans, a love of Freedom is the predominating feature, which marks and distinguishes the whole: and as an ardent is always a jealous affection, your Colonies become suspicious, restive, and untractable, whenever they see the least attempt to wrest from them by force, or shuffle from them by chicane, what they think the only advantage worth living for. This fierce spirit of Liberty is stronger in the English Colonies probably than in any other people of the earth; and this from a great variety of pow-

erful causes; which, to understand the true temper of their minds, and the direction which this spirit takes, it will not be amiss to lay open somewhat more largely.

First, the people of the Colonies are descendents of Englishmen. England, Sir, is a nation, which still I hope respects, and formerly adored, her freedom. The Colonists emigrated from you, when this part of your character was most predominant; and they took this biass and direction the moment they parted from your hands. They are therefore not only devoted to Liberty, but to Liberty according to English ideas, and on English principles. Abstract Liberty, like other mere abstractions, is not to be found. Liberty inheres in some sensible object; and every nation has formed to itself some favourite point, which by way of eminence becomes the criterion of their happiness. It happened, you know, Sir, that the great contests for freedom in this country were from the earliest times chiefly upon the question of Taxing. Most of the contests in the ancient commonwealths turned primarily on the right of election of magistrates; or on the balance among the several orders of the state. The question of money was not with them so immediate. But in England it was otherwise. On this point of Taxes the ablest pens, and most eloquent tongues, have been exercised; the greatest spirits have acted and suffered. In order to give the fullest satisfaction concerning the importance of this point, it was not only necessary for those who in argument defended the excellence of the English constitution, to insist on this privilege of granting money as a dry point of fact, and to prove, that the right had been acknowledged in ancient parchments, and blind usages, to reside in a certain body called an House of Commons. They went much further; they attempted to prove, and they succeeded, that in theory it ought to be so, from the particular nature of a House of Commons, as an immediate representative of the people; whether the old records had delivered this oracle or not. They took infinite pains to inculcate, as a fundamental principle, that, in all monarchies, the people must in effect themselves mediately or immediately possess the power of granting their own money, or no shadow of liberty could subsist. The Colonies draw from you as with their life-blood, these ideas and principles. Their love of liberty, as with you, fixed and attached on this specific point of taxing. Liberty might be safe, or might be endangered in twenty other particulars, without their being much pleased or alarmed. Here they felt its pulse; and as they found that beat, they thought themselves sick or sound. I do not say whether they were right or wrong in applying your general arguments to their own case. It is not easy indeed to make a monopoly of theorems and corollaries. The fact is, that they did thus apply those general arguments; and your mode of governing them, whether through lenity or indolence, through wisdom or mistake, confirmed them in the imagination, that they, as well as you, had an interest in these common principles.

They were further confirmed in this pleasing error by the form of their provincial legislative assemblies. Their governments are popular in an high degree; some are merely popular; in all, the popular representative is the most weighty; and this share of the people in their ordinary government never fails to inspire them with lofty sentiments, and with a strong aversion from whatever tends to deprive them of their chief importance.

If any thing were wanting to this necessary operation of the form of government, Religion would have given it a complete effect. Religion, always a principle of energy in this new people, is no way worn out or impaired; and their mode of professing it is also one main cause of this free spirit. The people are protestants; and of that kind, which is the most adverse to all implicit submission of mind and opinion. This is a persuasion not only favourable to liberty, but built upon it. I do not think, Sir, that the reason of this averseness in the dissenting churches from all that looks like absolute Government is so much to be sought in their religious tenets, as in their history. Every one knows, that the Roman Catholick religion is at least coeval with most of the governments where it prevails; that it has generally gone hand in hand with them; and received great favour and every kind of support from authority. The Church of England too was formed from her cradle under the nursing care of regular government. But the dissenting interests have sprung up in direct opposition to all the ordinary powers of the world; and could justify that opposition only on a strong claim to natural liberty. Their very existence depended on the powerful and unremitted assertion of that claim. All protestantism, even the most cold and passive, is a sort of dissent. But the religion most prevalent in our Northern Colonies is a refinement on the principle of resistance; it is the dissidence of dissent; and the protestantism of the protestant religion. This religion, under a variety of denominations, agreeing in nothing but in the communion of the spirit of liberty, is predominant in most of the Northern provinces; where the Church of England, notwithstanding its legal rights, is in reality no more than a sort of private sect, not composing most probably the tenth of the people. . . .

Sir, I can perceive by their manner, that some Gentlemen object to the latitude of this description; because in the Southern Colonies the Church of England forms a large body, and has a regular establishment. It is certainly true. There is however a circumstance attending these colonies, which in my opinion, fully counterbalances this difference, and makes the spirit of liberty still more high and haughty than in those to the Northward. It is that in Virginia and the Carolinas, they have a vast multitude of slaves. Where this is the case in any part of the world, those who are free, are by far the most proud and jealous of their freedom. Freedom is to them not only an enjoyment, but a kind of rank and privilege. Not seeing there, that freedom, as in countries where it is a common blessing, and as broad and general as the air, may be united with much abject toil, with great misery, with all the exterior of servitude, Liberty looks amongst them, like something that is more noble and liberal. I do not mean, Sir, to commend the superior morality of this sentiment, which has at least as much pride as virtue in it; but I cannot alter the nature of man. The fact is so; and these people of the Southern Colonies are much more strongly, and with an higher and more stubborn spirit, attached to liberty than those to the Northward. . . . In such a people the haughtiness of domination combines with the spirit of freedom, fortifies it, and renders it invincible.

Permit me, Sir, to add another circumstance in our Colonies, which contributes no mean part towards the growth and effect of this untractable spirit. I mean their education. In no country perhaps in the world is the law so general a study. The profession itself is numerous and powerful; and in most provinces it takes the lead. The greater number of the Deputies sent to the Congress were Lawyers. But all who read, and most do read, endeavour to ob-

tain some smattering in that science. I have been told by an eminent Bookseller, that in no branch of his business, after tracts of popular devotion, were so many books as those on the Law exported to the Plantations. The Colonists have now fallen into the way of printing them for their own use. I hear that they have sold nearly as many of Blackstone's Commentaries in America as in England. . . . This study renders men acute, inquisitive, dextrous, prompt in attack, ready in defence, full of resources. In other countries, the people, more simple and of a less mercurial cast, judge of an ill principle in government only by an actual grievance; here they anticipate the evil, and judge of the pressure of the grievance by the badness of the principle. They augur misgovernment at a distance; and snuff the approach of tyranny in every tainted breeze.

The last cause of this disobedient spirit in the Colonies is hardly less powerful than the rest, as it is not merely moral, but laid deep in the natural constitution of things. Three thousand miles of ocean lie between you and them. No contrivance can prevent the effect of this distance, in weakening Government. Seas roll, and months pass, between the order and the execution; and the want of a speedy explanation of a single point is enough to defeat an whole system. You have, indeed, winged ministers of vengeance, who carry your bolts in their pounces to the remotest verge of the sea. But there a power steps in, that limits the arrogance of raging passions and furious elements, and says, "So far shalt thou go, and no farther." Who are you, that should fret and rage, and bite the chains of Nature?—Nothing worse happens to you, than does to all Nations, who have extensive Empire; and it happens in all the forms into which Empire can be thrown. In large bodies, the circulation of power must be less vigorous at the extremities. Nature has said it. . . . This is the immutable condition; the eternal Law, of extensive and detached Empire.

Then, Sir, from these six capital sources; of Descent; of Form of Government; of Religion in the Northern Provinces; of Manners in the Southern; of Education; of the Remoteness of Situation from the First Mover of Government, from all these causes a fierce Spirit of Liberty has grown up. It has grown with the growth of the people in your Colonies, and encreased with the encrease of their wealth; a Spirit, that unhappily meeting with an exercise of Power in England, which, however lawful, is not reconcileable to any ideas of Liberty, much less with theirs, has kindled this flame, that is ready to consume us.

I do not mean to commend either the Spirit in this excess, or the moral causes which produce it. Perhaps a more smooth and accommodating Spirit of Freedom in them would be more acceptable to us. Perhaps ideas of Liberty might be desired, more reconcileable with an arbitrary and boundless authority. Perhaps we might wish the Colonists to be persuaded, that their Liberty is more secure when held in trust for them by us (as their guardians during a perpetual minority) than with any part of it in their own hands. But the question is, not whether their spirit deserves praise or blame;—what, in the name of God, shall we do with it? You have before you the object; such as it is, with all its glories, with all its imperfections on its head. You see the magnitude; the importance; the temper; the habits; the disorders. By all these considerations, we are strongly urged to determine something concerning it. We are called upon to fix some rule and line for our future conduct, which may give a little stability to our politics, and prevent the return of such unhappy deliberations as the present. Every such return will bring the matter before us in a still more untractable form. For, what astonishing and incredible things have we not seen already. What monsters have not been generated from this unnatural contention? Whilst every principle of authority and resistance has been pushed, upon both sides, as far as it would go, there is nothing so solid and certain, either in reasoning or in practice, that has not been shaken. Until very lately, all authority in America seemed to be nothing but an emanation from yours. Even the popular part of the Colony Constitution derived all its activity, and its first vital movement, from the pleasure of the Crown. We thought, Sir, that the utmost which the discontented Colonists could do, was to disturb authority; we never dreamt they could of themselves supply it; knowing in general what an operose business it is, to establish a Government absolutely new. But having, for our purposes in this contention, resolved, that none but an obedient Assembly should sit, the humours of the people there, finding all passage through the legal channel stopped, with great violence broke out another way. Some provinces have tried their experiment, as we have tried ours; and theirs has succeeded. They have formed a Government sufficient for its purposes, without the bustle of a Revolution, or the troublesome formality of an Election. Evident necessity, and tacit consent, have done the business in an instant. So well they have done it, that Lord Dunmore[19] . . . tells you, that the new institution is infinitely better obeyed than the antient Government ever was in its most fortunate periods. Obedience is what makes Government, and not the names by which it is

_____

[19]John Murray, fourth earl of Dunmore and governor of Virginia.

called: not the name of Governor, as formerly; or Committee, as at present. This new Government has originated directly from the people; and was not transmitted through any of the ordinary artificial media of a positive constitution. It was not a manufacture ready formed, and exported to them in that condition from England. The evil arising from hence is this; that the Colonists having once found the possibility of enjoying the advantages of order, in the midst of a struggle for Liberty, such struggles will not henceforward seem so terrible to the settled and sober part of mankind, as they had appeared before the trial.

Pursuing the same plan (of punishing disorders by the denial of Government) to still greater lengths, we wholly abrogated the antient Government of Massachuset. We were confident, that the first feeling, if not the very prospect of anarchy, would instantly enforce a compleat submission. The experiment was tried. A new, strange, unexpected face of things appeared. Anarchy is found tolerable. A vast province has now subsisted, and subsisted in a considerable degree of health and vigour, for near a twelve-month, without Governor, without public Council, without Judges, without executive Magistrates. How long it will continue in this state, or what may arise out of this unheard-of-situation, how can the wisest of us conjecture? Our late experience has taught us, that many of those fundamental principles, formerly believed infallible, are either not of the importance they were imagined to be; or that we have not at all adverted to some other far more important, and far more powerful principles, which entirely over-rule those we had considered as omnipotent. I am much against any further experiments, which tend to put to the proof any more of these allowed opinions, which contribute so much to the public tranquillity. In effect,

we suffer as much at home, by this loosening of all ties, and this concussion of all established opinions, as we do abroad. For, in order to prove, that the Americans have no right to their Liberties, we are every day endeavouring to subvert the maxims, which preserve the whole Spirit of our own. To prove that the Americans ought not to be free, we are obliged to depreciate the value of Freedom itself; and we never seem to gain a paltry advantage over them in debate, without attacking some of those principles, or deriding some of those feelings, for which our ancestors have shed their blood.

But, Sir, in wishing to put an end to pernicious experiments, I do not mean to preclude the fullest enquiry. Far from it. Far from deciding on a sudden or partial view, I would patiently go round and round the subject, and survey it minutely in every possible aspect. Sir, if I were capable of engaging you to an equal attention, I would state, that, as far as I am capable of discerning, there are but three ways of proceeding relative to this stubborn Spirit, which prevails in your Colonies, and disturbs your Government. These are—To change that Spirit, as inconvenient, by removing the Causes. To prosecute it as criminal. Or, to comply with it as necessary. I would not be guilty of an imperfect enumeration; I can think of but these three. Another has indeed been started, that of giving up the Colonies; but it met so slight a reception, that I do not think myself obliged to dwell a great while upon it. It is nothing but a little sally of anger; like the frowardness of peevish children; who, when they cannot get all they would have, are resolved to take nothing.

The first of these plans, to change the Spirit as inconvenient, by removing the causes, I think is the most like a systematic proceeding. It is radical in its principle; but it is attended with great difficulties, some of them little short, as I conceive, of impossibilities. This will appear by examining into the Plans which have been proposed.

As the growing population in the Colonies is evidently one cause of their resistance, it was last session mentioned in both Houses, by men of weight, and received not without applause, that, in order to check this evil, it would be proper for the crown to make no further grants of land. But to this scheme, there are two objections. The first, that there is already so much unsettled land in private hands, as to afford room for an immense future population, although the crown not only withheld its grants, but annihilated its soil. If this be the case, then the only effect of this avarice of desolation, this hoarding of a royal wilderness, would be to raise the value of the possessions in the hands of the great private monopolists, without any adequate check to the growing and alarming mischief of population.

But, if you stopped your grants, what would be the consequence? The people would occupy without grants. They have already so occupied in many places. You cannot station garrisons in every part of these deserts. If you drive the people from one place, they will carry on their annual Tillage, and remove with their flocks and herds to another. Many of the people in the back settlements are already little attached to particular situations. Already they have topped the Apalachian mountains. From thence they behold before them an immense plain, one vast, rich, level meadow; a square of five hundred miles. Over this they would wander, without a possibility of restraint; they would change their manners with the habits of their life; would soon forget a government, by which they were disowned; would become Hordes of English Tartars; and,

pouring down upon your unfortified frontiers a fierce and irresistible cavalry, become masters of your Governors and your Counsellors, your collectors and comptrollers, and of all the Slaves that adhered to them. Such would, and, in no long time, must be, the effect of attempting to forbid as a crime, and to suppress as an evil, the Command and Blessing of Providence, "Encrease and Multiply." Such would be the happy result of an endeavour to keep as a lair of beasts, that earth, which God, by an express Charter, has given to the children of men. Far different, and surely much wiser, has been our policy hitherto. Hitherto we have invited our people by every kind of bounty, to fixed establishments. We have invited the husbandman, to look to authority for his title. We have taught him piously to believe in the mysterious virtue of wax and parchment. We have thrown each tract of land, as it was peopled, into districts; that the ruling power should never be wholly out of sight. We have settled all we could; and we have carefully attended every settlement with government.

Adhering, Sir, as I do, to this policy, as well as for the reasons I have just given, I think this new project of hedging-in population to be neither prudent nor practicable.

To impoverish the Colonies in general, and in particular to arrest the noble course of their marine enterprizes, would be a more easy task. I freely confess it. We have shewn a disposition to a system of this kind; a disposition even to continue the restraint after the offence; looking on ourselves as rivals to our Colonies, and persuaded that of course we must gain all that they shall lose. Much mischief we may certainly do. The power inadequate to all other things is often more than sufficient for this. I do not look on the direct and immediate power of the Colonies to resist our violence, as very formidable. In this however, I may be mistaken. But when I consider, that we have Colonies for no purpose but to be serviceable to us, it seems to my poor understanding a little preposterous, to make them unserviceable, in order to keep them obedient. It is, in truth, nothing more than the old, and, as I thought, exploded problem of tyranny, which proposes to beggar its subjects into submission. But, remember, when you have compleated your system of impoverishment, that Nature still proceeds in her ordinary course; that discontent will encrease with misery; and that there are critical moments in the fortune of all states, when they, who are too weak to contribute to your prosperity, may be strong enough to complete your ruin. . . .

The temper and character which prevail in our Colonies, are, I am afraid, unalterable by any human art. We cannot, I fear, falsify the pedigree of this fierce people, and persuade them that they are not sprung from a nation, in whose veins the blood of freedom circulates. The language in which they would hear you tell them this tale, would detect the imposition; your speech would betray you. An Englishman is the unfittest person on earth, to argue another Englishman into slavery.

I think it is nearly as little in our power to change their republican Religion, as their free descent; or to substitute the Roman Catholick, as a penalty; or the Church of England, as an improvement. The mode of inquisition and dragooning, is going out of fashion in the old world; and I should not confide much to their efficacy in the new. The education of the Americans is also on the same unalterable bottom with their religion. You cannot persuade them to burn their books of curious science; to banish their lawyers from their courts of law; or to quench the lights

of their assemblies, by refusing to choose those persons who are best read in their privileges. It would be no less impracticable to think of wholly annihilating the popular assemblies, in which these lawyers sit. The army, by which we must govern in their place, would be far more chargeable to us; not quite so effectual; and perhaps, in the end, full as difficult to be kept in obedience.

With regard to the high aristocratic spirit of Virginia and the Southern Colonies, it has been proposed, I know, to reduce it, by declaring a general enfranchisement of their slaves. This project has had its advocates and panegyrists; yet I never could argue myself into any opinion of it. Slaves are often much attached to their masters. A general wild offer of liberty, would not always be accepted. History furnishes few instances of it. It is sometimes as hard to persuade slaves to be free, as it is to compel freemen to be slaves; and in this auspicious scheme, we should have both these pleasing talks on our hands at once. But when we talk of enfranchisement do we not perceive that the American master may enfranchise too; and arm servile hands in defence of freedom? A measure to which other people have had recourse more than once, and not without success, in a desperate situation of their affairs.

Slaves as these unfortunate black people are, and dull as all men are from slavery, must they not a little suspect the offer of freedom from that very nation which has sold them to their present masters? From that nation, one of whose causes of quarrel with those masters, is their refusal to deal any more in that inhuman traffick? An offer of freedom from England, would come rather oddly, shipped to them in an African vessel, which is refused an entry into the ports of Virginia or Carolina, with a cargo of three hundred Angola negroes.

It would be curious to see the Guinea captain attempting at the same instant to publish his proclamation of liberty, and to advertise his sale of slaves.

But let us suppose all these moral difficulties got over. The Ocean remains. You cannot pump this dry; and as long as it continues in its present bed, so long all the causes which weaken authority by distance will continue. "Ye gods, annihilate but space and time, and make two lovers happy!"—was a pious and passionate prayer;—but just as reasonable, as many of the serious wishes of very grave and solemn politicians.

If then, Sir, it seems almost desperate to think of any alterative course, for changing the moral causes (and not quite easy to remove the natural) which produce prejudices irreconcileable to the late exercise of our authority; but that the spirit infallibly will continue; and, continuing, will produce such effects, as now embarrass us; the second mode under consideration is, to prosecute that spirit in its overt-acts, as *criminal*.

At this proposition, I must pause a moment. The thing seems a great deal too big for my ideas of jurisprudence. It should seem, to my way of conceiving such matters, that there is a very wide difference in reason and policy, between the mode of proceeding on the irregular conduct of scattered individuals, or even of bands of men, who disturb order within the state, and the civil dissensions which may, from time to time, on great questions, agitate the several communities which compose a great Empire. It looks to me to be narrow and pedantic, to apply the ordinary ideas of criminal justice to this great public contest. I do not know the method of drawing up an indictment against an whole people. I cannot insult and ridicule the feelings of Millions of my fellow-creatures. . . . I am

not ripe to pass sentence on the gravest public bodies, entrusted with magistracies of great authority and dignity, and charged with the safety of their fellow-citizens, upon the very same title that I am. I really think, that for wise men, this is not judicious; for sober men, not decent; for minds tinctured with humanity, not mild and merciful.

Perhaps, Sir, I am mistaken in my idea of an Empire, as distinguished from a single State or Kingdom. But my idea of it is this; that an Empire is the aggregate of many States, under one common head; whether this head be a monarch, or a presiding republick. It does, in such constitutions, frequently happen (and nothing but the dismal, cold, dead uniformity of servitude can prevent its happening) that the subordinate parts have many local privileges and immunities. Between these privileges, and the supreme common authority, the line may be extremely nice. Of course disputes, often too, very bitter disputes, and much ill blood, will arise. But though every privilege is an exemption (in the case) from the ordinary exercise of the supreme authority, it is no denial of it. The claim of a privilege seems rather . . . to imply a superior power. For to talk of the privileges of a State or of a person, who has no superior, is hardly any better than speaking nonsense. Now, in such unfortunate quarrels, among the component parts of a great political union of communities, I can scarcely conceive any thing more compleatly imprudent, than for the Head of the Empire to insist, that, if any privilege is pleaded against his will, or his acts, that his whole authority is denied; instantly to proclaim rebellion, to beat to arms, and to put the offending provinces under the ban. Will not this, Sir, very soon teach the provinces to make no distinctions on their part? Will it not teach them that the Government, against which a claim of Liberty is tantamount to high-treason, is a Government to which submission is equivalent to slavery? It may not always be quite convenient to impress dependent communities with such an idea.

We are, indeed, in all disputes with the Colonies, by the necessity of things, the judge. It is true, Sir. But, I confess, that the character of judge in my own cause, is a thing that frightens me. Instead of filling me with pride, I am exceedingly humbled by it. I cannot proceed with a stern, assured, judicial confidence, until I find myself in something more like a judicial character. I must have these hesitations as long as I am compelled to recollect, that, in my little reading upon such contests as these, the sense of mankind has, at least, as often decided against the superior as the subordinate power. Sir, let me add too, that the opinion of my having some abstract right in my favour, would not put me much at my ease in passing sentence; unless I could be sure, that there were no rights which, in their exercise under certain circumstances, were not the most odious of all wrongs, and the most vexatious of all injustice. Sir, these considerations have great weight with me, when I find things so circumstanced; that I see the same party, at once a civil litigant against me in a point of right; and a culprit before me, while I sit as a criminal judge, on acts of his, whose moral quality is to be decided upon the merits of that very litigation. Men are every now and then put, by the complexity of human affairs, into strange situations; but Justice is the same, let the Judge be in what situation he will.

↬

In this situation, let us seriously and coolly ponder. What is it we have got by all our menaces, which have been many and fero-cious? What advantage have we derived from the penal laws we have passed, and which, for the time, have been severe and numerous? What advances have we made towards our object, by the sending of a force, which, by land and sea, is no contemptible strength? Has the disorder abated? Nothing less.—When I see things in this situation, after such confident hopes, bold promises, and active exertions, I cannot, for my life, avoid a suspicion, that the plan itself is not correctly right.

If then the removal of the causes of this Spirit of American Liberty be, for the greater part, or rather entirely, impracticable; if the ideas of Criminal Process be inapplicable, or, if applicable, are in the highest degree inexpedient, what way yet remains? No way is open, but the third and last—to comply with the American Spirit as necessary; or, if you please, to submit to it, as a necessary Evil.

If we adopt this mode; if we mean to conciliate and concede; let us see of what nature the concession ought to be? To ascertain the nature of our concession, we must look at their complaint. The Colonies complain, that they have not the characteristic Mark and Seal of British Freedom. They complain, that they are taxed in a Parliament, in which they are not represented. If you mean to satisfy them at all, you must satisfy them with regard to this complaint. If you mean to please any people, you must give them the boon which they ask; not what you may think better for them, but of a kind totally different. Such an act may be a wise regulation, but it is no concession: whereas our present theme is the mode of giving satisfaction.

Sir, I think you must perceive, that I am resolved this day to have nothing at all to do with the question of the right of taxation. Some gentlemen startle—but it is true: I put it totally out of the question. It is less than nothing in my consideration. I do not indeed wonder, nor will you, Sir, that gentlemen of profound learning are fond of displaying it on this profound subject. But my consideration is narrow, confined, and wholly limited to the Policy of the question. I do not examine, whether the giving away a man's money be a power excepted and reserved out of the general trust of Government; and how far all mankind, in all forms of Polity, are intitled to an exercise of that Right by the Charter of Nature. Or whether, on the contrary, a Right of Taxation is necessarily involved in the general principle of Legislation, and inseparable from the ordinary Supreme Power? These are deep questions, where great names militate against each other; where reason is perplexed; and an appeal to authorities only thickens the confusion. For high and reverend authorities lift up their heads on both sides; and there is no sure footing in the middle. This point is the *great Serbonian bog, betwixt Damiata and Mount Casius, old, where armies whole have sunk.*[20] I do not intend to be overwhelmed in that bog, though in such respectable company. The question with me is, not whether you have a right to render your people miserable; but whether it is not your interest to make them happy? It is not, what a lawyer tells me, I *may* do; but what humanity, reason, and justice, tell me, I ought to do. Is a politic act the worse for being a generous one? Is no concession proper, but that which is made from your want of right to keep what you grant? Or does it lessen the grace or dignity of relaxing in the exercise of an odious claim, because you have your evidence-room full of Titles, and your magazines stuffed with arms to enforce them? What signify all those titles, and all those arms? Of what avail are they, when the reason of the thing tells me, that the assertion of my title is the loss of my suit; and that I could do nothing but wound myself by the use of my own weapons?

Such is stedfastly my opinion of the absolute necessity of keeping up the concord of this empire by a Unity of Spirit, though in a diversity of operations, that, if I were sure the Colonists had, at their leaving this country, sealed a regular compact of servitude; that they had solemnly abjured all the rights of citizens; that they had made a vow to renounce all Ideas of Liberty for them and their posterity, to all generations; yet I should hold myself obliged to conform to the temper I found universally prevalent in my own day, and to govern two million of men, impatient of Servitude, on the principles of Freedom. I am not determining a point of law; I am restoring tranquility; and the general character and situation of a people must determine what sort of government is fitted for them. That point nothing else can or ought to determine.

My idea therefore, without considering whether we yield as matter of right, or grant as matter of favour, is *to admit the people of our Colonies into an interest in the constitution;* and, by recording that admission in the Journals of Parliament, to give them as strong an assurance as the nature of the thing will admit, that we mean for ever to adhere to that solemn declaration of systematic indulgence.

Some years ago, the repeal of a revenue act,[21] upon its understood principle, might have served to shew, that we intended an unconditional abatement of the exercise of a Taxing Power. Such a measure was then sufficient to remove all suspicion; and to give perfect content. But unfortunate events, since that time, may make

---

[20]From John Milton's *Paradise Lost* (1667).

[21]The 1766 repeal of the Stamp Act of 1765 by the Rockingham administration.

something further necessary; and not more necessary for the satisfaction of the Colonies, than for the dignity and consistency of our own future proceedings.

I have taken a very incorrect measure of the disposition of the House, if this proposal in itself would be received with dislike. I think, Sir, we have few American Financiers. But our misfortune is, we are too acute; we are too exquisite in our conjectures of the future, for men oppressed with such great and present evils. The more moderate among the opposers of Parliamentary Concession freely confess, that they hope no good from Taxation; but they apprehend the Colonists have further views, and if this point were conceded, they would instantly attack the Trade-laws.[22] These Gentlemen are convinced, that this was the intention from the beginning; and the quarrel of the Americans with Taxation was no more than a cloke and cover to this design. . . . I am, however, Sir, not a little surprized at this kind of discourse, whenever I hear it; and I am the more surprized, on account of the arguments which I constantly find in company with it, and which are often urged from the same mouths, and on the same day.

For instance, when we alledge, that it is against reason to tax a people under so many restraints in trade as the Americans, the Noble Lord in the blue ribband shall tell you, that the restraints on trade are futile and useless; of no advantage to us, and of no burthen to those on whom they are imposed; that the trade to America is not secured by the acts of navigation, but by the natural and irrestible advantage of a commercial preference.

Such is the merit of the trade laws in this posture of the debate. But when

strong internal circumstances are urged against the taxes; when the scheme is dissected; when experience and the nature of things are brought to prove, and do prove, the utter impossibility of obtaining an effective revenue from the Colonies; when these things are pressed, or rather press themselves, so as to drive the advocates of Colony taxes to a clear admission of the futility of the scheme; then, Sir, the sleeping trade laws revive from their trance; and this useless taxation is to be kept sacred, not for its own sake, but as a counterguard and security of the laws of trade.

Then, Sir, you keep up the revenue laws which are mischievous, in order to preserve trade laws that are useless. Such is the wisdom of our plan in both its members. They are separately given up as of no value; and yet one is always to be defended for the sake of the other. But I cannot agree with the Noble Lord, nor with the pamphlet from whence he seems to have borrowed these ideas,[23] concerning the inutility of the trade laws. For without idolizing them, I am sure they are still, in many ways, of great use to us; and in former times, they have been of the greatest. They do confine, and they do greatly narrow, the market for the Americans. But my perfect conviction of this, does not help me in the least to discern how the revenue laws form any security whatsoever to the commercial regulations; or that these commercial regulations are the true ground of the quarrel; or, that the giving way in any one instance of authority, is to lose all that may remain unconceded.

One fact is clear and indisputable. The public and avowed origin of this quarrel,

---

[22]The legislation regulating the commerce of the American colonies for the benefit of Britain.

[23]Burke is probably referring to Josiah Tucker's *Four Tracts, Together with Two Sermons, on Political and Commercial Subjects,* published in 1774, in which Tucker attacked the trade laws specifically and mercantilism as a trade policy generally.

was on taxation. This quarrel has indeed brought on new disputes on new questions; but certainly the least bitter, and the fewest of all, on the trade laws. To judge which of the two be the real radical cause of quarrel, we have to see whether the commercial dispute did, in order of time, precede the dispute on taxation? There is not a shadow of evidence for it. Next, to enable us to judge whether at this moment a dislike to the Trade Laws be the real cause of quarrel, it is absolutely necessary to put the taxes out of the question by a repeal. See how the Americans act in this position, and then you will be able to discern correctly what is the true object of the controversy, or whether any controversy at all will remain? Unless you consent to remove this cause of difference, it is impossible, with decency, to assert that the dispute is not upon what it is avowed to be. And I would, Sir, recommend to your serious consideration, whether it be prudent to form a rule for punishing people, not on their own acts, but on your conjectures? Surely it is preposterous at the very best. It is not justifying your anger, by their misconduct; but it is converting your ill-will into their delinquency.

But the Colonies will go further.—Alas! alas! when will this speculating against fact and reason end? What will quiet these panic fears which we entertain of the hostile effect of a conciliatory conduct? Is it true, that no case can exist, in which it is proper for the sovereign to accede to the desires of his discontented subjects? Is there any thing peculiar in this case, to make a rule for itself? Is all authority of course lost, when it is not pushed to the extreme? Is it a certain maxim, that, the fewer causes of dissatisfaction are left by government, the more the subject will be inclined to resist and rebel?

All these objections being in fact no more than suspicions, conjectures, divinations; formed in defiance of fact and experience; they did not, Sir, discourage me from entertaining the idea of a conciliatory concession, founded on the principles which I have just stated.

In forming a plan for this purpose, I endeavoured to put myself in that frame of mind, which was the most natural, and the most reasonable; and which was certainly the most probable means of securing me from all error. I set out with a perfect distrust of my own abilities; a total renunciation of every speculation of my own; and with a profound reverence for the wisdom of our ancestors, who have left us the inheritance of so happy a constitution, and so flourishing an empire, and what is a thousand times more valuable, the treasury of the maxims and principles which formed the one, and obtained the other.

. . . But, Sir, I am sure that I shall not be misled, when, in a case of constitutional difficulty, I consult the genius of the English constitution. Consulting at that oracle (it was with all due humility and piety) I found four capital examples in a similar case before me: those of Ireland, Wales, Chester, and Durham.

Ireland, before the English conquest, though never governed by a despotic power, had no Parliament. How far the English Parliament itself was at that time modelled according to the present form, is disputed among antiquarians. But we have all the reason in the world to be assured, that a form of Parliament, such as England then enjoyed, she instantly communicated to Ireland; and we are equally sure that almost every successive improvement in constitutional liberty, as fast as it was made here, was transmitted thither. The feudal Baronage, and the feudal Knighthood, the roots of our primitive constitution, were early transplanted into that soil; and grew and flourished there. Magna Charta, if it did not give us originally the House of Commons, gave us at least an House of Commons of weight and consequence. But your ancestors did not churlishly sit down alone to the feast of Magna Charta. Ireland was made immediately a partaker. This benefit of English laws and liberties, I confess, was not at first extended to *all* Ireland. Mark the consequence. English authority and English liberties had exactly the same boundaries. Your standard could never be advanced an inch before your privileges. Sir John Davis[24] shews beyond a doubt, that the refusal of a general communication of these rights, was the true cause why Ireland was five hundred years in subduing; and after the vain projects of a Military Government, attempted in the reign of Queen Elizabeth, it was soon discovered, that nothing could make that country English, in civility and allegiance, but your laws and your forms of legislature. It was not English arms, but the English constitution, that conquered Ireland. From that time, Ireland has ever had a general Parliament, as she had before a partial Parliament. You changed the people; you altered the religion; but you never touched the form or the vital substance of free government in that kingdom. You deposed kings; you restored them; you altered the succession to theirs, as well as to your own crown; but you never altered their constitution; the principle of which was respected by usurpation; restored with the restoration of Monarchy, and established, I trust, for ever, by the glorious Revolution.[25] This has made Ireland the great and flourishing

kingdom that it is; and from a disgrace and a burthen intolerable to this nation, has rendered her a principal part of our strength and ornament. This country cannot be said to have ever formally taxed her. . . . Your Irish pensioners would starve, if they had no other fund to live on than taxes granted by English authority. Turn your eyes to those popular grants from whence all your great supplies are come; and learn to respect that only source of public wealth in the British empire.

My next example is Wales. This country was said to be reduced by Henry the Third. It was said more truly to be so by Edward the First. But though then conquered, it was not looked upon as any part of the realm of England. Its old constitution, whatever that might have been, was destroyed; and no good one was substituted in its place. The care of that tract was put into the hands of Lords Marchers—a form of Government of a very singular kind; a strange heterogeneous monster, something between Hostility and Government; perhaps it has a sort of resemblance, according to the modes of those times, to that of commander in chief at present, to whom all civil power is granted as secondary. The manners of the Welsh nation followed the Genius of the Government: The people were ferocious, restive, savage, and uncultivated; sometimes composed, never pacified. Wales within itself was in perpetual disorder; and it kept the frontier of England in perpetual alarm. Benefits from it to the state, there were none. Wales was only known to England, by incursion and invasion.

Sir, during that state of things, Parliament was not idle. They attempted to subdue the fierce spirit of the Welsh by all sorts of rigorous laws. They prohibited by statute the sending all sorts of arms into Wales, as you prohibit by proclamation

---

[24]Author of *Discoverie of the True Causes Why Ireland Was Never Entirely Subdued Until the Beginning of His Majestie's Happy Reign,* published in 1612.

[25]The English Glorious Revolution of 1688, during which the protestant William of Orange was invited to take the throne of England to save England from the imposition of Catholicism by James II.

... the sending arms to America. They disarmed the Welsh by statute, as you attempted ... to disarm New England by an instruction. They made an act to drag offenders from Wales into England for trial, as you have done ... with regard to America. By another act, where one of the parties was an Englishman, they ordained, that his trial should be always by English. They made acts to restrain trade, as you do; and they prevented the Welsh from the use of fairs and markets, as you do the Americans from fisheries and foreign ports. In short, when the statute-book was not quite so much swelled as it is now, you find no less than fifteen acts of penal regulation on the subject of Wales.

Here we rub our hands—A fine body of precedents for the authority of Parliament and the use of it!—I admit it fully; and pray add likewise to these precedents, that all the while, Wales rid this kingdom like an *incubus;*[26] that it was an unprofitable and oppressive burthen; and that an Englishman travelling in that country, could not go six yards from the high road without being murdered.

The march of the human mind is slow. Sir, it was not, until after Two Hundred years, discovered, that by an eternal law, Providence had decreed vexation to violence; and poverty to rapine. Your ancestors did however at length open their eyes to the ill husbandry of injustice. They found that the tyranny of a free people could of all tyrannies the least be endured; and that laws made against an whole nation were not the most effectual methods for securing its obedience. Accordingly, in the Twenty-seventh year of Henry VIII. the course was entirely altered. With a preamble stating the entire and perfect rights of the crown of England, it gave to the

Welsh all the rights and privileges of English subjects. A political order was established; the military power gave way to the civil; the marches were turned into counties. But that a nation should have a right to English liberties, and yet no share at all in the fundamental security of these liberties, the grant of their own property, seemed a thing so incongruous; that Eight years after, that is, in the Thirty-fifth of that reign, a complete and not ill-proportioned representation by counties and boroughs was bestowed upon Wales, by act of Parliament. From that moment, as by a charm, the tumults subsided; obedience was restored; peace, order, and civilization, followed in the train of liberty—When the day-star of the English constitution had arisen in their hearts, all was harmony within and without. . . .

The very same year the county palatine of Chester received the same relief from its oppressions, and the same remedy to its disorders. Before this time Chester was little less distempered than Wales. The inhabitants, without rights themselves, were the fittest to destroy the rights of others; and from thence Richard II. drew the standing army of Archers, with which for a time he oppressed England. The people of Chester applied to Parliament in a petition. . . .

What did Parliament with this audacious address?—reject it as a libel? Treat it as an affront to government? Spurn it as a derogation from the rights of legislature? Did they toss it over the table? Did they burn it by the hands of the common hangman?—They took the petition of grievance, all rugged as it was, without softening or temperament, unpurged of the original bitterness and indignation of complaint; they made it the very preamble to their act of redress; and consecrated its principle to all ages in the sanctuary of legislation.

---

[26]An oppressive nightmare.

Here is my third example. It was attended with the success of the two former. Chester, civilized as well as Wales, has demonstrated that freedom and not servitude is the cure of anarchy; as religion, and not atheism, is the true remedy for superstition. Sir, this pattern of Chester was followed in the reign of Charles II. with regard to the county palatine of Durham, which is my fourth example. This county had long lain out of the pale of free legislation. So scrupulously was the example of Chester followed, that the style of the preamble is nearly the same with that of the Chester act; and without affecting the abstract extent of the authority of Parliament, it recognizes the equity of not suffering any considerable district in which the British subjects may act as a body, to be taxed without their own voice in the grant.

Now if the doctrines of policy contained in these preambles, and the force of these examples in the acts of Parliament, avail any thing, what can be said against applying them with regard to America? Are not the people of America as much Englishmen as the Welsh? The preamble of the act of Henry VIII. says, the Welsh speak a language no way resembling that of his Majesty's English subjects. Are the Americans not as numerous? If we may trust the learned and accurate Judge Barrington's account of North Wales,[27] and take that as a standard to measure the rest, there is no comparison. The people cannot amount to above 200,000; not a tenth part of the number in the Colonies. Is America in rebellion? Wales was hardly ever free from it. Have you attempted to govern America by penal statutes? You made Fifteen for Wales. But your legisla-

tive authority is perfect with regard to America; was it less perfect in Wales, Chester, and Durham? But America is virtually represented. What! does the electric force of virtual representation more easily pass over the Atlantic, than pervade Wales, which lies in your neighbourhood; or than Chester and Durham, surrounded by abundance of representation that is actual and palpable? But, Sir, your ancestors thought this sort of virtual representation, however ample, to be totally insufficient for the freedom of the inhabitants of territories that are so near, and comparatively so inconsiderable. How then can I think it sufficient for those which are infinitely greater, and infinitely more remote?

You will now, Sir, perhaps imagine, that I am on the point of proposing to you a scheme for a representation of the Colonies in Parliament. Perhaps I might be inclined to entertain some such thought; but a great flood stops me in my course. . . . I cannot remove the eternal barriers of the creation. The thing in that mode, I do not know to be possible. As I meddle with no theory, I do not absolutely assert the impracticability of such a representation. But I do not see my way to it; and those who have been more confident, have not been more successful. However, the arm of public benevolence is not shortened; and there are often several means to the same end. What nature has disjoined in one way, wisdom may unite in another. When we cannot give the benefit as we would wish, let us not refuse it altogether. If we cannot give the principal, let us find a substitute. But how? Where? What substitute?

Fortunately I am not obliged for the ways and means of this substitute to tax my own unproductive invention. I am not even obliged to go to the rich treasury of the fertile framers of imaginary common wealths; not to the Republick of Plato, not

---

[27]Burke is referring to a population estimate from 1770 of Daines Barrington, a judge in northern Wales.

to the Utopia of More; not to the Oceana of Harrington.[28] It is before me—It is at my feet, *and the rude swain treads daily on it with his clouted shoon.*[29] I only wish you to recognize, for the theory, the ancient constitutional policy of this kingdom with regard to representation, as that policy has been declared in acts of parliament; and, as to the practice, to return to that mode which an uniform experience has marked out to you, as best; and in which you walked with security, advantage, and honour, until the year 1763.[30]

My resolutions therefore mean to establish the equity and justice of a taxation of America, by *grant* and not by *imposition.* To mark the *legal competency* of the Colony assemblies for the support of their government in peace, and for public aids in time of war. To acknowledge that this legal competency has had a *dutiful and beneficial exercise;* and that experience has shewn the *benefit of their grants,* and the *futility of parliamentary taxation as a method of supply.*

These solid truths compose six fundamental propositions. There are three more resolutions corollary to these. If you admit the first set, you can hardly reject the others. But if you admit the first, I shall be far from sollicitous whether you accept or refuse the last. I think these six massive pillars will be of strength sufficient to support the temple of British concord. I have

---

[28]Plato, *The Republic* (c. 375 B.C.); Sir Thomas More, *Utopia* (1516), and James Harrington, *The Common-wealth of Oceana* (1656).

[29]From John Milton's *Comus* (1637).

[30]That year marked the end of the Seven Years' War between Britain and France for control of North America, which Britain followed with schemes to tax the American colonies. It first put these plans into practice with the Sugar Act of 1764 and the Stamp Act of 1765.

no more doubt than I entertain of my existence, that, if you admitted these, you would command an immediate peace; and with but tolerable future management, a lasting obedience in America. I am not arrogant in this confident assurance. The propositions are all mere matters of fact: and if they are such facts as draw irrestible conclusions even in the stating, this is the power of truth, and not any management of mine.

Sir, I shall open the whole plan to you together, with such observations on the motions as may tend to illustrate them where they may want explanation. The first is a resolution—"That the Colonies and Plantations of Great Britain in North America, consisting of Fourteen separate Governments, and containing Two Millions and upwards of free inhabitants, have not had the liberty and privilege of electing and sending any Knights and Burgesses, or others to represent them in the high Court of Parliament"—This is a plain matter of fact, necessary to be laid down, and (excepting the description) it is laid down in the language of the constitution; it is taken nearly *verbatim* from acts of Parliament.

The second is like unto the first—"That the said Colonies and Plantations have been liable to, and bounden by, several subsidies, payments, rates, and taxes, given and granted by Parliament, though the said Colonies and Plantations have not their Knights and Burgesses, in the said high Court of Parliament, of their own election, to represent the condition of their country; by lack whereof they have been oftentimes touched and grieved by subsidies given, granted, and assented to, in the said court, in a manner prejudicial to the common wealth, quietness, rest, and peace of the subjects inhabiting within the same."

Is this description too hot, or too cold, too strong, or too weak? Does it arrogate too much to the supreme legislature? Does it lean too much to the claims of the people? If it runs into any of these errors, the fault is not mine. It is the language of your own ancient acts of Parliament. . . . It is the genuine produce of the ancient rustic, manly, homebred sense of this country—I did not dare to rub off a particle of the venerable rust that rather adorns and preserves, than destroys the metal. It would be a profanation to touch with a tool the stones which construct the sacred altar of peace. I would not violate with modern polish the ingenuous and noble roughness of these truly constitutional materials. Above all things, I was resolved not to be guilty of tampering, the odious vice of restless and unstable minds. I put my foot in the tracks of our forefathers; where I can neither wander nor stumble. Determining to six articles of peace, I was resolved not to be wise beyond what was written; I was resolved to use nothing else than the form of sound words, to let others abound in their own sense; and carefully to abstain from all expressions of my own. What the law has said, I say. In all things else I am silent. I have no organ but for her words. This, if it be not ingenious, I am sure is safe.

↜

The next proposition is—"That, from the distance of the said Colonies, and from other circumstances, no method hath hitherto been devised for procuring a representation in Parliament for the said Colonies." This is an assertion of a fact. I go no further on the paper; though in my private judgement, an useful representation is impossible; I am sure it is not desired by them; nor ought it perhaps by us; but I abstain from opinions.

The fourth resolution is—"That each of the said Colonies hath within itself a body, chosen in part, or in the whole, by the freemen, freeholders, or other free inhabitants thereof, commonly called the General Assembly, or General Court, with powers legally to raise, levy, and assess, according to the several usage of such Colonies, duties and taxes towards defraying all sorts of public services."

This competence in the Colony assemblies is certain. It is proved by the whole tenour of their acts of supply in all the assemblies, in which the constant style of granting is, "an aid to his Majesty;" and acts granting to the Crown have regularly for near a century passed the public offices without dispute. Those who have been pleased paradoxically to deny this right, holding that none but the British parliament can grant to the Crown, are wished to look to what is done, not only in the Colonies, but in Ireland, in one uniform unbroken tenour every session. Sir, I am surprized, that this doctrine should come from some of the law servants of the Crown. I say, that if the Crown could be responsible, his Majesty—but certainly the ministers, and even these law officers themselves, through whose hands the acts pass, biennially in Ireland, or annually in the Colonies, are in an habitual course of committing impeachable offences. What habitual offenders have been all Presidents of the Council, all Secretaries of State, all First Lords of Trade, all Attornies and all Sollicitors General! However, they are safe; as no one impeaches them; and there is no ground of charge against them, except in their own unfounded theories.

The fifth resolution is also a resolution of fact—"That the said General Assemblies, General Courts, or other bodies legally qualified as aforesaid, have at sundry times freely granted several large subsidies and public aids for his Majesty's service, according to their abilities, when required thereto by letter from one of his Majesty's principal Secretaries of State; and that their right to grant the same, and their chearfulness and sufficiency in the said grants, have been at sundry times acknowledged by Parliament." To say nothing of their great expences in the Indian wars; and not to take their exertion in foreign ones, so high as the supplies in the year 1695; not to go back to their public contributions in the year 1710;[31] I shall begin to travel only where the Journals give me light; resolving to deal in nothing but fact, authenticated by parliamentary record; and to build myself wholly on that solid basis.

⤷

Sir, here is the repeated acknowledgement of Parliament, that the Colonies not only gave, but gave to satiety. This nation has formally acknowledged two things; first, that the Colonies had gone beyond their abilities, Parliament having thought it necessary to reimburse them; secondly, that they had acted legally and laudably in their grants of money, and their maintenance of troops, since the compensation is expressly given as reward and encouragement. Reward is not bestowed for acts that are unlawful; and encouragement is not held out to things that deserve reprehension. My resolution therefore does nothing more than collect into one proposition, what is scattered through your Journals. I give you nothing but your own; and you cannot

refuse in the gross, what you have so often acknowledged in detail. The admission of this, which will be so honourable to them and to you, will, indeed, be mortal to all the miserable stories, by which the passions of the misguided people have been engaged in an unhappy system. The people heard, indeed, from the beginning of these disputes, one thing continually dinned in their ears, that reason and justice demanded, that the Americans, who paid no Taxes, should be compelled to contribute. . . .

We see the sense of the Crown, and the sense of Parliament, on the productive nature of a *Revenue by Grant*. Now search the same Journals for the produce of the *Revenue by Imposition*—Where is it?—let us know the volume and the page?—What is the gross, what is the nett produce?—to what service is it applied?—how have you appropriated its surplus?—What, can none of the many skilful Index-makers, that we are now employing, find any trace of it?—Well, let them and that rest together.—But are the Journals, which say nothing of the Revenue, as silent on the discontent?—Oh no! a child may find it. It is the melancholy burthen and blot of every page.

I think then I am, from those Journals, justified in the sixth and last resolution, which is—"That it hath been found by experience, that the manner of granting the said supplies and aids, by the said General Assemblies, hath been more agreeable to the said Colonies, and more beneficial, and conducive to the public service, than the mode of giving and granting aids in Parliament, to be raised and paid in the said Colonies." This makes the whole of the fundamental part of the plan. The conclusion is irresistible. You cannot say, that you were driven by any necessity, to an exercise of the utmost Rights of Legislature. You cannot assert, that you took on yourselves the task of imposing Colony

---

[31]Burke is referring to the American colonists' participation in the Seven Years' War, the Nine Years' War (1689–1697) against France, and the War of the Spanish Succession (1701–1713), also against the French. British and American forces captured Port Royal from the French in 1710.

Taxes, from the want of another legal body, that is competent to the purpose of supplying the Exigences of the State without wounding the prejudices of the people. Neither is it true that the body so qualified, and having that competence, had neglected the duty.

The question now, on all this accumulated matter, is;—whether you will chuse to abide by a profitable experience, or a mischievous theory; whether you chuse to build on imagination or fact; whether you prefer enjoyment or hope; satisfaction in your subjects, or discontent?

&

Here, Sir, I should close; but that I plainly perceive some objections remain, which I ought, if possible, to remove. The first will be, that, in resorting to the doctrine of our ancestors, as contained in the preamble to the Chester act, I prove too much; that the grievance from a want of representation, stated in that preamble, goes to the whole of Legislation as well as to Taxation. And that the Colonies grounding themselves upon that doctrine, will apply it to all parts of Legislative Authority.

To this objection, with all possible deference and humility, and wishing as little as any man living to impair the smallest particle of our supreme authority, I answer, that *the words are the words of Parliament, and not mine;* and, that all false and inconclusive inferences, drawn from them, are not mine; for I heartily disclaim any such inference. I have chosen the words of an act of Parliament, which Mr. Grenville,[32] surely a tolerably zealous and very judicious advocate for the sovereignty of Parliament, formerly moved to have read at your table, in confirmation of his tenets. It is true that Lord Chatham[33] considered these preambles as declaring strongly in favour of his opinions. He was a no less powerful advocate for the privileges of the Americans. Ought I not from hence to presume, that these preambles are as favourable as possible to both, when properly understood; favourable both to the rights of Parliament, and to the privilege of the dependencies of this crown? But sir, the object of grievance in my resolution, I have not taken from the Chester, but from the Durham act, which confines the hardship of want of representation, to the case of subsidies; and which therefore falls in exactly with the case of the Colonies. But whether the unrepresented counties were *de jure,* or *de facto,* bound, the preambles do not accurately distinguish; nor indeed was it necessary; for, whether *de jure* or *de facto,* the Legislature thought the exercise of the power of taxing, as of right, or as of fact without right, equally a grievance and equally oppressive.

I do not know, that the Colonies have, in any general way, or in any cool hour, gone much beyond the demand of immunity in relation to taxes. It is not fair to judge of the temper or dispositions of any man, or any set of men, when they are composed and at rest, from their conduct, or their expressions, in a state of disturbance and irritation. It is besides a very great mistake to imagine, that mankind follow up practically any speculative principle, either of government or of freedom, as far as it will go in argument and logical illation. We Englishmen, stop very short of the principles upon which we support any given part of our constitution; or even the whole of it together. I could easily, if I had not already tired you, give you very striking

---

[32]George Grenville, prime minister when Parliament passed the Stamp Act of 1765.

[33]William Pitt the Elder, prime minister when Parliament imposed duties on America in 1767.

and convincing instances of it. This is nothing but what is natural and proper. All government, indeed every human benefit and enjoyment, every virtue, and every prudent act, is founded on compromise and barter. We balance inconveniences; we give and take; we remit some rights, that we may enjoy others; and, we chuse rather to be happy citizens, than subtle disputants. As we must give away some natural liberty, to enjoy civil advantages; so we must sacrifice some civil liberties, for the advantages to be derived from the communion and fellowship of a great empire. But in all fair dealings the thing bought must bear some proportion to the purchase paid. None will barter away the immediate jewel of his soul. Though a great house is apt to make slaves haughty, yet it is purchasing a part of the artificial importance of a great empire too dear, to pay for it all essential rights, and all the intrinsic dignity of human nature. None of us who would not risque his life, rather than fall under a government purely arbitrary. But, although there are some amongst us who think our constitution wants many improvements, to make it a complete system of liberty, perhaps none who are of that opinion, would think it right to aim at such improvement, by disturbing his country, and risquing every thing that is dear to him. In every arduous enterprize, we consider what we are to lose, as well as what we are to gain; and the more and better stake of liberty every people possess, the less they will hazard in a vain attempt to make it more. These are *the cords of man*. Man acts from adequate motives relative to his interest; and not on metaphysical speculations. Aristotle, the great master of reasoning, cautions us, and with great weight and propriety, against this species of delusive geometrical accuracy in moral arguments, as the most fallacious of all sophistry.

The Americans will have no interest contrary to the grandeur and glory of England, when they are not oppressed by the weight of it; and they will rather be inclined to respect the acts of a superintending legislature, when they see them the acts of that power, which is itself the security, not the rival, of their secondary importance. In this assurance, my mind most perfectly acquiesces; and I confess, I feel not the least alarm, from the discontents which are to arise, from putting people at their ease; nor do I apprehend the destruction of this empire, from giving, by an act of free grace and indulgence, to two millions of my fellow citizens, some share of those rights, upon which I have always been taught to value myself.

It is said indeed, that this power of granting vested in American assemblies, would dissolve the unity of the empire; which was preserved, entire, although Wales, and Chester, and Durham, were added to it. Truly, Mr. Speaker, I do not know what this unity means; nor has it ever been heard of, that I know, in the constitutional policy of this country. The very idea of subordination of parts, excludes this notion of simple and undivided unity. England is the head; but she is not the head and the members too. Ireland has ever had from the beginning a separate, but not an independent, legislature; which, far from distracting, promoted the union of the whole. Every thing was sweetly and harmoniously disposed through both Islands for the conservation of English dominion, and the communication of English liberties. I do not see that the same principles might not be carried into twenty Islands, and with the same good effect. This is my model with regard to America, as far as the internal circumstances of the two countries are the same. I know no other unity of this empire than I can draw from its example during these periods, when it seemed to my poor understanding more united than it is now, or than it is likely to be by the present methods.

⤷

. . . I have indeed tired you by a long discourse; but this is the misfortune of those to whose influence nothing will be conceded, and who must win every inch of their ground by argument. You have heard me with goodness. May you decide with wisdom! For my part, I feel my mind greatly disburthened, by what I have done to-day. I have been the less fearful of trying your patience, because on this subject I mean to spare it altogether in future. I have this comfort, that in every stage of the American affairs, I have steadily opposed the measures that have produced the confusion, and may bring on the destruction, of this empire. I now go so far as to risque a proposal of my own. If I cannot give peace to my country; I give it to my conscience.

But what (says the Financier) is peace to us without money? Your plan give us no Revenue. No! But it does—For it secures to the subject the power of REFUSAL; the first of all Revenues. Experience is a cheat, and fact a liar, if this power in the subject of proportioning his grant, or of not granting at all, has not been found the richest mine of Revenue ever discovered by the skill or by the fortune of man. It does not indeed vote you £152,750: II: 2 3/4ths, nor any other paltry limited sum.—But it gives the strong box itself, the fund, the bank, from whence only revenues can arise amongst a people sensible of freedom. . . . Cannot you in England; cannot you at this time of day; cannot you, an House of Commons, trust to the principle which has raised so mighty a rev-

enue, and accumulated a debt of near 140 millions in this country? Is this principle to be true in England and false every where else? Is it not true in Ireland? Has it not hitherto been true in the Colonies? Why should you presume that, in any country, a body duly constituted for any function, will neglect to perform its duty, and abdicate its trust? Such a presumption would go against all government in all modes. But, in truth, this dread of penury of supply, from a free assembly, has no foundation in nature. For first observe, that, besides the desire which all men have naturally of supporting the honour of their own government; that sense of dignity, and that security to property, which ever attends freedom, has a tendency to increase the stock of the free community. Most may be taken where most is accumulated. And what is the soil or climate where experience has not uniformly proved, that the voluntary flow of heaped-up plenty, bursting from the weight of its own rich luxuriance, has ever run with a more copious stream of revenue, than could be squeezed from the dry husks of oppressed indigence, by the straining of all the politic machinery in the world.

Next we know, that parties must ever exist in a free country. We know too, that the emulations of such parties, their contradictions, their reciprocal necessities, their hopes, and their fears, must send them in all their turns to him that holds the balance of the state. The parties are the Gamesters; but Government keeps the table, and is sure to be the winner in the end. When this game is played, I really think it is more to be feared, that the people will be exhausted, than that Government will not be supplied. Whereas, whatever is got by acts of absolute power ill obeyed, because odious, or by contracts ill kept, because constrained; will be narrow, feeble uncertain, and precarious. *"Ease would retract vows made in pain, as violent and void."*[34]

I, for one, protect against compounding our demands: I declare against compounding, for a poor limited sum, the immense, evergrowing, eternal Debt, which is due to generous Government from protected Freedom. And so may I speed in the object I propose to you, as I think it would not only be an act of injustice, but would be the worst oeconomy in the world, to compel the Colonies to a sum certain, either in the way of ransom, or in the way of compulsory compact.

But to clear up my ideas on this subject—a revenue from America transmitted hither—do not delude yourselves—you never can receive it—No, not a shilling. We have experience that from remote countries it is not to be expected. If, when you attempted to extract revenue from Bengal, you were obliged to return in loan what you had taken in imposition;[35] what can you expect from North America? for certainly, if ever there was a country qualified to produce wealth, it is India; or an institution fit for the transmission, it is the East-India company. America has none of these aptitudes. If America gives you taxable objects, on which you lay your duties here, and gives you, at the same time, a surplus by a foreign sale of her commodities to pay the duties on these objects which you tax at home, she has performed her part to the British revenue. But with regard to her own internal establishments; she may, I doubt not she will, contribute in moderation. I say in moderation; for she

ought not to be permitted to exhaust herself. She ought to be reserved to a war; the weight of which, with the enemies that we are most likely to have, must be considerable in her quarter of the globe. There she may serve you, and serve you essentially.

For that service, for all service, whether of revenue, trade, or empire, my trust is in her interest in the British constitution. My hold of the Colonies is in the close affection which grows from common names, from kindred blood, from similar privileges, and equal protection. These are ties, which, though light as air, are as strong as links of iron. Let the Colonies always keep the idea of their civil rights associated with your Government;—they will cling and grapple to you; and no force under heaven will be of power to tear them from their allegiance. But let it be once understood, that your Government may be one thing, and their Privileges another; that these two things may exist without any mutual relation; the cement is gone; the cohesion is loosened; and every thing hastens to decay and dissolution. As long as you have the wisdom to keep the sovereign authority of this country as the sanctuary of liberty, the sacred temple consecrated to our common faith, wherever the chosen race and sons of England worship freedom, they will turn their faces towards you. The more they multiply, the more friends you will have; the more ardently they love liberty, the more perfect will be their obedience. Slavery they can have any where. It is a weed that grows in every soil. They may have it from Spain, they may have it from Prussia. But until you become lost to all feeling of your true interest and your natural dignity, freedom they can have from none but you. This is the commodity of price, of which you have the monopoly. This is the true act of navigation, which binds to you the commerce of the Colonies, and through

---

[34]From John Milton's *Paradise Lost* (1667).

[35]Lord Chatham's administration imposed taxes on the East India Company in 1767, which triggered a financial crisis in the company, prompting a loan from the government in 1773.

them secures to you the wealth of the world. Deny them this participation of freedom, and you break that sole bond, which originally made, and must still preserve, the unity of the empire. Do not entertain so weak an imagination, as that your registers and your bonds, your affidavits and your sufferances, your cockets[36] and your clearances, are what form the great securities of your commerce. Do not dream that your letters of office, and your instructions, and your suspending clauses, are the things that hold together the great contexture of this mysterious whole. These things do not make your government. Dead instruments, passive tools as they are, it is the spirit of English communion that gives all their life and efficacy to them. It is the spirit of the English constitution, which, infused through the mighty mass, pervades, feeds, unites, invigorates, vivifies, every part of the empire, even down to the minutest member.

Is it not the same virtue which does every thing for us here in England? Do you imagine then, that it is the land tax act which raises your revenue? that it is the annual vote in the committee of supply, which gives you your army? or that it is the Mutiny Bill which inspires it with bravery and discipline? No! surely no! It is the love of the people; it is their attachment to their government from the sense of the deep stake they have in such a glorious institution, which gives you your army and your navy, and infuses into both that liberal obedience, without which your army would be a base rabble, and your navy nothing but rotten timber.

All this, I know well enough, will sound wild and chimerical to the profane herd of those vulgar and mechanical politicians,

who have no place among us; a sort of people who think that nothing exists but what is gross and material; and who therefore, far from being qualified to be directors of the great movement of empire, are not fit to turn a wheel in the machine. But to men truly initiated and rightly taught, these ruling and master principles, which, in the opinion of such men as I have mentioned, have no substantial existence, are in truth every thing, and all in all. Magnanimity in politicks is not seldom the truest wisdom; and a great empire and little minds go ill together. If we are conscious of our situation, and glow with zeal to fill our place as becomes our station and ourselves, we ought to auspicate all our public proceedings on America, with the old warning of the church, *Sursum corda!*[37] We ought to elevate our minds to the greatness of that trust to which the order of Providence has called us. By adverting to the dignity of this high calling, our ancestors have turned a savage wilderness into a glorious empire; and have made the most extensive, and the only honourable conquests; not by destroying, but by promoting, the wealth, the number, the happiness, of the human race. Let us get an American revenue as we have got an American empire. English privileges have made it all that it is; English privileges alone will make it all it can be.

⤚

---

[36]Documents certifying the payment of customs duties.

---

[37]"Lift up your hearts."

Introductory Note to
Letter to the Sheriffs of Bristol
(1777)

In Speech on American Taxation *(1774)* and Speech on Conciliation with America *(1775), Burke tried in vain to head off a rupture between the American colonies and Great Britain. Written after the outbreak of the American revolution,* Letter to the Sheriffs of Bristol *completes Burke's American thinking by expressing his thoughts on the consequences of the English civil war in America.*

Burke wrote Letter to the Sheriffs of Bristol *to justify his policy of abstention from Parliament during early 1777. At the time Burke wrote the letter (April 3, 1777), the British appeared to be winning the American campaign decisively, and Burke believed that his presence in Parliament would be "vain and frivolous." In his letter Burke critiqued two Parliamentary acts directed against the Americans, in which he found evidence that the policies that produced the war and the war itself were corrupting the British constitution and the character of the British people. This theme of domestic corruption of fundamental principles and manners by imperial misgovernment appears as well in Burke's Irish and Indian writings and speeches.*

Burke rejected the claim that the harsh (and in Burke's mind unconstitutional) measures adopted by Parliament during the war were justified by the Americans' rebellion. He argued that the British provoked the rebellion through unwise and oppressive policies. Diversity in unity was a central concept of Burke's notion of the imperial society. In Burke's view, the British abandoned their historical prudence toward America for a lust to make real Parliament's theoretical legislative supremacy. Burke lamented that the British had "triumphed in a dispute, whilst we lost an empire."

The abandonment of the approach advocated by Burke led the British nation down a dangerous path: "Contending for an imaginary power, we begin to acquire the spirit of domination, and to lose the relish of honest equality." Not only was the imperial society between the British and Americans dead as a result of British imperial policy, but the nature of civil society in Britain itself was in danger. ⌒

Letter to
the Sheriffs of Bristol
(1777)

GENTLEMEN,

I HAVE the honour of sending you the two last acts which have been passed with regard to the troubles in America.[38] These acts are similar to all the rest which have been made on the same subject. They operate by the same principle; and they are derived from the very same policy. I think they complete the number of this sort of statutes to nine. It affords no matter for very pleasing reflection, to observe, that our subjects diminish, as our laws encrease.

If I have the misfortune of differing with some of my fellow-citizens on this great and arduous subject, it is no small consolation to me, that I do not differ from you. With you, I am perfectly united. We are heartily agreed in our detestation of a civil war. We have ever expressed the most unqualified disapprobation of all the steps which have led to it, and of all those which tend to prolong it. And I have no doubt that we feel exactly the same emotions of grief and shame on

---

[38]The Letters of Marque Act and the American Treason Act, both passed in 1777.

all its miserable consequences; whether they appear, on the one side or the other, in the shape of victories or defeats; of captures made from the English on the continent, or from the English in these islands; of legislative regulations which subvert the liberties of our brethren, or which undermine our own.

Of the first of these statutes (that for the letter of marque) I shall say little. Exceptionable as it may be, and as I think it is in some particulars, it seems the natural, perhaps necessary result of the measures we have taken, and the situation we are in. The other (for a partial suspension of the *Habeas Corpus*) appears to me of a much deeper malignity. During its progress through the House of Commons, it has been amended, so as to express more distinctly than at first it did, the avowed sentiments of those who framed it: and the main ground of my exception to it is, because it does express, and does carry into execution, purposes which appear to me so contradictory to all the principles, not only of the constitutional policy of Great Britain, but even of that species of hostile justice, which no asperity of war wholly extinguishes in the minds of a civilized people.

It seems to have in view two capital objects; the first, to enable administration to confine, as long as it shall think proper, (within the duration of the act) those, whom that act is pleased to qualify by the name of *Pirates*. Those so qualified, I understand to be, the commanders and mariners of such privateers and ships of war belonging to the colonies, as in the course of this unhappy contest may fall into the hands of the crown. They are therefore to be detained in prison, under the criminal description of piracy, to a future trial and ignominious punishment, whenever circumstances shall make it convenient to execute vengeance on them,

under the colour of that odious and infamous offence.

To this first purpose of the law, I have no small dislike. Because the act does not (as all laws, and all equitable transactions ought to do) fairly describe its object. The persons, who make a naval war upon us, in consequence of the present troubles, may be *rebels;* but to call and treat them as *pirates,* is confounding, not only the natural distinction of things, but the order of crimes; which, whether by putting them from a higher part of the scale to the lower, or from the lower to the higher, is never done without dangerously disordering the whole frame of jurisprudence. Though piracy may be, in the eye of the law, a *less* offence than treason; yet as both are, in effect, punished with the same death, the same forfeiture, and the same corruption of blood, I never would take from any fellow-creature whatever, any sort of advantage, which he may derive to his safety from the pity of mankind, or to his reputation from their general feelings, by degrading his offence, when I cannot soften his punishment. The general sense of mankind tells me, that those offences, which may possibly arise from mistaken virtue, are not in the class of infamous actions. . . . The act prepares a sort of masqued proceeding, not honourable to the justice of the kingdom, and by no means necessary for its safety. . . .

↞

The second professed purpose of the act is to detain in England for trial, those who shall commit high treason in America.

↞

I take it for granted, gentlemen, that we sympathize in a proper horror of all punishment further than as it serves for an example. To whom then does the example of an execution in England for this American rebellion apply? Remember, you are told every day, that the present is a contest between the two countries; and that we in England are at war for *our own* dignity against our rebellious children. Is this true? If it be, it is surely among such rebellious children that examples for disobedience should be made. For who ever thought of instructing parents in their duty by an example from the punishment of a disobedient son? As well might the execution of a fugitive negro in the plantations, be considered as a lesson to teach masters humanity to their slaves. Such executions may indeed satiate our revenge; they may harden our hearts: and puff us up with pride and arrogance. Alas! this is not instruction.

If any thing can be drawn from such examples by a parity of the case, it is to shew, how deep their crime, and how heavy their punishment will be, who shall at any time dare to resist a distant power actually disposing of their property, without their voice or consent to the disposition; and overturning their franchises without charge or hearing. God forbid, that England should ever read this lesson written in the blood of *any* of her off-spring!

War is at present carried on, between the king's natural and foreign troops,[39] on one side, and the English in America, on the other, upon the usual footing of other wars; and accordingly an exchange of prisoners has been regularly made from the beginning. If, notwithstanding this hitherto equal procedure, upon some prospect of ending the war with success (which however may be delusive), administration prepares to act against those as *traitors* who remain in their hands at the end of the troubles, in my opinion we shall exhibit to the world as indecent a piece of injustice as ever civil fury has produced. If the prisoners who have been exchanged have not by the exchange been *virtually pardoned,* the cartel (whether avowed or understood) is a cruel fraud: for you have received the life of a man; and you ought to return a life for it, or there is no parity of fairness in the transaction.

If, on the other hand, we admit, that they, who are actually exchanged are pardoned, but contend that we may justly reserve for vengeance, those who remain unexchanged; then this unpleasant and unhandsome consequence will follow; that you judge of the delinquency of men merely by the time of their guilt, and not by the heinousness of it; and you make fortune and accidents, and not the moral qualities of human action, the rule of your justice.

These strange incongruities must ever perplex those, who confound the unhappiness of civil dissention, with the crime of treason. Whenever a rebellion really and truly exists, . . . government has not entered into such military conventions; but has ever declined all intermediate treaty, which should put rebels in possession of the law of nations with regard to war. Commanders would receive no benefits at their hands, because they could make no return for them. Who has ever heard of capitulation, and parole of honour, and exchange of prisoners, in the late rebellions in this kingdom? The answer to all demands of that sort was, "We can engage for nothing; you are at the king's pleasure." We ought to remember, that if our present enemies be, in reality and truth, rebels, the king's generals have no right to release them upon any conditions whatsoever; and they are themselves answerable to the law, and as much in want of a par-

---

[39]Britain was using German mercenary troops in the war against the American rebels.

don for doing so, as the rebels whom they release.

Lawyers, I know, cannot make the distinction, for which I contend; because they have their strict rule to go by. But legislators ought to do what lawyers cannot; for they have no other rules to bind them, but the great principles of reason and equity, and the general sense of mankind. These they are bound to obey and follow; and rather to enlarge and enlighten law by the liberality of legislative reason, than to fetter and bind their higher capacity by the narrow constructions of subordinate artificial justice. If we had adverted to this, we never could consider the convulsions of a great empire, not disturbed by a little disseminated faction, but divided by whole communities and provinces, and entire legal representatives of a people, as fit matter of discussion under a commission of oyer and terminer. It is as opposite to reason and prudence, as it is to humanity and justice.

This act, proceeding on these principles, that is, preparing to end the present troubles by a trial of one sort of hostility, under the name of piracy, and of another by the name of treason, and executing the act of Henry the eighth according to a new and unconstitutional interpretation, I have thought evil and dangerous, even though the instruments of effecting such purposes had been merely of a neutral quality.

But it really appears to me, that the means which this act employs are, at least, as exceptionable as the end. Permit me to open myself upon this subject, because it is of importance to me, when I am obliged to submit to the power without acquiescing in the reason of an act of legislature, that I should justify my dissent, by such arguments as may be supposed to have weight with a sober man.

The main operative regulation of the act is to suspend the common law, and the statute *Habeas Corpus,* (the sole securities either for liberty or justice,) with regard to all those who have been out of the realm or on the high seas, within a given time. The rest of the people, as I understand, are to continue as they stood before.

I confess, gentlemen, that this appears to me, as bad in the principle, and far worse in its consequence, than an universal suspension of the *Habeas Corpus* act; and the limiting qualification, instead of taking out the sting, does in my humble opinion sharpen and envenom it to a greater degree. Liberty, if I understand it at all, is a *general* principle, and the clear right of all the subjects within the realm, or of none. Partial freedom seems to be a most invidious mode of slavery. But, unfortunately, it is the kind of slavery the most easily admitted in times of civil discord. For parties are but too apt to forget their own future safety in their desire of sacrificing their enemies. People without much difficulty admit the entrance of that injustice of which they are not to be the immediate victims. In times of high proceeding, it is never the faction of the predominant power that is in danger; for no tyranny chastises its own instruments. It is the obnoxious and the suspected who want the protection of law; and there is nothing to bridle the partial violence of state factions, but this great, steady, uniform principle; "that whenever an act is made for a cessation of law and justice, the whole people should be universally subjected to the same suspension of their franchises." The alarm of such a proceeding would then be universal. It would operate as a sort of *call of the nation.* It would become every man's immediate and instant concern, to be made very sensible of *the absolute necessity* of this total eclipse of liberty. They would more carefully advert to every renewal, and more powerfully resist it. These great determined measures are not commonly so dangerous to freedom. They are marked with too strong lines to slide into use. No plea of pretence of mere *inconvenience or evil example* . . . can be admitted as a reason for such mighty operations. But the true danger is, when liberty is nibbled away, for expedients, and by parts. The *Habeas Corpus* act supposes (contrary to the genius of most other laws) that the lawful magistrate may see particular men with a malignant eye; and it provides for that identical case. But when men, *under particular descriptions, marked out by the magistrate himself,* are delivered over by parliament to this possible malignity, it is not the *Habeas Corpus* that is occasionally suspended, but its spirit that is mistaken, and its principle that is subverted. Indeed nothing is security to any individual but the common interest of all.

This act, therefore, has this distinguished evil in it, that it is the first *partial* suspension of the *Habeas Corpus* which has been made. The precedent, which is always of very great importance, is now established. For the first time a distinction is made among the people within this realm. Before this act, every man putting his foot on English ground, every stranger owing only a local and temporary allegiance, even a negro slave, who had been sold in the colonies and under an act of parliament, became as free as every other man who breathed the same air with him. Now a line is drawn, which may be advanced farther and farther at pleasure, on the same argument of mere expedience, on which it was first described. There is no equality among us; we are not fellow-citizens, if the mariner who lands on the quay does not rest on as firm legal ground, as the merchant who sits in his comptinghouse. Other laws may injure the community; this tends to dissolve it. It destroys *equal-*

ity, which is the essence of community. As things now stand, every man in the West Indies, every one inhabitant of three unoffending provinces on the continent, every person coming from the East Indies, every gentleman who has travelled for his health or education, every mariner who has navigated the seas, is, for no other offence, under a temporary proscription. Let any of these facts (now become presumptions of guilt) be proved against him, and the bare suspicion of the crown puts him out of the law. It is even by no means clear to me, whether the negative proof does not lie upon the person apprehended on suspicion, to the subversion of all justice.

I have not debated against this bill in its progress through the House; because it would have been vain to oppose, and impossible to correct it. It is some time since I have been clearly convinced, that in the present state of things, all opposition to any measures proposed by ministers, where the name of America appears, is vain and frivolous. . . .

. . . In declining my usual strict attendance, I do not in the least condemn the spirit of those gentlemen, who, with a just confidence in their abilities, . . . were of opinion that their exertions in this desperate case might be of some service. They thought, that by contracting the sphere of its application, they might lessen the malignity of an evil principle. Perhaps they were in the right. But when my opinion was so very clearly to the contrary, for the reasons I have just stated, I am sure *my* attendance would have been ridiculous.

I must add, in further explanation of my conduct, that, far from softening the features of such a principle, and thereby removing any part of the popular odium or natural terrors attending it, I should be sorry, that any thing framed in contradiction to the spirit of our constitution did not instantly produce in fact, the grossest of the evils, with which it was pregnant in its nature. It is by lying dormant a long time, or being at first very rarely exercised, that arbitrary power steals upon a people. On the next unconstitutional act, all the fashionable world will be ready to say— Your prophecies are ridiculous, your fears are vain, you see how little of the mischiefs which you formerly foreboded are come to pass. Thus, by degrees, that artful softening of all arbitrary power, the alledged infrequency or narrow extent of its operation, will be received as a sort of aphorism—and Mr. *Hume*[40] will not be singular in telling us, that the felicity of mankind is no more disturbed by it, than by earthquakes, or thunder, or the other more unusual accidents of nature.

The act of which I have said so much is among the fruits of the American war; a war, in my humble opinion, productive of many mischiefs of a kind, which distinguish it from all others. Not only our policy is deranged, and our empire distracted, but our laws and our legislative spirit are in danger of being totally perverted by it. We have made war on our Colonies, not by arms only, but by laws. As hostility and law are not very concordant ideas, every step we have taken in this business, has been made by trampling on some maxim of justice, or some capital principle of wise government. What precedents were established, and what principles overturned, (I will not say of English privilege, but of general justice), in the Boston Port, the Massachusets Charter, the Military Bill, and all that long array of hostile acts of parliament, by which the war with America has been begun and supported? Had the principles of any of these acts been first

[40]David Hume, the Scottish philosopher and a contemporary of Burke.

planted on English ground, they would probably have expired as soon as they touched it. But by being removed from our persons, they have rooted in our laws; and the latest posterity will taste the fruits of them.

Nor is it the worst effect of this unnatural contention, that our *laws* are corrupted. Whilst *manners* remain entire, they will correct the vices of law, and soften it at length to their own temper. But we have to lament, that in most of the late proceedings we see very few traces of that generosity, humanity, and dignity of mind, which formerly characterized this nation. War suspends the rules of moral obligation; and what is long suspended is in danger of being totally abrogated. Civil wars strike deepest of all into the manners of a people. They vitiate their politicus; they corrupt their morals; they pervert even the natural taste and relish of equity and justice. By teaching us to consider our fellow-citizens in an hostile light, the whole body of our nation becomes gradually less dear to us. The very names of affection and kindred, which were the bonds of charity whilst we agreed, become new incentives to hatred and rage, when the communion of our country is dissolved. We may flatter ourselves that we shall not fall into this misfortune. But we have no charter of exemption, that I know of, from the ordinary frailities of our nature.

What but that blindness of heart which arises from the phrenzy of civil contention, could have made any persons conceive the present situation of the British affairs as an object of triumph in themselves, or of congratulation to their sovereign? Nothing surely could be more lamentable to those who remember the flourishing days of this kingdom, than to see the insane joy of several unhappy people, amidst the sad spectacle which our affairs and conduct exhibit to the scorn of Europe. We behold (and it seems some people rejoice in beholding) our native land, which used to fit the envied arbiter of all her neighbours, reduced to a servile dependence on their mercy; acquiescing in assurances of friendship which she does not trust; complaining of hostilities which she dares not resent; deficient to her allies; lofty to her subjects; and submissive to her enemies; whilst the liberal government of this free nation is supported by the hireling sword of German boors and vassals; and three millions of the subjects of Great-Britain are seeking for protection to English privileges in the arms of France!

↜

Indeed our affairs are in a bad condition. I do assure those Gentlemen who have prayed for war, and obtained the blessing they have sought, that they are at this instant in very great straits. The abused wealth of this country continues a little longer to feed its distemper. As yet they, and their German allies of twenty hireling states, have contended only with the unprepared strength of our own infant colonies. But America is not subdued. Not one unattacked village, which was originally adverse, throughout that vast continent, has yet submitted from love or terror. You have the ground you encamp on; and you have no more. The cantonments of your troops and your dominions are exactly of the same extent. You spread devastation, but you do not enlarge the sphere of authority.

↜

There are many circumstances in the present zeal for civil war, which seem to discover but little of real magnanimity. The addressers offer their own persons; and they are satisfied with hiring Germans.

They promise their private fortunes, and they mortgage their country. They have all the merit of volunteers, without risque of person or charge of contribution; and when the unfeeling arm of a foreign soldiery pours out their kindred blood like water, they exult and triumph, as if they themselves had performed some notable exploit. I am really ashamed of the fashionable language which has been held for some time past; which, to say the best of it, is full of levity. You know, that I allude to the general cry against the cowardice of the Americans, as if we despised them for not making the King's soldiery purchase the advantages they have obtained, at a dearer rate. It is not, Gentlemen, it is not to respect the dispensations of Providence, not to provide any decent retreat in the mutability of human affairs. It leaves no medium between insolent victory and infamous defeat. It tends to alienate our minds further and further from our natural regards, and to make an eternal rent and schism in the British nation. Those who do not wish for such a separation, would not dissolve that cement of reciprocal esteem and regard, which can alone bind together the parts of this great fabrick. It ought to be our wish, as it is our duty, not only to forbear this style of outrage ourselves, but to make every one as sensible as we can of the impropriety and unworthiness of the tempers which gave rise to it, and which designing men are labouring with such malignant industry to difuse amongst us. It is our business to counteract them, if possible; if possible to awaken our natural regards; and to revive the old partiality to the English name. Without something of this kind I do not see how it is ever practicable really to reconcile with those, whose affections, after all, must be the surest hold of our government; and which are a thousand times more worth to us, than the mercenary zeal of all the circles of Germany.

I can well conceive a country completely over-run, and miserably wasted, without approaching in the least to settlement. In my apprehension, as long as English government is attempted to be supported over Englishmen by the sword alone, things will thus continue. I anticipate in my mind the moment of the final triumph of foreign military force. When that hour arrives, (for it may arrive) then it is, that all this mass of weakness and violence will appear in its full light. If we should be expelled from America, the delusion of the partizans of military government might still continue. They might still feed their imaginations with the possible good consequences which might have attended success. Nobody could prove the contrary by facts. But in case the sword should do all that the sword can do, the success of their arms and the defeat of their policy will be one and the same thing. You will never see any revenue from America. Some increase of the means of corruption, without any ease of the public burthens, is the very best that can happen. Is it for this that we are at war; and in such a war?

As to the difficulties of laying once more the foundations of that government, which, for the sake of conquering what was our own, has been voluntarily and wantonly pulled down by a court faction here, I tremble to look at them. Has any of these Gentlemen, who are so eager to govern all mankind, shewed himself possessed of the first qualification towards government, some knowledge of the object, and of the difficulties which occur in the tasks they have undertaken?

I assure you, that on the most prosperous issue of your arms, you will not be where you stood, when you called in war to supply the defects of your political establishment. Nor would any disorder or

disobedience to government, which could arise from the most abject concession on our part, ever equal those which will be felt after the most triumphant violence. You have got all the intermediate evils of war into the bargain.

I think I know America. If I do not, my ignorance is incurable, for I have spared no pains to understand it; and I do most solemnly assure those of my constituents who put any sort of confidence in my industry and integrity, that every thing that has been done there has arisen from a total misconception of the object: that our means of originally holding America, that our means of reconciling with it after quarrel, of recovering it after separation, or keeping it after victory, did depend, and must depend, in their several stages and periods, upon a total renunciation of that unconditional submission which has taken such possession of the minds of violent men. The whole of those maxims, upon which we have made and continued this war, must be abandoned. Nothing indeed . . . can place us in our former situation. That hope must be laid aside. But there is a difference between bad and the worst of all. Terms relative to the cause of the war ought to be offered by the authority of parliament. An arrangement at home promising some security for them ought to be made. By doing this, without the least impairing of our strength, we add to the credit of our moderation, which, in itself, is always strength more or less.

I know many have been taught to think, that moderation, in a case like this, is a sort of treason: and that all arguments for it are sufficiently answered by railing at rebels and rebellion, and by charging all the present or future miseries which we may suffer, on the resistance of our brethren. But I would wish them, in this grave matter, and if peace is not wholly removed from their hearts, to consider seriously, first,—that to criminate and recriminate never yet was the road to reconciliation, in any difference amongst men. In the next place, it would be right to reflect, that the American English . . . can, as things now stand, neither be provoked at our railing, or bettered by our instruction. All communication is cut off between us. But this we know with certainty; that though we cannot reclaim them, we may reform ourselves. If measures of peace are necessary, they must begin somewhere; and a conciliatory temper must precede and prepare every plan of reconciliation. Nor do I conceive that we suffer any thing by thus regulating our own minds. We are not disarmed by being disencumbered of our passions. Declaiming on Rebellion never added a bayonet, or a charge of powder, to your military force; but I am afraid that it has been the means of taking up many a musket against you.

This outrageous language, which has been encouraged and kept alive by every art, has already done incredible mischief. For a long time, even amidst the desolations of war, and the insults of hostile laws daily accumulated on one another, the American leaders seem to have had the greatest difficulty in bringing up their people to a declaration of total independence. But the Court Gazette accomplished what the abettors of independence had attempted in vain.[41] When that disingenuous compilation, and strange medley of railing and flattery, was adduced, as a proof of the united sentiments of the people of Great Britain, there was a great change throughout all America. The tide of popular affection, which had still set towards the parent country, began immedi-

ately to turn; and to flow with great rapidity in a contrary course. Far from concealing these wild declarations of enmity, the author of the celebrated pamphlet which prepared the minds of the people for independence, insists largely on the multitude and the spirit of these Addresses; and he draws an argument from them, which (if the facts were as he supposes) must be irresistible.[42] For I never knew a writer on the theory of government, so partial to authority, as not to allow, that the *hostile mind* of the rulers to their people, did fully justify a change of government. Nor can any reason whatever be given, why one people should voluntarily yield any degree of pre-eminence to another, but on a supposition of great affection and benevolence towards them. Unfortunately your rulers, trusting to other things, took no notice of this great principle of connexion. From the beginning of this affair, they have done all they could to alienate your minds from your own kindred; and if they could excite hatred enough in one of the parties towards the other, they seemed to be of opinion that they had gone half way towards reconciling the quarrel.

I know it is said, that your kindness is only alienated on account of their resistance; and therefore if the colonies surrender at discretion all sort of regard, and even much indulgence, is meant towards them in future. But can those who are partizans for continuing a war to enforce such a surrender, be responsible (after all that has passed) for such a future use of a power, that is bound by no compacts, and restrained by no terrors? Will they tell us what they call indulgences? Do they not at this instant call the present war and all its horrors, a lenient and merciful proceeding?

---

[41]The *London Gazette* published a number of addresses presented in late 1775 to the king supporting the British hard-line American policy.

[42]Burke is referring to Thomas Paine and his *Common Sense* (1776).

No conqueror, that I ever heard of, has *professed* to make a cruel, harsh, and insolent use of his conquest. No! The man of the most declared pride, scarcely dares to trust his own heart, with this dreadful secret of ambition. But it will appear in its time; and no man who professes to reduce another to the insolent mercy of a foreign arm, ever had any sort of good-will towards him. The profession of kindness, with that sword in his hand, and that demand of surrender, is one of the most provoking acts of this hostility. I shall be told, that all this is lenient, as against rebellious adversaries. But are the leaders of their faction more lenient to those who submit? Lord Howe and General Howe have powers under an Act of Parliament, to restore to the King's peace and to free trade any men, or district, which shall submit. Is this done? We have been over and over informed by the authorised Gazette, that the city of New York and the countries of Staten and Long Island have submitted voluntarily and cheerfully, and that many in these places are full even of zeal to the cause of Administration. Were they instantly restored to trade? Are they yet restored to it? . . . But we can see well enough to what the whole leads. The trade of America is to be dealt out in *private indulgences and graces;* that is, in jobbs to recompence the incendiaries of war. *They* will be informed of the proper time in which to send out their merchandise. From a national, the American trade is to be turned into a personal monopoly; and one set of Merchants are to be rewarded for the pretended zeal, of which another set are the dupes; and thus between craft and credulity, the voice of reason is stifled; and all the misconduct, all the calamities of the war are covered and continued.

If I had not lived long enough to be little surprized at any thing, I should have been in some degree astonished at the continued rage of several Gentlemen, who, not satisfied with carrying fire and sword into America, are animated nearly with the same fury against those neighbours of theirs, whose only crime it is, that they have charitably and humanely wished them to entertain more reasonable sentiments, and not always to sacrifice their interest to their passion. All this rage against unresisting dissent, convinces me, that at bottom they are far from satisfied they are in the right. For what is it they would have? A war? They certainly have at this moment the blessing of something that is very like one; and if the war they enjoy at present be not sufficiently hot and extensive, they may shortly have it as warm and as spreading as their hearts can desire. Is it the force of the Kingdom they call for? They have it already; and if they choose to fight their battles in their own person, nobody prevents their setting sail to America in the next transports. Do they think, that the service is stinted for want of liberal supplies? Indeed they complain without reason. The table of the House of Commons will glut them, let their appetite for expence be never so keen. And I assure them further, that those who think with them in the House of Commons are full as easy in the control, as they are liberal in the vote of these expences. If this be not supply or confidence sufficient, let them open their own private purse-strings, and give from what is left to them, as largely and with as little care as they think proper.

Tolerated in their passions, let them learn not to persecute the moderation of their fellow-citizens. If all the world joined them in a full cry against rebellion, and were as hotly inflamed against the whole theory and enjoyment of freedom, as those who are the most factious for servitude, it could not in my opinion answer any one end whatsoever in this contest. The leaders of this war could not hire ... one German more, than they do; or inspire him with less feeling for the persons, or less value for the privileges, of their revolted brethren. If we all adopted their sentiments to a man, their allies the savage Indians[43] could not be more ferocious than they are: They could not murder one more helpless woman or child, or with more exquisite refinements of cruelty torment to death one more of their English flesh and blood, than they do already. The public money is given to purchase this alliance;—and they have their bargain.

↬

When any community is subordinately connected with another, the great danger of the connexion is the extreme pride and self-complacency of the superior, which in all matters of controversy will probably decide in its own favour. It is a powerful corrective to such a very rational cause of fear, if the inferior body can be made to believe, that the party inclination or political views of several in the principal state, will induce them in some degree to counteract this blind and tyrannic partiality. There is no danger than any one acquiring consideration or power in the presiding state should carry this leaning to the inferior too far. The fault of human nature is not of that sort. Power in whatever hands is rarely guilty of too strict limitations on itself. But one great advantage to the support of authority attends such an amicable and protecting connexion, that those who have conferred favours obtain influence; and from the foresight of future events can persuade men who have received obligations

sometimes to return them. Thus, by the mediation of those healing principles, ... troublesome discussions are brought to some sort of adjustment; and every hot controversy is not a civil war.

But, if the Colonies ... could see, that in Great Britain the mass of the people is melted into its Government, and that every dispute with the Ministry must of necessity be always a quarrel with the nation; they can stand no longer in the equal and friendly relation of fellow-citizens to the subjects of this Kingdom. Humble as this relation may appear to some, when it is once broken, a strong tie is dissolved. Other sort of connexions will be sought. For, there are very few in the world, who will not prefer an useful ally to an insolent master.

Such discord has been the effect of the unanimity into which so many have of late been seduced or bullied, or into the appearance of which they have sunk through mere despair. They have been told that their dissent from violent measures is an encouragement to rebellion. Men of great presumption and little knowledge will hold a language which is contradicted by the whole course of history. *General* rebellions and revolts of an whole people never were *encouraged,* now or at any time. They are always *provoked.* But if this unheard-of doctrine of the encouragement of rebellion were true, if it were true, that an assurance of the friendship of numbers in this country towards the colonies, could become an encouragement to them to break off all connexion with it, what is the inference? Does any body seriously maintain, that, charged with my share of the public councils, I am obliged not to resist projects which I think mischievous, lest men who suffer should be encouraged to resist? The very tendency of such projects to produce rebellion is one of the chief reasons against them. Shall that reason not be given? Is it

---

[43]British forces attempted to use Indian tribes against the American rebels and settlers. Such practices angered Burke. See also *Speech on the Use of Indians, WSEB*, iii, 354–367.

then a rule, that no man in this nation shall open his mouth in favour of the Colonies, shall defend their rights, or complain of their sufferings? Or, when war finally breaks out, no man shall express his desires of peace? Has this been the law of our past, or is it to make the terms of our future, connexion? Even looking no further than ourselves, can it be true loyalty to any government, or true patriotism towards any country, to degrade their solemn councils into servile drawing-rooms, to flatter their pride and passions, rather than to enlighten their reason, and to prevent them from being cautioned against violence, lest others should be encouraged to resistance! By such acquiescence great Kings and mighty nations have been undone; and if any are at this day in a perilous situation from rejecting truth, and listening to flattery, it would rather become them to reform the errors under which they suffer, than to reproach those who have forewarned them of their danger.

But the rebels looked for assistance from this country. They did so in the beginning of this controversy most certainly; and they sought it by earnest supplications to Government, which dignity rejected, and by a suspension of commerce, which the wealth of this nation enabled you to despise. When they found that neither prayers nor menaces had any sort of weight, but that a firm resolution was taken to reduce them to unconditional obedience by a military force, they came to the last extremity. Despairing of us, they trusted in themselves. Not strong enough themselves, they sought succour in France.[44] In proportion as all encourage-

ment here lessened, their distance from this country encreased. The encouragement is over; the alienation is compleat.

In order to produce this favourite unanimity in delusion, and to prevent all possibility of a return to our antient happy concord, arguments for our continuance in this course are drawn from the wretched situation itself into which we have been betrayed. It is said, that being at war with the Colonies, whatever our sentiments might have been before, all ties between us are now dissolved; and all the policy we have left is to strengthen the hands of Government to reduce them. On the principle of this argument, the more mischiefs we suffer from any administration, the more our trust in it is to be confirmed. Let them but once get us into a war, their power is then safe, and an act of oblivion past for all their misconduct.

But is it really true, that Government is always to be strengthened with the instruments of war, but never furnished with the means of peace? . . .

When I was amongst my constituents at the last Summer Assizes,[45] I remember that men of all descriptions did then express a very strong desire for peace, and no slight hopes of attaining it from the commission sent out by my lord Howe. And it is not a little remarkable, that in proportion as every person shewed a zeal for the court measures, he was at that time earnest in circulating an opinion of the extent of the supposed powers of that commission. When I told them that lord Howe had no powers to treat, or to promise satisfaction on any point whatsoever of the controversy, I was hardly credited; so strong and general was the desire of terminating this

---

[44]Burke probably had in mind Benjamin Franklin's diplomatic mission to Paris in the winter of 1776–1777. The Americans eventually concluded an alliance with France in 1778.

[45]An assize was a session held periodically in all English and Welsh counties where civil and criminal justice was administered.

war by the method of accommodation. As far as I could discover, this was the temper then prevalent through the kingdom. . . . If such powers of treaty were to be wished, whilst success was very doubtful; how came they to be less so, since his Majesty's arms have been crowned with many considerable advantages? Have these successes induced us to alter our mind, as thinking the season of victory not the time for treating with honour or advantage? . . .

All the attempts made this session to give fuller powers of peace to the commanders in America, were stifled by the fatal confidence of victory, and the wild hopes of unconditional submission. There was a moment, favourable to the king's arms, when if any powers of concession had existed, on the other side of the Atlantick, even after all our errors, peace in all probability might have been restored. But calamity is unhappily the usual season of reflexion; and the pride of men will not often suffer reason to have any scope until it can be no longer of service.

I have always wished, that as the dispute had its apparent origin from things done in Parliament, and as the acts passed there had provoked the war, that the foundations of peace should be paid in Parliament also. I have been astonished to find, that those whose zeal for the dignity of our body was so hot, as to light up the flames of civil war, should even publickly declare, that these delicate points ought to be wholly left to the Crown. Poorly as I may be thought affected to the authority of Parliament, I shall never admit that our constitutional rights can ever become a matter of ministerial negociation.

I am charged with being an American. If warm affection, towards those over whom I claim any share of authority, be a crime, I am guilty of this charge. But I do assure you . . . that if ever one man lived,

more zealous than another, for the supremacy of Parliament, and the rights of this imperial Crown, it was myself. Many others indeed might be more knowing in the extent, or in the foundation of these rights. I do not pretend to be an Antiquary, or a lawyer, or qualified for the chair of Professor in Metaphysics. I never ventured to put your solid interests upon speculative grounds. My having constantly declined to do so has been attributed to my incapacity for such disquisitions; and I am inclined to believe it is partly the cause. I never shall be ashamed to confess, that where I am ignorant I am diffident. I am indeed not very sollicitous to clear myself of this imputed incapacity; because men, even less conversant than I am, in this kind of subtleties, and placed in stations to which I ought not to aspire, have, by the mere force of civil discretion, often conducted the affairs of great nations with distinguished felicity and glory.

When I first came into a publick trust, I found your Parliament in possession of an unlimited legislative power over the Colonies. I could not open the Statute-Book, without seeing the actual exercise of it, more or less, in all cases whatsoever. . . .

I had indeed very earnest wishes to keep the whole body of this authority perfect and entire as I found it, and to keep it so, not for our advantage solely, but principally for the sake of those, on those account all just authority exists; I mean, the people to be governed. For I thought I saw, that many cases might well happen, in which the exercise of every power, comprehended in the broadest idea of legislature, might become, in its time and circumstances, not a little expedient for the peace and union of the Colonies amongst themselves, as well as for their perfect harmony with Great-Britain. Thinking so, (perhaps erroneously) but being honestly of that opinion, I was at the same time very sure, that the authority of which I was so jealous, could not, under the actual circumstances of our Plantations, be at all preserved in any of its members, but by the greatest reserve in its application; particularly in those delicate points, in which the feelings of mankind are the most irritable. They who thought otherwise, have found a few more difficulties in their work, than (I hope) they were thoroughly aware of, when they undertook the present business.

I must beg leave to observe, that it is not only the invidious branch of taxation that will be resisted, but that no other given part of legislative rights can be safely exercised, without regard to the general opinion of those who are to be governed. That general opinion is the vehicle, and organ of legislative omnipotence. Without this, the extent of legislative power may be a theory to entertain the mind, but it is nothing in the direction of affairs. The compleatness of the legislative authority of Parliament *over this kingdom* is not questioned; and yet there are many things indubitably included in the abstract idea of that power, and which carry no absolute injustice in themselves, which, being contrary to the opinions and feelings of the people, can as little be exercised, as if Parliament in such cases had been possessed of no right at all. . . . In effect, to follow, not to force the publick inclination; to give a direction, a form, a technical dress and a specifick sanction, to the general sense of the community, is the true end of legislature. When it goes beyond this, its authority will be precarious, let its right be what they will.

It is so with regard to the exercise of all the powers, which our constitution knows in any of its parts, and indeed to the substantial existence of any of the parts themselves. The King's negative to bills is one of the most indisputed of the royal prerogatives; and it extends to all cases whatsoever. I am far from certain, that if several laws, which I know, had fallen under the stroke of that sceptre, that the publick would have had a very heavy loss. But it is not the *propriety* of the exercise which is in question. The exercise itself is wisely forborne. Its repose may be the preservation of its existence; and its existence may be the means of saving the constitution itself, on an occasion worthy of bringing it forth.

As the disputants, whose accurate and logical reasonings have brought us into our present condition, think it absurd that powers, or members of any constitution should exist, rarely if ever to be exercised, I hope, I shall be excused in mentioning another instance that is material. We know, that the Convocation of the Clergy had formerly been called and sat with nearly as much regularity to business as Parliament itself. It is now called for form only. It sits for the purpose of making some polite ecclesiastical compliments to the King; and when that grace is said, retires and is heard of no more. It is however *a part of the Constitution,* and may be called out into act and energy, whenever there is occasion; and whenever those, who conjure up that spirit, will choose to abide the consequences. It is wise to permit its legal existence; it is much wiser to continue it a legal existence only. So truly has Prudence (constituted as the God of this lower world) the entire dominion over every exercise of power, committed into its hands; and yet I have lived to see prudence and conformity to circumstances, wholly set at naught in out late controversies, and treated as if they were the most contemptible and irrational of all things. I have heard it a hundred times very gravely alledged, that in order to keep power in wind, it was necessary, by preference, to exert it in those very points in which it was most likely to be resisted, and the least likely to be productive of any advantage.

These were the considerations, Gentlemen, which led me early to think, that in the comprehensive dominion which the divine Providence had put into our hands, instead of troubling our understandings with speculations concerning the unity of empire, and the identity or distinction of legislative powers, and inflaming our passions with the heat and pride of controversy, it was our duty, in all soberness, to conform our Government to the character and circumstances of the several people who compose this mighty and strangely diversified mass. I never was wild enough to conceive, that one method would serve for the whole; I could never conceive that the natives of *Hindostan* and those of *Virginia* could be ordered in the same manner; or that the *Cutchery* Court[46] and the grand Jury of *Salem*[47] could be regulated on a similar plan. I was persuaded that Government was a practical thing, made for the happiness of mankind, and not to furnish out a spectacle of uniformity, to gratify the schemes of visionary politicians. Our business was, to rule, not to wrangle; and it would have been a poor compensation that we had triumphed in a dispute, whilst we lost an empire.

If there be one fact in the world perfectly clear, it is this, "That the disposition of the people of America is wholly averse to any other than a free Government;" and this known character of the people is indication enough to any honest statesman, how he ought to adapt whatever power he finds in his hands to their case. If any ask me what a free Government is? I answer, that, for any practical purpose, it is what the people think so; and that they, and not I, are the natural, lawful, and competent judges of this matter. If they practically allow me a greater degree of authority over them than is consistent with any correct ideas of perfect freedom, I ought to thank them for so great a trust, and not to endeavour to prove from thence, that they have reasoned amiss, and that having gone so far, by analogy, they must hereafter have no enjoyment but by my pleasure.

If we had seen this done by any others, we must have concluded them far gone in madness. It is melancholy as well as ridiculous, to observe the kind of reasoning with which the public has been amused, in order to divert our minds from the common sense of our American policy. There are people, who have split and anatomised the doctrine of free Government, as if it were an abstract question concerning metaphysical liberty and necessity; and not a matter of moral prudence and natural feeling. They have disputed, whether liberty be a positive or a negative idea; whether it does not consist in being governed by laws, without considering what are the laws or who are the makers; they have questioned whether man has any rights by nature; and whether all the property he enjoys, be not the alms of his government, and his life itself their favour and indulgence. Others corrupting religion, as these have perverted philosophy, contend, that Christians are redeemed into captivity; and the blood of the Saviour of mankind has been shed to make them the slaves of a few proud and insolent sinners. These shocking extremes provoking to extremes of another kind, speculations are let loose as destructive to all authority, as the former are to all freedom. In this manner the stirrers up of this contention, not satisfied with distracting our dependencies

---

[46]A Hindu courthouse with public seating.

[47]Salem, in the colony of Massachusetts.

and filling them with blood and slaughter, are corrupting our understandings: they are endeavouring to tear up, along with practical liberty, all the foundations of human society, all equity and justice, religion and order.

Civil freedom, gentlemen, is not, as many have endeavoured to persuade you, a thing that lies hid in the depths of abstruse science. It is a blessing and a benefit, not an abstract speculation; and all the just reasoning that can be upon it, is of so coarse a texture, as perfectly to suit the ordinary capacities of those who are to enjoy, and of those who are to defend it. Far from any resemblance to those propositions in Geometry and Metaphysics, which admit no medium, but must be true or false in all their latitude, social and civil freedom, like all other things in common life, are variously mixed and modified, enjoyed in very different degrees, and shaped into an infinite diversity of forms, according to the temper and circumstances of every community. The *extreme* of liberty (which is its abstract perfection, but its real fault) obtains no where, nor ought to obtain any where. Because extremes, as we all know, in every point which relates either to our duties or satisfactions in life, are destructive both to virtue and enjoyment. Liberty too must be limited in order to be possessed. The degree of restraint it is impossible in any case to settle precisely. But it ought to be the constant aim of every wise publick counsel, to find out by cautious experiments, and rational, cool endeavours, with how little, not how much of this restraint, the community can subsist. For liberty is a good to be improved, and not an evil to be lessened. It is not only a private blessing of the first order, but the vital spring and energy of the state itself, which has just so much life and vigour as there is liberty in it. But whether liberty be

advantageous or not, . . . none will dispute that peace is a blessing; and peace must in the course of human affairs be frequently bought by some indulgence and toleration at least to liberty. For as the Sabbath (though of divine institution) was made for man, not man for the Sabbath, government, which can claim no higher origin or authority, in its exercise at least, ought to conform to the exigencies of the time and the temper and character of the people, with whom it is concerned; and not always to attempt violently to bend the people to their theories of subjection. The bulk of mankind on their part are not excessively curious concerning any theories, whilst they are really happy; and one sure symptom of an ill conducted state, is the propensity of the people to resort to them.

But when subjects, by a long course of such ill conduct, are once thoroughly inflamed, and the state itself violently distempered, the people must have some satisfaction to their feelings, more solid than a sophistical speculation on law and government. Such was our situation; and such a satisfaction was necessary to prevent recourse to arms; it was necessary towards laying them down; it will be necessary to prevent the taking them up again and again. Of what nature this satisfaction ought to be, I wish it had been the disposition of Parliament seriously to consider. It was certainly a deliberation that called for the exertion of all their wisdom.

I am, and ever have been, deeply sensible, of the difficulty of reconciling the strong presiding power, that is so useful towards the conservation of a vast, disconnected, infinitely diversified empire, with that liberty and safety of the provinces, which they must enjoy, . . . or they will not be provinces at all. I know, and have long felt, the difficulty of reconciling the unwieldy haughtiness of a great ruling nation, habituated to command, pampered by enormous wealth, and confident from a long course of prosperity and victory, to the high spirit of free dependencies, animated with the first glow and activity of juvenile heat, and assuming to themselves as their birth-right, some part of that very pride which oppresses them. They who perceive no difficulty in reconciling these tempers . . . are much above my capacity, or much below the magnitude of the business. Of one thing I am perfectly clear, that it is not by deciding the suit, but by compromising the difference, that peace can be restored or kept. They who would put an end to such quarrels, by declaring roundly in favour of the whole demands of either party, have mistaken, in my humble opinion, the office of a mediator.

The war is now of full two years standing; the controversy of many more. In different periods of the dispute, different methods of reconciliation were to be pursued. I mean to trouble you with a short state of things at the most important of these periods, in order to give you a more distinct idea of our policy with regard to this most delicate of all objects. The Colonies were from the beginning subject to the legislative of Great-Britain, on principles which they never examined; and we permitted to them many local privileges, without asking how they agreed with that legislative authority. Modes of administration were formed in an insensible, and very unsystematick manner. But they gradually adapted themselves to the varying condition of things.—What was first a single kingdom stretched into an empire; and an imperial superintendency of some kind or other became necessary. Parliament, from a mere representative of the people, and a guardian of popular privileges for its own immediate constituents, grew into a mighty sovereign. Instead of

being a control on the Crown on its own behalf, it communicated a sort of strength to the Royal authority; which was wanted for the conservation of a new object, but which could not be safely trusted to the Crown alone. On the other hand, the Colonies advancing by equal steps, and governed by the same necessity, had formed within themselves, either by royal instruction, or royal charter, assemblies so exceedingly resembling a parliament, in all their forms, functions, and powers, that it was impossible they should not imbibe some opinion of a similar authority.

At the first designation of these assemblies, they were probably not intended for anything more, . . . than the municipal corporations within this Island, to which some at present love to compare them. But nothing in progression can rest on its original plan. We may as well think of rocking a grown man in the cradle of an infant. Therefore, as the Colonies prospered and encreased to a numerous and mighty people, spreading over a very great tract of the globe; it was natural that they should attribute to assemblies, so respectable in their formal constitution, some part of the dignity of the great nations which they represented. No longer tied to bye-laws, these assemblies made acts of all sorts and in all cases whatsoever. They levied money, not for parochial purposes, but upon regular grants to the Crown, following all the rules and principles of a Parliament, to which they approached every day more and more nearly. Those who think themselves wiser than Providence and stronger than the course of nature, may complain of all this variation, on the one side or the other, as their several humours and prejudices may lead them. But things could not be otherwise; and English Colonies must be had on these terms, or not had at all. In the mean time neither party felt any inconvenience from this double legislature, to which they had been formed by imperceptible habits, and old custom, the great support of all the governments in the world. Though these two legislatures were sometimes found perhaps performing the very same functions, they did not very grossly or systematically clash. In all likelyhood this arose from mere neglect: possibly from the natural operation of things, which, left to themselves, generally fall into their proper order. But whatever was the cause, it is certain, that a regular revenue by the authority of Parliament, for the support of civil and military establishments, seems not to have been thought of until the Colonies were too proud to submit, too strong to be forced, too enlightened not to see all the consequences which must arise from such a system.

If ever this scheme of taxation was to be pushed against the inclinations of the people, it was evident, that discussions must arise, which would let loose all the elements that composed this double constitution; would shew how much each of their members had departed from its original principles; and would discover contradictions in each legislature, as well to its own first principles, as to its relation to the other, very difficult if not absolutely impossible to be reconciled.

Therefore at the first fatal opening of this contest, the wisest course seemed to be, to put an end as soon as possible to the immediate causes of the dispute; and to quiet a discussion, not easily settled upon clear principles, and arising from claims, which pride would permit neither party to abandon, by resorting as nearly as possible to the old successful course. A mere repeal of the obnoxious tax, with a declaration of the legislative authority of this kingdom, was then fully sufficient to procure peace to *both sides*. Man is a creature of habit; and the first breach being of very short continuance, the Colonies fell back exactly into their antient state. The Congress has used an expression with regard to this pacification which appears to be truly significant. After the repeal of the Stamp Act, "the Colonies fell" says this assembly, "into their antient state of *unsuspecting confidence in the Mother Country*." This unsuspecting confidence is the true center of gravity amongst mankind, about which all the parts are at rest. It is this *unsuspecting confidence* that removes all difficulties, and reconciles all the contradictions which occur in the complexity of all antient puzzled political establishments. Happy are the rulers which have the secret of preserving it!

⁓

I had the happiness of giving my first votes in Parliament for that pacification. I was one of those almost unanimous members, who, in the necessary concessions of Parliament, would as much as possible have preserved its authority, and respected its honour. I could not at once tear from my heart prejudices which were dear to me, and which bore a resemblance to virtues. I had then, and I have still, my partialities. What Parliament gave up I wished to be given, as of grace, and favour, and affection, and not as a restitution of stolen goods. High dignity relented as it was soothed; and an act of benignity from old acknowledged greatness had its full effect on our dependencies. Our unlimited declaration of legislative authority produced not a single murmur. If this undefined power has become odious since that time, and full of horror to the Colonies, it is because the *unsuspicious confidence* is lost; and the parental affection, in the bosom of whose boundless authority they reposed their privileges, is become estranged and hostile.

It will be asked, if such was then my opinion of the mode of pacification, how I came to be the very person who moved, not only for a repeal of all the late coercive states, but for mutilating, by a positive law, the entireness of the legislative power of Parliament, and cutting off from it the whole right of taxation? I answer, because a different state of things requires a different conduct. When the dispute had gone to the last extremities (which no man laboured more to prevent than I did) the concessions which had satisfied in the beginning, could satisfy no longer; the violation of tacit faith required explicit security. The same cause, which has introduced all formal compacts and covenants among men, made it necessary: I mean, habits of soreness, jealousy, and distrust. I parted with it, as with a limb: but as with a limb to save the body; and I would have parted with more, if more had been necessary. Anything rather than a fruitless, hopeless, unnatural civil war. This mode of yielding would, it is said, give way to independency, without a war. I am persuaded from the nature of things, and from every information, that it would have had a directly contrary effect. But if it had this effect, I confess, that I should prefer independency without war, to independency with it; and I have so much trust in the inclinations and prejudices of mankind, and so little in anything else, that I should expect ten times more benefit to this Kingdom from the affection of America, though under a separate establishment, than from her perfect submission to the Crown and Parliament, accompanied with her terror, disgust, and abhorrence. Bodies tied together by so unnatural a bond of union, as mutual hatred, are only connected to their ruin.

One hundred and ten respectable Members of Parliament voted for that concession. Many, not present when the motion was made, were of the sentiments of those who voted. I knew it would then have made peace. I am not without hopes that it would do so at present, if it were adopted. No benefit, no revenue, could be lost by it. For be fully assured, that, of all the phantoms that ever deluded the fond hopes of a credulous world, a parliamentary revenue in the Colonies is the most perfectly chimerical. Your breaking them to any subjection, far from relieving your burthens (the pretext for this war,) will never pay that military force which will be kept up to the destruction of their liberties and yours. I risque nothing in this prophecy.

⮑

I am aware that the age is not what we all wish. But I am sure, that the only means of checking its precipitate degeneracy, is heartily to concur with whatever is the best in our time; and to have some more correct standard of judging what the best is, than the transient and uncertain favour of a court. If once we are able to find, and can prevail on ourselves to strengthen an union of such men, whatever accidentally becomes indisposed to ill-exercised power, even by the ordinary operation of human passions, must join with that society; and cannot long be joined, without in some degree assimilating to it. Virtue will catch as well as vice by contact; and the public stock of honest manly principle will daily accumulate. We are not too nicely to scrutinize motives as long as action is irreproachable. It is enough, . . . to deal out its infamy to convicted guilt and declared apostasy.

To act on the principles of the constitution, with the best men the time affords, has been from the beginning the rule of my conduct; and I mean to continue it, as long as such a body as I have described, can by any possibility be kept together. For I should think it the most dreadful of all offences, not only towards the present generation but to all the future, if I were to do any thing which could make the minutest breach in this great conservatory of free principles. Those who perhaps have the same intentions, but are separated by some little political animosities, will, I hope, discern at last, how little conducive it is to any rational purpose, to lower its reputation. For my part, Gentlemen, from much experience, from no little thinking, and from comparing a great variety of things, I am thoroughly persuaded, that the last hopes of preserving the spirit of the English Constitution, or of re-uniting the dissipated members of the English race upon a common plan of tranquility and liberty, does entirely depend on the firm and lasting union of such men; and above all on their keeping themselves from that despair, which is so very apt to fall on those, whom a violence of character, and a mixture of ambitious views, do not support through a long, painful, and unsuccessful struggle.

There never, Gentlemen, was a period in which the stedfastness of some men has been put to so sore a trial. It is not very difficult for well-formed minds to abandon their interest; but the separation of fame and virtue is an harsh divorce. Liberty is in danger of being made unpopular to Englishmen. Contending for an imaginary power, we begin to acquire the spirit of domination, and to lose the relish of honest equality. The principles of our forefathers become suspected to us, because we see them animating the present opposition of our children. The faults which grow out of the luxuriance of freedom, appear much more shocking to us, than the base vices which are generated from the rankness of servitude. Accordingly the least resistance to power appears more inexcuseable in our eyes than the greatest abuses of authority. All dread of a standing military force is looked upon as a superstitious panick. All shame of calling in foreigners and savages in a civil contest is worn off. We grow indifferent to the consequences inevitable to ourselves from the plan of ruling half the empire by a mercenary sword. We are taught to believe, that a desire of domineering over our countrymen, is love to our country; that those who hate civil war abet rebellion; and that the amiable and conciliatory virtues of lenity, moderation, and tenderness to the privileges of those who depend on this kingdom, are a sort of treason to the state.

It is impossible that we should remain long in a situation, which breeds such notions and dispositions, without some great alteration in the national character. Those ingenuous and feeling minds, who are so fortified against all other things, and so unarmed to whatever approaches in the shape of disgrace, finding the principles, which they considered as sure means of honour, to be grown into disrepute, will retire disheartened and disgusted. Those of a more robust make, the bold, able, ambitious men, who pay some part of their court to power through the people, and substitute the voice of transient opinion in the place of true glory, will give into the general mode. The superior understandings, which ought to correct vulgar prejudice, will confirm and aggravate its errors. Many things have been long operating towards a gradual change in our principles. But this American war has done more in a very few years than all the other causes could have effected in a century. It is therefore not on its own separate account, but because of its attendant circumstances, that I consider its continuance, or its ending in any way but that of an honourable and liberal accommodation, as the greatest evils which can befal us. For that reason I have troubled you with this long letter. For that reason I intreat you again and again, neither to be perswaded, shamed, or frighted out of the principles that have hitherto led so many of you to abhor the war, its cause, and its consequences. Let us not be amongst the first who renounce the maxims of our forefathers.

I have the honour to be, GENTLEMEN,
Your most obedient, and faithful humble Servant,

EDMUND BURKE
Beaconsfield, April 3, 1777

P.S. You may communicate this Letter in any manner you think proper to my Constituents.

On India

Introductory Note to
Speech on Fox's India Bill
(1783)

As indicated in Part 1, Burke's interest in the reform of British imperial policy in India took time to develop. He initially opposed efforts to reform the East India Company in the late 1760s and for most of the 1770s. In the late 1770s, Burke's attitude toward British policy and the behavior of the East India Company underwent a dramatic transformation. Burke became a leading figure in the parliamentary select committee charged with investigating the East India Company, and he wrote the famous Ninth *and* Eleventh Reports of the Select Committee. *Burke's involvement with the committee acted as a catalyst for his growing opposition to the practices of the East India Company and Parliament's acquiescence in such practices. In 1783 a coalition headed by Charles Fox and Lord North formed an administration that wanted to take action with regard to India. As the coalition's leading expert on India, Burke became the engine of Indian reform by drafting legislation known as Fox's India Bill to make the East India*

Company accountable to Parliament. His Speech on Fox's India Bill *was the first major parliamentary address in which Burke championed reform of the East India Company and British imperial policy in India; it thus represented the culmination of his shift away from his earlier opposition to reform.*

The themes of Speech on Fox's India Bill, *brought to life through vivid details and information about the abusive practices of the East India Company, include the undermining of Parliament's authority, the corruption of the British constitution engendered by the "instrument of influence" found in the ill-gotten fortunes of the company's agents, and the application of universal notions of human justice to British imperial policy.*

Fox's bill was defeated in Parliament, which played a major role in the fall of the Fox-North coalition in 1784. William Pitt won the general election that year with the financial backing of the East India Company and its supporters. Although this turn of events left Burke distraught because it reflected the power of those responsible for the destruction of India, Burke's determination to have justice for the Indian peoples gathered new strength in the face of rejection. ∿

Speech on
Fox's India Bill
(1783)

MR. SPEAKER,

I thank you for pointing to me. I really wished much to engage your attention in an early stage of the debate. I have been long very deeply, though perhaps ineffectually, engaged in the preliminary enquiries, which have continued without intermission for some years.[1] Though I have felt, with some degree of sensibility, the natural and inevitable impressions of the several matters of fact, as they have been successively disclosed, I have not at any time attempted to trouble you on the merits of the subject; and very little on any of the points which incidentally arose in the course of our proceedings. But I should be sorry to be found totally silent upon this day. Our enquiries are now come to their final issue:—It is now to be determined whether the three years of laborious parliamentary research,[2] whether the twenty years of patient Indian suffering,[3] are to produce a substantial reform in our Eastern administration; or whether our knowledge of the grievances has abated our zeal for the correction of them, and whether our very enquiry into the evil was only a pretext to elude the remedy which is demanded from us by humanity, by justice, and by every principle of true policy. Depend upon it, this business cannot be indifferent to our fame. It will turn out a matter of great disgrace or great glory to the whole British nation. We are on a conspicuous stage, and the world marks our demeanour.

I am therefore a little concerned to perceive the spirit and temper in which the debate has been all along pursued, upon one side of the House. The declamation of the Gentlemen who oppose the bill has been abundant and vehement, but they have been reserved and even silent about the fitness or unfitness of the plan to attain the direct object it has in view. By some gentlemen it is taken up . . . as a point of law on a question of private property, and corporate franchise; by others it is regarded as the petty intrigue of a faction at court, and argued merely as it tends to set this man a little higher, or that a little lower in situation and power. All the void has been filled up with invectives against coalition;[4] with allusions to the loss of America; with the activity and inactivity of ministers. The total silence of these gentlemen concerning the interest and well-being of the people of India, and concerning the interest which this nation has in the commerce and revenues of that country, is a strong indication of the value which they set upon these objects.

⮌

For my part, I have thought myself bound, when a matter of this extraordinary weight came before me, not to consider (as some Gentlemen are so fond of doing) whether the bill originated from a Secretary of State

---

[1]Burke is probably referring to his participation on the parliamentary select committee that investigated British practices in India in the early 1780s. A separate secret committee conducted inquiries as well. He may in addition be alluding to the study of the East India Company he began in the mid–1770s.

[2]The work of the parliamentary select and secret committees started in 1781.

[3]Burke was dating this suffering from the expansion of British power in India after the British military victories over native Indian forces at Plassey in 1757 and Buxar in 1764.

---

[4]The coalition administration overseen by Charles Fox and Lord North.

for the home department,[5] or from a Secretary for the foreign;[6] from a minister of influence or a minister of the people; from Jacob or from Esau. I asked myself, and I asked myself nothing else, what part it was fit for a member of parliament, who has supplied a mediocrity of talents by the extreme of diligence, and who has thought himself obliged, by the research of years, to wind himself into the inmost recesses and labyrinths of the Indian detail, what part, I say, it became such a member of parliament to take, when a minister of state, in conformity to a recommendation from the throne, has brought before us a system for the better government of the territory and commerce of the East. In this light, and in this only, I will trouble you with my sentiments.

It is not only agreed but demanded, by the Right Honourable gentleman,[7] and by those who act with him, that a *whole* system ought to be produced; that it ought not to be an *half measure;* that it ought to be no *palliative;* but a legislative provision, vigorous, substantial, and effective.—I believe that no man who understands the subject can doubt for a moment; that those must be the conditions of any thing deserving the name of a reform in the Indian government; that any thing short of them would not only be delusive, but, in this matter which admits no medium, noxious in the extreme.

⤺

But though there are no direct, yet there are various collateral objections made; objections from the effects, which this plan of reform for Indian administration may have on the privileges of great public bodies in England; from its probable influence on the constitutional rights, or on the freedom and integrity of the several branches of the legislature.

Before I answer these objections I must beg leave to observe, that if we are not able to contrive some method of governing India *well,* which will not of necessity become the means of governing Great Britain *ill,* a ground is laid for their eternal separation; but none for sacrificing the people of that country to our constitution. I am however far from being persuaded that any such incompatibility of interest does at all exist. On the contrary I am certain that every means, effectual to preserve India from oppression, is a guard to preserve the British constitution from its worst corruption. To shew this, I will consider the objections, which I think are four.

1st. That the bill is an attack on the chartered rights of men.

2dly. That it increases the influence of the crown.

3dly. That it does *not* increase, but diminishes, the influence of the crown, in order to promote the interests of certain ministers and their party.

4thly. That it deeply affects the national credit.

As to the first of these objections; I must observe that the phrase of "the chartered rights *of men,"* is full of affectation; and very unusual in the discussion of privileges conferred by charters of the present description. But it is not difficult to discover what end that ambiguous mode of expression, so often reiterated, is meant to answer.

The rights of *men,* that is to say, the natural rights of mankind, are indeed sacred

---

[5]Lord North.

[6]Fox.

[7]William Pitt (the Younger), who was at this time the House of Commons leader of the opposition to the Fox-North coalition.

things; and if any public measure is proved mischievously to affect them, the objection ought to be fatal to that measure, even if no charter at all could be set up against it. If these natural rights are further affirmed and declared by express covenants, if they are clearly defined and secured against chicane, against power, and authority, by written instruments and positive engagements, they are in a still better condition: they partake not only of the sanctity of the object so secured, but of that solemn public faith itself, which secures an object of such importance. Indeed this formal recognition, by the sovereign power, of an original right in the subject, can never be subverted, but by rooting up the holding radical principles of government, and even of society itself. The charters, which we call by distinction *great,* are public instruments of this nature; I mean the charters of King John and King Henry the Third.[8] The things secured by these instruments may, without any deceitful ambiguity, be very fitly called the *chartered rights of men.*

These charters have made the very name of a charter dear to the heart of every Englishman—But, Sir, there may be, and there are charters, not only different in nature, but formed on principles the *very reverse* of those of the great charter. Of this kind is the charter of the East India Company. *Magna charta* is a charter to restrain power, and to destroy monopoly. The East India charter is a charter to establish monopoly, and to create power. Political power and commercial monopoly are *not* the rights of men; and the rights to them derived from charters, it is fallacious and sophistical to call "the chartered rights of men." These chartered rights, . . . do at least suspend the natural rights of mankind at large; and in their very frame and constitution are liable to fall into a direct violation of them.

It is a charter of this latter description (that is to say a charter of power and monopoly) which is affected by the bill before you. The bill, Sir, does, without question, affect it; it does affect it essentially and substantially. But, having stated to you of what description the chartered rights are which this bill touches, I feel no difficulty at all in acknowledging the existence of those chartered rights, in their fullest extent. They belong to the Company in the surest manner; and they are secured to that body by every sort of public sanction. They are stamped by the faith of the King; they are stamped by the faith of Parliament; they have been bought for money, for money honestly and fairly paid; they have been bought for valuable consideration, over and over again.

I therefore freely admit to the East India Company their claim to exclude their fellow-subjects from the commerce of half the globe. I admit their claim to administer an annual territorial revenue of seven millions sterling; to command an army of sixty thousand men; and to dispose, (under the control of a sovereign imperial discretion, and with the due observance of the natural and local law) of the lives and fortunes of thirty millions of their fellow-creatures. All this they possess by charter and by acts of parliament, (in my opinion) without a shadow of controversy.

Those who carry the rights and claims of the Company the furthest do not contend for more than this; and all this I freely grant. But granting all this, they must grant to me in my turn, that all political power which is set over men, and that all privilege claimed or exercised in exclusion of them, being wholly artificial, and for so much, a derogation from the

---

[8]The Magna Carta, accepted by King John in 1215 and reissued by King Henry III in 1216, 1217, 1225, and 1264.

natural equality of mankind at large, ought to be some way or other exercised ultimately for their benefit.

If this is true with regard to every species of political dominion, and every description of commercial privilege, none of which can be original self-derived rights, or grants for the mere private benefit of the holders, then such rights, or privileges, or whatever else you choose to call them, are all in the strictest sense a *trust;* and it is of the very essence of every trust to be rendered *accountable;* and even totally to *cease,* when it substantially varies from the purposes for which alone it could have a lawful existence.

This I conceive, Sir, to be true of trusts of power vested in the highest hands, and of such as seem to hold of no human creature. But about the application of this principle to subordinate *derivative* trusts, I do not see how a controversy can be maintained. To whom then would I make the East India Company accountable? Why, to Parliament to be sure; to Parliament, from whom their trust was derived; to Parliament, which alone is capable of comprehending the magnitude of its object, and its abuse; and alone capable of an effectual legislative remedy. The very charter, which is held out to exclude Parliament from correcting malversation with regard to the high trust vested in the Company, is the very thing which at once gives a title and imposes a duty on us to interfere with effect, wherever power and authority originating from ourselves are perverted from their purposes, and become instruments of wrong and violence.

If Parliament, Sir, had nothing to do with this charter, we might have some sort of Epicurean excuse to stand aloof, indifferent spectators of what passes in the Company's name in India and in London. But if we are the very cause of the evil, we

are in a special manner engaged to the redress; and for us passively to bear with oppressions committed under the sanction of our own authority, is in truth and reason for this House to be an active accomplice in the abuse.

That the power notoriously, grossly, abused has been bought from us is very certain. But this circumstance, which is urged against the bill, becomes an additional motive for our interference; lest we should be thought to have sold the blood of millions of men, for the base consideration of money. We sold, I admit, all that we had to sell; that is our authority, not our controul. We had not a right to make a market of our duties.

I ground myself therefore on this principle—that if the abuse is proved, the contract is broken; and we re-enter into all our rights; that is, into the exercise of all our duties. Our own authority is indeed as much a trust originally, as the Company's authority is a trust derivatively; and it is the use we make of the resumed power that must justify or condemn us in the resumption of it. When we have perfected the plan laid before us by the Right Honourable mover,[9] the world will then see what it is we destroy, and what it is we create. By that test we stand or fall; and by that test I trust that it will be found in the issue, that we are going to supersede a charter abused to the full extent of all the powers which it could abuse, and exercised in the plenitude of despotism, tyranny, and corruption; and that, in one and the same plan, we provide a real chartered security for the *rights of men* cruelly violated under that charter.

This bill, and those connected with it, are intended to form the *Magna Charta* of Hindostan. Whatever the treaty of West-

---

[9]Fox.

phalia[10] is to the liberty of the princes and free cities of the empire,[11] and to the three religions there professed—Whatever the great charter, the statute of tallage, the petition of right, and the declaration of right,[12] are to Great Britain, these bills are to the people of India. Of this benefit, I am certain, their condition is capable; and when I know that they are capable of more, my vote shall most assuredly be for our giving to the full extent of their capacity of receiving; and no charter of dominion shall stand as a bar in my way to their charter of safety and protection.

The strong admission I have made of the Company's rights . . . binds me to do a great deal. I do not presume to condemn those who argue *a priori*, against the propriety of leaving such extensive political powers in the hands of a company of merchants.[13] I know much is, and much more may be said against such a system. But, with my particular ideas and sentiments, I cannot go that way to work. I feel an insuperable reluctance in giving my hand to destroy any established institution of government, upon a theory, however plausible it may be. My experience in life teaches me nothing clear upon the subject. I have known merchants with the sentiments and the abilities of great statesmen; and I have seen persons in the rank of statesmen, with the conceptions and character of pedlars. Indeed, my observation has furnished me

with nothing that is to be found in any habits of life or education, which tends wholly to disqualify men for the functions of government, but that, by which the power of exercising those functions is very frequently obtained, I mean, a spirit and habits of low cabal and intrigue; which I have never, in one instance, seen united with a capacity for sound and manly policy.

To justify us in taking the administration of their affairs out of the hands of the East India Company, on my principles, I must see several conditions. 1st. The object affected by the abuse should be great and important. 2d. The abuse affecting this great object ought to be a great abuse. 3d. It ought to be habitual, and not accidental. 4th. It ought to be utterly incurable in the body as it now stands constituted. All this ought to be made as visible to me as the light of the sun, before I should strike off an atom of their charter. A Right Honourable gentleman[14] has said, and said I think but once, and that very slightly . . . that "there are abuses in the Company's government." If that were all, the scheme of the mover of this bill, the scheme of his learned friend,[15] and his own scheme of reformation (if he has any) are all equally needless. There are, and must be, abuses in all governments. It amounts to no more than a nugatory proposition. But before I consider of what nature these abuses are, of which the gentleman speaks so very lightly, permit me to recall to your recollection the map of the country which this abused chartered right affects. This I shall do, that you may judge whether in that map I can discover any thing like the first of my con-

---

[10]The treaty of Westphalia of 1648 settled the Thirty Years' War in Europe and provided the foundation for the modern international system of sovereign states.

[11]The Holy Roman Empire.

[12]Magna Carta (1215), Statute of Tallage (1297), Petition of Right (1629), and Bill of Rights (1689).

[13]Burke may have had in mind here Adam Smith's opposition to the East India Company and its commercial and other activities.

[14]Pitt.

[15]Henry Dundas, who chaired the parliamentary secret committee that investigated the East India Company, tabled an East India Company reform bill in April 1783.

ditions; that is, Whether the object affected by the abuse of the East India Company's power be of importance sufficient to justify the measure and means of reform applied to it in this bill.

With very few, and those inconsiderable intervals, the British dominion, either in the Company's name, or in the names of princes absolutely dependent upon the Company, extends from the mountains that separate India from Tartary, to Cape Comorin, that is, one-and-twenty degrees of latitude!

In the northern parts it is a solid mass of land, about eight hundred miles in length, and four or five hundred broad. As you go southward, it becomes narrower for a space. It afterwards dilates; but narrower or broader, you possess the whole eastern and north-eastern coast of that vast country, quite from the borders of Pegu.—Bengal, Bahar, and Orissa, with Benares (now unfortunately in our immediate possession) measure 161,978 square English miles; a territory considerably larger than the whole kingdom of France. Oude, with its dependent provinces, is 53,286 square miles, not a great deal less than England. The Carnatic, with Tanjour and the Circars, is 65,948 square miles, very considerably larger than England; and the whole of the Company's dominion comprehending Bombay and Salsette, amounts to 281,412 square miles; which forms a territory larger than any European dominion, Russia and Turkey excepted. Through all that vast extent of country there is not a man who eats a mouthful of rice but by permission of the East India Company.

So far with regard to the extent. The population of this great empire is not easy to be calculated. When the countries, of which it is composed, came into our possession, they were all eminently peopled, and eminently productive; though at that time considerably declined from their antient prosperity. But since they are come into our hands!—! However if we take the period of our estimate immediately before the utter desolation of the Carnatic, and if we allow for the havoc which our government had even then made in these regions, we cannot, in my opinion, rate the population at much less than thirty millions of souls; more than four times the number of persons in the island of Great Britain.

My next enquiry to that of the number, is the quality and description of the inhabitants. This multitude of men does not consist of an abject and barbarous populace; much less of gangs of savages, like the Guaranies and Chiquitos, who wander on the waste borders of the river of Amazons, or the Plate; but a people for ages civilized and cultivated; cultivated by all the arts of polished life, whilst we were yet in the woods. There, have been (and still the skeletons remain) princes once of great dignity, authority, and opulence. There, are to be found the chiefs of tribes and nations. There is to be found an antient and venerable priesthood, the depository of their laws, learning, and history, the guides of the people whilst living, and their consolation in death; a nobility of great antiquity and renown; a multitude of cities, not exceeded in population and trade by those of the first class in Europe; merchants and bankers, individual houses of whom have once vied in capital with the Bank of England; whose credit had often supported a tottering state, and preserved their governments in the midst of war and desolation; millions of ingenious manufacturers and mechanicks; millions of the most diligent, and not the least intelligent, tillers of the earth. Here are to be found almost all the religions professed by men, the Bramincal, the Mussulmen, the Eastern and the Western Christians.

If I were to take the whole aggregate of our possessions there, I should compare it, as the nearest parallel I can find, with the empire of Germany. Our immediate possessions I should compare with the Austrian dominions, and they would not suffer in the comparison. The Nabob of Oude might stand for the King of Prussia, the Nabob of Arcot I would compare, as superior in territory, and equal in revenue, to the Elector of Saxony. Cheyt Sing, the Rajah of Benares, might well rank with the Prince of Hesse at least; and the Rajah of Tanjore (though hardly equal in extent of dominion, superior in revenue) to the Elector of Bavaria. The Polygars and the northern Zemindars, and other great chiefs, might well class with the rest of the Princes, Dukes, Counts, Marquisses, and Bishops in the empire; all of whom I mention to honour, and surely without disparagement to any or all of those most respectable princes and grandees.

All this vast mass, composed of so many orders and classes of men, is again infinitely diversified by manners, by religion, by hereditary employment, through all their possible combinations. This renders the handling of India a matter in an high degree critical and delicate. But oh! it has been handled rudely indeed. Even some of the reformers seem to have forgot that they had any thing to do but to regulate the tenants of a manor, or the shopkeepers of the next county town.

It is an empire of this extent, of this complicated nature, of this dignity and importance, that I have compared to Germany, and the German government; not for an exact resemblance, but as a sort of a middle term, by which India might be approximated to our understandings, and if possible to our feelings; in order to awaken something of sympathy for the unfortunate natives, of which I am afraid we are

not perfectly susceptible, whilst we look at this very remote object through a false and cloudy medium.

My second condition, necessary to justify me in touching the charter, is, Whether the Company's abuse of their trust, with regard to this great object, be an abuse of great atrocity. I shall beg your permission to consider their conduct in two lights; first the political, and then the commercial. Their political conduct (for distinctness) I divide again into two heads; the external, in which I mean to comprehend their conduct in their federal capacity, as it relates to powers and states independent, or that not long since were such; the other internal, namely their conduct to the countries either immediately subject to the Company, or to those who, under the apparent government of native sovereigns, are in a state much lower, and much more miserable, than common subjection.

⌣

With regard therefore to the abuse of the external federal trust, I engage myself to you to make good these three positions:— First, I say, that from Mount Imaus, (or whatever else you call that large range of mountains that walls the northern frontier of India) where it touches us in the latitude of twenty-nine, to Cape Comorin, in the latitude of eight, that there is not a *single* prince, state, or potentate, great or small, in India, with whom they have come into contact, whom they have not sold. I say *sold,* though sometimes they have not been able to deliver according to their bargain.—Secondly, I say, that there is not a *single treaty* they have ever made, which they have not broken—Thirdly, I say, that there is not a single prince or state, who ever put any trust in the Company, who is not utterly ruined; and that none are in any degree secure or flourishing, but in the exact proportion to their settled distrust and irreconcileable enmity to this nation.

These assertions are universal. I say in the full sense *universal*. They regard the external and political trust only; but I shall produce others fully equivalent, in the internal. For the present, I shall content myself with explaining my meaning; and if I am called on for proof whilst these bills are depending . . . I will put my finger on the Appendixes to the Reports, or on papers of record in the House, or the Committees, which I have distinctly present to my memory, and which I think I can lay before you at half an hour's warning.

The first potentate sold by the Company for money was the Great Mogul— the descendant of Tamerlane.[16] This high personage, as high as human veneration can look at, is by every account amiable in his manners, respectable for his piety according to his mode, and accomplished in all the Oriental literature. All this, and the title derived under his *charter,* to all that we hold in India, could not save him from the general *sale.* Money is coined in his name; In his name justice is administered; He is prayed for in every temple through the countries we possess—But he was sold.

It is impossible, Mr. Speaker, not to pause here for a moment, to reflect on the inconstancy of human greatness, and the stupendous revolutions that have happened in our age of wonders. Could it be believed, when I entered into existence, or when you, a younger man, were born, that on this day, in this House, we should be employed in discussing the conduct of those British subjects who had disposed of

the power and person of the Grand Mogul? This is no idle speculation. Awful lessons are taught by it, and by other events, of which it is not yet too late to profit.

This is hardly a digression; but I return to the sale of the Mogul. Two districts, Corah and Allahabad, . . . were reserved as a royal demesne to the donor of a kingdom, and the rightful ruler of so many nations.—After withholding the tribute of £260,000 a year, which the Company was, by the *charter* they had received from this prince,[17] under the most solemn obligation to pay, these districts were sold to his chief minister Sujah ul Dowlah.[18] . . . The descendant of Tamerlane now stands in need almost of the common necessities of life; and in this situation we do not even allow him, as bounty, the smallest portion of what we owe him in justice.

The next sale was that of the whole nation of the Rohillas, which the grand salesman,[19] without a pretence of quarrel, and contrary to his own declared sense of duty and rectitude, sold to the same Sujah ul Dowlah.[20] He sold the people to utter *extirpation,* for the sum of four hundred thousand pounds. Faithfully was the bargain performed upon our side. Hafiz Rhamet, the most eminent of their chiefs, one of the bravest men of his time, and as famous throughout the East for the elegance of his literature, and the spirit of his poetical compositions (by which he supported the name of Hafiz) as for his courage, was invaded with an army of an hundred thousand men, and an English

[16]Tamerlane ("Timur the Lame") established an empire in the fourteenth century that stretched from Mongolia to the Mediterranean and included Persia and India.

[17]The Treaty of Allahabad of 1765, under which the East India Company got control of Bengal.

[18]Sold by Warren Hastings, governor of Bengal, in 1773.

[19]Hastings.

[20]In 1774.

brigade. This man, at the head of inferior forces, was slain valiantly fighting for his country. His head was cut off, and delivered for money to a barbarian. His wife and children, persons of that rank, were seen begging an handful of rice through the English camp. The whole nation, with inconsiderable exceptions, was slaughtered or banished. The country was laid waste with fire and sword; and that land distinguished above most others, by the chearful face of paternal government and protected labour, the chosen seat of cultivation and plenty, is now almost throughout a dreary desert, covered with rushes and briars, and jungles full of wild beasts.

The British officer who commanded in the delivery of the people thus sold, felt some compunction at his employment. He represented these enormous excesses to the president of Bengal, for which he received a severe reprimand from the civil governor; and I much doubt whether the breach caused by the conflict, between the compassion of the military and the firmness of the civil governor, be closed at this hour.

In Bengal, Seraja Dowla was sold to Mir Jaffier; Mir Jaffier was sold to Mir Cossim; and Mir Cossim was sold to Mir Jaffier again. The succession to Mir Jaffier was sold to his eldest son;—another son of Mir Jaffier, Mobarech ul Dowla, was sold to his step-mother—The Maratta empire was sold to Ragoba; and Ragoba was sold and delivered to the Peishwa of the Marattas. Both Ragoba and the Peishwa of the Marattas were offered to sale to the Rajah of Berar. Scindia, the chief of Malva, was offered to sale to the same Rajah; and the Subah of the Decan was sold to the great trader Mahomet Ali, Nabob of Arcot. To the same Nabob of Arcot they sold Hyder Ali and the kingdom of Mysore. To Mahomet Ali they twice sold the kingdom of Tanjore. To the same Mahomet Ali they

sold at least twelve sovereign princes, called the Polygars. But to keep things even, the territory of Tinnivelly, belonging to their Nabob, they would have sold to the Dutch; and to conclude the account of sales, their great customer, the Nabob of Arcot himself, and his lawful succession, has been sold to his second son, Amir ul Omrah, whose character, views, and conduct, are in the accounts upon your table. It remains with you whether they shall finally perfect this last bargain.[21]

～

My second assertion is, that the Company never has made a treaty which they have not broken. This position is so connected with that of the sales of provinces and kingdoms, with the negotiation of universal distraction in every part of India, that a very minute detail may well be spared on this point. It has not yet been contended, by any enemy to the reform, that they have observed any public agreement. When I hear that they have done so in any one instance . . . I shall speak to the particular treaty. The governor general has even amused himself and the Court of Directors[22] in a very singular letter to that board, in which he admits he has not been very delicate with regard to public faith; and he goes so far as to state a regular estimate of the sums which the Company would have lost, or never acquired, if the rigid ideas of public faith entertained by his colleagues had been observed. The learned gentleman over against me[23] has

---

[21]These sales and resales of titles and territories took place between 1757 and 1783.

[22]Of the East India Company. The court of directors was the London-based organ responsible for operating the company.

[23]Dundas.

indeed saved me much trouble. On a former occasion he obtained no small credit, for the clear and forcible manner in which he stated what we have not forgot, and I hope he has not forgot, that universal systematic breach of treaties which had made the British faith proverbial in the East.

⤳

My third assertion, relative to the abuse made of the right of war and peace is, that there are none who have ever confided in us who have not been utterly ruined. ... There is proof more than enough in the condition of the Mogul; in the slavery and indigence of the Nabob of Oude; the exile of the Rajah of Benares; the beggary of the Nabob of Bengal; the undone and captive condition of the Rajah and kingdom of Tanjour; the destruction of the Polygars; and lastly, in the destruction of the Nabob of Arcot himself, who when his dominions were invaded was found entirely destitute of troops, provisions, stores, and (as he asserts) of money, being a million in debt to the Company, and four millions to others: the many millions which he had extorted from so many extirpated princes and their desolated countries having (as he has frequently hinted) been expended for the ground-rent of his mansion-house in an alley in the suburbs of Madras. Compare the condition of all these princes with the power and authority of all the Maratta states; with the independence and dignity of the Soubah of the Decan; and the mighty strength, the resources, and the manly struggle of Hyder Ali; and then the House will discover the effects, on every power in India, of an easy confidence, or of a rooted distrust in the faith of the Company.

These are some of my reasons, grounded on the abuse of the external political trust of that body, for thinking myself not only justified but bound to declare against those chartered rights which produce so many wrongs. I should deem myself the wickedest of men, if any vote of mine could contribute to the continuance of so great an evil.

Now, Sir, according to the plan I proposed, I shall take notice of the Company's internal government, as it is exercised first on the dependent provinces, and then as it affects those under the direct and immediate authority of that body. And here, Sir, before I enter into the spirit of their interior government, permit me to observe to you, upon a few of the many lines of difference which are to be found between the vices of the Company's government, and those of the conquerors who preceded us in India; that we may be enabled a little the better to see our way in an attempt to the necessary reformation.

The several irruptions of Arabs, Tartars, and Persians, into India were, for the greater part, ferocious, bloody, and wasteful in the extreme: our entrance into the dominion of that country was, as generally, with small comparative effusion of blood; being introduced by various frauds and delusions, and by taking advantage of the incurable, blind, and senseless animosity, which the several country powers bear towards each other, rather than by open force. But the difference in favour of the first conquerors is this; the Asiatic conquerors very soon abated of their ferocity, because they made the conquered country their own. They rose or fell with the rise or fall of the territory they lived in. Fathers there deposited the hopes of their posterity; and children there beheld the monuments of their fathers. Here their lot was finally cast; and it is the natural wish of all, that their lot should not be cast in a bad land. Poverty, sterility, and desolation, are not a recreating prospect to the eye of man; and there are very few who can bear to grow old among the curses of a whole people. If their passion or their avarice drove the Tartar lords to acts of rapacity or tyranny, there was time enough, even in the short life of man, to bring round the ill effects of an abuse of power upon the power itself. If hoards were made by violence and tyranny, they were still domestic hoards; and domestic profusion, or the rapine of a more powerful and prodigal hand, restored them to the people. With many disorders, and with few political checks upon power, Nature had still fair play; the sources of acquisition were not dried up; and therefore the trade, the manufactures, and the commerce of the country flourished. Even avarice and usury itself operated, both for the preservation and the employment of national wealth. The husbandman and manufacturer paid heavy interest, but then they augmented the fund from whence they were again to borrow. Their resources were dearly bought, but they were sure; and the general stock of the community grew by the general effort.

But under the English government all this order is reversed. The Tartar invasion was mischievous; but it is our protection that destroys India. It was their enmity, but it is our friendship. Our conquest there, after twenty years, is as crude as it was the first day. The natives scarcely know what it is to see the grey head of an Englishman. Young men (boys almost) govern there, without society, and without sympathy with the natives. They have no more social habits with the people, than if they still resided in England; nor indeed any species of intercourse but that which is necessary to making a sudden fortune, with a view to a remote settlement. Animated with all the avarice of age, and all the impetuosity of youth, they roll in one

after another; wave after wave; and there is nothing before the eyes of the natives but an endless, hopeless prospect of new flights of birds of prey and passage, with appetites continually renewing for a food that is continually wasting. Every rupee of profit made by an Englishman is lost for ever to India. With us are no retributory superstitions, by which a foundation of charity compensates, through ages, to the poor, for the rapine and injustice of a day. With us no pride erects stately monuments which repair the mischiefs which pride had produced, and which adorn a country, out of its own spoils. England has erected no churches, no hospitals, no palaces, no schools; England has built no bridges, made no high roads, cut no navigations, dug out no reservoirs. Every other conqueror of every other description has left some monument, either of state or beneficence, behind him. Were we to be driven out of India this day, nothing would remain, to tell that it had been possessed, during the inglorious period of our dominion, by any thing better than the ouran-outang or the tiger.

There is nothing in the boys we send to India worse than the boys whom we are whipping at school, or that we see trailing a pike, or bending over a desk at home. But as English youth in India drink the intoxicating draught of authority and dominion before their heads are able to bear it, and as they are full grown in fortune long before they are ripe in principle, neither nature nor reason have any opportunity to exert themselves for remedy of the excesses of their premature power. The consequences of their conduct, which in good minds, . . . might produce penitence or amendment, are unable to pursue the rapidity of their flight. Their prey is lodged in England; and the cries of India are given to seas and winds, to be blown about, in every breaking up of the monsoon, over a remote and unhearing ocean. In India all the vices operate by which sudden fortune is acquired; in England are often displayed, by the same persons, the virtues which dispense hereditary wealth. Arrived in England, the destroyers of the nobility and gentry of a whole kingdom will find the best company in this nation, at a board of elegance and hospitality. Here the manufacturer and husbandman will bless the just and punctual hand, that in India has torn the cloth from the loom, or wrested the scanty portion of rice and salt from the peasant of Bengal, or wrung from him the very opium in which he forgot his oppressions and his oppressor. They marry into your families; they enter into your senate; they ease your estates by loans; they raise their value by demand; they cherish and protect your relations which lie heavy on your patronage; and there is scarcely an house in the kingdom that does not feel some concern and interest that makes all reform of our eastern government appear officious and disgusting; and, on the whole, a most discouraging attempt. In such an attempt you hurt those who are able to return kindness or to resent injury. If you succeed, you save those who cannot so much as give you thanks. All these things shew the difficulty of the work we have on hand: but they shew its necessity too. Our Indian government is in its best state a grievance. It is necessary that the correctives should be uncommonly vigorous; and the work of men sanguine, warm, and even impassioned in the cause. But it is an arduous thing to plead against abuses of a power which originates from your own country, and affects those whom we are used to consider as strangers.

I shall certainly endeavour to modulate myself to this temper; though I am sensible that a cold style of describing actions which appear to me in a very affecting light, is equally contrary to the justice due to the people, and to all genuine human feelings about them. I ask pardon of truth and nature for this compliance. But I shall be very sparing of epithets either to persons or things. It has been said (and, with regard to one of them, with truth) that Tacitus and Machiavel,[24] by their cold way of relating enormous crimes, have in some sort appeared not to disapprove them; that they seem a sort of professors of the art of tyranny, and that they corrupt the minds of their readers by not expressing the detestation and horror that naturally belong to horrible and detestable proceedings. But we are in general, Sir, so little acquainted with Indian details; the instruments of oppression under which the people suffer are so hard to be understood; and even the very names of the sufferers are so uncouth and strange to our ears, that it is very difficult for our sympathy to fix upon these objects. I am sure that some of us have come down stairs from the committee-room, with impressions on our minds, which to us were the inevitable results of our discoveries, yet if we should venture to express ourselves in the proper language of our sentiments, to other gentlemen not at all prepared to enter into the cause of them, nothing could appear more harsh and dissonant, more violent and unaccountable, than our language and behaviour. All these circumstances are not, I confess, very favourable to the idea of our attempting to govern India at all. But

---

[24]Tacitus, a Roman public official and historian who wrote about the Roman Empire in his *Histories* (c. 109) and *Annals* (c. 117); and Niccolò Machiavelli, Florentine public official and writer, whose most famous works are *The Prince* (1513) and *Discourses* (1517).

there we are; there we are placed by the Sovereign Disposer: and we must do the best we can in our situation. The situation of man is the preceptor of his duty.

Upon the plan which I laid down, and to which I beg leave to return, I was considering the conduct of the Company to those nations which are indirectly subject to their authority. The most considerable of the dependent princes is the Nabob of Oude. . . .

In the year 1779 the Nabob of Oude represented, through the British resident at his court, that the number of Company's troops stationed in his dominions was a main cause of his distress; and that all those which he was not bound by treaty to maintain should be withdrawn, as they had greatly diminished his revenue, and impoverished his country. . . .

&

It was now to be seen what steps the governor general and council took for the relief of this distressed country, long labouring under the vexations of men, and now stricken by the hand of God. The case of a general famine is known to relax the severity even of the most rigorous government.—Mr. Hastings does not deny, or shew the least doubt of the fact. The representation is humble, and almost abject. On this representation from a great prince, of the distress of his subjects, Mr. Hastings falls into a violent passion; such as (it seems) would be unjustifiable in any one who speaks of any part of *his* conduct. He declares "that the *demands,* the *tone* in which they were asserted, and the *season* in which they were made, are all equally alarming, and appear to him to require an adequate degree of firmness in this board, in *opposition* to them." He proceeds to deal out very unreserved language, on the person and character of the Nabob and his

ministers. He declares, that in a division between him and the Nabob, *"the strongest must decide."* With regard to the urgent and instant necessity, from the failure of the crops, he says "that *perhaps* expedients *may be found* for affording a *gradual* relief from the burthen of which he so heavily complains, and it shall be my endeavour to seek them out:" and, lest he should be suspected of too much haste to alleviate sufferings, and to remove violence, he says, "that these must be *gradually* applied, and their complete *effect* may be *distant;* and this I conceive *is all* he can claim of right."

This complete effect of his lenity is distant indeed. Rejecting this demand (as he calls the Nabob's abject supplication) he attributes it, as he usually does of all things of the kind, to the division in their government; and says, "this is a powerful motive with *me* (however inclined I might be, *upon any other occasion,* to yield to some *part* of his demand) to give them an *absolute and unconditional refusal* upon the present; and even *to bring to punishment, if my influence can produce that effect, those incendiaries who have endeavoured to make themselves the instruments of division between us."*

Here, Sir, is much heat and passion; but no more consideration of the distress of the country, from a failure of the means of subsistence, and (if possible) the worse evil of an useless and licentious soldiery, than if they were the most contemptible of all trifles. A letter is written in consequence, in such a style of lofty despotism, as I believe has hitherto been unexampled and unheard of in the records of the East. The troops were continued. The *gradual* relief, whose effect was to be so *distant,* has *never* been substantially and beneficially applied—and the country is ruined.

&

The invariable course of the Company's policy is this: Either they set up some prince too odious to maintain himself without the necessity of their assistance; or they soon render him odious, by making him the instrument of their government. In that case troops are bountifully sent to him to maintain his authority. That he should have no want of assistance, a civil gentleman, called a Resident, is kept at his court, who, under pretence of providing duly for the pay of these troops, gets assignments on the revenue into his hands. Under his provident management, debts soon accumulate; new assignments are made for these debts; until, step by step, the whole revenue, and with it the whole power of the country, is delivered into his hands. The military do not behold without a virtuous emulation the moderate gains of the civil department. They feel that, in a country driven to habitual rebellion by the civil government, the military is necessary; and they will not permit their services to go unrewarded. Tracts of country are delivered over to their discretion. Then it is found proper to convert their commanding officers into farmers of revenue. Thus, between the well paid civil, and well rewarded military establishment, the situation of the natives may be easily conjectured. The authority of the regular and lawful government is every where and in every point extinguished. Disorders and violences arise; they are repressed by other disorders and other violences. Wherever the collectors of the revenue, and the farming colonels and majors move, ruin is about them, rebellion before and behind them. The people in crowds fly out of the country; and the frontier is guarded by lines of troops, not to exclude an enemy, but to prevent the escape of the inhabitants.

By these means, in the course of not more than four or five years, this once opulent and flourishing country, which, by the accounts given in the Bengal consultations, yielded more than three crore of Sicca rupees, that is, above three millions sterling, annually, is reduced, as far as I can discover, in a matter purposely involved in the utmost perplexity, to less than one million three hundred thousand pounds, and that exacted by every mode of rigour that can be devised. To complete the business, most of the wretched remnants of this revenue are mortgaged, and delivered into the hands of the userers at Benares ... at an interest of near *thirty per cent. per annum.*

The revenues in this manner failing, they seized upon the estates of every person of eminence in the country, and, under the name of *resumption,* confiscated their property. I wish, Sir, to be understood universally and literally, when I assert, that there is not left one man of property and substance for his rank, in the whole of these provinces, in provinces which are nearly the extent of England and Wales taken together. Not one landholder, not one banker, not one merchant, not one even of those who usually perish last, the *ultimum moriens* in a ruined state, no one farmer of revenue.

One country for a while remained, which stood as an island in the midst of the grand waste of the Company's dominion. My Right Honourable friend, in his admirable speech on moving the bill, just touched the situation, the offences, and the punishment, of a native prince, called Fizulla Khân. This man, by policy and force, had protected himself from the general extirpation of the Rohilla chiefs. He was secured (if that were any security) by a treaty. It was stated to you, as it was stated by the enemies of that unfortunate man— "that the whole of his country *is* what the whole country of the Rohillas *was,* cultivated like a garden, without one neglected spot in it."—Another accuser says,

"Fyzoolah Khan though a bad soldier [that is the true source of his misfortune] has approved himself a good aumil; having, it is supposed, in the course of a few years, at least *doubled* the population, and revenue of his country."—In another part of the correspondence he is charged with making his country an asylum for the oppressed peasants, who fly from the territories of Oude. The improvement of his revenue, arising from this single crime, (which Mr. Hastings considers as tantamount to treason) is stated at an hundred and fifty thousand pounds a year.

Dr. Swift[25] somewhere says, that he who could make two blades of grass grow where but one grew before, was a greater benefactor to the human race than all the politicians that ever existed. This prince, who would have been deified by antiquity, . . . was, for those very merits, by name attacked by the Company's government, as a cheat, a robber, a traitor. In the same breath in which he was accused as a rebel, he was ordered at once to furnish 5,000 horse. On delay, or (according to the technical phrase, when any remonstrance is made to them) *"on evasion,"* he was declared a violator of treaties, and every thing he had was to be taken from him—Not one word, however, of horse in this treaty.

The territory of this Fizulla Khân, Mr. Speaker, is less than the county of Norfolk. It is an inland country, full seven hundred miles from any sea port, and not distinguished for any one considerable branch of manufacture whatsoever. From this territory several very considerable sums had at several times been paid to the British Resident. The demand of cavalry, without a shadow or decent pretext of right,

amounted to three hundred thousand a year more, at the lowest computation; and it is stated, by the last person sent to negotiate, as a demand of little use, if it could be complied with; but that the compliance was impossible, as it amounted to more than his territories could supply, if there had been no other demand upon him—three hundred thousand pounds a year from an inland country not so large as Norfolk!

After a variety of extortions and vexations, too fatiguing to you, too disgusting to me, to go through with, they found "that they ought to be in a better state to warrant forcible means;" they therefore contented themselves with a gross sum of 150,000 pounds, for their present demand. They offered him indeed an indemnity from their exactions in future, for three hundred thousand pounds more. But he refused to buy their securities; pleading (probably with truth) his poverty: but if the plea were not founded, in my opinion very wisely; not choosing to deal any more in that dangerous commodity of the Company's faith; and thinking it better to oppose distress and unarmed obstinacy to uncoloured exaction, than to subject himself to be considered as a cheat, if he should make a treaty in the least beneficial to himself. Thus they executed an exemplary punishment on Fizulla Khân for the culture of his country. But, conscious that the prevention of evils is the great object of all good regulation, they deprived him of the means of encreasing that criminal cultivation in future, by exhausting his coffers; and, that the population of his country should no more be a standing reproach and libel on the Company's government, they bound him, by a positive engagement, not to afford any shelter whatsoever

---

[25]Jonathan Swift, author of *Gulliver's Travels* (1726).

to the farmers and labourers who should seek refuge in his territories, from the exactions of the British Residents in Oude. When they had done all this effectually, they gave him a full and complete acquittance from all charges of rebellion, or of any intention to rebel, or of his having originally had any interest in, or any means of rebellion.

These intended rebellions are one of the Company's standing resources. When money has been thought to be heaped up any where, its owners are universally accused of rebellion, until they are acquitted of their money and their treasons at once. The money once taken, all accusation, trial, and punishment ends. It is so settled a resource, that I rather wonder how it comes to be omitted in the Directors account; but I take it for granted this omission will be supplied in their next edition. The Company stretched this resource to the full extent, when they accused two old women,[26] in the remotest corner of India (who could have no possible view or motive to raise disturbances) of being engaged in rebellion, with an intent to drive out the English nation in whose protection, purchased by money and secured by treaty, rested the sole hope of their existence. But the Company wanted money, and the old women *must* be guilty of a plot. They were accused of rebellion, and they were convicted of wealth. Twice had great sums been extorted from them, and as often had the British faith guaranteed the remainder. A body of British troops, with one of the military farmers general at their head, was sent to seize upon the castle in which these helpless women resided. Their chief eunuchs, who were their agents, their guardians, protectors, persons of high rank according to the Eastern manners and of

great trust, were thrown into dungeons, to make them discover their hidden treasures; and there they lie at present. The lands assigned for the maintenance of the women were seized and confiscated. Their jewels and effects were taken, and set up to a pretended auction in an obscure place, and bought at such a price as the gentlemen thought proper to give. No account has ever been transmitted of the articles or produce of this sale. What money was obtained is unknown, or what terms were stipulated for the maintenance of these despoiled and forlorn creatures; for by some particulars it appears as if an engagement of the kind was made.

Let me here remark, once for all, that though the act of 1773[27] requires that an account of all proceedings should be diligently transmitted, that this, like all the other injunctions of the law, is totally despised; and that half at least of the most important papers are intentionally withheld.

I wish you, Sir, to advert particularly, in this transaction, to the quality and the numbers of the persons spoiled, and the instrument by whom that spoil was made. These ancient matrons called the Begums or Princesses, were of the first birth and quality in India, the one mother, the other wife, of the late Nabob of Oude, Sujah Dowlah, a prince possessed of extensive and flourishing dominions, and the second man in the Mogul empire. This prince (suspicious, and not unjustly suspicious, of his son and successor) at his death committed his treasures and his family to the British faith. That family and household, consisted of *two thousand women;* to which were added two other seraglios of near kindred, and said to be extremely numerous, and (as I am well in-

---

[26]The begums of Oudh.

[27]The Regulating Act of 1773 adopted to reform the East India Company's operations.

formed) of about fourscore of the Nabob's children, with all the eunuchs, the ancient servants, and a multitude of the dependants of his splendid court. These were all to be provided, for present maintenance and future establishment, from the lands assigned as dower, and from the treasures which he left to these matrons, in trust for the whole family.

So far as to the objects of the spoil. The *instrument* chosen by Mr. Hastings to despoil the relict of Sujah Dowlah was *her own son,* the reigning Nabob of Oude. It was the pious hand of a son that was selected to tear from his mother and grandmother the provision of their age, the maintenance of his brethren, and of all the ancient household of his father. [Here a laugh from some young members]—The laugh is *seasonable,* and the occasion decent and proper.

By the last advices something of the sum extorted remained unpaid. The women in despair refuse to deliver more, unless their lands are restored and their ministers released from prison: but Mr. Hastings and his council, steady to their point, and consistent to the last in their conduct, write to the Resident to stimulate the son to accomplish the filial acts he had brought so near to their perfection.—"We desire," say they in their letter to the Resident (written so late as March last) "that you will inform us if any, and what means, have been taken for recovering the balance due from the Begum [princess] at Fizabad; and that, if necessary, you *recommend* it to the Vizier to enforce *the most effectual means* for that purpose."

What their effectual means of enforcing demands on women of high rank and condition are, I shall shew you, Sir, in a few minutes; when I represent to you another of these plots and rebellions, which *always,* in India, though so *rarely* any where else,

are the offspring of an easy condition, and hoarded riches.

Benares is the capital city of the Indian religion. It is regarded as holy by a particular and distinguished sanctity; and the Gentûs in general think themselves as much obliged to visit it once in their lives as the Mahometans to perform their pilgrimage to Mecca. By this means that city grew great in commerce and opulence; and so effectually was it secured by the pious veneration of that people, that in all wars and in all violences of power, there was so sure an asylum, both for poverty and wealth, (as it were under a divine protection) that the wisest laws and best assured free constitution could not better provide for the relief of the one, or the safety of the other; and this tranquility influenced to the greatest degree the prosperity of all the country, and the territory of which it was the capital. The interest of money there was not more than half the usual rate in which it stood in all other places. The reports have fully informed you of the means and of the terms in which this city and the territory called Gazipour, of which it was the head, came under the sovereignty of the East India Company.

If ever there was a subordinate dominion pleasantly circumstanced to the superior power, it was this; a large rent or tribute, to the amount of two hundred and sixty thousand pounds a year, was paid in monthly instalments with the punctuality of a dividend at the Bank. If ever there was a prince who could not have an interest in disturbance, it was its sovereign, the Rajah Cheit Sing. He was in possession of the capital of his religion, and a willing revenue was paid by the devout people who resorted to him from all parts. His sovereignty and his independence, except his tribute, was secured by every tie. His territory was not much less than half of Ireland, and displayed in all parts a degree of cultivation, ease, and plenty, under his frugal and paternal management, which left him nothing to desire, either for honour or satisfaction.

This was the light in which this country appeared to almost every eye. But Mr. Hastings beheld it askance. Mr. Hastings tells us that it was *reported* of this Cheit Sing, that his father left him a million sterling, and that he made annual accessions to the hoard. Nothing could be so obnoxious to indigent power. So much wealth could not be innocent. . . .

Mr. Hastings, from whom I take the doctrine, endeavours to prove that Cheit Sing was no sovereign prince; but a mere Zemindar or common subject, holding land by rent. If this be granted to him, it is next to be seen under what terms he is of opinion such a land-holder, that is a British subject, holds his life and property under the Company's government. It is proper to understand well the doctrines of the person whose administration has lately received such distinguished approbation from the Company. His doctrine is—"that the Company, or the *person delegated by it,* holds *an absolute* authority over such Zemindars;—that he [such a subject] owes *an implicit* and *unreserved* obedience to its authority, at the *forfeiture* even of his *life* and *property,* at the DISCRETION of those who held *or fully represented* the sovereign authority;—and that *these* rights are *fully* delegated *to him* Mr. Hastings."

Such is a British governor's idea of the condition of a great Zemindar holding under a British authority; and this kind of authority he supposes fully delegated to *him;* though no such delegation appears in any commission, instruction, or act of parliament. At his *discretion* he may demand, of the substance of any Zemindar over and above his rent or tribute, even what he pleases, with a sovereign authority; and if he does not yield an *implicit unreserved* obedience to all his commands, he forfeits his lands, his life, and his property, at Mr. Hastings's *discretion.* . . .

But supposing the Rajah of Benares to be a mere subject, and that subject a criminal of the highest form; let us see what course was taken by an upright English magistrate. Did he cite this culprit before his tribunal? Did he make a charge? Did he produce witnesses? These are not forms; they are parts of substantial and eternal justice. No, not a word of all this. Mr. Hastings concludes him, *in his own mind,* to be guilty; he makes this conclusion on reports, on hear-says, on appearances, on rumours, on conjectures, on presumptions; and even these never once hinted to the party, nor publicly to any human being, till the whole business was done.

But the governor tells you his motive for this extraordinary proceeding, so contrary to every mode of justice towards either a prince or a subject, fairly and without disguise; and he puts into your hands the key of his whole conduct:—"I will suppose, for a moment, that I have acted with unwarrantable rigour towards Cheit Sing, and even with injustice.—Let my MOTIVE be consulted. I left Calcutta, impressed with a belief that *extraordinary means* were necessary, and those exerted with a *steady hand,* to preserve the Company's *interests from sinking under the accumulated weight which oppressed them.* I saw a *political necessity* for curbing the *overgrown* power of a great member of their dominion, and for *making it contribute to the relief of their pressing exigencies.*" This is plain speaking; after this, it is no wonder that the Rajah's wealth and his offence, the necessities of the judge, and the opulence of the delinquent, are never separated, through the whole of Mr. Hastings's apology. "The justice and *policy* of exacting *a large pecuniary mulct.*" The resolution "*to draw from his guilt* the means *of relief to the Company's distresses.*" His determination "to make him *pay largely* for his pardon, or to execute a severe vengeance for past delinquency." That "as his *wealth was great,* and the *Company's exigencies* pressing, he thought it a measure of justice and policy to exact from him a large pecuniary mulct for *their relief.*"—"The sum (says Mr. Wheler,[28] bearing evidence, at his desire, to his intentions) to which the governor declared his resolution to extend his fine; was forty or fifty lacks, *that is four or five hundred thousand pounds;* and that if he refused, he was to be removed from his zemindary entirely; or by taking possession of his forts, to obtain, *out of the treasure deposited in them,* the above sum for the Company."

Crimes so convenient, crimes so politic, crimes so necessary, crimes so alleviating of distress, can never be wanting to those who use no process, and who produce no proofs.

But there is another serious part . . . in this affair. Let us suppose that the power, for which Mr. Hastings contends, a power which no sovereign ever did, or ever can vest in any of his subjects, namely, his own sovereign authority, to be conveyed by the act of parliament to any man or body of men whatsoever; it certainly was never given to Mr. Hastings. The powers given by the act of 1773 were formal and official; they were given, not to the governor general, but to the major vote of the

board, as a board, on discussion amongst themselves, in their public character and capacity; and their acts in that character and capacity were to be ascertained by records and minutes of council. The despotic acts exercised by Mr. Hastings were done merely in his *private* character; and, if they had been moderate and just, would still be the acts of an usurped authority, and without any one of the legal modes of proceeding which could give him competence for the most trivial exertion of power. There was no proposition or deliberation whatsoever in council, no minute on record, by circulation or otherwise, to authorize his proceedings. No delegation of power to impose a fine, or to take any step to deprive the Rajah of Benares of his government, his property, or his liberty. The minutes of consultation assign to his journey a totally different object, duty, and destination. Mr. Wheler, at his desire, tells us long after, that he had a confidential conversation with him on various subjects, of which this was the principal, in which Mr. Hastings notified to him his secret intentions; "and that he *bespoke* his support of the measures which he intended to pursue towards him (the Rajah)." This confidential discourse, and *bespeaking* of support, could give him no power, in opposition to an express act of parliament, and the whole tenor of the orders of the Court of Directors.

In what manner the powers thus usurped were employed, is known to the whole world. All the House knows, that the design on the Rajah proved as unfruitful as it was violent. The unhappy prince was expelled, and his more unhappy country was enslaved and ruined; but not a rupee was acquired. Instead of treasure to recruit the Company's finances, wasted by their wanton wars and corrupt jobbs, they were plunged into a new war, which shook their

[28]Edward Wheler, a member of the Supreme Council of Bengal. The council had responsibilities for controlling the East India Company's operations in Bengal. Hastings was also a member of the council as governor-general of Bengal.

power in India to its foundation; and, to use the governor's own happy simile, might have dissolved it like a magic structure, if the talisman had been broken.

⤶

But here, Sir, mark the effect of all these *extraordinary* means, of all this policy and justice. The revenues which had been hitherto paid with such astonishing punctuality, fell into arrear. The new prince guardian was deposed without ceremony; and with as little, cast into prison. The government of that once happy country has been in the utmost confusion ever since such good order was taken about it. But, to complete the contumely offered to this undone people, and to make them feel their servitude in all its degradation, and all its bitterness, the government of their sacred city, the government of that Benares which had been so respected by Persian and Tartar conquerors, though of the Mussulman persuasion, that, even in the plenitude of their pride, power, and bigotry, no magistrate of that sect entered the place, was now delivered over by English hands to a Mahometan; and an Ali Ibrahim Khân was introduced, under the Company's authority, with power of life and death, into the sanctuary of the Gentû religion.

. . . It remains only to shew, through the conduct in this business, the spirit of the Company's government, and the respect they pay towards other prejudices not less regarded in the East than those of religion; I mean the reverence paid to the female sex in general, and particularly to women of high rank and condition. During the general confusion of the country of Gazypore, Panna, the mother of Cheit Sing, was lodged with her train in a castle called Bidgé Gur, in which were likewise deposited a large portion of the treasures of her son, or more probably her own. To whomsoever they belonged was indifferent; for, though no charge of rebellion was made on this woman (which was rather singular, as it would have cost nothing) they were resolved to secure her with her fortune. The castle was besieged by Major Popham.

. . . The Company's first civil magistrate discovered the greatest uneasiness lest the women should have any thing preserved to them. Terms, tending to put some restraint on military violence, were granted. He writes a letter to Mr. Popham, referring to some letter written before to the same effect, which I do not remember to have seen, but it shews his anxiety on this subject. Hear himself:—"I think *every* demand she has made on you, except that of safety and respect to her person, is unreasonable. If the reports brought to me are true, your rejecting her offers, or *any negotiation,* would soon obtain you the fort upon your own terms. I apprehend she will attempt to *defraud the captors of a considerable part of their booty, by being suffered to retire without examination.* But this is your concern, not mine. I should *be very sorry* that your officers and soldiers lost *any* part of the reward to which they are so well entitled; but you must be the best judge of the *promised* indulgence to the Ranny: what you have engaged for I will certainly ratify; but as to suffering the Ranny to hold the purgunna of Hurlich, or any other zemindary, without being subject to the authority of the Zemindar, *or any lands whatsoever,* or indeed making *any* condition with her for a *provision,* I will *never consent.*"

Here your governor stimulates a rapacious and licentious soldiery to the personal search of women, lest these unhappy creatures should avail themselves of the protection of their sex to secure any supply for their necessities; and he positively orders that no stipulation should be made for any provision for them. . . . I say, Sir, this antient lady was compelled to quit her house with three hundred helpless women, and a multitude of children in her train; but the lower sort in the camp it seems could not be restrained. They did not forget the good lessons of the governor general. They were unwilling "to be defrauded of a considerable part of their booty, by suffering them to pass without examination."—They examined them, Sir, with a vengeance, and the sacred protection of that awful character, Mr. Hastings's maitre d'hotel, could not secure them from insult and plunder. . . .

↬

It is only to complete the view I proposed of the conduct of the Company, with regard to the dependent provinces, that I shall say *any* thing at all of the Carnatic, which is the scene, if possible, of greater disorder than the northern provinces. . . . This country, in all its denominations, is about 46,000 square miles. It may be affirmed universally, that not one person of substance or property, landed, commercial, or monied, excepting two or three bankers, who are necessary deposits and distributors of the general spoil, is left in all that region. In that country the moisture, the bounty of Heaven, is given but at a certain season. Before the aera or our influence, the industry of man carefully husbanded that gift of God. The Gentûs preserved, with a provident and religious care, the precious deposit of the periodical rain in reservoirs, many of them works of royal grandeur; and from these, as occasion demanded, they fructified the whole country. To maintain these reservoirs, and to keep up an annual advance to the cultivators, for seed and cattle, formed a principal object of the piety and policy of the priests and rulers of the Gentû religion.

This object required a command of money; and there was no Pollam, or castle, which in the happy days of the Carnatic was without some hoard of treasure, by which the governors were enabled to combat with the irregularity of the seasons, and to resist or to buy off the invasion of an enemy. In all the cities were multitudes of merchants and bankers, for all occasions of monied assistance; and on the other hand, the native princes were in condition to obtain credit from them. The manufacturer was paid by the return of commodities, or by imported money, and not, as at present, in the taxes that had been originally exacted from his industry. In aid of casual distress, the country was full of choultries, which were inns and hospitals, where the traveller and the poor were relieved. All ranks of people had their place in the public concern, and their share in the common stock and common prosperity; but *the chartered rights of men,* and the right which it was thought proper to set up in the Nabob of Arcot, introduced a new system. It was their policy to consider hoards of money as crimes; to regard moderate rents as frauds on the sovereign; and to view, in the lesser princes, any claim of exemption from more than settled tribute, as an act of rebellion. Accordingly all the castles were, one after the other, plundered and destroyed. The native princes were expelled; the hospitals fell to ruin; the reservoirs of water went to decay; the merchants, bankers, and manufacturers disappeared; and sterility, indigence, and depopulation, overspread the face of these once flourishing provinces.

↬

The House perceives that the livery of the Company's government is uniform. I have described the condition of the countries indirectly, but most substantially, under the Company's authority. And now I ask, whether, with this map of misgovernment before me, I can suppose myself bound by my vote to continue, upon any principles of pretended public faith, the management of these countries in those hands. If I kept such a faith . . . with what is called the Company, I must break the faith, the covenant, the solemn, original, indispensable oath, in which I am bound, by the eternal frame and constitution of things, to the whole human race.

As I have dwelt so long on these who are indirectly under the Company's administration, I will endeavour to be a little shorter upon the countries immediately under this charter government.—These are the Bengal provinces. . . . I shall state to you, as shortly as I am able, the conduct of the Company;—1st, towards the landed interests;—next, the commercial interests;—3dly, the native government;—and lastly, to their own government.

Bengal, and the provinces that are united to it, are larger than the kingdom of France; and once contained, as France does contain, a great and independent landed interest, composed of princes, of great lords, of a numerous nobility and gentry, of freeholders, of lower tenants, of religious communities, and public foundations. So early as 1769, the Company's servants perceived the decay into which these provinces had fallen under English administration, and they made a strong representation upon this decay, and what they apprehended to be the causes of it. Soon after Mr. Hastings became president of Bengal. Instead of administering a remedy, upon the heels of a dreadful famine, in the year 1772, the succour which the new president and the council lent to this afflicted nation was—shall I be believed in relating it?—the landed interest

of a whole kingdom, of a kingdom to be compared to France, was set up to public auction! They set up (Mr. Hastings set up) the whole nobility, gentry, and freeholders, to the highest bidder. No preference was given to the ancient proprietors. They must bid against every userer, every temporary adventurer, every jobber and schemer, every servant of every European, or they were obliged to content themselves, in lieu of their extensive domains, with their house, and such a pension as the state auctioneers thought fit to assign. . . . Another reform has since come upon the back of the first; and a pension having been assigned to these unhappy persons, in lieu of their hereditary lands, a new scheme of oeconomy has taken place, and deprived them of that pension.

The menial servants of Englishmen, persons (to use the emphatical phrase of a ruined and patient Eastern chief) *"whose fathers they would not have set with the dogs of their flock,"* entered into their patrimonial lands. Mr. Hastings's banian[29] was, after this auction, found possessed of territories yielding a rent of one hundred and forty thousand pounds a year.

Such an universal proscription, upon any pretence, has few examples. Such a proscription, without even a pretence of delinquency, has none. It stands by itself. It stands as a monument to astonish the imagination, to confound the reason of mankind. I confess to you, when I first came to know this business in its true nature and extent, my surprise did a little suspend my indignation. I was in a manner stupified by the desperate boldness of a few obscure young men, who having obtained, by ways which they could not comprehend, a power of which they saw neither the purposes nor the limits, tossed about,

---

[29]Hastings's personal steward, Krishna Kanta Nandy.

subverted, and tore to pieces, as if it were in the gambols of a boyish unluckiness and malice, the most established rights, and the most ancient and most revered institutions, of ages and nations. Sir, I will not now trouble you with any detail with regard to what they have since done with these same lands and land-holders; only to inform you, that nothing has been suffered to settle for two seasons together upon any basis; and that the levity and inconstancy of these mock legislators were not the least afflicting parts of the oppressions suffered under their usurpation; nor will any thing give stability to the property of the natives, but an administration in England at once protecting and stable. The country sustains, almost every year, the miseries of a revolution. At present, all is uncertainty, misery, and confusion. . . .

I shall now say a word or two on the Company's care of the commercial interest of those kingdoms. As it appears in the Reports, that persons in the highest stations in Bengal have adopted, as a fixed plan of policy, the destruction of all intermediate dealers between the Company and the manufacturer, native merchants have disappeared of course. The spoil of the revenues is the sole capital which purchases the produce and manufactures; and through three or four foreign companies transmits the official gains of individuals to Europe. No other commerce has an existence in Bengal. The transport of its plunder is the only traffic of the country. . . .

As to the native government and the administration of justice, it subsisted in a poor tottering manner for some years. In the year 1781, a total revolution took place in that establishment. In one of the usual freaks of legislation of the council of Bengal, the whole criminal jurisdiction of these courts, called the Phoujdary Judicature, exercised till then by the principal

Mussulmen, was in one day, without notice, without consultation with the magistrates or the people there, and without communication with the directors or ministers here, totally subverted. A new institution took place, by which this jurisdiction was divided between certain English servants of the Company and the Gentû Zemindars of the country, the latter of whom never petitioned for it, nor, for ought that appears, ever desired this boon. But its natural use was made of it; it was made a pretence for new extortions of money.

⤶

An establishment of English government for civil justice, and for the collection of revenue, was planned and executed by the president and council of Bengal, subject to the pleasure of the Directors, in the year 1772. According to this plan, the country was divided into six great districts, or provinces. In each of these was established a provincial council, which administered the revenue; and of that council one member, by monthly rotation, presided in the courts of civil resort; with an appeal to the council of the province, and thence to Calcutta. In this system (whether, in other respects, good or evil) there were some capital advantages. There was in the very number of persons in each provincial council, authority, communication, mutual check, and controul. They were obliged, on their minutes of consultation, to enter their reasons and dissents; so that a man of diligence, of research, and tolerable sagacity, sitting in London, might, from these materials, be enabled to form some judgment of the spirit of what was going on on the furthest banks of the Ganges and Burrampûter.

The Court of Directors so far ratified this establishment, (which was consonant

enough to their general plan of government) that they gave precise orders, that
no alteration should be made in it, without their consent. So far from being ap-
prised of any design against this constitution, they had reason to conceive that on
trial it had been more and more approved
by their council general, at least by the
governor general, who had planned it. At
the time of the revolution, the council
general was nominally in two persons, virtually in one.[30] At that time measures of
an arduous and critical nature ought to
have been forborne, even if, to the fullest
council, this specific measure had not been
prohibited by the superior authority. It
was in this very situation, that one man
had the hardiness to conceive, and the
temerity to execute, a total revolution in
the form and the persons composing the
government of a great kingdom. Without
any previous step, at one stroke, the whole
constitution of Bengal, civil and criminal,
was swept away. The counsellors were recalled from their provinces. Upwards of
fifty of the principal officers of government were turned out of employ, and rendered dependent on Mr. Hastings for their
immediate subsistence, and for all hope of
future provision. The chief of each council, and one European collector of revenue,
was left in each province.

But here, Sir, you may imagine a new
government, of some permanent description, was established in the place of that
which had been thus suddenly overturned.
No such thing. Lest these chiefs without
councils should be conceived to form the
ground plan of some future government, it
was publicly declared, that their continuance was only temporary and permissive.
The whole subordinate British administra-

tion of revenue was then vested in a
committee in Calcutta, all creatures of the
governor general; and the provincial management, under the permissive chief, was
delivered over to native officers.

But, that the revolution, and the purposes of the revolution, might be complete, to this committee were delegated,
not only the functions of all the inferior,
but, what will surprize the House, those of
the supreme administration of revenue
also. Hitherto the governor general and
council had, in their revenue department,
administered the finances of those kingdoms. By the new scheme they are delegated to this committee, who are only to
report their proceedings for approbation.

The key to the whole transaction is
given in one of the instructions to the committee, "that it is not necessary that they
should enter dissents." By this means the
ancient plan of the Company's administration was destroyed; but the plan of concealment was perfected. To that moment
the accounts of the revenues were tolerably
clear; or at last means were furnished for
enquiries, by which they might be rendered satisfactory. In the obscure and silent
gulph of this committee every thing is now
buried. The thickest shades of night sur-
round all their transactions. No effectual
means of detecting fraud, mismanagement,
or misrepresentation, exist. The Directors,
who have dared to talk with such confidence on their revenues, know nothing
about them. What used to fill volumes is
now comprised under a few dry heads on a
sheet of paper. The natives, a people habit-
ually made to concealment, are the chief
managers of the revenue throughout the
provinces. I mean by natives, such wretches
as your rulers select out of them as most fitted for their purposes. . . .

As the whole revenue and civil administration was thus subverted, and a clandes-

---

[30]In 1781 Hastings and Wheler were the only
members of the Supreme Council of Bengal.

tine government substituted in the place of it, the judicial institution underwent a like revolution. In 1772 there had been six courts formed out of the six provincial councils. Eighteen new ones are appointed in their place, with each a judge, taken from the *junior* servants of the Company. To maintain these eighteen courts, a tax is levied on the sums in litigation, of 2 1/2 *per cent.* on the great, and of 5 *per cent.* on the less. This money is all drawn from the provinces to Calcutta. The chief justice[31] (the same who stays in defiance of a vote of this House, and of His Majesty's recal) is appointed at once the treasurer and disposer of these taxes, levied, without any sort of authority, from the Company, from the Crown, or from Parliament.

In effect, Sir, every legal regular authority in matters of revenue, of political administration, of criminal law, of civil law, in many of the most essential parts of military discipline, is laid level with the sound; and an oppressive, irregular, capricious, unsteady, rapacious, and peculating despotism, with a direct disavowal of obedience to any authority at home, and without any fixed maxim, principle, or rule of proceeding, to guide them in India, is at present the state of your charter-government over great kingdoms.

As the Company has made this use of their trust, I should ill discharge mine, if I refused to give my most chearful vote for the redress of these abuses, by putting the affairs of so large and valuable a part of the interests of this nation and of mankind, into some steady hands, possessing the confidence, and assured of the support of this House, until they can be restored to regularity, order, and consistency.

I have touched the heads of some of the grievances of the people, and the abuses of

government. But I hope and trust, you will give me credit, when I faithfully assure you, that I have not mentioned one fourth part of what has come to my knowledge in your committee; and further, I have full reason to believe, that not one fourth part of the abuses are come to my knowledge, by that or by any other means. Pray consider what I have said only as an index to direct you in your enquiries.

If this then, Sir, has been the use made of the trust of political powers internal and external, given by you in the charter, the next thing to be seen is the conduct of the Company with regard to the commercial trust. And here I will make a fair offer:—If it can be proved that they have acted wisely, prudently, and frugally, as merchants, I shall pass by the whole mass of their enormities as statesmen. That they have not done this their present condition is proof sufficient. Their distresses are said to be owing to their wars. This is not wholly true. But if it were, is not that readiness to engage in wars which distinguishes them, and for which the Committee of Secrecy has so branded their politics, founded on the falsest principles of mercantile speculation?

The principle of buying cheap and selling dear is the first, the great foundation of mercantile dealing. Have they ever attended to this principle? Nay, for years have they not actually authorized in their servants a total indifference as to the prices they were to pay?

A great deal of strictness in driving bargains for whatever we contract, is another of the principles of mercantile policy. Try the Company by that test! Look at the contracts that are made for them. Is the Company so much as a good commissary to their own armies? . . .

It is a third property of trading men, to see that their clerks do not divert the deal-

---

[31]Sir Elijah Impey.

ings of the master to their own benefit. It was the other day only, when their governor and council taxed the Company's investment with a sum of fifty thousand pounds, as an inducement to persuade only seven members of their board of trade to give their *honour* that they would abstain from such profits upon that investment as they must have violated their *oaths* if they had made at all.

It is a fourth quality of a merchant to be exact in his accounts. What will be thought, when you have fully before you the mode of accounting made use of in the treasury of Bengal? ... A new principle of account upon honour seems to be regularly established in their dealings and their treasury, which in reality amounts to an entire annihilation of the principle of all accounts.

It is a fifth property of a merchant, who does not mediate a fraudulent bankruptcy, to calculate his probable profits upon the money he takes up to vest in business. Did the Company, when they bought goods on bonds bearing 8 *per cent.* interest, at ten and even twenty *per cent.* discount, even ask themselves a question concerning the possibility of advantage from dealing on these terms?

The last quality of a merchant I shall advert to, is the taking care to be properly prepared, in cash or goods, in the ordinary course of sale, for the bills which are drawn on them. Now I ask, whether they have ever calculated the clear produce of any given sales, to make them tally with the four million of bills which are come and coming upon them, so as at the proper periods to enable the one to liquidate the other? No, they have not. They are now obliged to borrow money of their own servants to purchase their investment. ... Indeed no trace of equitable government is found in their politics; not one trace of commercial principle in their mer-

cantile dealing; and hence is the deepest and maturest wisdom of Parliament demanded, and the best resources of this kingdom must be strained, to restore them; that is, to restore the countries destroyed by the misconduct of the Company, and to restore the Company itself, ruined by the consequences of their plans for destroying what they were bound to preserve.

I required, if you remember, at my outset a proof that these abuses were habitual. But surely this is not necessary for me to consider as a separate head; because I trust I have made it evident beyond a doubt, in considering the abuses themselves, that they are regular, permanent, and systematical.

I am now come to my last condition, without which, for one, I will never readily lend my hand to the destruction of any established government; which is, That in its present state, the government of the East India Company is absolutely incorrigible.

Of this great truth I think there can be little doubt, after all that has appeared in this House. It is so very clear, that I must consider the leaving any power in their hands, and the determined resolution to continue and countenance every mode and every degree of peculation, oppression, and tyranny, to be one and the same thing. I look upon that body incorrigible, from the fullest consideration both of their uniform conduct, and their present real and virtual constitution.

If they had not constantly been apprized of all the enormities committed in India under their authority; if this state of things had been as much a discovery to them as it was to many of us; we might flatter ourselves that the detection of the abuses would lead to their reformation. I will go further: If the Court of Directors had not uniformly condemned every act which this House or any of its Committees had condemned; if the language in which they expressed their disapprobation against enormities and their authors had not been much more vehement and indignant than any ever used in this House, I should entertain some hopes. If they had not, on the other hand, as uniformly commended all their servants who had done their duty and obeyed their orders, as they had heavily censured those who rebelled; I might say, These people have been in an error, and when they are sensible of it they will mend. But when I reflect on the uniformity of their support to the objects of their uniform censure; and the state of insignificance and disgrace to which all of those have been reduced whom they approved; and that even utter ruin and premature death have been among the fruits of their favour; I must be convinced, that in this case, as in all others, hypocrisy is the only vice that never can be cured.

Attend, I pray you, to the situation and prosperity of Benfield,[32] Hastings, and others of that sort. The last of these has been treated by the company with an asperity of reprehension that has no parallel. They lament, "that the power of disposing of their property for perpetuity, should fall into such hands." Yet for fourteen years, with little interruption, he has governed all their affairs, of every description, with an absolute sway. He has had himself the means of heaping up immense wealth; and, during that whole period, the fortunes of hundreds have depended on his smiles and frowns. He himself tells you he is incumbered with two hundred and fifty young gentlemen, some of them of the best families in England, all of whom aim

at returning with vast fortunes to Europe in the prime of life. He has then two hundred and fifty of your children as his hostages for your good behaviour; and loaded for years, as he has been, with the execrations of the natives, with the censures of the Court of Directors, and struck and blasted with resolutions of this House, he still maintains the most despotic power ever known in India. He domineers with an overbearing sway in the assemblies of his pretended masters; and it is thought in a degree rash to venture to name his offences in this House, even as grounds of a legislative remedy.

⌐

Worse, far worse, has been the fate of the poor creatures, the natives of India, whom the hypocrisy of the Company has betrayed into complaint of oppression, and discovery of peculation. . . .

. . . So that there is none who hears me, that is not as certain as I am, that the Company, in the sense in which it was formerly understood, has no existence. The question is not, what injury you may do to the proprietors of India stock; for there are no such men to be injured. . . . The vote is not to protect the stock, but the stock is bought to acquire the vote; and the end of the vote is to cover and support, against justice, some man of power who has made an obnoxious fortune in India; or to maintain in power those who are actually employing it in the acquisition of such a fortune; and to avail themselves in return of his patronage, that he may shower the spoils of the East, "barbaric pearl and gold" on them, their families, and dependents. So that all the relations of the Company are not only changed, but inverted. The servants in India are not appointed by the Directors, but the Directors are chosen by them. The trade is carried on with their

---

[32]Paul Benfield, a prominent and controversial employee of the East India Company. Burke targeted Benfield in his *Speech on Nabob of Arcot's Debts,* *WSEB,* v, 478–617.

capitals. To them the revenues of the country are mortgaged. The seat of the supreme power is in Calcutta. The house in Leadenhall Street is nothing more than a change for their agents, factors, and deputies to meet in, to take care of their affairs, and support their interests; and this so avowedly, that we see the known agents of the delinquent servants marshalling and disciplining their forces, and the prime spokesmen in all their assemblies.

Every thing has followed in this order, and according to the natural train of events. I will close what I have to say on the incorrigible condition of the Company, by stating to you a few facts, that will leave no doubt of the obstinacy of that corporation, and of their strength too, in resisting the reformation of their servants. By these facts you will be enabled to discover the sole grounds upon which they are tenacious of their charter. It is now more than two years that, upon account of the gross abuses and ruinous situation of the Company's affairs, . . . that we instituted two Committees to enquire into the mismanagements by which the Company's affairs had been brought to the brink of ruin. These enquiries had been pursued with unremitting diligence; and a great body of facts was collected and printed for general information. In the result of those enquiries, although the Committees consisted of very different descriptions, they were unanimous. They joined in censuring the conduct of the Indian administration, and enforcing the responsibility upon two men, whom this House, in consequence of these reports, declared it to be the duty of the Directors to remove from their stations, and recal to Great Britain, *because they had acted in a manner repugnant to the honour and policy of this nation, and thereby brought great calamities on India, and enormous expences on the East India Company.*

Here was no attempt on the charter. Here was no question of their privileges. To vindicate their own honour, to support their own interests, to enforce obedience to their own orders; these were the sole object of the monitory resolution of this House. But as soon as the general court could assemble, they assembled to demonstrate who they really were. Regardless of the proceedings of this House, they ordered the Directors not to carry into effect any resolution they might come to for the removal of Mr. Hastings and Mr. Hornby.[33] The Directors, still retaining some shadow of respect to this House, instituted an enquiry themselves, which continued from June to October; and after an attentive perusal and full consideration of papers, resolved to take steps for removing the persons who had been the objects of our resolution; but not without a violent struggle against evidence. Seven Directors went so far as to enter a protest against the vote of their court. Upon this the general court takes the alarm; it re-assembles; it orders the Directors to rescind their resolution, that is, not to recal Mr. Hastings and Mr. Hornby, and to despise the resolution of the House of Commons. Without so much as the pretence of looking into a single paper, without the formality of instituting any committee of enquiry, they superseded all the labours of their own Directors, and of this House.

It will naturally occur to ask, how it was possible that they should not attempt some sort of examination into facts, as a colour for their resistance to a public authority, proceeding so very deliberately; and exerted, apparently at least, in favour of their own? The answer, and the only answer which can be given, is, that they were afraid that their true relation should be

---

[33]William Hornby, governor of Bombay.

mistaken. They were afraid that their patrons and masters in India should attribute their support of them, to an opinion of their cause, and not to an attachment to their power. They were afraid it should be suspected, that they did not mean blindly to support them in the use they made of that power. They determined to shew that they at least were set against reformation; that they were firmly resolved to bring the territories, the trade, and the stock of the Company, to ruin, rather than be wanting in fidelity to their nominal servants and real masters, in the ways they took to their private fortunes.

Even since the beginning of this session, the same act of audacity was repeated, with the same circumstances of contempt of all the decorum of enquiry, on their part, and of all the proceedings of this House. They again made it a request to their favourite, and your culprit, to keep his post; and thanked and applauded him, without calling for a paper which could afford light into the merit or demerit of the transaction, and without giving themselves a moment's time to consider, or even to understand, the articles of the Maratta peace. The fact is, that for a long time there was a struggle, a faint one indeed, between the Company and their servants. But it is a struggle no longer. For some time the superiority has been decided. The interests abroad are become the settled preponderating weight both in the Court of Proprietors, and the Court of Directors. Even the attempt you have made to enquire into their practices and to reform abuses, has raised and piqued them to a far more regular and steady support. The Company has made a common cause, and identified themselves, with the destroyers of India. They have taken on themselves all that mass of enormity; they are supporting what you have reprobated; those

you condemn they applaud; those you order home to answer for their conduct, they request to stay, and thereby encourage to proceed in their practices. Thus the servants of the East India Company triumph, and the representatives of the people of Great Britain are defeated.

I therefore conclude, what you all conclude, that this body, being totally perverted from the purposes of its institution, is utterly incorrigible; and because they are incorrigible, both in conduct and constitution, power ought to be taken out of their hands; just on the same principles on which have been made all the just changes and revolutions of government that have taken place since the beginning of the world.

I will now say a few words to the general principle of the plan which is set up against that of my Right Honourable friend. It is to re-commit the government of India to the Court of Directors. Those who would commit the reformation of India to the destroyers of it, are the enemies to that reformation. They would make a distinction between Directors and Proprietors, which, in the present state of things, does not, cannot exist. But a Right Honourable gentleman[34] says, he would keep the present government of India in the Court of Directors; and would, to curb them, provide salutary regulations;—wonderful! That is, he would appoint the old offenders to correct the old offences; and he would render the vicious and the foolish wise and virtuous, by salutary regulations. He would appoint the wolf as guardian of the sheep; but he has invented a curious muzzle, by which this protecting wolf shall not be able to open his jaws above an inch or two at the utmost. Thus his work is finished. But I tell the Right Honourable gentleman, that controuled

---

[34]Burke is probably referring to Pitt.

depravity is not innocence; and that it is not the labour of delinquency in chains, that will correct abuses. Will these gentlemen of the direction animadvert on the partners of their own guilt? Never did a serious plan of amending of any old tyrannical establishment propose the authors and abettors of the abuses as the reformers of them. If the undone people of India see their old oppressors in confirmed power, even by the reformation, they will expect nothing but what they will certainly feel, a continuance, or rather an aggravation, of all their former sufferings. They look to the seat of power, and to the persons who fill it; and they despise those gentlemen's regulations as much as the gentlemen do who talk of them.

~

If the government of India wants no reformation; but gentlemen are amusing themselves with a theory, conceiving a more democratic or aristocratic mode of government for these dependances, or if they are in a dispute only about patronage; the dispute is with me of so little concern, that I should not take the pains to utter an affirmative or negative to any proposition in it. If it be only for a theoretical amusement that they are to propose a bill; the thing is at best frivolous and unnecessary. But if the Company's government is not only full of abuse, but is one of the most corrupt and destructive tyrannies, that probably ever existed in the world (as I am sure it is) what a cruel mockery would it be in me, and in those who think like me, to propose this kind of remedy for this kind of evil!

I now come to the third objection, That this bill will increase the influence of the Crown. . . . But as to this bill, whether it encreases the influence of the Crown, or not, is a question I should be ashamed to ask. If I am not able to correct a system of oppression and tyranny, that goes to the utter ruin of thirty millions of my fellow-creatures and fellow-subjects, but by some increase to the influence of the Crown, I am ready here to declare, that I, who have been active to reduce it, shall be at least as active and strenuous to restore it again. I am no lover of names; I contend for the substance of good and protecting government, let it come from what quarter it will.

But I am not obliged to have recourse to this expedient. Much, very much the contrary. I am sure that the influence of the Crown will by no means aid a reformation of this kind; which can neither be originated nor supported, but by the uncorrupt public virtue of the representatives of the people of England. Let it once get into the ordinary course of administration, and to me all hopes of reformation are gone. I am far from knowing or believing, that this bill will encrease the influence of the Crown. We all know, that the Crown has ever had some influence in the Court of Directors; and that it has been extremely increased by the acts of 1773 and 1780. The gentlemen who, as part of their reformation, propose, "a more active controul on the part of the Crown," which is to put the Directors under a Secretary of State, specially named for that purpose, must know, that their project will increase it further. But that old influence has had, and the new will have, incurable inconveniences, which cannot happen under the parliamentary establishment proposed in this bill. . . . Ministers must be wholly removed from the management of the affairs of India, or they will have an influence in its patronage. The thing is inevitable. Their scheme of a new Secretary of State, "with a more vigorous control," is not much better than a repetition of the measure which we know by experience will not do. Since the year 1773 and the year 1780, the Company has been under the control of the Secretary of State's office, and we had then three Secretaries of State. If more than this is done, then they annihilate the direction which they pretend to support; and they augment the influence of the Crown, of whose growth they affect so great an horror. . . .

But, Sir, there is one kind of influence far greater than that of the nomination to office. This gentlemen in opposition have totally overlooked, although it now exists in its full vigour; and it will do so, upon their scheme, in at least as much force as it does now. That influence this bill cuts up by the roots; I mean the *influence of protection*. I shall explain myself:—The office given to a young man going to India is of trifling consequence. But he that goes out an insignificant boy, in a few years returns a great Nabob. Mr. Hastings says he has two hundred and fifty of that kind of raw materials, who expect to be speedily manufactured into the merchantable quality I mention. One of these gentlemen, suppose, returns hither, loaded with odium and with riches. When he comes to England he comes as to a prison or as to a sanctuary; and either are ready for him, according to his demeanor. What is the influence in the grant of any place in India, to that which is acquired by the protection or compromise with such guilt, and with the command of such riches, under the dominion of the hopes and fears which power is able to hold out to every man in that condition? That man's whole fortune, half a million perhaps, becomes an instrument of influence, without a shilling of charge to the Civil List; and the influx of fortunes which stand in need of this protection is continual. It works both ways; it influences the delinquent, and it may corrupt the minister. Compare the influence acquired by appointing for instance even a

governor general, and that obtained by protecting him. I shall push this no further. But I wish gentlemen to roll it a little in their own minds.

The bill before you cuts off this source of influence. Its design and main scope is to regulate the administration of India upon the principles of a Court of Judicature; and to exclude, as far as human prudence can exclude, all possibility of a corrupt partiality, in appointing to office or supporting in office, or covering from enquiry and punishment, any person who has abused or shall abuse his authority. At the board, as appointed and regulated by this bill, reward and punishment cannot be shifted and reversed by a whisper. That commission becomes fatal to cabal, to intrigue, and to secret representation, those instruments of the ruin of India. He that cuts off the means of premature fortune, and the power of protecting it when acquired, strikes a deadly blow at the great fund, the Bank, the capital stock of Indian influence, which cannot be vested any where, or in any hands, without most dangerous consequences to the public.

The third and contradictory objection, is, That this bill does not increase the influence of the Crown. On the contrary, That the just power of the Crown will be lessened, and transferred to the use of a party, by giving the patronage of India to a commission nominated by parliament, and independent of the Crown. The contradiction is glaring, and it has been too well exposed to make it necessary for me to insist upon it. But passing the contradiction, and taking it without any relation, of all objections that is the most extraordinary. Do not gentlemen know, that the Crown has not at present the grant of a single office under the Company, civil or military, at home or abroad? So far as the Crown is concerned, it is certainly rather a gainer;

for the vacant offices in the new commission are to be filled up by the King.

⤻

The fourth and last objection is, That the bill will hurt public credit. I do not know whether this requires an answer. But if it does, look to your foundations. The sinking fund is the pillar of credit in this country; and let it not be forgot, that the distresses, owing to the mismanagement of the East India Company, have already taken a million from that fund by the nonpayment of duties. The bills drawn upon the Company, which are about four millions, cannot be accepted without the consent of the treasury. The treasury, acting under a parliamentary trust and authority, pledges the public for these millions. If they pledge the public, the public must have a security in its hands for the management of this interest, or the national credit is gone. For otherwise it is not only the East India Company, which is a great interest, that is undone, but, clinging to the security of all your funds, it drags down the rest, and the whole fabric perishes in one ruin. If this bill does not provide a direction of integrity and of ability competent to that trust, the objection is fatal. If it does, public credit must depend on the support of the bill.

It has been said, if you violate this charter, what security has the charter of the Bank, in which public credit is so deeply concerned, and even the charter of London, in which the rights of so many subjects are involved? I answer, In the like case they have no security at all—No—no security at all. If the Bank should, by every species of mismanagement, fall into a state similar to that of the East India Company; if it should be oppressed with demands it could not answer, engagements which it could not perform, and with bills for which it could not procure payment; no charter should protect the mismanagement from correction, and such public grievances from redress. If the city of London had the means and will of destroying an empire, and of cruelly oppressing and tyrannizing over millions of men as good as themselves, the charter of the city of London should prove no sanction to such tyranny and such oppression. Charters are kept, when their purposes are maintained: they are violated when the privilege is supported against its end and its object.

Now, Sir, I have finished all I proposed to say, as my reasons for giving my vote to this Bill. If I am wrong, it is not for want of pains to know what is right. This pledge, at least, of my rectitude I have given to my country.

And now, having done my duty to the Bill, let me say a word to the author. I should leave him to his own noble sentiments, if the unworthy and illiberal language with which he has been treated, beyond all example of parliamentary liberty, did not make a few words necessary; not so much in justice to him, as to my own feelings. I must say then, that it will be a distinction honourable to the age, that the rescue of the greatest number of the human race that ever were so grievously oppressed, from the greatest tyranny that was ever exercised, has fallen to the lot of abilities and dispositions equal to the task; that it has fallen to one who has the enlargement to comprehend, the spirit to undertake, and the eloquence to support, so great a measure of hazardous benevolence. . . .

I have spoken what I think, and what I feel, of the mover of this Bill. . . . For my own part I am happy that I have lived to see this day; I feel myself overpaid for the labours of eighteen years, when, at this late period, I am able to take my share, by one humble vote, in destroying a tyranny that exists to the disgrace of this nation, and the destruction of so large a part of the human species.

Introductory Note to
Speech on Opening of Impeachment
(1788)

In his Speech on Nabob of Arcot's Debts *(1785), Burke reconfirmed his commitment to improving the lot of the Indian peoples. Legislation to reform the East India Company was not an option following Pitt's victory in the general election victory of 1784 because Burke was a member of a fragmented opposition. Burke decided to pursue justice for India by launching a campaign to impeach Warren Hastings. He filed his motion for papers on Hastings in February 1786 as the first step toward an investigation of Hastings's performance as governor-general of Bengal.*[35] *The Pitt ministry did not oppose Burke's motion. In April and May 1786, Burke delivered to the House of Commons twenty-two articles of charge of high crimes and misdemeanors. Hastings offered a defense to the House of Commons that played right into Burke's hands: Hastings asserted that he was beyond reproach and acted on the principles of government prevalent in Asia. After the examination of witnesses, the House of Commons debated and voted on each article of charge. By May 1787 the House of Commons had voted to impeach Hastings on seven charges. Burke had achieved a great victory, perhaps unthinkable a few years earlier, after the defeat of Fox's India Bill. The next test for Burke would be*

before the House of Lords, where the impeachment issue would be decided.

Speech on Opening of Impeachment *was Burke's four-day speech at the start of the Hastings's trial before the House of Lords. This massive effort is too long to reproduce in its entirety in this volume, so we have selected material primarily from the first and second days of the speech. On the first day, Burke set out to broaden the conception of justice he believed applied to the Hastings case, imploring the House of Lords not to try Hastings on narrow municipal conceptions of justice but under a more universal conception of justice befitting a great empire. Burke also traced the history of the East India Company and provided an analysis of the indigenous peoples and societies of India.*

Such background information set up the major objective of the second day of the speech: to show how the East India Company systematically destroyed Indian society through treachery, corruption, and greed and to condemn the principles under which Hastings justified his actions in India. The real meat of Speech on Opening of Impeachment *is found in Burke's rejection of what he called Hastings's "Geographical morality." Part of Hastings's defense was that he exercised arbitrary power in India because that was the ruling principle of Asiatic governments. Burke condemned the idea that a great part of the British Empire has been governed without adherence to or respect for British principles of government. He argued that actions in Asia and Europe bear the same moral qualities and that Hastings's notion that what would never stand in England is acceptable and praiseworthy in India should be rejected outright. Burke appealed to a universal moral framework that is one of the most interesting aspects of his thinking on India.*

The length of Speech on Opening of Impeachment *foreshadowed the long-drawn-*

---

[35] *Motion for Papers on Hastings, WSEB,* vi, 47–60.

out battle that the impeachment trial became. From 1788 until 1795, Burke toiled, increasingly on his own, in the proceedings. The House of Lords acquitted Hastings of all charges in 1795. Although Burke did not believe that the House of Lords would ever rule against Hastings, he never wavered in his determination to see justice done in India. Speech on Opening of Impeachment remains a pillar in Burke's "monument" of his "endeavours to save the Nation from the Shame and guilt" created by its treatment of the Indian peoples. ⌒

Speech on Opening of Impeachment (1788)

15 February 1788

Mr. Burke

My Lords, the Gentlemen who have it in command to support the Impeachment against Mr. Hastings, late Governor General of Bengal, have directed me to open a general view of the grounds upon which the Commons have proceeded in their charge against him; to open a general view of the extent, the magnitude, the nature, the tendency and effect of the crimes with which they have charged him; and they have also directed me to give such an explanation, as with their aid, I may be enabled to give of such circumstances preceding or concomitant with the crimes with which they charge him, as may tend to explain whatever may be found obscure in the charges as they stand. And they have further commanded me and enabled me, I hope and trust, to give to your Lordships such an explanation of any thing in the laws, customs, opinions and manners of

the people concerned, and who are the subjects of the crimes with which they charge him, as may tend to remove all doubt and ambiguity from the minds of your Lordships upon these subjects. . . .

My Lords, I confess that in this business I come before your Lordships with a considerable degree of animation, because I think it is a most auspicious circumstance in a prosecution like this, in which the honour of this Kingdom and that of many nations is involved, that from the commencement of our preliminary process to the hour of this solemn trial, not the smallest difference of opinion has arisen between the two Houses. My Lords, there were persons who, looking rather upon what was to be found in the Journals of Parliament, or what was to be expected from the public justice of Parliament, have formed hopes consolatory to them, and highly favourable to us; there were persons who entertained hopes that the corruptions of India should have escaped amongst the dissensions of Parliament, but they are disappointed: they will be disappointed in all the rest of their expectations which they had formed upon everything except the merits of the cause. The Commons will not have the melancholy and unsocial glory of having acted a right part in an imperfect work. What the greatest Inquest of the Nation has begun, its highest Tribunal will accomplish. Justice will be done to India. It is true your Lordships will have your full share in this great and glorious work; but we shall always consider that any honour that is divided with your Lordships will be more than doubled to ourselves.

My Lords, I must confess that, amongst all these encouraging prospects, the Commons do not approach your Lordships' Bar without some considerable degree of anxiety. I hope and trust that the magnitude of the interests which we have in hand will reconcile some degree of solicitude for the event with the undoubting confidence with which we impose ourselves upon your Lordships' justice. For we are so made, my Lords, that it is not only the greatness of the danger but the value of the stake that excites our concern in every undertaking, and I do assure your Lordships, for I am authorized to say it, that no standard is sufficient to estimate the value which the Commons set upon the fate of the Case which they now bring before you. . . . The question is, not solely whether the prisoner at the Bar be found innocent or be found guilty, but whether millions of mankind shall be miserable or happy. You do not decide the Case only; you fix the rule. For your Lordships will undoubtedly see in the course of this Case, that there is not only a long, connected, systematic, course of misdemeanors, but an equally connected system of maxims and principles invented to justify them, upon which your Lordships must judge. It is according to the Judgment that you shall pronounce upon the past transactions of India, connected with those principles, that the whole rule, tenure, tendency and character of our future government in India is to be finally decided. My Lords, it will take its course and work its whole impression from the business of this hour. My Lords, it is not only the interest of a great Empire which is concerned, which is now a most considerable part of the British Empire; but, my Lords, the credit and honour of the British nation will itself be decided by this decision. My Lords, they will stand or fall thereby. We are to decide by the case of this gentleman whether the crimes of individuals are to be turned into public guilt and national ignominy, or whether this nation will convert these offences, which have thrown a transient shade on its glory, into

a judgment that will reflect a permanent lustre on the honour, justice and humanity of this Kingdom.

My Lords, there is another consideration which has caused solicitude to the Commons, equal to those other two great interests that are affected. I mean the interest of our Empire in India, and the interest of the national character; something that if possible comes more home to the hearts and feelings of every Englishman. I mean the nature of our constitution itself, which is deeply involved in the event of this Cause. For the consequence and purport of an Impeachment for High Crimes and Misdemeanours before the Peers of this Kingdom, upon a charge of the Commons, will very much be decided by your decision. For, my Lords, if this tribunal should be found, as I hope it will always be found, too great for trifling and petty causes; if it should at the same time be found incompetent to one of the greatest which can come before you; if the lesser from their smallness escape you, and the greatest from their magnitude oppress you, it is impossible that the high end of this Judicature can be answered.

My Lords, I do not know whether it is owing to the polish of our times, less fertile perhaps in great offences than those that have gone before us, or whether it is from a sluggish apathy which has dulled and enervated public justice, I am not called upon to determine; but whatever the cause is, it is now 63 years since any impeachment, grounded on an abuse of authority and misdemeanour in office, has been brought before this tribunal. The last that I recollect is that of Lord Macclesfield in the year 1725. So that the oldest process known to the Constitution of this country has now upon its revival some appearance of novelty; and at this time, when all Europe is perhaps in a state of great agitation;

when antiquity has lost all its effect and reverence on the minds of men, and when novelty still retains the suspicions that always will be attached to novelty, we have been very anxious indeed, in a business like this, so to conduct ourselves that nothing in the revival of this great Parliamentary process should afford an excuse for its future disuse. Whatever does not stand with credit cannot stand long; and if the constitution should be deprived (I mean not in form, but virtually) of this resource, we should certainly be deprived of all its other valuable parts; because this is the cement which binds it all together. This is the individuating principle that makes England what England is. This it is by which the Magistracy and all other things are directed, and must be tried and controlled. It is by this tribunal that Statesmen who abuse their power are tried before Statesmen and by Statesmen, upon solid principles of State morality. It is here that those who by an abuse of power have polluted the spirit of all laws can never hope for the least protection from any of its forms. It is here that those who have refused to conform themselves to the protection of law can never hope to escape through any of its defects. Your Lordships have great and plenary power. You do not supersede, you do not annihilate, any subordinate jurisdiction. On the contrary, you are auxiliary and supplemental to them all. Here it is that no subject in any part of the Empire can be refused justice. Here it is that we provide for that which is the great, substantial, excellence of our Constitution. I mean that great circulation of responsibility, by which, excepting the Supreme power, no man in any condition can escape his responsibility to the laws of his Country.

꙲

My Lords, we say that, with very few interruptions indeed, the affairs of India have constantly engaged the attention of the House of Commons for more than fourteen years. We say that we tried every method of legislative provision before we had recourse to any thing that was a mode of punishment. . . . But when we found that our Laws, when we found that our admonitions, were despised, that enormities were increased in proportion to what was to be effected; when we found that legal authority seemed to skulk and conceal its head like outlawed guilt; when we found that those who were appointed by Parliament to assert the authority of this Kingdom were the most forward and most active in opposition to them; then it was time for the justice of the Nation to exert itself. To have forborne any longer would not have been patience, but illusion—a participation in guilt and almost party with the Criminal. . . .

꙲

My Lords, . . . with respect to the crime which we chose, we chose one which we contemplated in its nature, with all its circumstances, with all its extenuations, and with all its aggravations; and on that review we are bold to say that the crimes with which we charge the Prisoner at the Bar are substantial crimes; that they are no errors or mistakes, such as wise and good men might possibly fall into. They are crimes, my Lords, truly and properly and emphatically, crimes. The Commons are too liberal not to allow for the difficulties of a great and arduous public situation. They know too well that domineering necessities will frequently occur in all great affairs. They know that the exigencies of a great occasion, in its precipitate career, do not give time to have recourse to fixed principles, but that they oblige men frequently to decide in a manner that calmer reason would certainly have rejected. We know that, as we are to be served by men, the persons who serve us must be tried as men, and that there is a very large allowance indeed due to human infirmity and human error. This, my Lords, we knew and had weighed before we came to your Lordships' Bar. But the crimes which we charge in these Articles are not the lapses and defects and errors of common human nature and frailty, such as we know and feel, and can allow for. They are crimes which have their rise in the wicked dispositions of men. They are crimes that have their rise in avarice, rapacity, pride, cruelty, ferocity, malignity of temper, haughtiness, insolence. In short, my Lords, in everything that manifests a heart blackened to the very blackest, a heart dyed deep in blackness, a heart corrupted, vitiated and gangrened to the very core. If we do not plant the crimes in that we charge those vices which the breast of man is made to abhor and its laws to protect against, we desire no longer to be heard on this occasion. Let everything be pleaded that can be pleaded on the score of error and infirmity; we give up the whole. We stand on crimes that were crimes of deliberation. We charge him with nothing that he did not commit upon deliberation, that he did not commit against remonstrance. We charge him with nothing that he did not commit against command. We charge him with nothing that he did not commit contrary to the advice, contrary to the admonition and reprimand of those who were authorized by the laws to reprove and reprimand him. They were crimes, not against forms, but against those eternal laws of justice which you assembled here to assert, which forms are made to support and not to supersede in any instance whatever. They were, not in formal and technical language, but in real and absolute effect, High Crimes and Misdemeanours.

So far as to the crimes. Now as to the Criminal. We have not chosen to bring before you a poor, puny, trembling delinquent, misled perhaps by the example of those who ought to have kept him in awe, and afterwards oppressed by their power in order to make his punishment the means of screening the greater offences of those that were above him. We have not brought before your Lordships one of those poor, obscure, offenders, in an inferior situation, who, when his insignificance and weakness is weighed against the power of the prosecution, gives even to public justice something of the appearance of oppression. No, my Lords, we have brought before your Lordships the first man in rank, authority and station; we have brought before you the head, the chief, the captain-general in iniquity; one in whom all the frauds, all the peculations, all the violence, all the tyranny in India are embodied, disciplined and arrayed. This is the person, my Lords, that we bring before you. Then, if we have brought before you such a person, if you strike at him you will not have need of a great many more examples: you strike at the whole corps if you strike at the head.

My Lords, so far as to the crime, and so far as to the Criminal. Now, my Lords, I shall say a few words relative to the evidence that we have to bring to support such a charge, and which we think will be equal to the charge itself. And we say that the evidence that we have determined to bring before you is evidence of record, of weighty official, authentic record, and signed by the hand of the criminal himself in many instances. We have to bring before you his own letters, authenticated by his own hand. We shall bring before you also numbers of oral living witnesses, competent to speak to the points to which they are brought. This, my Lords, we are ready to bring before you, and I trust that the evidence will be found such as cannot leave the least doubt in your minds of the facts; and when you consider them, when the facts are proved, I believe, from their nature and effects you can have no doubt of their criminality.

My Lords, when we consider the late enormous power of the prisoner; when we consider the criminal and indefatigable assiduity in the destruction of evidence; when we consider the power that he had over all testimony, I believe your Lordships, and I believe the world, will be astonished that so much, so clear, so solid, and so conclusive a body of evidence has been obtained against him. My Lords, this I say, that I have no doubt that in nine instances out of ten it would satisfy the narrow precision which is supposed to prevail, and which really does prevail to a degree, in all subordinate and delegated jurisdictions. But your Lordships will maintain, what we assert and claim as the right of the subjects of Great Britain, that you are not bound by any rules whatever except those of natural, immutable and substantial justice. God forbid that the Commons should come before your Lordships and desire that anything should be received as proof which is not in its own nature adapted to prove the matter in question. God forbid that they should do so; for they would then overturn the very principles of that justice which they resort to your Lordships to obtain in favour of their constituents, and in favour of the people of India. They would be giving an evil example, that would redound to their own injury and bring mischief upon the heads of themselves and all their posterity. God forbid, on the other hand, that your Lordships should ever reject evidence on any

pretended nicety, which I am sure you will not. I have too much confidence in the learning with which you will be advised, and the liberality and the nobleness of the sentiments with which you were born. I have too much confidence to suspect, in the smallest degree, that you would, by any abuse of the forms and technical course of the proceedings, deny justice to so great a part of the world that claims it at your hand. For your Lordships always had a boundless power; I mean, always within the limits of justice. Your Lordships always had a boundless power and unlimited jurisdiction. You have now a boundless object. It is not from this Country or the other, from this district or the other, that relief is applied for, but from whole tribes of suffering nations, various descriptions of men, differing in language, in manners and in rights, men separated by every means from you. However, by the providence of God, they are come here to supplicate justice at your Lordships' Bar; and I hope and trust that there will be no rule, formed upon municipal maxims, which will prevent the Imperial justice which you owe to the people that call to you from all parts of a great disjointed empire. Situated as this Kingdom is—an object, thank God, of envy to the rest of the world for its greatness and its power—its conduct, in that very elevated situation to which it has arisen, will undoubtedly be scrutinized. It is well known that great wealth has poured into this country from India; and it is no derogation to us to suppose the possibility of being corrupted by that by which great Empires have been corrupted, and by which assemblies almost as respectable and as venerable as your Lordships' have been known to be indirectly shaken.

My Lords, when I say that forty millions of money have come from India to England, we ought to take great care that corruption does not follow, and we may venture to say that the best way to secure a man's reputation is, not by a proud defiance of public opinion, but by guiding one's actions in such a way as that public opinion may afterwards and not previously be defied. In such a situation, it is necessary that nothing in your Lordships' proceedings should appear to have the slightest trace, the faintest odour, of chicane. God forbid that, when you try the Cause of Asia in the presence of Europe, there should be the least suspicion that the Cause of Asia is not as good with you, because the abuse is committed by a British subject; that it should be supposed that that narrow partiality, so destructive of justice, should guide us; that a British subject in power should have rights which are denied to our humble allies, to our detached dependents, to those who at such a distance depend upon the breath of British justice, and have deprived themselves of every other resource under heaven.

My Lords, I do not say this from any fear, doubt or hesitation, as to what your Lordships will do, none in the world. God forbid I should. But I say it on the account of what you all know, what is disseminated abroad among the public, that those who cannot defend themselves upon their merits and their actions may defend themselves behind those fences and intrenchments that are made to secure the liberty of the people; that power and the abuses of power should cover themselves by those things which were made to secure liberty. But God forbid it should be bruited abroad that the laws of England are for the rich and the powerful; but that for the poor, the miserable, and defenceless they afford no resource at all. God forbid it should be said that we in this kingdom know how to confer the most extravagant and inordinate power upon public ministers; and that we are poor, helpless, deficient and impotent in the means of calling them to account for it. God forbid it should be said that no nation under heaven equals the British in substantial violence and informal justice. It shall never be said, and I trust that this Cause will put an end to all conjectures of that kind, which have been disseminated with so much industry through this kingdom and through foreign nations too, that, in order to cover our connivance and participation in guilt, and our common share in the plunder of the East, we have invented a set of scholastic distinctions abhorrent to the general sentiments of mankind, by which we are to deny ourselves the knowledge of all that the rest of the world knows, and what so great a part of the world both knows and feels. God forbid that appearance of that kind should happen. I do not deprecate it from any suspicion of the House; but I deprecate it from knowing that hitherto we have moved within the circle of municipal justice. I am afraid of moving within that circle. It may be suspected that we should endeavour to force nature into that, and not endeavour to enlarge the circle of justice to the necessities of the Empire that we have obtained.

This is the only thing which does create any doubt or difficulty upon the minds of the people. But if such a thing should happen, in my humble opinion it would be better a thousand times to give the short answer the Dey of Algiers gave to a British Ambassador, representing the rest of the British Merchants. "My friend", says he, . . . "do not you know that my subjects are a band of Robbers and that I am their Captain"; better far it would be, a thousand times more manly than an hypocritical process which, under a pretended reverence to punctilious ceremonies and observances of law, abandons mankind without help and resource to all the desolating consequences of arbitrary power. No, my Lords, I have not the least suspicion that such a thing will or can prevail in this House, nor prevail in this Kingdom. Your Lordships will exercise the great plenary powers with which you are invested in a manner that will do honour to your justice, to the protecting justice of this Kingdom, to the great people who are subjected to it. It shall not be squared by any rules, but by their necessities, and by that law of common justice which cements them to us and us to them. . . .

⤸

My Lords, the powers which Mr. Hastings is charged with having abused are the powers delegated to him by the East India Company. The East India Company itself acts under two sorts of powers, derived from two sources. The first source of its power is under a Charter which the Crown was authorized by Act of Parliament to grant it.[36] The next is from several grants and Charters indeed, as well as that great fundamental Charter, by several grants and charters which it derived from the Emperor of the Moguls, the person with whose domains they are chiefly conversant, particularly the great Charter by which they acquired the High Stewardship of the Kingdoms of Bengal, Bahar and Orissa in 1765.[37] Under those two Charters they act. As to the first, it is from that Charter that they derive the capacity by which they can be considered as a public body at all, or capable of any public function; it is from thence they acquire the capacity to take any other Charter, to acquire any other offices, or to hold any

other possessions. This being the root and origin of their power, makes them responsible to the party from whom that power is derived. As they have emanated from the supreme power of this kingdom, they themselves are responsible, their body as a corporate body, themselves as individuals, and the whole body and train of their servants are responsible to the high justice of this kingdom. In delegating great power to the India Company this kingdom has not released its sovereignty. On the contrary, its responsibility is increased by the greatness and sacredness of the power given. For this power they are and must be responsible; and I hope this day your Lordships will shew that this nation never did give a power without imposing a proportionable degree of responsibility.

As to the other power, which they derived from the Mogul Empire by various Charters from that Crown, and particularly by the Charter of 1765, by which they obtained the offices of Lord High Steward (as I said) Dewan or Dewannee of the Kingdoms of Bengal, Bahar and Orissa; by that Charter they bound themselves, and bound inclusively all their servants, to perform all the duties belonging to that new office. And by the ties belonging to that new relation they were bound to observe the laws, rights, usages and customs of the Natives, and to pursue their benefit in all things, which was the nature, institution and purpose, of the office which they received. If the power of the Sovereign from whom they derived these powers should be by any misfortune in human affairs annihilated or suspended, the duty to the people below, which they acquired under this Charter, is not suspended, is not annihilated, but remains in all its force; and, for the responsibility, they are thrown back upon that country from whence their original power, and

[36]Parliament began sanctioning the East India Company's royal charters in 1698.

[37]The Treaty of Allahabad.

along with it their responsibility, both emanated in one and the same act. For when the Company acquired that office in India, an English Corporation became an integral part of the Mogul Empire. When Great Britain assented to that grant virtually, and afterwards took advantage of it, Great Britain made a virtual act of union with that country, by which they bound themselves as securities for their subjects, to preserve the people in all rights, laws and liberties, which their natural original Sovereign was bound to enforce, if he had been in a condition to enforce it. So that the two duties flowing from two different sources are now united in one, and come to have justice called for them at the Bar of this House, before the Supreme Royal justice of this Kingdom, from whence originally their powers were derived.

⤺

Your Lordships will recollect that the India Company, and therefore I shall spare you a long history of that, hoping and trusting that your Lordships will think it is not to inform you, but to revive circumstances in your memory that I enter into this detail. Your Lordships will recollect the East India Company had its origin about the latter end of the reign of Elizabeth, a period when all sorts of Companies, inventions and monopolies were in fashion.[38] And at that time the Company was sent out with large extensive powers for increasing the commerce and the honour of this Country. For to increase its commerce without increasing its honour and reputation would have been thought at that time, and will be thought now, a bad bargain for the Country. But their powers were under that Charter confined merely to commercial affairs.

By degrees, as the theatre of the operation was distant, as its intercourse was with many great, some barbarous, and all of them armed nations, where not only the Sovereign but the Subjects were also armed in all places, it was found necessary to enlarge their powers. The first power they obtained was a power of naval disciplining their ships—a power which has since dropped. The next was a power of Law Martial. The next was a power of civil, and to a degree of criminal, Jurisdiction within their own Factory, within their settlements, over their own people and their own servants. The next was (and there was a stretch indeed) the powers of Peace and War; those great, high prerogatives of Sovereignty, which never were known before to be parted with to any Subjects, but those high sovereign powers were given to the East India Company. So that when it had acquired them all, which it did about the end of the reign of Charles the Second, the East India Company did not seem to be merely a Company formed for the extension of the British commerce, but in reality a delegation of the whole power and sovereignty of this kingdom sent into the East. In that light the Company began undoubtedly to be considered, and ought to be considered, as a subordinate sovereign power; that is, sovereign with regard to the objects which it touched, subordinate with regard to the power from whence this great trust was derived.

When the East India Company once appeared in that light, things happened to it totally different from what has happened in all other ordinary affairs, and from what has happened in all the remote mysteries of politicians, or been dreamed of in the world. For in all other Countries, a political body that acts as a Commonwealth is first settled, and trade follows as a necessary consequence of the protection

---

[38]The East India Company began through a royal charter granted in 1600.

obtained by political power. But there the affair was reversed. The constitution of the Company began in commerce and ended in Empire. And where powers of peace and war are given, it wants but time and circumstance to make this supersede every other and the affairs of commerce fall into their proper rank and situation. And accordingly it did happen that the possession and power of assertion of these great authorities coinciding with the improved state of Europe, with the improved state of arts and the improved state of laws, and (what is much more material) the improved state of military discipline; that coinciding with the general fall of Asia, and the relaxation and dissolution of its governments, with the fall of its warlike spirit, and the total disuse almost of all parts of military discipline. Those two coinciding, the India Company became to be what it is, a great Empire carrying on subordinately (under the public authority), a great commerce. It became that thing which was supposed by the Roman Law so unsuitable, the same power was a Trader, the same power was a Lord.

In this situation, the India Company however still preserved traces of its original mercantile character; and the whole exterior order of its service is still carried on upon a mercantile plan and mercantile principles. In fact, it is a State in disguise of a Merchant, a great public office in disguise of a Countinghouse. . . .

↜

My Lords, I must remark, before I go further that there is something peculiar in the service of the East India Company, and different from that of any other nation that has ever transferred its power from one Country to another. The East India Company in India is not the British Nation. When the Tartars entered into China and into Hindoostan, when all the Goths and Vandals entered into Europe, when the Normans came into England, they came as a Nation. The Company in India does not exist as a Nation. Nobody can go there that does not go in its Service. Therefore the English Nation in India is nothing but a seminary for the succession of Officers. They are a Nation of placemen. They are a Republic, a Commonwealth without a people. They are a State made up wholly of magistrates. The consequence of which is that there is no people to control, to watch, to balance against the power of office. The power of office, so far as the English Nation is concerned, is the sole power in the Country. There is no corrective upon it whatever. The consequence of which is that, being a Kingdom of Magistrates, the *Esprit du corps* is strong in it—the spirit of the body by which they consider themselves as having a common interest, and a common interest separated both from the Country that sent them out and from the Country in which they are; and where there is no control by persons who understand their language, who understand their manners, or can apply their conduct to the Laws of the Country. Such control does not exist in India. Therefore confederacy is easy, and had been general among them; and therefore your Lordships are not to expect that that should happen in such a body which never happened in the world in any body or Corporation, that they should ever be a proper check and control upon themselves; it is not in the nature of things. There is a monopoly with an *Esprit du corps* at home, called the India Company; there is an *Esprit du corps* abroad; and both those systems are united into one body, animated with the same spirit, that is, with the corporate spirit, which never was a spirit which corrected itself in any time or circumstance in the world, and which is such a thing as has not happened to the Moors, to the Portuguese, to the Romans (to go to any old or new examples). It has not happened in any one time or circumstance in the World, except in this. And out of that has issued a species of abuses, at the head of which Mr. Hastings has put himself against the authority of the East India Company at home and every authority in this Country.

My Lords, the next circumstance is—and which is curious too—that the emoluments of office do not in any degree correspond with the trust. For under the name of Junior Merchant and Senior Merchant and Writer, and those other little names of a Counting house, you have great Magistrates; you have the administrators of revenues truly royal; you have Judges civil, and in a great degree criminal, who pass judgments upon the greatest properties of the Country. You have all these under these names; and the emoluments that belong to them are so weak, so inadequate to the dignity of the character that it is impossible . . . for the subordinate parts of it to exist, to hope to exist, as Englishmen who look at their home as their ultimate resource, to exist in a state of incorruption. In that service the rule that prevails in many other Countries is reversed. In other Countries often the greatest situations are attended with but little emoluments because glory, family reputation, the love, the tears of joy, the honest applause, of their Country, pay those great and mighty labours which in great situations are sometimes required from the Commonwealth; but all other countries pay in money what cannot be paid in fame and reputation. But it is the reverse with the India Company. All the subordinate parts of the gradation are Officers, who, notwithstanding the weight and importance of the offices and dignities intrusted to them, are miserably provided for; and, the heads, the chiefs, have great emoluments, securing them against every

mode of temptation. And this is the thing Mr. Hastings has abused. He was at the head of the Service. He has corrupted his hands and sullied his government with bribes. He has used oppression and tyranny in the place of legal government; and instead of endeavouring to find honest, honourable, and adequate rewards for the persons who served the public, he has left them to prey upon it without the smallest degree of control. He has neither supplied nor taken care to supply, with that unbounded license which he used over the public revenues, to provide an honest scale of emoluments suited to the vastness of the power given to the Company's Service. He has not employed the public revenue for that purpose; but has left them at large to prey upon the Country, and find themselves emoluments as they could.

❧

My Lords, it is necessary for you, that you may the better judge of the abuse Mr. Hastings has made of the powers vested in him, to know who the people are over whom he has abused those powers. This is a little out of the way, but it will be necessary for me to explain it, and I shall explain it with as much brevity as is consistent with the distinctness, with which I mean to bring the whole before your Lordships. . . .

❧

Then, my Lords, there are two distinct people in India, totally distinct from each other in characters, lives and manners, for both of whom Mr. Hastings was bound to provide equally, agreeable to the terms of the Charter the Company received from the lawful governing power of the Country, which it had received at its own solicitation, which was not forced upon it by a superior power, but given at the immediate solicitation of the principal servant belonging to the

Company; accepted by the Company and by it, I am very sorry to say, little regarded, or at least by its principal servants.

The first set of people who are subjected virtually to the British Empire through those mediums which I have described to you, are the original inhabitants of Hindoostan, who have inhabited in all time, and beyond all the eras which we use ... have lived and been proprietors and inhabitants of that country, with manners, religion, customs and usages, appropriate to themselves and no ways resembling those of the rest of mankind. Those persons are commonly called Gentoos. The systems and principle of that Government is local; their laws, their manners, their religion are local.

Their legislator, whoever he was (for that is lost in the mists of a very obscure antiquity) had it as the great leading principle of his policy to connect the people with their soil. And accordingly, by one of those anomalies which time daily discovers, and which perhaps reflection would explain in the nature of man, these people who are the softest in their manners, approaching almost to feminine, who are the most benevolent, and of a larger circle of benevolence than our morals take in, who extend their benevolence to the whole animal creation; these people are the most unalliable to any other part of the creation. They cannot, the highest orders of them, touch that bond which is the bond of life, and which by supporting the individual unites them, in other cases—I mean conviviality. That bond of life cannot be had with these people. And there are some circumstances, relative to them, that exclude them still more than I have mentioned from all immediate commerce with this nation; namely, that that very element which, while appearing to disconnect, unites mankind—I mean the sea—the sea

is to them a forbidden element. None of their high castes can without great danger to his situation ... ever pass the sea. If it could be truly said that a great gulf is fixed between you and them, it is that gulf created by manners, opinions and laws, radicated in the very nature of the people, and which you can never efface from them. This forbids for ever all immediate communication between that country and this. And that, my Lords, makes it ten times more necessary for us to keep a strict eye upon all persons who go there, and so to conduct ourselves in our proceedings with regard to the knowledge of that country and all its affairs as may be conformable to their necessities and not to our inventions, that we, if we must govern such a Country, must govern them upon their own principles and maxims and not upon ours, that we must not think to force them to our narrow ideas, but extend ours to take in theirs; because to say that that people shall change their maxims, lives and opinions, is what cannot be. We know that empire of opinion is, I had almost said, human nature itself. It is however the strongest part of human nature; and more of the happiness and unhappiness of mankind resides in opinion than in all other external circumstances whatever. And, if it resides in us in opinion, much more does it reside in them in opinion. For sometimes our laws of religion differ from our laws of the land; sometimes our laws of the land differ from our laws of honour. But in that Country the laws of religion, the laws of the land and the laws of honour, are all united and consolidated in one, and bind a man eternally to the rules of what is called his *caste*.

I think it necessary to state to your Lordships what a *caste* is. These people from the oldest time have been distributed into the various orders, all hereditary, which are called castes. These castes are the fundamental part of the constitution of that Commonwealth, both in their Church and in their State.

Your Lordships are born to hereditary honours in the chief of your Houses; the rest mix with the people. But in the case of the Hindoos those who were born noble can never fall into any second rank. They are divided into four orders—the Brahmans, the Chehtrees, the Vissyas, and the Sooders.[39] They are divided into four Commonwealths. The higher cannot pass into the lower; the lower cannot rise into the higher. They have all their appropriate rank, place and situation, and their appropriate religion too, which, though they all go under one definition of religion, yet is different in its rites and ceremonies in each of those castes. And if a man who is in that caste which at once unites what we should call the dignity of the Peerage in this Country and the sanctity of Episcopacy, the Brahmans, falls out of it, he does not fall into the next order, the Chehtrees, the Vissyas, or the Sooders, but he falls out of all ranks of society, is excluded, an out cast, the most infamous of all mankind.

These people, bound by all laws, human and divine, to those principles of caste and which inveterate usage has grafted in them, in a manner in which no known prejudice in the world has been known to exist, these people are affected in their caste, not only by the crimes, the voluntary crimes by which they may lose it, but likewise by certain involuntary sufferings and involuntary disgraces, utterly out of their own power, which do affect them in their caste which is their everything. For speak to an Indian of his caste, and you speak to him of his all; when they lose that

caste they lose everything. The loss, as I said, is not only by voluntary crimes, but by the acts of other people. So that these miserable castes give one pledge more to fortune than any other nation was ever known to do. They are bound by new ties. Tyranny oppresses upon them. And, accordingly, those who have wished to oppress them, those who have stood imprisonment, those who have stood whips, those who have stood tortures, those who have stood the menaces of death itself, and they without any impression, have instantly given way when it has been attempted to bring upon them any of those pollutions by which they lose caste.

This shews us in what manner we ought to handle people so delicate in these respects. Now we shall shew you that Mr. Hastings made the full use, through several of his wicked and abominable instruments in that country, chosen from the Natives themselves, of not only all the wicked means of oppressing and abusing them, but striking at that which goes beyond life, which seems to affect them in other Worlds; which they conceive to themselves unknown, this power has been used to the destruction of that people. I shall prove that he has put his own menial domestic Servant, a wretch dependant, a wretch ignorant, a wretch vicious and corrupt, the instrument of his briberies, he has put him into that seat of Ecclesiastical Jurisdiction which was to decide upon the Castes of all these people, which contained their rank, their family and honour, their happiness here and their salvation hereafter. He put his own Servant to judge over them, and to get a new hold by which he brought the people under his tyranny and that nobody dare complain of him. Accordingly he says: Who complains of me? Who dare complain of me? No, your menial Servant has my caste in his power. I

---

[39]In modern spelling, the four castes, or *varnas*, are Brahmins, Ksatriyas, Vaisyas, and Sudras.

shall not trouble your Lordships with mentioning others. It was enough that Gentaboo,[40] and other names to which your Lordships are to be familiarized hereafter; it is enough that these persons had the Caste and character of the people in their hands; and by this means Mr. Hastings has taken care effectually that these people shall never complain.

My Lords, I am to mention to you circumstances relative to these people. They were the original people of Hindostan. They are still infinitely more numerous; I take for granted, twenty to one. The Musselmans are nothing like them. They are the old inhabitants of the Country, and still more numerous. Whatever fault they may have, God forbid we should go to pass judgment upon people who formed their Laws and Institutions prior to our insect origins of yesterday. That we should pass judgment upon them. They have two great principles which ought to be respected, that is to say, great force and stability, and great, glorious and excellent effects. Their stability has been proved by their holding on for a time and duration commensurate to all the Empires which History has made us acquainted with. And still they exist in a green old age, with all the reverence of antiquity and with all the affection to their own institutions that other people have to novelty and change. And accordingly they have stood firm in their own Country and cast their roots deep in their native soil, because they cast them nowhere else than in their native soil, and fixed their opinions in their native soil, and bound them together. Their religion has made no Converts; their dominion no conquests; and in proportion as they were concentred within and hindered

from spreading abroad, they have grown to double force and have existed against Bigotry, against persecution, against all the fury of Foreign Conquests, and almost against the fury and avarice of the English Dominion established among them.

↬

[Burke then reviews the history of India from the time before the Islamic invasions "till the unfortunate era of 1756," where he closes the first day of his speech. Eds.]

16 February 1788

↬

Having therefore wished your Lordships to keep steadily in your mind these circumstances of distinction—I shall beg leave to proceed to that period at which I closed—the great and memorable period which has given occasion to the Business of [this] day—a day which I hope will shine with distinguished Lustre in the annals of the British Justice.

My Lords to obtain empire has been a common thing—to govern it well has been more rare—but to chastise the guilt of those who have abused the power of the Country by its superintending justice is I hope a glory more peculiarly reserved to this Nation, to this time, and to this House.

The year 1756 is a memorable aera in the history of the world—It introduced a new power, with new manners, new customs, new opinions, new laws, into the Bosom of the East. And it would not only have been memorable as would have been for the history of Great Britain if it has shewn its virtue upon this occasion to be altogether equal to its fortune.

My Lords, that part of the Country which had its native government broken up

---

[40]Hastings's personal steward, Krishna Kanta Nandy.

which had fallen into a scene of confusion from being the prey and sport of the infernal ambition of its own grandees, if at that time a star had risen from the West that would have prognosticated order, peace, happiness and security to the Natives of that Country. And indeed some thing might have been expected of the kind. For when it was to come from a learned and enlightened part of Europe, in the most enlightened period of its time; when it was to come from a Nation the most enlightened of the enlightened part of Europe, it would have been a great deal to say that they came from the bosom of a free Country, which carried with it at least to a Country who had not the benefit of its forms, all the advantage of the liberty and spirit of a British constitution. It would have been glorious to this Country and would have saved the trouble of this day, in some measure at least. It would have been glorious to us too, that in an enlightened state of the world, possessing a religion an improved part of the religion of the World—I mean the reformed religion—that we had done honor to Europe, to our Cause, to our religion, done honor to all the circumstances of which we boast and pride ourselves at the moment of that revolution.

My Lords, it has happened otherwise; it is now for us to think how we are to repair it. And therefore resuming where I broke off, with your indulgence to my weakness yesterday, I shall beg leave to restate to you that Sujah Dowlah who was the adopted grandson of Ally Cawn, a cruel and ferocious tyrant, the manner of whose acquisition of power I have stated.[41] He came too young and inexperienced to that throne of usurpation. It was a usurpation yet green

in the Country; the Country felt uneasy under it. It had not the advantage of that prescriptive usage, that inveterate habit and opinion, which a long system of any government secures to it. The only security that it had was the security of an army. The prince of the Country had endeavored to supply the weakness of his government by the greatness of his purse and amassed treasures. But with all the more treasures they emassed, the more they felt the effects of poverty. For putting the money in the place of force, the consequences were that their armies were unpaid, and being unpaid or weakly paid, were undisciplined, disorderly and unfaithful. In this situation a young prince, confiding more in the appearances than in the reality of things, undertook from motives which the House of Commons, with all their industry to discover the circumstances of them, found some difficulty in making out, to attack a little miserable trading Fort that we had erected at Calcutta.[42] He succeeded in that attempt, because success in that attempt was easy; and there happened, in consequence of it, an imprisonment, not owing, I believe, to the direct will of the Prince, but what will always happen when the will of the Prince is but too much the law, that there was an abuse, a gross abuse, of his power by his lowest servants, by which 120 or more of your Country men perished miserably in a dungeon in that place, by a story too tragical for me to tell, too well known for me to need mention.[43] When the event happened, there happened at the same time a concurrence of other events which, in the midst of that weakness, displayed the

---

[41]Siraj al-Daula inherited the throne of Bengal from his grandfather, Alivardi Khan, who ruled Bengal from 1740 until his death in 1756.

---

[42]The attack occurred in 1756.

[43]Burke is referring to the British deaths in the infamous Black Hole of Calcutta.

strength of great Brittain in Asia. For some years before, upon the Coast of Coromandel, the French and English Troops began to exhibit the power, force and efficacy of European discipline in that part of the World; and, as we daily looked for a war with France,[44] the Country was to a degree armed there, and accordingly, My Lord Pigot,[45] the Preserver and the Victim[46] of the British domminion in Asia, detached a strong force, such of the Companies force as could be collected and such of his Majesty's ships on that station, to the assistance of that place and accordingly, to make short of this history, the daring and commanding genius of a Clive,[47] the patient, firm ability of a Watson,[48] the treachery of Mere Jaffier,[49] and the battle of Plassey, gave us the patronage of a Kingdom and the command of all its treasures. We negociated with Meere Jaffer, the Vice Roy, for the throne of his Master, upon which throne we seated him, and obtained immediately immense sums of money, a million sterling for the Company, upwards of a million £230,000 for individuals: in the whole, a sum of about two Millions, £230,000, for various purposes, from the Prince of that Country. We obtained too the Town of Calcutta more compleatly than We had it and the twenty four districts adjoining, which was the first small seminial principle of the great territorial acquisitions we since made in India.

Many circumstances of this acquisition I pass by. There is a secret veil to be drawn over the beginnings of all governments. They had their origin, as the beginning of all such things have had, in some matters that had as good be covered by obscurity. Time in the origin of most governments has thrown this mysterious veil over them. Prudence and discretion make it necessary to throw something of that veil over a business in which otherwise the fortune, the genius, the talents and military virtue of this Nation never shone more conspicuously. But a wise nation, when it has made a revolution itself, and upon its own principles, there rests. The first step is revolution to give it power; the next is good laws, good order, to give it stability. I am sorrow to say that the principle upon which the Gentlemen in India acted at that time was such as tended to make the new government as unstable as possible. For by the vast sums of money acquired by individuals upon this occasion, the immense, sudden, prodigious fortunes, it was discovered that a revolution in Bengal was a mine much more easily worked and infinitely more productive than the mine of Potosi and Mexico. But they found that the work was not only very lucretive, but not at all difficult. While Clive forded a deep water upon an unknown bottom, he left a bridge for his successors over which the lame could hobble and the blind might grope their way. There was not at that time a knot of Clerks in a Counting house, there was not a Captain of a band of ragged

---

[44]The Seven Years' War with France began in 1756.

[45]George Pigot, who defended Madras against the French in the Seven Years' War.

[46]Burke is referring to Lord Pigot's return to India in 1776 as governor of Madras, when he was imprisoned by subordinates of the East India Company who opposed his reforms of the company. Pigot died during his imprisonment. Pigot's treatment angered Burke. See *Speech on Restoring Lord Pigot, WSEB,* v, 35–40.

[47]Robert Clive, commander of British forces during the recapture of Calcutta and at the battle of Plassey in 1757.

[48]Charles Watson, rear admiral in the Royal Navy, who commanded British naval forces in the recapture of Calcutta.

[49]Mir Jafar, nabob of Bengal in 1757.

topassis,[50] that looked for any thing less than the deposition of Soubahs[51] and the sale of Kingdoms. Accordingly, this revolution that ought to have precluded other revolutions unfortunately become fruitful of them; and when my Lord Clive returned to Europe to enjoy his fame and fortune in this Country, there arose another set of people, who thought a revolution upon that revolution might be made as lucrative to [them] as this was to the first projectors. And accordingly, scarce was this Meere Jaffier seated upon this throne than they immediately, or in a short time, projected another revolution, a revolution which was to unsettle all the former revolution, to make way for new wars and disturbances, and for that train of peculation which ever since has vexed and oppressed that Country.

༄

[Burke describes in detail what he calls the "second" and "third" revolutions effected by the East India Company in Bengal. The "second" revolution involved, first, a plot between the East India Company and the nabob of Bengal to murder the emperor of the Mogul empire and, second, the usurpation of the nabob of Bengal's throne by the East India Company, which installed the ruthless and cruel nabob's son-in-law on the throne after the mysterious death of the nabob's son. To get the throne, the new nabob surrendered three southern provinces to the control of the East India Company. In the "third" revolution, the East India Company went to war against the nabob it installed and reinstated the original nabob on the throne of the by then truncated Bengal. Burke attempts to show how corrupt and

abusive the East India Company was after it first acquired substantial power after the battle of Plassey and to demonstrate that Hastings was a participant in this systematic corruption and abuse even as a junior officer in the East India Company. Eds.]

But the Company hearing of all these changes, hearing of such an incredible body of perfidy, knowing that there was a general market made of the Country and of the Company, that the flame of war spread from province to province, that in proportion as it spread the flame kindled, and that the rapacity which originally gave rise to it was following it in all its progress, the Company, my Lords, alarmed lest their very being should be destroyed, and finding themselves sinking by every victory they obtained, thought it necessary to come to some settlement. After having composed their differences with Lord Clive, they sent him out of that Country, about the year 1765, in order by his name, credit, and authority and weight in that Country to rectify the innumerable abuses which prevailed in it, and particularly that abuse which is the fundamental one of the whole, the abuse of presents. For all these bribes, all these rewards, had not the name of conditions or stipulations, but of presents. They were gratuities, given afterwards to the parties. They may give them what names they please, and your Lordships will think of them what you please. But they were the donations of misery to power, the gifts of wretchedness to the oppressors, and consequently left neither property nor security in permanence to any persons in the Country.

Lord Clive went out with new covenants. He went out to put an end to the practice of receiving presents. He himself had been a large receiver of them. Yet as it was in the moment of a revolution, the Company

---

[50]Mixed-race Indian soldiers.

[51]*Subahs* were provinces of the Mogul empire.

would have no more of it. They sent him out to reform. Whether they chose well or ill, does not signify. I think upon the whole they chose well; because his name, authority and weight would do a great deal. They sent him out to reform the grievances of that Country with such amazing powers as no servant of the Company ever had before. My Lords, I would not be understood here in my own character, much less in my delegated character, to stand up for any man in the totality of his conduct. I think that some of the measures which Lord Clive took were injudicious, and that some of them cannot be defended. But I do say that the plan which he laid down, and the course which he pursued were in general great and well imagined, that he settled great foundations, if they had been adhered to. For he first took strong measures below to put an end to a great many of the abuses that prevailed in the Country. And then he went up and did for a military man an act which will ever have great civil and political merit. He put a bound to the aspiring spirit of the Company. He limited its conquests, and prescribed bounds to its ambition. Quiet, says he, the minds of the Country, and what you have obtained regulate within; make it known to the Country that you resolve to acquire no more. Accordingly he settled every Prince that was concerned in a happy and easy settlement. He settled the Soubahdar of Oude, who had been driven from his dominions by the military arms and the great military merit of the British Commander. He with a generosity that astonished all Asia reinstated this enemy of his country peaceably upon his thrown, which did more towards quieting the minds of the people of Asia than any act that had been ever done by the English before. For the Mogul, the head of the Mussulman religion there and likewise of the Empire, a head honoured and esteemed even in its ruins, he obtained recognition by all the persons that were concerned. He got from him the Dewanee, which is the great grand period of the constitutional entrance of the Company into the affairs of India.[52] He quieted the minds of the people. He gave to the settlement of Bengal a constitutional form, and a legal right, acknowledged and recognized now for the first time by all the Princes of the Country, because given by the Charter of the Sovereign. He took care of Bulwant Sing, the Rajah of Benares, who had taken our part in the War.

⤶

In this manner he settled all the powers of Hindostan with which we were concerned and gave the country peace and form. . . .

⤶

My Lords, the fault in this settlement (which makes another period in our history) was, that Lord Clive did not stay long enough in that Country to give consistency to the settlement that he made. And the men that followed . . . had not weight enough to keep down and poize the country. Consequently many grievances arose: not such grievances as the sale and extirpation of a people; not such grievances as entirely subverting great and ancient families; not such grievances as changing instantly the settlements of the people; not the setting to farm the whole landed interest of a country; none of these. But certainly such grievances as made it necessary for the Company to send out a Commission in 1769, composed of Mr. Vansittart, Mr. Ford and Mr Scrafton. The unfortunate end of that commission is known to all the world.[53] But I mention it

---

[52] The Treaty of Allahabad.

[53] Henry Vansittart, Francis Forde, and Luke Scrafton were lost at sea en route to India.

in order to state the grievances which then prevailed in India, to state that the great order they gave the supervisors, with a view to give a force to the Service, was that they should upon no account whatever take presents. As soon as that Commission unfortunately perished ... the Company was preparing to send out another commission for the rectification of these grievances, but Parliament thought it necessary to supersede that Commission, to take the matter into their own hands, and to appoint another Commission in a Parliamentary way—of which Mr. Hastings was one—for the better government of that country. Mr. Hastings, on account of his local knowledge, on account of the number of friends he had here ... went out to India with great power indeed.

When this Government was settled, Moorshedabad still continued the seat of the Native Government and of all the Collections. Here the Company was not satisfied with putting a Resident at the Durbar, which was the first step to our assuming the Government in that Country. These steps must be traced by your Lordships. For I should never have given you this trouble, if it was not necessary to possess you clearly of the several progressive steps by which the Company's Government came to be established and to supersede the Native.

The next step that was made was the appointment of Supervisors in every Province, to oversee the Native Collector. The third was to establish a General Council of Revenue at Moorshedabad, to superintend the Great Steward Mahomed Reza Cawn. In 1772 that council by Mr Hastings was over turned, and the whole revenue brought to Calcutta. Mahomed Reza Cawn, by orders of the Company, was turned out of all his Offices, and turned out for reasons and principles

which your Lordships will hereafter see. And at last the Dewanee was entirely taken out of the Native hands and settled in the Supreme Council and Presidency itself in Calcutta. And so it remained until the year 1781, when Mr. Hastings made another revolution, took it out of the hands of the Council in which the orders of the Company, an Act of Parliament, and their own Act had vested it, and put it into a subordinate Council; that is, it was entirely vested in himself.

Now your Lordships see the whole of the revolutions. I have stated them—I trust with perspicuity; stated the grounds and principles upon which they were made; stated the abuses that grew upon them, and that every revolution produced its abuse. You saw the Native Government vanish away by degrees, until it is reduced to a situation fit for nothing but to become a private perquisite, as it has been to Mr Hastings to be granted to whom he pleased. The English Government succeeded. Mr Hastings was appointed to it by an Act of Parliament, having been appointed to the Presidency before to reform abuses.[54] And in those two periods of his Presidency and his appointment by Act of Parliament were those crimes committed of which he now stands accused. All this history is merely by way of illustration. His crimination begins with his nomination to the Presidency, and his subsequent nomination by Parliament.

The troubled period between the year 1756 and the settlement made in the year 1774 being passed, Mr Hastings having the Government in his hands, we are to consider how he comported himself in it.

---

[54]The East India Company appointed Hastings governor of Bengal in 1772. The Regulating Act of 1773 promoted him to governor-general of Bengal in 1774.

My Lords, the first thing in considering the character of any Governor is to have some test by which it may be tried. And we conceive here that when a British Governor is sent abroad, he is sent to pursue the good of the people as much as possible in the spirit of the Laws of this Country, which intend in all respects their conservation, their happiness, and their prosperity. These are the principles upon which Mr Hastings was bound to govern, and upon which he is to account for his conduct here.

The rule upon which you are to try him is this: what should a British Governor in such a situation do, or forbear to do? If he has done and if he has forborne in the manner in which a British Governor ought to do and to forbear, he has done his duty, and he is honourably acquitted. He resorts to other principles and to other maxims; but this Country will force him to be tried by its laws. The law of this Country recognizes that well known crime called misconduct in Office. It is a head of the Law of England and, so far as inferior Courts are competent to try it, it may be tried there. Here your Lordships are competent to every thing, and as you are competent in the power you are competent in the knowledge of the offence. And here I am bound to state to your Lordships, by the directions of those whose directions I am bound to follow, the principles upon which Mr Hastings declares he has conducted his Government, which principles he declares, first in several letters written to the East India Company, next in a paper of defence delivered to the House of Commons explicitly; and more explicitly, in his defence before your Lordships.

I am directed first to clear the way of all those grounds and principles upon which he frames his defence. For if those grounds are good and valid, they carry off a great deal at least, if not entirely, the foundation of our charge. My Lords, we contend that Mr Hastings, as a British Governor, ought to govern upon British principles, not by British forms. God forbid. For if ever there was a case in which the letter kills and the spirit gives life, it would be an attempt to introduce British forms and the substance of despotic principles together into any Country. No. We call for that spirit of equity, that spirit of justice, that spirit of safety, that spirit of protection, that spirit of lenity, which ought to characterise every British subject in power; and upon these and these principles only, he will be tried.

But he has told your Lordships in his defence, that actions in Asia do not bear the same moral qualities as the same actions would bear in Europe. My Lords, we positively deny that principle. I am authorized and called upon to deny it. And having stated at large what he means by saying that the same actions have not the same qualities in Asia and in Europe, we are to let your Lordships know that these Gentlemen have formed a plan of Geographical morality, by which the duties of men in public and in private situations are not to be governed by their relations to the Great Governor of the Universe, or by their relations to men, but by climates, degrees of longitude and latitude, parallels not of life but of latitudes. As if, when you have crossed the equinoctial line all the virtues die, as they say some animals die when they cross the line, as if there were a kind of baptism, like that practised by seamen, by which they unbaptize themselves of all that they learned in Europe, and commence a new order and system of things.

This Geographical morality we do protest against. Mr Hastings shall not screen himself under it. And I hope and trust not a great many words will be necessary to satisfy your Lordships. But we think it necessary in justification of ourselves to declare that the laws of morality are the same every where, and that there is no action which would pass for an action of extortion, of peculation, of bribery and of oppression in England, that is not an act of extortion, of peculation, of bribery and of oppression in Europe, Asia, Africa, and all the world over. This I contend for, not in the forms of it, but I contend for it in the substance.

Mr Hastings comes before your Lordships not as a British Governor, answering to a British Tribunal, but as a Soubahdar, as a Bashaw of three tails.[55] He says: I had an arbitrary power to exercise; I exercised it. Slaves I found the people; slaves they are. They are so by their Constitution; and if they are, I did not make it for them. I was unfortunately bound to exercise this arbitrary power, and accordingly I did exercise it. It was disagreeable to me, but I did exercise it, and no other power can be exercised in that Country. This, if it be true, is a plea in Bar. But I trust and hope your Lordships will not judge by Laws and institutions, which you do not know, against those Laws and institutions which you do know, and under whose power and authority Mr Hastings went out to India. Can your Lordships patiently hear what we have heard with indignation enough, and what, if there were nothing else, would call actions which are justified upon such principles to your Lordships Bar, that it may be known whether the Peers of England do not sympathize with the Commons in their detestation of such doctrine? Think of an English Governor tried before you as a British subject, and yet declaring that he governed upon the principles of arbitrary power. This plea is, that he did

govern there upon arbitrary and despotic, and, as he supposes, Oriental principles. And as his plea is boldly avowed and maintained and as, no doubt, all his conduct was perfectly correspondent to these principles, these principles and that conduct must be tried together.

If your Lordships will permit me, I will state one of the many places in which he has avowed these principles as the basis and foundation of all his conduct. "The sovereignty which they assumed, it fell to my lot, very unexpectedly to exert; and whether or not such power or powers of that nature were delegated to me by any provisions of any Act of Parliament I confess myself too little of a lawyer to pronounce. I only know that the acceptance of the sovereignty of Benares, &c is not acknowledged or admitted by any Act of Parliament; and yet, by the particular interference of the majority of the Council the Company is clearly and indisputably seized of that Sovereignty." So that this Gentleman, because he is not a lawyer nor clothed with those robes which distinguish and well distinguish the learning of this Country, is not to know anything of his duty; and whether he was bound by any, or what Act of Parliament, is a thing he is not lawyer enough to know. Now, if your Lordships will suffer the laws to be broken by those that are not of the long robe, I am afraid those of the long robe will have none to punish but those of their own profession. Mr Hastings therefore goes to a law which he knows better, that is, the law of arbitrary power and force, if it deserves to be called by any such name. "If therefore", says he, "the sovereignty of Benares, as ceded to us by the Vizier, have any rights what ever annexed to it, and be not a mere empty word without meaning, those rights must be such as are held, countenanced and established by the law,

---

[55] A subahdar was a provincial ruler in the Mogul empire, and a pasha was a provincial governor in the Ottoman Empire.

custom and usage, of the Mogul Empire, and not by the provisions of any British Act of Parliament hitherto enacted. These rights, and none other, I have been the involuntary instrument of enforcing. And if any future Act of Parliament shall positively, or by implication, tend to annihilate these very rights or their exertion, as I have exerted them, I much fear that the boasted sovereignty of Benares, . . . will be found a burthen instead of a benefit, a heavy clog rather than a precious gem to its present possessors; . . . The Hindoos, who never incorporated with their conquerors, were kept in order only by the strong hand of power. The constant necessity of similar exertions would increase at once their energy and extent; so that rebellion itself is the parent and promoter of despotism. Sovereignty in India implies nothing else—for I know not how we can form an estimate of its powers but from its visible effects—and these are every where the same from Cabool to Assam. The whole history of Asia is nothing more than precedents to prove the invariable exercise of arbitrary power. . . . "

My Lords, you have now heard the principles upon which Mr Hastings governs the part of Asia subjected to the British Empire. You have heard his opinion of "the mean and depraved state" of those who are subject to it. You have heard his lecture upon arbitrary power, which he states to be the constitution of Asia. You hear the application that he makes of it; and you hear the practices which he employs to justify it, and who the persons were the authority of whose examples he professes to follow. Do your Lordships really think that the nation would bear, that any human creature would bear, to hear an English Governor defend himself upon such principles? For, if he can defend himself upon such principles, no man has any security for anything but by

being totally independent of the British Government. Here he has declared his opinion that he is a despotic prince, that he is to use arbitrary power, and of course all his acts are covered with that shield. I know, says he, the constitution of Asia only from its practices. Will your Lordships ever hear the corrupt practices of mankind made the principles of Government? It will be your pride and glory to teach men that they are to conform their practices to principles, and not to draw their principles from the corrupt practices of any man whatever. Was there ever heard, or could it be conceived, that a man would dare to mention the practices of all the villains, all the mad usurpers, all the thieves and robbers in Asia, that he should gather them all up, and form the whole map of abuses into one code, and call it the duty of a British Governor? I believe that till this time so audacious a thing was never attempted by mankind.

He have arbitrary power. My Lords, the East India Company have not arbitrary power to give him; the King has no arbitrary power to give him; your Lordships have not, nor the Commons, nor the whole Legislature. We have no arbitrary power to give, because Arbitrary power is a thing which neither any man can hold nor any man can give away. No man can govern himself by his own will, much less can he be governed by the will of others. We are all born in subjection, all born equally, high and low, governors and governed, in subjection to one great, immutable, pre-existent law, prior to all our devices, and prior to all our contrivances, paramount to our very being itself, by which we are knit and connected in the eternal frame of the universe, out of which we cannot stir.

This great law does not arise from our conventions or compacts. On the contrary, it gives to our conventions and compacts all the force and sanction they can have. It does not arise from our vain institutions. Every good gift is of God; all power is of God; and He who has given the power and from whom it alone originates, will never suffer the exercise of it to be practised upon any less solid foundation than the power itself. Therefore, will it be imagined, if this be true, that He will suffer this great gift of Government, the greatest, the best that was ever given by God to mankind, to be the play thing and the sport of the feeble will of a man, who, by a blasphemous, absurd, and petulant usurpation, would place his own feeble, contemptible, ridiculous will in the place of the Divine wisdom and justice?

No. My Lords, it is not to be had by conquest; for by conquest, which is a more immediate designation of the hand of God, the conqueror only succeeds to all the painful duties and subordination to the power of God which belonged to the Sovereign that held the country before. He cannot have it by succession; for no man can succeed to fraud, rapine and violence; neither by compact, covenant or submission, nor by any other means can arbitrary power be conveyed to any man. Those who give and those who receive arbitrary power are alike criminal, and there is no man but is bound to resist it to the best of his power wherever it shall shew its face to the world. Nothing but absolute impotence can justify men in not resisting it to the best of their power.

Law and arbitrary power are at eternal enmity. Name me a Magistrate, and I will name property. Name me power, and I will name protection. It is a contradiction in terms, it is blasphemy in religion, it is wickedness in politics to say that any man can have arbitrary power. Judges are guided and governed by the eternal laws of justice to which we are all subject. We may bite our chains if we will, but we shall be made to know ourselves, and be taught that man is born to be governed by law; and he that will substitute will in the place of it is an enemy to God.

This idea of arbitrary power has arisen from a gross confusion and perversion of ideas, which your Lordships will know how to distinguish and to separate. It does so happen by the necessity of the case that the Supreme power in every Country is not legally and in any ordinary way subject to a penal prosecution for any of its actions. It is unaccountable. And it is not merely so in this Country or that country, but in all counties. The King in this Country is undoubtedly unaccountable for his actions. The House of Lords, if it should ever exercise (God forbid I should suspect it would ever do what it has never done), but if it should ever abuse its judicial power and give such a judgment as it ought not, whether from fear of popular clamour on the one hand or predilection to the prisoner on the other, if they should abuse their judgments there is no calling them to an account for it. And so if the Commons should abuse their power, nay, if they should have been so greatly delinquent as not to have prosecuted this offender, they could not be accountable for it—there is no punishing them for their acts, because they exercise a part of the Supreme power. But are they less criminal, less rebellious against the Divine Majesty? Are they less hateful to man, whose opinions they ought to cultivate as far as they are just? No. Till society fall into a state of dissolution, they cannot be accountable for their acts. But it is from confounding the unaccountable character inherent to the Supreme power with arbitrary power that all this confusion of ideas has arisen.

If my Lords you were to suppose an arbitrary power, which I deny totally and your Lordships will be the first and proudest to deny it, when absolute, supreme dominion was never given nor conferred and delegated from you. But if you suppose such a thing, I will venture to say that an intermediate arbitrary power, where the people below are subject to its possessor, but he is irresponsible to the power above, is a monster that never existed except in the wild imagination of some theorist. It cannot be, because it is a perversion of the principle that that power which is given for the protection of the people below should be responsible to the power above. It is to suppose that the people shall have no laws with regard to *him*, yet, when he comes to be tried, he shall claim the security of those laws that are made to secure the people from his violence; that he shall claim a fair Trial, an equitable hearing, every advantage of Counsel (God forbid he should not have them), yet that the people under him shall have none of those advantages.

My Lords, I will venture to say of the Governments of Asia that none of them ever had an arbitrary power. And if any Government had an arbitrary power, they cannot delegate it to any persons under them; that is they cannot so delegate it as not to leave them accountable upon the principles upon which it was given. As this is a contradiction in terms, a gross absurdity as well as a monstrous wickedness, let me say for the honour of human nature, that although undoubtedly we may speak it with the pride of England, that we have better institutions for the preservation of the rights of men than any other Country in the World, yet I will venture to say that no country has wholly meant, or ever meant, to give up this power.

I am to speak of Oriental Governments, and I do insist upon it that Oriental Governments know nothing of this arbitrary power. I have taken as much pains as I can to examine into the constitutions of them. I have been endeavouring to inform myself at all times to a certain degree; of late my duty has led me to a more minute inspection of them, and I do challenge the whole race of man to show me any of the Oriental Governors claiming to themselves a right to act by arbitrary will.

My Lords, the greatest part of Asia is under Mahometan Governments. To name a Mahometan Government is to name a Government by law. It is a law enforced by stronger sanctions than any law that can bind an European Sovereign, exclusive of the Grand Seignior.[56] The law is given by God, and it has the double sanction of law and of religion, with which the Prince is no more to dispense than any one else. And, if any man will produce the Khoran to me, and will but shew me one test in it that authorizes in any degree an arbitrary power in the Government, I will declare that I have read that book and been conversant in the affairs of Asia to a degree in vain. There is not such a syllable in it; but on the contrary, against oppressors by name every letter of that law is fulminated. There are Interpreters to explain that law. I mean that great priesthood established throughout all Asia, whom they call *men of the law*. These men are Conservators of the law, and, to enable them to preserve it to perfection, they are secured from the resentment of the Sovereign; for he cannot touch them. A man of the law is secured and indemnified against the Sovereign, acting, executive power.

My Lords, to bring this point a little nearer home, since we are challenged thus, since we are led into Asia, since we are called upon to make out our Case on the principles of the Governments there rather than of those here (which I trust your

---

[56]Sultan of the Ottoman Empire.

Lordships will oblige Mr Hastings finally to be governed by, puffed up as he is with the insolence of Asia), the nearest to us of the Governments he appeals to is the Government of the Grand Seignior, the Emperor of the Turks. He an arbitrary power? Why he has not the supreme power of his Country. Everyone knows that the Grand Seignior is exalted high in titles, as our prerogative Lawyers exalt an abstract sovereign, and they cannot exalt him too high in our books. But I say he misses the first character of Sovereign power. He cannot lay a tax upon his people. The next part in which he misses of a sovereign power is that he cannot dispose of the life, of the property, or of the liberty, of any of his subjects, but by what is called the Fetfa or sentence of the law. He cannot declare peace or war without the same sentence of the law; so much is he more than European sovereigns a subject of strict law, that he cannot declare war or peace without it. Then, if he can neither touch life nor property, if he cannot lay a tax upon his subjects, or declare peace or War, I leave it to your Lordships to say whether he can be called, according to the principles of that constitution, an arbitrary power. A Turkish sovereign, if he should be judged by the body of that law to have acted against its principles (unless he happens to be secured by a faction of the soldiery), is liable to be deposed upon the sentence of that law; and his successor comes in under the strict limitations of the ancient law of that Country. Neither can he hold his place, dispose of his succession, or take any one step whatever, without being bound by law. So far I say, when Gentlemen talk of the affairs of Asia, as to the nearest of Asiatic sovereigns; and he is more Asiatic than European. He is a Mahometan Sovereign; and no Mahometan is born who can exercise any arbitrary power at all agreeable to their consti-

tution. And that Magistrate who is the greatest executive power among them is the person who is by the constitution of the country the most fettered by law.

Corruption is the true cause of the loss of all the benefits of the constitution of that country. The practices of Asia, as the Gentleman at your Bar has thought fit to say, is what he holds to; the constitution he flies away from. Undoubtedly much blood, murder, false imprisonment, much peculation, cruelty and robbery are to be found in Asia; and if, instead of going to the sacred laws of the Country, Mr Hastings chooses to go to the iniquitous practices of it, and practices authorized only by public tumult, contention, war and riot, he will find as clear an acquittal in the practices, as he would find condemnation in the institutions. But if he disputes, as he does, the authority of an Act of Parliament, let him state to me that law to which he means to be subject, or any law which he knows that will justify his actions. I am not authorized to say that I shall even in that case give up what is not in me to give up, because I represent an authority of which I must stand in awe. But, for myself, I shall confess that I am brought to public shame and am not fit to manage the great interests committed to my charge before your Lordships. I therefore say of that Government which we best know, which has been constituted more in obedience to the laws of Mahomed than any other, that the Sovereign cannot agreeably to that constitution, exercise any arbitrary power whatever.

The next point for us to consider is whether or no the constitution of India authorizes that power. The Gentleman at your Lordships' Bar has thought proper to say that it will be happy for India (though soon after he tells you it is a happiness they can never enjoy) "when the despotic Institutes of Genghiz Khan, or Tamerlane, shall give place to the liberal spirit of a British Legislature; and", says he, "I shall be amply satisfied in my present prosecution, if it shall tend to hasten the approach of an event so beneficial to the great interests of mankind". My Lords, you have seen what he says about an Act of Parliament. Do not you now think it rather an extraordinary thing that any British subject should in vindication of the authority which he has exercised quote here the names and Institutes, as he calls them, of those men who were the scourges of mankind, whose power was a power which they held by great force?

As to the Institutes of Genghiz Khan, which he calls arbitrary Institutes, I never saw them. If he has that book he will oblige the public by producing it. I have seen a book existing called Yassa of Genghiz Khan. The other I never saw. If there be any part of it to justify arbitrary power, he will produce it. But if we may judge by those ten precepts of Genghiz Khan that we have, there is not a shadow of arbitrary power to be found in any one of them—Institutes of arbitrary power. Why if there is arbitrary power, there can be no Institutes. . . .

With regard to the Institutes of Tamerlane, here they are in their original, and here is a translation. I have carefully read every part of those Institutes, and if any one shews me one word in them in which the Prince claims in himself arbitrary power, I shall for my own part confess I have brought myself to great shame. There is no book in the world, I believe, which contains nobler, more just, more manly, more pious, principles of Government than this book called the Institutions of Tamerlane. Nor is there one word of arbitrary power in it, much less of that arbitrary power which Mr. Hastings supposed himself justified by, namely, a delegated, subordinate, arbitrary

power. So far are those great princes from permitting this gross, violent, arbitrary power, that I will venture to say the chief thing by which they have recommended themselves to posterity was a most direct declaration of all the wrath, indignation and powers of the Government against it.

↬

[Burke then reads a long passage from a 1783 translation of the Institutes of Tamerlane. Eds.]

But it is not here only that I must do justice to the East. I assert that their morality is equal to ours as regards the morality of Governors, fathers, superiors; and I challenge the world to shew, in any modern European book, more true morality and wisdom than is to be found in the writings of Asiatic men in high trusts, and who have been Counsellors to Princes. This is to be set against that geographical morality to which I have referred.

↬

Thus much concerning the laws of Asia: that the people of Asia have no laws, rights or liberties, is a doctrine that is to be disseminated wickedly through this country. But every Mahomedan Government, as I before stated, is by its principles a Government of law. I shall now state that it does not and cannot, from what is known of the Government of India, delegate (as Mr. Hastings has frequently declared) the whole of its powers and authority to him. If the Governments are absolute, as they must be, in the supreme power, they ought to be arbitrary in none. They were, however, never absolute in any of their subordinate parts; and I will prove it by the known provincial constitutions of Hindoostan, which shews that their power is never delegated by the proof that they are all descended of Mahomedans, under a law as clear, as explicit, and as learned, as ours.

The first foundation of their law is the Koran. The next part is the Fetfa, or adjudged cases by proper authority, well known there. The next is the written interpretation of the principles of jurisprudence; and their books are as numerous upon the principles of jurisprudence as in any country in Europe. The next part of their law is what they call the Kanon, which is equivalent to Acts of Parliament, being the law of the several powers of the Country, taken from the Greek word which was brought into their country, and it is well known. The next is the Rage ul Mulk, the Common Law or Custom of the Kingdom, equivalent to our Common Law. Therefore they have laws from more sources than we have, exactly in the same order, grounded upon the same authority, fundamentally fixed to be administered to the people upon these principles.

The next thing to shew is, that, having this law, they have subdelegated their power by parcels, and have not delegated the whole of it to any one man, who therefore cannot exercise it. In every Province the first person is the Soubahdar or Viceroy. He has the military power and the administration of criminal justice only. Then there is the Dewan or High Steward. He has the Revenue and all Exchequer Causes under him to be governed according to the Laws and Customs and institutions of the Kingdom.

The law of Inheritances, Successions, and every thing that relates to them, is under the Kadi, who judges in his court, but there there is another subdivision; that is to say, the Kadi cannot judge without having two Muftis[57] along with him. And though there is no appeal properly in the

Mahometan law, yet if they do not agree with him the Cause is removed. It is transferred to the general assembly, that is, the whole legal body united, consisting of all the men of law in the Kingdom. There are also, I will venture to say, other divisions and subdivisions. For there are the Kanongoes in the country, who hold their places for life, to be the Conservators of the Canons, customs and good usages in the Country. All these, as well as the Kadi and the Mufti, hold their places and situations, not during the wanton pleasure of the Prince, but upon permanent and fixed terms for life.

These powers of magistracy, revenue and law are all different and consequently are not delegated in the whole to any one. I say therefore that Mr. Hastings has no refuge there. Let him run from law to law; let him fly from the Common Law and the sacred institutions of the Country in which he was born; let him fly from Acts of Parliament, from which his power originated; let him plead his ignorance of them or fly in the face of them. Will he fly to the Mahometan law? That condemns him. Will he fly to the high magistracy of Asia to defend the taking of presents? Pad Sha[58] and the Sultan would condemn him to a cruel death. Will he fly to the Sophis,[59] to the laws of Persia, or to the practice of those monarchs? Oh, I cannot say the unutterable things that would happen to him if he was to govern there. Let him fly where he will; from law to law. Law thank God meets him everywhere; and the practice of the most impious tyrants which he quotes cannot justify his conduct. I would as willingly have him tried upon the law of the Koran, or the Institutes of Tamerlane, as

---

[57] Islamic legal experts.

[58] *Padishah*, a Persian term for "imperial ruler."

[59] *Safavi*, Persian rulers in the sixteenth and seventeenth centuries.

upon the Common Law or the Statute Law of this Kingdom.

My Lords, the next question is, whether the Gentoo Laws justify arbitrary power; and if Mr. Hastings finds any sanctuary there, he shall take sanctuary with the cow in the Pagoda. The Gentoos have a law accurately written, positively proscribing in Magistrates any idea of will; a law with which, or rather with extracts of which, that gentleman has himself furnished us. These people are governed, not by the arbitrary power of any one, but by laws and institutions in which there is the substance of a whole body of equity, diversified by the manners and customs of the people, but having in it that which makes law good for anything, a substantial body of equity and great principles of jurisprudence, both civil and criminal. I am ready to say that there are very few books, if we were to take them by a small body of extracts, that would exceed that book. I have given your Lordships some instances of Tamerlane's mode of proceeding; but every thing that Mr. Hastings has done, I believe, would be as severely punished as it is directly proscribed by the law of Tamerlane. In short, follow him where you will; let him have Eastern or Western Law; you find everywhere arbitrary power and peculation of Governors proscribed and horridly punished; more so than I should ever wish to punish any human creature.

If this then is the case, as I hope and trust it will be proved to your Lordships, that there is law in these Countries, that there is no delegation of power which exempts a Governor from the law, then I say at any rate a British Governor is to answer for his conduct, and cannot be justified by wicked examples and bad practices.

Another thing that Mr. Hastings says is that he was left to himself to govern himself by his own practice: that is to say, when he had taken one bribe, he might take another; when he had robbed one man of his property, he might rob another; when he had imprisoned one man arbitrarily and extorted money from him, he might do so by another. He resorts at first to the practice of barbarians and usurpers; at last he comes to his own. Now if your Lordships will try him upon those maxims and principles, he is clear, for there is no manner of doubt that there is nothing he has practised once which he has not practised again; and then the repetition of crimes becomes the means of his indemnity.

But, my Lords, he has given another softening to this business. He says, and with a kind of triumph, that the Ministry of this Country have great legal assistance, the lights of the commerce of the greatest commercial City in the world; the greatest Generals and Officers to guide and direct them in military affairs, whereas I, poor man, was sent almost a schoolboy from England, or at least little better, to find my way in that new world as well as I could.

Such a declaration would in some measure suit persons who had acted much otherwise than Mr Hastings. When a man pleads ignorance in justification of his conduct, it ought to be an humble, modest, unpresuming, ignorance, an ignorance which may have made him lax and timid in the exercise of his duty. But a bold, presuming, dogmatic, ferocious, active, ignorance is itself a crime; and the ignorance upon which it is founded aggravates the crime. Mr Hastings, if by ignorance he left some of the Directors' orders unexecuted because he did not understand them, might well say, I was an ignorant man, and these things were above my capacity. But when he understands them, and when he declares he will not obey them, positively and dogmatically, when he says, as he has said, and we shall prove it, that he never succeeds better than when he acts in an utter defiance of these orders, I believe this will not be thought the language of an ignorant man. But I beg your Lordships pardon; it is the language of an ignorant man. For no man who was not full of a bold, determined, wicked, ignorance, could ever think of such a system of defence. He quitted Westminster School almost a boy. We have reason to regret that he did not finish his education in that seminary which has given so many lights to the Church and ornaments to the State. Greatly have we to lament that he did not go to one of the Universities (where arbitrary power will I hope never be heard of; but the true principles of religion, of liberty, and law will ever be inculcated) instead of studying in the School of Cossim Ally Cawn.[60]

If he had lived with us, he would have quoted the example of Cicero[61] in his Government, he would have quoted several of the sacred and holy prophets, and made them his example. But he quotes every name of barbarism, tyranny and usurpation, that is to be found; and from these, he says, from the practice of one part of Asia or other, have I taken my rule. But your Lordships will shew him that in Asia as well as in Europe the same Law of Nations prevails, the same principles are continually resorted to, and the same maxims sacredly held and strenuously maintained; and however disobeyed, no man suffers from the breach of them, that does not know how to complain of that breach; that Asia is enlightened in that respect as well as Europe; but if it was totally blinded, that England would send out

Governors to teach them better; and that he might justify himself to the piety, the truth, the faith, of England, and not justify himself by having recourse to the barbarous tyranny of Asia, or any other part of the world.

↜

There is another topic which Mr. Hastings takes up more seriously, and as a general rebutter to the charge. Says he: After a great many of these practices, with which I am charged, Parliament appointed me to my trust, and consequently has acquitted me. Has it, my Lords? I am bold to say that the Commons are wholly guiltless of this charge. If they had re-appointed him to a great public trust, after they had known of his enormities, after they had had them before them, they would have participated in the guilt with him, and the public would have great reason to reprobate their conduct; and I admit that if that were the case there would be an indecorum in prosecuting him. But the House of Commons stand before your Lordships without shame; because they know that these crimes never were brought and proved before them. No. They lay buried in the records of the Company. Perhaps if we had examined them strictly, as we ought, Mr. Hastings would not have been re-appointed to that trust. But If any one will shew any part of the charge proved before the House of Commons we will take that part of the shame.

My Lords, at the time Mr. Hastings was reappointed we had not any knowledge of these transactions. Since they came to our knowledge we never ceased to attack, to condemn and prosecute them, and, as far as legal power was in us, to call him home to answer for them. Therefore we are as free from indecorum as from breach of duty in appointing such a person. But

---

[60]Alivardi Khan, the "cruel and ferocious tyrant" of Bengal from 1740 to 1756.

[61]Famous Roman statesman, lawyer, and orator known for his eloquence and wisdom.

even if that which he states were true, it does not rebut the greatest part of this charge. For a great number of these enormities and wickednesses were committed since his last appointment. But supposing it were true, think of the audacity of a man who will fly in the face of his Country and say: You trusted me when you ought not, therefore you are obliged to carry me through this matter, it being your own act. No. We return it upon him and say: It is not our own act; the wickedness was yours, the trust was yours. And if we, in a moment of inadvertence, or even from a breach of our duty, by neglect, appointed you, that ought to have been a lesson to you to forbear from these crimes on account of our lenity. But no. He has made use of that trust to redouble all those crimes and offences from the moment of his appointment to the moment of quitting that Country, as I hope we shall be able to prove fully before your Lordships.

My Lords, we have now gone through most of the general topics. But Mr. Hastings says he has had the thanks and approbation of the India Company for his services. We know too well here, I trust the world knows, and you will always assert, that a pardon from the Crown cannot bar the Impeachment of the Commons, much less a pardon of the East India Company; though it may involve them in guilt, which might induce us to punish them for such a pardon.

The East India Company it is true have thanked him. They ought not to have done it, and it is reflection upon their character that they did it. But if you come to this gentleman's actions, they are all, every one, censured one by one as they arise. I do not recollect any one transaction, few there are, I am sure, in the whole body of that train of crimes, which is now brought before you for your judgment, in which the India Company have not censured him. Then if for any fresh reasons they come and say, We thank you Sir for all your services; to that I answer, Yes, and I would thank him for his services too if I knew them. But I do not; perhaps they do. Let them thank him for those services. I am ordered to prosecute him for these crimes. Here, therefore, we are upon a balance with the India Company and your Lordships may perhaps think it some addition to his crimes that he has found means to obtain the thanks for the India Company for the whole of his conduct, at the same time that their records are full of constant, uniform, censure and reprobation of every one of those acts for which he now stands accused.

∽

My Lords, these are I believe the general grounds of our charge. I have now closed completely, and I hope to your Lordships' satisfaction, the whole body of history of which I wished to put your Lordships in possession. I do not mean that you will not know it more perfectly by your own inquiries, that many of your Lordships may not have known it more perfectly by your own previous inquiries. But bringing to your remembrance the state of the circumstances of the persons with whom he acted, the persons and power he has abused, I have gone to the principles he maintains, the precedents he quotes, the laws and authorities which he refuses to abide by, and those on which he relies; and at last I have refuted all those pleas in bar upon which he depends, and for the effect of which he presumes on the indulgence and patience of this Country, or the corruption of some persons in it.

And here I close what I have to say upon this subject, wishing and hoping that when I open the Case before your Lordships more particularly, so as to state rather a plan of the proceeding than the direct proof of the crimes, your Lordships will hear me with the same goodness and indulgence that I have hitherto experienced; that you will consider if I have detained you long, it was not with a view of exhausting my own strength, or putting your patience to too severe a trial; but from the sense I feel that it is the most difficult and the most complicated cause that was ever brought before any human tribunal. Therefore I was resolved to bring the whole substantially before you. And now, if your Lordships will permit me, I will state the method of my future proceeding and the future proceeding of the gentlemen assisting me.

I mean first to bring before you the crimes as they are classed, and which are of the same species and genus, and shew how they mutually arose from one another. I shall first shew that Mr. Hastings's crimes had root in that which is the root of all evil, I mean avarice; that avarice and rapacity were the groundwork and foundation of all his other vicious system; that he shewed it in setting to sale the native Government of the Country; in setting to sale the whole landed interest of the Country; in setting to sale the British Government and his own fellow servants to the basest and wickedest of mankind. I shall then shew your Lordships that when, in consequence of such a body of corruption and peculation, he justly dreaded the vengeance and indignation of the laws of his Country, in order to raise himself a faction embodied by the same guilt and rewarded in the same manner, he has with a most abandoned profusion thrown away the revenues of the Country to form such a faction here.

I shall next shew your Lordships that, having exhausted the Country and brought it to extreme difficulties within, he has looked to his external resources, as he calls them. He has gone up into the Country. I will shew that he has plundered, or attempted to plunder, every person dependent upon, connected or allied with this Country. I shall shew what infinite mischief has followed from it in the Case of Benares, upon which he first laid his hands; next in the Case of the Begums of Oude.

I shall then lay before you the wicked system by which he endeavoured to oppress that Country, first by Residents, next by spies under the name of British Residents. And, lastly, that, pursuing his way up to the mountains, he has found out one miserable chief, whose crimes were the prosperity of his Country, and him he endeavoured to torture and destroy; I do not mean in his body, but by exhausting the treasures which he kept for the benefit of his people.

My Lords, this is the plan on which I mean to go. If I should not be able to execute the whole of it (as I fear that I shall not), I shall go at least to the root of it, and so prepare it that the other gentlemen, with ten thousand times more ability than I, will be able to take up the part where I leave off, just when you find it proper. I shall shew your Lordships that Mr. Hastings's principle is, that no man who is under his power is safe from his arbitrary will; that no man, within or without, friend, ally, rival, anything, has been safe from him. Therefore I mean to bring the case to that point: to shew your Lordships the system of corruption which Mr. Hastings adopted, and the wicked, villanous, perfidious, means, which he calls external resources, of which he made use. And then, if I am not able in my own person immediately to go up into the Country and shew the ramifications of the system . . . , some other gentleman will take up each part in its proper order. . . .

The point I mean to bring before your Lordships first is the corruption of Mr.

Hastings, the system of peculation and bribery upon which he went; and to shew your Lordships the horrid consequences which resulted from it. For though at the first view bribery and peculation do not seem to be so horrid a matter, but may seem to be only transferring a little money out of one pocket into another, I shall shew that by such a system of bribery the Country is undone.

I shall inform your Lordships in the best manner I can and afterwards submit the whole, as I do with a cheerful heart and with an easy and assured security to that justice which is the security for all the other justice in the Kingdom.

[On the third day of the speech, Burke devotes his attention initially to the allegation that all Hastings's high crimes and misdemeanors had a common source: "pecuniary corruption and avarice." He details the system of bribery and corruption that Hastings controlled and upon which he based and exercised his power. Thereafter, Burke enters into a graphic description of cruelties and atrocities committed by agents of the East India Company in Rangpur, a northern district of Bengal. Burke describes scenes of horrific torture, rape, and mutilation carried out by those in the employ of the East India Company. Burke attempts to place the blame for such atrocities squarely at the feet of Hastings's system of bribery and corruption.

Burke continues with the Rangpur saga in the fourth day of the speech and delves further into the system of corruption in the collection of revenue in Bengal. This excerpt picks up with the final passages of the fourth day of the speech. Eds.]

In the name of the Commons of England, I charge all this villany upon Warren Hast-ings in this last moment of my application to you.

My Lords, what is it that we want here to a great act of national justice? Do we want a cause, my Lords? You have the cause of oppressed Princes, of undone women of the first rank, of desolated Provinces and of wasted Kingdoms.

Do you want a criminal, my Lords? When was there so much iniquity ever laid to the charge of any one? No. My Lords, you must not look to punish any delinquent in India more. Warren Hastings has not left substance enough in India to nourish such another delinquent.

My Lords, is it a Prosecutor that you want? You have before you the Commons of Great Britain as Prosecutors; and I believe, my Lords, that the sun in his beneficent progress round the world does not behold a more glorious sight than that of men, separated from a remote people by the material bounds and barriers of nature, united by the bond of a social and moral community, all the Commons of England resenting as their own, the indignities and cruelties that are offered to all the people of India.

Do you want a tribunal? My Lords, no example of antiquity, nothing in the modern world, nothing in the range of human imagination can supply us with a Tribunal like this. My Lords, here we see virtually, in the mind's eye, that sacred majesty of the Crown, under whose authority you sit and whose power you exercise. We see in that invisible authority, what we all feel in reality and life, the beneficent powers and protecting justice of His Majesty. We have here the Heir Apparent to the Crown, such as the fond wishes of the people of England wish an Heir Apparent of the Crown to be. We have here all the branches of the Royal Family, in a situation between Majesty and subjection, between the Crown and the subject, offering a pledge in that situation for the support of the rights of the Crown and the liberties of the people, both which extremities they touch. My Lords, we have a great hereditary Peerage here; those who have their own honour, the honour of their ancestors and of their posterity, to guard, and who will justify, as they have always justified, that provision in the constitution of which justice is made an hereditary office. My Lords, we have here a new nobility, who have risen and exalted themselves by various merits, by great military services which have extended the fame of this Country from the rising to the setting sun. We have those who, by various civil merits, and various civil talents, have been exalted to a situation which they well deserve, and in which they will justify the favour of their Sovereign and the good opinion of their fellow subjects, and make them rejoice to see those virtuous characters, that were the other day upon a level with them, now exalted above them in rank but feeling with them in sympathy what they felt in common before. We have persons exalted from the practice of the law, from the place in which they administered high, though subordinate, justice, to a seat here, to enlighten with their knowledge and to strengthen with their votes those principles which have distinguished the Courts in which they have presided.

My Lords, you have before you the lights of our religion; you have the Bishops of England. My Lords, you have that true image of the primitive Church in its ancient form, in its ancient ordinances, purified from the superstitions and the vices which a long succession of ages will bring upon the best institutions. You have the representatives of that religion which says that God is Love, that the very vital spirit of its institution is charity; a religion which so much hates oppression, that, when the God whom we adore appeared in human form, he did not appear in a form of greatness and majesty, but in sympathy with the lowest of the people, and thereby made it a firm and ruling principle that their welfare was the object of all Government, since the person who was the Master of Nature chose to appear himself in a subordinate situation. These are the considerations which influence them, which animate them, and will animate them against all oppression; knowing that He who is called first among them, and first among us all, both of the flock that is fed and of those who feed it, made Himself The Servant of all.

My Lords, these are the securities that we have in all the constituent parts of the body of this House; we know them, we reckon, we rest upon them, and commit safely the interests of India and of humanity into their hands. Therefore it is with confidence that, ordered by the Commons,

I impeach Warren Hastings, Esquire, of High Crimes and Misdemeanours.

I impeach him in the name of the Commons of Great Britain in Parliament assembled, whose parliamentary trust he has betrayed.

I impeach him in the name of all the Commons of Great Britain whose national character he has dishonoured.

I impeach him in the name of the people of India, whose laws, rights and liberties he has subverted, whose properties he has destroyed, whose Country he has laid waste and desolate.

I impeach him in the name and by virtue of those eternal laws of justice which he has violated.

I impeach him in the name of human nature itself, which he has cruelly outraged, injured and oppressed, in both sexes, in every age, rank, situation and condition of life.

↔ CHAPTER EIGHT ↔

On the French Revolution

Introductory Note to
Thoughts on French Affairs
(1791)

The French Revolution of 1789 and the principles ostensibly behind it occupied Burke for much of his remaining life. He considered the French Revolution "the greatest evil" he had confronted, and he responded with a body of writings and speeches that dominates his historical reputation. Burke's most famous work, Reflections on the Revolution in France *(1790), was his first published response to the events in France in 1789. Although* Reflections *examined the root causes and principles of the French Revolution from primarily a domestic perspective,* Thoughts on French Affairs *contains a more explicit treatment of the threat posed by the French Revolution to the security and civil society of European international society at large.*

Burke wrote Thoughts on French Affairs *as a memorandum to the Pitt ministry to spur Britain and other European powers to intervene militarily against the new French regime. In particular Burke analyzed the unique nature of the danger of the new regime in France, which was constituted by principles rather than armies. He proceeded to show how such "doctrine and theoretick dogma" harms a country as much through internal infection and corruption—"a sort of dry rot"—as through military threats and acts of war. Burke then went through the major states and principalities in Europe analyzing their vulnerability to the French disease. His descriptions toward the end of the piece of the "diplomacy" of Condorcet and Brissot indicated that Burke feared that the destruction by the revolutionaries of the manners, mores, and traditions of European states was the most serious menace that had ever befallen the commonwealth of Europe.*

In Thoughts on French Affairs, *then, Burke attempted to obliterate traditional notions of thinking separately about domestic and international politics. He expressed his "full conviction" that the greatest issue facing both the foreign and domestic policies of every European state was the condition and attitude of France. Burke did not explicitly advocate military intervention in* Thoughts, *but the reader is left in no doubt that Burke's solution to the French problem would be as encompassing as the threat itself.* ↔

Thoughts on
French Affairs
(1791)

In all our transactions with France, and at all periods, we have treated with that State on the footing of a Monarchy. Monarchy was considered in all the external relations of that kingdom with every Power in Europe as it's legal and constitutional Government, and that in which alone it's federal capacity was vested.

It is not yet a year since Monsieur de Montmorin, formally, and with as little respect as can be imagined, to the King, and to all crowned heads, announced a total revolution in that country. He has informed the British Ministry that it's frame of Government is wholly altered; that he is one of the Ministers of the new system; and in effect, that the King is no longer his master (nor does he even call him such) but the *"first of the Ministers"* in the new system.

The second notification was that of the King's acceptance of the new Constitution; accompanied with fanfaronades in the modern style of the French bureaus, things which have much more the air and character of the saucy declamations of their clubs, than the tone of regular office.

It has not been very usual to notify to foreign Courts, any thing concerning the internal arrangements of any State. In the present case, the circumstance of these two notifications, with the observations with which they are attended, does not leave it in the choice of the Sovereigns of Christendom to appear ignorant either of this French Revolution, or (what is more important) of it's principles.

↩

In this state of things (that is in the case of a *divided* kingdom) by the law of nations,[1] Great Britain, like every other Power, is free to take any part she pleases. She may decline, with more or less formality, according to her discretion, to acknowledge this new system; or she may recognize it as a Government *de facto,* setting aside all discussion of it's original legality, and considering the ancient Monarchy as at an end. The law of nations leaves our Court open to it's choice. We have no direction but what is found in the well-understood policy of the King and the kingdom.

This Declaration of a *new species* of Government, on new principles (such it professes itself to be) is a real crisis in the politicks of Europe. The conduct which prudence ought to dictate to Great Britain, will not depend (as hitherto our connexion or quarrel with other States has for some time depended) upon merely *external* relations; but, in a great measure also upon the system which we may think it right to adopt for the internal government of our own country.

If it be our policy to assimilate our Government to that of France, we ought to prepare for this change, by encouraging the schemes of authority established there. We ought to wink at the captivity and deposition of a Prince, with whom, if not in close alliance, we were in friendship. We ought to fall in with the ideas of Mons. Montmorin's circular Manifesto; and to do business of course with the functionaries who act under the new power, by which that King to whom his Majesty's Minister has been sent to reside, has been deposed and imprisoned. On that idea we ought also to with-hold all sorts of direct or indi-

---

[1]See Vattel, b. ii, c. 4, sect. 56, and b. iii, c. 18, sect. 296. [Burke's note]

rect countenance from those who are treating in Germany for the re-establishment of the French Monarchy and the ancient Orders of that State.[2] This conduct is suitable to this policy.

The question is, whether this policy be suitable to the interests of the Crown and subjects of Great Britain. Let us therefore a little consider the true nature and probable effects of the Revolution which, in such a very unusual manner, has been twice diplomatically announced to his Majesty.

There have been many internal revolutions in the Government of countries, but as to persons and forms, in which the neighbouring States have had little or no concern. Whatever the Government might be with respect to those persons and those forms, the stationary interests of the nation concerned, have most commonly influenced the new Governments in the same manner in which they influenced the old; and the Revolution, turning on matter of local grievance or of local accommodation, did not extend beyond it's territory.

The present Revolution in France seems to me to be quite of another character and description; and to bear little resemblance or analogy to any of those which have been brought about in Europe, upon principles merely political. *It is a Revolution of doctrine and theoretick dogma.* It has a much greater resemblance to those changes which have been made upon religious grounds, in which a spirit of proselytism makes an essential part.

The last Revolution of doctrine and theory which has happened in Europe, is the Reformation. It is not for my purpose to take any notice here of the merits of

that Revolution, but to state one only of it's effects.

That effect was *to introduce other interests into all countries, than those which arose from their locality and natural circumstances.* The principle of the Reformation was such, as by it's essence, could not be local or confined to the country in which it had it's origin. For instance, the doctrine of "Justification by Faith or by Works," which was the original basis of the Reformation, could not have one of it's alternatives true as to Germany, and false as to every other country. Neither are questions of theoretick truth and falsehood governed by circumstances any more than by places. On that occasion, therefore, the spirit of proselytism expanded itself with great elasticity upon all sides; and great divisions were every where the result.

These divisions however, in appearance merely dogmatick, soon became mixed with the political; and their effects were rendered much more intense from this combination. Europe was for a long time divided into two great factions, under the name of Catholick and Protestant, which not only often alienated State from State, but also divided almost every State within itself. The warm parties in each State were more affectionately attached to those of their own doctrinal interest in some other country than to their fellow citizens, or to their natural Government, when they or either of them happened to be of a different persuasion. These factions, wherever they prevailed, if they did not absolutely destroy, at least weakened and distracted the locality of patriotism. The publick affections came to have other motives and other ties.

It would be to repeat the history of the two last centuries to exemplify the effects of this Revolution.

---

[2] French royalist émigrés in Germany who were seeking support to restore the French monarchy.

Although the principles to which it gave rise, did not operate with a perfect regularity and constancy, they never wholly ceased to operate. Few wars were made, and few treaties were entered into in which they did not come in for some part. They gave a colour, a character, and direction to all the politicks of Europe.

These principles of internal, as well as external division and coalition, are but just now extinguished. But they who will examine into the true character and genius of some late events, must be satisfied that other sources of faction, combining parties among the inhabitants of different countries into one connexion, are opened, and that from these sources are likely to arise effects full as important as those which had formerly arisen from the jarring interests of the religious sects. The intention of the several actors in the change in France, is not a matter of doubt. It is very openly professed.

In the modern world, before this time, there has been no instance of this spirit of general political faction, separated from religion, pervading several countries, and forming a principle of union between the partizans in each. But the thing is not less in human nature. The antient world has furnished a strong and striking instance of such a ground for faction, full as powerful and full as mischievous as our spirit of religious system had ever been, exciting in all the States of Greece (European and Asiatick) the most violent animosities, and the most cruel and bloody persecutions and proscriptions. These ancient factions in each commonwealth of Greece, connected themselves with those of the same description in some other States; and secret cabals and publick alliances were carried on and made, not upon a conformity of general political interests, but for the support and aggrandizement of the two leading States which headed the Aristocratick and Democratick Factions.[3] For, as in later times, the King of Spain was at the head of a Catholick, and the King of Sweden of a Protestant interest, France, (though Catholick, acting subordinately to the latter,) in the like manner the Lacedemonians[4] were every where at the head of the Aristocratick interests, and the Athenians of the Democratick. The two leading Powers kept alive a constant cabal and conspiracy in every State, and the political dogmas concerning the constitution of a Republick, were the great instruments by which these leading States chose to aggrandize themselves. Their choice was not unwise; because the interest in opinions . . . when once they take strong hold of the mind, become the most operative of all interests, and indeed very often supercede every other.

‎ ﹏

The political dogma, which upon the new French system, is to unite the factions of different nations, is this, "That the majority told, by the head, of the taxable people in every country, is the perpetual, natural, unceasing, indefeasible sovereign; that this majority is perfectly master of the form, as well as the administration of the state, and that the magistrates, under whatever names they are called, are only functionaries to obey the orders, (general as laws or particular as decrees) which that majority may make; that this is the only natural government; that all others are tyranny and usurpation."

----

[3]Burke is referring to the Peloponnesian War between Sparta and Athens and their respective allies.

[4]Spartans.

In order to reduce this dogma into practice, the Republicans in France, and their associates in other countries, make it always their business, and often their publick profession, to destroy all traces of antient establishments, and to form a new commonwealth in each country, upon the basis of the French *Rights of Men*. On the principle of these rights, they mean to institute in every country, and as it were, the germe of the whole, parochial governments, for the purpose of what they call equal representation. From them is to grow, by some media, a general council and representative of all the parochial governments. In that representative is to be vested the whole national power; totally abolishing hereditary name and office, levelling all conditions of men, (except where money *must* make a difference) breaking all connexion between territory and dignity, and abolishing every species of nobility, gentry, and church establishments; all their priests, and all their magistrates being only creatures of election, and pensioners at will.

Knowing how opposite a permanent landed interest is to that scheme, they have resolved, and it is the great drift of all their regulations, to reduce that description of men to a mere peasantry, for the sustenance of the towns, and to place the true effective government in cities, among the tradesmen, bankers, and voluntary clubs of bold, presuming young persons;—advocates, attorneys, notaries, managers of newspapers, and those cabals of literary men, called academies. Their Republick is to have a first functionary, (as they call him) under the name of King, or not, as they think fit. This officer, when such an officer is permitted, is however, neither in fact nor name, to be considered as sovereign, nor the people as his subjects. The

very use of these appellations is offensive to their ears.

This system, as it has first been realized, dogmatically as well as practically, in France, makes France the natural head of all factions formed on a similar principle, wherever they may prevail, as much as Athens was the head and settled ally of all democratick factions, wherever they existed. The other system has no head.

This system has very many partizans in every country in Europe, but particularly in England, where they are already formed into a body, comprehending most of the dissenters of the three leading denominations; to these are readily aggregated all who are dissenters in character, temper, and disposition, though not belonging to any of their congregations—that is, all the restless people who resemble them, of all ranks and all parties—Whigs, and even Tories—the whole race of half-bred speculators;—all the Atheists, Deists, and Socinians;—all those who hate the Clergy, and envy the Nobility,—a good many among the monied people;—the East Indians almost to a man, who cannot bear to find that their present importance does not bear a proportion to their wealth.[5] . . .

&

What direction the French spirit of proselytism is likely to take, and in what order it is likely to prevail in the several parts of Europe, it is not easy to determine. The seeds are sown almost every where, chiefly by newspaper circulations, infinitely more efficacious and extensive than ever they were. And they are a more important instrument than generally is imagined. They are a part of the reading of all, they are the

---

[5]Men who made their fortunes through the East India Company.

whole of the reading of the far greater number. There are thirty of them in Paris alone. The language diffuses them more widely than the English, though the English too are much read. The writers of these papers indeed, for the greater part, are either unknown or in contempt, but they are like a battery in which the stroke of any one ball produces no great effect, but the amount of continual repetition is decisive. Let us only suffer any person to tell us his story, morning and evening, but for one twelvemonth, and he will become our master.

All those countries in which several States are comprehended under some general geographical description, and loosely united by some federal constitution; countries of which the members are small, and greatly diversified in their forms of government, and in the titles by which they are held—these countries, as it might be well expected, are the principal objects of their hopes and machinations. Of these, the chief are Germany and Switzerland: after them, Italy has it's place as in circumstances somewhat similar.

As to Germany . . . it appears to me to be from several circumstances, internal and external, in a very critical situation, and the laws and liberties of the Empire[6] are by no means secure from the contagion of the French doctrines and the effect of French intrigues; or from the use which two of the greater German powers may make of a general derangement, to the general detriment. I do not say that the French do not mean to bestow on these German States, liberties and laws too, after their mode; but those are not what have hitherto been understood as the laws and liberties of the Empire. These exist and have always existed under the principles of feudal tenure and succession,

under Imperial constitutions, grants and concessions of Sovereigns, family compacts and public treaties, made under the sanction, and some of them guaranteed by the Sovereign Powers of other nations, and particularly the old Government of France, the author and natural support of the treaty of Westphalia.[7]

In short, the Germanick body is a vast mass of heterogeneous States, held together by that heterogeneous body of old principles which formed the publick law positive and doctrinal. The modern laws and liberties which the new power in France proposed to introduce into Germany, and to support with all it's force, of intrigue and of arms, is of a very different nature, utterly irreconcileable with the first, and indeed fundamentally the reverse of it: I mean the *Rights and Liberties of the Man,* the *Droit de l'Homme.* That this doctrine has made an amazing progress in Germany, there cannot be a shadow of doubt. They are infected by it along the whole course of the Rhine, the Maese, the Moselle, and in the greater part of Suabia and Franconia. It is particularly prevalent amongst all the lower people, churchmen and laity, in the dominions of the Ecclesiastical Electors.[8] It is not easy to find or to conceive Governments more mild and indulgent than these Church Sovereignties; but good government is as nothing when the Rights of Man take possession of the mind. Indeed the loose rein held over the people in these provinces, must be considered as one cause of the facility with which they lend themselves to any schemes of innovation, by inducing them to think lightly of their governments, and to judge

---

[6]Holy Roman Empire.

[7]Of 1648, which ended the Thirty Years' War in Europe and provided the foundation for the modern international system of sovereign states.

[8]Cologne, Mainz, and Trier.

of grievances not by feeling, but by imagination.

It is in these Electorates that the first impressions of France are likely to be made, and if they succeed, it is over with the Germanick body as it stands at present. A great revolution is preparing in Germany; and a revolution, in my opinion, likely to be more decisive upon the general fate of nations than that of France itself; other than as in France is to be found the first source of all the principles which are in any way likely to distinguish the troubles and convulsions of our age. If Europe does not conceive the independence, and the equilibrium of the Empire to be in the very essence of the system of balanced power in Europe, and if the scheme of publick law, or mass of laws upon which that independence and equilibrium are founded, be of no leading consequence as they are preserved or destroyed, all the politicks of Europe for more than two centuries have been miserably erroneous.

If the two great leading Powers of Germany[9] do not regard this danger (as apparently they do not) in the light in which it presents itself so naturally, it is because they are powers too great to have a social interest. That sort of interest belongs only to those, whose state of weakness or mediocrity is such, as to give them greater cause of apprehension from what may destroy them, than of hope from any thing by which they may be aggrandized.

As long as those two Princes are at variance, so long the liberties of Germany are safe. But if ever they should so far understand one another as to be persuaded that they have a more direct and more certainly defined interest in a proportioned mutual aggrandizement than in a reciprocal reduction, that is, if they come to think that

they are more likely to be enriched by a division of spoil, than to be rendered secure by keeping to the old policy of preventing others from being spoiled by either of them, from that moment the liberties of Germany are no more.

That a junction of two in such a scheme is neither impossible nor improbable, is evident from the partition of Poland in 1773, which was effected by such a junction as made the interposition of other nations to prevent it, not easy. Their circumstances at that time hindered any other three States, or indeed any two, from taking measures in common to prevent it, though France was at that time an existing power, and had not yet learned to act upon a system of politicks of her own invention. The geographical position of Poland was a great obstacle to any movements of France in opposition to this, at that time unparalleled league. To my certain knowledge, if Great Britain had at that time been willing to concur in preventing the execution of a project so dangerous in the example, even exhausted as France then was by the preceding war,[10] and under a lazy and unenterprizing Prince,[11] she would have at every risque taken an active part in this business. But a languor with regard to so remote an interest, and the principles and passions which were then strongly at work at home, were the causes why Great Britain would not give France any encouragement in such an enterprize. At that time, however, and with regard to that object, in my opinion, Great Britain and France had a common interest.

⌐

---

[9]Prussia and the Austrian empire.

[10]Seven Years' War, 1756–1763.

[11]Louis XV.

France, the author of the treaty of West-phalia, is the natural guardian of the independence and balance of Germany. Great Britain . . . has a serious interest in preserving it; but, except through the power of France, *acting upon the common old principles of State policy,* in the case we have supposed, she has no sort of means of supporting that interest. It is always the interest of Great Britain that the power of France should be kept within the bounds of moderation. It is not her interest that that power should be wholly annihilated in the system of Europe. Though at one time through France the independence of Europe was endangered, it is and ever was through her alone that the common liberty of Germany can be secured against the single or the combined ambition of any other power. In truth, within this century the aggrandizement of other Sovereign Houses has been such that there has been a great change in the whole state of Europe, and other nations as well as France may become objects of jealousy and apprehension.

In this state of things, a new principle of alliances and wars is opened. The treaty of Westphalia is, with France, an antiquated fable. The rights and liberties she was bound to maintain are now a system of wrong and tyranny which she is bound to destroy. Her good and ill dispositions are shewn by the same means. *To communicate peaceably* the rights of men is the true mode of her shewing her *friendship;* to force Sovereigns to *submit* to those rights is her mode of *hostility.* So that either as friend or foe her whole scheme has been and is, to throw the Empire into confusion: and those Statesmen, who follow the old routine of politicks, may see in this general confusion, and in the danger of the *lesser* Princes, an occasion as protectors or enemies, of connecting their territories

to one or the other of the *two great* German Powers. They do not take into consideration that the means which they encourage, as leading to the event they desire, will with certainty not only ravage and destroy the Empire, but if they should for a moment seem to aggrandize the two great houses, will also establish principles, and confirm tempers amongst the people, which will preclude the two Sovereigns from the possibility of holding what they acquire, or even the dominions which they have inherited. It is on the side of the Ecclesiastical Electorates that the dykes, raised to support the German liberty, first will give way.

The French have begun their general operations by seizing upon those territories of the Pope, the situation of which was the most inviting to the enterprize.[12] Their method of doing it was by exciting sedition and spreading massacre and desolation thro' these unfortunate places, and then under an idea of kindness and protection, bringing forward an antiquated title of the Crown of France and annexing Avignon and the two cities of the Comtat with their territory to the French Republick. They have made an attempt on Geneva, in which they very narrowly failed of success. It is known that they hold out from time to time the idea of uniting all the other provinces of which Gaul was antiently composed, including Savoy on the other side, and on this side bounding themselves by the Rhine.

⤶

Switzerland and Germany are the first objects of the new French politicians. When I contemplate what they have done at home, which is in effect little less than an

----

[12]France seized the papal territories of Avignon and Comtat Venaissin in September 1791.

amazing conquest wrought by a change of opinion, in a great part (to be sure far from altogether) very sudden, I cannot help letting my thoughts run along with their designs, and without attending to geographical order, to consider the other States of Europe so far as they may be any way affected by this astonishing Revolution. If early steps are not taken in some way or other to prevent the spreading of this influence, I scarcely think any of them perfectly secure.

Italy is divided, as Germany and Switzerland into many smaller States, and with some considerable diversity as to forms of Government; but as these divisions and varieties in Italy are not so considerable, so neither do I think the danger altogether so imminent there as in Germany and Switzerland. Savoy I know that the French consider as in a very hopeful way, and I believe not at all without reason. They view it as an old member of the Kingdom of France which may be easily reunited in the manner, and on the principles of the re-union of Avignon. This country communicates with Piedmont; and as the King of Sardinia's dominions were long the key of Italy, and as such long regarded by France, whilst France acted on her old maxims, and with views on Italy; so in this new French empire of sedition, if once she gets that key into her hands, she can easily lay open the barrier which hinders the entrance in her present politicks into that inviting region. Milan, I am sure, nourishes great disquiets—and if Milan should stir, no part of Lombardy is secure to the present possessors—whether the Venetian or the Austrian. Genoa is closely connected with France.

↩

As to Spain, it is a nerveless country. It does not possess the use, it only suffers the abuse of a nobility. For some time, and even be-

fore the settlement of the Bourbon Dynasty, that body has been systematically lowered, and rendered incapable by exclusion, and for incapacity excluded from affairs. . . .

↩

It is a melancholy reflection that the spirit of melioration which has been going on in that part of Europe, more or less during this century, and the various schemes very lately on foot for further advancement are all put a stop to at once. Reformation certainly is nearly connected with innovation—and where that latter comes in for too large a share, those who undertake to improve their country may risque their own safety. In times where the correction, which includes the confession of an abuse, is turned to criminate the authority which has long suffered it, rather than to honour those who would amend it (which is the spirit of this malignant French distemper) every step out of the common course becomes critical, and renders it a task full of peril for Princes of moderate talents to engage in great undertakings. At present the only safety of Spain is the old national hatred to the French. How far that can be depended upon, if any great ferments should be excited, it is impossible to say.

↩

Denmark and Norway do not appear to furnish any of the materials of a democratick revolution, or the dispositions to it. Denmark can only be *consequentially* affected by any thing done in France; but of Sweden I think quite otherwise. The present power in Sweden is too new a system, and too green and too sore from it's late Revolution, to be considered as perfectly assured. The King[13] by his astonishing activity, his boldness, his decision, his ready

---

[13]Gustavus III.

versatility, and by rouzing and employing the old military spirit of Sweden, keeps up the top with continual agitation and lashing. The moment it ceases to spin, the Royalty is a dead bit of box. Whenever Sweden is quiet externally for some time, there is great danger that all the republican elements she contains will be animated by the new French spirit, and of this I believe the King is very sensible.

The Russian Government is of all others the most liable to be subverted by military seditions, by Court conspiracies and sometimes by headlong rebellions of the people, such as the turbinating movement of Pugatchef.[14] It is not quite so probable that in any of these changes the spirit of system may mingle in the manner it has done in France. The Muscovites are no great speculators—But I should not much rely on their uninquisitive disposition, if any of their ordinary motives to sedition should arise. The little catechism of the Rights of Men is soon learned; and the inferences are in the passions.

Poland, from one cause or another, is always unquiet. The new Constitution only serves to supply that restless people with new means, at least new modes, of cherishing their turbulent disposition. The bottom of the character is the same. It is a great question, whether the joining that Crown with the Electorate of Saxony, will contribute most to strengthen the Royal authority of Poland, or to shake the Ducal in Saxony. The Elector is a Catholick; the people of Saxony are, six sevenths at the very least, Protestants. He *must* continue a Catholick according to the Polish law, if he accepts that Crown. The pride of the Saxons, formerly flattered by having a Crown in the House of their Prince, though an

honour which cost them dear; the German probity, fidelity and loyalty; the weight of the Constitution of the Empire under the Treaty of Westphalia; the good temper and good nature of the Princes of the House of Saxony; had formerly removed from the people all apprehension with regard to their religion, and kept them perfectly quiet, obedient, and even affectionate. The seven years war made some change in the minds of the Saxons. They did not, I believe, regret the loss of what might be considered almost as the succession to the Crown of Poland, the possession of which, by annexing them to a foreign interest, had often obliged them to act an arduous part, towards the support of which that foreign interest afforded no proportionable strength. In this very delicate situation of their political interests, the speculations of the French and German *Oeconomists,* and the cabals, and the secret, as well as public doctrines of the *Illuminatenordens* and *Free Masons,*[15] have made considerable progress in that country; and a turbulent spirit under colour of religion, but in reality arising from the French Rights of Man, has already shewn itself, and is ready on every occasion to blaze out.

⤶

With regard to Holland and the ruling party there, I do not think it at all tainted, or likely to be so except by fear; or that it is likely to be misled unless indirectly and circuitously. But the predominant party in Holland is not Holland. The suppressed faction, though suppressed, exists. Under the ashes, the embers of the late commotions are still warm. This Anti-Orange party has from the day of it's origin been French, though alienated in some degree

---

[14]Emelyan Pugachev led an uprising in 1773–1774 against Catherine II.

[15]Secret societies believed to be promoting radical ideas.

for some time, through the pride and folly of Louis the Fourteenth. It will ever hanker after a French connexion; and now that the internal Government in France has been assimilated in so considerable a degree to that which the immoderate Republicans began so very lately to introduce into Holland, their connexion, as still more natural, will be more desired. . . .

These Provinces in which the French game is so well played, they consider as part of the Old French Empire: certainly they were amongst the oldest parts of it. These they think very well situated, as their party is well-disposed to a re-union. As to the greater nations, they do not aim at making a direct conquest of them, but by disturbing them through a propagation of their principles, they hope to weaken, as they will weaken them, and keep them in perpetual alarm and agitation, and thus render all their efforts against them utterly impracticable, whilst they extend the dominion of their sovereign anarchy on all sides.

As to England, there may be some apprehension from vicinity, from constant communication, and from the very name of Liberty, which, as it ought to be very dear to us, in it's worst abuses carries something seductive. It is the abuse of the first and best of the objects which we cherish. I know that many who sufficiently dislike the system of France, have yet no apprehensions of it's prevalence here. I say nothing to the ground of this security in the attachment of the people to their Constitution, and their satisfaction in the discreet portion of liberty which it measures out to them. Upon this I have said all I have to say, in the Appeal I have published.[16] That security is something, and

not inconsiderable. But if a storm arises I should not much rely upon it.

There are other views of things which may be used to give us a perfect (though in my opinion a delusive) assurance of our own security. The first of these is from the weakness and ricketty nature of the new system in the place of it's first formation. It is thought that the monster of a Commonwealth cannot possibly live—that at any rate the ill contrivance of their fabrick will make it fall in pieces of itself—that the Assembly must be bankrupt, and that this bankruptcy will totally destroy that system, from the contagion of which apprehensions are entertained.

For my part I have long thought that one great cause of the stability of this wretched scheme of things in France was an opinion that it could not stand; and, therefore, that all external measures to destroy it were wholly useless.

As to the bankruptcy, that event has happened long ago, as much as it is ever likely to happen. So soon as a nation compels a creditor to take paper currency in discharge of his debt, there is a bankruptcy. . . .

⤶

In my opinion there never was seen so strong a government internally as that of the French Municipalities. If ever any rebellion can arise against the present system, it must begin, where the Revolution which gave birth to it did, at the Capital. Paris is the only place in which there is the least freedom of intercourse. But even there, so many servants as any man has, so many spies, and irreconcileable domestick enemies.

But that place being the chief seat of the power and intelligence of the ruling faction, and the place of occasional resort for their fiercest spirits, even there a revolution is not likely to have any thing to feed

---

[16] *Appeal from the New to the Old Whigs*, published in 1791.

it. The leaders of the aristocratick party have been drawn out of the kingdom by order of the Princes, on the hopes held out by the Emperor and the King of Prussia at Pilnitz,[17] and as to the democratick factions in Paris, amongst them there are no leaders possessed of an influence for any other purpose but that of maintaining the present state of things. The moment they are seen to warp, they are reduced to nothing. They have no attached army—no party that is at all personal.

It is not to be imagined because a political system is, under certain aspects, very unwise in it's contrivance, and very mischievous in it's effects, that it therefore can have no long duration. It's very defects may tend to it's stability, because they are agreeable to it's nature. The very faults in the constitution of Poland made it last; the *veto* which destroyed all it's energy preserved it's life.[18] What can be conceived so monstrous as the Republick of Algiers?[19] and that no less strange Republick of the Mammalukes in Egypt?[20] They are of the worst form imaginable, and exercised in the worst manner, yet they have existed as a nuisance on the earth for several hundred years.

From all these considerations, and many more, that croud upon me, three conclusions have long since arisen in my mind—

First, that no counter-revolution is to be expected in France from internal causes solely.

Secondly, that the longer the present system exists, the greater will be it's strength; the greater it's power to destroy discontents at home, and to resist all foreign attempts in favour of these discontents.

Thirdly, that as long as it exists in France, it will be the interest of the managers there, and it is in the very essence of their plan, to disturb and distract all other governments, and their endless succession of restless politicians will continually stimulate them to new attempts.

Princes are generally sensible that this is their common cause; and two of them have made a publick declaration of their opinion to this effect. Against this common danger, some of them, such as the King of Spain, the King of Sardinia, and the Republick of Berne, are very diligent in using defensive measures.

If they were to guard against an invasion from France, the merits of this plan of a merely defensive resistance might be supported by plausible topicks; but as the attack does not operate against these countries externally, but by an internal corruption (a sort of dry rot); they who pursue this merely defensive plan, against a danger which the plan itself supposes to be serious, cannot possibly escape it. For it is in the nature of all defensive measures to be sharp and vigorous under the impressions of the first alarm, and to relax by degrees; until at length the danger, by not operating instantly, comes to appear as a false alarm; so much so that the next menacing appearance will look less formidable, and will be less provided against. But to those who are on the offensive it is not necessary to be always alert. Possibly it is more their interest not to be so. For their unforeseen attacks contribute to their success.

---

[17]At Pillnitz in August 1791, the Austrian emperor and king of Prussia requested other European powers to help them restore the king of France.

[18]In the Polish legislature, any member could exercise the *liberum veto* and stop any piece of legislation.

[19]Algiers was the home of Barbary pirates, who terrorized Mediterranean shipping.

[20]A reference to semiautonomous sultans in Egypt who became associated with barbaric rule.

In the mean time a system of French conspiracy is gaining ground in every country. This system happening to be founded on principles the most delusive indeed, but the most flattering to the natural properties of the unthinking multitude, and to the speculations of all those who think, without thinking very profoundly, must daily extend it's influence. A predominant inclination towards it appears in all those who have no religion, when otherwise their disposition leads them to be advocates even for despotism. . . .

Boldness formerly was not the character of Atheists as such. They were even of a character nearly the reverse; they were . . . rather an unenterprizing race. But of late they are grown active, designing, turbulent and seditious. They are sworn enemies to Kings, Nobility and Priesthood. We have seen all the Academicians at Paris, with Condorcet,[21] the friend and correspondent to Priestley,[22] at their head, the most furious of the extravagant Republicans.

The late Assembly, after the last captivity of the King, had actually chosen this Condorcet by a majority on the ballot, for Preceptor to the Dauphin, who was to be taken out of the hands and direction of his parents, and to be delivered over to this fanatick Atheist, and furious democratick Republican. His untractability to these leaders, and his figure in the Club of Jacobins, which at that time they wished to bring under, alone prevented that part of the arrangement, and others in the same style, from being carried into execution. Whilst he was candidate for this office, he produced his title to it by promulgating the following ideas of the title of his royal

pupil to the crown. In a paper written by him, and published with his name, against the re-establishment, even of the appearance of monarchy under any qualifications, He says, "Until now, they (the National Assembly) have prejudged nothing. Reserving to themselves a right to appoint a Preceptor to the Dauphin, they did not declare that *this child was* to reign; but only that *possibly* the Constitution *might* destine him to it: they willed that while education should efface from his mind all the prejudices arising from *the delusions of the throne* respecting his pretended birthright, it should also teach him not to forget, that it is *from the people* he is to receive the title of King, and that *the people do not even possess the right of giving up their power to take it from him.*

They willed that this education should render him worthy by his knowledge, and by his virtues, both to receive *with submission* the dangerous burden of a crown, and *to resign* it *with pleasure* into the hands of his brethren; that he should be conscious that the hastening of that moment when he is to be only a common citizen, constitutes the duty and the glory of a King of a free people.

They willed that the *uselessness of a King,* the necessity of seeking means to establish something in lieu of a *power founded on illusions,* should be one of the first truths offered to his reason; *the obligation of conforming himself to this, the first of his moral duties; and the desire of no longer being freed from the yoke of the law, by an injurious inviolability, the first and chief sentiment of his heart.* They are not ignorant that in the present moment the object is less to form a King than to teach him *that he should know how to wish no longer to be such."*

Such are the sentiments of the man who has occasionally filled the chair of the National Assembly, who is their perpetual

---

[21]The marquis de Condorcet was a leading figure among the French revolutionaries.

[22]Dr. Joseph Priestley, a British cleric and scientist who welcomed the French Revolution.

secretary, their only standing officer, and the most important by far. He leads them to peace or war. He is the great theme of the Republican faction in England. These ideas of M. Condorcet, are the principles of those to whom Kings are to entrust their successors, and the interests of their succession. This man would be ready to plunge the poignard in the heart of his pupil, or to whet the axe for his neck. Of all men, the most dangerous is a warm, hot-headed, zealous Atheist. This sort of man aims at dominion, and his means are, the words he always has in this mouth, "L'égalité naturelle des Hommes, et la Souverainté du Peuple."[23]

All former attempts grounded on these Rights of Men, had proved unfortunate. The success of this last makes a mighty difference in the effect of the doctrine. Here is a principle of nature, to the multitude, the most seductive, always existing before their eyes, *as a thing feasible in practice.* After so many failures, such an enterprize previous to the French experiment, carried ruin to the contrivers, on the face of it; and if any enthusiast was so wild as to wish to engage in the scheme of that nature, it was not easy for him to find followers: Now there is a party almost in all countries, ready made, animated with success, with a sure Ally in the very center of Europe. There is no cabal so obscure in any place, that they do not protect, cherish, foster, and endeavour to raise it into importance at home and abroad. From the lowest, this intrigue will creep up to the highest. Ambition, as well as enthusiasm, may find it's account in the party and in the principle.

In this state of general rottenness among subjects, and of delusion and false politicks in Princes, comes a new experiment. The King of France is in the hands of the Chiefs of the Regicide Faction, the Barnvaes, Lameths, Fayettes, Perigords, Duports, Robespierre's, Camus's, &c. &c. &c. They who had imprisoned, suspended, and conditionally deposed him, are his confidential counsellors. The next desperate of the desperate rebels, call themselves the *Moderate* Party. They are the Chiefs of the first Assembly, who are confederated to support their power during their suspension from the present, and to govern the existent body with as sovereign a sway as they had done the last. They have, for the greater part, succeeded; and they have many advantages towards procuring their success in future. Just before the close of their regular power, they bestowed some appearance of prerogatives on the King, which in their first plans they had refused to him; particularly the mischievous, and in his situation, dreadful prerogative of a *Veto*. This prerogative (which they hold as their bit in the mouth of the National Assembly for the time being) without the direct assistance of their Club, it was impossible for the King to shew even the desire of exerting with the smallest effect, or even with safety to his person. However, by playing through this *Veto,* the Assembly against the King, and the King against the Assembly, they have made themselves masters of both. In this situation, having destroyed the old Government by their sedition, they would preserve as much of order as is necessary for the support of their own usurpation.

It is believed that this, by far the worst party of the miscreants of France, has received direct encouragement from the counsellors who betray the Emperor. Thus strengthened by the possession of the cap-

_____

[23]"The natural equality of men, and the sovereignty of the people."

tive King (now captive in his mind as well as in body) and by a good hope of the Emperor, they intend to send their Ministers to every Court in Europe; having sent before them such a denunciation of terror and superiority to every nation without exception, as has no example in the diplomatick world. Hitherto the Ministers to foreign Courts had been of the appointment of the Sovereign of France *previous to the Revolution;* and either from inclination, duty or decorum, most of them were contented with a merely passive obedience to the new power. At present the King being entirely in the hands of his jailors, and his mind broken to his situation, can send none but the enthusiasts of the system. . . . These Ministers will be so many spies and incendiaries; so many active emissaries of Democracy. Their houses will become places of rendezvous here, as every where else, and centers of cabal for whatever is mischievous and malignant in this country, particularly among those of rank and fashion. As the Minister of the National Assembly will be admitted at this Court, at least with his usual rank, and as entertainments will be naturally given and received by the King's own Ministers, any attempt to discountenance the resort of other people to that Minister would be ineffectual, and indeed absurd, and full of contradiction. The women who come with these Ambassadors will assist in fomenting factious amoungst ours, which cannot fail of extending the evil. Some of them I hear are already arrived. There is no doubt they will do as much mischief as they can.

Whilst the publick Ministers are received under the general law of the communication between nations, the correspondences between the factious clubs in France and ours, will be, as they now are, kept up: but this pretended embassy will be a closer, more steady and more effectual link between the partizans of the new system on both sides of the water. I do not mean that these Anglo-Gallick clubs in London, Manchester, &c. are not dangerous in a high degree. The appointment of festive anniversaries has ever in the sense of mankind been held the best method of keeping alive the spirit of any institution. We have one settled in London; and at the last of them, that of the 14th of July, the strong discountenance of Government, the unfavourable time of the year, and the then uncertainty of the disposition of foreign Powers, did not hinder the meeting of at least nine hundred people, with good coats on their backs, who could afford to pay half a guinea a head to shew their zeal for the new principles. They were with great difficulty, and all possible address, hindered from inviting the French Ambassador. His real indisposition, besides the fear of offending any party, sent him out of town. But when our Court shall have recognized a Government in France, founded on the principles announced in Montmorin's Letter, how can the French Ambassador be frowned upon for an attendance on those meetings wherein the establishment of the Government he represents is celebrated? An event happened a few days ago, which in many particulars was very ridiculous; yet even from the ridicule and absurdity of the proceedings, it marks the more strongly the spirit of the French Assembly. I mean the reception they have given to the Frith-Street Alliance. This, though the delirium of a low, drunken alehouse-club, they have publicly announced as a formal alliance with the people of England, as such ordered it to be presented to their King, and to be published in every province in France. This leads more directly and with much greater force than any proceeding with a regular and rational appearance, to two very material considerations. First, it shews that they are of opinion that the current opinions of the English have the greatest influence on the minds of the people of France, and indeed of all the people in Europe, since they catch with such astonishing eagerness at every the most trifling shew of such opinions in their favour. Next, and what appears to me to be full as important, it shews that they are willing publickly to countenance and even to adopt every factious conspiracy that can be formed in this nation, however low and base in itself, in order to excite in the most miserable wretches here, an idea of their own sovereign importance, and to encourage them to look up to France, whenever they may be matured into something of more force, for assistance in the subversion of their domestick Government. This address of the alehouse club was actually proposed and accepted by the Assembly as an *alliance.* The procedure was in my opinion a high misdemeanor in these who acted thus in England, if they were not so very low and so very base, that no acts of theirs can be called high, even as a description of criminality; and the Assembly in accepting, proclaiming and publishing this forged alliance, has been guilty of a plain aggression, which would justify our Court in demanding a direct disavowal, if our policy should not lead us to wink at it.

Whilst I look over this paper to have it copied, I see a Manifesto of the Assembly, as a preliminary to a declaration of war against the German Princes on the Rhine. This Manifesto contains the whole substance of the French politicks with regard to foreign States. They have ordered it to be circulated amongst the people in every country of Europe—even previously to it's acceptance by the King and his new Privy Council. . . . Therefore, as a summary of

their policy avowed by themselves, let us consider some of the circumstances attending that piece, as well as the spirit and temper of the piece itself.

It was preceded by a speech from Brissot,[24] full of unexampled insolence towards all the Sovereign States of Germany, if not of Europe. The Assembly, to express their satisfaction in the sentiments which it contained, ordered it to be printed. This Brissot had been in the lowest and basest employ under the deposed Monarchy; a sort of thief-taker, or spy of police, in which character he acted after the manner of persons in that description. He had been employed by his master, the Lieutenant de Police, for a considerable time in London, in the same or some such honourable occupation. The Revolution which has brought forward all merit of that kind, raised him, with others of a similar class and disposition, to fame and eminence. On the Revolution he became a publisher of an infamous newspaper, which he still continues. He is charged, and I believe justly, as the first mover of the troubles in Hispaniola.[25] There is no wickedness, if I am rightly informed, in which he is not versed, and of which he is not perfectly capable. His quality of news-writer, now an employment of the first dignity in France, and his practices and principles, procured his election into the Assembly, where he is one of the leading members.— Mr. Condorcet produced on the same day a draft of a Declaration to the King, which the Assembly published before it was presented.

---

[24]Jean-Pierre Brissot, who was a leading advocate of war among the French revolutionaries.

[25]Brissot founded and served as an officer for the Amis des Noirs, a society promoting the rights and interests of blacks in the West Indies.

Condorcet . . . is a man of another sort of birth, fashion, and occupation from Brissot, but in every principle, and in every disposition to the lowest as well as the highest and most determined villainies, fully his equal. He seconds Brissot in the Assembly, and is at once his coadjutor and his rival in a newspaper, which in his own name and as successor to Mr. Garat, a Member also of the Assembly, he has just set up in that Empire of Gazettes. Condorcet was chosen to draw the first Declaration presented by the Assembly to the King, as a threat to the Elector of Treves, and the other Princes on the Rhine. In that piece, . . . they declared publickly, and most proudly and insolently, the principle on which they mean to proceed in their future disputes with any of the Sovereigns of Europe, for they say, "That it is not with fire and sword they mean to attack their territories, but by what will be *more dreadful* to them, the introduction of liberty."—I have not the paper by me to give the exact words—but I believe they are nearly as I state them. *Dreadful* indeed will be their hostility, if they should be able to carry it on according to the example of *their* modes of introducing liberty. They have shewn a perfect model of their whole design, very complete, though in little. This gang of murderers and savages have wholly laid waste and utterly ruined the beautiful and happy country of the Comtat Venaissin and the city of Avignon. This cruel and treacherous outrage the Sovereigns of Europe, in my opinion, with a great mistake of their honour and interest, have permitted even without a remonstrance to be carried to the desired point, on the principles on which they are now themselves threatened in their own States; and this, because, according to the poor and narrow spirit now in fashion, their brother Sovereign, whose

subjects have been thus traiterously and inhumanly treated in violation of the law of nature and of nations, has a name somewhat different from theirs, and instead of being styled King or Duke, or Landgrave, is usually called Pope.

The Electors of Treves and Mentz were frightened with the menace of a similar mode of war. The Assembly, however, not thinking that the Electors of Treves and Mentz had done enough under their first terror, have again brought forward Condorcet, preceded by Brissot, as I have just stated. The Declaration which they have ordered now to be circulated in all countries, is in substance the same as the first, but still more insolent, because more full of detail. There they have the impudence to state that they aim at no conquest; insinuating that all the old lawful Powers of the World had each made a constant open profession of a design of subduing his neighbours. They add, that if they are provoked, their war will be directed only against those who assume to be *Masters*. But to the *People* they will bring peace, law, liberty, &c. &c. There is not the least hint that they consider those whom they call persons *"assuming to be Masters,"* to be the lawful Government of their country, or persons to be treated with the least management or respect. They regard them as usurpers and enslavers of the people. If I do not mistake they are described by the name of tyrants in Condorcet's first draft. I am sure they are so in Brissot's speech, ordered by the Assembly to be printed at the same time and for the same purposes. The whole is in the same strain, full of false philosophy and false rhetorick, both however calculated to captivate and influence the vulgar mind, and to excite sedition in the countries in which it is ordered to be circulated. Indeed it is such, that if any of the lawful acknowledged Sovereigns of Europe had publickly ordered such a manifesto to be circulated in the dominions of another, the Ambassador of that power would instantly be ordered to quit every Court without an audience.

The powers of Europe have a pretext for concealing their fears, by saying that this language is not used by the King; though they will know that there is in effect no such person, that the Assembly is in reality, and by that King is acknowledged to be *the Master,* that what he does is but matter for formality, and that he can neither cause nor hinder, accelerate or retard any measure whatsoever, nor add to or soften the manifesto which the Assembly has directed to be published, with the declared purpose of exciting mutiny and rebellion in the several countries governed by these powers. By the generality also of the menaces contained in this paper (though infinitely aggravating the outrage) they hope to remove from each power separately the idea of a distinct affront. The persons first pointed at by the menace are certainly the Princes of Germany, who harbour the persecuted House of Bourbon and the Nobility of France; the declaration, however, is general, and goes to every state with which they may have a cause of quarrel. But the terror of France has fallen upon all nations. A few months since all Sovereigns seemed disposed to unite against her, at present they all seem to combine in her favour. At no period has the power of France ever appeared with so formidable an aspect. In particular the liberties of the Empire can have nothing more than an existence the most tottering and precarious, whilst France exists with a great power of fomenting rebellion, and the greatest in the weakest; but with neither power nor disposition to support the smaller states in

their independence against the attempts of the more powerful.

I wind up all in a full conviction within my own breast, and the substance of which I must repeat over and over again, that the state of France is the first consideration in the politicks of Europe, and of each state, eternally as well as internally considered.

Most of the topicks I have used are drawn from fear and apprehension. Topicks derived from fear or addressed to it, are, I well know, of doubtful appearance. To be sure, hope is in general the incitement to action. Alarm some men—you do not drive them to provide for their security; you put them to a stand; you induce them not to take measures to prevent the approach of danger, but to remove so unpleasant an idea from their minds; you persuade them to remain as they are, from a new fear that their activity may bring on the apprehended mischief before it's time. I confess freely that this evil sometimes happens from an overdone precaution; but it is when the measures are rash, ill chosen, or ill combined, and the effects rather of blind terror than of enlightened foresight. But the few to whom I wish to submit my thoughts, are of a character which will enable them to see danger without astonishment, and to provide against it without perplexity.

To what lengths this method of circulating mutinous manifestos, and of keeping emissaries of sedition in every Court under the name of Ambassadors, to propagate the same principles and to follow the practices, will go, and how soon they will operate, it is hard to say—but go on it will—more or less rapidly, according to events, and to the humour of the time. The Princes menaced with the revolt of their subjects, at the same time that they have obsequiously obeyed the sovereign mandate of the new Roman Senate, have received with distinction, in a publick character, Ambassadors from those who in the same act had circulated the manifesto of sedition in their dominions. This was the only thing wanting to the degradation and disgrace of the Germanick Body.

The Ambassadors from the Rights of Man, and their admission into the diplomatick system, I hold to be a new aera in this business. It will be the most important step yet taken to affect the existence of Sovereigns, and the higher classes of life— I do not mean to exclude it's effects upon all classes—but the first blow is aimed at the more prominent parts in the ancient order of things.

What is to be done?

It would be presumption in me to do more than to make a case. Many things occur. But as they, like all political measures, depend on dispositions, tempers, means, and external circumstances, for all their effect, not being well assured of these, I do not know how to let loose any speculations of mine on the subject. The evil is stated in my opinion as it exists. The remedy must be where power, wisdom and information, I hope are more united with good intentions than they can be with me. I have done with this subject, I believe for ever. It has given me many anxious moments for the two last years. If a great change is to be made in human affairs, the minds of men will be fitted to it; the general opinions and feelings will draw that way. Every fear, every hope, will forward it; and then they who persist in opposing this mighty current in human affairs, will appear rather to resist the decrees of Providence itself, than the mere designs of men. They will not be resolute and firm, but perverse and obstinate.

Introductory Note to
Heads for Consideration on the Present State of Affairs (1792)

Burke's warnings about the militaristic and expansionist potential of the revolutionary French regime began to ring true in 1792. France declared war on Austria and Prussia in April 1792, and its armies achieved a decisive victory over the Austrian and Prussian armies at Valmy in September 1792. Burke wrote Heads for Consideration on the Present State of Affairs *against this background of French success and expansion. As he did in* Thoughts on French Affairs, *he wrote* Heads for Consideration *in order to influence the Pitt ministry to take action against the Jacobin regime and to counter the noninterventionist stance of Charles Fox.*

In Heads for Consideration, *Burke acted as the quintessential foreign policy adviser, offering suggestions on military strategy and criticizing the Austrian and Prussian generals on their tactics leading to the Valmy debacle. He also counseled Great Britain, advising it to ally quickly with Spain to preserve some hope of maintaining a balance of power against French ambitions and to follow its ancient tradition of opposing French attempts to give the law to Europe. He advocated an offensive alliance designed not to contain French power but to cut out "this evil in the heart of Europe." Indeed, he argued that Britain must be the lead power and the soul of the offensive alliance.*

Heads for Consideration *in many ways constituted the plan for action against France that Burke declined to provide at the end of* Thoughts on French Affairs. *There is in* Heads for Consideration *an urgency that reflects Burke's sense that the evil he had long predicted was manifesting itself across Europe in full fury.* Heads for Consideration *did not, however, meet with any better reception from the Pitt ministry than did* Thoughts on French Affairs.⌒

Heads for Consideration on the Present State of Affairs (1792)

That France, by it's mere geographical position, independently of every other circumstance, must affect every State of Europe; some of them immediately, all of them through mediums not very remote.

That the standing policy of this kingdom ever has been to watch over the *external* proceedings of France (whatever form the *interiour* Government of that kingdom might take) and to prevent the extension of it's dominion or it's ruling influence, over other States.

That, there is nothing in the present *internal* state of things in France, which alters the national policy with regard to the exteriour relations of that country.

That there are, on the contrary, many things in the internal circumstances of France (and perhaps of this country too) which tend to fortify the principles of that fundamental policy; and which render the active assertion of those principles more pressing at this, than at any former time.

That, by a change effected in about three weeks, France has been able to penetrate into the heart of Germany; to make an absolute conquest of Savoy; to menace an immediate invasion of the Netherlands; and to awe and overbear the whole Helvetick Body,[26] which is in a most perilous situation. The great Aristocratick Cantons having, perhaps, as much or more to dread

from their own people whom they arm, but do not chuse or dare to employ, as from the foreign enemy, which against all publick faith has butchered their troops, serving by treaty in France.[27] To this picture, it is hardly necessary to add, the means by which France has been enabled to effect all this, namely the apparently entire destruction of one of the largest, and certainly the highest disciplined, and best appointed army ever seen, headed by the first military Sovereign in Europe, with a Captain under him of the greatest renown; and that without a blow given or received on any side.[28] This state of things seems to me, even if it went no further, truly serious.

Circumstances have enabled France to do all this by *land*. On the other element she has begun to exert herself; and she must succeed in her designs, if enemies very different from those she has hitherto had to encounter, do not resist her.

She has fitted out a naval force, now actually at sea, by which she is enabled to give law to the whole Mediterranean. It is known as a fact (and if not so known, it is in the nature of things highly probable) that she proposes the ravage of the Ecclesiastical State,[29] and the pillage of Rome, as her first object; that next she means to bombard Naples; to awe, to humble, and thus to command all Italy—to force it to a nominal neutrality, but to a real dependence—to compel the Italian Princes and Republicks to admit the free entrance of the French commerce, an open intercourse, and the sure concomitant of that inter-

---

[27]Hundreds of Swiss troops guarding the French royal family were killed in August 1792 when the palace of the Tuileries was stormed.

[28]French armies defeated Prussian forces commanded by Charles II, duke of Brunswick, at Valmy in September 1792.

---

[26]Switzerland.

[29]The Vatican.

course, the *affiliated societies,* in a manner similar to those she has established at Avignon, the Comtat, Chamberry, London, Manchester, &c. &c. which are so many colonies planted in all these countries, for extending the influence, and securing the dominion of the French Republick.

That there never has been hitherto a period in which this kingdom would have suffered a French fleet to domineer in the Mediterranean, and to force ITALY to submit to such terms as France would think fit to impose—to say nothing of what has been done upon land in support of the same system. The great object for which we preserved Minorca, whilst we could keep it, and for which we still retain Gibraltar, both at a great expence, was, and is, to prevent the predominance of France over the Mediterranean.

Thus far as to the certain and immediate effect of that armament upon the Italian States. The probable effect which that armament, and the other armaments preparing at Toulon, and other ports may have upon SPAIN, on the side of the Mediterranean, is worthy of the serious attention of the British councils.

That it is most probable, we may say, in a manner certain, that if there should be a rupture between France and Spain, France will not confine her offensive piratical operations against Spain, to her efforts in the Mediterranean; on which side, however, she may grievously affect Spain, especially if she excites Morocco and Algiers, which undoubtedly she will, to fall upon that power.

That she will fit out armaments upon the ocean, by which the flota itself may be intercepted,[30] and thus the treasures of all

Europe, as well as the largest and surest resources of the Spanish monarchy, may be conveyed into France, and become powerful instruments for the annoyance of all her neighbours.

That she makes no secret of her designs.

That, if the inward and outward bound flota should escape, still France has more and better means of dissevering many of the provinces in the West and East Indies, from the state of Spain, than Holland had when she succeeded in the same attempt. The French marine resembles not a little the old armaments of the Flibustriers,[31] which about a century back, in conjunction with pirates of our nation, brought such calamities upon the Spanish colonies. They differ only in this, that the present piratical force is, out of all measure and comparison, greater; one hundred and fifty ships of the line, and frigates being ready built, most of them in a manner new, and all applicable in different ways to that service. Privateers and Moorish corsaires possess not the best seamanship, and very little discipline, and indeed can make no figure in regular service, but in desperate adventures, and animated with a lust of plunder, they are truly formidable.

That the land forces of France are well adapted to concur with their marine in conjunct expeditions of this nature. In such expeditions, enterprize supplies the want of discipline, and perhaps more than supplies it. Both for this, and for other service . . . one arm is extremely good, the Engineering and Artillery branch. The old officer corps in both being composed for the greater part of those who were not gentlemen, or gentlemen newly such, few have abandoned the service, and the men are veterans well enough disciplined, and very expert. In this piratical way they must

---

[30]Burke is referring to the Spanish ships transporting goods to and from Spain's colonial possessions in the Americas.

[31]Pirates operating in the Caribbean.

make war with good advantage. They must do so, even on the side of Flanders, either offensively or defensively. This shews the difference between the policy of Louis the XIVth. who built a wall of brass about his kingdom; and that of Joseph the Second, who premeditatedly uncovered his whole frontier.

That Spain from the actual and expected prevalence of French power, is in a most perilous situation; perfectly dependent on the mercy of that Republick. If Austria is broken, or even humbled, she will not dare to dispute it's mandates.

In the present state of things, we have nothing at all to dread from the power of Spain by sea, or by land, or from any rivalry in commerce.

That we have much to dread from the connexions into which Spain may be forced.

From the circumstances of her territorial possessions, of her resources, and the whole of her civil and political state, we may be authorized safely, and with undoubted confidence to affirm, that

Spain is not a substantive Power.

That she must lean on France, or on England.

That it is as much for the interest of Great Britain to prevent the predominancy of a French interest in that kingdom, as if Spain were a province of the Crown of Great Britain, or a State actually dependent on it; full as much so as ever Portugal was reputed to be. This is a dependency of much greater value: and it's destruction, or it's being carried to any other dependency, of much more serious misfortune.

One of these two things must happen. Either Spain must submit to circumstances, and take such conditions as France will impose; or she must engage in hostilities along with the Emperor, and the King of Sardinia.

If Spain should be forced or awed into a treaty with the Republick of France, she must open her ports and her commerce, as well as the land communication for the French labourers, who were accustomed annually to gather in the harvest in Spain. Indeed she must grant a free communication for travellers and traders through her whole country. In that case it is not conjectural, it is certain, the Clubs will give law in the Provinces; Bourgoing,[32] or some such miscreant, will give law at Madrid.

In this England may acquiesce if she pleases; and France will conclude a triumphant peace, with Spain under her absolute dependence, with a broad highway into that, and into every State of Europe. She actually invites Great Britain to divide with her the spoils of the new world, and to make a partition of the Spanish Monarchy. Clearly it is better to do so, than to suffer France to possess those spoils, and that territory alone; which, without doubt, unresisted by us, she is altogether as able, as she is willing to do.

This plan is proposed by the French, in the way in which they propose all their plans; and in the only way in which indeed they can propose them, where there is no regular communication between his Majesty and their Republick.

What they propose is *a plan*. It is a *plan* also to resist their predatory project. To remain quiet, and to suffer them to make their own use of a naval power before our face, so as to awe and bully Spain into a submissive peace, or to drive them into a ruinous war, without any measure on our part, I fear is no plan at all.

However, if the plan of co-operation which France desires, and which her affiliated societies here ardently wish and are

---

[32]Baron de Bourgoing, diplomat sent in the spring of 1792 to represent France in Spain.

constantly writing up, should not be adopted, and the war between the Emperor[33] and France should continue, I think it not at all likely that Spain should not be drawn into the quarrel. In that case, the neutrality of England will be a thing absolutely impossible. The time is only the subject of deliberation.

Then the question will be, whether we are to defer putting ourselves into a posture for the common defence, either by armament, or negotiation, or both, until Spain is actually attacked; that is, whether our Court will take a decided part for Spain, whilst Spain on her side, is yet in a condition to act with whatever degree of vigour she may have; whilst that vigour is yet unexhausted;—or whether we shall connect ourselves with her broken fortunes; after she shall have received material blows, and when we shall have the whole slow length of that always unwieldy, and ill constructed, and then wounded and crippled body, to drag after us, rather than to aid us. Whilst our disposition is uncertain, Spain will not dare to put herself in such a state of defence as will make her hostility formidable, or her neutrality respectable.

If the decision is such as the solution of this question . . . conducts to—no time is to be lost. But the measures though prompt, ought not to be rash and indigested. They ought to be well chosen, well combined and well pursued. The system must be general; but it must be executed, not successively, or with interruption, but all together . . . in one melting, and one mould.

For this purpose, we must put Europe before us, which plainly is, just now, in all it's parts, in a state of dismay, derangement and confusion; and very possibly amongst all it's Sovereigns, full of secret heartburning, distrust, and mutual accusation. Perhaps it may labour under worse evils. There is no vigour any where, except the distempered vigour and energy of France. That country has but too much life in it, when every thing around is so disposed to tameness and languor. The very vices of the French system at home tend to give force to foreign exertions. The Generals *must* join the armies. They must lead them to enterprize, or they are likely to perish by their hands. Thus without law or government of her own, France gives law to all the Governments in Europe.

⟝

There seem indeed to have been several mistakes in the political principles on which the War was entered into, as well as in the plans upon which it was conducted; some of them very fundamental, and not only visibly, but I may say, palpably erroneous; and I think him to have less than the discernment of a very ordinary Statesman, who could not foresee from the very beginning, unpleasant consequences from those plans, though not the unparalleled disgraces and disasters which really did attend them: for they were, both principles and measures, wholly new and out of the common course, without any thing apparently very grand in the conception, to justify this total departure from all rule.

For, in the first place, the united Sovereigns very much injured their cause by admitting, that they had nothing to do with the interiour arrangements of France; in contradiction to the whole tenour of the publick Law of Europe, and to the correspondent practice of all it's States, from the time we have any history of them. In this particular, the two German Courts[34] seem to have as little consulted the Publicists of

---

[33]Of the Austrian empire.

[34]Prussia and Austria.

Germany, as their own true interests, and those of all the Sovereigns of Germany and Europe. This admission of a false principle in the Law of Nations, brought them into an apparent contradiction, when they insisted on the re-establishment of the Royal Authority in France. But this confused and contradictory proceeding gave rise to a practical error of worse consequence. It was derived from one and the same root; namely, that the person of the Monarch of France was every thing; and the Monarchy, and the intermediate orders of the State, by which the Monarchy was upheld, were nothing. So that, if the united Potentates had succeeded so far, as to re-establish the authority of that King, and that he should be so ill-advised as to confirm all the confiscations, and to recognize as a lawful body, and to class himself with, that rabble of murderers . . . there was nothing in the principle, or in the proceeding of the United Powers, to prevent such an arrangement.

An expedition to free a brother Sovereign from prison, was undoubtedly, a generous and chivalrous undertaking. But the spirit and generosity would not have been less, if the policy had been more profound, and more comprehensive; that is, if it had taken in those considerations, and those persons, by whom, and in some measure, for whom, Monarchy exists. This would become a bottom for a system of solid and permanent policy, and of operations conformable to that system.

The same fruitful error was the cause why nothing was done to impress the people of France . . . with an idea that the Government was ever to be really French, or indeed any thing else than the nominal government of a Monarch, a Monarch absolute as over them, but whose sole support was to arise from foreign Potentates, and who was to be kept on his throne by German forces; in short, that the King of

France was to be a Viceroy to the Emperor and the King of Prussia.

It was the first time that foreign Powers interfering in the concerns of a nation divided into parties, have thought proper to thrust wholly out of their councils, to postpone, to discountenance, to reject, and in a manner to disgrace the party whom those Powers came to support. The single person of a King cannot be a party. Woe to the King who is himself his party! The Royal party with the King or his Representatives at it's head, is the *Royal cause*. Foreign Powers have hitherto chosen to give to such wars as this, the appearance of a civil contest, and not that of an hostile invasion. When the Spaniards, in the sixteenth century, sent aids to the chiefs of the League, they appeared as Allies to that League, and to the imprisoned King (the Cardinal de Bourbon) which that League had set up.[35] When the Germans came to the aid of the Protestant Princes, in the same series of civil wars, they came as Allies. When the English came to the aid of Henry the Fourth, they appeared as Allies to that Prince.[36] So did the French always when they intermeddled in the affairs of Germany. They came to aid a party there. When the English and Dutch intermeddled in the succession of Spain, they appeared as Allies to the Emperor Charles the Sixth.[37] In short, the policy has been as uniform as it's principles were obvious to an ordinary eye.

---

[35]Burke is referring to Spanish support for the Holy Catholic League during the French civil war between Protestant and Catholic forces in the late sixteenth century.

[36]England supported the Protestant Henry IV during the French civil war.

[37]During the Wars of the Spanish Succession (1701–1713), England and Holland supported the claim of Charles VI of Austria to the throne of Spain.

According to all the old principles of law and policy, a regency ought to have been appointed by the French Princes of the Blood, Nobles, and Parliaments, and then recognized by the combined Powers. Fundamental law and antient usage, as well as the clear reason of the thing, have always ordained it during an imprisonment of the King of France; as in the case of John, and of Francis the First.[38] A Monarchy ought not to be left a moment without a Representative, having an interest in the succession. The orders of the State, ought also to have been recognized in those amongst whom alone they existed in freedom, that is, in the Emigrants.

Thus laying down a firm foundation on the recognition of the authorities of the Kingdom of France, according to nature and to it's fundamental laws, and not according to the novel and inconsiderate principles of the usurpation which the United Powers were come to extirpate. The King of Prussia and the Emperor, as Allies of the antient Kingdom of France, would have proceeded with dignity, first, to free the Monarch, if possible; if not, to secure the Monarchy as principal in the design; and in order to avoid all risques to that great object . . . they would of course avoid proceeding with more haste, or in a different manner than what the nature of such an object required.

Adopting this, the only rational system, the rational mode of proceeding upon it, was to commence with an effective siege of Lisle, which the French Generals must have seen taken before their faces, or be forced to fight. A plentiful country of friends, from whence to draw supplies, would have been behind them; a plentiful

country of enemies, from whence to force supplies, would have been before them. Good towns were always within reach to deposit their hospitals and magazines. The March from Lisle to Paris, is through a less defensible country, and the distance is hardly so great as from Longwy to Paris.

If the *old* politick and military ideas had governed, the advanced guard would have been formed of those who best knew the country and had some interest in it, supported by some of the best light troops and light artillery, whilst the grand solid body of an army disciplined to perfection, proceeded leisurely, and in close connexion with all it's stores, provisions, and heavy cannon, to support the expedite body in case of misadventure, or to improve and compleat it's success.

The direct contrary of all this was put in practice. In consequence of the original sin of this project, the army of the French Princes was every where thrown into the rear, and no part of it brought forward to the last moment, the time of the commencement of the secret negotiation. This naturally made an ill impression on the people, and furnished an occasion for the rebels at Paris to give out that the faithful subjects of the King were distrusted, despised, and abhorred by his allies. The march was directed through a skirt of Lorraine, and thence into a part of Champagne, the Duke of Brunswick leaving all the strongest places behind him; leaving also behind him, the strength of his artillery; and by this means giving a superiority to the French, in the only way in which the present France is able to oppose a German force.

In consequence of the adoption of those false politicks, which turned every thing on the King's sole and single person, the whole plan of the war was reduced to nothing by a *coup de main,* in order to set

---

[38]John II and Francis I were held captive during portions of their reigns as king of France in the fourteenth and fifteenth centuries, respectively.

that Prince at liberty. If that failed, every thing was to be given up.

The scheme of a *coup de main*, might (under favourable circumstances) be very fit for a partizan at the head of a light corps, by whose failure nothing material would be deranged. But for a royal army of eighty thousand men, headed by a King in person, who was to march an hundred and fifty miles through an enemy's country—surely this was a plan unheard of.

Although this plan was not well chosen, and proceeded upon principles altogether ill judged and impolitick, the superiority of the military force, might in a great degree have supplied the defects, and furnished a corrective to the mistakes. The greater probability was that the Duke of Brunswick would make his way to Paris, over the bellies of the rabble of drunkards, robbers, assassins, rioters, mutineers, and half-grown boys, under the ill-obeyed command of a theatrical, vapouring, reduced Captain of cavalry,[39] who opposed that great Commander and great army. But . . . [h]e began to treat, the winds blew, and the rains beat, the house fell—because it was built upon sand—and great was the fall thereof. . . .

≈

It is singular, and indeed, a thing, under all it's circumstances, inconceivable, that every thing should by the Emperor be abandoned to the King of Prussia. That Monarch was considered as principal. In the nature of things, as well as in his position with regard to the war, he was only an ally; and a new ally, with crossing interests in many particulars, and of a policy rather uncertain. At best, and supposing him to act with the greatest fidelity, the Emperor,

and the Empire, to him must be but secondary objects. Countries out of Germany, must affect him in a still more remote manner. France, other than from the fear of it's doctrinal principles, can to him be no object at all. Accordingly, the Rhine, Sardinia, and the Swiss, are left to their fate. The King of Prussia has no *direct* and immediate concern with France; *consequentially*, to be sure, a great deal; but the Emperor touches France *directly* in many parts: he is a near neighbour to Sardinia, by his Milanese territories; he borders on Switzerland; Cologne, possessed by his uncle, is between Mentz and Treves, the King of Prussia's territories on the Lower Rhine. The Emperor is the natural guardian of Italy and Germany; the natural balance against the ambition of France, whether Republican or Monarchical. His Ministers and his Generals, therefore, ought to have had their full share in every material consultation, which I suspect they had not. If he has no Minister capable of plans of policy, which comprehend the superintendancy of a war, or no General with the least of a political head, things have been as they must be. However, in all the parts of this strange proceeding, there must be a secret.

It is probably known to Ministers. I do not mean to penetrate into it. My speculations on this head must be only conjectural. If the King of Prussia, under the pretext, or on the reality of some information relative to ill practice on the part of the Court of Vienna, takes advantage of his being admitted into the heart of the Emperor's dominions in the character of an ally, afterwards to join the common enemy, and to enable France to seize the Netherlands, and to reduce and humble the Empire, I cannot conceive, upon every principle, any thing more alarming for this country, separately, and as a part of the

---

[39]Charles-François du Périer Dumouriez, commander of French forces at the battle of Valmy.

general system.[40] After all, we may be looking in vain in the regions of politicks, for what is only the operation of temper and character upon accidental circumstances—But I never knew accidents to decide the *whole* of any great business; and I never knew temper to act, but that some system of politicks, agreeable to it's peculiar spirit, was blended with it, strengthened it, and got strength from it. Therefore the politicks can hardly be put out of the question.

Great mistakes have been committed; at least I hope so. If there have been none, the case in future is desperate. I have endeavoured to point out some of those which have occurred to me, and most of them very early.

Whatever may be the cause of the present state of things, on a full and mature view and comparison of the historical matter, of the transactions that have passed before our eyes, and of the future prospect, I think I am authorized to form an opinion without the least hesitation.

That there never was, nor is, nor ever will be, or ever can be, the least rational hope of making an impression on France by any Continental Powers, if England is not a part, is not the directing part, is not the soul, of the whole confederacy against it.

This, so far as it is an anticipation of future, is grounded on the whole tenour of former history—In speculation it is to be accounted for on two plain principles.

First, That Great Britain is likely to take a more fair and equal part in the alliance, than the other Powers, as having less of crossing interest, or perplexed discussion with any of them.

Secondly, Because France cannot have to deal with any of these continental Sovereigns, without their feeling that nation, as a maritime Power, greatly superiour to them all put together; a force which is only to be kept in check by England.

England, except during the excentrick aberration of Charles the Second,[41] has always considered it as her duty and interest, to take her place in such a confederacy. Her chief disputes must ever be with France, and if England shews herself indifferent and unconcerned when these Powers are combined against the enterprizes of France, she is to look with certainty for the same indifference on the part of these Powers, when she may be at war with that nation. This will tend totally to disconnect this kingdom from the system of Europe, in which, if she ought not rashly to meddle, she ought never wholly to withdraw herself from it.

If then England is put in motion, whether by a consideration of the general safety, or of the influence of France upon Spain, or by the probable operations of this new system on the Netherlands, it must embrace in it's project the whole as much as possible, and the part it takes ought to be as much as possible a leading and presiding part.

I therefore beg leave to suggest,

First, That a Minister should forthwith be sent to Spain, to encourage that Court to persevere in the measures they have adopted against France; to make a close alliance and guarantee of possessions, as against France, with that power, and whilst the formality of the treaty is pending, to assure them of our protection, postponing any lesser disputes to another occasion.

Secondly, To assure the Court of Vienna, of our desire to enter into our antient con-

---

[40]Burke is referring to Prussia's efforts to come to terms with France after the defeat at Valmy.

[41]Burke has in mind the Treaty of Dover of 1670, under which England became a French ally in return for subsidy payments.

nexions with her, and to support her effectually in the war which France has declared against her.

Thirdly, To animate the Swiss, and the King of Sardinia, to take a part, as the latter once did on the principles of the Grand Alliance.[42]

Fourthly, To put an end to our disputes with Russia, and mutually to forget the past. I believe if she is satisfied of this oblivion, she will return to her old sentiments, with regard to this Court, and will take a more forward part in this business than any other Power.

Fifthly, If what has happened to the King of Prussia is only in consequence of a sort of panick or of levity, and an indisposition to persevere long in one design—the support and concurrence of Russia will tend to steady him, and to give him resolution. If he be ill disposed, with that power on his back, and without one ally in Europe, I conceive he will not be easily led to derange the plan.

Sixthly, To use the joint influence of our Court, and of our then Allied Powers, with Holland, to arm as fully as she can by sea, and to make some addition by land.

Seventhly, To acknowledge the King of France's next brother (assisted by such a Council and such Representatives of the Kingdom of France, as shall be thought proper) Regent of France, and to send that Prince a small supply of money, arms, cloathing and artillery.

Eighthly, To give force to these negociations, an instant naval armament ought to be adopted; one squadron for the Mediterranean; another for the Channel. The season is convenient, most of our trade being, as I take it, at home.

After speaking of a plan formed upon the antient policy and practice of Great Britain and of Europe; to which this is exactly conformable in every respect, with no deviation whatsoever, and which is, I conceive much more strongly called for by the present circumstances, than by any former, I must take notice of another which I hear, but cannot persuade myself to believe, is in agitation. This plan is grounded upon the very same view of things which is here stated, namely, the danger to all Sovereigns, and old Republicks, from the prevalence of French power and influence.

It is to form a Congress of all the European powers, for the purpose of a general defensive alliance, the objects of which should be,

First, The recognition of this new Republick (which they well know is formed on the principles, and for the declared purpose of the destruction of all Kings), and whenever the heads of this new Republick shall consent to release the Royal Captives, to make Peace with them.

Secondly, To defend themselves with their joint forces against the open aggressions or the secret practices, intrigues and writings, which are used to propagate the French principles.

It is easy to discover from whose shop this commodity comes. It is so perfectly absurd, that if that, or any thing like it, meets with a serious entertainment in any Cabinet, I should think it the effect of what is called a judicial blindness, the certain forerunner of the destruction of all Crowns and Kingdoms.

An *offensive* alliance, in which union is preserved, by common efforts in common dangers, against a common active enemy, may preserve it's consistency, and may pro-

---

[42]During the Wars of the Spanish Succession, the Grand Alliance, composed of England, Austria, and Holland, opposed Louis XIV's ambitions to expand French power in Europe.

duce for a given time, some considerable effect; though this is not easy, and for any very long period, can hardly be expected. But a *defensive* alliance, formed of long discordant interests, with innumerable discussions existing, having no one pointed object to which it is directed, which is to be held together with an unremitted vigilance, as watchful in peace as in war, is so evidently impossible, is such a chimera, is so contrary to human nature, and the course of human affairs, that I am persuaded no person in his senses, except those whose Country, Religion and Sovereign, are deposited in the French funds, could dream of it. There is not the slightest petty boundary suit, no difference between a family arrangement, no sort of misunderstanding, or cross purpose between the pride and etiquette of Courts, that would not entirely disjoint this sort of alliance, and render it as futile in it's effects, as it is feeble in it's principle. But when we consider that the main drift of that defensive alliance must be to prevent the operation of intrigue, mischievous doctrine and evil example, in the success of unprovoked rebellion, regicide, and systematick assassination and massacre, the absurdity of such a scheme becomes quite lamentable. Open the communication with France, and the rest follows of course.

How far the interiour circumstances of this country support what is said with regard to it's foreign politicks, must be left to better judgments. I am sure the French faction here is infinitely strengthened by the success of the assassins on the other side of the water.—This evil in the heart of Europe must be extirpated from that center, or no part of the circumference can be free from the mischief which radiates from it, and which will spread circle beyond circle, in spite of all the little defensive precautions which can be employed against it.

I do not put my name to these hints submitted to the consideration of reflecting men. It is of too little importance to suppose the name of the writer could add any weight to the state of things contained in this paper. That state of things presses irresistibly on my judgment, and it lies, and has long lain, with an heavy weight upon my mind. I cannot think that what is done in France, is beneficial to the human race. If it were, the English Constitution ought no more to stand against it than the antient Constitution of the kingdom in which the new system prevails. I thought it the duty of a man, not unconcerned for the publick, and who is a faithful subject to the King, respectfully to submit this state of facts at this new step in the progress of the French arms and politicks, to his Majesty, to his confidential servants, and to those persons who, though not in office, by their birth, their rank, their fortune, their character and their reputation for wisdom, seem to me to have a large stake in the stability of the antient order of things.

Bath, November 5, 1792.

Introductory Note to *Remarks on the Policy of the Allies* (1793)

Remarks on the Policy of the Allies *was the third private memorandum Burke wrote between 1791 and 1793 to try to influence the course of British policy toward France. The silence that* Thoughts on French Affairs *and* Heads for Consideration on the Present State of Affairs *received in official circles made Burke despondent, and he claimed in private correspondence that he wrote Re-marks on the Policy of the Allies "to relieve myself rather than to suggest any thing to others."[43] The subject and tone of* Remarks *are in fact more abstract and speculative than the prior two memoranda, as Burke discussed what should be done with France after the allies had defeated the Jacobins.*

Burke's prediction of regicide came true when the revolutionaries executed Louis XVI in early 1793. War between Britain and revolutionary France began shortly thereafter, generating a heated debate over war aims. Pitt's initial policy defined in April 1793 was to gain for Britain and its allies sufficient security and some measure of reparation from France. Pitt did not make the restoration of the French monarchy a condition of negotiating and concluding a settlement with the revolutionaries. Nor did his declarations against France lend any official support to the émigré cause. Burke did not agree with Pitt's formulation of Britain's war aims or its neglect of the royalist cause.

As indicated by his analysis of the nature of the French threat to European order and domestic stability in Thoughts on French Affairs *and* Heads for Consideration, *Burke believed that Britain had both a right and duty to intervene in the affairs of the French state. More specifically, Burke argued that the royalist émigré community contained the people capable of restoring France to its traditional forms of government and society and should therefore be the conduit for outside intervention. Nevertheless, he cautioned that the work of restoration must be the work of the French, for the French citizenry would never accept the imposition of a settlement by foreign powers. Here Burke demonstrated the same sensibility to diversity in his push for unity that he displayed in his efforts on Ireland and America. France was*

part of the commonwealth of Europe and therefore existed as part of a greater community. But it could not be restored to this community without French participation and leadership.

For Burke, any postwar settlement had not only to restore France's domestic political and social institutions but also to preserve France's role as a critical weight in the European balance of power. In passages that might have been useful to the leaders negotiating the Treaty of Versailles in 1919, Burke warned that a settlement that humiliated France and reduced its traditional role in international politics would only breed future conflict. Burke thus returned to the theme that the balance of power is a fundamental tenet of the commonwealth of Europe.

Although he urged the pursuit of a restrained punishment of revolutionaries based on the wisdom of historical experience, Burke concluded Remarks on the Policy of the Allies *with a warning about the limits of using history as a guide. History, wrote Burke, prepared no one for the French Revolution, and thus history cannot provide complete guidance for handling the aftermath of that cataclysm.*〜

Remarks on the Policy of the Allies (1793)

As the proposed manifesto is, I understand, to promulgate to the world the general idea of a plan for the regulation of a great kingdom, and through the regulation of that kingdom probably to decide the fate of Europe for ever, nothing requires a more serious deliberation with regard to the time of making it, the circum-

---

[43]*Corr.*, vii, 517.

stances of those to whom it is addressed, and the matter it is to contain.[44]

As to the time, . . . I have some doubts whether it is not rather unfavourable to the issuing any Manifesto, with regard to the intended government of France; and for this reason, that it is, (upon the principal point of our attack) a time of calamity and defeat. Manifestoes of this nature are commonly made when the army of some Sovereign enters into the enemy's country in great force, and under the imposing authority of that force employs menaces towards those whom he desires to awe; and makes promises to those whom he wishes to engage in his favour.

As to a party, what has been done at Toulon leaves no doubt, that the party for which we declare must be that which substantially declares for Royalty as the basis of the government.[45]

⌒

Speaking of this nation as part of a general combination of powers; are we quite sure, that others can believe us to be sincere, or that we can be even fully assured of our own sincerity in the protection of those who shall risque their lives for the restoration of Monarchy in France, when the world sees, that those who are the natural, legal, constitutional representatives of that

Monarchy, if it has any, have not had their names so much as mentioned in any one publick act; that in no way whatever are their persons brought forward, that their rights have not been expressly or implicitly allowed, and that they have not been in the least consulted on the important interests they have at stake.[46] On the contrary, they are kept in a state of obscurity and contempt, and in a degree of indigence at times boarding on beggary. They are in fact, little less prisoners in the village of Hanau,[47] than the Royal captives who are locked up in the tower of the Temple.[48] What is this, according to the common indications which guide the judgment of mankind, but, under the pretext of protecting the crown of France, in reality to usurp it?

I am also very apprehensive, that there are other circumstances which must tend to weaken the force of our declarations. No partiality to the allied powers, can prevent great doubts on the fairness of our intentions as supporters of the Crown of France, or of the true principles of legitimate Government in opposition to Jacobinism, when it is visible that the two leading orders of the State of France,[49] who are now the victims, and who must always be the true and sole supports of Monarchy in that country, are, at best, in some of their descriptions, considered only as objects of charity, and others are, when employed, employed only as mercenary solders; that they are thrown back out of all reputable service, are in a manner dis-

---

[44]Burke is alluding to a proposed statement of British policy toward the government of France after the defeat of the revolutionaries that eventually appeared in the declaration of King George III on October 29, 1793.

[45]British forces occupied Toulon at the end of August 1793, after the city declared its support for the French monarchy. Two months later, French republican forces began a siege of the city. In December the republican soldiers regained control of Toulon when the British and Spanish evacuated. Burke wrote *Remarks* after the British occupation but before the republican siege and recapture.

[46]Burke means the royalist émigrés.

[47]In the territory of the Landgrave Hesse-Kassel.

[48]The Temple was the prison in Paris in which the revolutionaries held the French royal family captive after August 1792.

[49]The clergy and aristocracy.

owned, considered as nothing in their own cause, and never once consulted in the concerns of their King, their country, their laws, their religion, and their property! We even affect to be ashamed of them. In all our proceedings we carefully avoid the appearance of being of a party with them. In all our ideas of Treaty we do not regard them as what they are, the two leading orders of the kingdom. If we do not consider them in that light, we must recognize the savages by whom they have been ruined, and who have declared war upon Europe, whilst they disgrace and persecute human nature, and openly defy the God that made them, as real proprietors of France.

I am much afraid, too, that we shall scarcely be believed fair supporters of lawful Monarchy against Jacobinism, so long as we continue to make and to observe cartels with the Jacobins, and on fair terms exchange prisoners with them, whilst the Royalists, invited to our standard, and employed under our publick faith, against the Jacobins, if taken by that savage faction, are given up to the executioner without the least attempt whatsoever at reprisal. For this, we are to look at the King of Prussia's conduct, compared with his Manifestoes about a twelvemonth ago. For this we are to look at the capitulations of Mentz and Valenciennes, made in the course of the present campaign.[50] By these two capitulations, the Christian Royalists were excluded from any participation in the cause of the combined powers. They were considered as the outlaws of Europe. Two armies were in effect sent against them. One of those armies (that which surrendered Mentz) was very near overpowering the Christians of Poitou, and the other (that which surrendered at Valenci-

ennes) has actually crushed the people whom oppression and despair had driven to resistance at Lyons, has massacred several thousands of them in cold blood, pillaged the whole substance of the place, and pursued their rage to the very houses, condemning that noble city to desolation, in the unheard of manner we have seen it devoted.

It is then plain by a conduct which overturns a thousand declarations, that we take the Royalists of France only as an instrument of some convenience in a temporary hostility with the Jacobins, but that we regard those atheistick and murderous barbarians as the bonâ fide possessors of the soil of France. It appears at least, that we consider them as a fair Government *de facto,* if not *de jure;* a resistance to which in favour of the King of France, by any man who happened to be born within that country, might equitably be considered by other nations, as the crime of treason.

For my part, I would sooner put my hand into the fire than sign an invitation to oppressed men to fight under my standard, and then on every sinister event of war, cruelly give them up to be punished as the basest of traitors, as long as I had one of the common enemy in my hands to be put to death in order to secure those under my protection, and to vindicate the common honour of Sovereigns. We hear nothing of this kind of security in favour of those whom we invite to the support of our cause. Without it, I am not a little apprehensive that the proclamations of the combined powers might (contrary to their intention no doubt) be looked upon as frauds, and cruel traps laid for their lives.

So far as to the correspondence between our declarations and our conduct, let the declaration be worded as it will, the conduct is the practical comment by which, and which alone it can be understood.

---

[50]Valenciennes and Mainz fell to allied forces in July 1793.

This conduct acting on the declaration, leaves a Monarchy without a Monarch; and without any representative or trustee for the Monarch, and the Monarchy. It supposes a kingdom without states and orders; a territory without proprietors; and faithful subjects, who are to be left to the fate of rebels and traitors.

The affair of the establishment of a Government is a very difficult undertaking for foreign powers to act in as *principals;* though as *auxiliaries and mediators,* it has been not at all unusual, and may be a measure full of policy and humanity, and true dignity.

The first thing we ought to do, supposing us not giving the law as conquerors, but acting as friendly powers applied to for counsel and assistance in the settlement of a distracted country, is well to consider the composition, nature, and temper of its objects, and particularly of those who actually do, or who ought to exercise power in that state. It is material to know who they are, and how constituted, whom we consider *as the people of France?*

The next consideration is, through whom our arrangements are to be made, and on what principles the Government we propose is to be established.

The first question on the people is this, Whether we are to consider the individuals *now actually in France, numerically taken and arranged into Jacobin Clubs,* as the body politick, constituting the nation of France? or, Whether we consider the original individual proprietors of lands, expelled since the Revolution, and the states and the bodies politick, such as the colleges of justice called parliaments, the corporations noble and not noble of balliages, and towns, and cities, the bishops and the clergy, as the true constituent parts of the nation, and forming the legally organized parts of the people of France?

In this serious concern it is very necessary that we should have the most distinct ideas annexed to the terms we employ; because it is evident, that an abuse of the term *people,* has been the original fundamental cause of those evils, the cure of which, by war and policy, is the present object of all the states of Europe.

If we consider the acting power in France in any legal construction of publick law, as the people, the question is decided in favour of the Republick one and indivisible. But we have decided for Monarchy. If so, we have a King and Subjects; and that King and Subjects have rights and privileges which ought to be supported at home; for I do not suppose that the Government of that kingdom can, or ought to be regulated, by the arbitrary Mandate of a foreign Confederacy.

As to the faction exercising power, to suppose that Monarchy can be supported by principled Regicides, Religion by professed Atheists, Order by Clubs of Jacobins, Property by Committees of Proscription, and Jurisprudence by Revolutionary Tribunals, is to be sanguine in a degree of which I am incapable. On them I decide, for myself, that these persons are not the legal Corporation of France, and that it is not with them we can (if we would) settle the Government of France.

Since, then, we have decided for Monarchy in that kingdom, we ought also to settle who is to be the Monarch, who is to be the Guardian of a Minor, and how the Monarch and Monarchy is to be modified and supported? If the Monarch is to be elected, who the Electors are to be: if hereditary, what order is established corresponding with an hereditary Monarchy, and fitted to maintain it? Who are to modify it in its exercise? Who are to restrain its powers where they ought to be limited, to strengthen them where they are to be supported, or to enlarge them, where the object, the time, and the circumstances, may demand their extension? These are things which, in the outline, ought to be made distinct and clear; for if they are not (especially with regard to those great points, who are the proprietors of the soil, and what is the corporation of the kingdom) there is nothing to hinder the compleat establishment of a Jacobin Republick, (such as that formed in 1790 and 1791) under the name of a Democracie Royale. Jacobinism does not consist in the having or not having, a certain Pageant under the name of a King, but "in taking the people as equal individuals, without any corporate name or description, without attention to property, without division of powers, and forming the government of delegates from a number of men so constituted, in destroying or confiscating property, and bribing the publick creditors, or the poor, with the spoils, now of one part of the community, now of another, without regard to prescription or possession."

I hope no one can be so very blind as to imagine that Monarchy can be acknowledged and supported in France upon any other basis than that of its property, *corporate and individual,* or that it can enjoy a moment's permanence or security upon any scheme of things, which sets aside all the antient corporate capacities and distinctions of the kingdom, and subverts the whole fabrick of its antient laws and usages, political, civil and religious, to introduce a system founded on the supposed *Rights of the Man, and the absolute equality of the human race.* Unless, therefore, we declare clearly and distinctly in favour of the *restoration* of property, and confide to the hereditary property of the kingdom, the limitation and qualifications of its hereditary Monarchy, the blood and treasure of Europe is wasted for the establishment of Jacobinism in France. There is no doubt that Danton and Robespierre, Chaumette and Barrere, that Condorcet, that Thomas Paine, that La Fayette, and the Exbishop of Autun, the Abbé Gregoire, with all the gang of the Syeyes's, the Henriots, and the Santerres, if they could secure themselves in the fruits of their rebellion and robbery, would be perfectly indifferent, whether the most unhappy of all infants, whom by the lessons of the shoemaker, his governour and guardian,[51] they are training up studiously and methodically to be an idiot, or what is worse, the most wicked and base of mankind, continues to receive his civic education in the Temple or the Thuilleries, whilst they, and such as they, really govern the kingdom.

It cannot be too often and too strongly inculcated, that Monarchy and property must, in France, go together; or neither can exist. To think of the possibility of the existence of a permanent and hereditary Royalty, *where nothing else is hereditary or permanent in point either of personal or corporate dignity,* is a ruinous chimera worthy of the Abbé Syeyes and those wicked Fools his Associates, who usurped Power . . . and who brought forth the Monster which they called Democracie Royale, or the Constitution.

I believe that most thinking men, would prefer infinitely some sober and sensible form of a Republick, in which there was no mention at all of a King, but which held out some reasonable security to property, life, and personal freedom, to a scheme of things like this Democracie Royale, founded on impiety, immortality, fraudulent currencies, the confiscation of innocent individuals, and the pretended Rights of Man; and which, in effect, excluding the

---

[51] In July 1793 the dauphin was placed in the care of Antoine Simon, a shoemaker by trade.

whole body of the nobility, clergy, and landed property of a great nation, threw every thing into the hands of a desperate set of obscure adventurers who led to every mischief, a blind and bloody band of Sans-Culottes. At the head, or rather at the tail of this system, was a miserable pageant as its ostensible instrument, who was to be treated with every species of indignity, till the moment, when he was conveyed from the Palace of Contempt to the Dungeon of Horrour, and thence led by a Brewer of his Capital through the applauses of an hired, frantick, drunken multitude, to lose his head upon a scaffold.[52]

This is the Constitution, or Democracie Royale; and this is what infallibly would be again set up in France to run exactly the same round, if the predominant power should so far be forced to submit as to receive the name of a King, leaving it to the Jacobins, (that is, to those who have subverted Royalty and destroyed Property) to modify the one, and to distribute the other as spoil. . . . As to any other party, none exists in that unhappy country. The Royalists (those in Poitou excepted) are banished and extinguished; and as to what they call the Constitutionalists, or *Democrats Royaux,* they never had an existence of the smallest degree of power, consideration or authority; nor, if they differ at all from the rest of the Atheistick Banditti . . . were they ever other than the temporary tools and instruments of the more determined, able, and systematick Regicides. . . .

In an Address to France, in an attempt to treat with it, or in considering any scheme at all relative to it, it is impossible we should mean the geographical, we must always mean the moral and political country. I be-

lieve we shall be in a great errour if we act upon an idea that there exists in that country any organized body of men who might be willing to treat on equitable terms, for the restoration of their Monarchy; but who are nice in balancing those terms, and who would accept such as to them appeared reasonable, but who would quietly submit to the predominant power, if they were not gratified in the fashion of some constitution which suited with their fancies.

I take the state of France to be totally different. I know of no such body, and of no such party. So far from a combination of twenty men (always excepting Poitou) I never yet heard, that a *single man* could be named of sufficient force or influence to answer for another man, much less for the smallest district in the country, or for the most incomplete company of soldiers in the army. We see every man that the Jacobins chuse to apprehend, taken up in his village, or in his house, and conveyed to prison without the least shadow of resistance; *and this indifferently,* whether he is suspected of Royalism or Federalism, Moderantism, Democracy Royal, or any other of the names of faction which they start by the hour. What is much more astonishing, (and if we did not carefully attend to the genius and circumstances of this Revolution, must indeed appear incredible) all their most accredited military men, from a generalissimo to a corporal, may be arrested, (each in the midst of his camp, and covered with the laurels of accumulated victories) tied neck and heels, thrown into a cart, and sent to Paris to be disposed of at the pleasure of the Revolutionary Tribunals.

As no individuals have power and influence, so there are no Corporations, whether of Lawyers or Burghers existing. The Assembly called Constituent, destroyed all such institutions very early. . . .

---

[52]Burke is referring to Louis XVI and his execution in 1793. The "Brewer" was Joseph Santerre, who was in charge of the king's execution.

The State of France is perfectly simple. It consists of but two descriptions—The Oppressors and the Oppressed.

The first have the whole authority of the State in their hands, all the arms, all the revenues of the publick, all the confiscations of individuals and corporations. They have taken the lower sort from their occupations and have put them into pay, that they may form them into a body of Janisaries to overrule and awe property.[53] The heads of these wretches they never suffer to cool. They supply them with a food for fury varied by the day—besides the sensual state of intoxication from which they are rarely free. They have made the Priests and people formally abjure the Divinity; they have estranged them from every civil, moral, and social, or even natural and instinctive sentiment, habit, and practice, and have rendered them systematically savages, to make it impossible for them to be the instruments of any sober and virtuous arrangement, or to be reconciled to any state of order, under any name whatsoever.

The other description, *the Oppressed*— are people of some property; they are the small reliques of the persecuted Landed Interest; they are the Burghers and the Farmers. By the very circumstance of their being of some property, though numerous in some points of view, they cannot be very considerable as a *number*. In cities the nature of their occupations renders them domestick and feeble; in the country it confines them to their farm for subsistence. . . .

⤣

As to the oppressed *individuals,* they are many; and as discontented as men must be under the monstrous and complicated

tyranny of all sorts, with which they are crushed. They want no stimulus to throw off this dreadful yoke: but they do want (not Manifestoes, which they have had even to surfeit, but) real protection, force and succour.

The disputes and questions of men at their ease, do not at all affect their minds, or ever can occupy the minds of men in their situation. These theories are long since gone by; they have had their day, and have done their mischief. The question is not between the Rabble of Systems, Fayetteism, Condorcetism, Monarchism, or Democratism or Federalism, on the one side, and the fundamental Laws of France on the other—or between all these systems amongst themselves. It is a controversy (weak indeed and unequal on the one part) between the proprietor and the robber; between the prisoner and the jailor; between the neck and the guillotine. Fourfifths of the French inhabitants would thankfully take protection from the Emperor of Morocco, and would never trouble their heads about the abstract principles of the power by which they were snatched from imprisonment, robbery, and murder. But then these men can do little or nothing for themselves. They have no arms, nor magazines, nor chiefs, nor union, nor the possibility of these things within themselves. On the whole therefore I lay it down as a certainty, that in the Jacobins, no change of mind is to be expected—and that no others in the territory of France have an independent and deliberative existence.

The truth is, that France is out of itself—The moral France is separated from the geographical. The master of the house is expelled, and the robbers are in possession. If we look for the *corporate people* of France existing as corporate in the eye and intention of public Law, (that corporate

---

[53] A janissary was a member of the Turkish infantry in the Ottoman Empire.

people, I mean, who are free to deliberate and to decide, and who have a capacity to treat and conclude) they are in Flanders, and Germany, in Switzerland, Spain, Italy, and England. There are all the Princes of the Blood, there are all the Orders of the State, there are all the Parliaments of the kingdom.

This being, as I conceive, the true state of France, as it exists *territorially,* and as it exists *morally,* the question will be, with whom we are to concert our arrangements; and whom we are to use as our instruments in the reduction, in the pacification, and in the settlement of France. The work to be done must indicate the workmen. Supposing us to have rational objects, we have two principal, and one secondary. The first two are so intimately connected as not to be separated even in thought; the re-establishment of Royalty, and the re-establishment of Property. One would think it requires not a great deal of argument to prove, that the most serious endeavours to restore Royalty, will be made by Royalists. Property will be most energetically restored by the antient proprietors of that kingdom.

When I speak of Royalists, I wish to be understood of those who were always such from principle. Every arm lifted up for Royalty from the beginning, was the arm of a man so principled. I do not think there are ten exceptions.

The principled Royalists are certainly not of force to effect these objects by themselves. If they were, the operations of the present great Combination would be wholly unnecessary. What I contend for is, that they should be consulted with, treated with, and employed; and that no Foreigners whatsoever are either in interest so engaged, or in judgment and local knowledge so competent, to answer all these purposes as the natural proprietors of the country.

Their number for an exiled party is also considerable. Almost the whole body of the landed proprietors of France, ecclesiastical and civil, have been steadily devoted to the Monarchy. This body does not amount to less than seventy thousand—a very great number in the composition of the respectable classes in any society.—I am sure, that if half that number of the same description were taken out of this country, it would leave hardly any thing that I should call the people of England. On the faith of the Emperor[54] and the King of Prussia, a body of ten thousand Nobility on horseback, with the King's two brothers at their head, served with the King of Prussia in the campaign of 1792, and equipped themselves with the last shilling of their ruined fortunes and exhausted credit.[55] It is not now the question how that great force came to be rendered useless and totally dissipated. I state it now, only to remark, that a great part of the same force exists, and would act if it were enabled. I am sure every thing has shewn us that in this war with France, one Frenchman is worth twenty foreigners. . . .

If we wish to make an impression on the minds of any persons in France, or to persuade them to join our standard, it is impossible that they should not be more easily led, and more readily formed and disciplined, (civilly and martially disciplined) by those who speak their language,

---

[54]Of the Austrian empire.

[55]Before the revolution the French Noblesse were so reduced in numbers, that they did not much exceed twenty thousand, at least of full grown men. As they have been very cruelly formed into entire corps of soldiers, it is estimated, that by the sword, and distempers in the field, they have not lost less than five thousand men; and if this course is pursued, it is to be feared, that the whole body of the French nobility may be extinguished. Several hundreds have also perished by famine and various accidents. [Burke's note]

who are acquainted with their manners, who are conversant with their usages and habits of thinking, and who have a local knowledge of their country, and some remains of antient credit and consideration, than with a body congregated from all tongues and tribes. Where none of the respectable native interests are seen in the transaction, it is impossible that any declarations can convince those that are within, or those that are without, that any thing else than some sort of hostility in the style of a conqueror is meant. At best it will appear to such wavering persons, (if such there are) whom we mean to fix with us, at best a choice whether they are to continue a prey to domestick banditti, or to be fought for as a carrion carcass, and picked to the bone by all the crows and vultures of the sky. They may take protection, (and they would I doubt not) but they can have neither alacrity nor real zeal in such a cause. When they see nothing but bands of English, Spaniards, Neapolitans, Sardinians, Prussians, Austrians, Hungarians, Bohemians, Sclavonians, Croatians, *acting as principals,* it is impossible they should think we come with a beneficent design. Many of those fierce and barbarous people have already given proofs how little they regard any French party whatsoever. Some of these nations the people of France are jealous of; such are the English, and the Spaniards—others they despise; such are the Italians—others they hate and dread; such are the German and Danubian powers. At best such interposition of antient enemies excites apprehension; but in this case, how can they suppose that we come to maintain their legitimate Monarchy in a truly paternal French Government, to protect their privileges, their laws, their religion, and their property, when they see us make use of no one person who has any

interest in them, any knowledge of them, or any the least zeal for them? On the contrary, they see, that we do not suffer any of those who have shewn a zeal in that cause, which we seem to make our own, to come freely into any place in which the Allies obtain any footing.

If we wish to gain upon any people, it is right to see what it is they expect. We have had a proposal from the Royalists of Poitou. They are well intitled, after a bloody war maintained for eight months against all the powers of anarchy, to speak the sentiments of the Royalists of France. Do they desire us to exclude their Princes, their Clergy, their Nobility? The direct contrary. They earnestly solicit that men of every one of these descriptions should be sent to them. They do not call for English, Austrian, or Prussian officers. They call for French emigrant officers. They call for the exiled priests. They have demanded the Comte d'Artois to appear at their head. These are the demands, (quite natural demands) of those who are ready to follow the standard of Monarchy.

The great means therefore of restoring the Monarchy which we have made *the main object of the war,* is to assist the dignity, the religion, and the property of France, to repossess themselves of the means of their natural influence. This ought to be the primary object of all our politicks, and all our military operations. Otherwise every thing will move in a preposterous order, and nothing but confusion and destruction will follow.

I know that misfortune is not made to win respect from ordinary minds. I know that there is a leaning to prosperity however obtained, and a prejudice in its favour; I know there is a disposition to hope something from the variety and inconstancy of villany, rather than from the tiresome uniformity of fixed principle. There have been, I admit, situations in which a guiding person or party might be gained over, and through him or them, the whole body of a nation. For the hope of such a conversion, and of deriving advantage from enemies, it might be politick for a while to throw your friends into the shade. But examples drawn from history in occasions like the present will be found dangerously to mislead us. France has no resemblance to other countries which have undergone troubles and been purified by them. If France, jacobinised as it has been for four full years, did contain any bodies of authority and disposition to treat with you, (most assuredly she does not) such is the levity of those who have expelled every thing respectable in their country, such their ferocity, their arrogance, their mutinous spirit, their habits of defying every thing human and divine, that no engagement would hold with them for three months; nor indeed could they cohere together for any purpose of civilized society, if left as now they are. There must be a means not only of breaking their strength within themselves, but of *civilizing* them; and these two things must go together, before we can possibly treat with them, not only as a nation, but with any division of them. Descriptions of men of their own race, but better in rank, superiour in property and decorum, of honourable, decent and orderly habits, are absolutely necessary to bring them to such a frame as to qualify them so much as to come into contact with a civilized nation. A set of those ferocious savages with arms in their hands, left to themselves in one part of the country, whilst you proceed to another, would break forth into outrages at least as bad as their former. They must, as fast as gained (if ever they are gained) be put under the

guide, direction and government of better Frenchmen than themselves, or they will instantly relapse into a fever of aggravated Jacobinism.

⤚

To administer the only cure for the unheard of disorders of that undone country, I think it infinitely happy for us, that God has given into our hands, more effectual remedies than human contrivance could point out. We have in our bosom, and in the bosom of other civilized states, nearer forty than thirty thousand persons, providentially preserved not only from the cruelty and violence, but from the contagion of the horrid practices, sentiments and language of the Jacobins, and even sacredly guarded from the view of such abominable scenes. If we should obtain in any considerable district, a footing in France, we possess an immense body of physicians and magistrates of the mind, whom we now know to be the most discreet, gentle, well tempered, conciliatory, virtuous, and pious persons, who in any order probably existed in the world. You will have a missioner of peace and order in every parish. Never was a wiser national oeconomy than in the charity of the English and of other countries. Never was money better expended than in the maintenance of this body of civil troops for re-establishing order in France, and for thus securing its civilization to Europe. This means, if properly used, is of value inestimable.

Nor is this corps of instruments of civilization confined to the first order of that state, I mean the clergy. The allied powers possess also, an exceedingly numerous, well informed, sensible, ingenious, high principled and spirited body of cavaliers in the expatriated landed interest of France,

as well qualified at least, as I, . . . ever expected to see in the body of any landed
gentlemen and soldiers by their birth.
France is well winnowed and sifted. Its virtuous men are, I believe, amongst the most
virtuous, as its wicked are amongst the
most abandoned upon earth. Whatever in
the territory of France may be found to be
in the middle between these, must be attracted to the better part. This will be
compassed, when every gentleman, every
where being restored to his landed estate,
each on his patrimonial ground, may join
the Clergy in reanimating the loyalty, fidelity and religion of the people; that these
gentlemen proprietors of land, may sort
that people according to the trust they sev-
erally merit, that they may arm the honest
and well affected, and disarm and disable
the factious and ill disposed. No foreigner
can make this discrimination nor these
arrangements. The antient corporations of
Burghers according to their several modes
should be restored; and placed, (as they
ought to be) in the hands of men of gravity and property in the cities or baillages,
according to the proper constitutions of
the commons or third estate of France.
They will restrain and regulate the seditious rabble there, as the gentlemen will
on their own estates. In this way, and *in
this way alone,* the country (once broken in
upon by foreign force well directed) may
be gained and settled. It must be gained
and settled by *itself,* and through the
medium of its *own* native dignity and
property. It is not honest, it is not decent,
still less is it politick, for foreign powers
themselves to attempt any thing in this
minute, internal, local detail, in which
they could shew nothing but ignorance,
imbecility, confusion and oppression. As
to the Prince who has a just claim to exercise the regency of France, like other men

he is not without his faults and his defects.[56] But faults or defects . . . are not
what in any country destroy a legal title to
Government. These princes are kept in a
poor obscure country town of the King of
Prussia's. Their reputation is entirely at the
mercy of every calumniator. They cannot
shew themselves, they cannot explain
themselves, as princes ought to do. After
being well informed, as any man here can
be, I do not find, that these blemishes in
this eminent person, are at all considerable, or that they at all affect a character,
which is full of probity, honour, generosity, and real goodness. In some points he
has but too much resemblance to his unfortunate Brother; who with all his weak-
nesses, had a good understanding and
many parts of an excellent man, and a
good King. But Monsieur, without supposing the other deficient, (as he was not)
excells him in general knowledge and in a
sharp and keen observation, with something of a better address, and an happier
mode of speaking and of writing. His conversation is open, agreeable and informed,
his manners gracious and princely. His
brother the Comte d'Artois sustains still
better the representation of his place. He is
eloquent, lively, engaging in the highest
degree, of a decided character, full of energy and activity. In a word he is a brave,
honourable, and accomplished cavalier.
Their brethren of Royalty, if they were
true to their own cause and interest, instead of relegating these illustrious persons
to an obscure town, would bring them forward in their courts and camps, and exhibit them to, what they would speedily
obtain, the esteem, respect, and affection
of mankind.

---

[56]The comte de Provence, who later became Louis
XVIII.

⌐

I think I have myself studied France, as much as most of those whom the allied courts are likely to employ in such a work. I have likewise of myself as partial and as vain as opinion as men commonly have of themselves. But if I could command the whole military arm of Europe, I am sure, that a bribe of the best province in that kingdom, would not tempt me to intermeddle in their affairs, except in perfect concurrence and concert with the natural legal interests of the country, composed of the Ecclesiastical, the Military, the several Corporate Bodies of Justice, and of Burghership, making under a Monarch (I repeat it again and again) *the French Nation, according to its fundamental Constitution*. No considerate Statesmen would undertake to meddle with it upon any other condition.

The Government of that kingdom is fundamentally Monarchical. The publick law of Europe has never recognized in it any other form of Government. The Potentates of Europe have by that law, a right, an interest, and a duty to know with what government they are to treat, and what they are to admit into the federative Society, or in other words into the diplomatick Republick of Europe. This Right is clear and indisputable.

What other and further interference they have a right to in the interior of the concerns of another people, is a matter on which, as on every political subject, no very definite or positive rule can well be laid down. Our neighbours are men; and who will attempt to dictate the laws, under which it is allowable or forbidden to take a part in the concerns of men, whether they are considered individually or in a collective capacity, whenever char-ity to them, or a care of my own safety, calls forth my activity. Circumstances perpetually variable, directing a moral prudence and discretion, the *general* principles of which never vary, must alone prescribe a conduct fitting on such occasions. The latest casuists of public law are rather of a Republican cast, and in my mind, by no means so averse as they ought to be to a Right in the people (a word which ill defined is of the most dangerous use) to make changes at their pleasure in the fundamental laws of their country. These writers, however, when a country is divided, leave abundant liberty for a neighbour to support any of the parties according to his choice.[57] This interference must indeed always be a Right, whilst the privilege of doing good to others, and of averting from them every sort of evil, is a Right: Circumstances may render that Right a Duty. It depends wholly on this, whether it be a *bona fide* charity to a party, and a prudent precaution with regard to yourself, or whether under the pretence of aiding one of the parties in a nation, you act in such a manner as to aggravate its calamities, and accomplish its final destruction. In truth it is not the interfering or keeping aloof, but iniquitous intermeddling, or treacherous inaction which is praised or blamed by the decision of an equitable judge.

It will be a just and irresistible presumption against the fairness of the interposing power, that he takes with him no party or description of men in the divided state. It is not probable, that these parties should all, and all alike, be more adverse to the true interests of their country, and less capable of forming a judgment upon them, than those who are absolute strangers to

---

[57]Vattel. [Burke's note]

their affairs, and to the character of the ac- tors in them, and have but a remote, fee- ble, and secondary sympathy with their in- terest. Sometimes a calm and healing arbiter may be necessary; but, he is to compose differences, not to give laws. It is impossible that any one should not feel the full force of that presumption. Even people, whose politics for the supposed good of their own country lead them to take advantage of the dissentions of a neighbouring nation in order to ruin it, will not directly propose to exclude the na- tives, but they will take that mode of con- sulting and employing them which most nearly approaches to an exclusion. In some particulars they propose what amounts to that exclusion, in others they do much worse. They recommend to Ministry, "that no Frenchman who has given a decided opinion, or acted a decided part in this great Revolution for or against it, should be countenanced, brought forward, trusted or employed, even in the strictest subordina- tion to the Ministers of the allied powers." Although one would think that this advice would stand condemned on the first proposition, yet as it has been made popu- lar, and has been proceeded upon practi- cally, I think it right to give it a full consid- eration.

And first, I have asked myself who these Frenchmen are, that, in the state their own country has been in for these last five years, of all the people of Europe, have alone not been able to form a decided opinion, or have been unwilling to act a decided part?

Looking over all the names I have heard of in this great Revolution, in all human affairs, I find no man of any distinction who has remained in that more than sto- ical apathy, but the Prince de Conti. This mean, stupid, selfish, swinish, and cow- ardly animal, universally known and de- spised as such, has indeed, except in one abortive attempt to elope, been perfectly neutral. However his neutrality, which it seems would qualify him for trust, and on a competition must set aside the Prince de Condé, can be of no sort of service. His moderation has not been able to keep him from a jail. The allied powers must draw him from that jail, before they can have the full advantage of the exertions of this great neutralist.[58]

Except him, I do not recollect a man of rank or talents, who by his speeches or his votes, by his pen or by his sword, has not been active on this scene. The time indeed could admit no neutrality in any person worthy of the name of man. . . .

It is however, out of these, or of such as these, guilty and impenitent, despising the experience of others, and their own, that some people talk of chusing their Negotia- tors with those Jacobins, who they suppose may be recovered to a sounder mind. They flatter themselves, it seems, that the friendly habits formed during their origi- nal partnership of iniquity, a similarity of character, and a conformity in the ground- work of their principles, might facilitate their conversion, and gain them over to some recognition of Royalty. But surely this is to read human nature very ill. The several Sectaries in this schism of the Ja- cobins, are the very last men in the world to trust each other. Fellowship in Treason, is a bad ground of confidence. The last quarrels, are the sorest; and the injuries re- ceived or offered by your own associates, are ever the most bitterly resented. . . .

---

[58]Burke is comparing Louis-François-Joseph de Bourbon, prince de Conti, with Louis-Joseph de Bourbon, prince de Condé. At the time Burke was writing *Remarks,* Conti was in prison in Paris after returning to France in 1792. Condé was an émigré leader who was very hostile toward the French revolutionaries.

The first description is that of the Christian Royalists, men who as earnestly wished for reformation, as they opposed innovation in the fundamental parts of their Church and State. *Their* part has been *very decided*. Accordingly they are to be set aside in the restoration of Church and State. It is an odd kind of disqualification where the restoration of Religion and Monarchy is the question. If England should (God forbid it should) fall into the same misfortune with France, and that the Court of Vienna should undertake the restoration of our Monarchy, I think it would be extraordinary to object to the admission of Mr. Pitt, of Lord Grenville, or Mr. Dundas into any share in the management of that business, because in a day of trial they have stood up firmly and manfully, as I trust they always will do, and with distinguished powers, for the Monarchy and the legitimate Constitution of their country. I am sure if I were to suppose myself at Vienna at such a time, I should, as a Man, as an Englishman, and as a Royalist, protest in that case, as I do in this, against a weak and ruinous principle of proceeding, which can have no other tendency, than to make those who wish to support the Crown, meditate too profoundly on the consequences of the part they take—and consider whether for their open and forward zeal in the Royal Cause, they may not be thrust out from any sort of confidence and employment, where the interest of crowned heads is concerned.

These are the *Parties*. I have said, and said truly, that I know of no neutrals. But as a general observation on this general principle of chusing neutrals on such occasions as the present, I have this to say—that it amounts to neither more nor less than this shocking proposition—that we ought to exclude men of honour and ability from serving theirs and our cause; and

to put the dearest interests of ourselves and our posterity into the hands of men of no decided character, without judgment to chuse, and without courage to profess any principle whatsoever.

Such men can serve no cause, for this plain reason—they have no cause at heart. They can at best work only as mere mercenaries. They have not been guilty of great crimes; but it is only because they have not energy of mind to rise to any height of wickedness. They are not hawks or kites; they are only miserable fowls whose flight is not above their dunghill or henroost. But they tremble before the authors of these horrors. They admire them at a safe and respectful distance. There never was a mean and abject mind that did not admire an intrepid and dexterous villain. In the bottom of their hearts they believe such hardy miscreants to be the only men qualified for great affairs: if you set them to transact with such persons, they are instantly subdued. They dare not so much as look their antagonist in the face. They are made to be their subjects, not to be their arbiters or controllers.

⤺

In all that we do, whether in the struggle or after it, it is necessary that we should constantly have in our eye, the nature and character of the enemy we have to contend with. The Jacobin Revolution is carried on by men of no rank, of no consideration, of wild savage minds, full of levity, arrogance and presumption, without morals, without probity, without prudence. What have they then to supply their innumerable defects, and to make them terrible even to the firmest minds? *One* thing, and *one* thing only—but that one thing is worth a thousand—they have *energy*. In France, all things being put into a universal ferment, in the decomposition of society, no man

comes forward but by his spirit of enterprize and the vigour of his mind. If we
meet this dreadful and portentous energy,
restrained by no consideration of God or
man, that is always vigilant, always on the
attack, that allows itself no repose, and
suffers none to rest an hour with impunity; if we meet this energy with poor
commonplace proceeding, with trivial
maxims, paltry old saws, with doubts,
fears and suspicions, with a languid, uncertain hesitation, with a formal, official
spirit, which is turned aside by every obstacle from its purpose, and which never
sees a difficulty but to yield to it, or at best
to evade it; down we go to the bottom of
the abyss—and nothing short of Omnipotence can save us. We must meet a vicious
and distempered energy with a manly and
rational vigour. As virtue is limited in its
resources—we are doubly bound to use all
that, in the circle drawn about us by our
morals, we are able to command.

I do not contend against the advantages
of distrust. In the world we live in it is but
too necessary. Some of old called it the
very sinews of discretion. But what signify
common-places, that always run parallel
and equal? Distrust is good or it is bad, according to our position and our purpose.
Distrust is a defensive principle. They who
have much to lose have much to fear. But
in France we hold nothing. We are to
break in upon a power in possession; we
are to carry every thing by storm, or by
surprize, or by intelligence, or by all. Ad-
venture therefore, and not caution, is our
policy. Here to be too presuming is the
better error.

The world will judge of the spirit of our
proceeding in those places of France which
may fall into our power, by our conduct in
those that are already in our hands. Our
wisdom should not be vulgar. Other times,
perhaps other measures: But in this awful

hour our politicks ought to be made up of
nothing but courage, decision, manliness,
and rectitude. We should have all the magnanimity of good faith. This is a royal and
commanding policy; and as long as we are
true to it we may give the law. Never can
we assume this command if we will not
risque the consequences. For which reason
we ought to be bottomed enough in principle not to be carried away upon the first
prospect of any sinister advantage. For depend upon it, that if we once give way to a
sinister dealing, we shall teach others the
game, and we shall be outwitted and over-
borne: the Spaniards, the Prussians, God
knows who, will put us under contribution at their pleasure; and instead of being
the head of a great confederacy, and the arbiters of Europe, we shall, by our mistakes,
break up a great design into a thousand little selfish quarrels; the enemy will triumph, and we shall sit down under the
terms of unsafe and dependent peace,
weakened, mortified, and disgraced, whilst
all Europe, England included, is left open
and defenceless on every part, to jacobin
principles, intrigues, and arms. . . .

↬

My clear opinion is, that Toulon ought to
be made, what we set out with, a royal
French city. By the necessity of the case, it
must be under the influence, civil and military, of the allies. But the only way of
keeping that jealous and discordant mass
from tearing its component parts to
pieces, and hazarding the loss of the
whole, is to put the place into the nominal
government of the regent, his officers
being approved by us. This, I say, is absolutely necessary for a poise amongst ourselves. Otherwise is it to be believed that
the Spaniards, who hold that place with us
in a sort of partnership contrary to our
mutual interest, will see us absolute mas-

ters of the Mediterranean, with Gibraltar on one side, and Toulon on the other, with a quiet and composed mind, whilst we do little less than declare that we are to take the whole West Indies into our hands, leaving the vast, unwieldy, and feeble body of the Spanish dominions in that part of the world, absolutely at our mercy, without any power to balance us in the smallest degree. Nothing is so fatal to a nation as an extreme of self-partiality, and the total want of consideration of what others will naturally hope or fear. Spain must think she sees, that we are taking advantage of the confusions which reign in France, to disable that country, and of course every country from affording her protection, and in the end to turn the Spanish Monarchy into a province. If she saw things in a proper point of light, to be sure, she would not consider any other plan of politicks as of the least moment in comparison of the extinction of jacobinism. But her ministers (to say the best of them) are vulgar politicians. It is no wonder that they should postpone this great point, or balance it, by considerations of the common politicks, that is, the questions of power between *state and state.* If we manifestly endeavour to destroy the balance, especially the maritime and commercial balance, both in Europe and the West Indies, (the latter their sore and vulnerable part) from fear of what France may do for Spain hereafter, is it to be wondered, that Spain, infinitely weaker than we are, (weaker indeed that such a mass of empire ever was,) should feel the same fears from our uncontroled power, that we give way to ourselves from a supposed resurrection of the antient power of France under a Monarchy? It signifies nothing whether we are wrong or right in the abstract; but in respect to our relation to Spain, with such principles followed up in practice, it is absolutely impossible that any cordial alliance can subsist between the two nations. If Spain goes, Naples will speedily follow. Prussia is quite certain, and thinks of nothing but making a market of the present confusions. Italy is broken and divided; Switzerland is jacobinized, I am afraid, completely. I have long seen with pain the progress of French principles in that country. Things cannot go on upon the present bottom. The possession of Toulon, which, well managed, might be of the greatest advantage, will be the greatest misfortune that ever happened to this nation. The more we multiply troops there, the more we shall multiply causes and means of quarrel amongst ourselves. I know but one way of avoiding it, which is to give a greater degree of simplicity to our politicks. Our situation does necessarily render them a good deal involved. And, to this evil, instead of increasing it, we ought to apply all the remedies in our power.

Another thing which I cannot account for is, the sending for the Bishop of Toulon, and afterwards forbidding his entrance. This is as directly contrary to the declaration, as it is to the practice of the allied powers. The King of Prussia did better. When he took Verdun, he actually reinstated the Bishop and his Chapter. When he thought he should be the master of Chalons, he called the bishop from Flanders, to put him into possession. The Austrians have restored the clergy wherever they obtained possession. We have proposed to restore Religion as well as Monarchy; and in Toulon we have restored neither the one nor the other. . . . If we give way to our Jacobins in this point, it is fully and fairly putting the government, civil and ecclesiastical, not in the

King of France, to whom, as the protector and governor, and in substance the head of the Gallican Church, the nomination to the bishopricks belonged, and who made the bishop of Toulon; it does not leave it with him, or even in the hands of the King of England, or the King of Spain; but in the basest Jacobins of a low sea-port, to exercise, *pro tempore,* the sovereignty. If this point of religion is thus given up, the grand instrument for reclaiming France is abandoned. We cannot, if we would, delude ourselves about the true state of this dreadful contest. *It is a religious war.* It includes in its object undoubtedly every other interest of society as well as this; but this is the principal and leading feature. It is through this destruction of religion that our enemies propose the accomplishment of all their other views. The French Revolution, impious at once and fanatical, had no other plan for domestick power and foreign empire. Look at all the proceedings of the National Assembly from the first day of declaring itself such in the year 1789, to this very hour, and you will find full half of their business to be directly on this subject. In fact it is the spirit of the whole. The religious system, called the Constitutional Church, was on the face of the whole proceeding set up only as a mere temporary amusement to the people, and so constantly stated in all their conversations, till the time should come, when they might with safety cast off the very appearance of all religion whatsoever, and persecute christianity throughout Europe with fire and sword. . . .

This religious war is not a controversy between sect and sect as formerly, but a war against all sects and all religions. The question is not whether you are to overturn the catholick, to set up the protestant. Such an idea in the present state of the world is too contemptible. Our busi-

ness is to leave to the schools the discussion of the controverted points, abating as much as we can the acrimony of disputants on all sides. It is for christian Statesmen, as the world is now circumstanced, to secure their common Basis, and not to risque the subversion of the whole Fabrick by pursuing these distinctions with an ill-timed zeal. We have in the present grand Alliance, all modes of Government as well as all modes of religion. In Government, we mean to restore that which, notwithstanding our diversity of forms we are all agreed in, as fundamental in Government. The same principle ought to guide us in the religious part; conforming the mode, not to our particular ideas . . . but to what will best promote the great general ends of the Alliance. As Statesmen we are to see which of those modes best suits with the interests of such a Commonwealth as we wish to secure and promote. There can be no doubt, but that the catholick religion, which is fundamentally the religion of France, must go with the Monarchy of France. . . .

⌁

Another political question arises about the mode of Government which ought to be established. I think the proclamation (which I read before I had proceeded far in this Memorial,) puts it on the best footing, by postponing that arrangement to a time of peace.

When our politicks lead us to enterprize a great, and almost total political revolution in Europe, we ought to look seriously into the consequences of what we are about to do. Some eminent persons discover an apprehension that the Monarchy, if restored in France, may be restored in too great strength for the liberty and happiness of the natives, and for the tranquillity of other States. They are therefore of opinion that terms ought to be made for the modification of that Monarchy. They are persons too considerable from the powers of their mind, and from their situation, as well as from the real respect I have for them, who seem to entertain these apprehensions, to let me pass them by unnoticed.

As to the power of France, as a State, and in its exterior relations, I confess my fears are on the part of its extreme reduction. There is undoubtedly something in the vicinity of France, which makes it naturally and properly an object of our watchfulness and jealousy, whatever form its Government may take. But the difference is great between a plan for our own security, and a scheme for the utter destruction of France. If there were no other countries in the political map but these two, I admit that policy might justify a wish to lower our neighbour to a standard which would even render her in some measure, if not wholly, our dependent. But the system of Europe is extensive and extremely complex. However formidable to us as taken in this one relation, France is not equally dreadful to all other States. On the contrary, my clear opinion is, that the Liberties of Europe cannot possibly be preserved, but by her remaining a very great and preponderating power. The design at present evidently pursued by the combined Potentates, or of the two who lead, is totally to destroy her as such a Power. For Great Britain resolves that she shall have no Colonies, no Commerce, and no Marine. Austria means to take away the whole frontier from the borders of Switzerland, to Dunkirk. It is their plan also to render the interiour Government lax and feeble, by prescribing by force of the arms of rival and jealous nations, and without consulting the natural interests of the kingdom; such arrangements as in the

actual state of Jacobinism in France, and the unsettled state in which property must remain for a long time, will inevitably produce such distraction and debility in Government, as to reduce it to nothing, or to throw it back into its old confusion. One cannot conceive so frightful a state of a Nation. A maritime country, without a marine, and without commerce; a continental country without a frontier, and for a thousand miles surrounded with powerful, warlike, and ambitious neighbours! It is possible, that she might submit to lose her commerce and her colonies; her security she never can abandon. . . .

༄

I am well aware how invidious a task it is to oppose any thing which tends to the apparent aggrandizement of our own country. But I think no country can be aggrandized whilst France is Jacobinised. This post removed, it will be a serious question how far her further reduction will contribute to the general safety which I always consider as included. Among precautions against ambition, it may not be amiss to take one precaution against our *own*. I must fairly say, I dread our *own* power and our *own* ambition; I dread our being too much dreaded. It is ridiculous to say we are not men; and that, as men, we shall never wish to aggrandize ourselves in some way or other. Can we say, that even at this very hour we are not invidiously aggrandized? We are already in possession of almost all the commerce of the world. Our Empire in India is an awful thing. If we should come to be in a condition not only to have all this ascendant in commerce, but to be absolutely able, without the least controul, to hold the commerce of all other Nations totally dependent upon our good pleasure, we may say that we shall not abuse this astonishing, and hitherto unheard of power. But every other Nation will think we shall abuse it. It is impossible but that sooner or later, this state of things must produce a combination against us which may end in our ruin.

As to France, I must observe that for a long time she has been stationary. She has, during this whole century, obtained far less by conquest or negotiation than any of the three great continental Powers. Some part of Lorraine excepted, I recollect nothing she has gained; no not a village. In truth, this Lorraine acquisition does little more than secure her Barrier. In effect and substance it was her own before.

However that may be, I consider these things at present chiefly in one point of view, as obstructions to the war on Jacobinism, which *must* stand as long as the Powers think its extirpation but a *secondary* object, and think of taking advantage under the name of *indemnity* and *security* to make war upon the whole Nation of France Royal, and Jacobin, for the aggrandizement of the Allies on the ordinary principles of interest, as if no Jacobinism existed in the world.

So far is France from being formidable to its neighbours for its domestick strength, that I conceive it will be as much as all its neighbours can do by a steady guarantee, to keep that Monarchy at all upon its basis. It will be their business to nurse France, not to exhaust it. France, such as it is, is indeed highly formidable. Not formidable, however, as a great Republick; but as the most dreadful gang of robbers and murderers that ever was embodied. But this distempered strength of France, will be the cause of proportionable weakness on its recovery. Never was a country so completely ruined; and they who calculate the resurrection of her power by former examples, have not sufficiently considered what is the present state

of things. Without detailing the inventory of what organs of Government have been destroyed, together with the very materials of which alone they can be recomposed, I wish it to be considered what an operose affair the whole system of taxation is in the old states of Europe. It is such as never could be made but in a long course of years. In France, all taxes are abolished. The present powers resort to the capital; and to the capital in kind. But a savage undisciplined people suffer a *robbery* with more patience than an *impost*. The former is in their habits and their dispositions. They consider it as transient, and as what, in their turn, they may exercise. But the terrours of the present power are such as no regular Government can possibly employ. They who enter into France do not succeed to *their* resources. They have not a system to reform, but a system to begin. The whole estate of Government is to be re-acquired.

What difficulties this will meet with in a country exhausted by the taking of capital, and among a people, in a manner new principled, trained, and actually disciplined to anarchy, rebellion, disorder, and impiety, may be conceived by those who know what Jacobin France is, and who may have occupied themselves by revolving in their thoughts, what they were to do if it fell to their lot to re-establish the affairs of France. What support, or what limitations the restored Monarchy must have, may be a doubt, or how it will pitch and settle at last: But one thing I conceive to be far beyond a doubt: that the settlement cannot be immediate; but that it must be preceded by some sort of power, equal at least in vigour, vigilance, promptitude and decision to a military Government. For such a *preparatory* Government, no slow-paced, methodical, formal, Lawyer-like system, still less that of a shewy, superficial, trifling, intriguing Court, guided by cabals of ladies, or of men like ladies; least of all, a philosophic, theoretic, disputatious school of sophistry. None of these ever will, or ever can lay the foundations of an order that can last. Whoever claims a right by birth to govern there, must find in his breast, or must conjure up in it, an energy not to be expected, perhaps not always to be wished for, in well ordered States. The lawful Prince must have, in every thing but crime, the character of an usurper. He is gone, if he imagines himself the quiet possessor of a throne. He is to contend for it as much after an apparent conquest as before. His task is to win it; he must leave posterity to enjoy and to adorn it. No velvet cushions for him. He is to be always (I speak nearly to the letter) on horseback. This opinion is the result of much patient thinking on the subject, which I conceive no event is likely to alter.

A valuable friend of mine, who I hope will conduct these affairs so far as they fall to his share, with great ability, asked me what I thought of acts of general indemnity and oblivion, as means of settling France, and reconciling it to Monarchy. Before I venture upon any opinion of my own in this matter, I totally disclaim the interference of foreign powers in a business that properly belongs to the Government which we have declared legal. That Government is likely to be the best judge of what is to be done towards the security of that kingdom, which it is their duty and their interest to provide for by such measures of justice or of lenity, as at the time they should find best. But if we weaken it, not only by arbitrary limitations of our own, but preserve such persons in it as are disposed to disturb its future peace, as they have its past, I do not know how a more direct declaration can be made of a dispo-

sition to perpetual hostility against a Government. The persons saved from the justice of the native Magistrate, by foreign authority, will owe nothing to his clemency. He will, and must, look to those to whom he is indebted for the power he has of dispensing it. A Jacobin faction, constantly fostered with the nourishment of foreign protection, will be kept alive.

⤳

If however I were asked to give an advice merely as such—here are my ideas. I am not for a total indemnity, nor a general punishment. And first, the body and mass of the people never ought to be treated as criminal. They may become an object of more or less constant watchfulness and suspicion, as their preservation may best require, but they can never become an object of punishment. This is one of the few fundamental and unalterable principles of politicks.

To punish them capitally would be to make massacres. Massacres only increase the ferocity of men, and teach them to regard their own lives and those of others as of little value; whereas the great policy of Government is to teach the people to think both of great importance in the eyes of God and the State, and never to be sacrificed or even hazarded to gratify their passions, or for any thing but the duties prescribed by the rules of morality, and under the direction of public law and public authority. To punish them with lesser penalties would be to debilitate the commonwealth, and make the nation miserable, which it is the business of Government to render happy and flourishing.

As to crimes too, I would draw a strong line of limitation. For no one offence, *politically an offence of rebellion,* by council, contrivance, persuasion or compulsion, for none properly a *military offence of rebel-*

lion, or any thing done by open hostility in the field, should any man at all be called in question; because such seems to be the proper and natural death of civil dissentions. The offences of war are obliterated by peace.

Another class will of course be included in the indemnity, namely, all those who by their activity in restoring lawful Government shall obliterate their offences. The offence previously known, the acceptance of service is a pardon for crimes. I fear that this class of men will not be very numerous.

So far as to indemnity. But where are the objects of justice, and of example, and of future security to the public peace? They are naturally pointed out, not by their having outraged political and civil laws, nor their having rebelled against the state, as a State, but by their having rebelled against the law of nature, and outraged man, as man. In this list, all the regicides in general, all those who laid sacrilegious hands on the King, who without any thing in their own rebellious mission to the convention to justify them, brought him to his trial and unanimously voted him guilty; all those who had a share in the cruel murder of the Queen, and the detestable proceedings with regard to the young King, and the unhappy Princesses; all those who committed cold-blooded murder any where, and particularly in their revolutionary tribunals, where every idea of natural justice and of their own declared Rights of Man, have been trod under foot with the most insolent mockery; all men concerned in the burning and demolition of houses or churches, with audacious and marked acts of sacrilege and scorns offered to religion; in general, all the leaders of Jacobin Clubs;—not one of these should escape a punishment suitable to the nature, quality and degree of their offence, by a steady but a measured justice.

In the first place, no man ought to be subject to any penalty, from the highest to the lowest, but by a trial according to the course of law, carried on with all that caution and deliberation which has been used in the best times and precedents of the French jurisprudence, the criminal law of which country, faulty to be sure in some particulars, was highly laudable and tender of the lives of men. In restoring order and justice, every thing like retaliation, ought to be religiously avoided; and an example ought to be set of a total alienation from the Jacobin proceedings in their accursed revolutionary tribunals. Every thing like lumping men in masses, and of forming tables of proscription ought to be avoided.

In all these punishments, any thing which can be alledged in mitigation of the offence should be fully considered. Mercy is not a thing opposed to justice. It is an essential part of it; as necessary in criminal cases, as in civil affairs equity is to law. It is only for the Jacobins never to pardon. They have not done it in a single instance. A council of mercy ought therefore to be appointed, with powers to report on each case, to soften the penalty, or entirely to remit it, according to circumstances.

↬

It is extraordinary that as the wicked arts of this regicide and tyrannous faction increase in number, variety, and atrocity, the desire of punishing them becomes more and more faint, and the talk of an indemnity towards them, every day stronger and stronger. Our ideas of justice appear to be fairly conquered and overpowered by guilt when it is grown gigantick. It is not the point of view in which we are in the habit of viewing guilt. The crimes we every day punish are really below the penalties we inflict. The criminals are obscure and feeble. This is the view in which we see ordinary crimes and criminals. But when guilt is seen, though but for a time, to be furnished with the arms and to be invested with the robes of power, it seems to assume another nature, and to get, as it were, out of our jurisdiction. This I fear is the case with many. But there is another cause full as powerful towards this security to enormous guilt, the desire which possesses people who have once obtained power, to enjoy it at their ease. It is not humanity, but laziness and inertness of mind which produces the desire of this kind of indemnities. This description of men love general and short methods. If they punish, they make a promiscuous massacre; If they spare, they make a general act of oblivion. This is a want of disposition to proceed laboriously according to the cases, and according to the rules and principles of justice on each case; a want disposition to assort criminals, to discriminate the degrees and modes of guilt, to separate accomplices from principals, leaders from followers, seducers from the seduced, and then by following the same principles in the same detail, to class punishments, and to fit them to the nature and kind of the delinquency. If that were once attempted, we should soon see that the task was neither infinite, nor the execution cruel. There would be deaths, but for the number of criminals, and the extent of France, not many. There would be cases of transportation; cases of labour to restore what has been wickedly destroyed; cases of imprisonment, and cases of mere exile. But be this as it may, I am sure that if justice is not done there, there can be neither peace or justice there, nor in any part of Europe.

∽

Among the ornaments of their place which eminently distinguish them, few people are better acquainted with the history of their own country than the illustrious Princes now in exile: but I caution them not to be led into errour by that which has been supposed to be the guide of life. I would give the same caution to all Princes. Not that I derogate from the use of history. It is a great improver of the understanding, by shewing both men and affairs in a great variety of views. From this source much political wisdom may be learned; that is, may be learned as habit, not as precept; and as an exercise to strengthen the mind, as furnishing materials to enlarge and enrich it, not as a repertory of cases and precedents for a lawyer: if it were, a thousand times better would it be that a Statesman had never learned to read. . . . This method turns their understanding from the object before them, and from the present exigencies of the world, to comparisons with former times, of which after all, we can know very little and very imperfectly; and our guides, the historians, who are to give us their true interpretation, are often prejudiced, often ignorant, often fonder of system than of truth. Whereas if a man with reasonable good parts and natural sagacity, and not the leading-strings of any master, will look steadily on the business before him, without being diverted by retrospect and comparison, he may be capable of forming a reasonable good judgment of what is to be done. There are some fundamental points in which nature never changes—but they are few and obvious, and belong rather to morals than to politicks. But so far as regards political matter, the human mind and human affairs are susceptible of infinite modifications, and of combinations wholly new and unlooked for. Very few, for instance, could have imagined that property, which has been taken for natural dominion, should, through the whole of a vast kingdom, lose all its importance and even its influence.

This is what history or books of speculation could hardly have taught us. How
many could have thought, that the most
complete and formidable Revolution in a
great empire should be made by men of
letters, not as subordinate instruments and
trumpeters of sedition, but as the chief
contrivers and managers, and in a short
time as the open administrators and sovereign Rulers? Who could have imagined
that Atheism could produce one of the
most violently operative principles of fa-
naticism? Who could have imagined that,
in a Commonwealth in a manner cradled
in war, and in an extensive and dreadful
war, military commanders should be of little or no account? That the Convention
should not contain one military man of
name? That administrative bodies in a state
of the utmost confusion, and of but a momentary duration, and composed of men
with not one imposing part of character,
should be able to govern the country and
its armies, with an authority which the
most settled Senates, and the most respected Monarchs scarcely ever had in the
same degree? This, for one, I confess I did
not foresee, though all the rest was present
to me very early, and not out of my apprehension even for several years.

I believe very few were able to enter into
the effects of mere *terrour*, as a principle
not only for the support of power in given
hands or forms, but in those things in
which the soundest political Speculators
were of opinion, that the least appearance
of force would be totally destructive,—
such is the market, whether of money,
provision, or commodities of any kind. Yet
for four years we have seen loans made,
treasuries supplied, and armies levied and
maintained, more numerous than France
ever shewed in the field, by the *effects of
fear alone*.

Here is a state of things of which, in its
totality, if history furnishes any examples
at all, they are very remote and feeble. I
therefore am not so ready as some are, to
tax with folly or cowardice, those who
were not prepared to meet an evil of this
nature. Even now, after the events, all the
causes may be somewhat difficult to ascertain. Very many are however traceable. But
these things history and books of speculation (as I have already said) did not teach
men to foresee, and of course to resist.
Now that they are no longer a matter of
sagacity, but of experience, of recent experience, of our own experience, it would be
unjustifiable to go back to the records of
other times, to instruct us to manage what
they never enabled us to foresee.

Introductory Note to
First Letter on a
Regicide Peace (1796)

*By 1796 Great Britain had been at war
with revolutionary France for three years. Although the Pitt ministry included intervention in the domestic constitution of revolutionary France in the declaration of King
George III of October 1793, Pitt continued
to keep open the possibility of coming to
terms with the French revolutionaries. Those
British ministers and politicians (such as
Charles Fox) who agreed with Pitt's flexibility on the issue of the nature of the French
regime took encouragement from the fall of
Robespierre in July 1794, which suggested
that France might become more moderate in
its behavior. The Pitt ministry began in late
1795 to explore the possibilities of negotiating a settlement with France. This develop-*

mcnt constituted the catalyst for the First
Letter on a Regicide Peace.

First Letter on a Regicide Peace *is one of
Burke's richest writings on foreign affairs.
Not only did he mount an attack against
Pitt's overtures for peace, but he also discussed
the relationship between the people and their
leaders in time of war; the historically
unique nature of the current war and the
struggle with revolutionary France; the threat
posed by France to the fundamental order of
European civilization; the existence of the
commonwealth of Europe; the importance in
international relations of a correspondence
among nations in laws, customs, manners,
and habits of life; the justification for intervention in the domestic affairs of another
state; the moral rather than geographical
essence of the nation; and the role of the
statesman.*

The scope, detail, and rhetoric of First
Letter on a Regicide Peace *suggest that
Burke intended not only to influence the direction of British policy toward France but
also to leave posterity a testament of his opposition to the French Revolution. In fact, at
the end of* First Letter on a Regicide Peace,
*Burke stated that what he had written was
"testamentary" and had the "sincerity of a
dying declaration." Less than a year after its
publication, Burke was dead. As Burke predicted in his* First Letter, *the war with
France was long and bloody. Even the
Younger Pitt, the target of the* First Letter on
a Regicide Peace, *did not live to see the termination of the war sparked by the revolution that Burke fiercely and consistently
resisted from its beginning until his own
death.*⁓

First Letter on
a Regicide Peace
(1796)

ON THE OVERTURES OF PEACE

MY DEAR SIR,

Our last conversation, though not in the
tone of absolute despondency, was far
from chearful. We could not easily account for some unpleasant appearances.
They were represented to us as indicating
the state of the popular mind; and they
were not at all what we should have expected from our old ideas even of the
faults and vices of the English character.
The disastrous events, which have followed one upon another in a long unbroken funereal train, moving in a procession,
that seemed to have no end, these were not
the principal causes of our dejection. We
feared more from what threatened to fail
within, than what menaced to oppress us
from abroad. To a people who have once
been proud and great, and great because
they were proud, a change in the national
spirit is the most terrible of all revolutions.

I shall not live to behold the unravelling
of the intricate plot, which saddens and
perplexes the awful drama of Providence,
now acting on the moral theatre of the
world. Whether for thought or for action, I
am at the end of my career. You are in the
middle of yours. In what part of it's orbit
the nation, with which we are carried along,
moves at this instant, it is not easy to conjecture. It may, perhaps, be far advanced in
its aphelion.—But when to return?

Not to lose ourselves in the infinite void
of the conjectural world, our business is
with what is likely to be affected for the
better or the worse, by the wisdom or

weakness of our plans. In all speculations upon men and human affairs, it is of no small moment to distinguish things of accident from permanent causes, and from effects that cannot be altered. It is not every irregularity in our movement that is a total deviation from our course. I am not quite of the mind of those speculators, who seem assured, that necessarily, and by the constitution of things, all States have the same periods of infancy, manhood, and decrepitude, that are found in the individuals who compose them. Parallels of this sort rather furnish similitudes to illustrate or to adorn, than supply analogies from whence to reason. The objects which are attempted to be forced into an analogy are not found in the same classes of existence. Individuals are physical beings, subject to laws universal and invariable. The immediate cause acting in these laws may be obscure: The general results are subjects of certain calculation. But commonwealths are not physical but moral essences. They are artificial combinations; and in their proximate efficient cause, the arbitrary productions of the human mind. We are not yet acquainted with the laws which necessarily influence the stability of that kind of work made by that kind of agent. There is not in the physical order . . . a distinct cause by which any of those fabricks must necessarily grow, flourish, or decay; nor, in my opinion, does the moral world produce any thing more determinate on that subject, than what may serve as an amusement . . . for speculative men. I doubt whether the history of mankind is yet compleat enough, if ever it can be so, to furnish grounds for a sure theory on the internal causes which necessarily affect the fortune of a State. I am far from denying the operation of such causes: But they are infinitely uncertain, and much more obscure, and much more difficult to trace,

than the foreign causes that tend to raise, to depress, and sometimes to overwhelm a community.

It is often impossible, in these political enquiries, to find any proportion between the apparent force of any moral causes we may assign and their known operation. We are therefore obliged to deliver up that operation to mere chance, or more piously (perhaps more rationally) to the occasional interposition and irresistible hand of the Great Disposer. We have seen States of considerable duration, which for ages have remained nearly as they have begun, and could hardly be said to ebb or flow. Some appear to have spent their vigour at their commencement. Some have blazed out in their glory a little before their extinction. The meridian of some has been the most splendid. Others, and they the greatest number, have fluctuated, and experienced at different periods of their existence a great variety of fortune. At the very moment when some of them seemed plunged in unfathomable abysses of disgrace and disaster, they have suddenly emerged. They have begun a new course and opened a new reckoning; and even in the depths of their calamity, and on the very ruins of their country, have laid the foundations of a towering and durable greatness. All this has happened without any apparent previous change in the general circumstances which had brought on their distress. . . .

Such, and often influenced by such causes, has commonly been the fate of Monarchies of long duration. They have their ebbs and their flows. This has been eminently the fate of the Monarchy of France. There have been times in which no Power has ever been brought so low. Few have ever flourished in greater glory. By turns elevated and depressed, that Power had been, on the whole, rather on the encrease; and it continued not only powerful but formidable to the hour of the total ruin of the Monarchy. This fall of the Monarchy was far from being preceded by any exterior symptoms of decline. The interior were not visible to every eye; and a thousand accidents might have prevented the operation of what the most clear-sighted were not able to discern, nor the most provident to divine. A very little time before its dreadful catastrophe, there was a kind of exterior splendour in the situation of the Crown, which usually adds to Government strength and authority at home. The Crown seemed then to have obtained some of the most splendid objects of state ambition. None of the Continental Powers of Europe were the enemies of France. They were all, either tacitly disposed to her, or publickly connected with her; and in those who kept the most aloof, there was little appearance of jealousy; of animosity there was no appearance at all. The British Nation, her great preponderating rival, she had humbled; to all appearance she had weakened; certainly had endangered, by cutting off a very large, and by far the most growing part of her empire.[59] In that it's acmé of human prosperity and greatness, in the high and palmy state of the Monarchy of France, it fell to the ground without a struggle. It fell without any of those vices in the Monarch, which have sometimes been the causes of the fall of kingdoms, but which existed, without any visible effect on the state, in the highest degree in many other Princes; and, far from destroying their power, had only left some slight stains on their character. The financial difficulties were only pretexts and instruments of those who accomplished

the ruin of that Monarchy. They were not the causes of it.

Deprived of the old Government, deprived in a manner of all Government, France fallen as a Monarchy, to common speculators might have appeared more likely to be an object of pity or insult, according to the disposition of the circumjacent powers, than to be the scourge and terror of them all: But out of the tomb of the murdered Monarchy in France, has arisen a vast, tremendous, unformed spectre, in a far more terrific guise than any which ever yet have overpowered the imagination, and subdued the fortitude of man. Going straight forward to it's end, unappalled by peril, unchecked by remorse, despising all common maxims and all common means, that hideous phantom overpowered those who could not believe it was possible she could at all exist, except on the principles, which habit rather than nature had persuaded them were necessary to their own particular welfare and to their own ordinary modes of action. But the constitution of any political being, as well as that of any physical being, ought to be known, before one can venture to say what is fit for it's conservation, or what is the proper means of it's power. The poison of other States is the food of the new Republick. That bankruptcy, the very apprehension of which is one of the causes assigned for the fall of the Monarchy, was the capital on which she opened her traffick with the world.

The Republick of Regicide with an annihilated revenue, with defaced manufactures, with a ruined commerce, with an uncultivated and half depopulated country, with a discontented, distressed, enslaved, and famished people, passing with a rapid, eccentrick, incalculable course, from the wildest anarchy to the sternest despotism, has actually conquered the

---

[59]Burke is referring to the role France played in the defeat of Britain in its war with the rebellious American colonies.

finest parts of Europe, has distressed, dis-
united, deranged, and broke to pieces all
the rest; and so subdued the minds of the
rulers in every nation, that hardly any resource presents itself to them, except that
of entitling themselves to a contemptuous
mercy by a display of their imbecility and
meanness. Even in their greatest military
efforts and the greatest display of their fortitude, they seem not to hope, they do not
even appear to wish, the extinction of
what subsists to their certain ruin. Their
ambition is only to be admitted to a more
favoured class in the order of servitude
under that domineering power.

This seems the temper of the day. At
first the French force was too much despised. Now it is too much dreaded. As inconsiderate courage has given way to irrational fear, so it may be hoped, that
through the medium of deliberate sober
apprehension, we may arrive at steady fortitude. Who knows whether indignation
may not succeed to terror, and the revival
of high sentiment, spurning away the
delusion of a safety purchased at the expence of glory, may not yet drive us to that
generous despair, which has often subdued
distempers in the State for which no remedy could be found in the wisest councils.

Other great States, having been without
any regular certain course of elevation, or
decline, we may hope that the British
fortune may fluctuate also; because the
public mind, which greatly influences that
fortune, may have it's changes. We are
therefore never authorized to abandon our
country to it's fate or to act or advise as if it
had no resource. There is no reason to apprehend, because ordinary means threaten
to fail, that no others can spring up. Whilst
our heart is whole, it will find means, or
make them. The heart of the citizen is a
perennial spring of energy to the State. Because the pulse seems to intermit, we must

not presume that it will cease instantly to
beat. The publick must never be regarded
as incurable. . . .

For one . . . I despair neither of the
publick fortune nor of the publick mind.
There is much to be done undoubtedly,
and much to be retrieved. We must walk
in new ways, or we can never encounter
our enemy in his devious march. We are
not at an end of our struggle, nor near it.
Let us not deceive ourselves, we are at the
beginning of great troubles. I readily acknowledge that the state of publick affairs
is infinitely more unpromising than at the
period I have just now alluded to, and the
position of all the Powers of Europe, in relation to us, and in relation to each other,
is more intricate and critical beyond all
comparison. Difficult indeed is our situation. In all situations of difficulty men will
be influenced in the part they take, not
only by the reason of the case, but by the
peculiar turn of their own character. The
same ways to safety do not present themselves to all men, nor to the same men in
different tempers. There is a courageous
wisdom: there is also a false reptile prudence, the result not of caution but of fear.
Under misfortunes it often happens that
the nerves of the understanding are so relaxed, the pressing peril of the hour so
completely confounds all the faculties,
that no future danger can be properly provided for, can be justly estimated, can be
so much as fully seen. The eye of the mind
is dazzled and vanquished. An abject distrust of ourselves, an extravagant admiration of the enemy, present us with no hope
but in a compromise with his pride, by a
submission to his will. This short plan of
policy is the only counsel which will obtain a hearing. We plunge into a dark
gulph with all the rash precipitation of
fear. The nature of courage is, without a
question, to be conversant with danger;

but in the palpable night of their terrors, men under consternation suppose, not that it is the danger, which, by a sure instinct, calls out the courage to resist it, but that it is the courage which produces the danger. They therefore seek for a refuge from their fears in the fears themselves, and consider a temporizing meanness as the only source of safety.

The rules and definitions of prudence can rarely be exact; never universal. I do not deny that in small truckling states a timely compromise with power has often been the means, and the only means, of drawling out their puny existence: But a great state is too much envied, too much dreaded, to find safety in humiliation. To be secure, it must be respected. Power, and eminence, and consideration, are things not to be begged. They must be commanded: and they who supplicate for mercy from others can never hope for justice thro' themselves. What justice they are to obtain, as the alms of an enemy, depends upon his character; and that they ought well to know before they implicitly confide.

Much controversy there has been in Parliament, and not a little amongst us out of doors, about the instrumental means of this nation towards the maintenance of her dignity, and the assertion of her rights. On the most elaborate and correct detail of facts, the result seems to be, that at no time has the wealth and power of Great Britain been so considerable as it is at this very perilous moment. We have a vast interest to preserve, and we possess great means of preserving it: But it is to be remembered that the artificer may be incumbered by his tools, and that resources may be among impediments. If wealth is the obedient and laborious slave of virtue and of publick honour, then wealth is in it's place, and has it's use: But if this order is changed, and hon-

our is to be sacrificed to the conservation of riches, riches which have neither eyes nor hands, nor any thing truly vital in them, cannot long survive the being of their vivifying powers, their legitimate masters, and their potent protectors. If we command our wealth, we shall be rich and free: If our wealth commands us, we are poor indeed. We are bought by the enemy with the treasure from our own coffers. Too great a sense of the value of a subordinate interest may be the very source of it's danger, as well as the certain ruin of interests of a superiour order. Often has a man lost his all because he would not submit to hazard all in defending it. A display of our wealth before robbers is not the way to restrain their boldness, or to lessen their rapacity. This display is made, I know, to persuade the people of England that thereby we shall awe the enemy, and improve the terms of our capitulation: it is made, not that we should fight with more animation, but that we should supplicate with better hopes. We are mistaken. We have an enemy to deal with who never regarded our contest as a measuring and weighing of purses. He is the Gaul that puts his *sword* into the scale.[60] He is more tempted with our wealth as booty, than terrified with it as power. But let us be rich or poor, let us be either in what proportion we may, nature is false or this is true, that where the essential publick force, (of which money is but a part,) is in any degree upon a par in a conflict between nations, that state which is resolved to hazard it's existence rather than to abandon it's objects, must have an infinite advantage over that which is resolved to yield rather than to carry it's resistance be-

---

[60]In an event related by the historian Livy, a Gallic chieftain placed his sword into the scales being used to weigh gold the Romans were giving to the Gauls to get them to lift a siege.

yond a certain point. Humanly speaking, that people which bounds it's efforts only with it's being, must give the law to that nation which will not push it's opposition beyond its convenience.

If we look to nothing but our domestick condition, the state of the nation is full even to plethory; but if we imagine that this country can long maintain it's blood and it's food, as disjoined from the community of mankind, such an opinion does not deserve refutation as absurd, but pity as insane.

I do not know that such an improvident and stupid selfishness, deserves the discussion, which, perhaps, I may bestow upon it hereafter. We cannot arrange with our enemy in the present conjuncture, without abandoning the interest of mankind. If we look only to our own petty peculium in the war, we have had some advantages; advantages ambiguous in their nature, and dearly bought. We have not in the slightest degree, impaired the strength of the common enemy, in any one of those points in which his particular force consists; at the same time that new enemies to ourselves, new allies to the Regicide Republick, have been made out of the wrecks and fragments of the general confederacy. So far as to the selfish part. As composing a part of the community of Europe, and interested in it's fate, it is not easy to conceive a state of things more doubtful and perplexing. When Louis the XIVth had made himself master of one of the largest and most important provinces of Spain; when he had in a manner over-run Lombardy, and was thundering at the gates of Turin; when he had mastered almost all Germany on this side the Rhine; when he was on the point of ruining the august fabrick of the Empire; when with the Elector of Bavaria in his alliance, hardly any thing interposed between him and Vienna; when the Turk

hung with a mighty force over the Empire on the other side; I do not know, that in the beginning of 1704 (that is in the third year of the renovated war with Louis the XIV) the state of Europe was so truly alarming.[61] To England it certainly was not. Holland (and Holland is a matter to England of value inestimable) was then powerful, was then independant, and though greatly endangered, was then full of energy and spirit. But the great resource of Europe was in England: Not in a sort of England detached from the rest of the world, and amusing herself with the puppet shew of a naval power . . . but in that sort of England, who considered herself as embodied with Europe; but in that sort of England, who, sympathetick with the adversity or the happiness of mankind, felt that nothing in human affairs was foreign to her. We may consider it as a sure axiom that, as on the one hand no confederacy of the least effect or duration can exist against France, of which England is not only a part, but the head, so neither can England pretend to cope with France but as connected with the body of Christendom.

Our account of the war, *as a war of communion,* to the very point in which we began to throw out lures, oglings, and glances for peace, was a war of disaster and of little else. The independant advantages obtained by us at the beginning of the war, and which were made at the expence of that common cause, if they deceive us about our largest and our surest interest, are to be reckoned amongst our heaviest losses.

The allies, and Great Britain amongst the rest, (and perhaps amongst the foremost) have been miserably deluded by this great fundamental error; that it was in our power to make peace with this monster of

---

[61]Burke is recounting events that happened in the first three years of the Wars of the Spanish Succession.

a State, whenever we chose to forget the crimes that made it great, and the designs that made it formidable. People imagined that their ceasing to resist was the sure way to be secure. This "pale cast of thought sicklied over all their enterprizes and turned all their politicks awry."[62] They could not, or rather they would not read, in the most unequivocal declarations of the enemy, and in his uniform conduct, that more safety was to be found in the most arduous war, than in the friendship of that kind of being. It's hostile amity can be obtained on no terms that do not imply an inability hereafter to resist it's designs. This great prolific error (I mean that peace was always in our power) has been the cause that rendered the allies indifferent about the *direction* of the war; and persuaded them that they might always risque a choice, and even a change in it's objects. They seldom improved any advantage; hoping that the enemy, affected by it, would make a proffer of peace. Hence it was, that all their early victories have been followed almost immediately with the usual effects of a defeat; whilst all the advantages obtained by the Regicides, have been followed by the consequences that were natural. The discomfitures, which the Republick of Assassins has suffered, have uniformly called forth new exertions, which not only repaired old losses, but prepared new conquests. The losses of the allies, on the contrary, . . . have been followed by desertion, by dismay, by disunion, by a dereliction of their policy, by a flight from their principles, by an admiration of the enemy, by mutual accusations, by a distrust in every member of the alliance of it's fellow, of it's cause, it's power, and it's courage.

Great difficulties in consequence of our erroneous policy, as I have said, press upon every side of us. Far from desiring to conceal or even to palliate the evil in the representation, I wish to lay it down as my foundation, that never greater existed. In a moment when sudden panick is apprehended, it may be wise, for a while to conceal some great publick disaster, or to reveal it by degrees, until the minds of the people have time to be re-collected, that their understanding may have leisure to rally, and that more steady councils may prevent their doing something desperate under the first impressions of rage or terror. But with regard to a *general* state of things, growing out of events and causes already known in the gross, there is no piety in the fraud that covers it's true nature; because nothing but erroneous resolutions can be the result of false representations. Those measures which in common distress might be available, in greater, are no better than playing with the evil. That the effort may bear a proportion to the exigence, it is fit it should be known; known in it's quality, in it's extent, and in all the circumstances which attend it. Great reverses of fortune, there have been, and great embarrassments in council: a principled Regicide enemy possessed of the most important part of Europe and struggling for the rest: within ourselves a total relaxation of all authority, whilst a cry is raised against it, as if it were the most ferocious of all despotism. A worse phaenomenon;—our government disowned by the most efficient member of it's tribunals; ill supported by any of their constituent parts; and the highest tribunal of all . . . deprived of all that dignity and all that efficiency which might enforce, or regulate, or if the case required it, might supply the

---

[62]An allusion to lines in the famous soliloquy in Shakespeare's *Hamlet* in which Hamlet ponders his indecision.

want of every other court.[63] Public prosecutions are become little better than schools for treason; of no use but to improve the dexterity of criminals in the mystery of evasion; or to shew with what compleat impunity men may conspire against the Commonwealth; with what safety assassins may attempt it's awful head.[64] Every thing is secure, except what the laws have made sacred; every thing is tameness and languor that is not fury and faction. Whilst the distempers of a relaxed fibre prognosticate and prepare all the morbid force of convulsion in the body of the State the steadiness of the physician is overpowered by the very aspect of the disease. The doctor of the Constitution, pretending to under-rate what he is not able to contend with, shrinks from his own operation. He doubts and questions the salutary but critical terrors of the cautery and the knife. He takes a poor credit even from his defeat; and covers impotence under the mask of lenity. He praises the moderation of the laws, as, in his hands, he sees them baffled and despised. Is all this, because in our day the statutes of the kingdom are not engrossed in as firm a character, and imprinted in as black and legible a type as ever? No! the law is a clear, but it is a dead letter. Dead and putrid, it is insufficient to save the State, but potent to infect, and to kill. Living law, full of reason, and of equity and justice, (as it is, or it should not exist) ought to be severe and awful too; or the words of menace, whether written on the parchment roll of England, or cut into the brazen tablet of Rome, will excite

nothing but contempt. How comes it, that in all the State prosecutions of magnitude, from the Revolution to within these two or three years, the Crown has scarcely ever retired disgraced and defeated from it's Courts? Whence this alarming change? By a connexion easily felt, and not impossible to be traced to it's cause, all the parts of the State have their correspondence and consent. They who bow to the enemy abroad will not be of power to subdue the conspirator at home. It is impossible not to observe, that in proportion as we approximate to the poisonous jaws of anarchy, the fascination grows irresistible. In proportion as we are attracted towards the focus of illegality, irreligion, and desperate enterprize, all the venomous and blighting insects of the State are awakened into life. The promise of the year is blasted, and shrivelled, and burned up before them. Our most salutary and most beautiful institutions yield nothing but dust and smut: the harvest of our law is no more than stubble. It is in the nature of these eruptive diseases in the State to sink in by fits and re-appear. But the fuel of the malady remains; and in my opinion is not in the smallest degree mitigated in it's malignity, though it waits the favourable moment of a freer communication with the source of Regicide to exert and to encrease it's force.

Is it that the people are changed, that the Commonwealth cannot be protected by its laws? I hardly think it. On the contrary, I conceive, that these things happen because men are not changed, but remain always what they always were; they remain what the bulk of us must ever be, when abandoned to our vulgar propensities, without guide, leader or controul: That is, made to be full of a blind elevation in prosperity; to despise untried dangers; to be overpowered with unexpected reverses; to

---

[63]This may be an oblique reference to the acquittal of Warren Hastings by the House of Lords in April 1795.

[64]Burke is referring to the unsuccessful prosecutions for treason of leading radicals that took place in 1794.

find no clue in a labyrinth of difficulties; to get out of a present inconvenience with any risque of future ruin; to follow and to bow to fortune; to admire successful though wicked enterprize, and to imitate what we admire; to condemn the government which announces danger from sacrilege and regicide, whilst they are only in their infancy and their struggle, but which finds nothing that can alarm in their adult state and in the power and triumph of those destructive principles. In a mass we cannot be left to ourselves. We must have leaders. If none will undertake to lead us right, we shall find guides who will contrive to conduct us to shame and ruin.

We are in a war of a *peculiar* nature. It is not with an ordinary community, which is hostile or friendly as passion or as interest may veer about; not with a State which makes war through wantonness, and abandons it through lassitude. We are at war with a system, which, by it's essence, is inimical to all other Governments, and which makes peace or war, as peace and war may best contribute to their subversion. It is with an *armed doctrine,* that we are at war. It has, by it's essence, a faction of opinion, and of interest, and of enthusiasm, in every country. To us it is a Colossus which bestrides our channel. It has one foot on a foreign shore, the other upon the British soil. Thus advantaged if it can at all exist, it must finally prevail. Nothing can so compleatly ruin any of the old Governments, ours in particular, as the acknowledgement, directly or by implication, of any kind of superiority in this new power. This acknowledgement we make, if in a bad or doubtful situation of our affairs, we solicit peace; of if we yield to the modes of new humiliation, in which alone she is content to give us an hearing. By that means the terms cannot be of our choosing; no, not in any part.

∽

In one point we are lucky. The Regicide has received our advances with scorn. We have an enemy, to whose virtues we can owe nothing; but on this occasion we are infinitely obliged to one of his vices. We owe more to his insolence than to our own precaution. The haughtiness by which the proud repel us, has this of good in it; that in making us keep our distance, they must keep their distance too. In the present case, the pride of the Regicide may be our safety. He has given time for our reason to operate; and for British dignity to recover from it's surprise. From first to last he has rejected all our advances. Far as we have gone he has still left a way open to our retreat.

There is always an augury to be taken of what a peace is likely to be, from the preliminary steps that are made to bring it about. We may gather something from the time in which the first overtures are made; from the quarter whence they come; from the manner in which they are received. These discover the temper of the parties. If your enemy offers peace in the moment of success, it indicates that he is satisfied with something. It shows that there are limits to his ambition or his resentment. If he offers nothing under misfortune, it is probable, that it is more painful to him to abandon the prospect of advantage than to endure calamity. If he rejects solicitation, and will not give even a nod to the suppliants for peace, until a change in the fortune of the war threatens him with ruin, then I think it evident, that he wishes nothing more than to disarm his adversary to gain time. Afterwards a question arises, which of the parties is likely to obtain the greater advantages, by continuing disarmed and by the use of time.

With these few plain indications in our minds, it will not be improper to reconsider the conduct of the enemy together with our own, from the day that a question of peace has been in agitation. In considering this part of the question, I do not proceed on my own hypothesis. I suppose, for a moment, that this body of Regicide, calling itself a Republick, is a politick person, with whom something deserving the name of peace may be made. On that supposition, let us examine our own proceeding. Let us compute the profit it has brought, and the advantage that it is likely to bring hereafter. A peace too eagerly sought, is not always the sooner obtained. The discovery of vehement wishes generally frustrates their attainment; and your adversary has gained a great advantage over you when he finds you impatient to conclude a treaty. There is in reserve, not only something of dignity, but a great deal of prudence too. A sort of courage belongs to negotiation as well as to operations of the field. A negotiator must often seem willing to hazard the whole issue of his treaty, if he wishes to secure any one material point.

The Regicides were the first to declare war. We are the first to sue for peace. In proportion to the humility and perseverance we have shewn in our addresses, has been the obstinacy of their arrogance in rejecting our suit. The patience of their pride seems to have been worn out with the importunity of our courtship. Disgusted as they are with a conduct so different from all the sentiments by which they are themselves filled, they think to put an end to our vexatious sollicitation by redoubling their insults.

⤶

In this intercourse, at least, there was nothing to promise a great deal of success in our future advances. Whilst the fortune of the field was wholly with the Regicides,

nothing was thought of but to follow where it led; and it led to every thing. Not so much as a talk of treaty. Laws were laid down with arrogance. The most moderate politician in their clan was chosen as the organ, not so much for prescribing limits to their claims, as to mark what, for the present, they are content to leave to others. They made, not laws, not Conventions, not late possession, but physical nature, and political convenience, the sole foundation of their claims. The Rhine, the Mediterranean, and the ocean were the bounds which, for the time, they assigned to the Empire of Regicide. . . . In truth, with these limits, and their principle, they would not have left even the shadow of liberty or safety to any nation. This plan of empire was not taken up in the first intoxication of unexpected success. You must recollect, that is was projected, just as the report has stated it, from the very first revolt of the faction against their Monarchy; and it has been uniformly pursued, as a standing maxim of national policy, from that time to this. It is, generally, in the season of prosperity that men discover their real temper, principles, and designs. But this principle suggested in their first struggles, fully avowed in their prosperity, has, in the most adverse state of their affairs, been tenaciously adhered to. The report, combined with their conduct, forms an infallible criterion of the views of this Republick.

In their fortune there has been some fluctuation. We are to see how their minds have been affected with a change. Some impression is made on them undoubtedly. It produced some oblique notice of the submissions that were made by suppliant nations. The utmost they did, was to make some of those cold, formal, general professions of a love of peace which no Power has ever refused to make; because they mean little, and cost nothing. The first paper I have seen (the publication at Hamburgh) making a shew of that pacific disposition, discovered a rooted animosity against this nation, and an incurable rancour, even more than any one of their hostile acts. In this Hamburgh declaration, they choose to suppose, that the war, on the part of England, *is a war of Government, begun and carried on against the sense and interests of the people;* thus sowing in their very overtures towards peace, the seeds of tumult and sedition: for they never have abandoned, and never will they abandon, in peace, in war, in treaty, in any situation, or for one instant, their old steady maxim of separating the people from their Government. Let me add—and it is with unfeigned anxiety for the character and credit of Ministers that I do add—if our Government perseveres, in its as uniform course, of acting under instruments with such preambles, it pleads guilty to the charges made by our enemies against it, both on it's own part, and on the part of parliament itself. The enemy must succeed in his plan for loosening and disconnecting all the internal holdings of the kingdom.

It was not enough, that the Speech from the Throne in the opening of the session in 1795, threw out oglings and glances of tenderness. Lest this coquetting should seem too cold and ambiguous, without waiting for it's effect, the violent passion for a relation to the Regicides, produced a direct Message from the Crown, and it's consequences from the two Houses of Parliament. On the part of the Regicides these declarations could not be entirely passed by without notice: but in that notice they discovered still more clearly the bottom of their character. The offer made to them by the message to Parliament was hinted at in their answer, but in an obscure and oblique manner as before. They accompanied their notice of the indications manifested on our side, with every kind of insolent and taunting reflection. The Regicide Directory, on the day which, in their gipsey jargon, they call the 5th of Pluviose, in return for our advances, charge us with eluding our declarations under "evasive formalities and frivolous pretexts." What these pretexts and evasions were, they do not say, and I have never heard. But they do not rest there. They proceed to charge us, and, as it should seem, our allies in the mass, with direct *perfidy;* they are so conciliatory in their language as to hint that this perfidious character is not new in our proceedings. However, notwithstanding this our habitual perfidy, they will offer peace "on conditions *as* moderate"—as what? as reason and as equity require? No! as moderate "as are suitable to their *national dignity.*" National dignity in all treaties I do admit is an important consideration. They have given us an useful hint on that subject: but dignity, hitherto, has belonged to the mode of proceeding, not to the matter of a treaty. Never before has it been mentioned as the standard for rating the conditions of peace; no, never by the most violent of conquerors. Indemnification is capable of some estimate; dignity has no standard. It is impossible to guess what acquisitions pride and ambition may think fit for their *dignity*. But lest any doubt should remain on what they think for their dignity, the Regicides in the next paragraph tell us "that they will have no peace with their enemies, until they have reduced them to a state, which will put them under an *impossibility* of pursuing their wretched projects;" that is, in plain French or English, until they have accomplished our utter and irretrievable ruin. This is their *pacific* language. It flows from their unalterable principle in whatever language they speak, or whatever steps they take, whether of real war, or of pretended pacification. They have never, to do them justice, been at much trouble in concealing their intentions. We were as obstinately resolved to think them not in earnest: but I confess jests of this sort, whatever their urbanity may be, are not much to my taste.

To this conciliatory and amicable publick communication, our sole answer, in effect, is this—"Citizen Regicides! whenever *you* find yourselves in the humour, you may have a peace with *us*. That is a point you may always command. We are constantly in attendance, and nothing you can do shall hinder us from the renewal of our supplications. You may turn us out at the door; but we will jump in at the window."

To those, who do not love to contemplate the fall of human greatness, I do not know a more mortifying spectacle, than to see the assembled majesty of the crowned heads of Europe waiting as patient suitors in the anti-chamber of Regicide. They wait, it seems, until the sanguinary tyrant *Carnot*,[65] shall have snorted away the fumes of the indigested blood of his Sovereign. Then, when sunk on the down of usurped pomp, he shall have sufficiently indulged his meditations with what Monarch he shall next glut his ravening maw, he may condescend to signify that it his pleasure to be awake; and that he is at leisure to receive the proposals of his high and mighty clients for the terms on which he may respite the execution of the sentence he has passed upon them. At the opening of those doors, what a sight it must be to behold the plenipotentiaries of royal impotence, in the precedency which

they will intrigue to obtain, and which will be granted to them according to the seniority of their degradation, sneaking into the Regicide presence, and with the reliques of the smile, which they had dressed up for the levee of their masters, still flickering on their curled lips, presenting the faded remains of their courtly graces, to meet the scornful, ferocious, sardonic grin of a bloody ruffian, who, whilst he is receiving their homage, is measuring them with his eye, and fitting to their size the slider of his Guillotine! These ambassadors may easily return as good courtiers as they went; but can they ever return from that degrading residence, loyal and faithful subjects; or with any true affection to their master, or true attachment to the constitution, religion, or laws of their country? There is great danger that they who enter smiling into this Trophonian Cave,[66] will come out of it sad and serious conspirators; and such will continue as long as they live. They will become true conductors of contagion to every country, which has had the misfortune to send them to the source of that electricity. At best they will become totally indifferent to good and evil, to one institution or another. This species of indifference is but too generally distinguishable in those who have been much employed in foreign Courts; but in the present case the evil must be aggravated without measure; for they go from their country, not with the pride of the old character, but in a state of the lowest degradation; and what must happen in their place of residence can have no effect in raising them to the level of

---

[65]Lazare-Nicolas-Marguerite Carnot, a leading figure in the French republic who voted to execute Louis XVI.

[66]Trophonius was the mythical builder of the Temple of Apollo at Delphi. After his death, he was worshiped as a god and had an oracle in a cave in Boeotia. It was believed that those who entered the cave of the Trophonian oracle would be filled with such awe that they would never smile again.

true dignity, or of chaste self estimation, either as men, or as representatives of crowned heads.

Our early proceeding, which has produced these returns of affront, appeared to me totally new, without being adapted to the new circumstances of affairs. I have called to my mind the speeches and messages in former times. I find nothing like these. You will look in the journals to find whether my memory fails me. Before this time, never was a ground of peace laid, (as it were, in a parliamentary record,) until it had been as good as concluded. This was a wise homage paid to the discretion of the Crown. It was known how much a negotiation must suffer by having any thing in the train towards it prematurely disclosed. But when those parliamentary declarations were made, not so much as a step had been taken towards a negotiation in any mode whatever. The measure was an unpleasant and unseasonable discovery.

I conceive that another circumstance in that transaction has been as little authorised by any example; and that it is as little prudent in itself; I mean the formal recognition of the French Republick. Without entering, for the present, into a question on the good faith manifested in that measure, or on it's general policy, I doubt, upon mere temporary considerations of prudence, whether it was perfectly adviseable. It is not within the rules of dexterous conduct to make an acknowledgement of a contested title in your enemy, before you are morally certain that your recognition will secure his friendship. Otherwise it is a measure worse than thrown away. It adds infinitely to the strength, and consequently to the demands of the adverse party. He has gained a fundamental point without an equivalent. It has happened as might have been foreseen. No notice whatever was taken of this recognition. In fact, the Directory never gave themselves any concern about it; and they received our acknowledgement with perfect scorn. With them, it is not for the States of Europe to judge of their title: The very reverse. In their eye the title of every other power depends wholly on their pleasure.

Preliminary declarations of this sort, thrown out at random, and sown, as it were, broad-cast, were never to be found in the mode of our proceeding with France and Spain, whilst the great Monarchies of France and Spain existed. I do not say, that a diplomatick measure ought to be, like a parliamentary or a judicial proceeding, according to strict precedent. I hope I am far from that pedantry: But this I know, that a great state ought to have some regard to it's antient maxims, especially where they indicate it's dignity; where they concur with the rules of prudence; and above all, where the circumstances of the time require that a spirit of innovation should be resisted, which leads to the humiliation of sovereign powers. . . .

At this second stage of humiliation, (I mean the insulting declaration in consequence of the message to both Houses of Parliament) it might not have been amiss to pause; and not to squander away the fund of our submissions, until we know what final purposes of publick interest they might answer. The policy of subjecting ourselves to further insults is not to me quite apparent. It was resolved however, to hazard a third trial. Citizen Barthelemi[67] had been established on the part of the new Republick, at Basle; where, with his proconsulate of Switzerland and the adjacent parts of Germany, he was appointed as a sort of factor to deal in the degrada-

---

[67]François Barthélemy, French minister to Switzerland.

tion of the crowned heads of Europe. At Basle it was thought proper, in order to keep others, I suppose, in countenance, that Great Britain should appear at this market, and bid with the rest, for the mercy of the People-King.

On the 6th of March 1796 Mr. Wickham,[68] in consequence of authority, was desired to sound France on her disposition towards a general pacification; to know whether she would consent to send Ministers to a Congress at such a place as might be hereafter agreed upon; whether there would be a disposition to communicate the general grounds of a pacification such as France (the diplomatick name of the Regicide power) would be willing to propose, as a foundation for a negociation for peace with his Majesty *and his allies;* or to suggest any other way of arriving at the same end of a general pacification; but he had no authority to enter into any negociation or discussion with Citizen Barthelemi upon these subjects.

On the part of Great Britain this measure was a voluntary act, wholly uncalled for on the part of Regicide. Suits of this sort are at least strong indications of a desire for accommodation. Any other body of men but the Directory would be somewhat soothed with such advances. They could not however begin their answer, which was given without much delay, and communicated on the 28th of the same month, without a preamble of insult and reproach. "They doubt the sincerity of the pacifick intentions of this Court." She did not begin, say they, yet to "know her real interests," "she did not seek peace *with good faith.*" This, or something to this effect, has been the constant preliminary observation, (now grown into a sort of office-form) on

all our overtures to this power: a perpetual charge on the British Government of fraud, evasion, and habitual perfidy.

⮌

This refusal of treating conjointly with the powers allied against this Republick, furnishes matter for a great deal of serious reflexion. They have hitherto constantly declined any other than a treaty with a single power. By thus dissociating every State from every other, like deer separated from the herd, each power is treated with, on the merit of his being a deserter from the common cause. In that light the Regicide power finding each of them insulted and unprotected, with great facility gives the law to them all. By this system for the present, an incurable distrust is sown amongst confederates; and in future all alliance is rendered impracticable. It is thus they have treated with Prussia, with Spain, with Sardinia, with Bavaria, with the Ecclesiastical State, with Saxony; and here we see them refuse to treat with Great Britain in any other mode. They must be worse than blind who do not see with what undeviating regularity of system, in this case and in all cases, they pursue their scheme for the utter destruction of every independent power; especially the smaller, who cannot find any refuge whatever but in some common cause.

Renewing their taunts and reflections, they tell Mr. Wickham, "that *their* policy has no guides but openness and good faith, and that their conduct shall be conformable to these principles." They say concerning their Government, that "yielding to the ardent desire by which it is animated to procure peace for the French Republick, and for all nations, it will not *fear to declare itself openly.*" Charged by the Constitution with the execution of the *laws,* it cannot *make* or *listen* to any pro-

---

[68] William Wickham, British minister to Switzerland.

posal that would be contrary to them. The constitutional act does not permit it to consent to any alienation of that which, according to the existing laws, constitutes the territory of the Republick.

"With respect to the countries *occupied by the French armies and which have not been united to France,* they, as well as other interests political and commercial, may become the subject of a negociation, which will present to the Directory the means of proving how much it desires to attain speedily to a happy pacification. That the Directory is ready to receive in this respect any overtures that shall be just, reasonable, and compatible *with the dignity of the Republick.*" On the head of what is *not* to be the subject of negotiation, the Directory is clear and open. As to what may be a matter of treaty, all this open dealing is gone. She retires into her shell. There she expects overtures from *you*— and you are to guess what she shall judge just, reasonable, and above all, *compatible with her dignity.*

In the records of pride there does not exist so insulting a declaration. It is insolent in words, in manner, but in substance it is not only insulting but alarming. It is a specimen of what may be expected from the masters we are preparing for our humbled country. Their openness and candour consist in a direct avowal of their despotism and ambition. We know that their declared resolution had been to surrender no object belonging to France previous to the war. They had resolved, that the Republick was entire, and must remain so. As to what she has conquered from the allies and united to the same indivisible body, it is of the same nature. That is, the allies are to give up whatever conquests they have made or may make upon France, but all which she has violently ravished from her neighbours and thought fit to appropriate,

are not to become so much as objects of negociation.

In this unity and indivisibility of possession are sunk ten immense and wealthy provinces, full of strong, flourishing and opulent cities, (the Austrian Netherlands,) the part of Europe the most necessary to preserve any communication between this kingdom and its natural allies, next to Holland the most interesting to this country, and without which Holland must virtually belong to France. Savoy and Nice, the keys of Italy, and the citadel in her hands to bridle Switzerland, are in that consolidation. The important territory of Leige is torn out of the heart of the Empire. All these are integrant parts of the Republick, not to be subject to any discussion, or to be purchased by any equivalent. Why? because there is a law which prevents it. What law? The law of nations? The acknowledged public law of Europe? Treaties and conventions of parties? No! not a pretence of the kind. It is a declaration not made in consequence of any prescription on her side, not on any cession or dereliction, actual or tacit, of other powers. It is a declaration *pendente lite*[69] in the middle of a war, one principal object of which was originally the defence, and has since been the recovery of these very countries.

This strange law is not made for a trivial object, not for a single port, or for a single fortress; but for a great kingdom; for the religion, the morals, the laws, the liberties, the lives and fortunes of millions of human creatures, who without their consent, or that of their lawful government, are, by an arbitrary act of this regicide and homicide Government, which they call a law, incorporated into their tyranny.

---

[69]"While the matter is unresolved."

In other words, their will is the law, not only at home, but as to the concerns of every nation. Who has made that law but the Regicide Republick itself, whose laws . . . they cannot alter or abrogate, or even so much as take into consideration? Without the least ceremony or compliment, they have sent out of the world whole sets of laws and law-givers. They have swept away the very constitutions under which the Legislatures acted, and the Laws were made. Even the fundamental sacred rights of man they have not scrupled to profane. They have set this holy code at nought with ignominy and scorn. Thus they treat all their domestick laws and constitutions, and even what they had considered as a Law of Nature; but whatever they have put their seal on for the purposes of their ambition, and the ruin of their neighbours, this alone is invulnerable, impassible, immortal. Assuming to be masters of every thing human and divine, here, and here alone, it seems they are limited, "cooped and cabined in;" and this omnipotent legislature finds itself wholly without the power of exercising it's favourite attribute, the love of peace. In other words, they are powerful to usurp, impotent to restore; and equally by their power and their impotence they aggrandize themselves, and weaken and impoverish you and all other nations.

⮑

Here therefore they and we were fixed. Nothing was left to the British Ministry but "to prosecute a war just and necessary"—a war equally just as at the time of our engaging in it—a war become ten times more necessary by every thing which happened afterwards. This resolution was soon, however, forgot. It felt the heat of the season and melted away. New hopes were entertained from supplication. No expectations, indeed, were then formed from renewing a direct application to the French Regicides through the Agent General for the humiliation of Sovereigns. At length a step was taken in degradation which even went lower than all the rest. Deficient in merits of our own, a Mediator was to be sought—and we looked for that Mediator at Berlin! The King of Prussia's merits in abandoning the general cause might have obtained for him some sort of influence in favour of those whom he had deserted;[70] but I have never heard that his Prussian Majesty had lately discovered so marked an affection for the Court of St. James's, or for the Court of Vienna, as to excite much hope of his interposing a very powerful mediation to deliver them from the distresses into which he had brought them.

⮑

The cup of bitterness was not, however, drained to the dregs. Basle and Berlin were not sufficient. After so many and so diversified repulses, we were resolved to make another experiment, and to try another Mediator. Among the unhappy gentlemen in whose persons Royalty is insulted and degraded at the seat of plebeian pride, and upstart insolence, there is a minister from Denmark at Paris. Without any previous encouragement to that, any more than the other steps, we sent through this turnpike to demand a passport for a person who on our part was to solicit peace in the metropolis, at the footstool of Regicide itself. It was not to be expected that any one of those degraded beings could have influence enough to settle any part of the terms in favour of the candidates for further degradation; besides, such intervention

---

[70]Prussia and France signed a peace treaty in April 1795.

would be a direct breach in their system, which did not permit one sovereign power to utter a word in the concerns of his equal.—Another repulse.—We were desired to apply directly in our persons.—We submitted and made the application.

It might be thought that here, at length, we had touched the bottom of humiliation; our lead was brought up covered with mud. But "in the lowest deep, a lower deep"[71] was to open for us still more profound abysses of disgrace and shame. However, in we leaped. We came forward in our own name. The passport, such a passport and safe conduct as would be granted to thieves, who might come in to betray their accomplices, and no better, was granted to British supplication. To leave no doubt of it's spirit, as soon as the rumour of this act of condescension could get abroad, it was formally announced with an explanation from authority, containing an invective against the Ministry of Great Britain, their habitual frauds, their proverbial, *punick* perfidy. No such State Paper, as a preliminary to a negociation for peace has ever yet appeared. Very few declarations of war have ever shewn so much and so unqualified animosity. . . .

I pass by all the insolence and contumely of the performance, as it comes from them. The present question is not how we are to be affected with it in regard to our dignity. That is gone. I shall say no more about it. Light lie the earth on the ashes of English pride. I shall only observe upon it *politically*, and as furnishing a direction for our own conduct in this low business.

The very idea of a negociation for peace, whatever the inward sentiments of the parties may be, implies some confidence in their faith, some degree of belief in the professions which are made concerning it. A temporary and occasional credit, at least, is granted. Otherwise men stumble on the very threshold. I therefore wish to ask what hope we can have of their good faith, who, as the very basis of the negociation, assume the ill faith and treachery of those they have to deal with? The terms, as against us, must be such as imply a full security against a treacherous conduct—that is, such terms as this Directory stated in it's first declaration, to place us "in an utter impossibility of executing our wretched projects." This is the omen, and the sole omen, under which we have consented to open our treaty.

The second observation I have to make upon it, (much connected undoubtedly with the first,) is, that they have informed you of the result they propose from the kind of peace they mean to grant you; that is to say, the union they propose among nations with the view, of rivalling our trade and destroying our naval power: and this they suppose (and with good reason too) must be the inevitable effect of their peace. It forms one of their principal grounds for suspecting our Ministers could not be in good earnest in their proposition. They make no scruple before hand to tell you the whole of what they intend; and this is what we call, in the modern style, the acceptance of a proposition for peace! In old language it would be called a most haughty, offensive, and insolent rejection of all treaty.

Thirdly, they tell you what they conceive to be the perfidious policy which dictates your delusive offer; that is, the design of cheating not only them, but the people of England, against whose interest and inclination this war is supposed to be carried on.

If we proceed in this business, under this preliminary declaration, it seems to me, that we admit, (now for the third time) by something a great deal stronger than

---

[71]From John Milton's *Paradise Lost* (1667).

words, the truth of the charges of every kind which they make upon the British Ministry, and the grounds of those foul imputations. The language used by us, which in other circumstances would not be exceptionable, in this case tends very strongly to confirm and realize the suspicion of our enemy. I mean the declaration, that if we do not obtain such terms of peace as suits our opinion of what our interests require, *then,* and in *that* case, we shall continue the war with vigour. This offer so reasoned, plainly implies, that without it, our leaders themselves entertain great doubts of the opinion and good affections of the British people; otherwise there does not appear any cause, why we should proceed under the scandalous construction of our enemy, upon the former offer made by Mr. Wickham, and on the new offer made directly at Paris. It is not, therefore, from a sense of dignity, but from the danger of radicating that false sentiment in the breasts of the enemy, that I think, under the auspices of this declaration, we cannot, with the least hope of a good event, or, indeed, with any regard to the common safety, proceed in the train of this negociation. I wish Ministry would seriously consider the importance of their seeming to confirm the enemy in an opinion, that his frequent use of appeals to the people against their Government has not been without it's effect. If it puts an end to this war, it will render another impracticable.

Whoever goes to the directorial presence under this passport, with this offensive comment, and foul explanation, goes, in the avowed sense of the Court to which he is sent; as the instrument of a Government dissociated from the interests and wishes of the Nation, for the purpose of cheating both the people of France and the people of England. He goes out the declared emissary of a faithless Ministry. He has perfidy for his credentials. He has national weakness for his full powers. I yet doubt whether any one can be found to invest himself with that character. If there should, it would be pleasant to read his instructions on the answer which he is to give to the Directory, in case they should repeat to him the substance of the Manifesto which he carries with him in his portfolio.

So much for the *first* Manifesto of the Regicide Court which went along with the passport. Lest this declaration should seem the effect of haste, or a mere sudden effusion of pride and insolence, on full deliberation, about a week after comes out a second. This manifesto, is dated the fifth of October, one day before the speech from the Throne, on the vigil of the festive day of cordial unanimity so happily celebrated by all parties in the British Parliament. In this piece the Regicides, our worthy friends, (I call them by advance and by courtesy what by law I shall be obliged to call them hereafter) our worthy friends, I say, renew and enforce the former declaration concerning our faith and sincerity, which they pinned to our passport. On three other points which run through all their declarations, they are more explicit than ever.

First, they more directly undertake to be the real representatives of the people of this kingdom: and on a supposition, in which they agree with our parliamentary reformers, that the House of Commons is not that Representative, the function being vacant, they, as our true constitutional organ, inform his Majesty and the world of the sense of the nation. They tell us that "the English people see with regret his Majesty's Government squandering away the funds which had been granted to him." This astonishing assumption of the publick voice of England, is but a slight foretaste of the usurpation which, on a peace, we may be assured they will make of all the powers in all the parts of our vassal constitution. . . .

Next they tell us as a condition to our treaty, that "this Government must abjure the unjust hatred it bears to them, and at last open it's ears to the voice of humanity."—Truely this is, even from them, an extraordinary demand. Hitherto it seems we have put wax into our ears to shut them up against the tender, soothing strains, in the *affettuoso*[72] of humanity, warbled from the throats of Reubel, Carnot, Tallien, and the whole chorus of Confiscators, domicilliary Visitors, Committee-men of Research, Jurors and Presidents of Revolutionary Tribunals, Regicides, Assassins, Massacrers, and Septembrizers. It is not difficult to discern what sort of humanity our Government is to learn from those syren singers. Our Government also, I admit with some reason, as a step towards the proposed fraternity, is required to abjure the unjust hatred which it bears to this body of honour and virtue. I thank God I am neither a Minister nor a leader of Opposition. I protest I cannot do what they desire. I could not do it if I were under the guillotine; or as they ingeniously and pleasantly express it, "looking out of the little national window." Even at that opening I could receive none of their light. I am fortified against all such affections by the declaration of the Government, which I must yet consider as lawful, made on the 29th of October 1793, and still ringing in my ears. This declaration was transmitted not only to all our commanders by sea and land, but to our Ministers in every Court of Europe. It is the most eloquent and highly finished in the style, the most judicious in the choice of topicks, the most orderly in the arrangement, and the most rich in the colouring, without employing the smallest degree of exaggeration, of any state paper that has ever yet appeared. An ancient writer, Plutarch, I think it is, quotes some verses on the eloquence of Pericles, who is called "the only orator that left stings in the minds of his hearers." Like his, the eloquence of the declaration, not contradicting, but enforcing sentiments of the truest humanity, has left stings that have penetrated more than skin-deep into my mind; and never can they be extracted by all the surgery of murder; never can the throbbings they have created, be assuaged by all the emollient cataplasms of robbery and confiscation. I *cannot* love the Republick.

The third point which they have more clearly expressed than ever, is of equal importance with the rest; and with them furnishes a complete view of the Regicide system. For they demand as a condition, without which our ambassador of obedience cannot be received with any hope of success, that he shall be "provided with full powers to negociate a peace between the French Republick and Great-Britain, and to conclude it *definitively* between the TWO powers." With their spear they draw a circle about us. They will hear nothing of a joint treaty. We must make a peace separately from our allies. We must, as the very first and preliminary step, be guilty of that perfidy towards our friends and associates, with which they reproach us in our transactions with them our enemies. We are called upon scandalously to betray the fundamental securities to ourselves and to all nations. In my opinion, . . . if we are meanly bold enough to send an ambassador such as this official note of the enemy requires, we cannot even dispatch our emissary without danger of being charged with a breach of our alliance. Government now understands the full meaning of the passport.

[72]"Tenderness."

↜

If the general disposition of the people be, as I hear it is, for an immediate peace with Regicide, without so much as considering our publick and solemn engagements to the party in France whose cause we had espoused, or the engagements expressed in our general alliances, not only without an enquiry into the terms, but with a certain knowledge that none but the worst terms will be offered, it is all over with us. It is strange, but it may be true, that as the danger from Jacobinism is increased in my eyes and in yours, the fear of it is lessened in the eyes of many people who formerly regarded it with horror. It seems, they act under the impression of terrors of another sort, which have frightened them out of their first apprehensions. But let their fears or their hopes, or their desires, be what they will, they should recollect, that they who would make peace without a previous knowledge of the terms, make a surrender. They are conquered. They do not treat; they receive the law. Is this the disposition of the people of England? Then the people of England are contented to seek in the kindness of a foreign systematick enemy combined with a dangerous faction at home, a security which they cannot find in their own patriotism and their own courage. They are willing to trust to the sympathy of Regicides, the guarantee of the British Monarchy. They are content to rest their religion on the piety of atheists by establishment. They are satisfied to seek in the clemency of practised murderers the security of their lives. They are pleased to confide their property to the safeguard of those who are robbers by inclination, interest, habit, and system. If this be our deliberate mind, truly we deserve to lose, what it is impossible we should long retain, the name of a nation.

In matters of State, a constitutional competence to act, is in many cases the smallest part of the question. Without disputing (God forbid I should dispute) the sole competence of the King and the Parliament, each in it's province, to decide on war and peace, I venture to say, no war *can* be long carried on against the will of the people. This war, in particular, cannot be carried on unless they are enthusiastically in favour of it. Acquiescence will not do. There must be zeal. Universal zeal in such a cause, and at such a time as this is, cannot be looked for; neither is it necessary. Zeal in the larger part carries the force of the whole. Without this, no Government, certainly not our Government, is capable of a great war. None of the ancient regular Governments have wherewithal to fight abroad with a foreign foe, and at home to overcome repining, reluctance, and chicane. It must be some portentous thing, like Regicide France, that can exhibit such a prodigy. Yet even she, the mother of monsters . . . shews symptoms of being almost effete already; and she will be so, unless the fallow of a peace comes to recruit her fertility. But whatever may be represented concerning the meanness of the popular spirit, I, for one, do not think so desperately of the British nation. Our minds, as I said, are light, but they are not depraved. We are dreadfully open to delusion and to dejection; but we are capable of being animated and undeceived.

It cannot be concealed. We are a divided people. But in divisions, where a part is to be taken, we are to make a muster of our strength. I have often endeavoured to compute and to class those who, in any political view, are to be called the people. Without doing something of this sort we must proceed absurdly. We should not be much wiser, if we pretended to very great accuracy in our estimate: But

I think, in the calculation I have made, the error cannot be very material. In England and Scotland, I compute that those of adult age, not declining in life, of tolerable leisure for such discussions, and of some means of information, more or less, and who are above menial dependence, (or what virtually is such) may amount to about four hundred thousand. There is such a thing as a natural representative of the people. This body is that representative; and on this body, more than on the legal constituent, the artificial representative depends. This is the British publick; and it is a publick very numerous. The rest, when feeble, are the objects of protection; when strong, the means of force. They who affect to consider that part of us in any other light, insult while they cajole us; they do not want us for counsellors in deliberation, but to list us as soldiers for battle.

Of these four hundred thousand political citizens, I look upon one fifth, or about eighty thousand, to be pure Jacobins; utterly incapable of amendment; objects of eternal vigilance; and when they break out, of legal constraint. On these, no reason, no argument, no example, no venerable authority, can have the slightest influence. They desire a change; and they will have it if they can. If they cannot have it by English cabal, they will make no sort of scruple of having it by the cabal of France, into which already they are virtually incorporated. It is only their assured and confident expectation of the advantages of French fraternity and the approaching blessings of Regicide intercourse, that skins over their mischievous dispositions with a momentary quiet.

This minority is great and formidable. I do not know whether if I aimed at the total overthrow of a kingdom, I should wish to be encumbered with a larger body of partizans. They are more easily disciplined and directed than if the number were greater. These, by their spirit of intrigue, and by their restless agitating activity, are of a force far superior to their numbers; and if times grew the least critical, have the means of debauching or intimidating many of those who are now found, as well as of adding to their force large bodies of the more passive part of the nation. This minority is numerous enough to make a mighty cry for peace, or for war, or for any object they are led vehemently to desire. By passing from place to place with a velocity incredible, and diversifying their character and description, they are capable of mimicking the general voice. We must not always judge of the generality of the opinion by the noise of the acclamation.

The majority, the other four fifths, is perfectly sound; and of the best possible disposition to religion, to government, to the true and undivided interest of their country. Such men are naturally disposed to peace. They who are in possession of all they wish are languid and improvident. With this fault, (and I admit it's existence in all it's extent) they would not endure to hear of a peace that led to the ruin of every thing for which peace is dear to them. However, the desire of peace is essentially the weak side of that kind of men. All men that are ruined, are ruined on the side of their natural propensities. There they are unguarded. Above all, good men do not suspect that their destruction is attempted through their virtues. This their enemies are perfectly aware of: And accordingly, they, the most turbulent of mankind, who never made a scruple to shake the tranquillity of their country to it's center, raise a continual cry for peace with France. Peace with Regicide, and war with the rest of the world, is their motto. From the beginning, and even whilst the French gave the blows, and we hardly opposed . . . their efforts, from that day to this hour, like importunate Guinea-fowls crying one note day and night, they have called for peace.

⌣

The minority I speak of, is not susceptible of an impression from the topics of argument, to be used to the larger part of the community. I therefore do not address to them any part of what I have to say. The more forcibly I drive my arguments against their system, so as to make an impression where I wish to make it, the more strongly I rivet them in their sentiments. As for us, who compose the far larger, and what I call the far better part of the people; let me say, that we have not been quite fairly dealt with when called to this deliberation. The Jacobin minority have been abundantly supplied with stores and provisions of all kinds towards their warfare. No sort of argumentative materials, suited to their purposes, have been withheld. False they are, unsound, sophistical; but they are regular in their direction. They all bear one way; and they all go to the support of the substantial merits of their cause. The others have not had the question so much as fairly stated to them.

There has not been in this century, any foreign peace or war, in it's origin, the fruit of popular desire; except the war that was made with Spain in 1739.[73] Sir Robert Walpole was forced into the war by the people, who were inflamed to this measure

by the most leading politicians, by the first orators, and the greatest poets of the time. For that war, Pope sung his dying notes. For that war, Johnson, in more energetic strains, employed the voice of his early genius. For that war, Glover distinguished himself in the way in which his muse was the most natural and happy. The crowd readily followed the politicians in the cry for a war, which threatened little bloodshed, and which promised victories that were attended with something more solid than glory. A war with Spain was a war of plunder. In the present conflict with Regicide, Mr. Pitt has not hitherto had, nor will perhaps for a few days have, many prizes to hold out in the lottery of war, to tempt the lower part of our character. He can only maintain it by an appeal to the higher; and to those, in whom that higher part is the most predominant, he must look the most for his support. Whilst he holds out no inducements to the wise, nor bribes to the avaricious, he may be forced by a vulgar cry into a peace ten times more ruinous than the most disastrous war. The weaker he is in the fund of motives which apply to our avarice, to our laziness, and to our lassitude, if he means to carry the war to any end at all, the stronger he ought to be in his addresses to our magnanimity and to our reason.

⌣

In my opinion, the present Ministry are as far from doing full justice to their cause in this war, as Walpole was from doing justice to the peace which at that time he was willing to preserve. They throw the light on one side only of their case; though it is impossible they should not observe, that the other side which is kept in the shade, has it's importance too. They must know, that France is formidable, not only as she is France, but as she is Jacobin France.

---

[73]Burke is referring to the so-called War of Jenkins' Ear (1739–1741) between Britain and Spain that arose from Anglo-Spanish difficulties in the Caribbean. Robert Jenkins, captain of a British ship, claimed before a House of Commons committee that the captain of a Spanish revenue ship had cut off his ear during a search of the British vessel. This story helped inflame public passions for war against Spain.

They knew from the beginning that the Jacobin party was not confined to that country. They knew, they felt, the strong disposition of the same faction in both countries to communicate and to co-operate. For some time past, these two points have been kept, and even industriously kept, out of sight. France is considered as merely a foreign Power; and the seditious English only as a domestick faction. The merits of the war with the former have been argued solely on political grounds. To prevent the mischievous doctrines of the latter, from corrupting our minds, matter and argument have been supplied abundantly, and even to surfeit, on the excellency of our own government. But nothing has been done to make us feel in what manner the safety of that Government is connected with the principle and with the issue of this war. For any thing, which in the late discussion has appeared, the war is entirely collateral to the state of Jacobinism; as truly a foreign war to us and to all our home concerns, as the war with Spain in 1739. . . .

Whenever the adverse party has raised a cry for peace with the Regicide, the answer has been little more than this, "that the Administration wished for such a peace, full as much as the Opposition; but that the time was not convenient for making it." Whatever else has been said was much in the same spirit. Reasons of this kind never touched the substantial merits of the war. They were in the nature of dilatory pleas, exceptions of form, previous questions. Accordingly all the arguments against a compliance with what was represented as the popular desire, (urged on with all possible vehemence and earnestness by the Jacobins) have appeared flat and languid, feeble and evasive. They appeared to aim only at gaining time. They never entered into the peculiar and dis-

tinctive character of the war. They spoke neither to the understanding nor to the heart. Cold as ice themselves they never could kindle in our breasts a spark of that zeal, which is necessary to a conflict with an adverse zeal; much less were they made to infuse into our minds, that stubborn persevering spirit, which alone is capable of bearing up against those vicissitudes of fortune, which all probably occur, and those burthens which must be inevitably borne in a long war. I speak it emphatically, and with a desire that it should be marked, in a *long* war; because, without such a war, no experience has yet told us, that a dangerous power has ever been reduced to measure or to reason. I do not throw back my view to the Peloponnesian war of twenty-seven years; nor to two of the Punick wars, the first of twenty-four, the second of eighteen, nor to the more recent war concluded by the treaty of Westphalia, which continued, I think, for thirty. I go to what is but just fallen behind living memory, and immediately touches our own country. Let the portion of our history from the year 1689 to 1713 be brought before us.[74] We shall find, that in all that period of twenty-four years, there were hardly five that could be called a season of peace; and the interval between the two wars was in reality, nothing more than a very active preparation for renovated hostility. During that period, every one of the propositions of peace came from the enemy: The first, when they were accepted, at the peace of Ryswick; The second, where they were rejected at the congress at Gertruydenburgh; The last, when the war ended by the treaty of Utrecht. Even then, a very great part of the nation, and that which contained by far the most

---

[74]During this period England fought the Nine Years' War and the Wars of the Spanish Succession.

intelligent statesmen, was against the conclusion of the war. I do not enter into the merits of that question as between the parties. I only state the existence of that opinion as a fact, from whence you may draw such an inference as you think properly arises from it.

It is for us at present to recollect what we have been; and to consider what, if we please, we may be still. At the period of those wars, our principal strength was found in the resolution of the people; and that in the resolution of a part only of the then whole, which bore no proportion to our existing magnitude. England and Scotland were not united at the beginning of that mighty struggle. When, in the course of the contest, they were conjoined, it was in a raw, an ill-cemented, an unproductive union.[75] . . . Ireland, now so large a source of the common opulence and power, and which wisely managed might be made much more beneficial and much more effective, was then the heaviest of the burthens. An army not much less than forty thousand men, was drawn from the general effort, to keep that kingdom in a poor, unfruitful, and resourceless subjection.

Such was the state of the empire. The state of our finances was worse, if possible. Every branch of the revenue became less productive after the Revolution.[76] . . .

As to our commerce, the imports and exports of the nation, now six and forty million, did not then amount to ten. The inland trade, which is commonly passed by in this sort of estimates, but which, in part growing out of the foreign, and connected with it, is more advantageous, and more substantially nutritive to the State, is not only grown in a proportion of near

five to one as the foreign, but has been augmented, at least, in a tenfold proportion. . . . Our naval strength in the time of King William's war was nearly matched by that of France; and though conjoined with Holland, then a maritime Power hardly inferior to our own, even with that force we were not always victorious. Though finally superior, the allied fleets experienced many unpleasant reverses on their own element. In two years three thousand vessels were taken from the English trade. On the continent we lost almost every battle we fought.

In 1697, (it is not quite an hundred years ago,) in that state of things, amidst the general debasement of the coin, the fall of the ordinary revenue, the failure of all the extraordinary supplies, the ruin of commerce and the almost total extinction of an infant credit, the Chancellor of the Exchequer himself . . . came forward to move a resolution, full of vigour, in which far from being discouraged by the generally adverse fortune, and the long continuance of the war, the Commons agreed to address the Crown in the following manly, spirited, and truly animating style.

"This is the EIGHTH year in which your Majesty's most dutiful and loyal subjects the Commons in Parliament assembled, have assisted your Majesty with large supplies for carrying on a just and necessary war, in defence of our religion, and preservation of our laws, and vindication of the rights and liberties of the people of England."

Afterwards they proceed in this manner:—"To shew to your Majesty and all Christendom, that the Commons of England will not be *amused* or diverted from their firm resolutions of obtaining by WAR, a safe and honourable peace, we do in the name of those we represent, renew our assurances to support your Majesty and your Government against all your en-

---

[75]England and Scotland were united under the name "Great Britain" in 1707.

[76]The English Glorious Revolution of 1688.

emies at home and abroad; and that we will effectually assist you in carrying on the war against France."

The amusement and diversion they speak of, was the suggestion of a treaty *proposed by the enemy,* and announced from the Throne. Thus the people of England felt in the *eighth,* not in the *fourth* year of the war. No sighing or panting after negociation; no motions from the Opposition to force the Ministry into a peace; no messages from Ministers to palsy and deaden the resolution of Parliament or the spirit of the nation. They did not so much as advise the King to listen to the propositions of the enemy, nor to seek for peace but through the mediation of a vigorous war. This address was moved in an hot, a divided, a factious, and in a great part, disaffected House of Commons, and it was carried *nemine contradicente.*

ھ

For what have I entered into all this detail? To what purpose have I recalled your view to the end of the last century? It has been done to shew that the British Nation was then a great people—to point out how and by what means they came to be exalted above the vulgar level, and to take that lead which they assumed among mankind. To qualify us for that pre-eminence, we had then an high mind, and a constancy unconquerable; we were then inspired with no flashy passions; but such as were durable as well as warm; such as corresponded to the great interests we had at stake. This force of character was inspired, as all such spirit must ever be, from above. Government gave the impulse. As well may we fancy, that, of itself the sea will swell, and that without winds the billows will insult the adverse shore, as that the gross mass of the people will be moved, and elevated, and continue by a steady and permanent direction to bear upon one point, without the influence of superior authority, or superior mind.

This impulse ought, in my opinion, to have been given in this war; and it ought to have been continued to it at every instant. It is made, if ever war was made, to touch all the great springs of action in the human breast. It ought not to have been a war of apology. The Minister[77] had, in this conflict, wherewithal to glory in success; to be consoled in adversity; to hold high his principle in all fortunes. If it were not given him to support the falling edifice, he ought to bury himself under the ruins of the civilized world. All the art of Greece, and all the pride and power of eastern Monarchs, never heaped upon their ashes so grand a monument.

There were days when his great mind was up to the crisis of the world he is called to act in.[78] His manly eloquence was equal to the elevated wisdom of such sentiments. But the little have triumphed over the great; an unnatural, (as it should seem) not an unusual victory. I am sure you cannot forget with how much uneasiness we heard in conversation, the language of more than one gentleman at the opening of this contest, "that he was willing to try the war for a year or two, and if it did not succeed, then to vote for peace." As if war was a matter of experiment! As if you could take it up or lay it down as an idle frolick! As if the dire goddess that presides over it, with her murderous spear in her hand, and her gorgon at her breast, was a coquette to be flirted with![79] We ought with reverence to approach that

---

[77]William Pitt the Younger, the prime minister.

[78]See the Declaration [of October 1793]. [Burke's note]

[79]The goddess Athena.

tremendous divinity, that loves courage, but commands counsel. War never leaves, where it found a nation. It is never to be entered into without a mature deliberation; not a deliberation lengthened out into a perplexing indecision, but a deliberation leading to a sure and fixed judgment. When so taken up it is not to be abandoned without reason as valid, as fully, and as extensively considered. Peace may be made as unadvisedly as war. Nothing is so rash as fear; and the counsels of pusillanimity very rarely put off, whilst they are always sure to aggravate, the evils from which they would fly.

In that great war carried on against Louis the XIVth, for near eighteen years, Government spared no pains to satisfy the nation, that though they were to be animated by a desire of glory, glory was not their ultimate object: but that every thing dear to them, in religion, in law, in liberty, every thing which as freemen, as Englishmen, and as citizens of the great commonwealth of Christendom, they had at heart, was then at stake. This was to know the true art of gaining the affections and confidence of an high-minded people; this was to understand human nature. A danger to avert a danger—a present inconvenience and suffering to prevent a foreseen future, and a worse calamity—these are the motives that belong to an animal, who, in his constitution, is at once adventurous and provident; circumspect and daring; whom his Creator has made, as the Poet says, "of large discourse, looking before and after."[80] But never can a vehement and sustained spirit of fortitude be kindled in a people by a war of calculation. It has nothing that can keep the mind erect under the gusts of adversity. Even where men are willing, as sometimes they

are, to barter their blood for lucre, to hazard their safety for the gratification of their avarice, the passion, which animates them to that sort of conflict, like all the shortsighted passions must see its objects distinct and near at hand. The passions of the lower order are hungry and impatient. Speculative plunder; contingent spoil; future, long adjourned, uncertain booty; pillage which must enrich a late posterity, and which possibly may not reach to posterity at all; these, for any length of time, will never support a mercenary war. The people are in the right. The calculation of profit in all such wars is false. On balancing the account of such wars, ten thousand hogsheads of sugar are purchased at ten thousand times their price. The blood of man should never be shed but to redeem the blood of man. It is well shed for our family, for our friends, for our God, for our country, for our kind. The rest is vanity; the rest is crime.

⤚

If the war made to prevent the union of two crowns upon one head was a just war, this, which is made to prevent the tearing all crowns from all heads which ought to wear them, and with the crowns to smite off the sacred heads themselves, this is a just war.

If a war to prevent Louis the XIVth from imposing his religion was just, a war to prevent the murderers of Louis the XVIth from imposing their irreligion upon us is just; a war to prevent the operation of a system, which makes life without dignity, and death without hope, is a just war.

If to preserve political independence and civil freedom to nations, was a just ground of war; a war to preserve national independence, property, liberty, life, and honour, from certain universal havock, is a

---

[80]From *Hamlet*.

war just, necessary, manly, pious; and we are bound to persevere in it by every principle, divine and human, as long as the system which menaces them all, and all equally, has an existence in the world.

You, who have looked at this matter with as fair and impartial an eye as can be united with a feeling heart, you will not think it an hardy assertion, when I affirm, that it were far better to be conquered by any other nation, than to have this faction for a neighbour. . . . They who are to live in the vicinity of this new fabrick, are to prepare to live in perpetual conspiracies and seditions; and to end at last, in being conquered, if not to her dominion, to her resemblance. But when we talk of conquest by other nations, it is only to put a case. This is the only power in Europe by which it is *possible* we should be conquered. To live under the continual dread of such immeasurable evils is itself a grievous calamity. To live without the dread of them is to turn the danger into the disaster. The influence of such a France is equal to a war; it's example, more wasting than an hostile irruption. The hostility with any other power is separable and accidental; this power, by the very condition of it's existence, by it's very essential constitution, is in a state of hostility with us, and with all civilized people.

A Government of the nature of that set up at our very door has never been hitherto seen, or even imagined, in Europe. What our relation to it will be cannot be judged by other relations. It is a serious thing to have a connexion with a people, who live only under positive, arbitrary, and changeable institutions; and those not perfected nor supplied, nor explained, by any common acknowledged rule of moral science. . . . France, since her Revolution, is under the sway of a sect, whose leaders have deliberately, at one stroke, demolished the whole body of that jurisprudence which France had pretty nearly in common with other civilized countries. In that jurisprudence were contained the elements and principles of the law of nations, the great ligament of mankind. With the law they have of course destroyed all seminaries in which jurisprudence was taught, as well as all the corporations established for it's conservation. I have not heard of any country, whether in Europe or Asia, or even in Africa on this side of Mount Atlas, which is wholly without some such colleges and such corporations, except France. No man, in a publick or private concern, can divine by what rule or principle her judgements are to be directed; nor is there to be found a professor in any University, or a practitioner in any Court, who will hazard an opinion of what is or is not law in France, in any case whatever. They have not only annulled all their old treaties; but they have renounced the law of nations from whence treaties have their force. With a fixed design they have outlawed themselves, and to their power outlawed all other nations.

Instead of the religion and the law by which they were in a great politick communion with the Christian world, they have constructed their Republick on three bases, all fundamentally opposite to those on which the communities of Europe are built. It's foundation is laid in Regicide; in Jacobinism; and in Atheism; and it has joined to those principles, a body of systematick manners which secures their operation.

If I am asked, how I would be understood in the use of these terms, Regicide, Jacobinism, Atheism, and a system of correspondent manners, and their establishment, I will tell you.

I call a commonwealth *Regicide,* which lays it down as a fixed law of nature, and a fundamental right of man, that all government, not being a democracy, is an usurpation. That all Kings, as such, are usurpers; and for being Kings, may and ought to be put to death, with their wives, families, and adherents. The commonwealth which acts uniformly upon those principles; and which after abolishing every festival of religion, chooses the most flagrant act of a murderous Regicide treason for a feast of eternal commemoration, and which forces all her people to observe it—This I call *Regicide by establishment.*

Jacobinism is the revolt of the enterprising talents of a country against it's property. When private men form themselves into associations for the purpose of destroying the pre-existing laws and institutions of their country; when they secure to themselves an army by dividing amongst the people of no property, the estates of the ancient and lawful proprietors; when a state recognizes those acts; when it does not make confiscations for crimes, but makes crimes for confiscations; when it has it's principal strength, and all it's resources in such a violation of property; when it stands chiefly upon such a violation; massacring by judgments, or otherwise, those who make any struggle for their old legal government, and their legal, hereditary, or acquired possessions—I call this *Jacobinism by Establishment.*

I call it *Atheism by Establishment,* when any State, as such, shall not acknowledge the existence of God as a moral Governor of the World; when it shall offer to Him no religious or moral worship;—when it shall abolish the Christian religion by a regular decree;—when it shall persecute with a cold, unrelenting, steady cruelty, by every mode of confiscation, imprisonment, exile, and death, all it's ministers;—when it shall generally shut up, or pull down, churches; when the few buildings which remain of this kind shall be opened only for the purpose of making a profane apotheosis of monsters, whose vices and crimes have no parallel amongst men, and whom all other men consider as objects of general detestation, and the severest animadversion of law. When, in the place of that religion of social benevolence, and of individual self-denial, in mockery of all religion, they institute impious, blasphemous, indecent theatric rites, in honour of their vitiated, perverted reason, and erect altars to the personification of their own corrupted and bloody Republick;—when schools and seminaries are founded at publick expence to poison mankind, from generation to generation, with the horrible maxims of this impiety;—when wearied out with incessant martyrdom, and the cries of a people hungering and thirsting for religion, they permit it, only as a tolerated evil—I call this *Atheism by Establishment.*

When to these establishments of Regicide, of Jacobinism, and of Atheism, you add the *correspondent system of manners,* no doubt can be left on the mind of a thinking man, concerning their determined hostility to the human race. Manners are of more importance than laws. Upon them, in a great measure the laws depend. The law touches us but here and there, and now and then. Manners are what vex or sooth, corrupt or purify, exalt or debase, barbarize or refine us, by a constant, steady, uniform, insensible operation, like that of the air we breathe in. They give their whole form and colour to our lives. According to their quality, they aid morals, they supply them, or they totally destroy them. Of this, the new French Legislators were aware; therefore, with the same method, and under the same authority, they settled a system of manners, the most licentious, prostitute, and abandoned that ever has been known, and at the same time the most coarse, rude, savage, and ferocious. Nothing in the Revolution, no, not to a phrase or a gesture, not to the fashion of a hat or a shoe, was left to accident. All has been the result of design; all has been matter of institution. . . .

～

The operation of dangerous and delusive first principles obliges us to have recourse to the true ones. In the intercourse between nations, we are apt to rely too much on the instrumental part. We lay too much weight upon the formality of treaties and compacts. We do not act much more wisely when we trust to the interests of men as guarantees of their engagements. The interests frequently tear to pieces the engagements; and the passions trample upon both. Entirely to trust to either, is to disregard our own safety, or not to know mankind. Men are not tied to one another by papers and seals. They are led to associate by resemblances, by conformities, by sympathies. It is with nations as with individuals. Nothing is so strong a tie of amity between nation and nation as correspondence in laws, customs, manners, and habits of life. They have more than the force of treaties in themselves. They are obligations written in the heart. They approximate men to men, without their knowledge, and sometimes against their intentions. The secret, unseen, but irrefragable bond of habitual intercourse, holds them together, even when their perverse and litigious nature sets them to equivocate, scuffle, and fight about the terms of their written obligations.

As to war, if it be the means of wrong and violence, it is the sole means of justice amongst nations. Nothing can banish it from the world. They who say otherwise, intending to impose upon us, do not im-

pose upon themselves. But it is one of the greatest objects of human wisdom to mitigate those evils which we are unable to remove. The conformity and analogy of which I speak, incapable, like every thing else, of preserving perfect trust and tranquillity among men, has a strong tendency to facilitate accommodation, and to produce a generous oblivion of the rancour of their quarrels. With this similitude, peace is more of peace, and war is less of war. I will go further. There have been periods of time in which communities, apparently in peace with each other, have been more perfectly separated than, in later times, many nations in Europe have been in the course of long and bloody wars. The cause must be sought in the similitude throughout Europe of religion, laws, and manners. At bottom, these are all the same. The writers on public law have often called this *aggregate* of nations a Commonwealth. They had reason. It is virtually one great state having the same basis of general law; with some diversity of provincial customs and local establishments. The nations of Europe have had the very same christian religion, agreeing in the fundamental parts, varying a little in the ceremonies and in the subordinate doctrines. The whole polity and oeconomy of every country in Europe has been derived from the same old Germanic or Gothic custumary; and the feudal institutions which must be considered as an emanation from and digested the whole has been by the Roman into system and the several orders, law. From every European country; with or of which, where Monarchy was never wholly extinguished or merged in despotism. In the few where Monarchy was cast off, the spirit of European Monarchy was still left. Those countries still continued countries of States; that is, of classes, orders, and distinctions, such as had before subsisted, or nearly so. Indeed the force and form of the institution called States, continued in greater perfection in those republican communities than under Monarchies. From all those sources arose a system of manners and of education which was nearly similar in all this quarter of the globe; and which softened, blended, and harmonized the colours of the whole. There was little difference in the form of the Universities for the education of their youth, whether with regard to faculties, to sciences, or to the more liberal and elegant kinds of erudition. From this resemblance in the modes of intercourse, and in the whole form and fashion of life, no citizen of Europe could be altogether an exile in any part of it. There was nothing more than a pleasing variety to recreate and instruct the mind; to enrich the imagination; and to meliorate the heart. When a man travelled or resided for health, pleasure, business or necessity, from his own country, he never felt himself quite abroad.

The whole body of this new scheme of manners in support of the new scheme of politics I consider as a strong and decisive proof of determined ambition and systematick ability. I defy the most refining ingenuity to invent any other cause for the total departure of the Jacobin Republick from every one of the ideas and usages, religious, legal, and social, of this civilized world, and its tearing herself from its communion, but from such studied violence, keeping no terms, as has resolution of the world. It has not been, as has been represented, and insidiously had only broke with miscreants ment. They made a schism in the govern- whole

universe; and that schism extended to almost every thing great and small. For one, I wish, since it is gone thus far, that the breach had been so compleat, as to make all intercourse impracticable; but partly by accident, partly by design, partly from the resistance of the matter, enough is left to preserve intercourse, whilst amity is destroyed or corrupted in it's principle.

This violent breach of the community of Europe, we must conclude to have been made, (even if they had not expressly declared it over and over again) either to force mankind into an adoption of their system, or to live in perpetual enmity with a community the most potent we have ever known. Can any person imagine, that in offering to mankind this desperate alternative, there is no indication of a hostile mind, because men in possession of the ruling authority are supposed to have a right to act without coercion in their own territories? As to the right of men to act any where according to their pleasure, without any moral tie, no such right exists. Men are never in a state of *total* independence of each other. It is not the condition of our nature: nor is it conceivable how any man can pursue a considerable course of action without it's having some effect upon others; or, of course, without producing some degree of responsibility for his conduct. The *situations* in which men relatively stand produce the rules and principles of that responsibility, and afford directions to prudence in exacting it.

Distance of place does not extinguish the duties or the rights of men; but it often renders their exercise impracticable. The same circumstance of distance renders the noxious effects of an evil system in any community less pernicious. But there are situations where this difficulty does not occur; and in which, therefore, these duties are obligatory, and these rights are to be asserted. It has ever been the method of publick jurists to draw a great part of the analogies on which they form the law of nations, from the principles of law which prevail in civil community. Civil laws are not all of them merely positive. Those which are rather conclusions of legal reason, than matters of statutable provision, belong to universal equity, and are universally applicable. . . . There is a *Law of Neighbourhood* which does not leave a man perfect master on his own ground. When a neighbour sees a *new erection,* in the nature of a nuisance, set up at his door, he has a right to represent it to the judge; who, on his part, has a right to order the work to be staid; or if established, to be removed. On this head, the parent law is express and clear; and has made many wise provisions, which, without destroying, regulate and restrain the right of *ownership,* by the right of *vicinage.* No *innovation* is permitted that may redound, even secondarily, to the prejudice of a neighbour. The whole doctrine . . . is founded on the principle, that no *new* use should be made of a man's private liberty of operating upon his private property, from whence a detriment may be justly apprehended by his neighbour. This law of denunciation is prospective. It is to anticipate . . . a damage justly apprehended but not actually done. Even before it is clearly known, whether the innovation be damageable or not, the judge is competent to issue a prohibition to innovate, until the point can be determined. This prompt interference is grounded on principles favourable to both parties. It is preventive of mischief difficult to be repaired, and of ill blood difficult to be softened. The rule of law, therefore, which comes before the evil, is amongst the very best parts of equity, and justifies the promptness of the remedy. . . . This right of denunciation

does not hold, when things continue, however inconveniently to the neighbourhood, according to the *antient* mode. For there is a sort of presumption against novelty, drawn out of a deep consideration of human nature and human affairs. . . .

Such is the law of civil vicinity. Now where there is no constituted judge, as between independent states there is not, the vicinage itself is the natural judge. It is, preventively, the assertor of it's own rights; or remedially their avenger. Neighbours are presumed to take cognizance of each other's acts. . . . This principle, which, like the rest, is as true of nations, as of individual men, has bestowed on the grand vicinage of Europe, a duty to know, and a right to prevent, any capital innovation which may amount to the erection of a dangerous nuisance.[81] Of the importance of that innovation, and the mischief of that nuisance, they are, to be sure, bound to judge not litigiously: but it is in their competence to judge. They have uniformly acted on this right. What in civil society is a ground of action, in politick society is a ground of war. But the exercise of that competent jurisdiction is a matter of moral prudence. As suits in civil society, so war in the political must ever be a matter of great deliberation. It is not this or that particular proceeding, picked out here and there, as a subject of quarrel, that will do. There must be an aggregate of mischief. There must be marks of deliberation; there must be traces of design; there must be indications of malice; there must be tokens of ambition. There must be

---

[81]"This state of things cannot exist in France without involving all the surrounding powers in one common danger, without giving them the right, without imposing it on them as a duty, to stop the progress of an evil which attacks the fundamental principles by which mankind is united in civil society." Declaration, 29th Oct. 1793. [Burke's note]

force in the body where they exist; there must be energy in the mind. When all these circumstances combine, or the important parts of them, the duty of the vicinity calls for the exercise of its competence; and the rules of prudence do not restrain, but demand it.

In describing the nuisance erected by so pestilential a manufactory, by the construction of so infamous a brothel, by digging a night cellar for such thieves, murderers, and house-breakers, as never infested the world, I am so far from aggravating, that I have fallen infinitely short of the evil. No man who has attended to the particulars of what has been done in France, and combined them with the principles there asserted, can possibly doubt it. When I compare with this great cause of nations, the trifling points of honour, the still more contemptible points of interest, the light ceremonies, the undefinable punctilios, the disputes about precedency, the lowering or the hoisting of a sail, the dealing in a hundred or two of wild cat-skins on the other side of the Globe, which have often kindled up the flames of war between nations, I stand astonished at those persons, who do not feel a resentment, not more natural than politick, at the atrocious insults that this monstrous compound offers to the dignity of every nation, and who are not alarmed with what it threatens to their safety.

I have therefore been decidedly of opinion, with our declaration at Whitehall, in the beginning of this war, that the vicinage of Europe had not only a right, but an indispensable duty, and an exigent interest, to denunciate this new work before it had produced the danger we have so sorely felt, and which we shall long feel. The example of what is done by France is too important not to have a vast and extensive influence; and that example backed with it's power, must bear with great force on those who are near it; especially on those who shall recognize the pretended Republick on the principle upon which it now stands. It is not an old structure which you have found as it is, and are not to dispute of the original end and design with which it had been so fashioned. It is a recent wrong, and can plead no prescription. It violates the rights upon which not only the community of France, but those on which all communities are founded. The principles on which they proceed are *general* principles, and are as true in England as in any other country. They who (though with the purest intentions) recognize the authority of these Regicides and robbers upon principle, justify their acts, and establish them as precedents. It is a question not between France and England. It is a question between property and force. The property claims; and it's claim has been allowed. The property of the nation is the nation. They who massacre, plunder, and expel the body of the proprietary, are murderers and robbers. The State, in it's essence, must be moral and just: and it may be so, though a tyrant or usurper should be accidentally at the head of it. This is a thing to be lamented: but this notwithstanding, the body of the commonwealth may remain in all it's integrity and be perfectly sound in it's composition. The present case is different. It is not a revolution in government. It is not the victory of party over party. It is a destruction and decomposition of the whole society; which never can be made of right by any faction, however powerful, nor without terrible consequences to all about it, both in the act and in the example. This pretended Republick is founded in crimes, and exists by wrong and robbery; and wrong and robbery, far from a title to any thing, is war with mankind. To be at peace with robbery is to be an accomplice with it.

Mere locality does not constitute a body politick. . . . The body politick of France existed in the majesty of it's throne; in the dignity of it's nobility; in the honour of it's gentry; in the sanctity of it's clergy; in the reverence of it's magistracy; in the weight and consideration due to it's landed property in the several bailliages; in the respect due to it's moveable substance represented by the corporations of the kingdom. All these particular *moleculae* united, form the great mass of what is truly the body politick in all countries. They are so many deposits and receptacles of justice; because they can only exist by justice. Nation is a moral essence, not a geographical arrangement, or a denomination of the nomenclator. France, though out of her territorial possession, exists; because the sole possible claimant, I mean the proprietary, and the government to which the propriety adheres, exists and claims. . . . Am I to transfer to the intruders, who not content to turn you out naked to the world, would rob you of your very name, all the esteem and respect I owe to you? The Regicides in France are not France. France is out of her bounds, but the kingdom is the same.

⸙

. . . This example we shall give, if instead of adhering to our fellows in a cause which is an honour to us all, we abandon the lawful Government and lawful corporate body of France, to hunt for a shameful and ruinous fraternity, with this odious usurpation that disgraces civilized society and the human race.

And is then example nothing? It is every thing. Example is the school of mankind, and they will learn at no other. This war is a war against that example. It is not a war for Louis the Eighteenth, or even for the property, virtue, fidelity of France. It is a war for George the Third, for Francis the Second, and for all the dignity, property, honour, virtue, and religion of England, of Germany, and of all nations.

⸙

It is no excuse at all for a minister, who at our desire, takes a measure contrary to our safety, that it is our own act. He who does not stay the hand of suicide, is guilty of murder. On our part I say, that to be instructed, is not to be degraded or enslaved. Information is an advantage to us; and we have a right to demand it. He that is bound to act in the dark cannot be said to act freely. When it appears evident to our governors that our desires and our interests are at variance, they ought not to gratify the former at the expence of the latter. Statesmen are placed on an eminence, that they may have a larger horizon than we can possibly command. They have a whole before them, which we can contemplate only in the parts, and often without the necessary relations. Ministers are not only our natural rulers but our natural guides. Reason clearly and manfully delivered, has in itself a mighty force: but reason in the mouth of legal authority, is, I may fairly say, irresistible.

I admit that reason of state will not, in many circumstances permit the disclosure of the true ground of a public proceeding. In that case silence is manly and it is wise. It is fair to call for trust when the principle of reason itself suspends it's public use. I take the distinction to be this: The ground of a particular measure, making a part of a plan, it is rarely proper to divulge; all the broader grounds of policy on which the general plan is to be adopted, ought as rarely to be concealed. They who have not the whole cause before them, call them politicians, call them people, call them what you will, are no judges. The difficulties of the case, as well as it's fair side, ought to be presented. This ought to be done: and it is all that can be done. When we have our true situation distinctly presented to us, if then we resolve with a blind and headlong violence, to resist the admonitions of our friends, and to cast ourselves into the hands of our potent and irreconcileable foes, then, and not till then, the ministers stand acquitted before God and man, for whatever may come.

Lamenting as I do, that the matter has not had so full and free a discussion as it requires, I mean to omit none of the points which seem to me necessary for consideration, previous to an arrangement which is for ever to decide the form and the fate of Europe. In the course, therefore, of what I shall have the honour to address to you, I propose the following questions to your serious thoughts. 1. Whether the present system, which stands for a Government in France, be such as in peace and war affects the neighbouring States in a manner different from the internal Government that formerly prevailed in that country? 2. Whether that system, supposing it's views hostile to other nations, possesses any means of being hurtful to them peculiar to itself? 3. Whether there has been lately such a change in France, as to alter the nature of it's system, or it's effect upon other Powers? 4. Whether any publick declarations or engagements exist, on the part of the allied Powers, which stand in the way of a treaty of peace, which supposes the right and confirms the power of the Regicide faction in France? 5. What the state of the other Powers of Europe will be with respect to each other, and their colonies, on the conclusion of a Regicide Peace? 6. Whether we are driven to the absolute necessity of making that kind of peace?

These heads of enquiry will enable us to make the application of the several matters of fact and topicks of argument, that occur in this vast discussion, to certain fixed principles. I do not mean to confine myself to the order in which they stand. I shall discuss them in such a manner as shall appear to me the best adapted for shewing their mutual bearings and relations. Here then I close the public matter of my Letter. . . .

Notes to
Part One

Chapter One

1. R. J. Vincent, "Edmund Burke and the Theory of International Relations," *Review of International Studies* 10 (1984), 206. Two more recent examinations of Burke's thinking on international relations can be found in J. M. Welsh, *Edmund Burke and International Relations: The Commonwealth of Europe and the Crusade Against the French Revolution* (New York, 1995), and J. M. Welsh, "Edmund Burke and the Commonwealth of Europe: The Cultural Bases of International Order," in *Classical Theories of International Relations*, ed. I. Clark and I. B. Neumann (London, 1996), 173.

2. Welsh, *Edmund Burke and International Relations*, 1.

3. Vincent, "Edmund Burke," 206.

4. Hazlitt commented that "to do him justice, it would be necessary to quote all his works; the only specimen of Burke is, *all that he wrote.*" W. Hazlitt, *Eloquence of the British Senate*, vol. 2 (London, 1808), 206.

5. Vincent, "Edmund Burke," 205.

6. Ibid.

7. Matthew Arnold believed that Burke was great "because, almost alone in England, he brings thought to bear upon politics, he saturates politics with thought." Quoted in ibid. Auerbach also wrote: "In spite of the fact that almost all of Burke's writings were directed to specific historical problems, they are interspersed with general formulations which can be put together to form a coherent ideology." M. Auerbach, *The Conservative Illusion* (New York, 1959), 34.

8. A. Cobban, *Edmund Burke and the Revolt Against the Eighteenth Century* (London, 1929), 75.

9. Burke regarded Montesquieu as "the greatest genius of the age." A. M. Osborn, *Rousseau and Burke: A Study of the Idea of Liberty in Eighteenth-Century Political Thought* (Oxford, 1940), 7. For a comparative study of the thought of Burke and Montesquieu, see C. P. Courtney, *Montesquieu and Burke* (Oxford, 1963).

10. *Reflections on the Revolution in France, WSEB*, viii, 58.

11. C. B. Macpherson, *Burke* (Oxford, 1980), 74.

12. Welsh, *Edmund Burke and International Relations*, 1.

13. Cobban, *Edmund Burke and the Revolt Against the Eighteenth Century*, 39.

14. Welsh, *Edmund Burke and International Relations*, 1.

15. Macpherson, *Burke*, 73.

16. I. Hampsher-Monk, "Introduction," in *The Political Philosophy of Edmund Burke*, ed. I. Hampsher-Monk (London, 1987), 15.

17. P. J. Stanlis, *Edmund Burke: The Enlightenment and Revolution* (New Brunswick, NJ, 1991), 64.

18. Vincent, "Edmund Burke," 216; Welsh, "Edmund Burke and the Commonwealth of Europe," 183–184. In Chapter 3 we define the international relations traditions of realism, rationalism, and revolutionism in connection with analyzing Burke as an international relations theorist.

Chapter Two

19. See generally W. O'Brien, *Edmund Burke as an Irishman* (Dublin, 2nd ed., 1926); T. H. D. Mahoney, *Edmund Burke and Ireland* (Cambridge, MA, 1960); and M. Fuchs, *Edmund Burke, Ireland, and the Fashioning of the Self* (Oxford, 1996).

20. S. Ayling, *Edmund Burke: His Life and Opinions* (London, 1988), 2.

21. See C. C. O'Brien, *The Great Melody: A Thematic Biography of Edmund Burke* (London, 1992), 3–14.

22. The only government post Burke had was paymaster general of the forces, which he held under the second Rockingham administration (1782) and the Fox-North coalition (1783).

23. *Letter to a Noble Lord*, WSEB, ix, 160.

24. Macpherson, *Burke*, 8–9. See also Fuchs, *Edmund Burke*, 45.

25. Macpherson, *Burke*, 9.

26. Ibid.

27. A. P. I. Samuels, *Early Life, Correspondence, and Writings of Edmund Burke* (Cambridge, 1923), 364.

28. Burke wrote to a friend in his second year at Middle Temple that the "law causes no difficulty to those who readily understand it, and to those who never will understand it; and for all between these extremes, God knows, they have a hard task of it." Quoted in P. Burke, *Public and Domestic Life of the Rt. Hon. Edmund Burke* (London, 1853), 13. Perhaps a key to Burke's frustration at Middle Temple may be found in a later speech on America, in which he said that law "does more to quicken and invigorate the understanding, than all the other kinds of learning put together; but it is not apt . . . to open and liberalize the mind exactly in the same proportion." *Speech on American Taxation*, WSEB, ii, 432.

29. J. Morley, *Burke* (London, 1879), 9.

30. Hampsher-Monk wrote that the English common law was "an institution which gives both legal and symbolic expression to custom and precedent, and was one of the sources from which Burke clearly 'abstracted' his political philosophy." Hampsher-Monk, "Introduction," 36.

31. *Speech on Conciliation with America*, WSEB, iii, 124.

32. *A Vindication of Natural Society, Works*, i, 1–48; *A Philosophical Inquiry into the Origin of Our Ideas of the Sublime and Beautiful, Works*, i, 49–181.

33. *An Abridgment of English History, Works*, vi, 184–422.

34. Osborn, *Rousseau and Burke*, 116–117.

35. On Burke's involvement with the *Annual Register*, see Fuchs, *Edmund Burke*, 245–264.

36. Osborn, *Rousseau and Burke*, 118.

37. Fuchs observed in the *Annual Register* a tempered approach to foreign affairs, as "in the thick of the Seven Years War repeated attempts were made to avoid fanning the national prejudices of the English against the French or the Spaniards. . . . Esteem between nations, as between individuals, has to be reciprocal." Fuchs, *Edmund Burke*, 251–252.

38. Quoted in Ayling, *Edmund Burke*, 17.

39. Quoted in ibid., 20.

40. Ibid., 17.

41. Quoted in ibid., 20.

42. Burke's efforts to become the personal assistant to the secretary of war, Charles Townshend, and to become the London agent to a group of West Indian islands produced no results. Ibid., 42.

43. Macpherson, *Burke*, 11.

44. Hampsher-Monk, "Introduction," 26.

45. *Tracts Relating to Popery Laws, WSEB*, ix, 434–482.

46 Ibid., 452.

47. Ibid., 453.

48. Ibid., 455.

49. Ibid.

50. Ibid.

51. Ibid., 463.

52. Ibid., 464.

53. *Letter to Sir Charles Bingham, WSEB*, ix, 487–495.

54. See O'Brien, *The Great Melody*, 70.

55. *Letter to Sir Charles Bingham, WSEB*, ix, 493.

56. Ibid., 489–490.

57. Ibid., 490, 488.

58. *Speech at the Conclusion of the Poll, WSEB*, iii, 69.

59. *Speech at Arrival at Bristol*, in ibid., 59–60.

60. R. Bisset, *Life of Edmund Burke* (London, 2nd ed., 1800), ii, 429. Canavan has, however, raised questions about Bisset's recording of Smith's declaration. See F. Canavan, *The Political Economy of Edmund Burke* (New York, 1995), 116–117. Nevertheless, Smith and Burke admired each other. After having read *Philosophical Inquiry*, Smith stated that Burke deserved a university chair. Ayling, *Edmund Burke*, 15. Burke reviewed in the *Annual Register* of 1759 Smith's *Theory of Moral Sentiments* and described it as "one of the most beautiful fabrics of moral theory that has perhaps ever appeared." Quoted in ibid., 16. Burke and Smith became personally acquainted when Smith was elected in 1775 to "the Club," which Joshua Reynolds and Dr. Johnson started in 1764 and that included Burke as one of the original members. The next year Smith published *Wealth of Nations* (1776). For more on Smith and Burke, see D. Wecter, "Adam Smith and Burke," *Notes and Queries* 174 (1938), 310–311; W. C. Dunn, "Adam Smith and Edmund Burke: Complementary Contemporaries," *Southern Economic Journal* 7 (1941), 330–346; C. R. Fay, *Burke and Adam Smith* (Belfast, 1956); and R. W. McGee, "Edmund Burke and Adam Smith: Pioneers in the Field of Law and Economics," *Australian Law Journal* 66 (1992), 262–269.

61. *Two Letters on the Trade of Ireland, WSEB*, ix, 509–510, 514–515.

62. Quoted in Ayling, *Edmund Burke*, 98. O'Brien wrote that Burke's "life was threatened, on several occasions during the riots, and witnesses attested his courageous conduct." O'Brien, *The Great Melody*, 77.

63. *Speech at Bristol Previous to the Election, WSEB*, iii, 620–664.

64. See O'Brien, *The Great Melody*, 81–85.

65. Quoted in Ayling, *Edmund Burke*, 116.

66. Ibid., 117. McDowell similarly noted that "Burke did not play a conspicuous part" in the legislative debates on the proposals for granting independence to the Irish Parliament. McDowell, "Introduction," *WSEB*, ix, 404.

67. Ayling, *Edmund Burke*, 116–117.

68. McDowell, "Introduction," *WSEB*, ix, 405.

69. Ibid.

70. Ibid.

71. *Speech on Irish Commercial Propositions, WSEB,* ix, 589–593.

72. The *Morning Herald* reported Burke as stating: "To consult the interests of England and Ireland, to unite and consolidate them in one, was a task which he would undertake." Ibid., 591.

73. Ibid., 592–593.

74. Burke stated "that he should be sorry it were to be so understood, that what was now to be done for Ireland should be conditional." Ibid.

75. Ibid., 589.

76. Ibid., 591.

77. O'Brien wrote that the *"Letter to Sir Hercules Langrishe,* by itself, constitutes most of that part of the Great Melody which is directly about Ireland." O'Brien, *The Great Melody,* 481.

78. *Letter to Sir Hercules Langrishe, WSEB,* ix, 628.

79. Ibid., 630.

80. Ibid.

81. Ibid., 631.

82. O'Brien, *The Great Melody,* 497.

83. Ibid., 513.

84. O'Brien wrote that for Burke "Fitzwilliam's recall was of course nothing less than the reversal of almost all Burke's hopes for Ireland." Ibid., 516.

85. Ibid., 525.

86. *Corr.,* ix, 162.

87. The confluence of Irish Catholic discontent and the expansionist ambitions of revolutionary France came dangerously close in late 1796, as Burke was writing to Hussey, when a French fleet carrying an army of 14,000 failed to land at Bantry Bay, Ireland, because of storms.

88. "It is difficult to imagine a more painfully complex dilemma both of head and heart, than Burke found himself in, while he helplessly contemplated the unfolding of the Irish tragedy, in the last months of his life." O'Brien, *The Great Melody,* 576.

89. Ayling, *Edmund Burke,* 281. Burke did not live to see his sorrow for Ireland's future confirmed in the 1798 Irish rebellion. The relative freedom gained by the Irish Parliament in the 1790s did not last long, as British fears of potential Irish complicity with Napoleon's imperialism led Britain to bring Ireland back under Westminster's control in the Act of Union of 1800, which created the United Kingdom. See H. Calvert, *An Introduction to British Constitutional Law* (London, 1985), 19–20.

90. Ayling wondered whether it was this proposal from Burke that "finally prompted his father to discontinue his allowance." Ayling, *Edmund Burke,* 13.

91. Quoted in Morley, *Burke,* 11.

92. His efforts with William on *Account* "aided Burke's subsequent master-display of knowledge on the American question." Burke, *Public and Domestic Life of the Rt. Hon. Edmund Burke,* 34.

93. Burke's first speech in the House of Commons was on America. See O'Brien, *The Great Melody,* 107–108.

94. *Short Account of a Late Short Administration, WSEB,* ii, 54, 55.

95. Hampsher-Monk, "Introduction," 20–21.

96. *Letter to Sir Hercules Langrishe, WSEB,* ix, 630.

97. As Burke said in his *Speech on American Taxation,* "[a]ll before this period stood on commercial regulation and restraint. The scheme of a Colony revenue by British authority appeared therefore to the Americans in the light of a great innovation." *Speech on American Taxation, WSEB,* ii, 428.

98. *Observations on a Late State of the Nation, WSEB,* ii, 200.

99. Ibid.

100. See A. O. Hirschman, *The Passions and the Interests* (Princeton, 1977), 77–81.

101. American Revenue Act of 1767.

102. *Speech on American Taxation, WSEB*, ii, 409.

103. See Hampsher-Monk, "Introduction," 28 for the distinction between substantive conservatism, which "identifies a particular society, set of institutions and practices as right and proper," and procedural conservatism, which "is identified with a disposition, and attitude towards the conduct of politics, rather than with any particular model of the good society."

104. *Speech on American Taxation, WSEB*, ii, 456.

105. Ibid., 458.

106. Ibid., 460.

107. Ibid.

108. Ibid.

109. Ibid.

110. Ibid.

111. Ibid., 459.

112. Ibid., 416.

113. Ibid.

114. Ibid.

115. *Speech on Conciliation with America, WSEB*, iii, 108.

116. Ibid.

117. Ibid., 109.

118. Ibid., 108.

119. Ibid., 118.

120. Ibid., 118–119.

121. Ibid., 119.

122. Ibid., 131.

123. Ibid., 132.

124. Ibid., 133.

125. Ibid., 134–135.

126. Ibid., 135.

127. Ibid., 136.

128. Ibid.

129. Ibid.

130. Ibid., 140. Burke made this statement when discussing the English conquest of Ireland. Burke's use of Ireland as an example of admitting colonial peoples into an interest in the British constitution rings false when considered against his Irish efforts. See O'Brien, *The Great Melody*, 151–152.

131. *Speech on Conciliation with America, WSEB*, iii, 164.

132. Toward the end of 1775, he tried three more times to head off war with the Americans, first in presenting King George III with a petition from Bristol merchants who opposed the war with the Americans; second in another speech in the House of Commons in which he urged that Britain at least recognize the Continental Congress; and third in seeking to encourage the Irish Parliament to offer to mediate the dispute or to withhold material and personnel for use in America. Ayling, *Edmund Burke*, 85–86.

133. Burke wrote that he did "not know how to wish success to those whose victory is to separate from us a large and noble part of our Empire. Still less do I wish success to injustice, oppression, and absurdity. . . . No good can come of any event in this war to any virtuous interest. We have forgot or thrown away all our antient principles." Quoted in ibid., 86.

134. *Address to the King, WSEB*, iii, 266.

135. Ibid., 258.

136. *Letter to the Sheriffs of Bristol, WSEB*, iii, 328–329.

137. "We grow indifferent to the consequences inevitable to ourselves from the plan of ruling half the empire by a mercenary sword. We are taught to believe, that a desire of domineering over our countrymen, is love to our country; that those who hate civil war abet rebellion; and that the amiable and conciliatory virtues of lenity, moderation, and tenderness to the privileges of those who depend on this kingdom, are a sort of treason to the state. It is impossible that we should remain long in a situation, which breeds such notions and dispositions, without some great alteration in the national character." Ibid., 329.

138. Ayling, *Edmund Burke*, 89.

139. O'Brien, *The Great Melody*, 225.

140. O'Brien described the "long battle of wills" between Burke and George III over American independence in ibid., 202–234.

141. *Corr.,* ix, 62.

142. F. G. Whelan, *Edmund Burke and India: Political Morality and Empire* (Pittsburgh, 1996), 1.

143. Marshall, "Introduction," *WSEB,* v, 1. At the end of the Hastings impeachment, Burke could claim to be "as conversant with the manners and customs of the East as most persons whose business has not directly led them into that country." Quoted in Marshall, "Introduction," *WSEB,* vi, 21.

144. Marshall, "Introduction," *WSEB,* vi, 20.

145. Ayling, *Edmund Burke*, 30.

146. Ibid., 67. As Ayling wrote, Burke's "attitude to the Clive affair stands indeed in remarkable contrast to the vendetta pursued later by him . . . against Warren Hastings." Ibid., 67–68.

147. See *Speech on North's East India Resolutions, WSEB,* ii, 390.

148. See Ayling, *Edmund Burke,* 68; O'Brien, *The Great Melody,* 265–266; and Whelan, *Edmund Burke and India,* 43.

149. *Speech on East India Settlement, WSEB,* ii, 220.

150. Ibid., 221.

151. *Speech on East India Regulating Bill, WSEB,* ii, 395.

152. Langford, "Introduction," *WSEB,* ii, 23.

153. Burke wrote in correspondence "that they only attack the Company, in order to transfer their wealth and Influence to the Court" and that "nothing further is meant, than to vest the immense patronage of Office, now in the hands of the Company in those of the Crown." *Corr.,* ii, 407, 399.

154. *Observations on a Late State of the Nation, WSEB,* ii, 102–219. *Thoughts on the Present Discontents, WSEB,* ii, 241–323.

155. For discussion of Burke's early speeches on India, see H. Furber, "Edmund Burke and India," *Bengal Past and Present* 76 (1957), 11–21; O'Brien, *The Great Melody,* 260–272; and Whelan, *Edmund Burke and India,* 43.

156. *Speech on East India Dividend Bill, WSEB,* ii, 64–67.

157. Ibid., 65.

158. *Speech on East India Settlement, WSEB,* ii, 221.

159. *Speech on East India Restraining Bill, WSEB,* ii, 378, 379.

160. Whelan, *Edmund Burke and India,* 43. The East India Company even offered to have Burke "chair a committee of supervisors that would go out to Calcutta and set things straight." Ibid. O'Brien concluded that this offer to so friendly a politician as Burke was intended to facilitate "a whitewash" for the East India Company. O'Brien, *The Great Melody,* 264.

161. Langford, "Introduction," *WSEB,* ii, 23; Whelan, *Edmund Burke and India,* 43.

162. *Speech on North's East India Resolutions, WSEB,* ii, 391.

163. Ibid.

164. Ibid.

165. *Speech on East India Settlement, WSEB,* ii, 220.

166. *Speech on North's East India Resolutions, WSEB,* ii, 392.

167. Ibid.

168. Ibid., 393.

169. Marshall suggested that Burke was complacent on India prior to 1778. Marshall, "Introduction," *WSEB,* v, 4. Ayling commented that Burke's opposition was "both factious and ill-conceived." Ayling, *Edmund Burke,* 69. Whelan argued that "[a]s a newcomer, Burke naturally followed his party and feared [Lord] North's partial control of India affairs." Whelan, *Edmund Burke and India,* 43, n. 40.

170. Marshall further commented that "[i]n an age when many intellectuals prided themselves on the interest which they took in accounts of the peoples of the world, Burke's study of India was probably more intensive and more prolonged than any study of a non-European people undertaken by any of his contemporaries." Marshall, "Introduction," *WSEB,* vi, 20.

171. *Speech on Restoring Lord Pigot, WSEB,* v, 36.

172. "*Government* as *Government* was immediately interested in it. . . . All its fundamental principles were at stake. It was just whether the *subordinate* was to depose the *superior*—whether the *Military* was to mount over the *Civil*—Whether a *foreign* prince was to dictate in *Domestick* Councils." Ibid., 39.

173. "Some people [are] great lovers of uniformity—They are not satisfied with a rebellion in the West. They must have one in the East: They are not satisfied with losing one Empire—they must lose another—Lord N[orth] will weep that he has not more worlds to lose." Ibid., 40.

174. Ibid.

175. Ibid.

176. Marshall, "Introduction," *WSEB,* v, 8.

177. *Policy of Making Conquests for the Mahometans, WSEB,* v, 41–124.

178. Ibid., 112–113.

179. Ibid., 113.

180. Ibid.

181. Ibid., 113–114.

182. Ibid., 114.

183. Ibid.

184. Quoted in Marshall, "Introduction," *WSEB,* v, 18. A secret committee chaired by Henry Dundas was formed at the same time.

185. *Ninth Report* and *Eleventh Report of the Select Committee* are found in *WSEB,* v, 194–333 and 334–378.

186. *Ninth Report, WSEB,* v, 197.

187. Ibid., 241.

188. Ibid., 246.

189. "This System of Government appears to Your Committee to be at least as much disordered, and as much perverted from every good Purpose, for which lawful Rule is established, as the trading System has been from every just Principle of Commerce." Ibid., 306.

190. "The Disobedience of Mr. Hastings has of late . . . become uniform and systematical in Practice." Ibid., 311.

191. Ibid., 221.

192. Marshall, "Introduction," *WSEB,* v, 20.

193. Whelan, *Edmund Burke and India,* 44, 55.

194. *Speech on Fox's India Bill, WSEB,* v, 381.

195. Ibid., 389.

196. Ibid., 390.

197. Ibid., 385.

198. Ibid., 403.

199. Ibid., 386, 384.

200. In this speech Burke stated that if he allowed East India Company oppression to continue, "I must break the faith, the covenant, the solemn, original, indispensable oath, in which I am bound, by the eternal frame and constitution of things, to the whole human race." Ibid., 425.

201. See B. P. Frohnen and C. J. Reid Jr., "Diversity in Western Constitutionalism: Chartered Rights, Federated Structure and Natural-Law Reasoning in Burke's Theory of Empire," *Pacific Law Journal* 29 (1997), 27.

202. *Speech on Fox's India Bill, WSEB,* v, 381.

203. Ibid., 402.

204. Ibid., 415.

205. "If I am not able to correct a system of oppression and tyranny, that goes to the utter ruin of thirty millions of my fellow-creatures and fellow-subjects, but by some increase to the influence of the Crown, I am ready here to declare, that I, who have been active to reduce it, shall be at least as active and strenuous to restore it again." Ibid., 442.

206. Ibid., 383.

207. Ibid.

208. Marshall, "Introduction," *WSEB,* v, 26.

209. Ibid., vi, 1.

210. *Speech on Nabob of Arcot's Debts, WSEB,* v, 478–617.

211. "I believe, after this exposure of facts, no man can entertain a doubt of the collusion of ministers with the corrupt interest of the delinquents in India." Ibid., 547.

212. Marshall, "Introduction," *WSEB,* v, 26.

213. Burke asked: "India in debt to *them!* For what? . . . What are the articles of commerce, or the branches of manufacture which those gentlemen have carried hence to enrich India? What are the sciences they beamed out to enlighten it? What are the arts they introduced to chear and adorn it? What are the religious, what the moral institutions they have taught among that people as a guide to life, or as a consolation when life is to be no more, that there is an external debt, a debt 'still paying, still to owe,' which must be bound on the present generation in India, and entailed on their mortgaged posterity forever?" *Speech on Nabob of Arcot's Debts, WSEB,* v, 494.

214. "He! the mover! the chairman! the reporter of the Committee of Secrecy! He that brought forth in the utmost detail, in several vast printed folios, the most recondite parts of the politics, the military, the revenues of the British empire in India." Ibid., 550.

215. Ibid., 548–549.

216. Ibid., 549.

217. In the final lines of the speech, Burke dedicated himself to "[w]hoever . . . shall at any time bring before you any thing towards the relief of our distressed fellow-citizens in India, and towards a subversion of the present most corrupt and oppressive system for its government." Ibid., 552.

218. Marshall wrote that "[b]y the winter of 1785 Burke had decided that moves against Hastings should take the form of initiating an impeachment." Marshall, "Introduction," *WSEB,* vi, 2.

219. *Corr.,* v, 243.

220. Marshall, "Introduction," *WSEB,* vi, 1.

221. *Motion for Papers on Hastings, WSEB,* vi, 47–65.

222. Marshall, "Introduction," *WSEB,* vi, 6.

223. Ibid., 7.

224. *Speech on Rohilla War Charge, WSEB,* vi, 91–113.

225. "In this business the question is not between me and Mr. H[astings]. . . . The question is about the fundamental principles of the English Government, the expectations of India and a Rule to future Governors." Ibid., 93.

226. Ibid., 96.

227. Ibid., 108.

228. Ibid., 105.

229. *Speech on Opening of Impeachment, WSEB*, vi, 348–349.

230. *Speech on Rohilla War Charge, WSEB*, vi, 107.

231. Ibid., 109.

232. Ibid. This statement echoes arguments Burke made in his early *Tracts Relating to Popery Laws*. Marshall, "Introduction," *WSEB*, vi, 18. There Burke wrote of an immutable, superior law impressed on human nature by the benevolence of God. See *Tracts Relating to Popery Laws, WSEB*, ix, 455. The importance of a conception of universal justice in imperial policy alluded to in *Tracts* and the Rohilla war speech receives more prominent treatment further along the path to impeachment. See, for example, *Speech on Opening of Impeachment, WSEB*, vi, 350.

233. Marshall, "Introduction," *WSEB*, vi, 14–15.

234. *Speech on Opening of Impeachment, WSEB*, vi, 270.

235. Ibid., 271.

236. Ibid., 271, 272, 276.

237. Ibid., 277, 278.

238. Ibid., 279.

239. Ibid., 345.

240. Ibid., 350.

241. Burke observed that "these Gentlemen have formed a plan of Geographical morality, by which the duties of men in public and private situations are not to be governed by their relations to the Great Governor of the Universe, or by their relations to men, but by climates, degrees of longitude and latitude, parallels not of life but of latitudes. . . . This Geographical morality we do protest against." Ibid., 346. As Marshall observed, "[c]entral to everything in this part of the speech is Burke's total rejection of any kind of moral relativism." Ibid., 268.

242. Ibid., 279.

243. Ibid., 302.

244. "My Lords, I will venture to say of the Governments of Asia that none of them ever had an arbitrary power . . . that Oriental Governments know nothing of this arbitrary power." Ibid., 352, 353.

245. *Speech on Opening of Impeachment, WSEB*, vi, 361. Later in the speech on the second day, Burke also stated "that in Asia as well as in Europe the same Law of Nations prevails, the same principles are continually resorted to, and the same maxims sacredly held and strenuously maintained; and however disobeyed, no man suffers from the breach of them, that does not know how and where to complain of that breach; that Asia is enlightened in that respect as well as Europe." Ibid., 367.

246. "The title of conquest makes no difference at all." Ibid., 350–351.

247. "Let him fly where he will; from law to law. Law, thank God meets him everywhere. . . . I would as willingly have him tried by the law of the Koran, or the Institutes of Tamerlane, as upon the Common Law or the Statute Law of this Kingdom." Ibid., 365.

248. Marshall, "Introduction," *WSEB*, vi, 28.

249. *Speech on Opening of Impeachment, WSEB*, vi, 457–458.

250. Marshall, "Introduction," *WSEB*, vi, 13.

251. O'Brien noted that although Burke failed to impeach Hastings, his efforts on India had resonance and impact after his death when Parliament again turned its attention to reform of the empire in India. O'Brien, *The Great Melody*, 382–383. Kirk wrote that "Burke's eloquence contributed much to the pattern of English imperial administration which endured—though vastly diminished—until recent times. Still more important, Burke expressed principles of justice, universal in

their application, that have lost nothing with the passing of years." R. Kirk, *Edmund Burke: A Genius Reconsidered* (Wilmington, DE, rev. ed., 1997), 97.

252. *Corr.*, viii, 254.

253. Ibid., vi, 10.

254. Ibid.

255. Ibid.

256. Burke wrote in this letter, "I must delay my congratulations on your acquisition of Liberty. You may have made a Revolution, but not a Reformation. You may have subverted Monarchy, but not recover'd freedom." Ibid., 46.

257. O'Brien, *The Great Melody*, 394.

258. Ibid., 397. The stance conflicted with the official policy of Prime Minister Pitt's government, which insisted on a noninterventionist approach to the internal upheavals in France. For a discussion of Pitt's foreign policy in these years, see J. Ehrman, *The Younger Pitt: The Reluctant Transition* (Stanford, 1983). The debate on British involvement in the French Revolution can also be followed in the House of Commons. See in particular the *Debate on the Army Estimates, Parl. Hist.*, xxviii, 323–374.

259. See *Parl. Hist.*, xxviii, 356–357.

260. *Reflections on the Revolution in France, WSEB*, viii, 53–293.

261. Ibid., 81.

262. Ibid., 72. Burke's sympathy with the American colonists also stemmed from his belief that what the Americans wanted was not the abstract "rights of man" but the ancient rights and privileges of Englishmen. His suggestions for reform with respect to Ireland and America similarly contain the principles of reverence for antiquity, of conservation, and of correction.

263. For discussion of Burke's theory regarding rebellion, revolution, and reformation, see M. Freeman, "Burke and the Theory of Revolution," *Review of Politics* 6 (1978), 277–299.

264. *Reflections on the Revolution in France, WSEB*, viii, 86.

265. Ibid., 85–86.

266. Ibid., 216.

267. See *Parl. Hist.*, xxviii, 357, 358.

268. *Reflections on the Revolution in France, WSEB*, viii, 266.

269. Ibid., 189–190.

270. Ibid., 190.

271. See, for example, Thomas Paine's *Rights of Man* (1791) and Mary Wollstonecraft's *Vindication of the Rights of Man* (1790).

272. *Parl. Hist.*, xxix, 249. Fox's admiration for the republican ideals of 1789 led him to oppose any proposals for British involvement in a counterrevolutionary war. Later, when the war in Europe had begun, Fox urged a foreign policy stance that would formally recognize the revolutionary regime in France and enter into peace negotiations with it. See *Parl. Hist.*, xxx, 80–81.

273. O'Brien, *The Great Melody*, 415.

274. *Parl. Hist.*, xxix, 384.

275. Ibid.

276. In particular, Burke singled out religious dissenters, domestic reform movements, and political pamphleteers supportive of the ideas of Thomas Paine. See, for example, Burke's speech against the repeal of the Corporation and Test Acts, a piece of legislation that would have lifted the ban on dissenters from holding public office. *Parl. Hist.*, xxviii, 432–443. For a general discussion of the British government's attempt to address popular turbulence and reform demands during this period, see C. Emsley, *British Society and the French Wars: 1793–1815* (London, 1979); and I. Christie, *Stress and Stability in Late Eighteenth-Century Britain: Reflections on the British Avoidance of Revolution* (Oxford, 1984).

277. See, for instance, Burke's *Observations on the Conduct of the Minority*, *WSEB*, viii, 402–451.

278. *Corr.*, vii, 305.

279. Britain's concern over French absorption of the Austrian Netherlands is treated in T. C. W. Blanning, *The Origins of the French Revolutionary Wars* (London, 1986).

280. *Corr.*, vi, 211.

281. Burke wrote to Britain's foreign representative at Turin, John Trevor, that "I cannot persuade myself that any thing whatsoever can be effected without a great force from abroad." Ibid., 217. Burke believed that France's neighbors had to "act in concert, with all their forces" to restore the ancien régime. Ibid., 218.

282. *Letter to a Member of the National Assembly*, *WSEB*, viii, 294–335.

283. O'Brien, *The Great Melody*, 439.

284. Thomas Jefferson, *The Papers of Thomas Jefferson*, ed. J. P. Boyd (Princeton, 1982), xx, 391.

285. *An Appeal from the New to the Old Whigs*, *Works*, iii, 1–115.

286. *Corr.*, vi, 242.

287. Burke had written to Calonne to provide advice on the size, composition, and purpose of the French émigré army. See ibid., 257.

288. Ibid., 343. The French translates as "to Mr. Burke."

289. Quoted in Marshall, "Introduction," *WSEB*, viii, 44. Marshall commented that "[i]t was not that what might be called Burke's foreign policy had failed that struck contemporaries. It was rather that a private family should have a foreign policy at all." Ibid., 45. See also O'Brien, *The Great Melody*, 467.

290. *Corr.*, vi, 421–422.

291. Ibid., 422.

292. *Thoughts on French Affairs*, *WSEB*, viii, 338–386.

293. Ibid., 340.

294. Ibid., 341.

295. Ibid.

296. Ibid., 342.

297. Ibid., 368.

298. Ibid., 384–385. Burke appealed to the authority of prominent international lawyers such as Emer de Vattel to prove the legality of such an interventionary policy. See Chapter 3.

299. O'Brien recorded that "Lord Grenville, the Foreign Secretary, returned *Thoughts on French Affairs*, 'without a word of Observation'. Pitt, who also had a copy, said nothing either. Burke was hurt, and very much alone." O'Brien, *The Great Melody*, 454. See also *Corr.*, vii, 81.

300. Quoted in O'Brien, *The Great Melody*, 485.

301. *Heads for Consideration on the Present State of Affairs*, *WSEB*, viii, 392. This work followed the French victory over Prussia at Valmy in September 1792 and Prussia's willingness to negotiate with the revolutionaries.

302. Ibid., 399.

303. *Corr.*, vii, 309.

304. As we show later, Burke referred to the French Revolution as a "civil war in Europe."

305. O'Brien, *The Great Melody*, 489.

306. Ibid., 502–503.

307. Sir Gilbert Elliot has left us an account of one meeting between Burke and Pitt in March 1793: "Burke gave him [Pitt] a little political instruction, in a very respectful and cordial way, but with the authority of an old and most informed statesman; and although nobody ever takes the whole of Burke's advice, yet he often, or rather always, furnishes very important and useful matter, *some part* of which sticks and does good. Pitt took it all very patiently and cordially." *Corr.*, vii, 349, n. 4.

308. Burke retired from the House of Commons in 1794, but he continued to be a leading figure in British and European affairs. For his part, Pitt could neither ignore Burke now that the revolution had unfolded as Burke predicted nor stomach the prospect of having Burke's ideas control the policy of his government. Pitt's recall of Fitzwilliam from the viceroyalty in Ireland strained the already tense relationship between Pitt and Burke, but Burke was committed to Pitt as long as Pitt continued to wage war with revolutionary France.

309. Mitchell, "Introduction," *WSEB*, viii, 50. For more on Burke's arguments in support of the émigrés, see Welsh, *Edmund Burke and International Relations*, 150–151.

310. Cited in *Selected Letters of Edmund Burke*, ed. H. C. Mansfield Jr. (Chicago, 1984), 356.

311. The four *Letters on a Regicide Peace* are in *WSEB*, ix: *First Letter* (1796), 187–264; *Second Letter* (1796), 264–296; *Third Letter* (1797), 296–386; and *Fourth Letter* (1795), 44–119.

312. *Fourth Letter on a Regicide Peace*, *WSEB*, ix, 50.

313. *First Letter on a Regicide Peace*, *WSEB*, ix, 199.

314. *Fourth Letter on a Regicide Peace*, *WSEB*, ix, 75.

315. *Third Letter on a Regicide Peace*, *WSEB*, ix, 340.

316. *Second Letter on a Regicide Peace*, *WSEB*, ix, 267.

317. *Letter to a Member of the National Assembly*, *WSEB*, viii, 320. For more on Burke's depiction of "Holy War," see Welsh, *Edmund Burke and International Relations*, 157–161.

318. *Second Letter on a Regicide Peace*, *WSEB*, ix, 290.

319. Quoted in O'Brien, *The Great Melody*, 587.

Chapter Three

320. M. Wight, "Why Is There No International Theory?" in *Diplomatic Investigations*, ed. H. Butterfield and M. Wight (London, 1960), 20. The number of references to Burke in Wight's lectures suggests that Wight considered Burke an important source in his own quest for international theory. See *International Theory: The Three Traditions*, ed. G. Wight and B. Porter (Leicester, 1992).

321. For a summary of this position, see Q. Skinner, "Meaning and Understanding in the History of Ideas," in *Meaning and Context: Quentin Skinner and His Critics*, ed. J. Tully (Cambridge, 1988), 29–67.

322. Q. Skinner, *The Foundations of Modern Political Thought*, vol. 1 (Cambridge, 1978), x.

323. See also Welsh, *Edmund Burke and International Relations*, 12–19; and Bull, "Martin Wight and the Theory of International Relations," in *The Three Traditions*, xix.

324. Ricoeur referred to this objective meaning as the "surplus meaning" of a text. See P. Ricoeur, *Interpretation Theory: Discourse and the Surplus of Meaning* (Fort Worth, TX, 1976).

325. Those such as Harle focus on Burke's Manicheanism and its influence on cold war "images of the enemy." See V. Harle, "Burke the International Theorist—or the War of the Sons of Light and the Sons of Darkness," in *European Values in International Relations*, ed. V. Harle (London, 1990), 58–79. Others draw on Burke in order to develop certain traditions of international theory. Boucher, for example, cited Burke as an archetype for his school of "historical reason." See D. Boucher, "The Character of the History of the Philosophy of International Relations and the Case of Edmund Burke," *Review of International Studies* 17 (1990), 127–148. Notable exceptions are Vincent, "Edmund Burke and the Theory of International Relations"; Welsh, *Edmund Burke and International Relations;* and Welsh, "Edmund Burke and the Commonwealth of Europe."

326. See Wight, *The Three Traditions*, 7–24.

327. See, for example, T. Dunne, *Inventing International Society: A History of the English School* (London, 1998).

328. T. Dunne, "Mythology or Methodology? Traditions in International Theory," *Review of International Studies* 19 (1993), 306.

329. Ibid., 307.

330. Wight, *The Three Traditions*, 15.

331. Ibid., 17.

332. Ibid., 13.

333. Ibid., 8.

334. Ibid., 12.

335. *Corr.*, vi, 48; Letter to the Sheriffs of Bristol, WSEB, iii, 316. See Welsh, *Edmund Burke and International Relations*, 25–26; and B. Frohnen, *Virtue and the Promise of Conservatism: The Legacy of Burke and Tocqueville* (Lawrence, KS, 1993), 76–80 (analyzing the importance of prudence in Burke's thinking).

336. Quoted in Courtney, *Montesquieu and Burke*, 156.

337. According to Auerbach, Burke's emphasis on balance and equilibrium derives from his aesthetic preference for "harmonious proportion." See Auerbach, *The Conservative Illusion*, 35. For further discussion of Burke's aesthetic theory, see C. Reid, *Edmund Burke and the Practice of Political Writing* (Dublin, 1985), 34–50.

338. *Annual Register* (1762), 227.

339. *Reflections on the Revolution in France*, WSEB, viii, 293.

340. *Appeal from the New to the Old Whigs*, *Works*, iii, 110.

341. See Welsh, *Edmund Burke and International Relations*, 26–29.

342. B. T. Wilkins, *The Problem of Burke's Political Philosophy* (Oxford, 1967), 91.

343. Burke believed that passion and emotion often take control of the rational faculty. "Men often act right from their feelings," he stated, "who afterwards reason but ill on them from principle." *Philosophical Inquiry*, *Works*, i, 86. As a result, reason plays a subordinate part to sentiment and emotion in Burke's political theory.

344. Ibid., 84–85. See C. Murphy, "The Grotian Vision of World Order," *American Journal of International Law* 76 (1982), 483.

345. Quoted in C. Parkin, *The Moral Basis of Burke's Political Thought* (Cambridge, 1956), 22.

346. See Stanlis, *Edmund Burke*, 45–46.

347. *Reflections on the Revolution in France*, WSEB, viii, 109.

348. *Speech on Opening of Impeachment*, WSEB, vi, 316–317.

349. For Burke's views on contract theory, see H. C. Mansfield Jr., "Introduction," in *Selected Letters of Edmund Burke*, 12–13.

350. *Observations on the Conduct of the Minority*, WSEB, viii, 439.

351. Cobban, *Edmund Burke and the Revolt Against the Eighteenth Century*, 51.

352. *First Letter on a Regicide Peace*, WSEB, ix, 253.

353. "The truth is that France is out of itself—The moral France is separated from the geographical. The master of the house is expelled, and the robbers are in possession." *Remarks on the Policy of the Allies*, WSEB, viii, 465.

354. F. H. Hinsley, *Nationalism and the International System* (London, 1973), 41. Burke's view of nation is more than territorial or administrative, but it stops short of the romantic ideas associated with the later doctrine of national self-determination. In particular, although he recognized that each nation possesses a certain distinguishable "character" (*Reflections on the Revolution in France*, WSEB, viii, 137), it is nationality (as opposed to nationalism) that influenced his thinking. For Burke, national character was the outcome of living under shared institutions and social practices rather than an objective or preordained fact. For more on Burke's idea of nation and nationality, see Welsh, *Edmund Burke and International Relations*, 53–55; and Cobban, *Edmund Burke and the Revolt Against the Eighteenth Century*, 130.

355. Quoted in Parkin, *The Moral Basis of Burke's Political Thought*, 59. We use the terms "nation" and "state" interchangeably since Burke seems to have made little analytical distinction between them.

356. *Reflections on the Revolution in France*, *WSEB*, viii, 146–147.

357. Ibid., 147.

358. Ibid., 291.

359. *Letter to Sheriffs of Bristol*, *WSEB*, iii, 318.

360. Vincent, "Edmund Burke," 212. See also Welsh, *Edmund Burke and International Relations*, 115–140.

361. *Corr.*, vii, 176–177.

362. See Welsh, *Edmund Burke and International Relations*, 32–34.

363. *Annual Register* (1772), 3; *First Letter on a Regicide Peace*, *WSEB*, ix, 248.

364. Ibid.

365. Wight, *The Three Traditions*, 206–207.

366. *First Letter on a Regicide Peace*, *WSEB*, ix, 237.

367. *Parl. Hist.*, xxii, 229.

368. Ibid., 228.

369. *Letter to the Sheriffs of Bristol*, *WSEB*, iii, 301, 308.

370. See Welsh, *Edmund Burke and International Relations*, 34–38.

371. *Third Letter on a Regicide Peace*, *WSEB*, ix, 338.

372. *Annual Register* (1772), 2. Burke noted that the same balance of power had contributed to the "fortune and glory" of ancient Greece.

373. *Third Letter on a Regicide Peace*, *WSEB*, ix, 339; *Thoughts on French Affairs*, *WSEB*, viii, 351–352.

374. "It is always the interest of Great Britain that the power of France should be kept within the bounds of moderation. It is not her interest that the power should be wholly annihilated in the system of Europe." *Remarks on the Policy of the Allies*, *WSEB*, viii, 352.

375. Here Burke was following Vattel. See Hinsley, *Nationalism and the International System*, 79–80.

376. For the difference between a "natural" and "contrived" balance of power, see E. V. Gulick, *Europe's Classical Balance of Power* (New York, 1967), 35.

377. *Annual Register* (1772), 3.

378. M. Wight, "The Balance of Power," in *The Bases of International Order*, ed. A. James (London, 1973), 108.

379. *Annual Register* (1760), 2; ibid., (1772), 3.

380. Ibid., 2.

381. Vincent, "Edmund Burke," 210.

382. See Welsh, *Edmund Burke and International Relations*, 30–31.

383. J. Coniff, "Burke on Political Economy: The Nature and Extent of State Authority," *Review of Politics* 49 (1987), 490–491; and J. Coniff, *The Useful Cobbler: Edmund Burke and the Politics of Progress* (Albany, NY, 1994), 114. Those who interpret Burke as a "market liberal" include D. P. M. Barrington, "Edmund Burke as an Economist," *Economica* 21 (1954), 252–258; F. Petrella Jr., "Edmund Burke: A Liberal Practitioner of Political Economy," *Modern Age* 8 (1963–1964), 52–60; P. Stanlis, *Edmund Burke and the Natural Law* (Ann Arbor, MI, 1958); I. Kramnick, *The Rage of Edmund Burke* (New York, 1977); Macpherson, *Burke;* and G. Himmelfarb, *The Idea of Poverty* (New York, 1984).

384. *Speech on Economical Reform*, *Works*, ii, 55–126; *Thoughts and Details on Scarcity*, *WSEB*, ix, 119–145.

385. Barrington, "Edmund Burke as an Economist," 252.

386. See Wecter, "Adam Smith and Burke"; Dunn, "Adam Smith and Edmund Burke: Complementary Contemporaries"; Barrington, "Edmund Burke as Economist," 258; and Fay, *Burke and Adam Smith*.

387. Welsh, *Edmund Burke and International Relations*, 31.

388. In this respect Burke parted company with Smith, who recommended that the East India Company's monopoly on trade be replaced with a system open to other foreign merchants. See *Ninth Report of the Select Committee, WSEB*, v, 196.

389. As Coniff wrote, "[T]hough Burke usually favored free trade and a free economy, he did so as a matter of pragmatic policy choice not one of abstract principle." Coniff, "Burke on Political Economy," 493. See also Coniff, *The Useful Cobbler*, 116 (arguing that "Burke usually favored free trade and a free economy, but he did so as a matter of utilitarian policy choice rather than abstract principle").

390. See *Letter to the Rt. Hon. Hen. Dundas with the Sketch of Negro Code, Works*, v, 521–544.

391. Coniff, "Burke on Political Economy," 507.

392. As Coniff argued, Burke's "economics was both sophisticated and consistent with his politics." Coniff, *The Useful Cobbler*, 136.

393. *Speech on Opening of Impeachment, WSEB*, vi, 350. Although this passage suggests Burke's adherence to an idea of natural law, the specific nature of his appeals to that law should be clarified. In this regard, many neoconservative interpretations of Burke as a disciple of Thomas Aquinas read too much into Burke's texts. See, for example, Stanlis, *Edmund Burke and the Natural Law*. When Burke appropriated natural law vocabulary, he was contributing to the secularization of the term. Though he maintained that natural law was binding because it ultimately reflected God's will, he discovered its content through human custom and precedent—the "wisdom of the species." For more on the debate over Burke's attitude to natural law, see F. O'Gorman, *Edmund Burke: His Political Philosophy* (London, 1973), 12–13; and Coniff, *The Useful Cobbler*, 37–48.

394. Following Grotius, Burke diverged from a purely positivist view of international law as the sum of those rules expressly consented to by states. See H. Bull, "The Importance of Grotius in the Study of International Relations," in *Hugo Grotius and International Relations*, ed. H. Bull, B. Kingsbury, and A. Roberts (Oxford, 1990), 78–80.

395. *Parl. Hist.*, xxii, 228–229.

396. J. Davidson, "Natural Law and International Law in Burke," *Review of Politics* 21 (1959), 485. In this sense, Burke was engaged in the same balancing act as his contemporaries, Wolff and Vattel. Both created a voluntary law of nations as a link between natural and positive law, locating its content in the rules devised to regulate European interstate relations. See Welsh, *Edmund Burke and International Relations*, 44–45.

397. As Stanlis wrote, "In considering the individual differences and circumstances of mankind at large, India excepted, this common law of the European commonwealth is the broadest frame of reference Burke ever made." Stanlis, *Edmund Burke and the Natural Law*, 89.

398. *First Letter on Regicide Peace, WSEB*, ix, 240.

399. "All writers on the science of policy are agreed, and they agree with experience, that all governments must frequently infringe the rules of justice to support themselves; that truth must give way to dissimulation; honesty to convenience; and humanity itself to the reigning interest." *A Vindication of Natural Society, Works*, i, 21.

400. H. Bull, "Martin Wight and the Theory of International Relations," *British Journal of International Studies* 2 (1976), 105.

401. *Remarks on the Policy of the Allies, WSEB*, ix, 490.

402. M. Wight, "Western Values in International Relations," in *Diplomatic Investigations*, ed. H. Butterfield and M. Wight (London, 1960), 123. As Wight explained, "It follows that the whole conception of policy is broadened and capable of being suffused with moral value. Political expedience

itself has to consult the moral sense of the politician himself. Thus it is softened into prudence, which is a moral virtue." Ibid., 128.

403. "All persons possessing any portion of power ought to be strongly and awefully impressed with an idea that they act in trust; and that they are to account for their conduct in that trust to the one great master, author and founder of society." *Reflections on the Revolution in France, WSEB*, viii, 143.

404. On Burke's theory of trusteeship, see Coniff, *The Useful Cobbler*, 137–160.

405. Vincent, "Edmund Burke," 205; and Cobban, *Edmund Burke and the Revolt Against the Eighteenth Century*, 256. For analysis on Burke and medievalism, see Welsh, *Edmund Burke and International Relations*, 49–69.

406. According to Nisbet, a fundamental feature of the feudal political structure was its synthesis of diversity and unity. This reconciliation was achieved through a dissolution of power and a toleration for intermediate institutions (church, family, guild, etc.) and sources of authority. See R. Nisbet, *Conservatism* (Milton Keynes, UK, 1986). In Burke's theory it is in these latter organizations— "the little platoons"—that individuals first experience community: "To be attached to the little subdivision is the first principle . . . of public affection. It is the first link in the series by which we proceed towards a love to our country, and to mankind." *Reflections on the Revolution in France, WSEB*, viii, 97–98.

407. For analysis of Burke's theory of empire, see Frohnen and Reid, "Diversity in Western Constitutionalism," 27.

408. *Speech on Conciliation with America, WSEB*, iii, 132.

409. Ibid., 125.

410. Contrast this interpretation of Burke with Rousseau's claim that empire gained by force and deception remains forever illegitimate. See *First Version of the Social Contract*, in J. J. Rousseau, *Rousseau on International Relations*, ed. S. Hoffmann and D. P. Fidler (Oxford, 1991), 116.

411. *First Letter on a Regicide Peace, WSEB*, ix, 248. For a full treatment of this Burkean concept, see Welsh, *Edmund Burke and International Relations*, 70–80.

412. Vincent, "Edmund Burke," 211.

413. *First Letter on a Regicide Peace, WSEB*, ix, 248.

414. Stanlis, *Edmund Burke*, 65–66.

415. S. Hoffmann and D. P. Fidler, "Introduction," in *Rousseau on International Relations*, xlvi.

416. See generally I. Crowe, "Edmund Burke on Manners," *Modern Age* 39 (1997), 389.

417. *Reflections on the Revolution in France, WSEB*, viii, 127. In fact, Burke's attempt to distinguish the commonwealth of Europe from the non-European societies in Asia, the New World, and the Ottoman Empire forms an integral part of the definition of the commonwealth. See Marshall, "Introduction," *WSEB*, vi, 20.

418. *First Letter on a Regicide Peace, WSEB*, ix, 242.

419. Ibid., 249.

420. Ibid., 247.

421. Ibid., 248.

422. See H. Bull, "The Grotian Conception of International Society," in *Diplomatic Investigations*, ed. H. Butterfield and M. Wight (London, 1960), 51–73. On Vattel see A. Hurrell, "Vattel: Pluralism and Its Limits," in *Classical Theories of International Relations*, ed. I. Clark and I. B. Neumann (London, 1996), 233.

423. Hinsley, *Nationalism and the International System*, 71. The peace project of Saint Pierre is discussed in F. H. Hinsley, *Power and the Pursuit of Peace* (Cambridge, 1963), 33–45.

424. Wight, "Western Values in International Relations," 113.

425. See R. J. Vincent, *Nonintervention and International Order* (Princeton, 1974), 69.

426. This noninterventionist stance most commonly derives from an analogy between the autonomy and equality of states with the autonomy and equality of individuals. Alternatively, nonin-

terventionism can be the product of a contractarian philosophy. In this case, the state is granted an autonomous moral character by virtue of its role in safeguarding the rights and liberties of individuals, which have been transferred to the sovereign through the social contract. See C. Beitz, *Political Theory and International Relations* (Princeton, 1979), 75–77.

427. This position was also exemplified by the Austrian chancellor Klemens von Metternich at the Congress of Vienna in 1815. See H. Kissinger, *A World Restored* (London, 1957).

428. *First Letter on a Regicide Peace*, WSEB, ix, 199.

429. Ibid., 249.

430. See M. S. Anderson, "Eighteenth Century Theories of the Balance of Power," in *Studies in Diplomatic History: Essays in Memory of David Bayne Horn*, ed. R. Hatton and M. S. Anderson (London, 1970), 183–198.

431. Hinsley, *Nationalism and the International System*, 82.

432. *Annual Register* (1772), 1.

433. *Third Letter on a Regicide Peace*, WSEB, ix, 306; and *Corr.*, vii, 176.

434. See E. Vattel, *Le Droit des gens*, bk. 2, chap. 4, para. 53. Extracts from Vattel's *Droit*, complete with Burke's annotations, are included as an appendix in an older edition of the *Thoughts on French Affairs*. See *Three Memorials on French Affairs Written in the Years 1791, 1792 and 1793. By the Late Right Hon. Edmund Burke* (London, 1797).

435. Appendix to *Three Memorials* (*Le Droit des gens*, bk. 2, chap. 4, para. 70).

436. *First Letter on a Regicide Peace*, WSEB, ix, 239.

437. Appendix to *Three Memorials* (*Le Droit des gens*, bk. 2, chap. 4, para. 56). In letters to his son, Richard, Burke advised him to consult Vattel's works on the legality of armed intervention. See *Corr.*, vi, 317. Burke advanced the same argument about the legality of intervention in civil conflict fifteen years earlier to justify French involvement in the American rebellion.

438. *Remarks on the Policy of the Allies*, WSEB, viii, 474 (emphasis added).

439. *Corr.*, vii, 176.

440. Ibid.

441. *Heads for Consideration*, WSEB, viii, 394. Again, Burke invoked historical precedents for this kind of intervention: German assistance to the Protestant princes, English support for Henry IV of France, and English and Dutch intervention to support Charles VI of Spain.

442. *First Letter on a Regicide Peace*, WSEB, ix, 250.

443. Ibid.

444. Ibid., 251.

445. See, for example, Welsh, *Edmund Burke and International Relations*, 172–173.

446. As Davidson wrote, what "saved Burke from a Hobbesian view of international affairs was his belief in the existence of a community beyond the nation capable of a moralizing influence." Davidson, "Natural Law and International Law in Burke," 491.

447. Wight himself stated that if Burke is "apparently marching sturdily along the road" of rationalism, "his movements are erratic." See Wight, *The Three Traditions*, 15.

448. *First Letter on a Regicide Peace*, WSEB, ix, 247.

449. See generally Dunne, *Inventing International Society*.

450. H. Bull, *The Anarchical Society* (London, 1977), 13.

451. Welsh, *Edmund Burke and International Relations*, 173 (citing *First Letter on a Regicide Peace*, WSEB, ix, 247).

452. Vincent, "Edmund Burke," 205.

453. See, for example, Bull, *The Anarchical Society*, 13–16.

454. See generally I. Neumann and J. M. Welsh, "The 'Other' in European Self-Definition: An Addendum to Literature on International Society," *Review of International Studies* 17 (1991), 327.

455. *First Letter on a Regicide Peace*, WSEB, ix, 247.

456. The issue of "cultural bonding" can be seen in debates over European identity in the context of the European Union. According to some scholars, the frontiers of "economic Europe" should be brought more into line with those of "cultural Europe" if the engine of European integration is to keep moving. See W. Wallace, *The Transformation of Western Europe* (London, 1990).

457. Welsh, "Edmund Burke and the Commonwealth of Europe," 182.

458. See *First Letter on a Regicide Peace, WSEB,* ix, 242–244. Comparison of Europe with other societies is further explored in Neumann and Welsh, "The 'Other' in European Self-Definition."

459. *Parl. Hist.,* xxix, 76–78.

460. See generally H. Bull and A. Watson, eds., *The Expansion of International Society* (Oxford, 1984).

461. S. Murden, "Cultural Conflict in International Relations: The West and Islam," in *The Globalization of World Politics,* ed. J. Baylis and S. Smith (Oxford, 1997), 378.

462. B. Kingsbury, "Confronting Difference: The Puzzling Durability of Gentili's Combination of Pragmatic Pluralism and Normative Judgment," *American Journal of International Law* 92 (1998), 713.

463. For analysis on liberalism, see M. A. Zacher and R. A. Matthew, "Liberal International Theory: Common Threads, Divergent Strands," in *Controversies in International Relations Theory,* ed. C. Kegley (New York, 1995), 107; S. Burchill, "Liberal Internationalism," in *Theories of International Relations,* ed. S. Burchill and A. Linklater (London, 1996), 28; and T. Dunne, "Liberalism," in *The Globalization of World Politics,* ed. J. Baylis and S. Smith (Oxford, 1997), 147.

464. S. Smith, "New Approaches to International Theory," in *The Globalization of World Politics,* ed. J. Baylis and S. Smith (Oxford, 1997), 168.

465. Ibid., 172–183.

466. Ibid., 172.

467. C. Brown, *International Relations Theory: New Normative Approaches* (Hemel Hempstead, UK, 1992), 3–4.

468. Smith, "New Approaches," 173 (citing C. Brown).

469. According to Smith, "[c]osmopolitanism is the view that any normative theory of world politics should focus on either humanity as a whole or on individuals; on the other hand, communitarians maintain that the appropriate focus is the political community (the state)." Ibid.

470. See *Articles of Impeachment, WSEB,* vi, 147–156; *Speech on Opening the Impeachment,* in ibid., 420–421; and *Evidence on the Begums of Oudh,* in ibid., 474–479. On Marie Antoinette, see *Reflections on the Revolution in France,* in ibid., viii, 126–127.

471. L. M. G. Zerilli, *Signifying Woman: Culture and Chaos in Rousseau, Burke, and Mill* (Ithaca, 1994), 60.

472. M. Freeman, *Edmund Burke and the Critique of Political Radicalism* (Oxford, 1980), 100.

473. P. J. Marshall, "Introductory Note," to *Evidence on the Begums of Oudh, WSEB,* vi, 475.

474. Kramnick, *The Rage of Edmund Burke,* 137.

475. For more on feminist international relations theory, see J. True, "Feminism," in *Theories of International Relations,* ed. S. Burchill and A. Linklater (London, 1996), 210–251; and J. J. Pettman, "Gender Issues," in *The Globalization of World Politics,* ed. J. Baylis and S. Smith (Oxford, 1997), 483–497.

476. R. Devetak, "Critical Theory," in *Theories of International Relations,* ed. S. Burchill and A. Linklater (London, 1996), 147, 151.

477. Ibid., 155–156.

478. Ibid., 156.

479. Ibid., 173.

480. Ibid., 150.

481. Ibid., 169.

482. Smith, "New Approaches," 178.

483. Ibid., 179.

484. Ibid., 180 (citing M. Mann).

485. Ibid., 183. On postmodernism see also R. Devetak, "Postmodernism," in *Theories of International Relations*, ed. S. Burchill and A. Linklater (London, 1996), 179–209.

486. Smith, "New Approaches," 181.

487. A. Wendt, "Anarchy Is What States Make of It: The Social Construction of Power Politics," *International Organization* 46 (1992), 395.

488. Ibid., 394.

Chapter Four

489. Quoted in O'Brien, *The Great Melody*, 47.

490. Quoted in ibid., 590.

491. Macpherson, *Burke*, 74. See, for example, P. J. Stanlis, "Edmund Burke in the Twentieth Century," in *The Relevance of Edmund Burke*, ed. P. J. Stanlis (New York, 1964), 53; M. Almond, "Burke After the Cold War: Bourgeois Triumphalist or Cassandra?" in *Edmund Burke: His Life and Legacy*, ed. I. Crowe (Dublin, 1997), 169; Frohnen and Reid, "Diversity in Western Constitutionalism," 27; and J. McCue, *Edmund Burke and Our Present Discontents* (London, 1997), 9.

492. For a recent example of this kind of debate, see T. Eagleton, "Saving Burke from the Tories," *New Statesman* 126 (July 4, 1997), 52 (arguing that the left needs "to reclaim" Burke from the conservative right).

493. Address at Trinity College, March 1947.

494. O'Brien, *The Great Melody*, lxi. For a different treatment of Burke's legacy as a crusader, see Welsh, *Edmund Burke and International Relations*, 173–179. Welsh showed that Burke's thinking is relevant for understanding not only crusading anti-Communists such as John Foster Dulles but also realists such as George Kennan.

495. J. R. Bolton, "The Prudent Irishman," *National Interest* (December 1997), 74.

496. Ibid., 74.

497. Ibid. See also R. Dahrendorf, *Reflections on the Revolution in Europe* (London, 1990), 164 (praising Burke's prudence and moderation as guides for statecraft).

498. *Remarks on the Policy of the Allies*, WSEB, viii, 490–491.

499. *First Letter on a Regicide Peace*, WSEB, ix, 253.

500. See S. Huntington, "Clash of Civilizations?" *Foreign Affairs* (Summer 1993), 22.

501. Murden, "Cultural Conflict," 378.

502. B. R. Barber, *Jihad vs. McWorld: How the Planet Is Both Falling Apart and Coming Together and What It Means for Democracy* (New York, 1995).

503. F. Zakaria, "Culture Is Destiny: A Conversation with Lee Kuan Yew," *Foreign Affairs* (March/April 1994), 125.

504. N. J. Wheeler and T. Dunne, "Hedley Bull's Pluralism of the Intellect and Solidarism of the Will," *International Affairs* 72 (1996), 91–107.

505. Bull, *The Anarchical Society*, 317.

506. M. W. Doyle, "Kant, Liberal Legacies, and Foreign Affairs," *Philosophy and Public Affairs* 12 (1983), 205, 323; and F. Fukuyama, *The End of History and the Last Man* (New York, 1992).

507. Kingsbury has argued that the construction of "a universal justification on the basis of the rectitude of the moral and political theory of the West . . . faces profound normative challenges that have scarcely been considered, let alone resolved, and in any case is far from materializing in practice." Kingsbury, "Confronting Difference," 723. See also Dunne, "Liberalism," 160–162 (pointing to a crisis of liberalism in the 1990s).

508. Murden, "Cultural Conflict," 378.

509. Ibid., 377–378.

510. See, for example, S. Marks, "Guarding the Gates with Two Faces: International Law and Political Reconstruction," *Indiana Journal of Global Legal Studies* 6 (1999), 457–495.

511. Murden, "Cultural Conflict," 378.

512. On the challenge of cultural relativism to human rights theory, see R. J. Vincent, *Human Rights and International Relations* (Cambridge, 1986), 37–57. See also C. Brown, "Human Rights," in *The Globalization of World Politics,* ed. J. Baylis and S. Smith (Oxford, 1997), 479–480 (analyzing cultural challenges to the universalism of human rights).

513. Vincent, *Human Rights and International Relations,* 55.

514. *Speech on Opening of Impeachment, WSEB,* vi, 365.

515. Brown, "Human Rights," 480 (arguing "it may be that an apparently principle rejection of universalism is, in fact, no more than a rationalization for tyranny").

516. *Corr.,* vii, 176–177.

517. Welsh, *Edmund Burke and International Relations,* 139.

518. For a statement of the principle of universal jurisdiction, see I. Brownlie, *Principles of Public International Law* (Oxford, 4th ed., 1990), 304–305.

519. J. R. Bolton, "The Global Prosecutors: Hunting War Criminals in the Name of Utopia," *Foreign Affairs* 78, 1 (1999), 160.

520. Ibid., 162.

521. On the first point, see *Remarks on the Policy of the Allies, WSEB,* ix, 493–498. See also Welsh, *Edmund Burke and International Relations,* 165–166.

522. *Remarks on the Policy of the Allies, WSEB,* ix, 493.

523. Ibid., 494–497.

524. Ibid., 495. See also Welsh, *Edmund Burke and International Relations,* 166.

525. R. Tooze, "International Political Economy in an Age of Globalization," in *The Globalization of World Politics,* ed. J. Baylis and S. Smith (Oxford, 1997), 226–227.

526. G. R. Walker and M. A. Fox, "Globalization: An Analytical Framework," *Indiana Journal of Global Legal Studies* 3 (1996), 380.

527. See Tooze, "International Political Economy," 226–227.

528. C. W. Maynes, "Squandering Triumph: The West Botched the Post–Cold War World," *Foreign Affairs* 78, 1 (1999), 16.

529. Ibid., 16–17.

530. These features of Burke's thought, according to O'Neil, make Burke a better guide to economic development for developing countries than Marx. See D. J. O'Neil, "Edmund Burke, Karl Marx, and the Contemporary Third World," *Modern Age* 34 (1992), 349.

531. Almond, "Burke After the Cold War," 169.

532. See N. J. Wheeler, "Guardian Angel or Global Gangster: A Review of the Ethical Claims of International Society," *Political Studies* 44 (1996), 123 (discussing the growing importance of moral claims to the international society tradition).

533. Ibid., 127.

534. Wheeler and Dunne, "Hedley Bull's Pluralism of the Intellect and Solidarism of the Will," 107.

535. Wheeler, "Guardian Angel or Global Gangster," 128.

536. Murden, "Cultural Conflict," 377.

537. *Speech on Nabob of Arcot's Debts, WSEB,* v, 494.

538. *Remarks on the Policy of the Allies, WSEB,* viii, 499.

Bibliography

Primary Sources

Annual Register 1760, 1762, 1772.

Burke, Edmund. *The Correspondence of Edmund Burke.* 10 vols. Ed. T. W. Copeland. Chicago, 1958–1978.

_____. *Selected Letters of Edmund Burke.* Ed. H. C. Mansfield Jr. Chicago, 1984.

_____. *Three Memorials on French Affairs Written in the Years 1791, 1792 and 1793. By the Late Right Hon. Edmund Burke.* London, 1797.

_____. *The Works of the Right Honourable Edmund Burke.* 6 vols. Bohn's British Classics. London, 1854–1856.

_____. *The Writings and Speeches of Edmund Burke.* Vols. 2, 3, 5, 6, 8, and 9 published to date. Gen. ed. P. Langford. Oxford, 1981– .

Cobbett, W., ed. *The Parliamentary History of England from the Earliest Period to the Year 1803.* 36 vols. London, 1806–1820.

Burke Biographies

Ayling, S. *Edmund Burke: His Life and Opinions.* London, 1988.

Bisset, R. *Life of Edmund Burke.* 2nd ed. London, 1800.

Burke, P. *Public and Domestic Life of the Rt. Hon. Edmund Burke.* London, 1853.

Morley, J. *Burke.* London, 1879.

O'Brien, C. C. *The Great Melody: A Thematic Biography of Edmund Burke.* London, 1992.

Samuels, A. P. I. *Early Life, Correspondence, and Writings of Edmund Burke.* Cambridge, 1923.

Secondary Sources on Burke

Almond, M. "Burke After the Cold War: Bourgeois Triumphalist or Cassandra?" In *Edmund Burke: His Life and Legacy,* ed. I. Crowe. Dublin, 1997, 159.

Auerbach, M. *The Conservative Illusion.* New York, 1959.

Barrington, D. P. M. "Edmund Burke as an Economist." *Economica* 21 (1954), 252.

Bolton, J. R. "The Prudent Irishman." *National Interest,* December 1997, 67.

Boucher, D. "The Character of the History of the Philosophy of International Relations and the Case of Edmund Burke." *Review of International Studies* 17 (1990), 127.

Canavan, F. *The Political Economy of Edmund Burke.* New York, 1995.

Cobban, A. *Edmund Burke and the Revolt Against the Eighteenth Century.* London, 1929.

Coniff, J. "Burke on Political Economy: The Nature and Extent of State Authority." *Review of Politics* 49 (1987), 490.

_____. *The Useful Cobbler: Edmund Burke and the Politics of Progress.* Albany, NY, 1994.

Courtney, C. P. *Montesquieu and Burke.* Oxford, 1963.

Crowe, I. "Edmund Burke on Manners." *Modern Age* 39 (1997), 389.

Davidson, J. "Natural Law and International Law in Burke." *Review of Politics* 21 (1959), 485.

Dunn, W. C. "Adam Smith and Edmund Burke: Complementary Contemporaries." *Southern Economic Journal* 7 (1941), 330.

Eagleton, T. "Saving Burke from the Tories." *New Statesman* 126 (July 4, 1997), 32.

Fay, C. R. *Burke and Adam Smith.* Belfast, 1956.

Freeman, M. "Burke and the Theory of Revolution." *Review of Politics* 6 (1978), 277.

_____. *Edmund Burke and the Critique of Political Radicalism.* Oxford, 1980.

Frohnen, B. *Virtue and the Promise of Conservatism: The Legacy of Burke and Tocqueville.* Lawrence, KS, 1993.

Frohnen, B. P., and Reid, C. J., Jr. "Diversity in Western Constitutionalism: Chartered Rights, Federated Structure and Natural-Law Reasoning in Burke's Theory of Empire." *Pacific Law Journal* 29 (1997), 27.

Fuchs, M. *Edmund Burke, Ireland, and the Fashioning of the Self.* Oxford, 1996.

Furber, H. "Edmund Burke and India." *Bengal Past and Present* 76 (1957), 11.

Hampsher-Monk, I. "Introduction." In *The Political Philosophy of Edmund Burke,* ed. I. Hampsher-Monk. London, 1987, 1.

Harle, V. "Burke the International Theorist—or the War of the Sons of Light and the Sons of Darkness." In *European Values in International Relations,* ed. V. Harle. London, 1990, 58.

Kirk, R. *Edmund Burke: A Genius Reconsidered.* Rev. ed. Wilmington, DE, 1997.

Kramnick, I. *The Rage of Edmund Burke.* New York, 1977.

Langford, P. "Introduction." In *The Writings and Speeches of Edmund Burke,* ii, ed. P. Langford. Oxford, 1981, 1.

Macpherson, C. B. *Burke.* Oxford, 1980.

Mahoney, T. H. D. *Edmund Burke and Ireland.* Cambridge, MA, 1960.

Mansfield, H. C., Jr. "Introduction." In *Selected Letters of Edmund Burke,* ed. H. C. Mansfield Jr. Chicago, 1984.

Marshall, P. J. "Introduction." In *The Writings and Speeches of Edmund Burke,* v, ed. P. J. Marshall. Oxford, 1981, 1.

_____. "Introduction." In *The Writings and Speeches of Edmund Burke,* vi, ed. P. J. Marshall. Oxford, 1991, 1.

McCue, J. *Edmund Burke and Our Present Discontents.* London, 1997.

McDowell, R. B. "Introduction." In *The Writings and Speeches of Edmund Burke,* ix, ed. R. B. McDowell. Oxford, 1991, 1.

McGee, R. W. "Edmund Burke and Adam Smith: Pioneers in the Field of Law and Economics." *Australian Law Journal* 66 (1992), 262.

Mitchell, L. G. "Introduction." In *The Writings and Speeches of Edmund Burke,* viii, ed. L. G. Mitchell. Oxford, 1989, 1.

O'Brien, W. *Edmund Burke as an Irishman.* 2nd ed. Dublin, 1926.

O'Gorman, F. *Edmund Burke: His Political Philosophy.* London, 1973.

O'Neil, D. J. "Edmund Burke, Karl Marx, and the Contemporary Third World." *Modern Age* 34 (1992), 349.

Osborn, A. M. *Rousseau and Burke: A Study of the Idea of Liberty in Eighteenth-Century Political Thought.* Oxford, 1940.

Parkin, C. *The Moral Basis of Burke's Political Thought.* Cambridge, 1956.

Petrella, F., Jr. "Edmund Burke: A Liberal Practitioner of Political Economy." *Modern Age* 8 (1963–1964), 52.

Reid, C. *Edmund Burke and the Practice of Political Writing.* Dublin, 1985.

Stanlis, P. J. *Edmund Burke and the Natural Law.* Ann Arbor, MI, 1958.

———. "Edmund Burke in the Twentieth Century." In *The Relevance of Edmund Burke,* ed. P. J. Stanlis. New York, 1964, 21.

———. *Edmund Burke: The Enlightenment and Revolution.* New Brunswick, NJ, 1991.

Vincent, R. J. "Edmund Burke and the Theory of International Relations." *Review of International Studies* 10 (1984), 206.

Wecter, D. "Adam Smith and Burke." *Notes and Queries* 174 (1938), 310.

Welsh, J. M. *Edmund Burke and International Relations: The Commonwealth of Europe and the Crusade Against the French Revolution.* New York, 1995.

———. "Edmund Burke and the Commonwealth of Europe: The Cultural Bases of International Order." In *Classical Theories of International Relations,* ed. I. Clark and I. B. Neumann. London, 1996, 173.

Whelan, F. G. *Edmund Burke and India: Political Morality and Empire.* Pittsburgh, 1996.

Wilkins, B. T. *The Problem of Burke's Political Philosophy.* Oxford, 1967.

Zerilli, L. M. G. *Signifying Woman: Culture and Chaos in Rousseau, Burke, and Mill.* Ithaca, 1994.

General Secondary Sources

Anderson, M. S. "Eighteenth Century Theories of the Balance of Power." In *Studies in Diplomatic History: Essays in Memory of David Bayne Horn,* ed. R. Hatton and M. S. Anderson. London, 1970, 183.

Barber, B. R. *Jihad vs. McWorld: How the Planet Is Both Falling Apart and Coming Together and What It Means for Democracy.* New York, 1995.

Beitz, C. *Political Theory and International Relations.* Princeton, 1979.

Blanning, T. C. W. *The Origins of the French Revolutionary Wars.* London, 1986.

Bolton, J. R. "The Global Prosecutors: Hunting War Criminals in the Name of Utopia." *Foreign Affairs* 78, 1 (1999), 157.

Brown, C. "Human Rights." In *The Globalization of World Politics,* ed. J. Baylis and S. Smith. Oxford, 1997, 469.

———. *International Relations Theory: New Normative Approaches.* Hemel Hempstead, UK, 1992.

Brownlie, I. *Principles of Public International Law.* 4th ed. Oxford, 1990.

Bull, H. *The Anarchical Society.* London, 1977.

———. "The Grotian Conception of International Society." In *Diplomatic Investigations,* ed. H. Butterfield and M. Wight. London, 1960, 51.

———. "The Importance of Grotius in the Study of International Relations." In *Hugo Grotius and International Relations,* ed. H. Bull, B. Kingsbury, and A. Roberts. Oxford, 1990, 78.

———. "Martin Wight and the Theory of International Relations." *British Journal of International Studies* 2 (1976), 105.

Bull, H., and Watson, A., ed. *The Expansion of International Society.* Oxford, 1984.

Burchill, S. "Liberal Internationalism." In *Theories of International Relations,* ed. S. Burchill and A. Linklater. London, 1996, 28.

Calvert, H. *An Introduction to British Constitutional Law.* London, 1985.

Christie, I. *Stress and Stability in Late Eighteenth-Century Britain: Reflections on the British Avoidance of Revolution.* Oxford, 1984.

Dahrendorf, R. *Reflections on the Revolution in Europe.* London, 1990.

Devetak, R. "Critical Theory." In *Theories of International Relations,* ed. S. Burchill and A. Linklater. London, 1996, 145.

_____. "Postmodernism." In *Theories of International Relations,* ed. S. Burchill and A. Linklater. London, 1996, 179.

Doyle, M. W. "Kant, Liberal Legacies, and Foreign Affairs." *Philosophy and Public Affairs* 12 (1983), 205, 323.

Dunne, T. *Inventing International Society: A History of the English School.* London, 1998.

_____. "Liberalism." In *The Globalization of World Politics,* ed. J. Baylis and S. Smith. Oxford, 1997, 147.

_____. "Mythology or Methodology? Traditions in International Theory." *Review of International Studies* 19 (1993), 305.

Ehrman, J. *The Younger Pitt: The Reluctant Transition.* Stanford, 1983.

Emsley, C. *British Society and the French Wars: 1793–1815.* London, 1979.

Fukuyama, F. *The End of History and the Last Man.* New York, 1992.

Gulick, E. V. *Europe's Classical Balance of Power.* New York, 1967.

Hazlitt, W. *Eloquence of the British Senate.* London, 1808.

Himmelfarb, G. *The Idea of Poverty.* New York, 1984.

Hinsley, F. H. *Nationalism and the International System.* London, 1973.

_____. *Power and the Pursuit of Peace.* Cambridge, 1963.

Hirschman, A. O. *The Passions and the Interests.* Princeton, 1977.

Huntington, S. "The Clash of Civilizations?" *Foreign Affairs,* Summer 1993, 22.

Hurrell, A. "Vattel: Pluralism and Its Limits." In *Classical Theories of International Relations,* ed. I. Clark and I. B. Neumann. London, 1996, 233.

Jefferson, Thomas. *The Papers of Thomas Jefferson.* Ed. J. P. Boyd. Princeton, 1982.

Kingsbury, B. "Confronting Difference: The Puzzling Durability of Gentili's Combination of Pragmatic Pluralism and Normative Judgment." *American Journal of International Law* 92 (1998), 713.

Kissinger, H. *A World Restored.* London, 1957.

Marks, S. "Guarding the Gate with Two Faces: International Law and Political Reconstruction." *Indiana Journal of Global Legal Studies* 6 (1999), 457.

Maynes, C. W. "Squandering Triumph: The West Botched the Post–Cold War World." *Foreign Affairs* 78, 1 (1999), 15.

Murden, S. "Cultural Conflict in International Relations: The West and Islam." In *The Globalization of World Politics,* ed. J. Baylis and S. Smith. Oxford, 1997, 374.

Murphy, C. "The Grotian Vision of World Order." *American Journal of International Law* 76 (1982), 483.

Neumann, I., and Welsh, J. M. "The 'Other' in European Self-Definition: An Addendum to Literature on International Society." *Review of International Studies* 17 (1991), 327.

Nisbet, R. *Conservatism.* Milton Keynes, UK, 1986.

Pettman, J. J. "Gender Issues." In *The Globalization of World Politics,* ed. J. Baylis and S. Smith. Oxford, 1997, 483.

Ricoeur, P. *Interpretation Theory: Discourse and the Surplus of Meaning.* Fort Worth, TX, 1976.

Rousseau, J. J. *Rousseau on International Relations.* ed. S. Hoffman and D. P. Fidler. Oxford, 1991.

Skinner, Q. *The Foundations of Modern Political Thought.* Cambridge, 1978.

_____. "Meaning and Understanding in the History of Ideas." In *Meaning and Context: Quentin Skinner and His Critics,* ed. J. Tully. Cambridge, 1988, 29.

Smith, S. "New Approaches to International Theory." In *The Globalization of World Politics,* ed. J. Baylis and S. Smith. Oxford, 1997, 165.

Tooze, R. "International Political Economy in an Age of Globalization." In *The Globalization of World Politics,* ed. J. Baylis and S. Smith. Oxford, 1997, 212.

True, J. "Feminism." In *Theories of International Relations,* ed. S. Burchill and A. Linklater. London, 1996, 210.

Vincent, R. J. *Human Rights and International Relations.* Cambridge, 1986.

_____. *Nonintervention and International Order.* Princeton, 1974.

Walker, G. R., and Fox, M. A. "Globalization: An Analytical Framework." *Indiana Journal of Global Legal Studies* 3 (1996), 380.

Wallace, W. *The Transformation of Western Europe.* London, 1990.

Wendt, A. "Anarchy Is What States Make of It: The Social Construction of Power Politics." *International Organization* 46 (1992), 391.

Wheeler, N. J. "Guardian Angel or Global Gangster: A Review of the Ethical Claims of International Society." *Political Studies* 44 (1996), 123.

Wheeler, N. J., and Dunne, T. "Hedley Bull's Pluralism of the Intellect and Solidarism of the Will." *International Affairs* 72 (1996), 91.

Wight, M. "The Balance of Power." In *The Bases of International Order,* ed. A. James. London, 1973.

_____. *International Theory: The Three Traditions.* Ed. G. Wight and B. Porter. Leicester, 1992.

_____. "Western Values in International Relations." In *Diplomatic Investigations,* ed. H. Butterfield and M. Wight. London, 1960, 91.

_____. "Why Is There No International Theory?" In *Diplomatic Investigations,* ed. H. Butterfield and M. Wight. London, 1960, 20.

Zacher, M. A., and Matthew, R. A. "Liberal International Theory: Common Threads, Divergent Strands." In *Controversies in International Relations Theory,* ed. C. Kegley. New York, 1995, 107.

Zakaria, F. "Culture Is Destiny: A Conversation with Lee Kuan Yew." *Foreign Affairs,* March/April 1994, 125.

Index